James and John Stuart Mill

JAMES AND JOHN STUART MILL

Father and Son in the Nineteenth Century

BRUCE MAZLISH

Basic Books, Inc., Publishers

NEW YORK

Library of Congress Cataloging in Publication Data

Mazlish, Bruce, 1923–
James and John Stuart Mill : father and son in the nineteenth century.

Includes bibliographical references and index.
1. Mill, James 1773–1836. 2. Mill, John Stuart, 1806–1873.
B1606.M39 192 [B] 74-79278
ISBN 0-465-03630-9

Printed in the United States of America
DESIGNED BY VINCENT TORRE
75 76 77 78 10 9 8 7 6 5 4 3 2 1

TO MY PARENTS

AND

MY CHILDREN

"[T]he women, of all I have known, who possessed the highest measure of what are considered feminine qualities, have combined with them more of the highest masculine qualities than I have ever seen in any but one or two men, & those one or two men were also in many respects almost women. I suspect it is the second-rate people of the two sexes that are unlike—the first-rate are alike in both—except —no, I do not think I can except anything—but then, in this respect, my position has been and is, what you say every human being's is in many respects 'a peculiar one.' "

J. S. Mill to Thomas Carlyle,
5 October 1833

"It would be a mistake to suppose that a science consists entirely of strictly proved theses, and it would be unjust to require this. Only a disposition with a passion for authority will raise such a demand, someone with a craving to replace his religious catechism by another, though it is a scientific one. Science has only a few apodeictic propositions in its catechism: the rest are assertions promoted by it to some particular degree of probability. It is actually a sign of a scientific mode of thought to find satisfaction in these approximations to certainty and to be able to pursue constructive work further in spite of the absence of final confirmation."

Sigmund Freud, Third Lecture,
Introductory Lectures on Psycho-Analysis

CONTENTS

Contents

ACKNOWLEDGMENTS

I LIKE TO THINK that with this book I have made a contribution to psychohistory, a new field where history and psychology meet. I have tried to broaden its concerns and means of approach, to re-examine some classical psychoanalytic concepts per se, and to revitalize the figures of James and John Stuart Mill, breathing fresh life especially into the latter and his works. Whatever the actual success of this effort, it has rested on the assistance of innumerable persons and institutions, and I would like to make here a general acknowledgment of my thanks and appreciation.

The initial research work, done mainly in Great Britain in 1967–1968, was made possible by a faculty fellowship from the Social Science Research Council. A year as a Visiting Member at the Institute for Advanced Study in Princeton, New Jersey (1972–1973) then gave me the essential time and setting for the actual writing of this book. I am deeply grateful to Carl Kaysen, Director, and to Clifford Geertz, head of the Social Science Program, not only for their invitation to me but for providing an ideal combination of catered isolation and intellectual stimulation. Part of my support at the Institute was provided by the National Science Foundation under Grant GS-31730X1, and I would like gratefully to acknowledge it. Anna Marie Holt, who headed the secretarial staff of the Social Science Program, was somehow always able to produce chapters or assistance when neeeded, and I tend her and her staff my admiration.

The Boston Psychoanalytic Society and Institute was kind enough to invite me to deliver a version of what is now Chapter 2 of this book at one of its scientific meetings, and I gained a good deal from that session, especially from the commentaries of Professors Abraham Zaleznik and John Demos. To my friend, Abe Zaleznik, I owe additional debts with which he will be familiar. To my colleagues at the Group for Applied Psychoanalysis (Boston) I also extend thanks for their general inspiration and criticisms.

Others who have helped by readings, specific suggestions, or assistance are Professors J. H. Burns, Joseph Frank, Albert Hirschman, Norman Holland, Dr. O. Mannoni, Arnaldo Momigliano, Robert C. Tucker, Fred Weinstein, Perez Zagorin, and, of course, my wife Anne. In my efforts to make some of the translations from the French correct and literate I have called upon Professors Richard M. Douglas and George Kelly. Professors Michael Laine, and John Robson have kindly responded to factual inquiries, but, more than that, everyone working on Mill is indebted to Professors Priestley and Robson for their magnificent editing of the *Collected Works of John Stuart Mill.* Unfortunately, much of my writing was done before key volumes were published and my references, therefore, are often to earlier editions or to the original collections in the British Museum and the London School of Economics.

My publisher, Basic Books, Inc., has been a source of great support throughout. I should like to express my appreciation to Erwin Glikes, President, and Julie DeWitt, Project Editor. As for Martin Kessler, Vice President and Editorial Director, and my personal editorial mentor, he has once again put me under obligation to him by his patient assistance and wise counseling.

FATHER AND SON

1

Introduction

Book and Boy

"I WAS BORN in London on the 20th of May, 1806," John Stuart Mill begins his *Autobiography*, "and was the eldest son of James Mill, the author of the History of British India." Most readers, and this includes most scholars, have not noticed what an extraordinary statement this is. It invokes a new version of an immaculate conception, in which the mother is entirely missing; indeed, John Stuart Mill never mentions her throughout the published version of his work. Instead, we have "book and boy" both produced by James Mill, seemingly acting alone. The rest of the *Autobiography* appears to bear out this conception. It is as much about James Mill, the father, as it is about the son. Taken together, the relations of the two make up one of the great father and son stories of the nineteenth century. It is in these terms that we shall deal with the case of James and John Stuart Mill; for us, however, the unnamed mother, epitomizing all women of the period, will also figure largely in the matter, haunting us, so to speak, throughout this book.

The other extraordinary thing about John Stuart Mill that catches one's immediate attention is the episode of his mental crisis. At the age of twenty, a faithful disciple of his father's belief in strict rationality, John Stuart Mill underwent an experience that saw him teetering on the edge of seeming irrationality. For months, and even years, he hovered on the brink of the darkest despair, sometimes falling victim to his feelings of profound melancholy, and then painfully pulling himself back to healthier emotions. Out of this descent into self-awareness, Mill emerged with a personal, as well as intellectual, need to reconcile thought and feeling, the "rational" and the seeming "irrational." In the synthesis that he now painstakingly constructed, he forged a new and much broader definition of liberalism than was envisioned in his father's constricted Utilitarianism. Thus, his mental crisis, itself related to his deepest feelings about both his father and his mother, resulted in a kind of "new birth," of John Stuart Mill the person and of liberalism the doctrine.

A Short Story

APART FROM BEING the author of *The History of British India*, who exactly was James Mill, the father? What sort of son was John Stuart Mill, and what sort of mother did he have? What was the character of the time and society in which they all lived and which shaped their lives and the lives of those around them, and which they in turn shaped?

We shall devote our entire book to answering these and related questions. Here, however, let us start with a brief glimpse, a review and overview of the entire personal story. The external facts are fairly simple. James Mill was born in Scotland in 1773 of humble parentage. Spurred on by his ambitious mother, the bright young boy devoted himself to study. Fortunate enough to attract the patronage of Sir John Stuart and his wife, Mill was sent to the University of Edinburgh to prepare for the ministry. By 1802, unable to find a parish and disillusioned with a religious career, he "emigrated" to London. There he quickly obtained a position as editor and writer, married, and began to raise a family. To secure his position, he started to write a great work, *The History of British India*, in 1806, the same year as his first-born, John Stuart, arrived on the scene. The writing of the book and the education of the boy—four or five hours each day devoted to this latter enterprise—went on together, at the same time as James Mill slaved over his articles and periodicals in order to earn a necessary living. The education seems an act of unusual parental devotion.

Devoted as he was to the education of the boy, James Mill, after a year of marital bliss, began to disparage and scorn his wife, Harriet. This did not prevent him, however, from fathering on her eight more children, in spite of his being perhaps the earliest public advocate of birth control. Meanwhile, James finally finished *The History of British India*, and on the basis of it secured the post of an examiner at the East India Company, rising to the top in a few years. By about 1818 he had become a successful and comfortable civil servant, a friend of the rich and mighty.

He was also a Utilitarian reformer. Enrolling himself in 1808 as a disciple of Jeremy Bentham, the famous Utilitarian philosopher, James Mill rapidly became a power on his own, writing tracts and books on all aspects of knowledge as well as lending a practical political basis to the doctrine and organizing support for its aims inside and outside of Parliament. A man of forceful character, he played a significant role in British intellectual, political, and economic life, until his death in 1836.

As a Utilitarian, James Mill made sure that John Stuart Mill's education conformed to the tenets and aims of that school. Starting with Greek (at age three) and Latin, the child prodigy—for so John Stuart Mill seems to have been—was made to work through arithmetic and much of history and literature by twelve. At that time he was also given a rigorous training by his father in logic and political economy. The boy had no peers or playmates aside from his siblings. All feelings were disparaged, and the sole emphasis was on hard work and cold rationality. A trip to France when he was fourteen seemed a mere hiatus in this education, for on his return John Stuart Mill went, not to Cambridge University as contemplated at one time, but back to his books and the teaching of his siblings. All seemed placid enough; John Stuart Mill accepted his father's Utilitarian views as his own, and at seventeen dutifully accepted a post next to his father in the East India Company. The only sign of his autonomous growing up was the gathering of a peer group around him that was independent of the father. Then, suddenly, in 1826 at age twenty, John Stuart Mill underwent a severe mental crisis, characterized by profound melancholia and depression. He now felt a loss of faith in his chosen career as a Utilitarian moral reformer, and an awareness of how joyless and devoid of feelings was his own life. Silently he suffered through this "crisis," finally reconstituting his balance around 1830, though with constant relapses throughout the rest of his life. Intellectually he then began to explore new avenues of thought, and to make friends with men like Carlyle, of whom his father would disapprove. Outwardly still subservient and devoted to his father, John Stuart Mill had inwardly moved a great distance away, though he never entirely broke the ties that bound him.

At about the same time that he had worked his way through his crisis, the young and handsome John Stuart Mill met the beautiful and vivacious Harriet Taylor, and the two fell deeply in love. The only problem was that Harriet Taylor was married and the mother of two children (with a third to follow almost immediately). What occurred now is an amazing love story. For nineteen years John Stuart Mill, Harriet Taylor, and her husband lived in a kind of *ménage à trois*, to the scandal of all their "Victorian" friends. Yet, if we can trust the evidence, the two lovers never consummated their love sexually. Then, on the death of John Taylor, John Stuart Mill and Harriet were at last free to marry each other, which they did in 1851. At this point John Stuart Mill broke with his mother and remaining siblings, accusing them in raucous fashion of not accepting his new wife.

When Harriet died in 1859, Mill mourned extravagantly, and devoted the rest of his life to her memory. In this devotion he was joined by Harriet's daughter, Helen, who came to live with and take care of her stepfather. John Stuart Mill lived for almost fifteen more years, working at his writings and causes, and even entering Parliament for a few years. When he died in 1873 he left behind a rich legacy of works and a reputation as the foremost liberal thinker of his times. At this point his father's life and work lay in shadow, obscured by the greater fame of the son.

Such, in scandalous brevity, is the bare outline of the story of James and John Stuart Mill. What are we to make of it? Why do we bother with it? After all, James Mill is a half-forgotten figure, unknown any longer in his native Scotland, and remembered elsewhere only by fusty scholars.[1] One could paraphrase a statement about Herbert Spencer, and ask "Who now reads James Mill's *History of British India*, or his *Essay on Government*?" True, the son is more important. While one could raise the Spencerian question about John Stuart Mill's *System of Logic* or *Principles of Political Economy*, it would not hold for the classic *On Liberty*, a staple reading today as it was in 1859, or *The Subjection of Women*, which, with the advent of Woman's Liberation, is also rapidly becoming a popular classic.

With this said, however, one might still wonder what importance the two men together might have, aside from their works, read or unread. To further whet the reader's curiosity, let me pose a series of questions: How do we explain the fact that James Mill, perhaps the earliest exponent of birth control by artificial means, nevertheless produced nine children with a woman whom he had ceased to love? What sort of character did this "self-made man" have, and how did it affect the way he treated his family? What kind of education did he give his first-born son, whom he "made" as he did his books, and to what effect? What really happened during John Stuart Mill's mental crisis? How can we explain satisfactorily the fact that the highly restrained and virtuous John Stuart Mill entered into a shocking relationship with a married woman? What actual shape did his intellectual development take, as he broke with his father, and yet remained tied to him? Why the cankered and unnecessary break with his surviving family after his marriage to Harriet Taylor? And how do we account for his over-extravagant mourning at her death? These are some of the seemingly titillating questions, and there are many more like them.

Fathers and Sons

OUR PRIMARY AIM in dealing with James and John Stuart Mill, however, is not to describe the story alone, dealing with specific biographical questions as they arise, but to seek to understand its whole meaning and significance in terms of generational relations, specifically the father–son conflict encased in the concept of the Oedipus complex. We are starting from the view that man, though an animal with "instincts," has few that are invariant. The direction and satisfaction of these instincts is extremely plastic, and largely controlled by culture. The cultural cues are something that must be learned by each individual. They are learned through "symbolic" rather than genetic inheritance. Moreover, they change over time. This change is facilitated by the fact that, with few exceptions, men are born and then die within less than a century. The new "generation" is less ossified than its parents, and is open to fresh cultural innovations. Thus, generational change becomes, potentially, a prime mechanism of social change.

If men lived forever, they would undoubtedly become quite fixed in their ways. "Learned behavior" would take on the rigid quality of a "programmed instinct." Death of the individual, and new birth, offer the possibility of regeneration. Society, of course, must retain a large degree of constancy in order to remain a "society," that is, a constellation of relatively permanent relations. Hence, in most cases, generations greatly resemble one another—that is what the socialization process is about—and cultural change can often be minute. One thinks of so-called "traditional" or "primitive" societies. At critical moments, however, for whatever reasons, the pace of change accelerates dramatically. At this point generational change often becomes the prime vehicle for social change.

It is my thesis that in the nineteenth-century Western world (and perhaps elsewhere, too), generational change as the means of social change suddenly became pivotal. Industrial and scientific revolutions, along with political ones, posed a problem of cultural transmission that was new in its intensity and placed an enormous strain on parent-child relations. In the nineteenth century the most dramatic form this took was in a heightened sense of father-son, i.e., generational, conflict.[2] Much attention has been given, and rightly so, to class conflict at this time as a mechanism of social change. I am suggesting that generational conflict is at least of equal importance. Here, in actual human beings, external experience of the new social and cultural developments met with internal, psychological experience. The result, a total experience of the person, had enormous social consequences. It is the interplay of the personal and the social, of the individual psychic development and the general political and economic evolution—with each "causing" and influencing the other in what I call "corresponding processes"—that makes for the powerful social change that we call history.

If this be granted, how can we approach effectively this subject of generational change? One good way, I believe, is to start with detailed case studies, and work out from them. Such a case study is the present one: the father-son relations of James and John Stuart Mill. It has the great advantage of dealing with two famous men, at least in their own time, whose intellectual works are available to us, and about whose lives we have relatively abundant documentary evidence.[3] Moreover, one of the participants in the conflict has left us an autobiographical account of his "mental crisis," which stands at the heart of his generation's experience. As key figures in the political and intellectual changes of their time, both father and son become prototypic protagonists in what Freud was later to call the Oedipal conflict. They allow us to see not only into their own hearts and minds, but symbolically into the heart of their times.

Our approach will emphasize both analysis and synthesis. We shall go freely from the microscopic to the macroscopic. We shall indulge in both minute, detailed statements concerning the Mills and those around them, and bold, soaring speculations concerning all of nineteenth-century man and society. Thus, for example, our next chapter will offer a macroscopic speculation about the nature of the Oedipus complex in the whole of the nineteenth century.

At the other extreme, when we come to our detailed account of Mill's mental crisis (Chapter 10), we offer a microscopic analysis of his experience, as presented by himself. Here we shall largely proceed by a "classic" Freudian analysis of the 1920s, which comes perilously close, at least initially, to "reducing" its subject to a patient, a psychopathic "case." However, John Stuart Mill is not a patient, and psychohistory, as we seek to practice it, does not wish to treat him as one. In this, psychohistory differs greatly from clinical psychoanalysis. Thus, our intention in this particular use of the microscopic treatment is partly to show precisely how psychohistory moves from classic analysis to a wider, more broadly historical and creative kind of analysis, and so to force the reader to feel this progression, when and if it comes, for himself. In Chapter 10, then, we seek to show, by actual doing and then undoing, what are the limits of the purely psychoanalytic approach.

As for the macroscopic analysis of father-son conflict in the nineteenth century, it has the further virtue of introducing us to the basic analytic concept which will inform our study. Thus equipped, we can plunge fully into all aspects of the James and John Stuart Mill relationship. First we deal with James Mill, and this time we give a detailed analysis of his life, seen especially from a psychological perspective. Next we turn to his life work, and devote separate chapters to his conceptions of government, economics, and India. Here our aim is not merely to offer a descriptive, or even critical, account of James Mill's views on these topics, but to see them as complete "thought-worlds," involving his deepest feelings as well as his ratiocinations about "life," and thus his own life. We use the same approach, of course, with John Stuart Mill, where our documentation is even greater, and even more significant. Thus, we divide the account of John Stuart Mill's personal development, his life, into chapters on his family, his childhood, his "adolescence," his "mental crisis" (a microscopic analysis, as we have indicated), and then his early intellectual development. After this, we have separate chapters on his involvement with Harriet Taylor, who presents in flesh and blood terms the problems of sex and women, which Mill will then etherealize and make abstract in his theoretical writings. Next, we compare his treatment of economics and government with that of his father, and add a final chapter on John Stuart Mill's conception of social science. Such, in bare outline, is the framework on which we place our detailed treatment of generational conflict in the nineteenth century, as manifested in the case of James and John Stuart Mill. As the reader will see, it is in many ways a frame for extended "free associations" to an enormous range of topics.

Psychohistory

THROUGHOUT we shall try to use psychological concepts, especially psychoanalytic ones, to gain increased understanding and insight. Such an effort often goes under the label "psychohistory," a term originally made famous by Erik H. Erikson, but now under some attack. It has, in fact, taken on some of the polemical connotations of the word "sex" in Freud's time, with many of his contemporary supporters urging him to drop it as unnecessarily provocative. So, too, "psychohistory" seems to make many people bristle, as if one had uttered an indefensible word. It smacks of "psycho," and one thinks, perhaps, of Hitchcock's film. Although psychohistorians protest that they are not trying to reduce great, creative figures to sick patients, on the unconscious level the term itself seems for many people to undercut the better intention.

Rational or irrational as such objections may be, they must give one pause. Why not accept the "rose by any other name" response? One reason is that no better term has been suggested. In Political Science there does exist a subfield, called "Personality and Politics," but its name indicates its clear limits. Some have suggested "Psychology and History," or "Psychological History," and at one point I myself recommended the unwieldy term, "Psycho-social History," partly to take the curse off the first part of the phrase.[4] But psychohistory does have the undoubted merit of pointing directly to the application of *psycho*analysis to history. There is no "rational" reason why, any more than economic history or social history, psychohistory cannot be considered a subfield of general history, one that adds to rather than reduces the latter. In fact, there may be a virtue in the term if it forces us to confront our "irrational" dislike for it; as Freud said, to tone down his remarks about sex might make people more comfortable, but would scarcely advance the field of psychoanalysis. The important thing is to recognize that we are trying to gain enlightenment by using psychoanalytic theory and concepts in relation to fairly traditional historical materials; the test is not what name we use, but what results we obtain.

Our aim, however, is not merely to apply Freudian psychoanalysis to a study of the Mills. It is also to reexamine Freudian concepts in the light of our general historical materials. Freud was a late nineteenth-century figure, only a few generations after John Stuart Mill. How culture-bound was Freud, and therefore his ideas? Universal in its pretension to being a science, is psychoanalysis simply a parochial outgrowth of a particular period of Central European history, limited in its range and applicability? Hopefully, we shall be able to reexamine a few key components of psychoanalysis, such as the Oedipus complex, mourning and melancholia, death feelings, and the psychology of woman, and emerge with satisfactory answers. In short, we are as concerned with examining anew the psychoanalytic "tools" we are about to use as we are with using them.

There are, of course, clear dangers in the use of psychoanalysis, even reexamined, in biography or history. Richard Ellmann puts one such danger well. Discussing psychobiography, he warns:

> As we push back into the mind of a writer, we are apt to lose sight of his conscious direction, of all that gives shape to what might otherwise be his run-of-the-mill phobias or obsessions and that distinguishes his grand paranoia from our own small squirmy one. It is relevant, though already suspiciously pat, to point out the existence of an Oedipal situation in childhood, but in the works of a writer's maturity this is usually so overlaid with more recent and impinging intricacies that we run the danger of being too simple about the complexes. We may reduce all achievement to a web of causation until we cannot see the Ego for the Id.[5]

We are very concerned about the Oedipal situation in the lives of the Mills. Our problem, therefore, is not to be "too simple about the complexes," not to reduce complicated and complex works of maturity to a single childhood impulse. Further, we must exercise great caution not to see only the psychological line in isolation from the manifold influences normally dealt with under the heading of political, social, economic, intellectual, and cultural history. In reality, individual life-history, family history, and the history of the group, for example, are all commingled.

With all the dangers involved in this sort of work, and with all the demands made on the psychohistorical investigator, the effort still seems eminently worthwhile. As one analyst has put it, once one has become used to "listening with the third ear," traditional history appears thin; it is like listening to music on single-track after one has heard stereo. Nor is it just "identity," the life-histories of great individuals, that are illuminated; ideas also yield new and fresh meaning to the psychoanalytic inquisitor. We have known for a long time that ideas are related to the social context in which they are conceived; now we can add the personal context, and see the baffling and complex ways in which these relationships work themselves out.[6]

In the end, our answers can never be simple. They must be built in complicated fashion, out of numerous, often seemingly trivial details. The exact words of our subjects must be scrupulously and repetitiously examined, for they are our primary clues. What we are putting together, to repeat Freud, is a puzzle, and only after we have assembled the entire puzzle do we see the actual picture.[7] To use another image, our analysis of James and John Stuart Mill is not so much a psychoanalytic case study as a "detective case." Our solution, i.e., our full analysis, comes only at the end, often after we have been misled by various single clues. Only then, after we have carefully analyzed each piece and synthesized all the evidence, can we feel that we have solved the "case."

Universal Men

JAMES AND JOHN STUART MILL were impressively educated men. The range of their interests and, moreover, of their writings is extraordinary. To live with them and to share in their intellectual concerns is itself a form of liberal education. For an age trembling on the edge of professionalization, they were "universal" men, ranging freely over philosophy, political economy, political science, social science, history, psychology, pedagogy, science, religion, and literature, and making contributions of a high level of sophistication. They wrote on logic and poetry, morals and legislation, mind and matter. They were also men who often acted on what they wrote, shaping domestic and colonial policy, espousing specific reform measures, editing periodicals, and leading the Radical opposition in Parliament.

In trying to deal with such a variety of talent and concern, we must be sorely taxed. There is, so to speak, a whole Mill industry, even to the extent of a *Mill News Letter*.[8] Some scholars may be disturbed by the fact that we omit whole sections of the Mills' work on sundry topics: missing from our account, for example, is any systematic treatment of such choice items as John Stuart Mill's philosophy of mathematics, his views on religion, and his and his father's prolonged consideration of the correct nature of pedagogy. Our answer can only be that we are not attempting a formal "life and works" of either James or John Stuart Mill, but rather a psychohistorical study of the two men, seen as a father-son case symbolic of nineteenth-century generational change. While we hope that the portraits of our two major subjects—and of the people who surround them—are interesting and true in themselves, our further intent is the presentation of these portraits as part of a larger museum gallery, or historical exhibit: Western society in the period of rapid social and cultural change surrounding the first industrial revolution.

To this end, we have resorted to work done in a wide range of areas other than the traditional Mill studies. We have, as already stated, appealed to psychoanalytic theories and concepts; here again we run the risk of being faulted by experts in the field. The psychoanalytic literature on, for example, the Oedipus complex is vast. Have we been faithful to Freud's interpretation? Have we taken sufficient cognizance of the changed thought on the subject by post- and neo-Freudians? Then there is family history, one of the fastest-growing branches on Clio's tree. Have we managed to keep up with the latest evidence and views on the existence of the nuclear family? Is the nuclear family a new entry on the domestic scene, appearing with the advent of industrial society, or is it the norm as far back as we can trace it? Similar problems and questions arise with childhood history, a study related to but nonetheless separate from family history. Medical history, the history of economics, class stratification, the history of the women's rights movement, the history of the social sciences, and many other areas have lured us into their specialized and secret compartments, with what results the professional and general reader alike must decide.

The Divine Comedy

IN MY FIRST ATTEMPT to relate psychoanalysis and history, I concluded that psychoanalysis was "like the figure of Virgil in Dante's *Divine Comedy*, indicating the way to the circles of man's underground life." I then quoted W. H. Auden's poem, "In Memory of Sigmund Freud":

> *. . . he went his way,*
> *Down among the Lost People like Dante, down*
> *To the stinking fosse where the injured*
> *Lead the ugly life of the rejected.*

As I pointed out then:

> Freud himself had recognized the comparison. At one point he remarked in a mood of deep pessimism to his friend Fliess, "it will be a fitting punishment for me that none of the unexplored regions of the mind in which I have been the first mortal to set foot will ever bear my name or submit to my laws." Then, later, defiantly, he said of his psychoanalytic work: "It is an intellectual hell, layer upon layer of it, with everything fitfully gleaming and pulsating; and the outline of Lucifer-Amor coming into sight at the darkest corner.

My conclusion at the time was that:

> In the light of this fitful gleaming we can see that only by man's pushing on to the "darkest corner" of his being, by experiencing the "divine comedy"

of his past, can he rise to the heights of his noblest aspirations. This is the promise held out to us by the union of psychoanalysis and history. At the moment, we stand, at best, "Nel mezzo del cammin di nostra vita . . . per una selva oscura."[9]

At this point, I like to think that we have advanced some way out of the "dark forest." Recent developments in psychohistory suggest that our concern is not limited to the "injured," leading the "ugly life of the rejected," but that, as was true of Freud himself, we have gone beyond the sharp dichotomy between the normal and the abnormal, the "healthy" and the "injured," and now treat of the complex, creative, and elusive "human, all too human" being, great or small, in all his depths and heights. Such is our ideal as we enter upon the study of James and John Stuart Mill.

In their lives we shall find whole "thought-worlds" encased. With the mental submarine (or should it be called a "spaceship"?) of psychohistory, we shall attempt to enter these spheres of thought and feeling, ranging from the "lowest" to the "highest" elements. In this new space, perhaps we shall find that such hierarchical terms are meaningless, and that we must navigate in both our inner and outer worlds with a new psychological gyroscope. To go "down" in this world may also be to go "up." Only actual entrance into the "thought-world," conscious and unconscious, of James and John Stuart Mill will tell us whether we have lost our bearings completely, or entered upon a more abundant and ever-expanding universe of human meaning.

2

Fathers and Sons: The Nineteenth Century and the Oedipus Complex

A Nineteenth-Century Compulsion

THERE IS abundant evidence that, in the course of the nineteenth and early twentieth centuries, the Western imagination became almost compulsively concerned with the conflict of fathers and sons. In comparison with, say, Turgenev's *Fathers and Sons* (1861), or Edmund Gosse's *Father and Son* (1907), John Stuart Mill's attention to the subject in his chapter, "Mental Crisis," must be seen as merely a side glance, although a herald of what was to come. Surrounding Mill and for many years afterward, the novels and autobiographies overtly on the father-son relation became legion.

When Sigmund Freud took up the subject, then, he was hardly the first to notice the phenomenon. His unique contribution was to encase the father-son conflict in the amber of scientific concept, by elaborating the notion of an Oedipus complex. In his elaboration, Freud made of the Oedipus complex a universal, eternal generalization. *All* fathers and *all* sons, presumably, had to encounter one another in this conflict, irrespective of the historical period or society in which they found themselves. The intensity and the resolution might be different, but the basic conflict was the same. Freud's task, therefore, was to extend the particular nineteenth-century awareness of the conflict into a universal law, and to analyze the conflict itself in detail.

Was Freud right? To answer this with any conviction, we need first to have a relatively detailed view of Freud's conception of the Oedipus complex. That will come a bit later. Provisionally, however, we shall take the following position. In spite of the criticisms by antagonists such as Bronislaw Malinowski, and the qualifications correctly introduced by protagonists such as Anne Parsons, the Oedipus complex does exist *more or less* as Freud perceived it, in the sense that all children in the course of their development go through a stage—indeed, two stages, one in childhood and one at puberty—during which they have strongly evident libidinal attachments to parental (not necessarily the actual parents) figures of both sexes.[1] We shall proceed, therefore, on the conviction that there is a piece of relatively unchanging human nature—the Oedipus complex (see p. 301 for details of what forms this "constant" may take, as well as the limitations of Freud's original formulation in neglecting the aggressive impulses)—but with no fixed pattern of human behavior that necessarily emerges from it. In short, there are biopsychological givens of development, such as the Oedipus complex, but the way in which those givens actually manifest themselves is determined by the social and cultural conditions—or, to put it another way, the historical circumstances—which surround the individual. As we remarked earlier, psychohistory seeks to study both parts of this claim: the psychoanalytic "constant" and the historic "conditioning."

Our concern in this chapter is primarily with the historical circumstances surrounding father-son relations, especially as they can be illuminated by the concept of the Oedipus complex, in the nineteenth-century Western world; thus we wish to move from the particular father-son relation of the Mills to broader considerations. John Stuart Mill's account of that relation, however, offers us a cautionary note as we proceed. His omission of any mention of his mother reminds us how easy it is to lose sight of mothers, and of women in general, as we deal with fathers and sons. Mothers, it would almost appear, are merely objects of libidinal strife between father and sons, instead of being formative influences at least equal in importance to fathers, with a character and individuality in their own right. We must remember that, while father and son conflict is highly dramatic, it is not as all-encompassing as it sometimes appeared to the inflamed imagination of some nineteenth-century sons and writers.

2 / The Nineteenth Century and the Oedipus Complex

Anticipations

OF ALL THE FORMS of conflict in the nineteenth century, the conflict between fathers and sons has received the least *historical* analysis, though it has been given a great deal of literary attention and, through the genius of Freud, exquisite *psychological* analysis. A pioneer study in this area has been an article by Howard R. Wolf.[2] Wolf's thesis is as follows. In the late eighteenth century British literature, both popular and esoteric, still portrayed sons as submissive to fathers. True, sons did rebel against heavy-handed fathers, but they then submitted, and received as their reward the Christian sense of virtuous humility and the positive awareness of a righteous authority rooted in Roman patriarchy. The exiled son, as in a typical account such as the eighteenth-century French writer Marmontel's *Les Incas*, returned to his father's embrace in a mood of righteous acceptance and received grace (this is the same Marmontel who is to play such an important role in Mill's mental crisis—see Chapter 10).

The power of this "myth," according to Wolf, carried over into the early nineteenth century, causing severe depression and anxiety in those who, like Mill, went further in their rebellions. For Wolf, however, Mill is only a transitional figure. Gradually, some sons went even further, and the rebellion became a Darwinian struggle (as in Gosse) in which the son does not return to the father for forgiveness, but defeats him. This is the classic father-son struggle; in fantasy, the truly murderous Oedipal conflict. Or, as Wolf puts it, "The son is a 'survivor,' the Darwinian victor in a psychological struggle for autonomy."

By the beginning of the twentieth century, according to Wolf, the father-figure was fading away, and the son's relations were predominantly with the mother. The father was no longer perceived particularly as an authoritarian mentor or fierce competitor. The son had won in the fight for the mother, but this victory brought its own anxieties: an overinvolvement with the mother, a fear of oversubmission to her, and a need to reject her, too, in order to maintain autonomy, identity, and self. The woman now threatened totally to absorb the son—a partly desired "return to the generous bosom where *I* and *Thou* are indistinguishable"—a threat which, Wolf claims, is dealt with by turning to a "communion with nature," an allowable and acceptable merger.

Wolf's work is undoubtedly sketchy, as he would be the first to acknowledge. Wolf has dealt only with British literature, and within that only with a few key figures.[3] More detailed studies of the development in Great Britain are needed, as well as innumerable comparative studies. Was the eighteenth century quite as submissive as Wolf suggests? One thinks of the younger Mirabeau and his violent rebellion against his unforgiving father, and of the Marquis de Sade and the lengths to which his rebellion went. Did American mothers in the eighteenth century play a stronger and different role, as frontier women, from their European counterparts? Erikson seems to suggest this in his article on American Character.[4]

Nevertheless, partial as they are, I believe that Wolf's theses point substantially in the right direction (although I am less sure of his thesis concerning the centrality of the mother by the early twentieth century). Somewhere between the late eighteenth and early nineteenth centuries, sons began to adopt a different posture toward their fathers (and therefore mothers?). The Oedipus complex was handled at first in a slightly different, and eventually in a totally new way. A relationship, formerly patterned and secure, became problematic. Filial rebellions became more intense, and their fizzling out into submission less common and complete. The psychic price, in anxiety and guilt, became acute, and its prevalence increasingly epidemic—at least among selected members of the upper and middle class. Moreover, the fathers too must be seen as suffering, almost as much as the sons, though without the public lamentations. A relationship expressing an eternal biological aspect of development—for "sons" succeeding "fathers" is a constant of human life—now became shifting, dubious, and open to critical reflection.

Social Causes

WHY DID this happen? What produced these widespread and deep changes in the relations between fathers and sons? Until further, detailed research is undertaken, we can only hazard some informed speculations. These speculations can best be handled under two broad headings: structural change and ideational change.

The structural change must cover the whole movement compassed by what we may refer to as the dual revolutions, involving the Democratic and the Industrial Revolutions, or, more broadly, modernization, in its political and economic aspects.[5] In any comparative study we should expect that Great Britain, the first to experience the Industrial Revolution, should also be the first to manifest the new father-son relations, but the evidence does not obviously support such a simple conclusion. We can, however, observe certain important features of the modernization process at work, differentially, in all of Western Europe. Thus we can make certain general observations.

One of the key processes in the late eighteenth to the early nineteenth century was the population change, generally referred to as the Demographic Revolution. In the Western European countries especially, population increased dramatically—in England from about 6.3 million in 1750 to about 15.9 million in 1840, and in France from twenty million in 1750 to twenty-nine million in 1820. Most of this rise appears due to the increase in the number of births and the decline of infant mortality (owing to changes in diet, sanitation, medical care, and so on), though some could also be accounted for by the prolongation of adult life. As we shall see later, this population change brought to the fore the entire question of birth control and sexual relations. But for our immediate purposes, the important aspect of this population change lay in the emergence of young people as a proportion of the population (for, although exact figures do not exist, it is unquestionable that a rise in the birth rate a few generations earlier made for a significant bulge in the fifteen to thirty age group). Thus, in France in 1789, persons in the age group fifteen to thirty numbered sixty-one for every one hundred persons who fell outside of this age range (a figure whose full significance we realize when we note that it fell to thirty-seven in 1964!). In England in 1840 the age group fifteen to thirty accounted for seventy-seven compared to every one hundred of those outside it (dropping to thirty-seven in 1965). These bellwether figures show us how strong, demographically, was the emergence of youth.[6]

These large numbers of young people, moreover, came into existence at a time of rapid industrial and social change. The French Revolution had propagated the notion of "careers open to talent"; the Industrial Revolution opened a nonmilitary manner of achieving widespread social mobility. Together, these Democratic and Industrial Revolutions encouraged young people to compete, against their elders as well as against one another, in what appeared to be a boundlessly expanding world. In reality, of course, their path was often blocked by entrenched bureaucrats and "philistines," leading to frustration and sometimes rage. The rage itself was often complicated by growing awareness that the young rebel would generally exchange his early idealism for the philistinism of his elders as he himself grew older.[7] Only those who died young—a Keats or a Novalis—seemed sure to escape this fate.

In any case, a new society began to emerge in the nineteenth century, in which role and position, instead of being primarily ascribed, could more readily be achieved. Literary observers at the time, and many sociologists ever since, have lamented the fact that a society based on contract began to succeed a society based on status, or, as Tönnies put it, *Gesellschaft* replaced *Gemeinschaft.* For those who achieved a better position, this change meant freedom; presumably for those who suffered in the struggle, it meant alienation; and for those who thought of themselves as above the struggle, the aristocrats, it meant insubordination. What it meant for John Stuart Mill can be seen in his comment that the most distinctive feature of modern life was that "human beings are no longer born to their place in life . . . but are free to employ their faculties . . . to achieve the lot which may appear to them most desirable."[8] As we shall see more fully later, Mill was aware of the actual limitations to that freedom—female status, working-class existence, parental tyranny—but at this point he was content to make the observation that self-development required the possibility of social mobility.

The Industrial Revolution meant change and expansion. In this new society, novel occupations came into existence—textile entrepreneurs, railroad engineers, inventors of all sorts—and training and knowledge of a different sort from the old became obligatory. Fathers were no longer necessarily wiser than their sons, and sons did not as frequently have to wait for their parents to die in order to inherit their land or craft or business.

Geographic mobility also played its role in the new society. The vast movement of population from rural to urban areas accelerated rapidly at this time. The figures for the growth of cities illustrate one aspect of this migration: London went from a population of about 959,000 in 1800 to about 2,681,000 in 1850, and Paris from about 600,000 to about 1,422,000.[9] Qualitative accounts, such as Goldsmith's *Deserted Village* or Corbett's *Rural Rides*, suggest what was happening in the deserted countryside. In the cities, individuals and families existed, as the familiar litany has it, unknown to their neighbors, and thus not bound by the old ties of morality, custom, and sentiment. Urban people tended to be less religious than their rural counterparts, and we shall see later what role this shift may have played in father-son relations. Overcrowding, in certain areas, may have exacerbated the spirit of ruthless competitiveness; certainly it seems to have led to an enormous increase in tuberculosis, generally called consumption, the effects of which we shall also study later.

As for the family, it was either in the process of further giving up its extended kinship nature, and turning into the nuclear family with which we are all so familiar, *or* of remaining nuclear, but with increased affective ties.[10] Both kinds of changes seem to have incalculable effects on the relations of its members, some of which we shall seek to study in terms of the Mills. One function the family now took on, more grimly, was the preparation of its children to go out in the world and surpass their own parents; the nuclear family, giving up many of its previous formal educational functions, took on with a vengeance the task of offering its young an education in what has been called the Achievement Motive.

Ideas as Causes

THUS FAR, we have sought to sketch with very broad strokes some of the features of the emerging social world of the nineteenth century in Western Europe. These features—population growth, shifts in age strata, geographic movement, social mobility, family structure—we have been suggesting, opened up the possibility that "fathers" and "sons" might often find themselves in direct competition with one another, and thus in a new situation in which sons, generically speaking, instead of "replacing" their fathers, might simply "displace" them. In fact, this possibility appears to have been seldom realized during the early nineteenth century. Fathers enjoyed an entrenched position. The tradition of children being bound to parental control and authority still persisted. Much of the potentially threatening turbulence from the increased number of young people was drawn away from the "mother country" by emigration. Those who remained had plenty of scope for their ambition in an expanding economy. Thus, our broad speculations about the changing nature of early nineteenth-century modernizing society are meant only to suggest the possibility of "psychic" rebellion. Whether it was realized in particular cases, and in how widespread a fashion, is a matter for specific study.

It is the general thesis, however, of two scholars, Gerald Platt and Fred Weinstein, that these structural changes, even if only partially successful in bringing about effective filial rebellion in specific instances, did make possible what they call "The Introspective Revolution," that is, the work of Freud.[11] Only *after* these changes in society, Weinstein and Platt insist, could "Freud's discovery of the Oedipal complex, a result of his own self-analysis . . . [be] acceptable to ego." According to their analysis, it is the changes in the family that permit the father's position and authority to be examined critically; the father, for example, because he is working outside of the house, in some obscure, meaningless world as far as his children are concerned, is now perceived as illegitimately authoritative.

In their view, critical knowledge of the mother is still repressed because she continues directly to raise the children; they are therefore still fully dependent on her. As Weinstein and Platt put it, the father

> made the same demands as before for authority, respect, submission, and loyalty. But the demands could no longer be morally justified; the father did not play a nurturant role, he had an entirely different (instrumental) function in relation to his children. The identifications and attachments that had attended the former affectual exchange were broken, and the father's demands appeared oppressive. The need to repress hostile sentiments lapsed, and the guilt resulting from the expression of aggressive feelings and thoughts, though never entirely overcome, was sufficiently diminished that the son could express the fantasied desire for independence.

This analysis glimpses part of what was happening. As Weinstein and Platt also point out, "The son's demand for parity was facilitated by another development that followed upon the preceding social change. It became necessary to develop systematically the characteristics of personal autonomy in the son, so that he might be able to compete effectively in the abstract economic and political markets." Here I would only add that the apparently oppressive father may also be a new aspect of the situation; we must at least allow for the possibility that the father is himself a new type—the self-made, hard, autonomous, rebellious son of a previous "struggle," one generation earlier. Indeed, as I shall try to suggest shortly, the original Oedipal conflict of the nineteenth century may all too often have first involved "soft," loving fathers.

What of the ideational changes that accompany the structural changes that we have been discussing? Once again we can merely speculate on a few of the changes involved. The most pervasive ideational change probably involves the idea of progress. In the seventeenth century, the battle of the ancients and the moderns offers the first really impressive victory over the weight of the past. It is a very complicated struggle, with two points of special importance. The first is that a major shift in time perspective occurred. As Francis Bacon triumphantly pointed out, if one looked from the perspective of the present, then it was the "ancients" who were, in fact, the earlier, younger, newborn members of the human race, not his seventeenth-century contemporaries. Thus the earlier position was to be reversed, and it was the moderns who now had the advantage of experience and age.[12] Such a shift in time perspective prepares the way for our second point, one with which most readers will be familiar. It is simply that, for seventeenth-century man, additional experience brought additional knowledge, most obviously in the area of the natural sciences. Thus, not only are the moderns superior in age to the "ancients" but, more importantly, they have surpassed them in wisdom, and new wisdom at that.

By the eighteenth century, and with the Enlightenment, the conviction that modern man had progressed, and was destined to progress even further, was widespread and fundamental. It must be seen as the backdrop against which the whole drama and struggle of human life was henceforth to be played out. Condorcet's *Sketch for a Historical Picture of the Progress of the Human Mind* merely gave "classic" form to this basic world-view.

It must be noted that the progress being talked about was *man's* progress; women seem somehow not to figure in the great cosmic drama being enacted on earth. This was true even for mid-nineteenth-century versions of the idea of progress, as with Marx's materialist conceptions. As Marx points out repeatedly, "*Man* [italics added] makes his own history"; women were merely an appendage to his efforts. It is this basically male version of the idea of progress that serves as the context in which sons come to displace, and eventually perhaps eliminate, their fathers in the name of progress. Women, presumably, are merely the prizes of the contest, or at most the cheering spectators.

At the very time the Industrial Revolution was first gathering strength, however, a challenge to the entire notion of progress was issued by the movement of thought and feeling broadly known as romanticism. We shall not attempt to encapsulate so complex and many-faceted a subject as romanticism here; we shall merely seek to extract from this profound ideational change a few observations for our purposes. A preliminary observation: Romanticism undoubtedly helped to prepare the way for the Introspective Revolution. From Rousseau on, the romantics emphasized the value of introspection, and focused attention on the importance of memory. Unsystematically, they plumbed the depths of what later was to be called the unconscious. Part of their work, of course, was an attack on rationalism. Yet their antirationalism had the paradoxical effect of freeing the "irrational" sufficiently from repression so as to make it available for rational attention and treatment.

The romantics' challenge to rationalism also led to an attack on the general idea of progress. The products of men's minds and hands, they pointed out, might be improving, but there was no evidence that men's feelings were in any way being perfected. Indeed, as many romantics, including Rousseau, emphasized, advances in science and technology seemed to have harmful rather then beneficial effects on morality. At the very least, the romantic challenge suggested that the values of modern civilization were, if not worse, at least not better than those of earlier cultures, only different. Thus in place of the idea of progress, many romantics offered the notion of historicism, that is, the idea that all cultures were to be judged in their own terms (and, it was implied, to be found "equal"), instead of by a present-minded linear measure.

By attacking the idea of progress, the romantics would seem to be undercutting one of the changes that we earlier identified as favoring emergence of father-son conflict, and thereby weakening an attitude that fostered this form of generational change. However, because they were in fact attacking the very "fathers" who were in process of constructing the new, industrial society that undergirded the idea of progress, the romantics were themselves often engaged in an intense father-son conflict. The rebellion of the romantic "sons," in short, was as much a rejection of the fathers as that undertaken by those who went beyond their fathers in the name of progress; the romantics were simply taking another direction.

Interestingly, one of the key romantic complaints was that the new world of self-made men had broken all ties: with the past, with one another, with nature. The lament at the lack of "connection"—"only connect the landscape with the sky," Wordsworth implored—was omnipresent. Mediated through Carlyle, the general theme passed into Karl Marx's accusation that the "bourgeoisie had broken all ties between man and man except for the 'callous' cash nexus!"

For our purposes, what is most important is that authoritarian fathers are seemingly put to one side by many of the romantics. As Howard Wolf had suggested, Roman attitudes to the family had helped support the authority of eighteenth-century fathers. The romantic rejection of classicism thus indirectly sapped one of the foundations of parental power (as did, ironically, the new science and technology which, for different reasons, *also* attacked the classical past). It must be noted, however, that the romantic rejection of the past was selective; there was also romantic nostalgia for various pasts. Many of the romantics appealed to the Middle Ages, with its presumed harmony and sense of belonging: this is connection achieved vertically, through a well-defined, stable hierarchy. (Note that in this medieval hierarchy the romantics did not imagine authority in terms of stern, despotic fathers; rather, the "rulers" were benevolent, loving, cherishing parental types.) On the other hand, many of them glorified a putative communal past, when all men were brothers, sharing a common simplicity: here the connection is achieved horizontally, by means of a brotherhood of equality.

Thus the romantics appear to have simply avoided conflict with father, either by picturing him as a distant, though loving, figure, by replacing him with the mother, or by substituting for both parents a sort of brotherhood (along the lines of Freud's primal bond?). Paradoxically, in fact, by rejecting both the modern (i.e., scientific) and the classical world, they were rejecting the stern, authoritarian father-figure of their own time, and thus encouraging the emergence of even more pronounced Oedipal conflicts.

Romanticism, then, seems initially to have encouraged young men to run away from a fight with strong fathers even though in fact it fostered a subtle form of rejection. A later movement of thought in the nineteenth century, Darwinism, appears to have justified their staying to compete, openly. Darwin, of course, published his *Origin of Species* in 1859. For our purposes, the most important aspect of Darwinism was that, in effect, it announced the destruction of the father, that is, of the highest father-figure, God.[13] In essence, Darwin's evolutionary scheme left behind a feeling of "fatherlessness" in a purely chance universe. The Christian concept of creation—by a Father, note, not a Mother—was now broken, with a "self-making" process left behind in its place. The emotional effects of this change in thought were necessarily shattering (even if at first repressed by most people). The basic psychological prop of parental authority was destroyed.[14]

We are all familiar with the loss of religious faith that followed the Darwinian Revolution, and the turmoil that the break with accepted faith caused in all sorts of people. Less familiar is the realization that, with religious belief gone, real fathers were now confronted directly by their sons. Displacement of feelings to God the Father—in which, for example, the child's image of the father as perfect and all-powerful could be maintained—was no longer possible. Now actual fathers, with clay feet, stood before critical sons, without any buffers to protect them from the disappointment that, as Freud said, would almost inevitably arise in the maturing child. Henceforth the fight would be direct, with no mediation.

In the form of Social Darwinism, moreover, Darwin's theories seemed to justify displacement of the fathers through the "survival of the fittest." Since fitness was generally equated with progress, the "fittest" could fight in good conscience; their victory could now also be morally justified. In fact, Darwin himself was ambiguous on the question of whether evolution entailed progress. In deference to the leading idea of his time he did mumble words to that effect, as when at the end of the *Origin of Species* he dutifully intoned: "And as natural selection works solely by and for the good of each being, all corporeal and mental endowments will tend to progress towards perfection." Nevertheless, the whole substance of Darwin's theory worked against such a happy conclusion. Change by chance, not progress, ruled the world of nature. At best, differentiation and complexity seemed to be the outcome. But why should this be called "Progress"?

August Strindberg, who wrote one of the better autobiographical accounts of a child's relations with his family, and especially with his father, *The Son of a Servant* (1886), perceived the problem clearly. "I'm sure," he wrote a friend in 1886, "that there is such a thing as evolution, development, change, but not that this equals progress." In fact, Strindberg added, anticipating Freud, he thought his own work would "show that civilized man is screwy, sick from being conscious. . . ." It was "progress," ironically, as we have tried to show earlier in discussing various structural changes that had helped prepare the way for man's increasing consciousness—and thus sickness.[15]

Whatever the ultimate effect of Darwin's thought on the idea of progress—it would, in fact, help to call it into question—it initially, especially in the form of Social Darwinism, seemed to support it strongly, and thus encouraged whatever effect it had on father-son relations. More to the point, Darwin's ideas undermined the fundamental metaphysical support given to authoritarian fatherhood by orthodox Christian religious conceptions. As one consequence, man, in the person of sons, could be more confident and "righteous" in the fight against his own preceding generation—in the literal sense. Yet the sense of "righteousness" was only on the surface. Deeper down in each son was also a "bad conscience" as he displaced as well as replaced his father. It was this awareness, unconscious even more than conscious, that tended to make men of the nineteenth century "sick." It was to be the genius of Sigmund Freud to analyze that particular sickness in terms of the Oedipus complex.

Freud's Theory

FREUD did his work as a scientist, and not as an artist. While he used some of the same data as literary artists, and had an artistic eye, it is crucial to realize that he placed his materials and gifts in the service of science. For this reason he was able to turn his own Oedipal "sickness" to scientific account, rather than merely falling victim to it, or simply "experiencing" and then reporting it. As Weinstein and Platt remind us:

> It is clear that the great introspective artists—Baudelaire, Kafka, Strindberg, Nietzsche, Dostoevsky—all suffered from the failure of repression, the lack of control, the "too easy" communication with unconscious materials. Dostoevsky said that it was to his horror that he understood these things; Kafka's work can sometimes be so obscure, so virtually autistic, that one can infer a dangerous proximity to the loss of control; and Nietzsche too paid a high price for his insights. . . . Their impulses were not acceptable, conflict was not mitigated, and there is manifest, among the many invariable results, a good deal of self-hatred.[16]

How did Freud manage to acquire knowledge of the unconscious without severe personal dislocation, without, as Nietzsche put it, falling into the abyss? For Weinstein and Platt the answer lies primarily in the fact that "Freud escaped the threat of isolation and rejection; he did not become one more introspective intellectual or artist whose work is of only academic interest." The reason for this was "favorable circumstances in the environment. The changes that had transpired in the family structure allowed Freud to be recognized and accepted by the culture—if not by his own middle-class society than at least by those societies that had survived the pressures of differentiation, England and the United States."

We have already referred to many of these "favorable circumstances" in our discussion of structural and ideational changes. To these *must* be added Freud's unique situation *as a scientist* concerned with introspective materials who, moreover, took his own inner life as a prime subject for his work. Others, such as Charcot and Breuer, helped to prepare the way, but one has the feeling that only the happy accident of a Freud, able to combine their scientific interests with the artistic insights of a Schopenhauer and a Nietzsche, could have brought about the synthesis required for the founding of psychoanalysis. Unlike the differential calculus, with Newton and Leibniz, or even the theory of evolution, with Darwin and Wallace, there seemed to be no "Dopplegänger" of discovery next to Freud on the horizon. If ever a major scientific discovery seemed to be a "chance" occurrence, not in the natural and determined line of development, it seems to have been the "evolution" of psychoanalytic knowledge.[17]

A major inspiration for Freud as a scientist was, in fact, the father of evolution, Charles Darwin; we have already remarked upon the way in which his theories destroyed the entire cosmic backdrop to the relations of fathers and sons in nineteenth-century Europe and America. Darwin's theories must additionally be seen as the metaphysical, as well as physical, prerequisite for Freud's work. On a more limited scale, Freud took as his inspiration the physicalistic theories of Brücke, Helmholtz, and Du Bois-Reymond, but it was Darwin's conception of man *as an evolutionary animal*, and therefore subject to normal scientific inquiry, that Freud needed to inspire his own inquiries. Directly, Darwin influenced Freud in his decision to enter medicine (in his autobiography Freud gives the credit to Darwin and Goethe), and supplied the theory of the primal horde from which Freud elaborated his book, *Totem and Taboo*. In essence, Darwin offered to Freud the pervasive, all-enveloping way of thinking about man as a natural animal who had evolved in an "unnatural" way.

Freud, partly inspired by Darwin, entered science. There is no need for us to trace his route toward a scientific career in any more detail; that has been done abundantly and well by many others.[18] We shall concentrate instead on some aspects of Freud's discovery and elaboration of the Oedipus complex. It emerged, strikingly enough, from his own self-analysis, a novel kind of Archimedean lever for the inner world. As he wrote to his friend Fliess in 1897, his self-analysis had revealed to him the overwhelming knowledge of "love of the mother and jealousy of the father in my own case too." Moreover, Freud concluded, this was "a general phenomenon of early childhood." To this phenomenon, Freud attributed the "gripping power of Oedipus Rex."

In his *Interpretation of Dreams* (1900), Freud spreads before us the dreamlike details of his own Oedipal experience. As he himself realized, the recent death of his father reactivated ancient feelings and made them more available to his own observation. Thus, in the preface to the second edition of the book, he wrote that it was "a portion of my own self-analysis, my reaction to my father's death." It is interesting to note that Freud's Oedipal opponent in real life, his father, was a sweet, gentle man—hardly the stern, authoritarian image of the nineteenth-century Victorian parent! Yet, in the alchemy of the unconscious, he had nevertheless played the role of Laius in the story of Oedipus Rex.

Work with patients confirmed Freud in his discovery of the Oedipus complex and its significance. It is not clear, however, exactly what role the patients played in the actual discovery itself. On the basis of his writings, Freud's earliest patients appear to have been mainly women. Thus, in his first book, *The Study of Hysteria*, with Josef Breuer, we are presented with five case studies of hysterical women. Indeed, the classic Freudian patient seems (but see further, p. 29) to have been the upper-class Viennese woman, freed from household tasks and child rearing (which appears to put her in the same category as the man, no longer nurturant, and therefore vulnerable to challenge by her pubescent children?), and suffering from sexual frustration. In sociological terms she is the dissatisfied, functionless, hypochondriac female of capitalist society; the Veblenite leisure-class woman. In psychoanalytic terms she is the patient par excellence, clearly demonstrating symptoms of physical impairment—paralysis, tics, and so on—without organic cause, curable by depth psychology.

It is worth pausing for a moment over the hysteric woman patient. Hysterical symptoms are a common occurrence in many societies over a vast range of time, and are manifest in numerous phenomena. Freud wrote of hysterical possession in medieval demonology, and others have noted its occurrence in antiquity, in religious conversions, in military episodes, and so on. Is it, therefore, a universal, eternal characteristic of mankind? The answer seems to be "yes," in the sense that the propensity to hysterical behavior seems present in all of us at all times. Yet, as a definite character type of social significance, the actual hysteric woman patient seems to be a product almost solely of the nineteenth-century European and American world. If my practicing psychoanalytic friends can be believed, an actual case of an hysteric female patient is today a rarity which training analysts will travel hundreds of miles to observe. Thus, when we come to consider the question of the universal nature of the Oedipus complex, we may wish to bear in mind the phenomenon of female hysteria, as manifested in Freud's first analytic patients.[19]

In any case, Freud's reported cases, at least until 1900, focus on women, and do not seem predominantly to feature male patients.[20] The first of his classic male cases concerns "Little Hans" (1909), a boy five to six years old. Where else had Freud found confirmation of his self-analysis, as far as concerns the Oedipus complex, before this? We are in the dark on this subject.[21]

We are clear, however, as to Freud's theories. At a very young age the male child takes his mother as his libidinal object. Generally this will be between the ages of three and five, when the child has entered upon his phallic stage of development, after earlier oral and anal stages (the pre-Oedipal stage). The father is then perceived as a rival for the boy's total possession of the mother's love and attention. As a rival he is, of course, terribly threatening, for he is perceived as all-powerful and therefore all-punishing. Castration is his ultimate possible weapon. To make the matter more complicated, the boy not only hates and fears his father, but, quite naturally, also loves him. Torn between his ambivalences, the son suffers through the Oedipus complex, eventually reaching the satisfactory equilibrium whereby he identifies himself with the father, gives up the mother as a love object, and is psychologically prepared later in life to find a woman of his own. This is the ideal pattern. In fact, the Oedipus complex may be experienced in an inverted form—in which the son identifies with the mother, seeking thereby to obtain the father's love—or it may not be experienced in any psychologically significant form at all.

Freud's emphasis was decidedly on the libidinal nature of the Oedipus complex. More recently, psychoanalysts have called attention to another component of the Oedipus complex: the impulse of aggression, involving a fight over authority. As the *Oedipus Rex* story itself reminds us, Oedipus not only secures possession of his mother by killing his father; he also gains the father's kingly powers. Freud, however, especially in his early work, played down the aggressive impulse, and understood the Oedipus complex largely in terms of his discoveries about infantile sexuality. (For this reason, because we are trying to reexamine classic Freudian theory in an historical context, as well as the Mills, we shall continue the discussion here mainly in libidinal terms, while bearing constantly in mind the other aspect.)[22]

In any case, the Oedipal fight, when it occurs, goes on mainly in the realm of the unconscious, though anyone who watches carefully a child's behavior and utterances will find many overt expressions of his desires. At around six or seven, the child enters a latency period, unique to human beings, during which sexuality is temporarily suspended. Then at about fourteen (though this varies among groups, and among individuals in the group, and can be affected by diet, and so on), comes puberty, when true genitality manifests itself. Now the reawakened Oedipus complex rages fiercely, at least in nineteenth-century Western culture, and the classic Oedipal conflict takes place in earnest. By the late teens or early twenties, in most cases, the struggle is decided. For some, as for a Kafka or a Max Weber, the conflict is never satisfactorily resolved, and they are "sick" for the rest of their lives.[23]

Freud was less sure about what happened with girls. In fact, Freud never explored the "Electra complex" in its own right in any detail, and it is clear that its claims rested almost completely on his analysis of the Oedipus complex.[24]

It must be clear by now that the Oedipus complex is not itself a sickness. In fact, passing through it is a necessary means to maturity and health. In Freud's view, with successful passage of the Oedipus complex the boy learns to become a man by identifying with his father and achieving libidinal autonomy from his mother. No society, according to Freud, could hand on its culture and structure, and allow for their evolution, except through generational change. As Freud declared, "The whole progress of society rests upon the opposition between successive generations. . . ."[25] Or again: "Everything that is hopeful, as well as everything that is unwelcome, in the new generation is determined by this detachment from the father."[26]

The "unwelcome" reminds us that there is no guarantee that "detachment from the father" will be successful. Individuals, and even a whole generation it seems, may become "stuck" in the Oedipal conflict. Was this the case in late nineteenth-century Europe? Had the structural and ideational changes that we have discussed earlier created a situation in which the Oedipus complex no longer functioned in a "hopeful" fashion? In his most pessimistic moments, Freud himself seems to imply this conclusion.

Let us return to the question of the universality of the Oedipus complex in societies which have been fully formed and about which reasonably extensive data exists. Anthropologist Bronislaw Malinowski challenged Freud's theory by pointing out that the Trobriand Islanders have their children raised by the father's brother, rather than by the father. This, of course, can be answered in terms of displacement: the son will place upon the uncle, as father-figure, the same feelings that he would have toward his real father. The same is true if the child is raised by a nurse rather than its own mother. In short, the Oedipus complex must be construed figuratively, not literally.

More to the point is Anne Parson's examination of the Oedipus complex. Studying the South Italy family structure at first hand, she concludes two things: The Oedipus complex does exist, but significantly modified in its expression by the particular family rearing habits of the South Italians, and the Oedipus complex is not the major, or "nuclear," complex in South Italian family life; rather, that role is played by what she calls the *Madonna complex*, in which feelings are directed toward an asexual, ideal mother figure.[27]

In sum, most of the evidence, from diverse sources, suggests that the Oedipus complex *is* universal, in the sense that all sons do show "love of the mother and jealousy of the father," if we expand this definition to mean mother- and father-figures. Moreover, myth and legend from innumerable cultures confirm this finding.[28] The evidence also suggests firmly that different individuals will manifest the Oedipus complex to very different degrees. Even more important, the way in which societies rear their children markedly affects expression of the Oedipus complex, as well as its role in the individual and in the culture. Lastly, the centrality of the Oedipus complex in the development of character in a particular culture is by no means assured; in that sense, nineteenth-century Europe and America may be "pathological."

One other consideration may be important here. The Oedipus complex, as we have said earlier, manifests itself first in the phallic stage, and then in puberty. Both, as physiological "givens," make for the universality of the Oedipus complex.[29] The *psychological* importance, as we have tried to suggest, depends on the culture. My own suspicion is that the phallic stage of the Oedipus complex would show more "universality" than the puberty stage, if by the latter we mean the "Sturm und Drang" of nineteenth-century "adolescence." Adolescence is really a cultural rather than a physiological stage, and appears uniquely related to the structural and ideological changes that we described earlier. Child rearing, on the other hand, has exigencies of its own which almost necessarily are common to all societies: children must be nursed, tended to, toilet trained, and gradually socialized. While patterns of child rearing vary enormously, we can assume a greater "constant" for the Oedipus complex, from the "nature" of things. By the time of puberty, however, the "spread" of cultural differences will have become greater and greater.

Needless to say, the patterns first laid down in the phallic stage are fundamental for later developments. Experiences in the puberty stage are *in terms of* the earlier patterns. Nevertheless, the puberty stage in various cultures adds another differentiating element to the manifestation and significance of the Oedipus complex. One must study the Oedipus complex separately and then together both at the phallic and the puberty stage, and in terms both of the specific culture and universally. Our presumption here is that the Oedipus complex, for some of the many and complicated reasons that we have touched upon, played a uniquely important and significant role in father-son relations in nineteenth-century Europe and America. Thus placed in historical context, the possibility is opened before us that, like the classic hysteric female patient, the "sick" victim of the Oedipus complex may eventually become a rarity on the psychoanalyst's couch as well as in Western culture.

The Father's Due

IN NINETEENTH-CENTURY European culture, the Oedipus complex has generally been looked upon only from the side of the son. Surely it is time now to think more about the father's side of the relationship.[30] After all, in the original Oedipal play, *Oedipus Rex*, it is the father who is killed by his son (though originally, under the sway of prophecy, the father and mother jointly decide to abandon the child to its death). As the myth suggests, fathers may have as much to fear from their sons as vice versa. We must also remember that fathers, having once themselves been Oedipal sons, "know," if only unconsciously, the hostility and rage generated toward them in the breast of their own sons.

Yet few great works of art have been written from the father's side of the conflict. True, that good nineteenth-century Victorian, Matthew Arnold, aged thirty-one, wrote his narrative poem, *Sohrab and Rustum* (1853), in which the son, Sohrab, is killed in battle by his father, each combatant, as in *Oedipus Rex*, ignorant of the other's identity. But then, as Howard Wolf points out, once their identities are revealed, the son offers grateful submission to the now tender father.[31] This hardly amounts to offering the father's side of the "complex." There are hints of that side in Arnold Bennett's *Clayhanger* (1910), and more recently and with less pretension to "greatness" in Howard Spring's *My Son, My Son* (1938). One ought also to mention Arthur Miller's play, *Death of a Salesman* (1949). All in all, however, the neglect in the literature mirrors the fact that in *Oedipus Rex* only the relation of son and mother is developed, while the father's dead body is simply removed from the stage, and from further consideration. Let us here, however, try to render unto the father what is his due.

What is the possible impact of the Oedipus complex on the father? We need to deal with this question by separating the two stages, phallic and pubic. Both stages, when they occur in the son, are bound to reawaken the father's own generally deeply repressed Oedipal struggle; if that struggle has been severe, the reawakening may be painful. In any case, at the birth of his child the father will probably be faced in a more dramatic way than usual with the possibility of his own death. The coming of the son, while bringing with it the promise of symbolically continuing and immortalizing the father's existence, also brings an awareness that the son is there to "replace" (and perhaps to "displace") the father.

These death anxieties are intensified, or reawakened, when the son enters the phallic stage. At this point, we can assume, the son also reactivates the sexual threat to his father that first occurs when the child is born. The mother is at that time usually absorbed in his care, and all her love and attention are generally devoted to him rather than to the father. She is bound to be less "sexual" in her attitude to the father, and, in any case, less available to him sexually. If the child is a boy, the jealousy will have a special unconscious meaning for the father. Thus, when the son is actually weaned, goes through the oral and anal stages, and enters the phallic stage, the way is prepared for unconscious hostility on the part of the father as well as the son. Perhaps the boy is right, unconsciously, to fear his father. If we are correct that the father unconsciously wishes to get rid of his "rival," that is, the child clamoring for the mother's attention and love in the oral stage, and then also in the phallic stage (as well as, of course, loving his son intensely), then we can also speculate that there will be deep guilt feelings on *his* side of the complex, as well as on the son's side, about forbidden death wishes.

Freud himself unknowingly suggests this possibility to us. He tells us it was the death of his own father that prompted him toward discovery of the Oedipus complex. We know, however, that in the 1890s, when Freud was struggling through to his concept, he was also experiencing what it was to be a father. He and Martha Bernays had been married in 1886. Freud was aged 30. Within a year, a daughter, Mathilde, had been born. By 1897 Freud had five more children: three sons, Martin, born 1889, Oliver, born 1891, and Ernst, born 1892, and daughters Sophie, born 1893, and the youngest, Anna, born 1895. Thus his sons ranged in age at that time from about eight to five, and either had just passed through the Oedipus complex or were in the middle of it. Is it too much to assume that Freud's awareness of "love for the mother and jealousy of the father" was overdetermined, in the sense that he stood between the generations, gradually becoming conscious of his own feelings toward his father and of his children's feelings toward *him*—and of his *own* reawakened feelings toward them? Or were the latter too painful and shocking to be acknowledged?

The second phase of the Oedipus complex, at puberty, also brings its problems for the father. At this stage, at least in its nineteenth-century form of adolescence, the child must seek his own "identity." Erik Erikson has made this search familiar to us in terms of the "identity crisis." What has not been made clear is that the son's prolonged and often tumultuous effort at achieving his own identity frequently calls into question *the father's* identity. Fathers in nineteenth-century Western society often needed their sons' approval of their achievement, almost as much as the sons needed the approval of the fathers. By refusing to take over the father's craft, business, or profession, to follow his values, or to honor his work, the adolescent may be not only rejecting the parent but undermining his need for assurance of "immortality." Moreover, to use Erikson's terms, the initiative and industry of the father may be as much at stake, symbolically, as they are for the son. Following Erikson's lead, we can see that in such a situation, an identity crisis for the son is what can be called a generativity crisis for the father.

Rejection of the father and his "creativity" can be made even more acute by the son's search for a new, or "second," father to replace his real father. In *Gandhi's Truth*, Erikson celebrates the fact that Gandhi had become an ideal, second, or stepfather to his followers (although a poor father in actuality to his own children). Quite correctly, Erikson sees this as a major part of Gandhi's leadership and as a source of gratification to his disciples. One could expand this further and see Gandhi as providing a new ego-ideal that allows for the "progress" between the generations described by Freud. However, there is a price to be paid for this which even Erikson seems to overlook: the real fathers "lose" their sons and the confirmation of their generativity that the latter would bring if they were to follow in the footsteps of their parent. Thus, while perhaps necessary for progress, one cannot always rejoice at the consequences of "second fathers."

Thus, sons passing through the period of adolescence in nineteenth-century Europe not only reawakened earlier death and sexual anxieties in their fathers, but brought into question their generativity. Christ's injunction, "Follow me, and abandon thy fathers and mothers," appeared to have taken on a new life, though perhaps in a paradoxical sense. In any event, as Freud pointed out so well for the nineteenth century, sons often suffered grievously in the stage of puberty by this developmental "necessity," in the form of adolescence; what he made less obvious was that the fathers could also be badly hurt in the Oedipal conflict.

Of course, fathers, unlike sons, did not have to contend with the onrushing libidinal impulses suddenly awakened at puberty. They did not have to cope with those threatening physiological changes whose psychological impact has been so well described by Anna Freud in her book, *The Ego and Its Mechanisms of Defense*. Nor, in general, did they have to contend with problems of identity and work. In theory, at least, these would be behind the father. But at this point we would have to raise certain questions: What physiological changes would fathers be experiencing? Male menopause? Loss of physical strength and vitality? These lead to another set of questions: How old were fathers generally, in the nineteenth century, when their children were going through the phallic stage and the stage of puberty? Does it make a difference whether the father is twenty or forty when the child is born, or whether his own identity is still to be formed at the child's phallic stage, and his own career still be to successfully defined at the puberty stage?[32]

Such questions will remind us that structural, along with cultural, factors shape the way in which the Oedipus complex is experienced, in this case, by both the fathers and the sons. We must also remind ourselves that, in any Oedipal situation, the father has gone through the conflict with his own father, and brings the results of that encounter to his renewal of the struggle with the new generation. Thus, father and son, along with their whole culture, interact with one another; it is not simply the son who unilaterally undergoes and works through an Oedipus complex. In a different context, Erikson has wisely remarked:

> A baby's presence exerts a consistent and persistent domination over the outer and inner lives of every member of a household. Because these members must reorient themselves to accommodate his presence, they must also grow as individuals and as a group. It is as true to say that babies control and bring up their families as it is to say the converse.[33]

No less is true of the Oedipus complex. Sons struggle, and in the process control and, hopefully, teach their fathers as much as the latter do them. Relations between the two, and among the whole family, may thereby be reoriented. In this interaction presumably lies the "progress of the generations," the possibilities for all that is "hopeful" or "unwelcome," which Freud saw as stemming from the Oedipus complex.

Turgenev's Fathers and Sons

AT THE END of the century Freud tried to summarize father-son relations in terms of the Oedipus complex, a scientific concept. Earlier, nearer the middle of the century, Turgenev sought to delineate its features in his great novel, *Fathers and Sons* (1861), an artistic creation.[34] Both efforts may be seen as prototypic, with Turgenev's dominating the imaginations of the nineteenth century, and Freud's gradually coming to control our perceptions in the twentieth century.

Indeed, if any novel may be said to epitomize father-son relations in the nineteenth century, it is surely *Fathers and Sons.* As a novel it vastly transcends any simple Oedipal relation, though elements of that relationship are undoubtedly present. (Turgenev's short novel, *First Love* [1860], is, however, a classic statement of the Oedipal theme.) It will therefore be useful and right to consider *Fathers and Sons*, in its own terms, as a revelation of father-son relations as perceived at the time of John Stuart Mill's publication of *On Liberty*.

But first we must remember that Turgenev is writing about Russia, a Russia that is lagging behind Western Europe in structural, though not ideational, changes by about two generations. Thus it will be our thesis that Bazarov, the hero of Turgenev's novel, is analogous not to John Stuart Mill but to James Mill and the early Utilitarians.

In our interpretation, there are two major themes in the novel. The first is Turgenev's awareness of a general social movement toward greater equality (exactly as de Tocqueville had seen it earlier in France, and then America). As Pavel, the aristocratic representative, comments about one of the younger generation, "his feeling of equality will be flattered. And really why should there be castes in the *dix-neuvième siècle*?" [p. 316] The second theme is that in Russia, with its rigid social structure, this equality will only be achieved by sons breaking with their fathers, that is, by generational conflict and thus progress. What is striking here is that the sons are not rebelling against hard, unyielding fathers, as in the classic Oedipal picture, but rather are forcing themselves to become hard and unyielding in order to reject their soft, loving fathers! It is, in short, the reality of Freud's own parental situation, rather than the fantasied and unconscious version of his Oedipus complex.[35]

Turgenev reveals a tremendous awareness of generational shifts and tremors. Nikolai Piotrovich, the loving father who is initially threatened by the loss of his son, Arkady, owing to the influence of the latter's friend, Bazarov, is forced to remember his own break with family (in this case, in the person of his mother). As he tells his brother: "One day I quarreled with our mother: she started to shout and wouldn't listen to me. . . . At last I told her that she couldn't understand me: we belonged to two different generations. She was terribly annoyed, but I thought: 'It can't be helped. It's a bitter pill, but it has to be swallowed.' And now our turn has come, and our heirs can say to us: 'You are not of our generation; swallow the pill.' " Pavel, in turn, says to Bazarov openly: "Why, you have come to take our places." [p. 270] By the end of the book it is clear that even Bazarov is shortly to be put on the shelf by the younger generation (although he himself is not yet thirty). As Anna Sergeevna, the woman with whom he allows himself temporarily, and unwillingly, to become involved, reminds him, "neither of us is any longer in our first youth." Driving the point home, she remarks of his friend Arkady, "I am old enough to be his aunt." [p. 329]

The generational lines are hardly clear-cut, and in this Turgenev comes close to the multiplicities and ambiguities of real life. Thus, one of the fathers, Nikolai Piotrovich, is forty-four, while his son Arkady is twenty-three. Moreover, Nikolai Piotrovich has just taken a mistress, after his first wife's death, by whom he has had a baby boy; at the end of the novel he marries his twenty-three-year-old mistress *at the same ceremony* at which his son Arkady finally marries a girl of roughly his own age. The other father, Bazarov's, is sixty-two, while Bazarov, as we have said, is somewhere just under thirty. Thus the two fathers are really of two separate generations, though neither is the stern, authoritarian Victorian parent.

The real father-son fight is displaced onto the uncle, Pavel, one year older than his brother Nikolai Piotrovich; it is with Pavel that Bazarov carries on the quarrel. A handsome, supremely self-confident man, a captain in the army at the age of twenty-eight, with a brilliant career in front of him, Pavel had suddenly fallen in love with "a certain woman." Sacrificing everything, he had pursued her through all Europe, until finally she left him in the lurch forever. A true victim of romantic love—the one "flaw" in his otherwise domineering personality—Pavel lives out a wasted life, and at the time of the story has settled down to live with his brother.

The conflict with Bazarov, who comes to visit the family as a guest of Arkady, is really between "likes." Bazarov, too, is a strong, supremely self-confident, and domineering man, with a rigid adherence to his own views. The romantic impulse is also terribly threatening to him, for it represents "love," which he cannot really tolerate, and loss of control, which is even more overwhelming.

In the conflict, which ultimately takes potentially murderous physical shape in the form of a duel (though this, in turn, leads to a kind of understanding and reconciliation between the two men—shades of the earlier "submission with grace" pattern!), Pavel states his aristocratic position. "We, the people of the older generation," he tells Bazarov, "we assume that without principles . . . taken, as you put it, on trust, it is impossible to move a single step forward, or to breathe." [p. 183] He insists that civilization is precious, not to be destroyed by savagery and violence.

Against Pavel's "principles" and "civilization" Bazarov sets his "nihilism." The nihilist, a word first given wide circulation by Turgenev, "recognizes nothing" and "respects nothing," he is "a man who does not bow to any authorities, who does not take any principle on trust, no matter with what respect that principle is surrounded." [p. 183] Nihilism, then, is the vehicle for rebelling against the authority and unequal society of the older generation. We can see the highly personal aspect of this rebellion in the confession of one of Bazarov's disciples, Sitnikov. "I am an old acquaintance of Yevgeny Vasilich [Bazarov]," he tells Arkady, "and, I can even say, his pupil. I am obliged to him for my regeneration. . . .[36] Will you believe that when Yevgeny Vasilich said for the first time in my hearing that *one should not recognize any authorities*, I felt such exultation—*as though I had come to maturity*. Now, I thought, *at last I have found a man* [italics added]!" [p. 220] In short, before one can come to maturity, or be a man, one must reject, and not introject, existing authority—and that means fathers (even loving fathers).

Bazarov is undeniably a nihilist. He is also a Utilitarian, a counterpart of acknowledged contemporary Russian Utilitarians, such as Chernyshevsky, and very much a James Mill type.[37] For example, Bazarov embraces the crude version of Utilitarian psychology: Refusing to accept abstractions, or what he calls principles, he announces that there are only "sensations. Everything depends on them." [p. 282] As he says to Pavel, "You, I hope, have no need for logic [again, in the sense of abstractions] in order to put a piece of bread into your mouth when you're hungry. What do we need these abstractions for?" [p. 207] So, too, Bazarov appeals constantly to the standard of utility. "We act by the force of what we recognize as beneficial," he announces. "At the present time rejection is the most beneficial of all things, and so we reject." [p. 208] Or, more directly, "A decent chemist is twenty times more useful than any poet" (reminiscent of Bentham's comment that push-pin is as good as poetry). [p. 186] Further, we are told that Bazarov "could not endure excursions without a purpose." [p. 203] He is always talking only about "useful" things; as he tells the beautiful Anna Sergeevna, "I endeavor to talk with you about useful subjects." [p. 250]

Like James Mill, Bazarov worked hard. He had no time for idle feelings, and least of all for "romantic" notions, which he scorned. "The important thing is that twice two are four, and nothing else matters in the least." When Arkady asks, "Including nature?" Bazarov snaps back, "Even nature doesn't matter, in the sense in which you mean it at this moment. Nature isn't a temple, but a workshop, and man is the workman in that workshop." [p. 202] Carrying the workman image even further, Bazarov reminds us of the caricature of the Utilitarian as a "mechanical" man when he snorts, "As I thought . . . the cigar doesn't taste pleasant. The machine's gone wrong." [p. 264]

In relation to women also, Bazarov's attitude resembles that of James rather than John Stuart Mill. Bazarov scorns the emancipated woman, Yevdoksia, who, incidentally, is ugly, and sarcastically responds to her rhetoric of "rights of women" with the assertion that "A whip is a good thing." [p. 225] His need to dominate, with women as well as men, is constantly made clear to us; he does so either through coldness, rudeness, or, one suspects, by "dissecting" the subject. Bazarov, like James Mill, seems unable to love. Toward women he appears able to entertain only "bestial" passion, "a passion, strong and oppressive, that was struggling within him—a passion resembling malice and, perhaps, akin to it." [p. 258] In such a passion we recognize aggression, not libido in genital form.

Why is Bazarov unable to love? The answer seems to be that he has received too much love from his parents! Our first introduction to Bazarov's parents comes midway through the book, when he returns home to them with Arkady. It is worth quoting the entire scene:

> "Yevgeny, my dear little Yevgeny," a woman's quavering voice was heard. The door was flung wide open, and on the threshold appeared a round little, short little old woman, in a white mobcap and a short, varicolored jacket. She groaned, stumbled, and would certainly have fallen if Bazarov had not supported her. Her swollen little arms were at once wound round his neck, her head nestled against his chest, and there was a silence. Only her convulsive sobbing was to be heard.
>
> Old Bazarov breathed deeply and screwed up his eyes even more.
>
> "Well, that's enough, that's enough, Arina my dear! Stop it!" he said, exchanging glances with Arkady, who was standing motionless by the tarantass, while the peasant on the box even turned away. "That's quite unnecessary, do please stop it!"
>
> "Ah, Vasily Ivanich!" the old woman murmured, "at last, my dear, I see my little one, my little Yevgeny . . ." and, without unclasping her arms, she drew her wet, tearstained, crushed, and beaming face away from Bazarov, gazed at him with beatific and absurd eyes, then fell on his chest again.
>
> "Well, yes, of course, that's all in the nature of things," Vasily Ivanovich said, "only we'd better go into the house. Here's a guest arrived with Yevgeny. You mustn't mind," he added, turning to Arkady, and slightly scraping one foot, "you understand, it's just a woman's weakness and a mother's heart, you know. . . ."
>
> But his own lips and eyebrows were twitching, and his chin was quivering—though he obviously was trying to master himself and to appear all but unconcerned. Arkady bowed. [p. 267]

In the face of so much cloying love, which threatens to overwhelm him, Bazarov erects a stony defense. We are given only one hint as to a possible Oedipal connection. When Bazarov temporarily, and in spite of himself, becomes involved with Anna Sergeevna, the widowed Mme. Odintsova, he suffers feelings "that tormented and enraged him." [p. 246] One night, we are told, "he was tormented by disjointed dreams . . . Mme. Odintsova hovered around him, and she was his mother too." [p. 305] Love must have seemed terribly threatening and "suffocating" to Bazarov. It was a giving way to "weakness," to that romanticism which he called "nonsense, an unforgivable stupidity." [p. 246] Bazarov, then, cannot permit himself to love, because he is afraid of loving too much, and thus losing all control of himself.

Afraid to love, Bazarov rejects his parents. He literally "deserts" them, staying only three days (after an interval of some years) and then abruptly departing, to their intense dismay. It is not only by isolating himself physically that Bazarov rejects his doting parents; he does it psychologically as well. Thus, he fantasies himself a self-made man. "Upbringing?" Bazarov lashes out, "Every man should bring himself up—well, as I have, for instance." [p. 192] His thoughts, too, he owes to no man. Accused of sharing Proudhon's opinions, "Bazarov drew himself up haughtily. 'I share no one's opinions; I have my own.' " His sycophantic disciple, Sitnikov, catches the spirit of what is involved when he shouts, "Down with the authorities," abasing himself before his master. [p. 225]

Self-made, forced to deny his parents and any feeling of love and gratitude toward them, Bazarov ends up unable to love himself either. His hatred of others becomes self-hatred as well. To Arkady's "Strange! I don't hate anybody," Bazarov responds, "But I hate so many people." [p. 281] He hates even the Russian peasants, for whose betterment he is wearing himself out. Then, in an unguarded moment, Bazarov confesses to a feeling of being "self-humiliated." [p. 280] We can see clearly that Bazarov is turning his destructive feelings, his hatred, onto himself when he makes the philosophical nihilist point, "Having decided to mow everything down, then mow yourself down too!" [p. 282] It is the prelude to his actual later self-destruction, for that is what his "accidental" poisoning of himself in the course of an autopsy of a typhoid patient amounts to. The accident occurs, interestingly enough, when Bazarov returns to be with his parents—thus, symbolically as well as actually, having to be with his family "kills" him (along with the backwardness of the Russian countryside, for the availability of silver nitrate in time would have saved his life). In this father and son "conflict," it is the son who is destroyed; no "progress" has taken place.

I / *Father and Son*

Loving and Unloving Fathers

THERE IS, of course, much more to Turgenev's *Fathers and Sons*. And while Bazarov resembles James Mill and the Utilitarians in many ways, as our detailed account of James Mill will show, there are also many differences that we have not stressed. Nevertheless, our account of the novel does confirm three things: first, Freud's concept of the Oedipus complex, while a crucial insight, does not exhaust the nature of father-son relations in general; second, the conflict is often with loving fathers, instead of stern authoritarians, in order to free the son's aggression against the established authority of society; and third, the Oedipal conflict in the nineteenth century manifested itself at a variegated rate in different countries and took differing forms at particular points in time.

The virulence of the Oedipus complex seems related to the onset of the structural and ideational changes whose features we tried to recognize earlier, such as population growth, age distribution, geographic and social mobility, progressive ideas, romantic notions, and Darwinian theories. Modernization, we contend, brought with it a new emphasis on a particular eternal and universal feature of father-son relations: the Oedipus complex. It was Freud's genius to recognize this development and to give it scientific form. In so doing he may have both overgeneralized it—not allowed sufficiently for its varied historical manifestations—and overnarrowed it—concentrated too heavily on the specific father-son struggle of late authoritarian Victorian family life, to the exclusion of mothers and loving fathers.

Against this last, simplistic view, we maintain that men like James Mill and Bazarov, in order to bring about and to cope with the structural changes of an industrial society, had to toughen themselves, and to reject softness and emotions; they had, in their Oedipal experience, to reject identification with the tender, loving father. Then, as typically self-made men, they could also make the new, modernized society. As authoritarians in turn, they threatened to crush their sons, this time not by too much love but by its absence. Thus, for example, John Stuart Mill's Oedipal conflict had to take the classic form of a struggle against a strong, domineering father, with momentous consequences in terms of intellectual formulations concerning the need for free development and personal liberty. In short, we can witness at least two kinds of Oedipal conflict occurring in the nineteenth century, with vastly different implications for the nature of autonomy and authority relations, and a whole host of other aspects of men's, and women's, relations to one another. In order to give specificity to our assertions, we must now turn to the full details of the stories of James and John Stuart Mill.

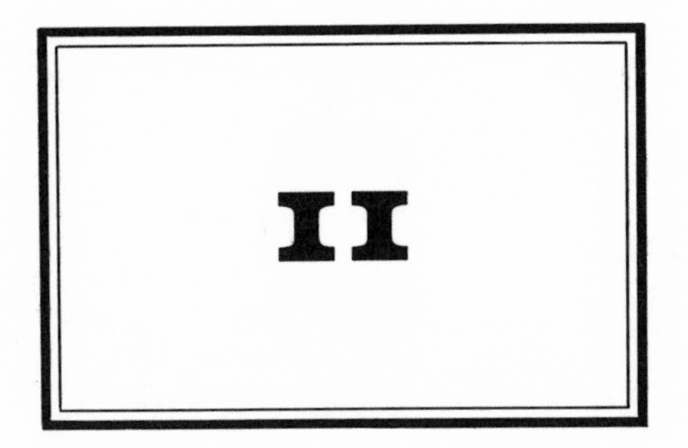

JAMES MILL

3

The Person

A Man of Flesh and Blood

JAMES MILL is not just John Stuart Mill's father. He is a person in his own right, with a life of his own: with his own father and mother, and eventually with a wife, and with other children besides John. Moreover, James Mill was a man of great accomplishments, intellectual and otherwise, even if it has been his fate to have his merits and importance overshadowed for us (though not his contemporaries) by the success of his son.

There are few good sources on James' early life. We have no autobiography, there are no published collections of his letters, and there is only one full-scale biographical treatment. Fortunately, that biography, by Alexander Bain, is a useful one, for Bain interviewed many of those who knew Mill during his youth, as well as during the course of his life, and also used a number of unpublished letters; alas, some of those letters have been destroyed or lost, and we must therefore rely principally on Bain's excerpts.[1]

Two main reasons account for the paucity of data on James Mill's early life. The first is that he came from humble circumstances and, by the time he became successful and famous, time had washed away the unkept records of his early days. The second reason is that James Mill resolutely turned his back on his past, and made no effort to preserve its evidences. Indeed, as we shall shortly see, he became a prototype of the "self-made man," who sought to pose as one practically sprung from his own loins.

In James Mill's life-history, caricature almost comes to take the place of character. He became the epitome of Utilitarian man: a "reasoning machine," calculating, cold, unfeeling, who exhibited in his own existence the "mechanical" nature of his doctrine. Both Carlyle and Dickens had him in mind when, in "Signs of the Times" and in *Hard Times*, they attacked and satirized the tendency of the Industrial Revolution to make men grow, as Carlyle put it, "mechanical in head and in heart, as well as in hand."

While acknowledging the reality behind it, we shall try to go beyond the caricature. James Mill was, in fact, a man of flesh and blood and feeling. However, his way of handling his feelings, his defenses, were reasonably typical of many in his generation, which was the first full generation of the Industrial Revolution, and much of his importance as a "character" derives from that fact. But Mill was also an individual, and I hope to show how, in the course of his personal development, he reached an identity that corresponded fittingly with the ideology which he both took on from others, such as Bentham, and helped to develop on his own. In short, caricature and character, identity and ideology interlocked in a way significant and representative of much that was critical for his entire generation, while intensely personal for Mill as an individual.

Early Life

THE FACTS about James Mill's early life can be briefly stated. He was born in 1773 in Logie Pert, a Scottish parish of about nine hundred inhabitants. His father, James, was a shoemaker. His mother, Isabel Fenton, had been a servant girl in Edinburgh when, at age seventeen, she had married James Milne. Isabel was the daughter of a farmer, and with a legend of better times in her background, she was proud and even haughty. Changing her husband's undistinguished family name of Milne to the less common Mill, she sought to realize her ambitions in her first-born son, James. (To him, for example, was allotted one of the three rooms in the house for a study, and here he was commanded to study.) A younger brother, Will, was set to the shoemaking trade, and a sister, May, was made to take care of the cow.

James Mill was gifted by nature. Pushed on by his mother, he soon came to the attention of the parish minister. At some point he attended Montrose Academy. At the age of eighteen he came to the notice of Sir John and Lady Jane Stuart, who sponsored him at the

University of Edinburgh. At the university Mill took special training in divinity, while reading widely on his own in the secular authors of the Enlightenment (we must recall that, entering in 1790, Mill was living through the stirring events of the French Revolution and its aftermath). In 1798, licensed as a preacher, Mill gave itinerant sermons and waited for a permanent post, without success. Finally, in 1802, approaching thirty and still unable to earn a living, Mill decided to seek his fortune outside barren Scotland. Sir John Stuart, off to attend to his duties in Parliament, gave his protégé a seat to London in his carriage.

Let us pause for some comments. The first concerns James Mill's father. Though we have little information about him, we know he was a shoemaker. As such, he was part of an artisan class notorious for being above the average in intelligence and interest in political affairs. Of all those in a village, the shoemaker was often the source and communication conduit of broader views and knowledge. Thus, at least by trade, Mill's father was in a tradition stretching from Thomas Hardy and the Corresponding Society to George Odger, first President of the International Workingmen's Association. He was also, on the eve of the Industrial Revolution, a part of what in France was to become the sans-culottes of the French Revolution.

We know nothing of what influence he may have had on his son. We do not even know whether he was typical of the shoemakers, as I have described them. Bain tells us: "In general character, all we can say is, that he was industrious and steady in his calling, good-natured in disposition, pious, and devout, but with no special claim to intelligence or any high mental quality." [p. 3] But Bain offers us no evidence for these assertions. He adds only that Mill's father "was very strict in all observances of a religious nature: but as regards the discipline of the children, he and his wife were (in their eldest son's judgement) blameably lax." [p. 32] James Mill's one recorded view of his father was that the latter tended to "spoil" and pet James' sister May, a strange accusation as we shall see in a moment.

Otherwise, the father seems nonexistent as a formative influence in James' life. Only at the end, shortly before dying a bankrupt, did he enter his son's life again, for James, at that time at the beginning of his career in London, had to step in to help support his father and pay off his debts.

It is the mother, Isabel Fenton, who dominates the picture of James Mill's early life. Clearly, Bain believes her to be the source of her son's intelligence and drive; perhaps Bain's prejudice is at work. In any case, she was certainly ambitious for James, treated him in an extraordinarily favored way—as Bain remarks, "nurtured and petted" him (shades of his accusation of his father's treatment of his sister)—and drove him on his way to achievement. She also seems to be the model for his pride. Bain comments that all his informants "admit that she was a proud woman . . . [and] was the object of no small spite among the villagers from her presumption in bringing up her eldest son to be a gentleman." [p. 5]

James appears to have accepted both his mother's ambitions and pride. Later in life he wrote that "My pleasure shall consist . . . in establishing to myself that name in the world for wisdom and knowledge which was the darling object even of my infant years to think I should one day attain. . . ." [p. 9] The pride showed itself in various instances, most dramatically in the story that, as a tutor in an aristocratic household, he asserted his equality and "gave offense to the heads of the family by drinking the health at table of one of the junior female members of the house." In consequence, Mill "gave up his situation, and determined to trust to his pen and his own exertions." [p. 29]

This particular story may be apocryphal, but the general point is well taken.[2] James Mill was one of numerous proud and climbing young men at the end of the eighteenth century forced to take situations as tutors in noble homes, and occupying a precarious social situation as a result. Julien Sorel, in Stendhal's *The Red and the Black*, may be considered the prototype of what, along with the governess, was one of the major social types of the time. Generally more intelligent than their patrons, often more sensitive in feelings, forced into intimate relations with members of the family, frequently involved with pupils, boys and girls, almost their own ages, and open to emotional attachments (James Mill, for example, may have been in such a situation with the Stuart's daughter, Wilhelmina), the tutor nevertheless was incessantly uncertain whether he sat "above or below the salt."

One result, for Mill as well as for Julien Sorel, was hatred for the class of aristocrats. Although James Mill honored the Stuarts and was enormously indebted to their kind offices, and although in later life he associated freely with members of the best families in Great Britain, he was notorious for his detestation of the aristocrats as a group. As he remarks under the heading *Aristocracy* in his *Commonplace Book*: "It is one of the properties of an aristocrat to hate that any persons should come among them, but of their own choosing."[3] Personal pique, stemming from the experiences of his life, undoubtedly seems to support Mill's later ideological opposition to aristocrats.

Out of the mists of James Mill's early life one fact seems to stand out. He was never really a child. At a time when Rousseau was calling attention to the child as something different from a little adult, and, if we are to believe Philippe Ariès, the "nuclear family" was coming into sharper focus, with a definite role reserved for the "child," James Mill's upbringing proceeded as if he were born a little man (is this part of the syndrome of the "self-made" man?). As Bain puts it, his "sole occupation was study." Unlike his siblings, he "neither assisted in his father's trade, nor took any part in the labour of the fields." [p. 7] We can surmise that he had no childhood friends, nor partook in the usual childish games around him; confirmation of this surmise is indirectly afforded by the way he denied a real childhood to his own son, John Stuart Mill.[4]

How did James react to his upbringing? We can only speculate. We know that his mother lavished attention and effort on the young James, calculated to appeal to his narcissistic feelings. Her successful efforts to push and to harden him for struggle by rigid discipline undoubtedly made him feel special—but not necessarily loved for himself. We can conjecture that, unconsciously, Mill in part resented his mother without ever being able openly to express such feelings. In later life Mill treated his own wife harshly; an assumption such as we have been making allows us better to understand this fact—was he getting his "own" back?—as well as the fact of his stern disciplining of his own children (especially John, his first-born), who, in any case, perceived *him* as unloving. The assumption that James Mill was, so to speak, "identifying with the aggressor," his mother, would make sense out of parts of his later life.

Yet we must make clear that this is all mere speculation. In truth, we know almost nothing about James' early life and feelings. We do know that women, in the shape first of his mother and then of Lady Jane Stuart, who was the prime instrument of his being sent to the University of Edinburgh and destined for a career in divinity (we are told it was her special wish), played a major role in inspiring and supporting him in his ambitions. We also know that when he married, his mother-in-law bought a small house for him (although he paid her a rent of fifty pounds a year). [p. 60] Women were apparently greatly attracted to him, and admired him greatly. James Mill's scornful treatment of his wife, therefore, seems inexplicable on ordinary grounds, offending even his closest friends, even if his general disparagement of women could be written off as merely the typical attitude of his time.

II / *James Mill*

A Self-Made Man

THE SHADOWY ASPECT of James Mill's early life accords well with the "self-made man" stereotype which may be used to describe him. Thus, we can apply to James Mill the words he used to eulogize his own friend, David Ricardo, on the latter's death. "Mr. Ricardo had everything to do for himself, and he did everything. . . . He had his fortune to make, he had his mind to form, he had even his education to commence and to conduct." [p. 212] James Mill, too, thought of himself as starting in "humble circumstances" and making his way independently in the world.

One result of this self-image was that James Mill largely rejected his Scottish past. Come south to London to make his fortune, as so many other Scots were doing at the time, he apparently kept his love for Scotch songs, but carefully lost his accent. We catch the flavor of his ambivalence toward his past in the anecdote recorded by Bain of a visit in 1810 by a Scotch friend. "Mrs. Mill and a young boy (John, 4 years old) were at dinner. While they were present, not a word was said of Scotland; but the moment they left the room, Mill burst out in eager inquiry after everybody in Logie Pert." [p. 110]

The son, John Stuart Mill, knew almost nothing of his father's Scottish background or origins, even though James spent an incredible amount of time with him. Thus, after the father's death in 1836, we see John Stuart Mill writing a curious letter to one of his father's youthful friends, asking for information to serve for a biography of James in the *Encyclopedia Britannica*. He asks:

> The chief points are the time and place of his birth; who and what his parents were, and anything interesting that there may be to state about them: what places of education he went to: for what professions he was educated. I believe he went through a medical course, and also that for the Church, and I have heard that he was actually licensed as a preacher, but I never heard him say so himself, and never heard of it till after his death. I do not know whether it is true or not; perhaps you do. How long did he remain at the University, or prosecute his studies for the Church? The history of his connection with the late Sir John Stuart. [p. 11]

Such ignorance by a son about his father's origins is astounding. Why did James Mill place before his son, and almost all his English acquaintances, the image of a man who came from nowhere? On a superficial level one can say that James Mill wished to play down or hide his humble beginnings, out of social shame. This would certainly be an understandable prudential reason, but it runs against the grain of James Mill's assertive pride.

In fact, the self-made aspect of James Mill begs for an explanation in Oedipal terms, even though we have no direct evidence to sustain our speculations. Psychoanalytic theory tells us that, in the basic Oedipal fantasy, catered to in this case by the excessive attention and hopes centered on James by his mother, the child wishes to become his father in relation to his mother, and also to become his *own* father. The child gives "back" life to the father, thus denying the wish to kill him, and as a result purchases his own life afresh. One thinks of Mill's paying his father's bankruptcy debts.

In short, there is a quality of myth—the Oedipal myth—to the concept of the self-made man. There seems to be a psychological need to deny one's origins, dismiss the past, and assert one's independence. We see this trait in pronounced caricature in the character of Mr. Bounderby, in Dickens' 1854 novel, *Hard Times* (in which, incidentally, a composite of James Mill and Bentham seems to be embodied in the characters of Mr. Gradgrind and Mr. Bounderby). Dickens describes Mr. Bounderby as "A man who could never sufficiently vaunt himself a self-made man. A man who was always proclaiming . . . his old ignorance and his old poverty."[5] Successful in business, Bounderby spreads the myth that he had been deserted by his parents, left in the gutter, and had thus risen all on his own. There is, however, a delicious denouement to the book when Bounderby's mother, whom, in fact, *he* had deserted, accidentally appears.

James Mill, of course, never went to such lengths, although he did seem to share with Bounderby the psychological need to cover up his origins.[6] We have tried to hint at the nature of that psychological need, despite the little direct evidence at our disposal. In the case of James Mill, there appears to be an "ideological" aspect to this denial of origins. It relates to his eventual views on religion, as reported by John Stuart Mill in the draft version of his *Autobiography*. "My father," John Stuart Mill informs us, "educated in the creed of Scotch presbyterianism, had, by his own studies and reflections been early led to reject . . . the belief in a supreme governor of the world. . . . He yielded to the conviction, *that of the origin of things nothing whatever can be known* [italics added]." It is only owing to "*the infantine state* of the general intellect of mankind" that this truth is not apparent, that people are not aware "that the question '*Who made me?*' [italics added] cannot be answered."[7]

II / *James Mill*

A Family Romance

"WHO MADE ME?" One answer is to say that I am "self-made," as the Oedipus myth suggests. There is, however, another way that the Oedipus complex may express itself in fantasy, in what Freud called a "family romance." There is some evidence that, at some level in the unconscious, James Mill adopted the Stuarts as his "real" family (having effectively denied his own, psychologically). Bain, for example, offers us an intriguing footnote.

It was surmised by Dr. Thomas Thomson, and, on his authority, believed by various friends of Mill in London, that he was related to Sir John Stuart by blood. The insinuation admits of positive disproof. Sir John did not acquire the property of Fettercairn, so as to be resident in the neighbourhood, till 1777, when Mill was four years old. I could mention other decisive circumstances, but refrain from giving more importance to what was a mere creation of Thomas Thomson's cynical fancy. [p. 10]

Can this story simply be dismissed? Thomas Thomson, a celebrated chemist, was a classmate of James Mill at Edinburgh and, as Bain himself remarks, "all through life an intimate friend." [p. 20] What is more, Bain adds, "the intimacy subsisting between Mill and Dr. Thomson makes a large part of his early biography." [p. 27] Is it more likely that Thomson would make up such a story out of whole cloth, or that Mill, unintentionally perhaps, led him to believe that a blood relationship existed with the Stuarts? Even if not "factually" true, does Thomson's "fancy" point to a "psychic reality" of great intensity and importance for Mill?

We do know that James Mill (incidentally, named after *his* father), called his first-born son John Stuart, after his patron, and his first-born daughter Wilhelmina Forbes (the latter a marriage name), after Sir John Stuart's daughter (and, later, another daughter, Jane, after Lady Jane Stuart). Now, we must be careful about the significance of "naming" at this period. A good deal of flexibility prevailed, and people changed names readily, for various reasons. Thus, Sir John Stuart himself had been born John Belsches and had changed his name only as a condition of inheriting a title. Mill, as we have seen, was originally spelled Milne until changed for reasons of social pride by the mother. James Mill, in naming his son after his patron, was following a time-honored custom (he also named another son James Bentham, and yet another George Grote, after other upper-class "patrons" or friends).

Nevertheless, with this said, we must not underestimate the psychological significance of "naming." There is power in a name, as the fairy tale of Rumpelstiltskin reminds us. When David Hume, Mill's Scottish contemporary, changed the spelling of his name from David Home, it was an assertion of autonomy from his family. Closer to the present, Thomas Woodrow Wilson, by dropping his first name, tried to get out from under the weight of his father's "Little Tommy" designation. On a larger scene, American blacks shifting from upper-class Anglo-Saxon planter names—Cassius Marcellus Clay—to so-called Muslim names—Muhammed Ali—are also trying to say something on the psychological level.

In short, for the psychohistorian "names" are of major significance. Often they involve a kind of "omnipotence of thought": If I have the power to use a name, I have a power over the object involved (the "boss" addresses his workmen by their first name, while they must call him Mr.). Even more frequently they involve a form of identification (Sigmund Freud yielded to this temptation, as when, out of admiration for the English, he named one of his sons Oliver, after Oliver Cromwell). In this light, we cannot simply pass by James Mill's naming of his children after the Stuarts as a mere result of social convention; it was that in part, but also a good deal more. It represented, I am suggesting, another element in Mill's "family romance."

There is one more piece of evidence that must be presented, though it comes from fairly late in James Mill's life. In 1817 Francis Place, Mill's friend since around 1811, wrote to him a sort of rambling letter in which he spoke of making satisfactory progress in learning the practices of our ancestors, manners, and habits of thinking, "all leading to a more correct knowledge of Jurisprudence," went on to a touching and intimate account of his asking himself, while walking, about his life, and then asked casually, "Tell me something of that old friend of yours. Baron Sir *Jno.* Stewart [sic] whose name you never before mentioned to me but of whom I have heard in relation to you although I cannot recollect from whom."[8]

James Mill responded with an uncharacteristically revealing letter, which we quote at length.

> As for Sir John Stuart, he is one of the Barons of the Exchequer in Scotland, and his estate and residence was near my father's. I was at an early age taken notice [of] by him and Lady Jane. When the time came for my going to college, it was my father's intention to send me to Aberdeen, as both nearer and less expensive than Edinburgh. Sir John, however, and Lady Jane insisted that he should let them take me to Edinburgh, which was the more celebrated university; that they would look after me, and take care that the

expense to my father should not be greater than at Aberdeen. I went to Edinburgh, and from that time lived as much in their house as in my father's, and there had many advantages, saw the best company, and had an educated man to direct my education, and who paid for several expensive branches of education, but which for him I must have gone without, and above all, had unlimited access in both town and country to well-chosen libraries. So you see I owe much to Sir John Stuart, who had a daughter, one only child, about the same age as myself, who, besides being a beautiful woman, was in point of intellect and disposition one of the most perfect human beings I have ever known. We grew up together and studied together from children, and were about the best friends that either of us ever had. She married Sir William Forbes, and after producing him six children died a few years ago of a decline. Her poor mother told me with her heart ready to break that she spoke about me with almost her last breath, and enjoined them never to allow the connection which subsisted between us to be broken. So much for the old friendship with Sir J. Stuart, which it is very proper you should know, but which I do not wish to be talked about.[9]

"I . . . lived as much in their house as in my father's," "I owe much to Sir John Stuart," "but which I do not wish to be talked about." Why not? Mill was not so far gone in fantasy as to believe that the Stuarts were his real family. There is some evidence, however, that he nourished the notion that, somehow, they had taken the place of his father (and mother?) and that in that sense, psychologically, they were indeed his own family.

Thus far we have been trying to establish (out of necessity in all too sketchy fashion) the picture of Mill as a "self-made man," and to suggest the psychological dynamics that may have gone into this conception. Let us reflect briefly on the broader psychohistorical dimensions of this attribute of Mill's personality. When, in fact, is the notion of the "self-made man" first in evidence? The data suggest that in Great Britain and America the term was in common currency by at least 1848. We need a comparative study of the concept of the self-made man, assuming it exists, in other countries such as France and Germany. We also need to raise further questions. Is the notion of the self-made man a nineteenth-century "proletarianization" or "embourgeoisement" of the Renaissance idea of the "genius," who also emerges full-blown from nowhere? Is there any notion of a self-made woman? Is there a set psychological relationship of the self-made man to the notion of motherhood and womanhood, and, if so, what is it?

O. Mannoni, a French analyst, has suggested that seventeenth-century European man's insistence on conceiving of himself as totally independent and cut off from all other humans should be regarded as compensation for deep-rooted feelings of anxiety. Thus, for example, Descartes postulated a world created solely by our rational faculties (in imitation of God), where we exist separate from all sensual intake. As Mannoni informs us, Descartes "never knew his mother and was firmly convinced that she had died at his birth [in fact an error]." Hence, he constructed a psychological as well as physical world "in which a man could do without both the help and the authority of others."[10] Indeed, Descartes deliberately placed himself in a position of abandonment in order to confront his fears that he might, in fact, *be* abandoned by his parents and other nurturant figures.

Defoe's Robinson Crusoe offers us another classic case. According to Mannoni, the book embodies the child's fantasy of a "world without men."[11] In such a world of solitude, the child has escaped from parental figures and all their prohibitions. He can people his world with obedient, childlike Fridays who obey *him*. He has become his own father.

Summing up Mannoni's work in this connection, can we see the "self-made man" of the nineteenth century as a psychological conclusion to the Descartes and Robinson Crusoes of the preceding two centuries? In all three cases there appears to be a severe rebellion against parental authority (along with an implicit defense, the claim of "independence," against the threat of removal of parental nurturance). This would fit with the gathering challenge to patriarchical political authority, as manifested in Locke's *First Treatise on Government*, with its preemptory "Who Heir?" query, and culminating with the late eighteenth-century emphasis on new beginnings, the *Novum Orbis* of the American Revolution. Throughout there is a sense of a new "generation," a fresh making, as embodied in the Constitutional Conventions of America and France, where political order will be established *de novo*, as on a blank tablet.

In a difficult but fascinating article, Judith Shklar has argued at length that "the search for origins [i.e., social and political ancestries] will be subversive."[12] Monarchy and aristocracy are clearly based on genealogical claims. In a democracy, where all are presumed equal, there is no need to know or to vaunt one's ancestors. As Shklar reminds us, "a lack of respect for one's parents was for Plato also one of the vices peculiar to democracy." On the other side, we are all familiar with the ways in which social snobbery tends to be grounded in the possession of "illustrious" ancestors (even to the point, if necessary, of manufacturing one's genealogy).

Seen in this light, the "self-made man" becomes part of a general attack on ancestry as a justification for political or social power. One denies one's own ancestors as a preliminary to denying the ancestry of others. "All men are created equal" when no one has parents. Mill's rejection of his own past permits him, in good conscience, to reject the past of the aristocrats, and their resultant claims to preeminence. No wonder that Burke, an admirer of aristocrats, rose to the defense of a prescriptive past and genealogy!

The "self-made man" should be seen as reflecting a widespread movement against existing governmental and social authority. This movement provided the psychological underpinning for the assertion of political independence. It also corresponded with the early stages in England and America of the Industrial Revolution, with its vaunted claims to laissez faire, as if the new, thrusting entrepreneurs could have made their way without nurturance or support from the rest of society. In sum, while the particular concept of the "self-made man" flourished most ostensibly in relation to the economic and social world, I have been trying to suggest that, psychologically, it was equally related to the political world. In this light, James Mill, both as character and caricature, is a prototype of both sorts of protest against authority based on ancestry. The claim to be "self-made," in short, is an enormously potent psychological form of "subversive genealogy."

Life in London

ONCE ARRIVED in London, Mill never really looked back. Like other thrusting young men of the time, he was delighted with his new possibilities. He secured a job as a hack writer, within a year persuaded a publisher to set him up as editor of a new periodical, and two years later was also editing a newspaper. As he wrote to a friend back in Scotland:

> I am extremely ambitious to remain here, which I feel to be much the best scene for a man of letters. . . . You get an ardour and a spirit of adventurousness, which you can never get an idea of among our overcautious countrymen at home. Here everybody applauds the most romantic scheme you can form. In Scotland, everybody represses you, if you but propose to step out of the beaten track.[13]

There was nothing to hold him any longer to Scotland. His mother, worn out by cares, had died of consumption (as had his brother Will). In any case, she had trained James Mill to go on without her; it was her ambition at work as much as it was his. As for his father, he had become paralyzed as well as bankrupt, and Mill's only future filial act was to pay off all the family debts. His sister May had never meant much to him in any case, and her subsequent marriage to a journeyman shoemaker retained her in a way of life that was no longer Mill's. Small wonder that Mill turned his back so completely on his origins.

At this point he began to create his own family. Soon after coming to London, Mill somehow became acquainted with a family named Burrow. Mrs. Burrow, a widow with two sons and three daughters (we never hear anything further about his future in-laws from Mill), kept an establishment for lunatics, which brought in a good income. The eldest daughter, Harriet, an admired beauty, became engaged to Mill in 1804, and they were married the next year. She was twenty-three, and he, as we know, was thirty-two.

One surviving letter from the courtship, Bain tells us, shows Mill filled with affection and tender love. Alas, within a year or so of the marriage, and shortly after the birth in 1806 of his first child, John Stuart, James Mill's feelings began to change, and he now poured scorn on his young wife as a mere unintelligent *hausfrau*. He maintained this harsh attitude, whose outer expression he was unable to control even in the presence of his friends, through the rest of the marriage and the birth of eight more children. It is the one overwhelming breakdown in James Mill's otherwise almost total control over his intimate feelings, and it enormously affected the attitude of his son, John, toward his own mother and women in general in complicated ways we shall need to explore later.

For James Mill, the period 1802–1805 represented a major turning point in his life. In leaving Scotland physically, he also left it psychologically. As we have seen, he became something of a "self-made man," taking on now a new identity as an Englishman. Fortunately for Mill, there was no "nationality crisis" connected with this step. England, unlike, say, Germany, was set in its self-definition, and Mill had a ready-made identity which he could assume.

More importantly, Mill also gave up the ministerial calling for which he had been intended by both his mother and his first patrons, the Stuarts (especially Lady Jane). This marked, it would seem, the first rejection of the women who had helped and pushed him in his career; while retaining the psychological direction of his ambitious mother's training, Mill rebelled against the specific form she had imposed upon it. Mill's emigration also marked a shift from a religious to a secular career, and in this he was prototypic of a whole wave of opinion and movement of social change engulfing the late eighteenth and early nineteenth centuries. Like the fictional Julien Sorel, and the real Adam Smith, G. F. Hegel, and innumerable others, James Mill participated in perhaps the most important long-term transformation of the nineteenth century: the increasing secularization of life and thought.

Mill now became a "man of letters," a generalized intellectual. At a time when professionalization and specialization were beginning to spread in numerous fields, James Mill still felt competent to write and preach in depth on a wide range of topics: government, jurisprudence, economics, logic, psychology, history, pedagogy, and so on.[14] In this, of course, he was still quite typical of his age; by John Stuart Mill's time such virtuosity had become something of an exceptional feat rather than a normal function.

As a generalized man of letters and social critic, James Mill may be compared with similar types in Russia, where by the 1830s a class later to be known as the "intelligentsia" came into being. In autocratic Russia the intelligentsia were forced to operate outside of existing society and government, harassed by censorship and poverty. In England, however, unlike Russia, there was a large and growing middle class desirous of supporting a man such as Mill within the Establishment, rather than forcing him into revolutionary activity. In fact, the middle class needed men like Mill, steeled to lead it *into* the Establishment. Thus, the relation was reciprocal.

In any event, within a year of coming to London Mill was able to earn a decent living by his pen, and it was as a journalist-editor that he continued to support his large and growing family. Still, his position was precarious, dependent on the day-to-day success of his writings. He knew that he could not have his valued independence unless he established a more solid basis for his fame and fortune. So he began to write the *History of British India*, expecting to finish it in about three years. Conceived around the same time as John Stuart, the book appeared not in three years, but only at the end of twelve long, arduous years. Boy and book, it seems, developed into maturity together. In the end the book was to make James Mill's reputation, and help to secure for him the well-paid post of examiner at the East India Company. At that point James Mill finally moved from the precarious life of an intellectual, a man of letters, to the established position of a high civil servant.

But that is to anticipate our story. If 1802 can be seen as one point in James Mill's continuing "crisis of identity," 1808 would seem to represent a second.[15] In that year he met Bentham and became his disciple; at the same time he began firmly and even publicly to renounce his previous religious views. Although he had given up the ministerial career in 1802, Mill had at first held on to the religion. He still went to church, and he had all his children baptized. But with the influence and support of Bentham he now began to attack the clerical establishment, although not Christianity itself, fiercely and stridently (though modulated in print for reasons of prudence). Thus, by the age of thirty-five he had finally revolted against the specific content as well as the form of his mother and Lady Jane Stuart's original ambitions for him.

James Mill had become a Utilitarian. What Bentham confirmed for him was a complete ideology to go with his new identity (and vice versa). In its simplest, most provisional terms, Utilitarianism (or Philosophical Radicalism, as it came to be called) advocated a radical legal reform, based on the codifications of Bentham, which insisted that laws and legislation ought to aim at, and be measured by, the principle of "the greatest good of the greatest number." In the economic sphere, Utilitarian doctrine espoused rigorous free trade and industry, appealing to the theories of Malthus, Ricardo, Bentham, and James Mill as well. We can turn to John Stuart Mill for a summary of two other major points of the Utilitarian creed: it meant, he tells us, "In politics, an almost unbounded confidence in the efficacy of two things: representative government and complete freedom of discussion. In psychology . . . the formation of all human character by circumstances, through the universal Principle of Association, and the consequent unlimited possibility of improving the moral and intellectual condition of mankind by education."[16]

As we have already mentioned, the publication in 1817 of the *History of British India* established Mill's reputation firmly, while also turning him into an important civil servant. Thus he was now in a strengthened position to implement his Utilitarian theories as a movement as well as a doctrine. On this basis, he exerted, as we shall see, a tremendous influence on the governance of India. He also gave leadership in domestic politics (see Chapter 4), culminating in the Reform Bill of 1832. Bain has caught the flavor of his leadership: "Mill, I take it, while so daring as to be accounted revolutionary, was really the safest politician of his age. In the first French Revolution, no such man was to be found."[17] In sum, Mill had achieved his full identity: He was a revolutionary leader whose energies and ambitions were safely channeled in the ways of reform. Character and circumstance, personality and party, individual and class—all combined in Mill and the Utilitarians in a special and mutually advantageous symbiosis.

Hard Work

ONE DOMINANT TRAIT in Mill's character was his overwhelming dedication to hard work. He both preached and practiced the ethic of hard work, the need to labor. "He who works more than all others," Mill admonished his son, "will in the end excel all others."[18] And Mill suited his actions to his words, putting in prodigious hours at his writing and editing. For a few months during the final stages of preparing his *History*, he "got up at four in the morning, and worked till twelve at night," according to Mrs. Mill.[19] This, of course, was extraordinary, but not all that different from Mill's normal work schedule. "Mill is beyond comparison the most diligent fellow I ever knew or heard of," declared Francis Place, whose own early life was one of unremitting toil; "almost any other man would tire and give up teaching, but not so he; three hours every day, frequently four, are devoted to the children, and there is not a moment's relaxation."[20] All this, needless to say, was in addition to Mill's required journalistic and literary labors.

Freud has defined the good life as "Liebe und Arbeit" (love and work). Certainly Mill tried to pursue the good life in terms of the second quality (though without the first). Like so many others in nineteenth-century England and Scotland, having rejected religion and the Calvinist dogmas, Mill retained the Calvinist ethos in a secularized form. True to his Utilitarian convictions, Mill believed that one educated and shaped oneself—and others—through that same dedication to hard work. Character was "produced" just as was any other commodity. One was not "self-made" just by wishing; one had to work hard at it.

Frequently, it must be admitted, there is a touch of self-pity in Mill's descriptions of his labors. He often complains, as in his letter to Macvey Napier, publisher of the *Encyclopedia Britannica*, of the "heavy load which I have long had upon my shoulders." There are, surprisingly, also gaps in his compulsive work habits. Mill appears, from his own comments, to have been frequently dilatory in answering his correspondence, and his replies are filled with such statements as "on turning to your letter, for the purpose of answering it, and observing the date, I have reason to be ashamed of myself," and "I ought to have replied to your kind letter before this time. . . ."[21]

All of this would seem to make Mill more human, at least to us, since his work habits apparently could falter. But his own view of himself is better reflected in his comment to Henry Brougham: "I hope you will make the best use of the little time you have for recruiting [i.e., proselytizing]. You must remember that the best machine is impossible of being worn out."[22] Like his enemies, Mill seemed to prefer the caricature of himself as a "machine" which never wore out, but worked incessantly. In this case, the caricature was dangerously close to the true character.

In the largest context, work, as all good Calvinists knew, justified one's existence to God. Freudians would add that it entitled one to nurturance, for it fulfilled parental ambitions for achievement as well as serving as a form of sublimation of both libido and aggression. Mill preferred to look at the matter in good Utilitarian terms. Work was one's duty to the community. Those who did not work betrayed their duty to society in two ways. They were parasites, and they were likely to be stupid. In his *Essay on Government*, he put the matter succinctly:

There may be a strong presumption that any aristocracy monopolizing the powers of government would not possess intellectual powers in any very high perfection. Intellectual powers are the offspring of labor. But a hereditary aristocracy are deprived of the strongest motives to labor. The greater part of them will, therefore, be defective in those mental powers.[23]

Fortunately, in place of the "defective" aristocracy there were men like Mill himself: self-made, hard-working individuals of the "middle rank." Mill announced their claim to rule in no uncertain terms:

There can be no doubt that the middle rank, which gives to science, to art, and to legislation itself their most distinguished ornaments, and is the chief source of all that has exalted, and refined human nature, is that portion of the community of which, if the basis of representation were ever so far extended, the opinion would ultimately decide.[24]

In back of this view lay Mill's and the Utilitarians' general conception of government. The purpose of government is to attain the "greatest possible happiness of the greatest possible number," and the way to attain this end is to protect men in the fruits of their labor; government has no other function. Only a representative government, whose interests are identical with those of the community at large, can be expected to protect and not prey on the generality of citizens. How happy a conclusion for Mill and the Utilitarians that the one group whose interests are identical with all is the middle class (whose "wisdom" the lower classes will always allow to guide them)!

Anxiety

THE COMPULSION to work arose from many elements of Mill's early life and fulfilled many functions in his psychic economy, one of which, surely, was to allay his sense of anxiety. That he was anxious there seems no doubt. In 1807, still with his fortune and place to make, he wrote a Scottish friend nostalgically: "Have you no good Kirk yet in your neighborhood which you could give me, and free me from this life of toil and anxiety which I lead here? . . . I know not how it is: but I toil hard, spend little, and yet am never the more forward."[25] Nothing appears to have changed seven years later, when Edward Wakefield wrote Place that their mutual friend, Mill, "says he is very well, but looks otherwise—thin in the face; and I misread him if he is not in a state of anxiety." To this Place replied, "Shall such a man be left to the chance of sickness to reduce him to absolute want?[26] Shall he be destroyed by anxiety and corroding cares, which the firmest mind cannot always repel when no prospect of better days presents itself?" Place then proposed a scheme (which came to nought) for raising £300 among Mill's friends, to be put anonymously to his credit at the bank.[27]

To his friends, Mill's situation was clearly precarious. Thus, even on the eve of his success, with the *History of British India* published and a lucrative and settled future about to open before him in the East India House, Mill was still tempted by the prospect of a professorial chair at a Scottish university which would offer him security and comfort.[28]

One suspects that Mill also still felt anxious about being a Scotsman in England. In 1802, as we have seen, he wrote to a friend in Scotland extolling the English openness to achievement in contrast to Scottish repression of the innovator. It is, therefore, with great surprise that we see him writing in 1818 to Macvey Napier (true, a Scotsman) about a mutual acquaintance: "Englishly educated people . . . are all hostile to him, as they (at least the greater part of them) are hostile to everybody who seeks to advance the boundaries of human knowledge, which they have sworn to keep where they are."[29]

Obviously, Mill felt himself surrounded by enemies, a fact which added to his financial and other anxieties. Incredible as it may seem, James Mill is even able to make the formation of opinions a matter of the greatest anxiety. Writing in 1826, now successful and established, Mill argues that actions are based on opinions, and opinions formed on evidence. Therefore, the weighing of evidence is crucial. This is how Mill puts it: "The habit of the neglect of evidence, therefore, is the habit of disregarding the good and evil of our fellow-creatures. It is the habit of hard-heartedness and cruelty, on the largest scale, and rooted in the deepest part of the mind . . . of what is viscious and degraded in human character." His sweeping conclusion is: "One of the grand objects of education should be, to generate a *constant and anxious concern* about evidence . . ." [italics added].[30]

There is a kind of transplanted Calvinistic concern and anxiety manifested here. The "evidences" are not about one's salvation directly, but, in good Utilitarian fashion, about the "saving" of one's fellow men by having the correct opinions. Michael Walzer has discussed the strong role of anxiety in Calvin and among the Puritans in his book, *The Revolution of the Saints*, and tried to indicate how Calvinist doctrine sought to allay its followers' fears. He has suggested, in a preliminary article, that Calvinist personalities can be "best explained in terms of the actual experiences of exile, alienation, and social mobility" which led to discipline, self-control, and acceptance of aloneness, and to the "bold effort to shape a personality amidst 'chaos.' "[31] Mill's "exile" was self-imposed, but, added to the stresses of social mobility, alienation, and insecurity, it seems to have evoked the same feeling of anxiety. Hard work could serve as the basis not only for social mobility but as an anodyne for the fears and anxieties awakened in Mill by the unknown threats surrounding him in a new and changing society.

Controlled Emotions

WHAT OTHER character traits besides hard work would be helpful in steeling a man trying to make his way in an anxious world? In general, it seems, Mill needed intense self-control and repression of feeling. The intense self-control, mainly, one suspects, of aggressive impulses, was exhibited by Mill to perfection in public. As Bain tells us, "He could exercise perfect self-control in his intercourse with the world." At home the control broke down; here Mill did not need to feel threatened through retaliation by his own loss of control. In Bain's words, "at home he did not care to restrain the irritability of his temperament . . . the thing that has left the most painful memories was the way that he allowed himself to speak and behave to his wife and children before visitors."[32]

Mill's political and intellectual success was undoubtedly due in major part to his rigid public control of his emotions. He impressed others with his steellike qualities. Some of his power and control were also exerted in relation to sex. For example, Mill warmly congratulated a friend on being "past the hey-day of the blood when the solid qualities are apt to be overlooked for the superficial"; he opposed dances "such as slide into lasciviousness"; and he, who had nine children of his own, extended his personal and psychological needs to public ones and became one of the first exponents of birth control. Here the connection of bourgeois economics and sexuality, so handily linked in Malthus, becomes obvious, and the mechanism of sublimation is brought evidently into play. As Peter Cominos has shown for a later period, the abstraction of *Homo Economicus* required a tandem mate in an abstraction of *Homo Sensualis*; part of Mill's "moral superiority" over his contemporaries was the strength of his control in the areas of both work and sex.[33]

Soft and affectionate feelings, as well as sexual impulses, were also severely repressed by Mill. As Bain admits, though he tries to defend his subject from the accusations, local tradition in Logie Pert censured Mill's conduct toward his paternal family. "He is commonly styled 'a hard unfeeling man,'" Bain reports.[34] Place, too, in spite of his loyalty to Mill, attests to the fact that Mill starved the affection of his friends as well as that of his family. "He could help the mass," Place wrote, "but he could not help the individual, not even himself, or his own."[35] Well might Place have been thinking of the tragic moments when, with his wife dying of cancer, Mill could only talk callously of their meeting as usual.[36]

Mill's defense against the accusation that he was an unloving, ungiving, and unaffectionate man in his personal relations is implicitly made in a passage he wrote in his *Commonplace Book*.

> Love institutions! Oh yes. Agreed. But what is the best way of loving? Does the man who applauds and encourages all the vices of his children, or the man who vigorously detects, and rigidly prohibits them, take the best way of loving his children? Love institutions! You may as well say to us, love women! There is no great danger of our failing in that, though we may not all love them in the right way.[37]

Here we have the same "judging" attitude that Mill believed to be the prime requirement of an historian. One chastizes and judges even what one likes. Mill was "hard" on himself; how else could he show love to others than by behaving in the same way to them as to himself? This, in any case, was James Mill's only way of loving, and we can guess that it was derived from his mother and her treatment of him.

But, as Place has reminded us, Mill could feel for and "help the mass." He was undeniably an effective leader, aiming at the "greatest good of the greatest number" in the abstract, though unable to love in the particular. A hint at this sort of personality is given us by Freud, who describes the ideal leader, the "father of his people" (that is, of the primal horde). Asserting that the will of the leader needed no reinforcement from others, Freud declares that "his ego had few libidinal ties; he loved no one but himself, or other people only insofar as they served his needs. To objects his ego gave away no more than was barely necessary." Freud's conclusion is most interesting: "He, at the very beginning of the history of mankind, was the 'superman' whom Nietzsche only expected from the future."[38]

How does Mill measure up to this picture of the "superman"? "He loved no one but himself." Certainly Mill had no overt love for his original family, except perhaps for his mother, and his love for her was hardly demonstrative. His wife, after the first year or so, he treated with disdain. His first-born, John, lamented the absence of a loving parent and admitted that he respected but did not love his father. As John tells us in the *Autobiography*, "For passionate emotions of all sorts, and for everything which has been said or written in exaltation of them, he [his father] professed the greatest contempt. He regarded them as a form of madness."[39] Of all James Mill's friends, only Ricardo seems to have awakened strong and tender feelings; it was his death that Mill lamented openly. Otherwise, Mill's reputation and much of his power were seen to lie in his absence of feelings—in short, of libidinal ties. Even Mill's friendly biographer, Bain, admitted as much:

> It is a consequence of the determined pursuit of one or two all-comprehending ends, that a man has to put aside many claims of mere affection, feeling, or sentiment. Not that he is necessarily devoid of the warm, social emotions: he may have them, in fair measure; not, however, in an overpowering degree. It is that they stand in his way to other things; and so are, on certain occasions, sacrificed; leading thereby to the reproach of being of a nature hard and unfeeling. Such was Pitt, and such was Mill.[40]

An Independent Man

AS a self-made man, dedicated to hard, anxious work, free from the normal ties of love and affection, Mill also vaunted himself as an independent man. Another way of putting this is to say that he strongly feared dependency and dependent relations. (The threat is that the source of supply may disappear; as psychoanalyst Otto Fenichel puts it, dependency fear involves "The fear that the external means of satisfaction might possibly fail to arrive. It is the 'fear over loss of love' or rather loss of help and protection.")[41]

We have already recounted how, out of pride, Mill presumably asserted his independence when a tutor in a noble family, and how the resulting quarrel supposedly occasioned his leaving Scotland to go to England. We have also quoted his encomium of Ricardo. In the *Commonplace Book*, discussing the impropriety of theatricals, Mill gave some of his intimate reasons for deprecating the career of an actor:

> In the choosing of a line of life, it is always a sign of an erect and *manly* character to choose those employments, however poor, which are least allied to *dependence* . . . where it is necessary for them to court the favour of others, and to dread the frown, which they must endeavor to escape by way out of submission and compliance . . . [italics added].[42]

Note that manliness is equated with independence. In Mill's *Commonplace Book*, in an entry marked "Effeminacy," he also cites Schlegel to the effect that "effeminacy has become the characteristic of the English people, among whom any marks of the manly mind so rarely appears." Then Mill concludes, "This a fertile subject."[43]

Oddly enough, with all the stress on independence and manliness, James Mill, the self-made man, was always being helped, *being patronized*, by others. As we have already noted, first he received special attention from his mother. Next the Stuarts were, in fact, his patrons. Once in London, Mill married a girl above his own station who brought him a dowry and whose mother bought him a house. Later he became the acknowledged discipline of Jeremy Bentham and lived advantageously with his "master" for a number of summers. Francis Place, the master tailor, lent him money.

Moreover, Mill was not above fulsome flattery on occasions. Thus he boastfully writes the Swiss publicist, Dumont, praising his work, and adding: "Bentham himself now feels no small share of the opinion which I am here expressing; and he has had no want of urging to bring him to that state." Writing to his friend Brougham, who was Lord Chancellor at the time, Mill asserts: "I know not when the time was, in the history of our species, that more depended on the health of one man, than depends at this moment on yours. The progress of mankind would lose a century by the loss of you." A perusal of Mill's correspondence with Macvey Napier will show how Mill's initial assertions of independence grow mild and are retracted out of reasons of convenience.[44]

Mill seemed oblivious to these unconscious lapses of his into "courting the favor of others." But threats to his independence he acknowledged overtly, and tried to deal with vigorously. Scrupulously he paid off his debt to Place. When his own father went bankrupt, as we have noted, he paid off these debts as well. In 1814, when Bentham took umbrage at one of Mill's actions, Mill wrote him that "it has been one of the great purposes of my life to avoid pecuniary obligations, even in the solicitation or acceptance of ordinary advantages—hence the penury in which I live." Then Mill added rather cryptically: "To receive obligations of any sort from you was not a matter of humiliation to me, but of pride. And I only dreaded it from the danger to which I saw that it exposed our friendship."[45] Bentham, however, disregarded Mill's suggestion that he move out of Bentham's house, and the two families lived together for another four years. As for Mill's "repayment" to his wife, we have seen what form that took.

Dependence and independence—these were the poles of Mill's relation to all figures of authority and sustenance. Such a personal pattern fitted consistently with wider, ideological needs, corresponding beautifully with the Utilitarian stress on individualism. In both cases, we would suggest, the true state of affairs was being masked. Mill himself was extremely ambivalent in his feelings and behavior, constantly putting himself, or allowing himself to be put, in the position of a protégé or disciple. In the case of economic liberalism, the vaunted independence asserted by the commercial and industrial proponents of laissez faire was, in fact, based on the covert if not overt protection, patronage, and support of the state.[46] Mill's character and Utilitarian ideology (political as well as economic) were both part of what Erikson has penetratingly characterized as "co-determined Processes."[47]

Patron and Protégé

MILL'S RELATIONS with Bentham brought into sharpest relief his psychological reactions to dependency and independency. When the two men first met in 1808, Bentham was sixty years old, yet still scarcely known to the English public; Mill was thirty-five, struggling to support a growing family, and with only some small reputation as a writer and journalist, his major work on the history of India still ahead of him. Bentham needed an intelligent disciple and a forceful man to make a political philosophy and party out of his Utilitarian doctrines; Mill needed—psychologically and economically—a patron and a philosophical mentor under whom he could serve with security. As Elie Halévy says of Bentham: "It seems as though the intrusion into his life of James Mill was needed to make him a democrat. . . . It was to James Mill that this hermit, this maniac owed the fact that he became the popular chief of a party that was half philosophical and half political." As Bentham himself saw the relation, writing about Mill in 1828 to a friend: "For these three or four-and-twenty years he has numbered himself among my disciples; for upwards of twenty years he has been receiving my instructions; for about the half of each of five years, he and his family have been my guests." And Mill, in a letter to Bentham of 1814, spoke of "the cause [Utilitarianism] which has been the great bond of connection between us . . . that system of important truths of which you have the immortal honour to be the author, but of which I am a most faithful and fervent disciple . . . nobody at all so likely to be your real successor as myself. . . . I am pretty sure you cannot think of any other person whose whole life will be devoted to the propagation of the system."[48]

As a self-proclaimed disciple of Bentham, James Mill not only provided the key political leadership for the radicals, but synthesized a number of diverse currents of thought into one cohesive doctrine: Utilitarianism. "It was James Mill," as Halévy observes, "who, having become a Benthamite, perceived the logical link which connected the ideas of Bentham and Malthus, became a Malthusian and made use of Ricardo to incorporate the ideas of Malthus with the tradition of Adam Smith."[49]

Mill had had one other major spiritual mentor before Bentham: Dugald Stewart, a teacher and philosopher at the University of Edinburgh. As Mill wrote Macvey Napier, "I never knew anything nearly so eloquent as some of the lectures of Mr. Stewart. I never heard anything like so fine speaker [sic]. The taste for the studies which have formed my favorite pursuits, and which will be so to the end of my life I owe to Mr. Stewart."[50] There can be no question of Stewart's profound intellectual effect on Mill. Through Stewart, the interests and ways of thinking summed up in the phrase "Scottish Enlightenment" were brought to bear on the young James Mill. So, too, Stewart provided Mill with a model, a figure with which to identify.

Stewart, however, never took on the qualities of patron or, more importantly perhaps, father-figure for Mill. (In fact, as Mill said, Stewart would at best only be familiar with his face, from the lecture hall.) "I was the spiritual father of Mill," declared Bentham, and we are prepared to agree with him.[51] (It is also worth noting that Mill first met Bentham in 1808, the same year that his own father died.)

Bentham was a sort of spiritual or second father to many of his disciples—for example, Francis Place's habitual mode of address to him was "My dear old Father"—but we must assume a special quality in this paternal relation with Mill.[52] It must have taken the place not only of his own father, but, to some extent, of his "family romance" parent, Sir John Stuart. Mill's "parentage" problem, I am suggesting, was acute and overdetermined.

The apostolic laying on of hands was further reinforced when James Mill placed his own son, John, then six years old, under Bentham as a sort of godfather. Bentham appears to have made the first overture when he declared:

If you will appoint me guardian to Mr. John Stuart Mill, I will, in the event of his father's being disposed of elsewhere [James Mill had just had an acute attack of gout, and thus the possibility suddenly seemed real], take him to Q.S.P. [Queen's Square Place, Bentham's residence] and there or elsewhere, by whipping or otherwise [humorous remark, needless to say], do whatsoever may seem most necessary and proper, for teaching him to make all proper distinctions, such as between the Devil and the Holy Ghost, and how to make Codes and Encyclopaedias, and whatsoever else may be proper to be made, so long as I remain an inhabitant of this vale of tears.

In a letter of July 28, 1812, Mill responded to his patron in the same somewhat jocular vein:

I am not going to die, notwithstanding your zeal to come in for a legacy. However, if I were to die any time before this poor boy is a man, one of the things that would pinch me most sorely, would be, the being obliged to leave his mind unmade to the degree of excellence of which I hope to make it. But another thing is, that the only prospect which would lessen that pain, would be the leaving him in your hands. I therefore take your offer quite seriously, and stipulate, merely, that it shall be made as good as possible; and then we may perhaps leave him a successor worthy of both of us.[53]

Bentham had indeed become interested in the boy. A child prodigy himself, he might well have rejoiced at the chance of exercising paternal solicitude for another such prodigy. In any case, he wished both his spiritual "son," James, and godson, John, to be near him. A few years later he let a house very near his own advantageously to Mill, and there the growing family resided for the next sixteen years. At the same time, upon acquiring a grand summer residence, Ford Abbey, he insisted on having the society of the Mills there, too; as Bain informs us: "The whole family went there every year, for four years, and spent, not the summer merely, but nine or ten months at a stretch."[54]

Mill's services to his patron were numerous and critical. He did many small favors for him, helped manage his affairs, edited his papers, and generally served as an amanuensis. (John's services were mustered as late as 1825 to help in editing Bentham's papers on *The Rationale of Judicial Evidence*, a long and technical book.) In turn, he insisted on his position as Bentham's foremost disciple and, moreover, pushed his mentor on to increased efforts even in the face of approaching old age.

It was a symbiotic relation, mutually advantageous. But it contained great dangers for James Mill. It both satisfied his unacknowledged dependency wishes—we have seen how deeply the patron theme ran through his life—and threatened to reawaken his dependency fears. The latter element appears to have gained the upper hand some time around 1818, when a definite coolness seems to have arisen between the two men.

Others had noticed Mill's dependency even earlier. As Wakefield wrote Place in 1814: "I am deeply interested about Mill, for, with all my admiration of Mr. Bentham, he is too good a man to become a dependent upon any individual; and I fear that the increasing expenses of his young family must render him so."[55] James Mill himself had momentarily, and, at the beginning of his residence with Bentham, openly admitted to the danger. In a long letter to Bentham (September 19, 1814) he signaled his pride and independence. We must quote extensively from it:

I see that you have extracted umbrage from some part of my behaviour; and have expressed it by deportment so strongly, that I have seriously debated with myself whether propriety permitted that I should remain any longer in your house. I considered, however, that I could not suddenly depart, without proclaiming to the world that there was a quarrel between us; and this, I think, for the sake of both of us, and more especially the cause which has been the great bond of connexion between us, we should carefully endeavour to avoid. . . . In reflecting upon the restraint which the duty which we owe to our principles—to that system of important truths of which you have the immortal honour to be the author, but of which I am a *most faithful and fervent disciple*—and hitherto, I have fancied, my *master's favourite disciple* [italics added]; in reflecting, I say, upon the restraint which regard for the interest of our system should lay upon the conduct of both of us, I have considered that there was nobody at all so likely to be your real successor as myself. . . . It is this relation, then, in which we stand to the grand cause—to your own cause—which makes it one of the strongest wishes of my heart that nothing should occur which may make other people believe there is any interruption to our friendship.

For this purpose, I am of opinion that it will be necessary not to live so much together. . . .

My experience has led me to observe that there are two things which are peculiarly fatal to friendship, and these are great intimacy and pecuniary obligations. It has been one of the great purposes of my life to avoid pecuniary obligations, even in the solicitation or acceptance of ordinary advantages—hence the penury in which I live. To receive obligations of any sort from you was not a matter of humiliation to me, but of pride. . . . At your solicitation, that I might be near to you, I came to live in a house of which, as the expense of it was decidedly too great for my very small income, part of the expense was to be borne by you. . . . As it would be ruinous for me to bear the whole expense of the house, of course I must leave it. . . .

As I propose all this most sincerely, with a view of preserving our friendship—and as the only means, in my opinion, of doing so—the explanation being thus made, I think we should begin to act towards one another without any allusion whatsoever towards the past; talk together, and walk together, looking forward solely, never back. . . . For my part, I have been at pains to conceal even from my wife that there is any coldness between us. I am strongly in hopes that the idea of the limitation will give an additional interest to our society, and overbalance the effects of a too long and uninterrupted intimacy, which I believe to be the great cause—for there is such a disparity between the apparent cause, my riding out a few times in the morning with Mr. Hume, to take advantage of his horses in seeing a little of the country, instead of walking with you, and the great umbrage which you have extracted—that the disposition must have been prepared by other causes, and only happened first to manifest itself on that occasion.

I remain, with an esteem which can hardly be added to, and which, I am sure, will never be diminished, my dear Friend and Master, most affectionately yours.[56]

Though expressed in cold and restrained terms, one senses the power of Mill's feelings. For Bentham, one suspects, it was merely the ill humor of one of his spiritual sons, of a disciple—he had many, after all. For Mill the issue touched on his most intimate emotions. At any rate, as Bain puts it, "The dose so effectually purged Bentham's humours, that a full reconciliation followed, and the two lived together for four years, in the intimacy that Mill accounted so hazardous."[57] The relationship was indeed emotionally hazardous, and it continued its up and down course throughout its remaining years.

We can guess that the successful publication of the *History*, and Mill's subsequent entrance on a secure and comfortable career in the East India House in 1818, must have made him less willing than ever to be dependent on Bentham, or to accept umbrage from him. Bain's account is that "There was . . . a growing coolness latterly [after 1818], of which I cannot describe the steps for want of exact information."[58] The real break, however, finally came in 1827. Bentham had his nephew enter Mill's house without warning and take out books presumably lent by Bentham. We know of the occasion from Mill's letter to Bentham of February 22, 1827, written in white heat, with a compressed fury.

Mr. Mill presents his respects to Mr. Bentham, and begs to be furnished with a list of the books which his nephew took from Mr. Mill's house this morning. Without this list, which, if Mr. Bentham's nephew could have waited till Mr. M. [sic] had been present, and could have told what books were and were not his, would not have been necessary, it is impossible for Mr. Mill to tell how many of his books have been taken away under the guise of being Mr. Bentham's. Mr. Mill, even by the glance which he has taken of his shelves, can [mention?] several of his which have been taken away—Macpherson's Hist. [sic] of Commerce [from [?] four?] [vo?] vol. 4 [th?], unbound, Mr. Bentham's copy being bound and on his own shelves—Colebrooke's Digest of Hindu Law, of which Mr. Bentham's own copy will also be found on his shelves—Nichol's Anecdotes, 8 or 10 vol. 8vo., of which Mr. Bentham never had a copy—and several large volumes of Parl. Papers from the top shelves between the windows in Mr. M.'s room. Among the virtues which Mr. B. has discovered in his nephew, Mr. M. cannot forbear adding his testimony to the handsome manner he has of doing things.

Another glance shows Mr. Mill that Mad. du Deffand's Letters have been taken away, which are not Mr. Bentham's but his: also a number of volumes of the *New* Annual Register.[58]

There is no signature. James Mill was obviously livid. This particular adoptive father-son relationship has dissolved in acrimony.[59] As always, Mill restrained his feelings in public. So as not to injure the Utilitarian "cause," he covered over the extent of his rupture with Bentham. The quiet tone reasserted itself, as when he responded to Dumont on July 31, 1828: "The old Philosopher precisely the same—but little seen by me. Writing letters is now his great occupation, on the various occasions which excite him, many of them very small ones."[60] On Bentham's death in 1832, there is no evidence of any deep emotional reaction by Mill. His son, John, did write a commemorative notice in the *Examiner*.[61] Otherwise, the "foundations of attachment" seemed completely eroded.

Character and Caricature

ALTHOUGH the emotional attachment between James Mill and Bentham ultimately dissolved, the intellectual alliance held. Mill was, as he had confessed, a true spiritual son of the old philosopher. It was Mill, in fact, who took over leadership of the Utilitarian movement, providing not only a synthesis of the doctrine and, as we shall see in Chapter 4, a method by which to propagate it, but also a prototype of the personality and character of the men who were to live by and for it. To quote Halévy:

A new type of humanity, with its virtues and its failings, began to be sketched out around Bentham, thanks not to Bentham but to James Mill. . . . He was nothing more than the man of abstract convictions, a living example of the Utilitarian morality and of the absolute identification of private interest with the good of humanity . . . without eyes or ears for the beauties of nature and art, having systematically destroyed in himself the spontaneous impulses of feeling.[62]

It was intellect and intellectuality, not feelings, that Mill emphasized. We can understand this overvaluation of intellect when we remember that it was the indispensable means of Mill's rise from humble beginnings. We can also remember that his disdain for his wife was based on her lack of intellectuality, and we shall see that intellectuality was his main link to his son, John Stuart Mill. As best he could, James Mill tried to make the world rational, not least by seeking to behave as if he were a rational machine. Such an attitude and attempt must be seen as a measure, not of the absence of feelings, but of their strength. Powerful feelings, which were unacceptable, required massive repression and the creation of rigid defenses.

So, too, Mill's stress on his independence, on his being a "self-made man," masked a pervasive need to be taken care of, to be loved and patronized. In a threatening and anxious universe, a world of emotional scarcity sat side by side with one of material scarcity. As we have seen, Mill's abilities and laborious activity succeeded in mitigating the latter; he was characterologically incapable, as a result of the indelible imprinting of his childhood, of doing anything to change the former.

In studying Mill's life we have tried to focus attention on the formation of his character, to offer a sketch of his life-history. We have also attempted to indicate the coherence between his character traits —the emphasis on self-control and hard work, rejection of the past, the claim to being "self-made," and the fear of dependency coupled with the ambivalence thereto—and some of the doctrines of Utilitarianism (especially the espousal of laissez faire and the hatred of hereditary aristocracy as giving political or social power). In the chapters to come we shall highlight other features of Utilitarian doctrine. Our assertion of coherence, however, must not be mistaken for an assertion of causation; we are talking here about what I have called "corresponding processes."

To use Eriksonian terms, we are asserting that Identity has become intrinsic to Ideology. Moreover, our thesis is that, in the course of developing his own identity, James Mill was able to offer an important type of leadership to a significant number of his contemporaries who were searching for an ideology and an identity of their own. We remember James Mill mainly as the father of John Stuart Mill; his contemporaries knew him, on the one hand, as a caricature—the picture held of him by his enemies—and, on the other, as a strong, dynamic, and almost charismatic character—the view taken of him by his followers. Mill, in our judgment, was equally important as both caricature and character.

4

Government and Leadership

Mill's Utilitarianism

TREATISES or essays in political science frequently claim to offer universal knowledge, transcending any particular society, and are as frequently perceived by their readers as primarily contributions to pressing political problems of the moment. James Mill's *Essay on Government* has long been looked at in both ways. It is less usual, however, to view a treatise on political science as also being based on the person of the author, on the way his pressing problems and needs shape the way he conceives and perceives the political world. Yet surely we have already seen enough of James Mill to realize how strongly his feelings were interwoven with his ratiocinations. Moreover, his own assertion in the *Essay* that "The whole science of human nature must be explored to lay a foundation for the science of government," underlines the critical importance of psychology in relation to politics for Mill; thus, though our psychology is rather different from his, it would appear to follow in the path he himself took.[1]

Mill's theory, needless to say, was Utilitarian theory; we shall examine it in detail in a moment. Here we need only remark that, while the theory pretended to universality—as a science—Mill's own expression of it was occasioned by the debates over parliamentary reform agitating England in the first third of the nineteenth century, a debate itself strongly affected by the ideas and practice of the French Revolution.

The original lines had been laid down by Bentham. He wished reform, and envisioned the Legislator as his vehicle for destroying the political relics of the feudal system which were still cluttering up the late eighteenth-century landscape. Thus, Bentham at first offered his various reforms and codifications of the law to any enlightened despot who would listen. When the French Revolution came, he initially saw it as offering him another opportunity to implement his ideas. But the reign of terror soon disillusioned him, and recalled him to his earlier conviction that a revolution in the name of natural rights was bound to go astray. During the period of the Revolution and its immediate aftermath, Bentham not only reemphasized Utilitarianism, but also muted his advocacy of parliamentary reform in England. He wrote nothing on the subject between 1790 and 1809.[2]

Bentham's return to public reform coincided with his meeting with James Mill. "Left to himself," as Burns puts it, "Bentham would never have founded a school or launched a movement, for all his ambitions and dreams."[3] Only the drive and character of someone like James Mill could turn dreams into political reality.[4] Mill took Bentham's theory, by and large, and made it his own; by simplifying and dogmatizing it, he also made it the ideology of a whole movement.

The immediate occasion for the *Essay on Government* was a request for Mill to write on the subject for the *Encyclopedia Britannica.* He set to work in 1819, and we catch the spirit of his approach in a letter he wrote to David Ricardo (whom he was urging to write an article on the Sinking Fund for the *Encyclopedia*). "An article in an Encyclopedia," Mill declared, "should be to a certain degree didactic, and also elementary—as being to be [sic] consulted by the ignorant as well as the knowing; but the matter that has been often explained, may be passed over very shortly, to leave more space for that which is less commonly known."[5] But as Halévy points out, the demands of the *Encyclopedia* form for didacticism was not the only constraint on Mill; the *Encyclopedia* was not a Benthamite publication, and Mill "was obliged to be careful concerning both the publisher who printed it, and the public to whom it was addressed."[6] Thus, to some extent the message was both oversimple—a caricature of the Utilitarian position —and less direct than it might have been. The political caricature, however, corresponded with the caricature of Mill's character; in any case, Mill's true character was too strong for him to water down his beliefs to any appreciable degree for propagandistic reasons.

Published in 1820, the *Essay* was so popular with the Utilitarians that they had it, along with a number of Mill's other articles for the *Encyclopedia*, reprinted in 1828 and distributed gratis.

At the time it was published, the *Essay* not only seemed to espouse successfully a universal theory of political science, but to strike a blow for the cause of parliamentary reform. There were three key issues in the 1820s: Who should have the suffrage (with universal manhood suffrage as the most extreme goal)? How often should parliament be elected? Should the vote be secret (what was called "the ballot")? Mill argued a position somewhere in the mainstream of Utilitarian intention, though not as radical as Bentham's own theories dictated. Practical considerations obviously influenced Mill in the writing of the *Essay*, but, as we have suggested, only to a minimal degree. Thus, our thesis is that there is really no sharp dichotomy between universal theory and practical politics, political ideology and personal identity, as we come to consider Mill's basic views on government.

A Science?

MILL BEGINS *An Essay on Government* by defining the fundamental question of government as "the adaptation of means to an end." [p. 47] Government is a mere means, a contrivance, and not an organic unity, a linking of generations, or a psychological communion, as some other writers have asserted. The end, according to Mill, is to secure "the happiness of the greatest number of men." [p. 48] Happiness, in good Utilitarian terms, is measured by the amount of pleasure obtained and the amount of pain avoided. Thus Mill can say confidently that the science of government depends for its foundation on the science of human nature.

Mill devotes only a little over three pages to his discussion of the end of government and its foundation in human nature, so much does he take his assumptions for granted. In those opening three pages, however, Mill adds another important notion to his conception of the end of government: He insists that government is required primarily because of economics, that is, because of scarcity, and the need of every man to work. In short, government exists to protect the fruits of labor. As Mill puts it, "if nature had produced spontaneously all the objects which we desire, and in sufficient abundance for the desires of all, there would have been no source of dispute or of injury among men, nor would any man have possessed the means of ever acquiring authority over another." [p. 48]

At this point, Mill seems to be reducing psychology to economics, as if the only source of man's desire for authority lay in that field; it is the same position later adopted by Karl Marx.

What strikes one most in Mill's exposition is the air of total conviction with which he expounds his doctrine. Everything appears to follow logically (and for Mill, even psychologically) from his initial premises. All is a matter of "calculation" [p. 56], of a "chain of inferences" [p. 59], of making sure that a "conclusion is demonstrated." [p. 64] Government for Mill seems to be a simple exercise in geometry. The style of his writing supports this conception, and one is tempted to write after each of his paragraphs, Q.E.D.[7]

Mill can speak with such conviction because he is propounding a *science*, offering universal knowledge, though it is being applied to a local situation: parliamentary reform in nineteenth-century England. J. H. Burns has put beautifully the defense of such an attempt:

> It seems to me that the belief in the possibility of devising a science of society—and specifically a science of legislation—grounded in the laws of individual psychology was one of the principal liberating factors in the intellectual life of late eighteenth-century Europe. More than anything else, that belief enabled the legislative scientists to take over from the godlike legislators of the past with no sense of inferiority. It led directly to the belief that rational institutions could, here and now, be substituted for the irrational, inefficient, and often oppressive tangle of the existing order, and thus it gave a new dimension to an old dream. The legislator had passed from the world of ancient myth to the world of modern Enlightenment.[8]

Privately, Mill's friend Ricardo, although he was prepared to work with Mill in making a science out of economics, had serious reservations as to the feasibility of a science of government. He wrote to Mill (November 9, 1817):

> Legislation would be comparatively an easy science if it were not so much influenced by the characters and dispositions of the people for whom it is to be undertaken. However well we may have examined the end to which all our laws should tend, yet when they are to influence the actions of a different people we have to acquire a thorough knowledge of the peculiar habits, prejudices and objects of desire of such people, *which is itself almost an unattainable knowledge, for I am persuaded that from our own peculiar habits and prejudices we should frequently see these things through a false medium, and our judgements would err accordingly* . . . [italics added].[9]

What is merely implicit in Ricardo becomes a scathing indictment in Thomas Babington Macaulay. Describing Mill, in a review of his book in 1824, as "an Aristotelian of the fifteenth century, born out of due season," Macaulay derides even his opponent's logic, accusing him at one point of "that slovenliness of thinking which is often concealed beneath a peculiar ostentation of logical neatness."[10] But what disturbs him is not Mill's errors in logic so much as his erroneous reduction of government to logic. Macaulay declares:

The fact is that, when men, in treating of things which cannot be circumscribed by precise definitions, adopt this mode of reasoning, when once they begin to talk of power, happiness, misery, pain, pleasure, motives, objects of desire, as they talk of lines and numbers, there is no end to the contradictions and absurdities into which they fall. There is no proposition so monstrously untrue in morals or politics that we will not undertake to prove it, by something which shall sound like a logical demonstration, from admitted principles. [p. 294]

Thus it is Mill's "science of human nature" which is faulty, according to Macaulay, and with this rotten foundation the whole science of government comes crashing to the ground. Mill had argued that government's only end was to protect men in the fruits of their labor, and, as we shall see, he based this necessity on the supposed "law of human nature, that a man if able will take from others anything which they have and he desires."[11] Wrong, says Macaulay. "Mr. Mill has chosen to look only at one-half of human nature, and to reason on the motives which impel men to oppress and despoil others, as if they were the only motives by which men could possibly be influenced." [p. 295] He has ignored the fact "that every man has some desires which he can gratify only by hurting his neighbours, and some which he can gratify only by pleasing them." [p. 295] Respect for the good opinion of others, desire for love and approbation: these are also motives animating men.

Macaulay's attack here is a root and branch one. It questions Mill's foundation of government, his science of human nature. Why, we in turn may ask, does Mill insist on his "law of human nature"? That law, put simply, is man's desire to dominate others. Domination, defined as power over others, gives maximum pleasure, or so it seems. For Mill, this desire has no limits. "The demand," he declares, "of power over the acts of other men is really boundless." [p. 57] Macaulay points out that history shows few, if any, verifications of Mill's assertion; even absolute monarchs have not sought to dominate without limit over their subjects. Our concern here, however, is not to settle the empirical argument between Mill and Macaulay, but to explore a bit further the psychological springs of Mill's conviction.

We shall speculate that Mill's "unipassion" view of man is overdetermined. Among other things, it is related to his intense need for an assertion of independence, which we have already studied. And that need, in turn, is so intense because Mill believes that the threats to his independence are "boundless." All of this, as we have seen, is compounded because of Mill's latent desire to be "dependent," to submit to "domination."

Mill's world is also threatening. Everywhere he seems to see enemies out to destroy him. The picture we have is colored over by lack of trust. Those entrusted with political power are sure to abuse their trust. Even "trusted" friends cannot really be trusted; a letter of Mill's to Ricardo shows the suspicious side of his nature. Ricardo had just praised the *History of British India*, and Mill responded:

> I shall need to be supported by the good opinion of such men as you. For you will see by and bye how I shall be treated by the men and the creatures of party, and by all those who aim at being the great ones of this world, upon whose craft I have endeavoured to let in some light more than ordinary. You will see how I shall be treated by some of my own friends and yours; and it will amuse you to contemplate the awkward shifts they will be put to, between the necessity they may think themselves under to speak somewhat in praise, and the real hearty inclination to backbite, and undervalue.[12]

Erikson has spoken movingly of what he calls "mutuality." By this he means the mutual giving and taking, starting with the infant at the mother's breast, in which the actions of one affect and regulate the actions of the other. This pattern of "mutuality" then persists through all the stages of an individual's development. Such mutuality must be rooted in what Erikson calls "basic trust." The child must gain a sense of "moral responsibility" whereby he does not overmanipulate, or control, others, and also a sense of his own autonomy, not overly dominated by others. Erikson comments that in the adolescent stage, when genital sexuality manifests itself, "Neurotic people, deep down, would rather incorporate or retain, eliminate or intrude, than enjoy the mutuality of genital patterns. Many others *would rather be or make dependent, destroy or be destroyed, than love maturely* [italics added], and this often without being overtly neurotic in any classifiable, diagnosable, and curable sense." Exploitation, Erikson stresses, in the shape of Male and Female, Ruler and Ruled, is the opposite of mutuality.[13]

Thus defined, one cannot help feeling that Mill, while certainly not overtly neurotic about it, had little sense of what was involved in mutuality. His imagination, and his unconscious, stressed boundless domination, either as threat or, it may be, desire. Mill's most basic *logical* assumption for his science of government was really *psychological*, and personally so, in nature. This is the best explanation for his otherwise gratuitous assumption concerning man's limitless lust for domination over the person and property of his fellow creatures.

That assumption is even more gratuitous if we realize that it implicitly contradicted Mill's other fundamental assumption: that man was rational and could be "trusted" in the use of his reason, if rightly educated. How could man be both a "reasoning machine" and, as Macaulay put it, describing Mill's first assumption, a "yahoo fighting for carrion"?[14] The answer, as Macaulay overtly recognized, is that man is both. Mill, needless to say, at various moments also recognized both parts of human nature. Personal psychological needs—the threat of the yahoo in himself, as well as in others, forcing him first toward a denial of any bounds to aggressive impulses and then toward a denial of any limits to the rational restraints on such impulses—and pressing polemical necessity caused him to alternate between both sides of his feelings, without being able to bring the two together in a single image.

Interest Politics

HAVING dogmatically "demonstrated" the end of government, Mill took as his next task in the *Essay* the problem of how to restrain those "in whose hands are lodged the powers necessary for the protection of all." [p. 50] As we have seen, he assumed that the power holders would have a boundless desire to dominate others. Only the community as a whole, he believed, could not desire its own misery; thus it alone could be trusted not to abuse its own powers. Unfortunately, the whole community could hardly assemble to effect the business of government democratically without suspending the labor, hence property, which it is the business of government to protect. The alternatives are an aristocracy or a monarchy. Mill's objections to the first are of two kinds, and revealing of his own psychology. "There may be a strong presumption," he informs us, "that any aristocracy monopolizing the powers of government would not possess intellectual powers in any very high perfection. Intellectual powers are *the offspring of labor* [italics added]. But a hereditary aristocracy are deprived of the strongest motives to labor. The greater part of them will, therefore, be defective in those mental powers." His second objection reverts to a point we have already discussed. "And if powers are put into the hands of a comparatively small number, called an aristocracy. . . . They will take from the rest of the community as much as they please of the objects of desire." [p. 53] Monarchy, too, falls victim to the same criticisms. In most respects, Mill claims, it "agrees with the aristocratical and is liable to the same objections." [pp. 53–54]

The only solution is a representative government. This, however, only defers the problems, for how are the representatives to be kept from turning against the community? They must be made to identify their interests with the community. Mill's way of assuring this seems simplistic and anticlimactic. He advocates short terms and frequent elections! By this arrangement, it would be impossible for the representative "to do himself so much good by misgovernment as he would do himself harm in his capacity of member of the community." [p. 69] Though Mill does not set the actual duration, it is clear that he has in mind the contemporary debate over annual, triennial, and septennial elections.

Let us concentrate on the assumption underlying Mill's entire theory of representative government. It is what I call "interest politics."

Interest politics, based on the assumption that there existed a landed-, a middle-, and a working-class interest, dominated the theory of nineteenth-century parliamentary government. It allowed for rationality and calculation. It was unsentimental. In theory, it could offer a "scientific" basis for legislative action. Perhaps paradoxically, it could also offer a basis for compromise; after all, interests could be traded, just as could property. It is easy to see why such a theory and practice should appeal to men like Mill. It "fitted" both their character and their political needs in the 1820s.

For Mill, interest politics was also identified with independence, i.e., freedom, and we have already seen how deep and ambivalent in him was this latter need. Both the depth and the ambivalence can be seen in this statement, in the *History of British India:*

> A voter may be considered as subject to the operation of two sets of interests: the one, interests arising out of the good or evil for which he is dependent upon the will of other men: the other interests in respect to which he cannot be considered as dependent upon any determinate man or men. . . . Those interests of each of the individuals composing the great mass of the people, for which he is not dependent upon other men, compose the interests of the nation.[15]

Dependence equaled the "sinister interests"; independence equaled the "interests of the nation."

Interest politics, we can now see, corresponded fairly well with a nineteenth-century British parliament in which "landed-" and "middle-class" interests were represented in a middling fashion and could strike the necessary bargains. It can even be said to have functioned passably well. What it ignored, or at least tried to ignore, was what today we call "cultural" or "status politics." As late nineteenth- and early twentieth-century politics have shown all too starkly, people do not necessarily vote their "rational" and "calculable" economic interest, but rather their "cultural" emotions, their "status anxieties." Ethnic affiliations, "ways of life," ideologies, and *Weltanschauungs* seem to outweigh mere interest politics. As deeper interests (if one can so regard them), they are "irrational" and seemingly do not allow for compromises.

But Mill was prevented by his definition of government as a mere contrivance from seeing even the possibility of cultural politics. Government was not a cultural product or a means of fostering the cultivation of the community and its individuals. With all his stress on education, Mill did not perceive what Coleridge, Matthew Arnold, and a host of others, including his own son John, had come to recognize: that government was more than a mere mechanical policeman over "interests," that it was a source of cultivation of all that was deepest and most valued in the society. For good or for ill, moral value, not exchange value, was the grave concern of government in cultural politics.

In stressing abstract, calculable interests, Mill ignored the need of individuals for what today we would call "identity," the confirmation of the individual's sense of selfhood by his membership in the community. By stressing rationality and dismissing sentiment, Mill closed his eyes to the sort of emotional ties that underlie the whole fabric of government. His friend Ricardo caught a glimpse of one part of the trouble with pure interest politics as espoused in the Utilitarian pleasure-pain theory. "The difficulty," Ricardo wrote Mill, "of the doctrine of expediency or utility is to know how to balance one object of utility against another—there being no standard in nature, it must vary with the tastes, the passions and the habits of mankind. This is one of the subjects on which I require to be enlightened."[16] Mill tried to enlighten his friend, most thoroughly and broadly, in the *History of British India*, and then more dogmatically in the *Essay on Government*. The evidence suggests that Ricardo was never completely convinced, though he put a good face on his continuing doubts. A twentieth-century reader may be permitted more open doubts.

II / *James Mill*

Choosing Representatives

MILL BROUGHT his interest theory of politics squarely to bear on the then crucial question of who shall choose the representatives. Obviously, choice by the entire community would be congruent with the community's interests. But is there a portion of the community that would be equally congruent? In terms of pure theory, it is not clear why Mill is driven to this question, and away from Bentham's universal suffrage. One reason, surely, is the pressure of practical politics in 1820. Other reasons may lie more deeply in his own emotional disposition.

In any case, for Mill in the *Essay*:

> One thing is pretty clear, that all those individuals whose interests are indisputably included in those of other individuals may be struck off without inconvenience. In this light may be viewed all children, up to a certain age, whose interests are involved in those of their parents. In this light, also, women may be regarded, the interest of almost all of whom is involved in that of their fathers or in that of their husbands. [pp. 73–74]

Subtly, though clearly, there is the implication that women are like children. As for those few women whose interests are not involved with some man's, Mill has no word about them. The term "indisputably" covers the entire argument, one with which most of Mill's contemporaries agreed.

Mill, then, is left with males as the right portion of the community to choose the representatives (assumed, without any overt statement, also to be males). But not all males. They must have the correct mental qualities. However, "As degrees of mental qualities are not easily ascertained, outward and visible signs must be taken to distinguish, for this purpose, one part of these males from another." In this new version of the Calvinist elect, Mill lists three signs: age, property, and profession or mode of life. [p. 74] On the property qualification Mill is properly ambiguous; he is willing to have a low qualification, as long as it does not exclude a bare majority of the males. As to representation by profession or mode of life, he opposes it as bound to create a "motley aristocracy." It is on the age qualification that Mill takes an apparently surprising position. Suppose the age of forty were prescribed, he asks; would this not serve the requisite purpose? After all:

> The men of forty have a deep interest in the welfare of the younger men, for otherwise it might be objected with perfect truth, that, if decisive power were placed in the hands of men of forty years of age, they would have an

interest, just as any other detached portion of the community, in pursuing that career which we have already described—for reducing the rest of the community to the state of abject slaves. *But the great majority of old men have sons, whose interest they regard as an essential part of their own. This is a law of human nature* [italics added]. [p. 75]

James Mill was thirty-seven when he wrote this; his son, John, was fourteen. One can only wonder what sort of understanding of father-son relations, as they were unfolding in the early nineteenth century, James Mill can be said to have had. Most commentators on Mill's qualifications for the suffrage have focused on his remarks about women, and assumed these to have had the major effect on John Stuart Mill. Macaulay asked rhetorically and indignantly: "Is then the interest of a Turk the same with that of the girls who compose his harem? Is the interest of a Chinese the same with that of the woman whom he harnesses to his plough?"[17] John Stuart Mill, according to his most recent biographer, Michael St. John Packe, felt there was much truth in what Macaulay wrote. As Packe puts it: "The passage about the position of women struck him particularly hard: throughout his life, that question was so much a passion with him that he often made it the final issue, the test on which depended his acceptance or rejection of a philosophic system. In this case, it was the means of doubling the gap between his father and himself. . . ."[18]

This is true, of course. But the greater truth, surely, is that John Stuart Mill was even more radically struck by his father's assumption of paternal domination over him until he would reach the age of forty; the "indisputable" notion that John could have no "interests" of his own, separate from his father's.[19] In 1820, aged fourteen, he might have sensed these matters only dimly. By 1829, when Macaulay's critique appeared and John was just barely emerging from his mental crisis, he must have felt keenly the arrogance and lack of understanding in his father's presumed "law of human nature." For a man who so savagely proclaimed his own independence, James Mill seems to have had little understanding or sympathy for the autonomous needs of others. But this, of course, is only to say that his own desperate inner need to escape domination by others (a domination which also had its attraction for him) led James Mill to seek domination over others: women and sons.

Middle Class

ONE OTHER important notion advanced by James Mill in his *Essay on Government* involves his eulogy of the middle class, and his faith that the lower class would follow its lead. The middle class, he tells us, is universally described "as both the most wise and the most virtuous part of the community." [p. 89] They are numerous and "form a large proportion of the whole body of the people."[20] By a definitional sleight of hand, Mill seems to enlarge their numbers by declaring the "middle rank . . . wholly included in that part of the community which is not aristocratical." [p. 89] He simply means that he does not want to contaminate the "middle rank" with any aristocrats, however middle class their sympathies; he does not mean to confound the middle class with the lower, as in a pre-1789 Third Estate.

In any case, Mill then goes on with a sweeping assertion which needs to be quoted in its entirety:

> Another proposition may be stated, with a perfect confidence of the concurrence of all those men who have attentively considered the formation of opinions in the great body of society, or, indeed, the principles of human nature in general. It is, that the opinions of that class of the people who are below the middle rank are formed, and their minds are directed by that intelligent, that virtuous rank who come the most immediately in contact with them, who are in the constant habit of intimate communication with them, to whom they fly for advice and assistance in all their numerous difficulties, upon whom they feel an immediate and daily dependence in health and in sickness, in infancy and in old age; to whom their children look up as models for their imitation, whose opinions they hear daily repeated and account it their honor to adopt. There can be no doubt that the middle rank, which gives to science, to art, and to legislation itself their most distinguished ornaments, and is the chief source of all that has exalted and refined human nature, is that portion of the community of which, if the basis of representation were ever so far extended, the opinion would ultimately decide. Of the people beneath them a vast majority would be sure to be guided by their advice and example. [p. 90]

Coming a few years after the Peterloo massacres (Mill began to write his *Essay* a month after Peterloo), this was an astounding statement. Most of his readers would also have memories of the Gordon Riots of 1780, the French Revolutionary insurrections, and the ominous beginnings of English working-class politics. Mill sought to answer them directly when he concluded his *Essay* with the following paragraph:

The incidents which have been urged as exceptions to this general rule, and even as reasons for rejecting it, may be considered as contributing to its proof. What signify the irregularities of a mob, more than half composed, in the greater number of instances, of boys and women, and disturbing for a few hours or days a particular town? What signifies the occasional turbulence of a manufacturing district, peculiarly unhappy from a very great deficiency of a middle rank, as there the population almost wholly consists of rich manufacturers and poor workmen—with whose minds no pains are taken by anybody, with whose afflictions there is no virtuous family of the middle rank to sympathize, whose children have no good example of such a family to see and to admire, and who are placed in the highly unfavorable situation of fluctuating between very high wages in one year and very low wages in another? It is altogether futile with regard to the foundation of good government to say that this or the other portion of the people may at this or the other time depart from the wisdom of the middle rank. It is enough that the great majority of the people never cease to be guided by that rank; and we may, with some confidence, challenge the adversaries of the people to produce a single instance to the contrary in the history of the world. [pp. 90–91]

It is an audacious conclusion, even for his own day, much less for ours.

Why did Mill set himself against the middle-class fear of the masses, seen as the mob? One answer is that, by and large, the lower class *was* prepared to follow the middle class in the agitation for parliamentary reform in England in the 1820s. A figure such as Mill's friend, Francis Place, must have been very reassuring as to the willingness of lower-class individuals either to aspire to be middle class or to follow in its lead. Mill, unlike many of his contemporaries, thought of Place, not of Peterloo.

Another reason was political necessity: Without trust in the lower class, the choice for the middle class lay either in acceptance of aristocratic rule or the frightening specter of violent revolution. As we know, scared by the latter, middle classes elsewhere, as in Germany, for example, lay largely quiescent. Forces of public order, such as police, were hardly existent and not to be depended on by the middle class. Mill and his followers, therefore, literally required their faith in the lower class.

Yet all of these objective reasons might not have been enough for Mill, as they were not for many others in the middle class, if they had not been supported by equally strong subjective reasons. By placing the lower class with women and children as "dependent" people, Mill could feel secure. The lower class "fly for advice and assistance" and their children (only the children?) "look up as models for their imitation" to that intelligent and virtuous rank, the middle class. Their "interests" are necessarily subsumed in that of the middle-class male, and Mill and his followers could therefore claim the right to rule with a good conscience—a vital psychological necessity.

True, there is a necessary ambivalence to Mill's view of the lower class. Like unruly, irrational "boys and women," or poor workmen "whose children have no good example of such a family [middle class] to see and to admire," they may occasionally have a tantrum and behave as a rioting mob. But such an outburst merely calls for a little discipline, a little patience, and renewed efforts at educating them correctly. Basically, the lower class will behave as they should. We are in the presence of a theory of government which sees the lower class as children![21]

It was a comforting view. Taken all in all, logically and psychologically, Mill's *Essay on Government*, and related works on politics, provided his followers with an ideology which could lead them to the Reform Bill of 1832, allowing middle-class "domination" of England without any feeling of their being oppressors. Quite the contrary. For most Marxists, of course, Mill's views merely mask an economic position, or interest (for the orthodox Marxist thinks in the same terms). This, however, is a simple view. The complicated reality is that James Mill came to and held his views on government and related subjects at least as much for personal, psychological reasons, deriving from his family upbringing, Calvinist heritage, and early experiences in life, as he did for economic and class reasons. Put thusly, this is still a poor way of understanding the matter. What really happened was that Mill emerged from corresponding processes of personal "givens": a family fostering that itself encased developing personal and social conditions, accelerating economic, social, and political change, and widespread intellectual currents, none of which is sole or prime cause of the others.

One specific result, as we have just seen, was Mill's views on government. These provided his followers with a happy conjoining of two elements: a "science" of human nature and government that gave them total certainty and good conscience as to the rightness of what they were up to, and a specific defense of certain features of desired parliamentary reform (a secret ballot, more frequent parliaments, and an extended but still partial suffrage). Carried too far in one direction, the science could become a dogma, which, as William Thomas so well puts it, "was very much at variance with their [Utilitarians'] democratic pretensions; or to put it another way, they were so convinced that they knew what was best for the people that they tended to underrate or ignore the operation of actual public opinion."[22] Taken too far in the other direction, the democratic pretensions could be overly responsive to actual public opinion and wash away any claim to a central core of meaning and intellectual conviction, around which a continuing political movement could form. Mill provided just the needed mixture for the Utilitarians. It was one major reason for his unique position of leadership among them.

Leadership in Politics

WE HAVE thus far centered our attention on Mill's doctrines on government. At this point we need to shift our focus a bit and examine his implementation of those doctrines in the actual political movement of Utilitarianism. Mill the doer, and not just the thinker, becomes our concern. In order to study him as a leader, we need to establish a context for his leadership. What, for example, was the social and political structure of England in which leadership could be exercised? Who were the members of the Utilitarian movement? Why did James Mill, and not someone else, become the leader of the movement? What particular methods did he use to implement his leadership? In short, we need to bring the party into correspondence with the personality.[23]

Let us first take the question of political and social structure. A cliché of political philosophy at the time was that public opinion ruled political life, if not at first, then ultimately. Hence, whoever shaped public opinion at large might be thought to shape the politics of England. In a gross sense, one might claim that a John Wesley, a William Cobbett—men who might be labeled demagogues (with the Greek meaning of the word in mind)—appealed to the country at large. James Mill was certainly not this sort of leader, nor were the Utilitarians interested in appealing to this sort of audience.

Actually, in nineteenth-century England there was no such thing as an undifferentiated public. Wesley, for example, appealed mainly to lower middle-class and laboring groups left untouched by the Church of England, and Cobbett to dispossessed agricultural workers and others of the lower classes who were uprooted by the growing industrialization of the country. To all intents and purposes, aside from mob actions, the working classes of early nineteenth-century England might be dismissed from consideration as serious participants in the political process. That process went on mainly in Parliament, dominated as it was before the Reform Bill by the "landed interest"; in the law courts, reflecting largely the interests and desires of those already in power;

and in the local government of the counties, administered by and for this same group.

To the "landed interest" we must add the beneficed clergy of the Church of England, often appointed to their well-endowed posts by the "landed interest"; the members of the professions: army, navy, and bar; and the class of very rich men who hoped to become part of the landed aristocracy, either for themselves or their children. Generally known as Tories, these constituted the factions or groups that controlled Parliament, hence the sources of legislation, and whom Mill's son John called the Privileged Classes.[24] Clearly this was not the audience for Utilitarian ideas and persuasions.

Against the aristocracy and their privileges stood the middle class, but generally with only a partial vote and therefore only a partial possibility of making their voices heard in Parliament; certain individuals from the aristocratic class "whom some circumstance of a personal nature has alienated from their class" (to quote John Stuart Mill again); and, in the background, the working classes.

Parliament, of course, met in London. Of outstanding importance in the political history of the time was the county of Westminster (thus matching the county of Middlesex, scene of Wilkes' activities in the 1770s). Until 1807 its seventeen thousand electors had dutifully elected one Whig and one Tory, the two faces of aristocratic parliamentary control. Then, sensationally, it elected Sir Francis Burdett as a popular and independent candidate (another Radical, Lord Cochrane, was elected with him), supported by such "democrats" as William Cobbett and Francis Place. This accidental spark was flamed into a permanent political conflagration by the fortunate meeting of Bentham and Mill the next year and the gradual formation around them of a Utilitarian, or Radical, party. Basing themselves pragmatically on the shopkeepers and tradesmen of Westminster, the Utilitarians used Westminster as the pivot for their lever on Parliament and as the model for their arguments in favor of parliamentary reform.

In this hasty perusal we have our answer as to the target population at whom the Utilitarians aimed their appeal: the electors of Westminster, as "representatives" of the ten-pound middle-class electors of the towns of England, and, above them in station and intellect, the men of the aristocratic and professional classes "whom some circumstance of a personal nature has alienated from their class." Let us look at this last group closely, for they, of necessity (with some additions, of course), had to constitute the politically active "leadership cadres" of the Utilitarian movement as well as its primary "audience."

It must be noted initially that the Utilitarians were not a highly structured, well-knit group. Mill deplored this state of affairs constantly. Sir Francis Burdett, for example, scion of an aristocratic family, married to the daughter of a banker, became a radical of sorts after 1807, only to end his political life as a Tory. At the other end of the social scale, William Cobbett started out as an anti-Jacobin journalist and demagogue, only to switch around in 1807 by supporting Burdett and then, though in undependable fashion, the Radicals thereafter.

So amorphous and shifting a group as the Radicals is hard to bring into focus. For convenience, however, we can fix the political kaleidoscope at one or two patterns. A group of identifiable "members" can be made out from, say, 1808 to 1824, led and influenced primarily by James Mill. In the latter year, new young men were recruited to the movement, circling around James Mill's son John, who served mainly as his father's alter ego. A final formation can be discerned in the first reformed Parliament, only to fall apart disastrously after 1835.

In our first group portrait we would have, of course, Bentham and Mill. With them is the exemplary and unique Francis Place, a self-made working man (he rose to be a master tailor, head of a thriving business) with unusual connections and organizational skills and, moreover, the only real contact with the artisan population of London. As Radical M.P.s we can cite Mill's dearest friend, David Ricardo, Joseph Hume (whose 1813 meeting with Place brought him into the fold), Henry Brougham (a boyhood friend of Mill's and mostly a Whig rather than a Radical), Sir Francis Burdett, and John Cam Hobhouse (Lord Broughton). As journalists and editors there are Albany Fonblanque (who took over the editorship of the *Examiner* in 1830), Dr. Southwood Smith (contributor to the *Westminster Review*), Colonel Perronet Thompson (a long-time Radical who kept the ailing *Westminster Review* going for five years, from 1830 on), and of course, William Cobbett. As intellectuals and theorists, note George Grote, the historian (introduced to Mill by Ricardo in 1818), J. R. M'Culloch, the economist, and John Austin, the legal philosopher. Hovering just outside this group seems to have been the eminent legalist Sir Samuel Romilly (actually a Whig), and transcending it, though part of it, the old reforming warhorse, Major John Cartwright.

In our second picture we must add some new faces surrounding John Stuart Mill: the M.P. John Arthur Roebuck, the Unitarian minister and editor of the *Monthly Repository*, William J. Fox, Charles Austin (brother of John), Edward Strutt (Lord Belper), Hyde and Charles Villiers, John Romilly (son of Sir Samuel), George John Graham, and Charles Buller.

These form more or less the hard core of the Utilitarian movement. After the Reform Bill, Tory alarmists claimed that Radicals in the Parliament of 1835 numbered about 190. But this included, in addition to about twenty-one of the foremost Radicals, the leaders of the Political Unions of 1831–1832, a number of mere time-serving Whig-Radicals, and about a hundred Irish members, functioning as what is called O'Connell's "tail."[25] Such a diverse gathering had no common creed or political platform and was a "Radical group" only for expediency. By the time of Mill's death in 1836, the coalition was already in the process of falling apart.

Why was it James Mill who led the Utilitarians? His contemporaries amply attest to the fact that he was the leader and hint at the reasons why. As his son tells us:

By his writings and his personal influence he was a great centre of light to his generation. During his later years he was quite as much the head and leader of the intellectual radicals in England, as Voltaire was of the *philosophes* in France. . . . In the power of influencing by mere force of mind and character, the conviction and purposes of others, and in the strenuous exertion of that power to promote freedom and progress, he left, as far as my knowledge extends, no equal among men.[26]

Is this a hyperbolic view offered out of filial devotion? It would seem not. Typical of many other such comments are those by the journalist Albany Fonblanque:

One of our master-minds . . . one that has given the most powerful impulse, and the most correct direction to thought. . . . His conversation was so energetic and complete in thought, so succinct, and exact *ad unguem* in expression, that, if reported as uttered, his colloquial observations or arguments would have been perfect compositions. . . . It was hardly possible for an intelligent man to know James Mill without feeling an obligation for the profit derived from his mind.[27]

As Bain sums it up:

In spite of all that is said of his arrogant manner, he made his way in society, and gained over people his superiors in rank. . . . Whether, as John Mill said, he was pre-eminently adapted for a prime minister, he was at all events a born leader—a king of men.[28]

Did Mill gain over people "his superiors in rank"—and a look at the 1808 or 1824 list of Utilitarians reveals how many of them were upper class—because he "represented" them in some way, or because he was "marginal" to them? The case looks suspiciously like Edmund Burke's earlier ascendancy over the Whig aristocrats whom he, as the "outsider," admired so extravagantly and whose unarticulated views he formulated so persuasively. For example, Burke was Irish, Mill Scottish; both were marginal to English politics. Both had their fame and fortune to make, and both made it into the company, if not the ranks, of the upper class.

But there the analogy stops. Burke eulogized the aristocracy and abandoned his possible leadership of the middle class. Mill fiercely attacked the aristocracy and never pretended, as Burke did, to their way of life; instead, he was middle class to his marrow and representative of that class in its most intimate traits of sobriety, hard work, and moral commitment. True, Bentham putatively impugned Mill's motives in attacking the aristocracy: "His creed of politics results less from love for the many than from hatred of the few. It is too much under the influence of social and dissocial affection." We catch an echo of this criticism in Grote's first impression of Mill:

> His mind has, indeed, all that cynicism and asperity which belongs to the Benthamian school, and what I chiefly dislike in him is, the readiness and seeming preference with which he dwells on the *faults and defects* of others —even of the greatest men![29]

Nevertheless, for whatever reasons and in whatever modes, Mill's dislike of the aristocracy was representative of himself and his middle-class identity. It allowed him, as Bain remarks, to get "hold of the more intelligent minds of the growing middle class in our great centres of industry."[30]

As for the aristocrats in the Utilitarian movement, those "whom some circumstance of a personal nature has alienated from their class" —the Sir Francis Burdetts of the time—with them Mill's position was obviously "marginal." Yet, as Grote has told us, he won them over in a sweeping and profound way. Surely this was because, out of strength of mind and character, Mill voiced better than they could their own highest aspirations for society and the good of man. He offered them a total ideology—a psychology that gave certainty to their hopes and views on education and knowledge, a morality that could be calculated scientifically, an economic theory that left no doubts as to its rightness, and a political philosophy that justified their most earnest efforts at reform—and exemplified that ideology in his person.

No one else could have done it, or so we are told by Bain: "Had Mill not appeared on the stage at the opportune moment, the whole cast of political thinking at the time of the Reform settlement must have been very inferior in point of sobriety and ballast to what it was. His place could not have been taken by any other man that we can fix upon."[31] In the words of Packe: "James Mill, by reason of his long influence on the works of Bentham, as well as of his own steady service for the cause during the last twenty years, stood at the conflux of many tributaries and currents, contrary and unruly though they often were, as they flowed towards the great sea of democratic progress."[32] It is exactly because he was both representative and marginal, leader and disciple, that Mill was able to stand at the "conflux" of the many currents that brought reform, and not revolution, to England in 1832.

Mill never ran for Parliament, however. Instead he persuaded others, such as Ricardo, to enter it. Mill's power was always behind the scenes, exercised directly only over those who formed the circle of his acquaintances. His was a force that could spur others, with his help, to start journals, launch educational experiments, publish their own work (he had this effect on both Bentham and Ricardo), and strive to put together a political coalition. It was a leadership exercised more by character and intellect than by organizational or oratorical abilities; these were in Mill's possession, but he seems not to have used them to the fullest extent. In all of this, he was true to the deepest elements of his personality, if not always to the immediate needs of his political party.

5

The Economic World

A New World

IN A SENSE, the late eighteenth century first created what we can call an economic world. Of course, as far back as one can go in the history of society, men had labored, exchanged, and consumed. But they had not done so in a self-conscious manner, aware that they were moving in what I call an economic world. Quesnay and the Physiocrats seem to have been the first to try to establish a rational science of economics and thereby to create such a world. Quesnay postulated an annual circulation of wealth, subject to precise natural laws. This was the new economic world.

It was Adam Smith, combining the Physiocrats' stress on a rational system with previous work in "political arithmetic"—on practical, empirical problems of banking, currency, balance of payments, and so on—who placed the new "science" on a secure footing. Smith's *Wealth of Nations*, however, was as much an historical disquisition on economics as it was a deductive system; much of the work that followed him wrestled with this potential division.

Meanwhile, in the late eighteenth and early nineteenth centuries, Western Europe, and especially Great Britain, was moving into an entirely new social and economic system which was first labeled "Industrialism" by Thomas Carlyle in 1833 (in *Sartor Resartus*). The importance and magnitude of this development, which is still going on, can hardly be exaggerated. Its significance and scope can only be compared to the Agricultural Revolution of ten thousand years ago, when man began to move from hunting-gathering bands into settled communities tilling the land. It is this immense change in economic-social conditions that supplied the bricks and mortar, the reality behind the intellectual construction of the new economic world depicted by the political economy (as it was then called) of the time.

This political economy postulated not only a new world, but a new man to inhabit it: economic man. The postulate quickly became a prescription, indicating how men *should* behave. Thus, the economic laws of nature took on the aspect of a self-fulfilling prophecy. Such a development touched on psychology—what are the traits of "economic man" and how can he be reared by family and society?—as much as on economics. In what follows, we shall be as much interested in that relationship as in any economic theories per se.[1]

Elementary, My Dear Watson

JAMES MILL was in the forefront of those who occupied themselves with the new science of political economy. In this, of course, he was not unique among the Utilitarians. Bentham, too, devoted much of his attention to political economy, publishing his *Defence of Usury* as early as 1787, and eventually writing a *Manual of Political Economy* in 1811. James Mill's particular accomplishments were twofold: he became the schoolmaster of Utilitarian economics, publishing his *Elements of Political Economy* in 1821, and he pushed and prodded David Ricardo into writing and publishing his major works in economic science. Together, Mill, Ricardo, and a few others such as Malthus and M'Culloch took Adam Smith's work and developed it into what we know as classical economics. In so doing, I have tried to suggest, they created a new economic world in men's minds and souls, as well as in their material environment.

The impetus for this creation was especially strong after 1815 and the end of the Napoleonic Wars. The wars had left a number of problems for Great Britain which suddenly made economic questions a matter of popular discussion instead of an esoteric subject. There were the problems of unemployment, made acute by returning soldiers and displaced markets; inflation, caused partly by a depreciated paper currency; a huge national debt; a newly created income tax; badly administered poor laws relief; and a protectionist agricultural policy, now anchored in the controversial revised Corn Laws. Suddenly wages, profits, and rent, and the laws regulating them, leaped out of the dusty pages of abstruse thinkers and entered lustily into the marketplace of ideas.

It was in this atmosphere that James Mill's *Elements of Political Economy* made its appearance.[2] The word "elements" in the title really has a double meaning. Mill's work is "elementary," for his object as he tells us, was "to compose a school-book of Political Economy" that could be read profitably by "persons of either sex, of ordinary understanding." [p. iii] He pretends to nothing new, and makes claim to no discovery. Having gotten Ricardo to publish his *Principles of Political Economy* in 1817, Mill needed only offer a precise summary and synthesis of accepted truths.

Mill's other use of the word "elements" is in the sense of reduction to simple parts. For Mill, economics is a matter of logical propositions, of proceeding as in geometry, from demonstration to demonstration. It is a deductive science, and it is not for nought that the title page has a quotation from Hobbes. It was Hobbes, of course, who in *Leviathan* insisted that political science, or what he called Civil Philosophy, was not a matter of historical experience, and therefore uncertainty, but of geometrical demonstration, the construction of an artificial figure, and therefore apodictic. Now Mill was doing the same thing for political economy, ridding it of Smith's historical disquisitions and turning it strictly into a branch of logic. (Even Mill's style, in its didactic aridness, is reminiscent of Hobbes.) In this effort Mill was aided and indeed further prompted by his friend Ricardo, who wrote him about Malthus that "Another of his [Malthus'] great mistakes is I think this: Political Economy he says is not a strict science like the mathematics, and therefore thinks he may use words in a vague way. . . . No proposition can surely be more absurd."[3]

By thus removing economics from the historical realm and making it a matter of "strict science," Mill in effect did two things: (1) he detached, or at least tried to detach, his economic findings from the practical, time-bound, socially rooted problems surrounding him in emergent capitalist-industrialist society, thus denying to himself the "interest" roots of his economic "laws"; and (2) he set up a kind of mechanical model of the economic world in which the system is "closed" to other influences. By postulating a free movement of men and materials in this closed system, he took no theoretical account of the fact that men do *not* operate in the manner prescribed for them by the model. For example, in a completely free market men ought to shift immediately to another job when there is an oversupply of labor in their field. Alas, as reality shows, considerations of family ties, geography, job training, ego investment, and a host of other factors keep individuals from acting as they "should." Mill and his followers ignored such considerations, or, if acknowledging them finally, disdainfully put them aside as aberrations from correct theory and behavior. In short, classical economics needed a "mechanical" man to go along with its strict science, and Carlyle was not far from the mark when he accused Industrialism, and its Utilitarian spokesmen, of making men "mechanical in head and in heart, as well as in hand."[4]

The Economics of Class

MILL BEGINS his *Elements* in a rather odd way. He asserts that "Political Economy is to the State, what domestic economy is to the family." [p. 1] Then he adds, "the family consumes; and, in order to consume, it must supply." Since the desire for consumption is endless —"There is no end to the desire of enjoyment" (compare with Mill's view of government, as similarly based on an unlimited desire for domination)—the problem of political economy is to increase the supply.

This is practically the last time we hear of the family as the microcosm for economic activity. Was Mill momentarily thinking overmuch of his own family and its consumption needs? What would have been the results for his theory if he had kept the family as his model of economic life? Was this an obvious impossibility for a "self-made man"? In any case, Mill rapidly abandons this model and moves immediately to the model of economic individualism. He conjures up in his imagination a state of nature—"That simple state of things, in which society may be conceived to have originated"—and postulates an individual savage procuring his subsistence. This, he claims, is Labor—man's "naked powers"—without the aid of Capital. [p. 8]

Labor, however, can be improved as regards its productive powers in two ways: by the use of "instruments which form one of the portions of capital," and by the division of labor. [p. 10] Capital itself, of course, is originally derived from labor and is simply a result of saving, or delayed gratification. Mill wastes no further time in examining how capital is first acquired—a comparison with Karl Marx's work on primary accumulation shows the gap—or, indeed, on division of labor (a subject carefully dealt with by Adam Smith).[5] Instead he proceeds directly to a class analysis based on his economic theory.

In a fashion to gladden the heart of any Marxist, Mill tells us that production involves two classes, "The rich men who supply the materials and instruments of production, and that of the workmen, who supply the labour." [p. 21] Moreover, "the share of the one cannot be increased without a corresponding diminution of the share of the other." [p. 79] Mill even goes to the point of overtly comparing the capitalist to the slave owner, with the difference that the latter owns both the capital and the labor, i.e., the laborer. [p. 21] Thus it was only a short step for Marx, who had read Mill's *Elements* carefully, to be able to talk of wage slavery.

But Mill's analysis, while logically seeming to entail the possibility of class conflict, came to a different conclusion. Mill postulated what Halévy calls the principle of the identity of interests.[6] He did this by trying to demonstrate that an increase in capital, made possible by profits, and thus an increase in the instruments of production, is the only basis for an increase in wages. [p. 86] Thus the greatest happiness of the laboring class was bound up with the success of capitalism, for the middle class, unlike the aristocrats, can defer immediate gratification, and thus save moderate sums of capital. Because of the middle class, then, the worker's lot can improve.

As in his *Essay on Government*, Mill waxed lyrical in *Elements* about the middle class. Here, however, it is not their dedication to hard work (as opposed to aristocratic parasitism) that Mill primarily extols, but their capacity for leisure—and thus knowledge! In Mill's words:

> All the blessings, which flow from that grand and distinguishing attribute of our nature, its progressiveness, the power of advancing continually from one degree of knowledge, one degree of command over the means of happiness, to another, seem, in a great measure, to depend upon the existence of a class of men who have their time at their command; that is, who are rich enough to be freed from all solicitude with respect to the means of living in a certain state of enjoyment. . . .
>
> It will not probably be disputed, that they who are raised above solicitude for the means of subsistence and respectability, without being exposed to the vices and follies of great riches, the men of middling fortunes, in short, the men to whom society is generally indebted for its greatest improvements, are the men, who, having their time at their own disposal, freed from the necessity of manual labour, subject to no man's authority, and engaged in the most delightful occupations, obtain, as a class the greatest sum of human enjoyment. [pp. 63–64]

Mill's conclusion is that "To enable a considerable portion of the community to enjoy the advantages of leisure, the return to capital must evidently be large." (For Mill, incidentally, this was one more argument against a heavy income tax.)

What of the laborers? Would they see things this way? As in his writings on government, Mill has a touching faith in the willingness of the working class to follow their betters, that is, the middle class, when properly led. After all, his demonstration of the requisite economic laws was simple enough even for ordinary minds, and its arguments were scientifically unanswerable. Of course the correct leadership was essential, and Mill frequently worried about its absence. As he wrote Ricardo in 1821:

It is very curious that almost every body you meet with—whig and tory—agree in declaring their opinion of one thing—that a great struggle between the two orders, the rich and poor, is in this country commenced—and that the people must in the end prevail;—and yet that the class of the rich act as if they were perfectly sure of the contrary—for if the people must gain the victory, but are made to suffer intensely in the gaining of it, what can these people mean who would enrage the victors to the utmost? The old adage seems to be true; that when God wants to destroy a set of men, he first makes them mad.

Ricardo was more sanguine in his remarks, and, as the Reform Bill of 1832 eventually showed, more right in his estimate:

The only prospect we have of putting aside the struggle which they say has commenced between the rich and the other classes, is for the rich to yield what is justly due to the other classes, but this is the last measure which they are willing to have recourse to. I cannot help flattering myself that justice will prevail at last, without a recurrence to actual violence; but if it does, it will only be because the event of the struggle will be so obvious to all eyes that expediency, the expediency of the rich, will make it necessary even in their view.[7]

The real enemy of the laboring class, according to Mill in *Elements*, was a third class, the "Owners of the Land." [p. 27] Strictly speaking, Mill's economic analysis, in this case of rent, really relieves the landowner of the onus of guilt later to be placed upon him. Thus, following Ricardo, Mill claims that "in considering what regulates wages and profits, rent may be left altogether out of the question." [p. 70] Rent itself is determined by the pressure of population upon the fertility of land, with increased population causing less fertile land to be brought into production. The more fertile portions can now demand a monthly payment, called a rent.

But if pure economic analysis does not seem to indict the landlord, contemporary political questions, in the form of the Corn Laws, do. Here the landlord's interests are against the general interest, because the higher the price of corn, "The smaller a portion of the produce will suffice to replace with its profits, the capital of the farmer; and all the rest belongs to himself [the landlord]." [p. 207] In short, whereas in Adam Smith's view the landowners are the one class whose interests are generally the same as the general interest, and the manufacturers the most opposite, Mill reverses the formula. Disliking aristocrats, i.e., landowners, (and never, like Burke, aspiring himself to own land), Mill chastised the landowner as "not a producer, not a capitalist." Separating him from the farmer, who is both "a producer and a capitalist," Mill also separated him from the other two classes of society, and their economic interests. Class conflict, if it existed in nineteenth-century England, linked the middle and laboring classes against a common enemy: the landowner. For Mill this was a happy fit between both the logical and the psychological needs of his political economy.

Productive Consumption

THE PSYCHOLOGICAL seems to dominate the logical analysis when Mill takes up the subject of productive and unproductive consumption. Productive consumption occurs when expenditures are made only "for the sake of something to be produced." [p. 220] In short, "men consume for the sake of production." Unproductive consumption, then, occurs when men consume without producing, e.g., using wine at the table, giving wages to a footman, and so on. Though Mill does not offer the following as illustrations, we can readily see that music, poetry, and, one would suppose, even philosophy are unproductive consumptions. As he concludes, "The commodity perishes in the using, and all that is derived is the good, the pleasure, the satisfaction, which the using of it yields." [p. 222]

"*All* that is derived" [italics added]! There is an unconscious tone of presumption to these words. Did not much of John Stuart Mill's mental crisis revolve around exactly this issue? Was not much of his difficulty that he had to learn to "yield" to his needs for "unproductive consumption"? The very terms used by James Mill are pejorative and suggest a mere giving way to immediate impulse, instead of obeying the stern virtue of eternally delayed gratification.

That this is what Mill had in mind is made clearer for us when he intones, "To use for ultimate profit, is to consume productively. To use for immediate enjoyment, is to consume unproductively." [p. 226] As for productive consumption, there can never be too much of it. Man is voracious in his desires. In Mill's words, "It appears, therefore, by accumulated proof, that production can never be too rapid for demand," and this is by definition because production "never furnishes supply, without furnishing demand."

This argument has the happy consequence of doing away, again by definition, of a supposed glut. Increased production will, *after a lapse of time*, automatically call forth increased demand, and Mill concludes that "The doctrine of the glut, therefore, seems to be disproved by reasoning perfectly conclusive." [p. 240] It never seems to occur to Mill to take seriously the *social* consequences of the dislocations of laborers that occur in the real world if not in his hermetically sealed economic model, or to concede that time elapsed in the life of a person is different from time elapsed in an economic graph.

Or, rather, it does not occur to him until it is the life and time of men like himself, and their heirs. Generalizing against the use of taxation to change the condition of the different classes of contributors, Mill concludes:

> It may be said, that if the class who live upon salaries are loaded with more than their due share of the burden, the balance will adjust itself; because, the situation having been rendered less desirable, fewer people will go into it, and the salaries will rise. This does not remove the objection. For, first of all, why should legislation disturb the natural proportion, in order that the force of things may restore it? In the next place, the restoration of the equilibrium in this case is a slow operation. It requires a generation to pass away before the diminution of the numbers of those who live upon salaries can raise their condition. A whole generation is therefore sacrificed. [pp. 274–275]

The sacrifice of a "whole generation" suddenly becomes meaningful to Mill when it is his own.

Generally, glut, as we have seen, cannot exist. There cannot be too much of that good thing, productive consumption. Mill's terms are obviously tendentious, and it is clear that he was inveighing against such unproductive consumption as gaming, the arts, and other such enjoyments. His inclusion of government expenditures under unproductive consumption confirms this general view.

How then can he justify his own existence? Are James Mill's writings a species of "productive consumption"? To what further production do they lead? Mill avoids dealing with this question directly, but there is a curious paragraph in which he seems to broach the subject. He informs us:

> Though a very accurate conception may thus be formed of the two species of consumption; and the two species of labour; productive, and unproductive; it is not easy to draw the line precisely between them. Almost all our classifications are liable to this inconvenience. Between things, which differ the most widely, there are almost always orders of things, which approach

by insensible gradations. We divide animals into two classes, the rational and irrational: and no two ideas can be more clearly distinguished. Yet beings may be found, of which it would be difficult to say, to which of the two classes they belonged. In like manner, there are consumers, and labourers, who may seem, with some propriety, to be capable of being ranked, either in the productive, or the unproductive class. Notwithstanding this difficulty, it is absolutely necessary, for the purposes of human discourse, that classification should be performed, and the line drawn somewhere. This may be done, with sufficient accuracy both for science and for practice. It is chiefly necessary that the more important properties of the objects classified should be distinctly marked in the definition of the class. It is not difficult, after this, to make allowance, in practice, for those things which lie, as it were, upon the confines of two classes; and partake, in some degree, of the properties of both. [pp. 224–225]

One has the feeling that Mill, if pushed, would place himself somewhere on the "confines of two classes."

But why is it "absolutely necessary . . . that classification should be performed, and the line drawn somewhere"? In what way is this essential for Mill's economic analysis?[8] There seems to be no good answer to that question. The classification into productive and unproductive consumption—and thus a new sort of class analysis?—seems to supply political and psychological needs rather than economic ones.

True, Mill could claim that increased production is essential for human happiness. But if "push-pin is as good as poetry," to cite Bentham's famous adage, why aren't both as good as an extra piece of linen (Mill's example)? If happiness is the criterion, then enjoyment, whether immediate or deferred, is the objective aimed at. Of course a certain amount of deferred gratification is necessary, for strictly prudential reasons and to avoid the life of the improvident grasshopper, but this, it could be argued, is to provide a basis from which we can then "enjoy" life. Mill himself paints the leisured state of the middle class as desirable. In short, only if one assumes unending desire for consumption, and eternal dedication to deferred gratification, do Mill's views on productive and unproductive consumption make sense. And such a view presupposes a man much like Mill himself—or at least the caricature of him.

Population and Birth Control

MILL HAD "demonstrated" that only an increase in middle-class capital could lead to increased productive consumption and improvement in the lot of the laboring class. One great specter that hovered over this prospect was the threat of increased population growth. Increased population meant an increase in the demand for food, and thus a recourse to land of second quality (or "a second dose of capital, less productively, upon land of the first quality"). [p. 31] This, in turn, meant increased rent, a decrease in available capital, and a decrease in wages. The result would be poverty, misery, and increased mortality among the laboring class. Only the landlord could benefit; the capitalist and laborer alike would suffer.

Mill, of course, drew his gloomy picture from Malthus' *Essay on Population.* But whereas Malthus had claimed to draw his conclusion—that food tended to increase arithmetically while population grew geometrically—by induction from the evidence, Mill, typically, based his conclusions on logical deduction. In a matter-of-fact way he examines the physiological basis of reproduction in the human female—her period of gestation, the suckling of the infant, span of possible child bearing—and concludes that, even making allowances, there is a child-bearing period from twenty to forty years of age, permitting a child every two years, or a total of ten during the normal woman's life. Even cutting this figure in half, Mill continues, means that the population would double itself in a small number of years.

For Mill, actual statistics on births and deaths ought not to figure in the argument. Even if they show population actually to be stationary, they prove nothing. For Mill has demonstrated the *natural tendency* of population to increase, unless checked. What then are the checks that operate? One is poverty, by which "all but a certain number undergo a premature destruction." The other "is prudence; by which either marriages are sparingly contracted, or care is taken that children, beyond a certain number, shall not be the fruit." [p. 50] In this last, seemingly innocuous statement, Mill has buried a time bomb: the idea of birth control!

We shall see shortly the centrality of birth control to the principle of population, which had become the pivot of Mill's, and the Utilitarians', science of political economy. First, however, let us pursue Mill's analysis further. Population growth would not be worrisome if capital tended to increase just as rapidly. Unfortunately, the disposition in mankind to save is less than the disposition to spend. Only in that small set of men "in whom the reasoning power is strong, and who are able to resist a present pleasure for a greater one hereafter" [p. 52] is the disposition to save strong. Thus, capital accumulation cannot keep up with population "expenditure," and the result for the mass of laborers will be "premature destruction" by poverty.

However, there is the alternative of "prudence." Implicit in Mill's discussion is the conviction that the sexual impulse is stronger than the saving one. "Spending," incidentally, was the Victorian term for sexual emission. As Steven Marcus reminds us, general medical opinion held that the expenditure of semen was debilitating, liable to waste away the body (as well as lead to mental difficulties). As Marcus comments about Dr. Acton's physiology, "The fantasies that are at work here have to do with economics; the body is regarded as a productive system with only a limited amount of material at its disposal."[9] Here, it seems, the economic world has served as the model for the sexual. With Mill, we are suggesting, the sexual serves as the model for the economic.

There is evidence that Mill and his friends were speaking out of personal experience, as well as out of "deductive" necessity. Mill had nine children, one short of the "physiological" unchecked norm. While writing the *Elements* and strenuously arguing the need for population control, Mill, bordering on age fifty, had his seventh child, Henry, in 1820, and his eighth child, Mary, in 1822! In fact, as his friend and fellow advocate of birth control, Francis Place, himself the father of fifteen (five of whom died in childhood), pointed out sarcastically, "moral restraint" had failed completely. It "has served so well in the instances of you and I," he wrote his friend, Ensor, "Mill and Wakefield—mustering among us no less I believe than 36 children—rare fellows we to teach moral restraint."[10] For men like Mill and Place, who prided themselves on their rigid self-control, such a failure was traumatic. It meant not only that lesser men could not be expected to regulate and repress the sexual impulse and thus "spend" less, but that they, themselves, needed a new, more scientific form of discipline. The answer was "birth control" by artificial means as a substitute for insufficient "self-control." Only in this way could the requirements of a scientific political economy be met, capital be made to exceed population growth, and men saved from the consequences of their otherwise unreasoning and impulsive behavior.

Birth control, I am suggesting, is deeply rooted in psychohistorical considerations. It stands as a symbol of the intimate connection between sex and economics, especially in the nineteenth-century unconscious. The symbolic connection must not blind us to the reality factors behind Mill's notions; it illuminates them, as well as him. The evidence is clear to us, though a matter of debate for contemporaries, that a great Demographic Revolution was occurring in the late eighteenth century. The first three English censuses—and we note the introduction of a modern tool of social science into the new world of Industrialism—of 1801, 1811, and 1821 gradually made the fact clear to all willing to see.

Before the Demographic Revolution, we can now perceive that preindustrial population was not static, in the sense of never changing, but stagnant. As Phyllis Deane puts it: "When population rose in pre-industrial England, product per head fell: and if, for some reason (a new technique of production or the discovery of a new resource, for example, or the opening up of a new market), output rose, population was not slow in following and eventually levelling out the original gain in incomes per head. Alternately raised by prosperity and depressed by disease, population was ultimately contained within relatively narrow limits by static or slowly growing food supplies."[11] And as William Langer confirms for us: "This much is certain: The rate of marriage fluctuated everywhere in constant response to economic situations. A good harvest would invariably produce a rich crop of marriages, and lean years were marked by a sharp decline in new unions."[12] Thus, unhappily, the classical economists from Smith to Ricardo had empirical grounds for their "analysis" of laboring man as a "commodity," produced, like any other commodity, by the laws of supply and demand.

The Demographic Revolution, however, broke through this stagnant situation. In a mere one hundred years, from 1750 to 1850, the population of Europe more or less doubled. The reasons are still not totally clear. J. T. Krause, for example, sees the population growth as the result of an increased birth rate rather than a declining death rate, and adduces as evidence that "fertility was highest in the 1810's in the industrial counties, which probably had the highest infant and child mortality rates in England. Also, fertility was higher than average in the Poor Law counties, which were certainly not prosperous." In short, "early industrialization and the Poor Law were the major causes of high fertility."[13]

Other scholars, such as William Langer, suggest that more varied causes were at work. In his fascinating article, "Checks on Population Growth: 1750–1850," Langer indicates how the age-old checks of war, famine, and disease were steadily whittled away toward the end of the eighteenth century and the beginning of the nineteenth century. Improved communications and trade meant relief of famine in local areas. War, though still present in the Revolutionary and Napoleonic periods, seemed not to bring with it the usual epidemics following in the army's wake. The incidence of smallpox, which had attacked ninety-six out of every one hundred persons, and was fatal in about one case in seven, began to yield to inoculation and vaccination. Thus, the death rate apparently declined as a check on population growth.

There were other, less obvious checks at work as well. "The upper classes," as Langer informs us, "restricted marriages other than their own." Their domestic servants either were not allowed to or did not wish to give up steady, secure posts in order to marry. And not least of the checks was the practice of infanticide, whether illegal or under the legal pretense of placing unwanted children in Foundling Hospitals, where about 80 to 90 percent of them died before reaching their first year.

All of these checks (and more) appear to have been inadequate against the sexual impulses feared so strongly by Mill and his friends. According to Langer, a fundamental change in the European food supply—the introduction from America in the middle of the eighteenth century of the potato and maize—made it possible for 100 million new mouths to be fed, no matter how poorly (though Ireland, in 1846–1848, showed how fragile this was as a solution). Although Mill seems not to have recognized this new causal element in population growth, he was more than aware of the growth itself. The specter of uncontrolled reproduction haunted him and his classical economics, as I have tried to show, for reasons of both economic logic and psycho-logic.

Mill, however, was timid, or rather "prudent" about making known his advocacy of artificial birth control. He first hinted at his thoughts in his article, "Colony," for the Supplement (1818) to the eighth edition of the *Encyclopedia Britannica.* Here he said:

> What are the best means of checking the progress of population . . . it is not now the time to inquire. It is, indeed, the most important practical problem to which the wisdom of the politician and moralist can be applied. It has, till this time, been miserably evaded by all those who have meddled with the subject. . . . And yet, if the superstitions of the nursery were discarded, and the principles of utility kept steadily in view, a solution might not be very difficult to be found; and the means of drying up one of the most copious sources of human evil . . . might be seen to be neither doubtful nor difficult to be applied.[14]

He was even more circumspect, as we have seen, in his veiled allusion to the subject in the *Elements.*

It remained for Francis Place to broach the subject openly in his book, *Illustrations and Proofs of the Principle of Population* (1822), and to make the first effort at birth control as a social movement. In his own life Place had experienced the problem at first hand. At nineteen, an impecunious journeyman breeches maker, he married seventeen-year-old Elizabeth Chadd. Place thought of himself as a dissolute youth; as one commentator puts it, marriage "proved the great moral influence of his life, and lifted him, smirched but not deeply stained from the mire of his past surroundings."[15] While lifting the moral burden, marriage brought economic ones, especially in the form of children. As James Field has observed, "His own early marriage had been salvation. He had failed to live decently in celibacy even to the age of 19: and for the man of the laboring class who awaited assured means of supporting a family before taking a wife, the horror of this youthful experience foretold to him hopeless immorality. But experience no less emphatically warned him that early marriage meant many children."[16]

Out of his own bitter experience, then, even after becoming a successful master tailor, Place was aware that neither celibacy nor marriage *without some form of artificial birth control* was a realistic solution to the Malthusian problem. He became a dedicated advocate of some kind of contraception. Setting out to teach the laboring class that the cause of their low wages was excessive population, he exhorted them to control the former by controlling the latter. In the *Illustrations*, he argued that:

> If, above all, it were clearly understood, that it was not disreputable for married persons to avail themselves of such precautionary means as would, without being injurious to health, or destructive of female delicacy, prevent conception, a sufficient check might at once be given to the increase of population beyond the means of subsistence; vice or misery, to a prodigious extent, might be removed from society, and the objective of Mr. Malthus, Mr. Godwin, and of every philanthropic person, be promoted, by the increase of comfort, of intelligence and of moral conduct, in the mass of the population.

Then, in a very interesting remark, reminiscent of Mill's comment about the "superstitions of the nursery," Place added, "It is childish to shrink from proposing or developing any means, however repugnant they may at first appear to be" to achieve the aim of limiting births.[17]

What were these means, however repugnant? Place left the matter in complete obscurity, though in an 1823 letter to the editor he talked of "the use of the sponge."[18] Nevertheless, for his public espousal of contraception, Place was condemned as promoting immorality and even prostitution (though as his followers pointed out, one consequence of birth control was to reduce the need for prostitutes). As his biographer Graham Wallas tells us, "Good men refused to be introduced to him, and in 1834, his help was declined on this ground alone by the strongly liberal 'Society for the Promotion of Useful Knowledge.' "[19]

Place, however, did not stop with his publication of the *Illustrations*. He reduced its essentials into handbills on contraception, and caused these to be distributed among the working class. Thus began birth control agitation as a social movement. One of those who distributed the handbills was seventeen-year-old John Stuart Mill. He had been shocked a short time earlier when, on his way to work, he had stumbled on a bundle containing a strangled newborn child in St. James's Park. The experience, and his discipleship to his father's economics, made John a ripe convert for Place's work. Handing out the bills to "maid-servants," he was arrested and brought up on charges of distributing obscenity. The entire episode is murky, but it appears that the magistrate, on discovering who it was he was sentencing, dismissed the case. The episode was hushed over, and, according to Michael St. John Packe, only a not very definite verse by poet Thomas Moore, a professional lampoonist, hinted at the affair:

> *There are two Mr. M . . ls, too, whom those who like reading*
> *What's vastly unreadable, call very clever*
> *And whereas M . . l senior makes war on good breeding*
> *M . . l junior makes war on all breeding whatever.*[20]

Friendship with Ricardo

MANY of Mill's ideas of population, wages, rent, and so on, came from David Ricardo. Ricardo was more than just a theorist for James Mill. He was, in fact, his closest friend, the one person for whom Mill had truly warm and loving feelings. It is a relationship which we need to explore more deeply.

The two men were first brought together as a result of Mill's essay of 1808, "Commerce Defended." As John Stuart Mill later wrote about his father's pamphlet, it was "the first of his writings which attained any celebrity, and which he prized more as having been his first introduction to the friendship of David Ricardo, the most valued and most intimate friendship of his life."[21] When their extant correspondence begins, at the end of 1810, the two men were already fast friends.

Almost all attention has understandably been paid either to the influence of Ricardo's economic theories on Mill, or, more recently, to the influence of Mill's character on forcing Ricardo to write out and publish his ideas, and even to run for Parliament. Sraffa's edition of

Ricardo's correspondence supplies the evidence and, as T. W. Hutchison puts it, shows convincingly how Mill "got the modest, unlettered paterfamilias and wealthy retired-stockbroker-turned-country-gentlemen, first to publish to the world a treatise on the *Principles of Political Economy* and then, following up the written with the spoken message, how he pushed the still reluctant Ricardo into Parliament to proclaim the new politico-economic doctrines from the stage of the House of Commons."[22]

Mill took on the role of teacher and master to Ricardo, just as he had with his own son. In November 1815, Mill wrote to his friend: "As I am accustomed to wield the authority of a schoolmaster, I therefore, in the genuine exercise of this honourable capacity, lay upon you my commands, to begin to the first of the three heads of your proposed work, rent, profit, wages—viz. *rent*, without an hours delay." A month later, Mill cautioned: "You must not tell Mrs. Ricardo how I am thus acting the pedagogue over you. She will think (what I think myself) that my impudence truly is not small."[23]

One senses an almost maternal role being played here. Mill is acting to Ricardo as his own mother acted to him. This was a kind of "love" he could understand. Ricardo, in turn, was willing to play his part. As he wrote to Mill in August 1816, apologizing for the state of some papers he had sent, "but you are absolute, and it is my business to obey you. They shall therefore be copied and sent and you will then be convinced that however tractable the dispositions of your pupils may be there is a vast difference in directing the energies and talents of a young mind whose habits are not formed, and an old one whose pursuits have been in no way favourable to the objective you wish to attain." When Ricardo a few years later (September 1819) showed himself less amenable to one of Mill's suggestions, the latter sternly replied: "You are not a puling sentimentalist—a thing that must be *governed by*, not govern, its fine feelings!" and continued: "So now I hope you are properly scolded and having kissed the rod [had James Mill's mother beaten him? had his teachers?] like a good disciple, are taking seriously to your task."[24]

How strange, after reading Mill's stricture on being "a puling sentimentalist" to go back to a letter of his to Ricardo in October 1816: "You do not doubt that I have a *good* deal of friendship for you, and I do not doubt that you have a *good* deal for me. But know that I have a *great* deal for you, and wish you to have a *great* deal for me." Abashed at his own display of emotion, Mill then hastily adds: "But not to lay too much stress upon this ground, *lest I begin to be sentimental* [italics added]," and immediately places the discussion on a more detached plane.[25] Surely, it seems, it is the threat in Mill of giving way to sentimental feelings, not the absence of them, that can explain his utterances.

What was there in Ricardo that led *him* to accept the role of obedient student when he was a successful financier, far wealthier than Mill? How best can we explain the total relationship, which had such important consequences for the development of economic theory and practice? Hutchison offers one explanation:

> Partly, it was a case of the attraction of opposites. As a writer Ricardo always felt himself something of an amateur, at any rate outside the narrower field of monetary and banking problems, and he admired the strenuous professional intellectual (or "hackneyed stager" as Mill called himself), who wielded such a fluent and incisive pen on any subject from India to Education. Mill, on the other hand, respected the practical, successful, financial acumen and expertise of Ricardo. But it was not contrasts but close intellectual affinities which made possible their partnership, and which made Ricardo such a "natural" for Mill's great project or promotion.[26]

Apparently Ricardo needed a strong, confident man to dominate over him, to quiet his doubts, and to jolt him out of his passivity. Mill supplied that need. Outwardly, Mill never wavered. As he typically wrote in 1817: "I have *no doubt* [italics added] about removing all your difficulties. . . ." Ricardo, in response to this assertion of self-confidence, answered: "If I before had had doubts of what legislation might do, to improve society, I should have none after reading what I have read of your book. . . ." Such general certainty of purpose and conviction prodded Ricardo into writing his *Principles of Political Economics* and then securing a seat in Parliament. Well could Mill exult: "You are now beyond all dispute at the head of Political Economy. Does not that gratify your ambition? And who prophesied all this? Tell me that! And scolded you on, coward that you are? Tell me that!"[27]

If Ricardo was attracted to Mill as a sort of "opposite" figure, his attraction for Mill seems to have been of a far more complicated nature. In reading the correspondence one cannot avoid noticing that the intensity of feeling, surprisingly, was more on Mill's side. Even if we cannot offer the correct interpretation of what was actually involved, it still seems useful to cite some of the puzzling data. Unfortunately, it comes only in intriguing bits and pieces.

For example, as early as August 1815 Mill speaks of Ricardo's family as "making on him" the highest claims "to his love." A year later, Mill underlines that "love" in a somewhat strange and teasing comment, when he remarks of Ricardo's sister, Esther: "As for that noble Esther—I know not how to express my admiration of her . . . I wish I knew a husband worthy of her—*and since I cannot have her myself, that I had a son ready to become a candidate for those affections* which are composed of so precious a metal [italics added]."[28] Mill here, it seems to me, is not being unfaithful to his own wife, even unconsciously; rather, I believe, he is unconsciously wishing in some way to enter Ricardo's family.

There is a revealing comment about that family in a letter of August 1817, especially if we recall the unloving nature of James Mill's own family as viewed by his son John. James Mill wrote to Ricardo: "I know how well you are beloved by all who belong to you. And *yours is a family that seem to have the knack of loving one another* [italics added]." Mill, in my judgment, wished to belong to what he saw as an ideal, loving family. As he writes a few paragraphs after the sentence quoted above, "you must hold it a religious duty to work—to work and perseveringly—if I had a cottage within a couple of miles of you, how I would keep you to it!"[29] Doubly interesting for our purposes is that Mill makes this comment about the cottage shortly after he had commented on the fact that Ricardo was finding a cottage for his own son, Osman, within a mile of the paternal residence!

What I am suggesting, in short, is that Mill's relations to Ricardo fit in with another variant of his "family romance" longings. As with the Stuarts and with Bentham, Ricardo and his family offer Mill a fantasied other, and better, family than his own. Perhaps this is the tragedy of a "self-made man." In part, Ricardo allowed Mill to play the mother-as-pedagogue to him. Ricardo also served as the loving and wealthy father, spoiling his children (an accusation Mill brings to bear on him, as a possible danger arising from his children living a "fashionable life") in a manner Mill may have wished for from his father. Ricardo was possibly also Mill's fantasied sibling, since the two men were born only a year apart. There is a kind of identification seemingly played out at various points, as when Mill writes in August 1817: "Oh, yes—I should like vastly well to have a purse as full as yours. . . . Give me £20,000 a year, and I will show you a parliament radically reformed, in one half of twenty years," and then pushes Ricardo into Parliament.[30]

Whatever the correct analysis, we need some such speculation as the above to explain the strange bits of quotations cited, and to allow us to understand the loving relation to Ricardo, which appears so out of character for Mill. On Ricardo's death in 1823, Mill was visibly distraught, to the surprise of his friends. As Mrs. Grote said: "As to Ricardo's death . . . Mill was terribly affected—far more so than you would have supposed it likely. The heart of him was touched, and his nature revealed more tenderness on this occasion than I had believed to reside within his philosophic frame. I am woman enough to feel greater admiration for him than before, on this account."[31]

In the case of Ricardo, Mill seems to have given way to unusual feelings of "love." The reasons are unusual, and we have had a difficult time securing even a vague glimpse of them. Yet, vague as they are, they suggest that the intellectual collaboration of Mill and Ricardo, with its fateful contributions to economic science as one result, had a strong, unconscious emotional foundation. In short, there is here, too, as we have been trying to show throughout this chapter, a psychohistorical basis to the abstract economics of the *Elements of Political Economy*.

6

India and Colonial Attitudes

A Philosophy of History

"I WAS BORN in London. . . . The eldest son of James Mill, the author of the History of British India." So announced John Stuart Mill in his *Autobiography*. We have already touched on the significance of this statement for the son; now we need to explore it further, especially for the father. As John continues, his father undertook his task weighed down with a growing family whose pecuniary needs he sought to satisfy with his writings, and whose pedagogic requirements he supplied by instruction at his own hands. "But he," John finishes his eulogy, "with these burthens on him, planned, commenced, and completed the History of India; and this in the course of about ten years, a shorter time than has been occupied (even by writers who had no other employment) in the production of almost any other historical work of equal bulk."[1]

James shared his son's view that his superhuman effort was as much his "child" as John. As he wrote his friend, David Ricardo, at its completion: "[I am] very anxious to hear what you think of this offspring."[2] However, looked at from another point of view, the *History* was not just a sibling to John, but a part of paternal solicitude, "nourishing" the family by providing Mill Senior with an established, secure position in the East India Company, and, later, his son John with a similar post.[3] The *History*, then, must be seen as playing a major and complex role in the lives of both Mills.

Why did James Mill take on the heavy task of writing his *History*, and why a history of India? In many ways it was a foolish choice. Misjudging his almost impossibly large task, he had originally estimated that it would take him two or three years to finish! Only his compulsive habits of labor and iron will brought him out of the jungle of materials in ten years. The most obvious reason for James' choice was undoubtedly ambition. He saw a chance to fill a void, for there was no reputable book on India, and to achieve established fame, and perhaps fortune, as well. India was growing in the British consciousness; the trial of Hastings had resounded throughout the Isle, and nabobs and the Indian "interest" played a prominent role in Parliament.

Had Mill thought about India as a child? It is interesting to note that, scattered throughout John Galt's *Annals of the Parish*, which we may take as an accurate picture of Scottish life at the time of Mill's growing up, are numerous references to ambitious and adventurous young men going off to India. We are told of one parishioner who got a "legacy from a cousin that died among the Hindoos"; of another, buying the main house in the village, who was "a nabob from India"; of how tea became a staple of local smuggling; of how a client of the local lord was "sent out as a cadet" to India; and so on.[4]

We can only conjecture that some early impressions had disposed Mill toward the choice of India, for on the face of it it seemed an unlikely assignment. Mill had never been to India, and he knew none of the native languages. With characteristic force and arrogance, however, he transformed these faults into virtues. Mill claimed that the power of induction from the "facts" was, philosophically, more important than firsthand observation. As for languages, all the "facts" that he needed "to ascertain every important point, in the history of India" were already available in the European languages.[5]

For Mill, in short, India posed no problems different from any other historical endeavor. In an age when professional specialization was yet on the horizon, a scholar could still profess general abilities and knowledge. There seemed no reason why Mill could not write equally well on India as he did on economics, government, and jurisprudence. Indeed, he felt that his lack of firsthand acquaintance with India guaranteed a certain impartiality.

Mill felt additionally justified because of his Utilitarian convictions as to the "science of human nature." In 1806, when he started his

History, Mill had not yet met Jeremy Bentham, but he already shared many of his convictions. One was a faith in Associationalist psychology, which offered a model of universal human behavior that could only be exemplified by the particulars of Indian life and history. Because Mill wrote his book over the course of ten years, during which his personal relationship to Bentham formed and then grew in significance, it is difficult to say where Bentham's specific influence actually enters into Mill's writing. Bentham himself, as Eric Stokes reminds us,

> had always been eager to take a hand in framing the law system of India. In 1793 he had made an offer of his services, as a sort of Indian Solon, to Dundas, at this time President of the Board of Control; and Bentham's papers show that he toyed with the notion of constructing an Indian constitutional code. The important essay *On the Influence of Time and Place in Matters of Legislation* was composed with the object of considering what modifications were required in order to transplant his system of law codes to Bengal.

Bentham was later to boast that he had become the philosopher-king for India's teeming population: "Mill will be the living executive—I shall be the dead legislative of British India."[6]

There can be little question that Mill's *History* showed Utilitarian principles in action; his was truly a history defined in the Enlightenment sense of "philosophy teaching by examples." In addition, as we shall see shortly, by disparaging the Hindu culture and literally stripping the Hindus of any pretense to civilization, Mill could treat India, *in part*, as a blank continent on which the Utilitarian legislator could impose his ideas. In America in 1789, and France in 1789–1793, constitutional conventions sought to construct a new political order freed from the irrational, unplanned vestiges of the past. India posed a more difficult problem, but Mill sought to reduce the challenge to something like the same terms.

In doing so, he appealed not only to Utilitarian principles, and thus perhaps to Bentham, but to something not in Bentham: a philosophy of history. While the conventional view (held even by John Stuart Mill) that Bentham and the Enlightenment were antihistorical is not true—though Bentham's interests were mainly in identifying and then destroying what he called "antiquities"—it is correct to assert that "he rejected all claims that history discloses laws of development."[7] For Bentham there existed universal law, but not universal history. His science of legislation was ahistorical. For the law giver:

> The great outlines, which require to be drawn, will be found to be the same for every *territory*, for every *race*, and for every *time*: only in this or that

territory, only for this or that *race*, only for this or that *time*, as distinguished from this or that other, will the *filling* up of those lines be found to require to be, on this or that point, more or less different.[8]

Mill accepted this dictum, but added to it a belief in the laws of historical development, a belief he had derived from his Scottish education and from his teachers who preached and practiced what is called "conjectural history."[9] Conjectural history gave to James Mill a flexibility, lacking in Bentham, that was to stretch Utilitarianism almost to the breaking point when carried further by John Stuart Mill in terms that went far beyond, though in the same direction as, his father's philosophy of history.

The Lessons of History

HISTORY may recapture the past, but it may also be used to destroy it. Historical writing reveals one's attitude to time gone by, and time to come, as well as the present. We have already seen how important was the time reversal in the Battle of the Ancients and the Moderns. The ties that bind one to revered ancestors may be strengthened or snapped; in the eighteenth century many of these ties were frayed. It is one part of the coming Romantic lament at the lack of connection. Yet, for people who wish to move into a future different from the past, it is psychologically necessary to attenuate certain ties (and/or to fantasize new ones).

It is in these terms that we can see Mill's *History* as part of the continuing battle of the moderns versus the ancients; in this case, ancient Indian civilization. Mill was fairly typical of the Enlightenment attitude toward history, especially of the Scottish Enlightenment. Two words can best sum up his approach: critical and conjectural. Critical history meant, as Mill said, "a judging history." [1:v] At the very beginning of his work, Mill cites Beausobre, *Histoire de Manichée*, as the first author to have a distinct conception of critical, or judging, history. Isaac de Beausobre was a refugee pastor who wrote the two-volume *Histoire critique de Manichée et du Manicheisme* (Amsterdam, 1734–1739), vaguely defending Socinian views. Of little or no importance today, he had obviously impressed James Mill by his critical attitude toward revealed religion. A few pages later, Mill also cites Pierre Bayle as "a great judge," [1:xxvi] and this citation confirms our judgment. Bayle, of course, is still well known as the pioneering author of the *Dictionnaire historique et critique* (1697). It is Bayle's *Diction-*

ary, with its mingling of religious skepticism and "critical" method (i.e., "doubting" his Biblical sources), and its emphasis on the past as a record of crimes and errors, which became the model for Diderot's *Encyclopedia* and the *philosophes*' thinking about history.[10]

To these liberal or radical Protestant historians, Mill added the name of Gibbon as his inspiration. Such attribution makes clear Mill's strong anticlerical feelings, and these are confirmed for us in numerous pages of his *History*. His satire and criticism, of course, are directed toward the Hindu religion, a safe target, but obviously the intelligent reader is expected to extend the criticism to beliefs and institutions nearer to home as well.

Mill made clear his view of history as a "judging" matter in a book review. "The course of history," Mill declared, "should be so directed as to present in clear and instructive light the natural rewards of virtue and the punishments of vice. In this important quality the modern historians, we are sorry to say, are almost all defective, and shamefully defective."[11]

History was to "instruct," and Mill intended to be a better teacher than the defective modern historians around him. His particular judgments were often carefully and even painfully worked out; for example, he leaned over backward to be fair to Warren Hastings. What Mill really had in mind was "useful" history. Like Voltaire, referring to a clouded point in Greek antiquity, Mill would have said "Let us not lose time in fathoming these useless obscurities." Like Condorcet, Mill would have added, "It is enough to assemble and order the facts and to show the *useful truths* [italics added] that can be derived from their connections and from their totality."[12]

Mill's useful history was also Utilitarian history. As Mill insisted, utility was the measure of civilization. "Exactly in proportion as Utility is the objective of every pursuit," Mill announced, "may we regard a nation as civilized. Exactly in proportion as its ingenuity is wasted on contemptible or mischievous objects . . . The nation may safely be dominated barbarous." [2:134] Exactly the same measure applied to history as to civilization, and Mill in his *History* wished to offer only "what was useful." [1:ii]

This intention linked directly with what today we would call present-mindedness. Mill, as so many of the *philosophes*, was not interested in history for its own sake, but only as it had a "lesson" for his own time. In fact, of course, the lesson came from his own time. Thus Mill, who detested the aristocracy of his contemporary England, read back into India the lesson that aristocracy was detestable. Voltaire and Montesquieu before him had used a China and a Persia to satirize and criticize eighteenth-century France; Mill used India for the same purpose in reference to early nineteenth-century England. Unless we understand this fully, we shall not understand Mill's history of India.

Mill claimed to derive his useful knowledge from correct deduction from the facts. The facts, in turn, were derived from written records, and to sift through them Mill utilized the rules of evidence (as in legal matters) and logic. He insisted that "facts" must be sharply differentiated from mere "matters of opinion."

Facts, correct deductions, useful truths—these were the key elements forming Mill's critical history. To the latter, however, he added what we have referred to as conjectural history. In the most limited sense, conjectural history "only applied to periods where there was a lack of evidence, where, although annals were lacking, 'philosophy' could conjecture the succession of the states of society."[13] More broadly interpreted, conjectural history offered a scale of development whereby particular societies could be measured as to their barbarous or civilized state (and we have already seen that for Mill this equates with their level of "utility").

As for the "canons" called for by Mill, these remained even in his hands still rather indistinct. "Utility" was the chief canon, but as a measure it needed to be applied in detail. One detail seemed to be the tools used by a society, and Mill throws out an anticipation of Karl Marx almost as an aside. [2:31] The level of agriculture, closely related to the tools used in it, is another. Then there are the arts and architecture, though Mill warns us not to be misled by mere largeness, for rude civilization can easily produce these. Language is another sign, for the more language avoids ambiguity, and has one name for one thing, the closer it is to indicating a civilized people. Surprisingly, Mill also offers the status of women as a test of civilization, and cites Millar's *Origin of Ranks* as his authority in this matter.

The major canons, as to be expected, were the nature and level of government, economics, morality, and religion. These Mill judged in the particular case in good Benthamite fashion. On such a basis, it seems, Hindu and Chinese civilizations were inferior to the Turkish—an assertion Mill makes without any effort at demonstration or examination. We shall see shortly, in detail, his objections to Hindu civilization. Chinese civilization, praised so highly by Voltaire, was dismissed by Mill as barbarous. Both Chinese agriculture and government were rude. Mill declared:

> The information we now have concerning China, however defective in marking the particular aspect which, among them, a particular stage of

civilization exhibits, is yet abundantly sufficient to prove that they are in the very infancy or very little advanced beyond the infancy, of fixed, or agricultural society. It is not possible for a people, deriving their subsistence from the culturation of the soil, and spread over a very considerable extent of country, to be held together by means less artificial, and less favourable to human happiness than the Chinese are. Their government is a despotism in the very simplest and rudest form.[14]

Voltaire had seen this Chinese despotism as a model for "enlightened" government; Mill saw it in terms that are more familiar to us today as "hydraulic" society, to use the Marxist terminology, or "Oriental despotism," to use the phrase of Karl Wittfogel.[15] Mill's insight into the true nature of Chinese government, however, did not prevent him from making a great error as to the rest of Chinese civilization. In his eagerness to show Europe more advanced than China, he dismissed its arts, crafts, and general culture as barbarous, when, in fact, recent scholarship shows that it equaled or led Europe in many of these areas, at least until Mill's time.

China was never at the center of Mill's interests, as India was. In terms of his scale of civilizations, the two countries seemed equally barbarous. But Great Britain was involved with India in a large-scale and dramatic way (which was not true of its relationship with China), and with repercussions for British politics and government itself. Mindful of Great Britain's duties toward India, Mill drew a surprisingly historicist conclusion from his belief in the scale of nations. He announced:

To ascertain the true state of the Hindus in the scale of civilization is not only an object of curiosity in the history of human nature; but to the people of Great Britain, charged as they are with the government of that great portion of the human species, it is an object of highest practical importance. No scheme of government can happily conduce to the ends of government, unless it is adopted to the state of the people for whose use it is intended. [2:135]

It is true, as Duncan Forbes points out, that Mill's historicism, if such it can be called, is blunted by the very scale of nations that calls it into being. Thus, as Bentham had suggested, the Utilitarian legislator need not take into account, for example, the climate of a particular country because "the savage is listless and indolent under every climate."[16] For Mill, Hindus were savages, and therefore he could ignore the climate. However, it is noteworthy how often Mill does pay attention to particulars of this sort; what vitiates his historicism in practice is that he is at least as often interested in drawing a "lesson" from India for British purposes, as he is in governing India by adapting Utilitarian principles to its particular level of civilization.

What is more, it never seems to have occurred to him that Utilitarian principles themselves were merely representative of one stage in the evolution of human society, and not therefore of eternal validity. Canning, for example, as President of the Board of the East India Company, was able to rise to a humility that Mill, Examiner in the Company, could not reach. Admitting ignorance at one point, Canning concluded: "I apprehend nothing to be so little useful as reasoning by analogy from Europe to India."[17] More fundamental is the later criticism by Sir Henry Maine in his *Ancient Law* (1861). As Eric Stokes so well sums it up: "Holding the entire range of Utilitarian dogma to be the product not of intellectual discovery but of long institutional growth, Maine denied that they were of absolute and universal validity. The Utilitarian postulates in jurisprudence or political economy could never be more than conditional truths, relative to a particular stage in the development of human society."[18] Mill could not see that the very "scale"—Utilitarianism—by which he measured the achievements of other civilizations was itself only the product of a time-bound, nineteenth-century European civilization. Nor could he see to what an extent his own thought and character was conditioned by that fact, a fact which is one of the main subjects of our present inquiry into the relations of James and John Stuart Mill.

History as Personality Revealed

UP TO NOW we have concentrated on the public, conscious reasons why James Mill chose to write his history of India in the way he did. Good histories are usually thought of as relatively objective handling of agreed upon facts, and this was certainly Mill's view. In our sophisticated age we are aware that subjective factors also enter into the account: the historians' class, nationality, political views, and so on. In general, however, these subjective factors are considered solely on the conscious level. Psychohistory introduces the possibility of looking at a piece of historical writing as a palimpsest in which unconscious factors also show through. The unconscious does not replace the conscious; it deepens it, and adds corresponding material.

Literary texts, of course, have been treated in this way for quite some time. Erik Erikson has recently taken an enormous qualitative step forward in his suggestions about how to approach autobiographical texts. He has pointed our attention to the problem of transferences and countertransferences in the use of such material, and offered typologies whereby to fix the positions of what he calls the complementarity of the recorder and the reviewer, both on the individual and the communal level.[19] Tremendously suggestive, there is no reason why Erikson's scheme cannot be extended to historical writings per se.

It is interesting to note that Eric Stokes, author of the most important book on the English Utilitarians and India, intuitively senses what is involved in his subject. Thus, in his Preface he declares: "It has been my conviction that British rule in India was not a disconnected and meaningless fragment of English history, but that even from the most insular standpoint it holds a mirror up to nature, reflecting the English character and mind in a way that often escapes the Englishman confined within his domestic setting." A little further on, Stokes suggests:

> The transformation of the Englishman from nabob to sahib was also fundamentally an English and not an Indian transformation, however much events assisted the process. Indian experience undoubtedly hardened certain traits in the English character, but for their origin one needs to penetrate to the genesis of the nineteenth-century English middle class, and to the hidden springs setting its type.

Hastily, Stokes even sees the connection between the "hidden springs" and the changes to which I have referred to earlier as "structural changes." As he announced:

> The transformation of the English in India from suppliant merchants to a ruling caste, consciously isolated and imbued with a sense of racial superiority, was a natural consequence of their career of conquest. The growth of a considerable European population, in particular of the number of English women, also made for a more regular and settled mode of life, and diminished contact between the races. Yet the change that was everywhere noted as taking shape after Cornwallis came out to Bengal in 1786 was much more than a response to changed political circumstances. The improvement in moral tone was not a merely local phenomenon. It was a change being wrought in the character of the Englishman at his centre; the product of advancing industrialism, of the ascendancy of the new middle classes, and of the emergence of a new ethic for a new society.[20]

More recently, Francis Hutchins has sought to develop Stokes' notion of a change in English character in India. Psychological insight is very consciously present in his discussion, though exhibited without any of the jargon. Thus we have such subtle remarks as "Englishmen conceived that to govern India was their duty and were further convinced of this by how little they enjoyed doing it and how little they

were appreciated for it," and "If one were ashame
one's own sexuality, it was a psychological relief to c
still relatively superior state with the presumably ur
of those one disliked."[21]

With such predecessors in mind, we can take cou
more closely at James Mill as he reveals to us himself
tarian colleagues, rather than the Indians, his ostensible
himself strikes the personal note in his Preface, whe rather lachrymosely talks of "The whole of my life, which I may, without scruple, pronounce to have been a laborious one." [1:xiv] Moreover, while Mill eulogizes the virtues of hard work, it is clear that he has reservations about his "labor of love." "To watch, to scrutinize," he tells us, "to inquire, is labour, and labour is pain." [2:5] Now, according to his own pleasure-pain principles, Mill should hardly be one to praise labor. After all, man's aim is to maximize pleasure and reduce pain. Mill's way out of this dilemma is in terms of deferred gratification; that is, painful labor now prevents greater pain (or offers greater pleasure) later.

Mill's argument really goes beyond this, and relates his feelings about labor to his hatred of aristocracy. As in his *Essay on Government*, Mill believed that aristocracy, leisure, and stupidity went together, whereas hard work and ability cohered on the other side. He constantly cites "that voluptuousness and neglect of the business of government, which so uniformly accompany the continued possession of power." [2:389] Was there any real evidence that "voluptuousness" led to stupidity? Were not the glories of European civilization themselves in large part due to leisure? Mill never debated such questions. Himself having to labor out of necessity, idleness loomed as a great threat. Softness, idleness, voluptuousness—these were attributes of the aristocracy, which Mill hated intensely. Does Mill's one recorded comment on his sister, in which he called her "spoiled," give us an insight to a personal dimension of his feelings?

Labor meant duty, and duty offered a warm sense of virtue. Writing from the East India offices to Ricardo in 1819, Mill protested: "Though I might procure leave of absence for the asking, there are so many despatches to answer, and the happiness and misery of so many millions are affected by what I write, that I cannot find it in my heart to abstract a day from the labours of this place till I have got towards an end of my arrears."[22] The "millions," of course, would not even know of Mill's labors, and even if they did would not love him for it. We have already noted Hutchins' comment on this matter, and we need only recall Kipling's famous lines:

Take up the White Man's burden—
And reap his old reward:
The blame of those ye better,
The hate of those ye guard—

For Mill, it was not only to India, but to all of life that these lines could apply.

Others might thirst for the plaudits and appreciation of the crowd. Not so Mill. Speaking of Edmund Burke, he is really speaking at the end about himself. "Edmund Burke lived upon applause—upon the applause of the men who were able to set a fashion; and the applause of such men were not to be hoped for by him who should expose to the foundation the iniquities of the judicial system." [5:231–232] Instead, as Mill informs us in his Preface, he will eschew the well-trodden paths to "immediate applause" and the "acquisition of fame" [1:xxvii], and offer only materials for the "improvement of the mind." He boasts, too, of having formed his own opinions—a familiar note—and of expressing them with "manly plainness." [1:xxv–xxvi] The note of "manliness" is one we shall encounter again.

Without expressly intending it, then, Mill has sketched a brief portrait of himself—or at least of his virtues. He labors hard, and expects no rewards or love for it. He shuns voluptuousness and idleness, and this in itself is proof of his capacities and abilities, as opposed to aristocratic nullity. He thinks for himself, that is, he is self-formed, and he is manly. With these qualities among others in the man, and the man the measure of the civilization he is studying, it will be interesting to see what sort of transferences occur in Mill's *History of India.*

Villains and Heroes

IN INDIA Mill perceived a villain, the Hindus, and a hero of sorts, the Mohammedans. In psychological terms, he seems to have loaded all the elements of what Erikson has called "negative identity" on the former, and reserved for the latter the positive features. The result is a sort of historical Punch and Judy show which seems to have established or confirmed lasting stereotypes about India in the British mind.[23]

Mill's litany of the Hindu vices was long and comprehensive; even traits that in other peoples seemed virtues turned into dross or mere appearance when exhibited by the Hindus. Thus, even the Hindu "gentleness of manner" does not win Mill's approbation; it is a sign of their feminineness and timidity, which he reprobates. [1:399] The Hindus are indolent, weak, profligate, and passive. Mill's dislike for anything that is not "manly" comes through clearly in his comments, and is confirmed by his unexpected admiration for the mogul warrior-rulers, in spite of their admitted cruelty and their killing of sibling rivals, and his scorn for their opponents, the "effeminate," i.e., nonmilitaristic, Hindu princes. Yet this is the Mill who, as a typical member of the Enlightenment, is antimilitaristic and humanitarian (one might note in passing the numerous pages that Mill accords to a narrative of various battles, all well done and with great reader interest).

Similar paradoxes appear in his comments on women and on flattery. Mill, who in his own life exhibited such scorn to his own wife as to offend his friends and mar his child, John, held it against the Hindus that they kept the weaker sex in "a state of dependence . . . strict and humiliating." "No thing," he added "can exceed the habitual contempt which the Hindus entertain for their women." [1:385–386] Moreover, the prudish Mill showed a suspect interest in stories about Hindu pornography and the immoderate desires of the women. So, too, Mill, who flattered Bentham and other friends without ever being aware of it, accused the Hindus of being "remarkably prone to flattery; the most prevailing mode of address from the weak to the strong, while men are still ignorant and unreflecting." [1:405]

For Mill, the Hindus were in a rude state of savagery. This was equivalent to being childlike, though they were fortunately taking the "first feeble steps in improvement." [1:421] Not for Mill the Rousseau-like adulation of the childish state as an entity in itself, with virtues lost to adult men. The child, for Mill, was merely a little adult, defective at first in all the manly virtues, but with the possibility of maturing into possession of them with the right education. This was the attitude he took toward his son, as we have seen, and it is the same attitude he took to the Hindus.

To give Mill his due, though he looked upon the Hindus as childlike, he did allow for their growing up; in fact, his task, at which he labored mightily (just as with John's education), was to foster that maturation. His immediate disciples and followers pursued the path of Indian reform with this goal in mind. In 1838, someone like C. E. Trevelyan could still speak with confidence of the moment when Indians would "grow to man's estate."[24] By the time of the Indian Mutiny (1857), British opinion had largely swung over to the belief that the Indian's childlike state was rooted in his character and could never be changed. A "racist" view, which we shall discuss more fully later, had taken the place of Mill's pedagogy.

Meanwhile, in Mill's view, the childlike Hindus showed "wild imagination" and had elaborated a "wild mythology." [1:143, 310] Their worship of animals provoked Mill's puzzlement. [1: 367] He deprecated their poetry as violating the confines of "reason and taste," [2:47] and disapproved of their preferring it to history. Their art and architecture alike earned no favor in his eyes. Only the work of the loom in India and the Hindu knowledge of dyeing evoked his admiration, but he mitigated his praise by pointing out that these achievements were typical of a "rude" people. [2:19]

There is no need to go on with Mill's animadversions on the Hindus. It should be clear by now how massive was his disdain for childishness, uncontrolled imagination, weakness, effeminacy, and passiveness, and how much this is a tribute to his own anxieties on these matters, and his own desperate need to defend against the temptation to indulge these qualities in himself. It is a familiar psychoanalytic picture, masked by him as objective, rational scholarship. The Hindus had become, for Mill, a scapegoat.

Vehemently turning from the Hindus, Mill extolled the Mohammedans for the opposite virtues. Thus, in a typical outburst, he claimed to see "in the manners of the Mahomedan conquerers of India, an activity, a manliness, an independence, which rendered it less easy for despotism to sink among them, to that disgusting state of weak and profligate barbarism, which is the natural condition of government among such a passive people as the Hindus." [2:434] Even Mohammedan law came in for Mill's praise, allowing him in the process to score points against the existing state of English law. [2:445] Nowhere, incidentally, does Mill mention the flagrant religious intolerance exhibited by the Moslems in India.

It is ironic that it was the Hindus who accepted Mill's reforming ideas, and the Muslims who ignored them almost completely! For example, Ram Mohan Roy (1774–1833), the "father of modern India," founded the Calcutta Book Society in 1817 and the Calcutta School Society in 1818, and helped launch the Hindu College (later Presidency College), on the basis of the new ideas. Then, in 1830 he traveled to England to testify about the East India Company, and mingled among the Radical and Utilitarian leaders there till his death.[25] Taking the West as his model, Ram Mohan Ray attacked Hindu abuses with the zeal of Mill himself.

There is a further delightful irony in Mill's preference for the Mohammedans over the Hindus, for it was his own reforms that helped to displace the former from their traditional place in the administration of Indian law. In the 1830s, under pressure of the Utilitarian zeal for reform, Persian was officially replaced by English in the law courts and administration. Thus, the Muslims, with their monopolistic knowledge of Persian and Arabic, were displaced by a new, English-speaking Hindu middle-class elite who had learned their language in the Utilitarian-inspired colleges disdained by the Muslims![26]

Before we laugh too heartily at Mill and his eulogistic elevation of the Muslims over the Hindus (though, in fact, his work had the opposite effect), we might reflect for a moment over the life of Mahatma Gandhi. Following the account in his *Autobiography*, we see how Gandhi, as a young boy, became consciously ashamed of his Hindu weakness and femininity, in contrast to Mohammedan and British "masculinity." Seeking to imitate a Mohammedan friend, Gandhi ate meat—forbidden by his Hindu religion—for meat eaters were "strong," tried to be a virile male among the women, smoked, and, in general, sought to "grow up" on the British model, mediated through the Mohammedanism which seemed so close to it. In short, young Gandhi presents us with a picture of himself as "identifying with the aggressor," of having introjected the values so stridently proclaimed by James Mill.

As Suzanne Rudolph, as well as Erikson, points out, only by accepting his own "feminine" and "maternal" qualities was Gandhi able to rise to a new, self-sustained courage. In turning his "passivity" into passive resistance, Gandhi gained a strength to defy the British and to lead India to independence.[27] It is striking to see how, on a national scene a hundred years later, Gandhi, in his own way, was to repeat the efforts of John Stuart Mill at true self-development. Redefining "manly" so that it could embrace "gentleness of manners," "effeminacy," softness, and lovingness, both John Stuart Mill and Gandhi matured in a way that went beyond the "pseudomanliness" set before them as the preferred type. In so doing they became their own man, able to offer a new kind of intellectual and political leadership to their fellow men and women.

But Gandhi was well in the future when James Mill wrote his *History of India*. In 1818 Mill was still recommending that India be "civilized" on the Utilitarian model, that is, in terms of *reformed* English values. Munro, an administrator in India opposed to this plan, missed the point when he wrote:

> Englishmen are as great fanatics in politics as Mahomedans in religion. They suppose that no country can be saved without English institutions. The natives of this country have enough of their own to answer every useful object of internal administration, and if we maintain and protect them, the country will in a very few months settle itself.[28]

Mill did not wish "English institutions" in India; he wished to reform them at home, and to introduce uncorrupted versions into India.

Mill's general reputation is as one opposed to the teaching of Hindu culture and language in India. In one sense he was an opponent, for, as we have seen, he was convinced that they were not very worthy of respect. His real objection to them, however, was not for themselves, but because they did not offer *useful* knowledge. We must not let the stereotype of Mill, the fanatic reformer, blind us to the stringent logical demands he could make on himself when his own "projections" could be controlled. We see the full qualities of his mind at work in an East India Company dispatch of February 18, 1824, concerning the establishment of a Sanscrit College at Calcutta:

> The great end should not have been to teach Hindoo learning or Mahomedan learning, but useful learning. No doubt in teaching useful learning to the Hindoos or Mahomedans, Hindoo *media*, or Mahomedan *media*, as they were found the most effectual would have been proper to be employed, and Hindoo and Mahomedan prejudices would have needed to be consulted, while everything which was useful in Hindoo or Mahomedan literature it would have been proper to retain. . . .[29]

Lest we have any doubt of Mill's position, we need only add his comment about Warren Hastings: "He was the first, or among the first of the servants of the Company, who attempted to acquire any language of the natives, and who set on foot those liberal inquiries into the literature and institutions of the Hindus, which have led to the satisfactory knowledge of the present day." [4:454–455]

True, Mill drew opposite conclusions than did Hastings from "satisfactory knowledge." Hastings, who had, in fact, become fluent in Bengali, and knowledgeable in Urdu and Persian, protested constantly that India had an ancient civilization not inferior to the European. "The inhabitants of this land," he declared, "are not in the savage state in which they have been unfairly represented." In his old age, Hastings wrote to the Marquis of Hastings what can stand as a direct rebuttal to Mill's assertions:

> Our Indian subjects have been represented as sunk in the grossest brutality, and defiled with every abomination that can debase humanity; and it is therefore said that we possess the power, so it is our duty to reform them, nay to "coerce" them into goodness by introducing our faith amongst them. If the debasement of their moral character is the only plea for the positive intervention of our Government to bring about their reformation, indeed, my Lord, it will be better to leave them as they are, especially that race of them, the Hindoos, against which these aspersions are particularly fulminated. These I dare to pronounce . . . are as exempt from the worst propensities of human nature as any people upon the face of the earth,

ourselves not excepted. They are gentle, benevolent, more susceptible of gratitude for kindness shewn them than prompt to vengeance for wrongs sustained, abhorrent of bloodshed, faithful and affectionate in service and submission to legal authority. They are superstitious; but they do not think ill of us for not behaving as they do. Coarse as the modes of their worship are, the precepts of their religion are admirably fitted to promote the peace and good order of society; and even from their theology arguments, which no other can afford, may be drawn to support the most refined mysteries of their own.[30]

Hastings' reference to "introducing our faith among them" must remind us that Mill faced a competing "faith" to Utilitarianism in India, other than the Hindu. That other faith was Evangelical. The Evangelicals also took it as their mission to civilize India. Their justification for their mission, like Mill's, was also the presumed detestable condition of native Indian civilization. Thus, for Wilberforce, the Hindu divinities were "absolute monsters of lust, injustice, wickedness and cruelty. In short, their religious system is one grand abomination." Charles Grant, eventually a director of the East India Company, though resident in India in 1792 when he wrote *Observations* (privately printed 1797), issued a sweeping condemnation, as when he concluded that:

Upon the whole then, we cannot avoid recognizing in the people of Hindostan, a race of men lamentably degenerate and base; retaining but a feeble sense of moral obligation; yet obstinate in their disregard of what they know to be right, governed by malevolent and licentious passions, strongly exemplifying the effects produced on society by a great and general corruption of manners, and sunk in misery by their vices, in a country peculiarly calculated by its natural advantages, to promote the prosperity of its inhabitants.[31]

The Evangelicals, at one with Mill in their view of Indian depravity, saw conversion, rather than legislation, as the civilizing means. In 1813 Wilberforce made the first breech by securing admission of Christian missionaries into the Company's territories. Aiming at a total Reformation, the Evangelicals put their stress on education as the vehicle for cleansing the Indian mind of error and superstition and preparing it for the redeeming message. Happily, as in Europe, the proposed Protestant Reformation for India would bring economic growth as well as salvation. Thus, after declaring India "providentially" placed in English hands, Grant rhetorically asks:

Is it not necessary to conclude that they were given to us, not merely that we might draw an annual profit from them, but that we might diffuse among their inhabitants, long sunk in darkness, vice and misery, the light and benign influence of the truth, the blessings of well-regulated society, the improvements and comforts of active industry? . . . In every progressive step of this work, we shall also serve the original design with which we visited India, that design still so important to this country—the extension of our commerce.[32]

James Mill, of course, had come out of the same Calvinist background as many of the Evangelists. Indeed, he had first trained to be a preacher, but poor prospects and a loss of faith had turned him into an anticleric. Looked at closely, however, we can see that Mill is merely "secularizing" many of the original Calvinist aims and values. He and the Evangelicals are at one in their missionary impulse for India; it is only the particular outcome and the method that are different.

Needless to say, we must not lose sight of the difference: Bentham is a very eccentric version of Jesus Christ. When Mill recommends in his *History* a "Panopticon penitentiary house" for Bengal, which in a remarkably felicitous phrase he calls "hospitals for the mind," he is being a true disciple to his own master. [5:532] Moreover, the recommendation seems to have become reality in the prisons constructed at Poona and Ratnagiri; in the suggestions by Elphinstone (the first British resident at Poona, and later Governor of Bombay) for building one, contained in an 1819 report on Decca and eventually put into effect; and in a Punjab Administration Report, written as late as 1849–1851.[33] So, too, the content of the education proposed by Mill was vastly different in intent from that envisaged by the Evangelicals. And in the whole realm of government and legislation, the Utilitarian voice sounded alone.

Racism?

WHAT WAS the inner message of that voice? Were Mill and the Evangelicals merely disguising British Imperialism in pious and lofty language? Did Mill's extraordinary denunciation of Hindu depravity amount to a racist position? Were his feelings toward the Hindus a form of racial prejudice? He certainly projected onto them many of his own fears about indolence, childishness, passivity, and effeminacy. Picturing the Hindus in a degraded condition undoubtedly served to support Mill's unconscious defenses against similar impulses. Yet Mill's racism—for so it seems in its starkest form—was attenuated by his conviction that the Hindus' benighted state was due to their place on the scale of civilization, and not to their innate nature. Thus they were redeemable, and with the proper education might grow up—to be like the virtuous Mill!

Unfortunately, Mill's prejudices about the Hindus prepared the way for an even more nefarious British racism after 1857. From about 1818 to 1838 there was a golden age of Utilitarian reform in India. Though Mill himself did not believe the Indians were yet mature enough to participate in self-government, some of his followers were more sanguine and hastened to prepare the way for such an eventuality. However, within a few years of the death of Bentham (1832) and Mill (1836), that first reform wave crested. With Dalhousie in the 1850s there was a second reform wave. Then in 1857, with the Indian Mutiny, while various Benthamite-type legal codes were introduced in a renewed paternalism, a new racist spirit entered the British Raj. In what one scholar, Hutchins, has termed "The Illusion of Permanence," the British decided that the native Indians could never grow up—they were children forever—and must be ruled (for their own good, of course) permanently by the British. As Stokes summarizes the change: "Now reform was to be carried in the spirit of racial conquest that succeeded the Mutiny. . . ."[34]

The Mutiny focused and gave reality to what had been a growing British feeling. Disliking the natives, partly along the lines of Mill's inspiration, the British assumed, by projection, a similar dislike in their subjects. The latter feeling, in a perversion of the reality, then justified the former. Thus the Mutiny merely confirmed the rightness of British perception and of British rule. As Hutchins so well puts it: "The change was the result of the influence of revulsion and fear, shame and insecurity, of the attempt to justify dislike and defensiveness by the perception of an imagined threat; in other words, of changes in British attitudes for which Indians could scarcely be held responsible."[35]

Mill had never lived in India. Thus, he took no cognizance of what we may call the "confrontation" aspect of psychohistory, the way in which one personality impinges on another, and calls forth certain "characteristic" responses and defenses in both. Sir Walter Scott knew what was involved when he wrote Southey in 1818:

> The history of colonies has in it some points of peculiar interest as illustrating human nature. On such occasions the extremes of civilized and savage life are suddenly and strongly brought into contact with each other and the results are as interesting to the moral observer as those which take place on the mixture of chemical substances are to the physical investigator.[36]

More recently, O. Mannoni has tried to describe in detail one such encounter, between the "savages" of Madagascar and the "civilized" colonialists of Europe.[37] Mannoni claims that the colonialist brings to the encounter his need to feel superior, based on his fear of inferiority (these are Adlerian categories), while the native brings to it his need to feel dependent, based on his fear of the dead. Both play a needed role for the other, though there are consequent misunderstandings, such as the colonialists' disdain for the seeming lack of gratitude by the natives, in the form of their propensity to "take" things not belonging to them (from the native point of view, as "dependents," they are entitled to them), and the natives' bewilderment when the colonialists force them into measures of independence, which are perceived as desertion. Also of great interest is Mannoni's effort to trace the European need to be superior, which entails self-sufficiency and independence, from Descartes to the present (an inquiry which we mentioned earlier; see pp.).

Partly inspired by Mannoni's work, Philip Mason, who had served for many years as an administrator in India, has written an intriguing little book called *Prospero's Magic*.[38] I shall single out two of his themes. The first is that the European has managed to maintain his domination over the vastly larger number of natives, not so much by his advanced techniques and military prowess—as an Indian wit irreverently remarked, "If all the Indians pissed together at one time, they would wash all the British out to sea"—as by his claim to moral superiority. By establishing his own values as the higher ones, and getting the natives to accept this claim, the colonialist has placed the native in a position of "identifying with the aggressor." He has made the native internalize the values that established the native's inferiority to the colonialist. How, then, can the native rise up in rebellion with a good heart? It would be as if he were rebelling against his own better self.

Mason's second thesis is that the same techniques used to establish racial superiority are also employed in the maintenance of class superiority. On his return to England, Mason noted that the same devices of language (e.g., Oxford accent), clothes, clubs, even separate bathroom facilities were employed to emphasize the differences between masters and servants (in England, read workers)—almost as if the two classes belonged to different races. Once again the "lower" class had been brought to "identify with the aggressor" and to internalize the latter's values.

Both of these themes are enormously suggestive. It is worth viewing Frantz Fanon, for example, in the light of Mason's first theme as well as of Mannoni's general observations. In his own life Fanon had first tried to assimilate himself completely to the European "way of life." He took its values for his own. Only when he discovered that he could never really "pass," that European racism insisted on keeping him in his place as a "nigger," did he turn against his master and mentor. By a massive effort of will and of love turned to hate, he broke partially through the internalized values of his upbringing (in this case, French colonial). The master was no longer perceived as a nurturer; in hopeless disappointment Fanon eventually turned to his message of violence as the only means of breaking his bonds. If we read Fanon carefully,[39] we see that the violence is primarily directed at destroying the bonds within himself, which tie him emotionally to the colonizer, rather than at the latter per se.

In his way, Fanon is repeating the experience of Gandhi before him (even though his violence is ostensibly the reverse of Gandhi's nonviolence): he is seeking to free himself from the internalized values implanted in him by the colonizers. (We have already suggested that this colonial experience is the large-scale version of what we shall be studying, *mutatis mutandis*, in the microscopic case of John Stuart Mill.) Fanon seeks to recover his *self*-respect.

What of the colonizer? In India, the original colonizers, if such they should be called, like Warren Hastings, went out primarily for trading purposes, to make a fortune. To this end they did not need to deprecate the natives, or feel that they had to replace their ancient civilization. Moreover, their aim was to return to England; they were mere visitors. Accidental expansion of a trading company into a political empire—for such was the result of the conquests of Clive, Hastings, and others—made for a change that was ultimately to turn the nabob into the sahib.

James Mill, with the best conscious intentions in the world, signalized the beginning of the shift. Along with the Evangelicals, he propagated the view that the Indians were to be reformed and governed in new ways. Out of his own inner needs he projected a picture of them as childlike and depraved. Such a portrait, created mainly out of Mill's unconscious, served the conscious function of justifying British rule over India. That rule became fully racist after the Indian Mutiny, at which point Philip Mason's second theme reenters the picture. It is the *home* conditions—the British class structure—that turns Mill's strictures on the Hindus into a vicious racism.

As Francis Hutchins suggests, "The English created for themselves in India a social world intended to be as much like life in England as possible."[40] By the mid-nineteenth century, Englishmen who went to India no longer expected to return home quickly, with large fortunes, as nabobs. They recognized that their whole careers would be spent in India, with English womenfolk sharing life with them there. The aim was to play out in India the aristocratic life their predecessors had enjoyed on their return to England.

Ensconced in their own little social colonies, limiting the Indians with whom they mixed almost solely to menials (thus confirming the British picture of their invincible ignorance and "lowness"), the English in India closed ranks and thought of themselves all as aristocrats versus the "niggers." The lowest Englishman was superior to the most cultured, respected Hindu. United in disdain against the Indians, the English assumed a reciprocity of feeling, which then additionally justified their disdain of their "subjects." With the dissolution of the East India Company in 1858, and the devolution of its "empire" to the British nation as a whole, the entire home country could now fancy itself as aristocrats versus the, at best, Gunga Dins of India.

How would James Mill have reacted to such developments? Mill, as we know, was stridently opposed to "aristocrats" of any sort, and we can only assume that he would have disliked heartily the "sahibs" created by the actual confrontation in India of the colonizer and the native. Mill generally lived up to his own stern principles, and there is no reason to believe that he would have wavered in this instance. Mill's views on the Hindus unfortunately came to serve racist needs, but Mill himself, if, in fact, a racist, was of a very special breed. We must remember that he passed the same strictures on indolence and depravity among English aristocrats as among distant Hindus. Mill's heart beat to the sound of a different drummer from that of the English racist of the second half of the nineteenth century.

The Drum of Modernization

THE DRUM to which Mill listened was what we today would call "modernization." Mill was really the first conscious "modernizer." Whereas he spoke of India as a "rude" civilization, we would talk of it as an "underdeveloped" nation. While he wished to reform India along Utilitarian lines, we would seek to "Westernize," or at least "industrialize" the country. By now, of course, it is not only we, but many of the "native" Indian leaders who wish to tread the path of modernization. Mill's values, insofar as they were the values of the Industrial Revolution of his time, and his favored type of character structure, have become internalized in certain elite segments of Indian society.[41]

Against the general opinion of his time, which still thought of India in mythlike terms as a fabulously wealthy civilization—the "riches of India" theme that had led Columbus on his voyage of discovery—Mill insisted on the basic nature of India as a poverty-stricken country. Taking great pains to make his point, Mill stood firm in his view: "Though no body should believe it; India, like other countries, in which the industrious arts are in their infancy, and in which law is too imperfect to render property secure, has always been poor." [3:389] Mill was right, of course, if we allow for the fact that he was measuring riches by the new standard reached in the early nineteenth century by the "advanced" nations of the west. As with the earlier battle of the ancients and the moderns, Mill reversed the old perspective that saw the former as both wiser and wealthier than the present generations.

From his new perspective, Mill went on to write what is really a pioneering history of colonialism, that encounter of two civilizations described by Sir Walter Scott. Others, such as Adam Smith, had written on colonies and their history, but almost solely in terms of economic contact. Mill widened this effort so as to offer a broad, encompassing frame of cultural confrontation. Moreover, Smith, Ricardo, and others had tended to concentrate on the effects of the relationship on the "mother country." Mill, while holding up India as a negative example to England, really was equally or more concerned with the latter's impact on her newly acquired Asian empire.

The *History of British India* delves deep into the origins of India before the coming of the British. It is interesting to note that Mill, who disdained any reflection on his own origins, feeling himself a "self-made" man, transferred his persistent interest in origins to history. Surely, in this instance and many others, the search for collective origins is a displaced way of finding out about one's self. In any case, in the first few volumes especially, Mill traced the various Hindu and Muslim conquests that had surged across India before the coming of the British. Thus, the East India Company invasion takes its place in a deeply furrowed continent.

Mill was basically opposed to that invasion. He was not an imperialist, but a Little Englander. He would have preferred that the English had never begun their conquest of India. Once begun, he would have wished it limited. There is no rejoicing in Mill when he quotes Clive in 1765 as announcing: "We have at last arrived at that critical period, which I have long foreseen . . . Sujah Dowla is beat from his dominion; we are in possession of it, and it is scarcely hyperbole to say, tomorrow the whole Mogul empire is in our power. . . . We must indeed become Nabobs ourselves, in fact, if not in name." [3:332]

Further, Mill repeatedly stated that he did not believe India could be well-governed from Great Britain. Discussing a particular abuse, he declares it "another proof (we shall find an abundance of them as we proceed) of the impossibility of governing any country well from the distance of half the circumference of the globe." [3:230] Holding true to his Utilitarian belief that only the ruled know fully what is to their own advantage, Mill reiterated "the obvious and neglected truth, that the knowledge requisite for good government in India cannot be possessed by rulers sitting and deliberating in Europe." [3:389]

Even more fundamental in its challenge to British dominion over India was this comment of Mill's:

> The most flagitious perhaps of all the crimes which can be committed against human nature, [is] the imposing upon a nation, by force of foreign armies, and for the pleasure or interest of foreign rulers, a government composed of men, and involving principles, which the people for whom it is destined have either rejected from experience of their badness, or repel from the experience or expectation of better. Even where the disparity of civilization and knowledge were very great; and where it were beyond dispute, that a civilized country was about to bestow upon a barbarous one the greatest of all possible benefits, a good and beneficent government; even there, it would require the strongest circumstances to justify the employment of violence or force. [4:334–335]

Nevertheless, Mill faced the fact that India *was* being governed from Europe, and by force. The problem, therefore, was to give it the best possible government; because it could be treated as something of a blank tablet, by deprecating the existing Hindu civilization, it could, in theory, be given an even better government than Great Britain. India, for example, was free of the feudal remnants that still plagued England. Once again placing himself against the received wisdom, Mill remarked:

> Such a thing as a feudal system or a liege lord, never had a moment's existence in India, nor was ever supposed to have, except by a few pedantic and half-lettered Englishmen, who knew little more of the feudal system than the name. [4:102]

Instead, India was correctly perceived by Mill as an "Asiatic Society," an "Oriental Despotism" whose village communities formed a sort of beehive underneath the ruler. Into this timeless, replicative society broke the English power; Mill's vision of Indian society and what then took place is the inspiration for Marx's later views on the revolutionary impact of the British on India.[42]

Mill's plans to modernize India by giving it new values and institutions meant a dramatic shift from the rule of custom to the rule of law. They embodied the *Gemeinschaft-Gesellschaft* transformation so dear to the hearts of late nineteenth-century German sociologists.

Writing in 1883, J. Fitzjames Stephens percipiently summed up what was involved when he wrote that the British endeavor in India "is nothing less than the management and guidance of the most extensive and far-reaching revolution recorded in history. It involves the radical change of the ideas and institutions of a vast population which has already got ideas and institutions to which it is deeply attached."[43]

By calling for the suppression of customs such as "suttee" and infanticide, attacking the Indian treatment of women, advocating free trade and a different land revenue system, insisting on the need for a free press, establishing colleges on the European model, and numerous other suggested "reforms," Mill and his followers in India were really promoting the "far-reaching revolution" mentioned by Stephens. Such a "revolution" is what is involved in modernization, and Mill was the first clearly to indicate its nature and to apply his analysis of the elements constituting it to India.

One fundamental part of present-day modernization efforts was totally overlooked by Mill. He ignored completely the force of nationalism. "For the aversion to a government," he declared, "because in the hands of foreigners; that is, of men who are called by one rather than some other name, without regard to the qualities of the government, whether better or worse; is a prejudice which reason disclaims."[2:428] What is startling about Mill's view is that he announced it at a time when the effects of the French Revolution in the direction of national feeling were becoming more and more evident. In 1806, when Mill began his *History*, the seeds of Prussian nationalism were just beginning to sprout; by 1815, and the Congress of Vienna, all of Europe had become fertile soil for the new plant. Perhaps unable to see the growing identity problem facing individuals in a time of modernization, Mill was equally unable to recognize it in relation to groups.

In any case, national feeling played no role in Mill's vision of modernizing India. He attacked the British government for its opposition to the settlement of Englishmen in India, "foresooth, lest Englishmen, if allowed to settle in India, should detest and cast off its [Great Britain's] yoke," [5:503–504], without a thought for how Indians might react to this suggestion; Mill's mind was obviously on the recent American Revolution.

By overlooking the growing force of nationalism, Mill overlooked what we can perceive as the major dynamism behind the forced-draft modernization of contemporary "underdeveloped" countries. Yet such ignorance on his part should not blind us to one of his major achievements. Mill took economics and political science and combined them into a theory of economic development. With all its limitations and, from our point of view, primitive notions, Mill, in his *History of British India*, offers what is probably the first major discussion and analysis of the values and institutions necessarily involved in the modernization of a "rude" civilization. This is no mean achievement for a man who never visited India, except in his imagination.

India and the Mills

JAMES MILL exerted a direct influence on India, both through his *History* and by his appointment in the Examiner's Office of the East India Company, brought about by the publication of his great work. A few years after James Mill's appointment, his son John joined him at the East India Company, where he worked for the next thirty-five years. Did father and son manifest generational differences in regard to India, and in relation to the colonial situation? This is a question we shall seek to explore shortly. Before that, however, we ought to look more closely at the role of the East India Company in the lives of the Mills.

Publication of Mill's *History* coincided with a need in the East India House, because of retirements and press of business, for men of unusual intelligence and literary abilities to prepare the dispatches. Thus, in 1819 three outsiders were brought in as Assistants to the Examiners: Edward Strachey, aged forty-five, a retired Bengal judge reputed to be "Utilitarian and Democratic by creed," at £1000 per year; James Mill, aged forty-six, at £800; and Thomas Love Peacock, the novelist, aged thirty-four, at £600. (Another novelist, Charles Lamb, was a clerk in the Company.) Strachey had the judicial branch, Mill the revenue, and Peacock the miscellaneous subjects.[44] These were probationary appointments till 1821, when they were made permanent. Two years later, in 1823, Mill had outdistanced his competitors and was made Assistant Examiner, while Strachey and Peacock were called Assistants Under the Examiner (Strachey resigned over this move, but reconsidered a few weeks later). James Mill had won out because of his extraordinary capacity for, and ability at, work.

From that year on, Mill also won annual salary increases and/or gratuities. Then in 1831 he was made chief Examiner at a salary of £1900 a year. To put his position in perspective, we must realize that his post during all these years was equivalent to a Secretary, or Assistant Secretary, of State for the East India Company, in a sort of private version of a foreign office administering a huge empire. In short, Mill in the East India Company had become a very high-ranking civil servant with a very respectable salary, able now to afford his own house, summer vacations, and a most comfortable style of living. His was, indeed, a success story.

Mill's enemies accused him of having sold his principles for the porridge of the East India Company. For example, the Radical newspaper of Calcutta, *The Bengal Hurkaru*, assailed his defection:

> He is a man of the highest order of intellect, and would doubtless have done much for this country, and among other things would have finished his long promised supplementary volumes of his history [of British India], but for one slight impediment, which does honor to the sagacity of at least one party to the bargain. He has now a retainer from the other side. Honor, gratitude, and complacent self-love have won him, and kept him on the non-popular side of one great public question—that between the Company and England.[45]

There is undeniably a grain of truth to such criticisms. To a reader of the *History*, a perceptible change of tone creeps into the last volume, when Mill must have learned from his friends that they were pushing his name forward for an appointment in the Company. In the earlier volumes Mill was sharply critical of many of the Company's actions in India. By volume 6 he judiciously sums up his position:

> In regard to *intention*, I know no government, either in past or present times, that can be placed equally high with that of the East India Company. . . . in the highly important part of the servants . . . there is nothing in the world to be compared with the East India Company, whose servants, as a body, have not only exhibited a portion of talent which forms a contrast with that of the ill-chosen instruments of other governments, but have, except in some remarkable instances . . . maintained a virtue which, under the temptations of their situation, is worthy of the highest applause. [6:17–18]

Mill, who condemned flattery in the Indians, was not above it in his own interests. However, I believe there was a greater spur than mere pecuniary interest to Mill's desire to enter the East India Company. It was ambition for power. With power Mill could do good, could bring "happiness" to millions of his fellow creatures. We must not underestimate the missionary impulse, in its secularized form of modernization, that animated Mill. As he wrote his friend Dumont as early as 1819, describing his duties and powers:

> The business, though laborious enough, is to me highly interesting. It is the very essence of the internal government of 60 millions of people with whom I have to deal; and as you know that the government of India is carried on by correspondence; and that I am the only man whose business it is, or who

has the time to make himself master of the facts scattered in a most voluminous correspondence, on which a just decision must rest, you will conceive to what an extent the real decision on matters belonging to my department rests with the man who is in my situation.

Mill adds, "The idea of being useful, as far as that is capable of animating a man's labour, can hardly be enjoyed in greater perfection. . . . There is motive, therefore, in abundance for one's best exertions. So much for *Ego*."[46]

Pursuing egoistic motives of interest and service, Mill left his mark on the administration of India. Indeed, he was Bentham's living legislator there. Especially through Lord William Bentinck, the Governor-General of Bombay from 1827 to 1835, who succeeded Montstuart Elphinstone's reforming rule (1819–1827), did Utilitarianism come to dominate Indian policy. "I am going to British India," James Mill reported Bentinck as saying at the farewell dinner given for him by the Benthamites, "but I shall not be Governor-General. It is you that will be Governor-General."[47]

On two issues—land revenue and peasant proprietorship—Mill laid his hand with heavy authority. He insisted that the original rights to the soil belonged, not to the *zemindars*, whom he disliked as Indian versions of the English aristocrats, but to the *ryot* or peasant. Whatever "rights" the *zemindars* claimed, Mill declared, were merely artificial rights set up by the State, and as easily removed. He took his stand firmly on the side of peasant proprietorship, a system which in fact entailed a social revolution in India, or, as one critic put it, a scheme to "flatten the whole surface of society."[48]

On top of peasant proprietorship, Mill imposed his land revenue system. The State was to fix and collect all rents. This, in effect, was to advocate State ownership of the soil, a startling piece of socialism for Mill. Mill's position derived from his views on rent. Following Malthus and his friend Ricardo, as we have seen, Mill believed rent to be the consequence of population outgrowing food supplies, and thus driving men to cultivate increasingly poorer soils. The differential between the better and poorer soils constituted rent. It was, therefore, an unearned value, arising from a monopoly, so to speak, and consequently not a "right" belonging to a private landlord. Mill insisted that, in India, the State undertake the entire assessment and collection from each peasant proprietor.

To these major economic decisions Mill added measures for judicial and administrative reform, governmental reorganization, and educational institutions. Until his death in 1836, his views, and those of his disciples, played a prominent role in the governance of India. For almost eighteen years, from his entrance in 1818 into the East India Company, Mill's life and its policies were intimately tied together.

Appointment of John Stuart Mill as a clerk in the Examiner's Department in 1823, when he had just turned seventeen, made the ties between the Mill family and the Company even stronger. Eventually, in 1835, a writership in the Bengal Presidency was procured for James Mill's second son, James Bentham Mill (what a fitting name!), who served the Company until his retirement in 1852. A younger son, George Grote Mill, was appointed a clerk in 1844, but gave up his post in 1850, having contracted a lung disease, and died three years later at Madeira. Such was the fruit of Mill's writing his *History of British India*: a post for himself with the East India Company, and three of his sons appointed to positions with him.

For Mill's son John it meant his official vocation. For thirty-five years India House was the scene of John Stuart Mill's labors from ten to four every weekday. Did he follow closely in his father's steps, or strike out on his own? The fact is that John never rivaled his father either in achievement or influence at the East India Company, and formulated no new policies for India. As Stokes puts it: "Although he [John Stuart Mill] was to remain in high administrative office in the Company until its abolition in 1858, eventually succeeding to the examinership, he had neither his father's opportunities nor his bent for the practical realization of the Utilitarian theories." Continuing, Stokes asserts that "perhaps the real secret why John Stuart Mill left relatively so small a mark on Indian policy was that he was unfitted by temperament or belief to take over the leadership of the doctrinaire programme laid down by his father."[49]

There can be little question of John Stuart Mill's intellectual capabilities (like his father, he was jumped over those above him; in 1828, the eleventh clerk in the Examiner's Office, he passed over ten clerks to become Assistant to the Examiner).[50] Yet most of his work at India House seems to have been rather humdrum. A glance at the list of dispatches prepared by him gives an indication of his concerns. The first entry, dated April 7, 1824, in the Bengal Political Department, is an answer to a letter dated January 15, 1820! Thus, initially, John Stuart Mill's task was to catch up on arrears of letters. The subjects of future letters ranged from those dealing with the Persian Gulph [sic] and Insurrection at Kittoor (1828) to Affairs of the Myhee Caunta; Affairs of Cutch; Salaries, Allowances, and Pecuniary Grants; Case of Lt. Colonel Ballantine: Allowances of Lt. Colonel Barnewall, and appointment of his successor; and Grants of land to natives, all written in a beautiful, flowing hand.[51]

The crucial factors in his lack of inspiration were the loss of power of the East India Company from about 1833, when the Government took over many of its functions, and John Stuart Mill's temperament, as indicated by Stokes. While John Stuart Mill did not mind too much his regular hours and work at India House, one has the distinct impression that his interests lay elsewhere (see Chap. 9, p. 199). What had been for his father an achievement was for John Stuart Mill a sinecure. In general he followed his father's policies, but without involving himself in a modification of them, as he did in other areas more vital to him. John Stuart Mill also favored peasant proprietorship, and devoted a long section of his *Principles of Political Economy* to defending it in France and Ireland, as well as in the North-Western Provinces. Referring in the book to his father as "the philosophical historian of India," he quoted him with approval on the relations of *ryot* and *zemindar*. Adopting his father's views on the land revenue, John Stuart Mill pushed the notion that the State might lay its hands on private landed property further toward a full-blown socialism covering the industrial as well as the agricultural sector. Even on the issue of admitting Indians to high office and eventually granting self-government to them, which John Stuart Mill favored more in practice than did his father, the son did not consider, as Stokes puts it, "that the time was ripe in 1853 for the introduction of a single Indian member into the Legislative Council."[52]

John Stuart Mill, in fact, was true to his father's position on India to the very end. Defending the East India Company in 1858 against the threat of dissolution by Parliament, Mill, the opponent of monopoly, put forward anew the argument for the Company's exclusive rule. He claimed that that rule was in the interests of India, and that British government rule would entail the opposite. Mill's arguments, however, were dismissed, and the Company's rule ended in 1858. John Stuart Mill retired, though he was asked to stay on. His "job" was done. He had written no major work on India, as his father had done, and seemed to hold himself aloof from Indian affairs, perhaps because of his official position: there are no significant reviews, articles, or even allusions on the subject. In this one area he appeared not to want to challenge his father (or was it his twin sibling?).

It is odd that an intimate knowledge of colonial rule did not prompt John Stuart Mill into a profound examination of questions of liberty and self-development in this increasingly important context although he touched on these subjects briefly in his *Considerations on Representative Government*. After his retirement from the India House, he led an attack in 1866 on Governor Eyre for alleged brutalities in Jamaica. There is no comparable episode in his life in relation to India. The Indian Mutiny meant a vast increase in Mill's burden of work at India House, but this was only for a brief time, until the Company was taken over the next year by the Government. In any case, the Mutiny appears not to have moved John Stuart Mill to significant reflection.

In short, India represents a curious lacunae in John Stuart Mill's intellectual life (exemplified by the few pages devoted to it by Packe, Mill's most eminent biographer, in a work of over 500 pages). What was absolutely central for James Mill's life—indeed, the area in which he truly pioneered—was peripheral for his son, though the latter put in almost twice as many years at the desk in the East India Company. In this area, John Stuart Mill was content to leave his father's heritage as he found it. India was *par excellence* the domain of James Mill, author of the *History of British India*, and the father of John Stuart Mill, for whom he secured a position in India House.

JOHN STUART MILL

7

The Family

Apologia Pro Vita Sua

IN HIS *Autobiography* John Stuart Mill places great stress on his life as an example of education, a pedagogic saga. He also suggests that, in an "age of transition in opinions," his life is prototypic. In hindsight we can see that his personal development symbolized the clash of reason and feeling, of scientific and moral attitudes, that characterized the "Spirit of the Age." As John Stuart Mill saw it, it was a fight between the eighteenth and nineteenth centuries, and in that sense a recognized generational conflict. Otherwise, he declared, his was an "uneventful" life, worthy of little or no attention.

Contemporaries and later commentators have added to this modest list an emphasis on John Stuart Mill's importance as the prototypic spokesman for the liberal position. More recently he has been hailed as the pioneer of Women's Liberation. Other claims for him, diminishing as time goes on, are as a logician, a political economist, and a moral philosopher. Through all these estimates of John Stuart Mill's importance runs one theme: The crucial role of his own personal development, his education, as both mirroring and inspiring the intellectual doctrines and positions that he espoused.

The initial locus for that development was his family. And that family, as we have seen, appeared, certainly in young John's imagination, totally to circle about and be dominated by his father, James Mill. In the centrifugal force of *that* family, John Stuart Mill's character *and* ideas, indissolubly linked, were formed, until eventually he was whirled out into the larger world of men and women.

III / *John Stuart Mill*

Unto the Third Generation

WHAT WAS the reality of John Stuart Mill's family? We have said of James Mill that he was a "self-made man." Such a man, psychologically, claims to have no family as progenitors, and in fact, once James Mill was in London he had no family around him other than the one he created after his marriage to Harriet Burrow.

What was the effect of this family without a past on John Stuart Mill? We have stated earlier that he was ignorant, even at the time of his father's death, of the simplest details of his parent's earlier life. As he wrote in 1836 to David Barclay, an early friend of his father's, in order to obtain information for a projected biography (by Andrew Bisset; it appeared in 1837):

> The chief points are the time and place of his birth; who and what his parents were, and anything interesting that there may be to state about them: what places of education he went to: for what professions he was educated. I believe he went through a medical course, and also that for the Church, and I have heard that he was actually licensed as a preacher, but I never heard him say so himself, and never heard of it till after his death. I do not know whether it is true or not; perhaps you do. How long did he remain at the University, or prosecute his studies for the Church? The history of his connection with the late Sir John Stuart.[1]

Surely at some point John Stuart Mill must have wondered why he was named after Sir John Stuart. We have no word, however, as to his feelings on the matter, or whether he had ever asked his father whence his name had come. It seems, at least at first, that John Stuart Mill accepted without curiosity his father's "self-made" quality, at the same time as he accepted rather unreflectively his own "made" nature. (As we shall see shortly, it was also clear to the boy that his father had had poor materials with which to work.) As late as the 1830s, this was the impression John Stuart Mill was still creating on those around him, for as his friend Sterling told him, "he and others had been accustomed to look upon me as a 'made' or manufactured man, having had a certain impress of opinion stamped upon me which I could only reproduce."[2]

The stamp, of course, was perceived by John Stuart Mill and his friends as coming only from the author of the *History of British India*. But, in fact, John Stuart Mill did have other family. If he had no kin from his father's side, he did have a maternal grandmother, Mrs. Harriet Burrow, who had supplied the dowry and a house for James Mill and his bride at the time of their marriage, and at least two cousins, Harriet Burrow, ten years younger than he, and her brother, John, who was a clerk in Edwin Chadwick's office.[3] Then there was his own mother, also named Harriet (we shall see the significance of so many Harriets on the maternal side of John Stuart Mill), and, eventually, eight siblings. Although none of these relations is mentioned in the *Autobiography*, we can assume that at least some of them also had an effect on the boy, as well as the later man. Lastly, we might also think of Bentham in these terms, for he served as sort of unofficial godfather to young John, and had the whole Mill family living on terms of intimacy with him for a number of John's formative years. As a kind of honorary grandfather, we shall deal with him later.

The importance of grandparents, as a possible alternative identity to the actual parents, is well known in the psychoanalytic literature. (Conversely, parents may also identify their own children with the grandparents, i.e., their own parents.)[4] As Erikson, for example, has pointed out, grandparents may serve as either negative or positive models for the child: there may be the skeleton-in-the-closet grandparent, who was a drunkard, or the revered grandparent, who was a successful doctor or lawyer. Thus, the child may be solemnly warned not to follow grandfather's drinking habits (with the frequent result that the child rebelling against its own parents may seize upon this negative image), or be encouraged by the mother to be the doctor she had wished herself to be. In Mill's case, the vacuum surrounding both paternal grandparents, as well as the absence of a maternal grandfather—for his mother's father had been dead at the time of her marriage to James Mill—and the seemingly tenuous presence of his maternal grandmother, threw him ever more strongly upon his father as the only possible model.

What we know of the grandmother is slight. John Stuart Mill's biographer, Packe, describes her as "a strikingly handsome Yorkshire widow." We are also told that at the time she kept a "prosperous establishment for lunatics," left to her by her husband.[5] We do not seem to know her maiden name or anything about her husband, Mr. Burrow. Bain, in his 1882 biography of John Stuart Mill, never even mentions the grandparents, but in his biography of James Mill, published in the same year, he informs us that Mrs. Burrow had two sons and two daughters in addition to Harriet, her eldest daughter. This appears to be the sum total of our knowledge of John Stuart Mill's grandmother.

Was the private asylum for the insane continued after 1805 by Mrs. Burrow? Had James Mill or his son ever visited the establishment, whose inmates represented another extreme deviation from the strict rationality of the Utilitarians? All is silence. We wonder whether Mrs. Burrow may have been living, or on an extended visit, with the family in 1820, for John Stuart Mill wrote from France to his father: "I hope my mother, James and my sisters are very well, as well as my grandmother, etc. and that the scholars [i.e., his siblings] all make good progress."[6] And we have a childish letter of October 27, 1817, written by John from Ford Abbey to his "Dear Grandmother," who was presumably somewhere in London. He informs her that he has little news to convey, other than about his siblings, their studies, games, and health. He does add one statement of special interest to us: "I hope that all my aunts and uncles are very well. I did not know that I had a little cousin, till Willie [his sister] saw it in the paper." The letter is signed, "Your affectionate Grandson."[7]

The only other evidence we have about John's grandmother is the statement many years later of his sister Harriet (again the name), who recalled:

> My grandmother [Mrs. Burrow] was a truly excellent and religious woman and taught us to pray, etc. I remember her giving me 6d. for learning my catechism! My father never interfered and as quite children we girls used to go to church.[8]

In sum, whatever extended family John Stuart Mill had came through his grandmother, but his uncles, aunts, and cousins seem to have played no real role in his life. As for the grandmother herself, she presumably gave young John a certain amount of affection. It is clear, however, that her religiosity had no effect, or else a negative one, on him. In this, as in so much else, he was strictly his father's child. As John Stuart Mill informs us in his *Autobiography*, "I was brought up from the first without any religious belief."[9]

Mother and Child

FROM Mill's *Autobiography*, one would think that he was also brought up without a mother. The truth, of course, is different, and the lack of public mention of his mother (although there are a few passages, as we shall see, in the early draft) gives testimony to intense feelings. One does not offer a new version of the immaculate conception, with only the father and a book at the birth, without having extraordinary emotions about one's mother. This is especially so if one goes on to be a pioneer in the feminist movement!

Father and Son

I. James Mill (1773–1836) by Perugini.

II. John Stuart Mill (1806–1873) from a cameo ca. 1840.

III. 39 Rodney Street, Islington, formerly 12 Rodney Terrace, Pentonville, where John Stuart Mill was born on May 20, 1806.

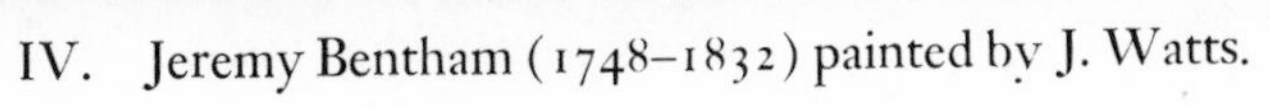

IV. Jeremy Bentham (1748–1832) painted by J. Watts.

Harriet Burrow Mill (1782?–1854). There is no surviving portrait of Harriet Mill, John's mother. Symbolically, this accords with the fact that he never once mentions her in his published *Autobiography*. Although Mill's relationship with his mother was ambivalent, other women fulfilled his need for a strong mother-figure, among them Lady Jeremy Bentham, and . . .

V. Sarah Austin (nee Taylor, 1793–1807) whom Mill called "Mütterlein."

John Stuart Mill in Maturity

VI.

Fellow Intellectuals

VII. Auguste Comte (1798–1857)

VIII. Thomas Carlyle (1795–1881).

X. Alexis de Tocqueville (1805–1859).

X. Samuel Taylor Coleridge (1772–1834).

XI. John Taylor (1796?–1849), Harriet's husband.

XII. Harriet Taylor, John's wife.

XIII. John Stuart Mill, with his step-daughter, Helen Taylor (1831–1907).

In any case, John Stuart Mill did have a mother. Harriet Burrow was twenty-two when she became engaged in 1804 to thirty-one-year-old James Mill, then entering his third year in London. All accounts tell us that she was an exceedingly pretty woman who passed on her aquiline face to her first-born, John.[10] Although the accounts agree that she had a fine figure, they disagree as to whether she was small or tall[11] (and we shall find this same surprising inaccuracy of observation about John Stuart Mill's size).

At first the marriage was a love match (though the obscure and poor James Mill can be said to have done well in the marriage, financially). Bain tells us that Harriet Mill had preserved a letter from her husband, filled with strong affectionate outpourings. Unfortunately, Bain does not quote any of it, but tells us simply that "The depth and tenderness of the feeling could not well be exceeded."[12] Alas, these deep and tender feelings did not last long. One year after the birth of John, the father had fallen out of love with his wife, whom he came to regard as a stupid woman. The disdain with which he now began to treat her shocked all his friends. Such behavior was not typical English patriarchal authority, as we can see from a comment by a young friend of the family, Henry Solly:

> Accustomed as I was to my father's behaviour to my mother, and that of other gentlemen whom I had observed in similar relations, I could not help being rather pained at his manner occasionally to Mrs. Mill. She was a tall, handsome lady, sweet-tempered, with pleasant manners, fond of her children: but I think not much interested in what the elder ones and their father talked about.[13]

Years after their father's death, John Stuart Mill's third sister Harriet commented:

> Here was an instance of two persons, as husband and wife, living as far apart, under the same roof, as the north pole from the south; from no "fault" of my poor mother most certainly; but how was a woman with a growing family and very small means (as in the early years of the marriage) to be anything but a German Hausfrau? How could she "intellectually" become a companion for such a mind as my father?

Such a comment unwittingly reflects the nasty remark of Mrs. Grote, a friend of the family, that "He married a stupid woman, 'a housemaid of a woman,' and left off caring for her and treated her as his squah but was always faithful to her."[14]

Was Harriet Mill stupid? If so, how could James Mill have been so "stupid" as to marry her? Was it uncontrollable sexual impulse that caused him, a proponent of birth control, to have eight more children with her after John's birth?

The charge of stupidity hardly seems fitting to one who reads Harriet Mill's letters, which are legible, literate, and sensible. She was not, of course, an intellectual, and to one who prizes only cold rationality and logic she might appear a mere "housemaid." As such, she seems to have been highly effective, for even Francis Place, the friend of her husband, admiringly wrote to his wife:

> Since I have been here [Ford Abbey] there has not been one single instance of crying among the children, who certainly give less trouble . . . than any I ever knew, notwithstanding they have a plentiful lack of manners, and as much impertinence, sometimes called impudence, as any children need have.

More revealing is Place's further observation that "Mrs. Mill is both good-natured and good-tempered, two capital qualities in a woman; she is, however, not a little vain of her person, and would be thought to be still a girl."[15]

Of course, she was a bit of a girl compared to Mill. (We have already speculated on whether she reminded him of his sister, of whom James Mill's one memory was that she was spoiled.) Our concern here, however, is the effect of the increasingly loveless and ill-assorted marriage on the first-born, John Stuart Mill. There can be no question that, as he grew up, he completely took his father's side, and blamed his mother for the failed relationship.

What is striking is that John not only accepted his father's verdict on the mother as stupid, but blamed her for the absence of love in the family! In an important passage in the early draft of the *Autobiography*, rejected completely in the published version, John Stuart Mill gave vent to his feelings:

> That rarity in England, a really warm hearted mother, would in the first place have made my father a totally different being, & in the second would have made the children grow up loving & being loved. But my mother with the very best intentions, only knew how to pass her life in drudging for them. Whatever she could do for them she did, & they liked her, because she was kind to them, but to make herself loved, looked up to, or even obeyed, required qualities which she unfortunately did not possess.[16]

Moreover, he declared:

> Personally I believe my father to have had much greater capacities of feeling than were ever developed in him. He resembled almost all Englishmen in being ashamed of the signs of feeling, & by the absence of demonstration, starving the feelings themselves. In an atmosphere of tenderness & affection he would have been tender & affectionate; but his ill assorted marriage & his asperities of temper disabled him from making such an atmosphere.[17]

Yet, as we have already noted, all our other evidence suggests that John's mother was warm-hearted and affectionate, and that the lack of ability to love (or at least difficulty in loving consistently) was deeply ingrained in James Mill even before his marriage. The son's touching faith that a "really warmhearted mother" (how curious that he does not say "wife" here) would have made his father "a totally different being" appears strangely misplaced. He is obviously seeing only through the eyes of his father.

The situation becomes even more complicated when we realize that James Mill subjected young John to the same strictures as his mother. He, too, was treated as stupid. In another passage of his *Autobiography* rejected for inclusion in the final published version, John Stuart Mill confesses that "I was, as my father continually told me, like a person who had not the organs of sense. . . . He could not endure stupidity, nor feeble and lax habits, in whatever manner displayed, and I was perpetually exciting his anger by manifestations of them." Rather than sympathizing with his mother, John "identified with the aggressor," his father, and took his views as his own. As in all other early instances, the young boy "acquired a habit," as the *Autobiography* tells us, "of leaving my responsibility as a moral agent to rest on my father, *my conscience never speaking to me except by his voice* [italics added]."[18]

Although Place had remarked on the good behavior of the children under Mrs. Mill's regime, John reproached his mother for not being able to have herself "obeyed" (a trait which he later admired in other women). Commenting on the fact that as a child he was disputatious with adults and thought to be conceited, behavior uncorrected by his father, who appeared to overlook it, John Stuart Mill remarks in a sentence later deleted from his *Autobiography*: "My mother did tax me with it, but for her remonstrances I never had the slightest regard." So, too, there is an implicit complaint in John Stuart Mill's observation that "I had also the great misfortune of having, in domestic matters, everything done for me. . . . This discipline, I presume my father did not see the necessity of; and it would never have occurred to my mother, who without misgivings of any sort worked from morning till night for her children."[19] What is a virtue in the father—work from morning till night—becomes in the mother a pure vice.

Did John Stuart Mill have any positive feelings toward his mother? Erikson has talked about the importance of the initial stage in child rearing in terms of "Basic Trust." We have no direct evidence of John's first year of life—if he was breast-fed (probably), how old he was when weaned, and so on—and only a comment in his late twenties to Carlyle that "mine is a trustful nature, and I have an unshakeable faith in others though not in myself."[20] The "others," however, would seem to be those such as his father, and eventually Harriet Taylor who dominated him and whom he could "obey" almost without question. At least, as we shall see, this obedience continued until a point at which he suddenly needed to withdraw his trust and abandon his unquestioning discipleship. As for his mother, we can only speculate that she gave much love and attention to her first-born, nursing and tenderly caring for him, until the arrival of her second child, Wilhelmina Forbes, followed soon after by two more daughters, and then other sons and daughters as well. The withdrawal of the mother and her overt love must surely have had a strong effect on John. At hand, however, was the father, ready now to claim his first-born and to give him almost unparalleled attention as he educated him to be a true-born Utilitarian.

Still, in his early thirties, John Stuart Mill was writing to his mother as "Dear Mammy." But this may have been a regression of sorts to an earlier feeling, for the letter swells out of his feelings of seasickness and a disordered stomach; in the next letter that we have to his mother he uses the more formal salutation, "My Dear Mother."[21] It is only in the turbulence and discord created by his marriage in 1851 to Harriet Taylor that his relations with his mother seem finally to slide into real acrimony, in spite of her efforts to maintain whatever emotional ties had existed. In the end, as in the beginning, that eminent friend of the female species, John Stuart Mill, appears to an outside observer to have rejected his mother unfeelingly. Or was it that his feelings were too strong and too complicated for him to understand correctly? In this he may have been repeating, though in reversed form, his father's experience. If so, then the absent grandmother, Isobel Fenton Mill (incidentally, the full name of one of James Mill's daughters was Harriet Isabelle), may actually have played a more important role in the formation of John Stuart Mill than Mrs. Harriet Burrow, the "Dear Grandmother." Such are the vagaries of family life.

The Intrusive Parent

THERE IS little need to say much here about the father, James Mill. We have already dealt with him as an individual as well as one of the protagonists in an epic father-son relation. Here we need only highlight certain aspects of James Mill as a father.

The major point to note is the inordinate attention showered on young John by his father. The fact is clear. For three or four hours a day, amidst all his other heavy labors, James Mill labored with his son's studies. As the son recalled in his dry prose, "a considerable part of almost every day was employed in the instruction of his children; in the case of one of whom, myself, whatever may be thought of his success, he exerted an amount of labour, care and perseverance rarely if ever employed for a similar purpose, in endeavouring to give according to his own conception the highest order of intellectual education."[22]

Why did James Mill do it? We sense elements of a repetition of his own upbringing, far more intense and sophisticated, with James Mill assuming his own mother's role. Was it the birth of his first-born that led in some way to the withdrawal of James Mill's affection from his wife, and its loading totally on the child? Certainly there is a coincidence of time. Or was it her seeming withdrawal from him in order to give attention and love to the newborn child that drove him to his negative feelings toward her, and a rivalry for the son? Clinical experience tells us that both of these reactions, and similar ones, were possible, but we cannot tell at this remove how what happened, happened. We only know that the reaction described took place.

James Mill's attention to his child was extraordinary; no comparable case for the times comes to mind. It can, however, be seen as prototypic of what we may call the "intrusive parent," a type which seems to have become more common in the nineteenth century. Such a parent, instead of largely ignoring his child, as most Western European parents can be said to have done until the late eighteenth century, "intrudes" himself completely into his child's life. The child becomes a vehicle for the parent's second life, another opportunity to achieve what the parent has been unable to accomplish. Immortality through children has been a commonplace in many times and cultures. What is new for the nineteenth century, I suggest, is the growing dissociation of such immortality desires from religion (frequently a discarded belief, as with James Mill), and their intimate connection with achievement. The child becomes an extension of the parent's "achieving" personality. And at a time when individualism is praised and asserted, the ground is further laid for an intense father-son conflict.

The result of James Mill's "intrusive" parentage is the lengthy story of John Stuart Mill's effort to free himself from his father, while at the same time retaining him inside himself. The narcissistic consequences of James Mill's extraordinary attention to his son should be obvious. "If my father is so concerned with me, I must be something special," and identified closely with him, is the natural thought. Thus the desire to imitate the father, to a degree precocious beyond the usual, should not be surprising. We understand fully when John Stuart Mill informs us in the *Autobiography*, for example, that "A voluntary exercise to which I was throughout my boyhood much addicted, was what I called writing histories: of course in imitation of my father—who used to give me the manuscript of part of his history of India to read. Almost as soon as I could hold a pen I must needs write a history of India too."[23] Needless to say, it is not that other children do not also identify with their fathers, and have strong narcissistic feelings; it is the strength of John Stuart Mill's identification and narcissism that is special.

There is abundant evidence that John Stuart Mill thought his father the most wonderful and intelligent, the strongest and wisest, person in the world, and that he continued in this belief beyond the age of most adoring children. Indeed, in his unconscious this image of his father prevailed for John Stuart Mill for the rest of his life.[24] Yet, gradually and consciously, John Stuart Mill became very aware of other traits in his father. We shall identify three which seem to loom largest in the *Autobiography*.

The first is his father's temper, or what John Stuart Mill called "asperities of temper." Indeed, until the *History of British India* was finished, bringing with it success and security, James Mill's impatience seemed to mount. As the younger sister Harriet confirmed of her father, "*His* great want was 'temper.' "[25] As we shall see shortly in more detail, it was exercised against John, as well as his siblings, with terribly damaging effects to the young boy's self-esteem.

The second noticeable trait in his father was his joylessness. "He had . . . scarcely any belief in pleasure," his son tells us. "He deemed very few pleasures worth the price which at all events in the present state of society, must be paid for them." Strange feelings for a Utilitarian? Or are they? In any event, as John Stuart Mill continued: "He thought human life a poor thing at best, after the freshness of youth and of unsatisfied curiosity had gone by." Then comes a most interesting comment: "He would sometimes say that if life were made what it might be, by good government and good education, it would then be worth having: *but he never spoke with anything like enthusiasm even of that possibility* [italics added]."[26] Do we not sense here the seed of John Stuart Mill's mental crisis? When it came in one prolonged, traumatic experience, as psychic time stood still, John Stuart Mill wrestled with the futility of Utilitarian reform, and the values behind it, experienced so poignantly and despairingly by his father. For the father it was a matter stoically and joylessly to be endured; for the son it became a crisis to be broken through at whatever price.

7 / The Family

Of all the emotions denied to or by his father, the one that distressed his son most was the lack of love. Display of tender feelings was forbidden to the stern, rational James Mill (except in the case of Ricardo), and the education not "of love but of fear" had a searing effect on the young boy. Sealed up altogether were "the fountains of frank and spontaneous communicativeness" in the childish character of John Stuart Mill. As an adolescent and young man, John tried desperately to start the fountain of emotion and love flowing again, with enormous consequences for his intellectual as well as his personal life. We see how curious and twisted the problem was for John Stuart Mill in this 1833 letter to Carlyle:

> You wonder at "the boundless capacity Man has of loving"—boundless indeed it is in some natures, immeasurable and inexhaustible: but I also wonder, judging from myself, at the limitedness and even narrowness of that capacity in others. That seems to me the only really insuperable calamity in life; the only one which is not conquerable by the power of a strong will. It seems the eternal barrier between man and man; the natural and impassable limit both to the happiness and to the spiritual perfection of (I fear) a large majority of our race.[27]

Even his father, the most perfect man in the world for John Stuart Mill, was unable to conquer that calamity "by the power of a strong will." How ironic, then, that the weaker son, for so John Stuart Mill perceived himself, could make a more powerful effort in this direction than the father! Perhaps a "strong will" is a more complicated matter than revealed at first glance.

Family History

FAMILY HISTORY is a relatively new field. While there has long been a general kind of intuitive knowledge that the family is the basic molecule of society in which the individual takes shape, and on whose basis the state, for example, models itself, until recently there has been little detailed examination of how this takes and has taken place. The most important formative institution in society has been accorded the neglect we reserve for those things closest to us, averting our eyes from what is most obvious because it is also most critical to our psyches and sense of self.

Fortunately, this situation is beginning to change. Historians have finally joined psychologists and sociologists, who are also recent arrivals, and have become concerned not only with illustrious families—

dynasties—from the outside, but with average families from the inside. Thus, the new history of the family, at its best, seeks to utilize and unify the concern of the psychoanalyst with intrapersonal dynamics on the unconscious as well as conscious level; of the sociologist with formal properties of the family as a social system; and of the historian, newly enlightened, with the possibility of change over time in all the aspects of the family.

One account of the long-term movement of the family in, say, the last 500 years, depicts a shift from the traditional family system of extended kinship ties to a "conjugal" family pattern, in which there are "fewer kinship-ties with distant relatives and a greater emphasis on the 'nuclear' family unit of couple and children."[28] First appearing in the West, it is now a worldwide movement as a result of the spread of industrialization and urbanization.

The assumed change or evolution of the family (if it actually occurred, and scholars argue vehemently over the matter) *may* be viewed as "progressive."[29] The conjugal family seems rooted in the values of Protestant individualism. It asserts the right of the individual to enter into marriage on his own accord, to seek his own happiness therein, and to dissolve it by divorce if disappointed. The values of such a family pattern appear to accord with a number of nineteenth-century developments: the Utilitarian stress on happiness as the measure of social institutions; the Romantic call to love as the basis of marital relations; and the Liberal's emphasis on personal choice and freedom. We have little reason, therefore, to assume that John Stuart Mill would not approve of such a general trend as "progressive." In fact, as we shall see, he played a strong role in advancing the values, the ideology, that shaped such a family.

There is one other major point to be made before we proceed to judge the Mill family in the context of this putative general trend. It is that the emotional ties of the conjugal family, rather than diminishing from the extended kinship pattern, have grown appreciably stronger. Ironically, in this sense, it can be maintained that the increasingly "Gesellschaft" tendency of the modern family, to use Tönnies' famous phrase, coheres with stronger rather than weaker affective ties. It can be further suggested that exactly this fact is responsible for the supposed "breakdown" of the family, as manifested in divorce or delinquency rates.

If this view of the family's changing character is accepted, we can see that John Stuart Mill's tremendous emphasis on love, or rather the lack of it, in his family is a new development, a modern expectation. It is doubtful whether a boy growing up in a family a hundred years earlier would have expected such love, and thus suffered an almost traumatic sense of disappointment and loss in not having received it. We can probably say something similar about James Mill's feelings toward his wife, Harriet. And we can see even more plausibly that John Stuart Mill's "infatuation" with Harriet Taylor had as its background the romantic conception of marriage.[30]

Within this general picture of family evolution that we are portraying, there are certain reinforcing, or corresponding, processes to be discerned (even if not exemplified in James Mill). For example, when the stress on individualism, freedom, and equality is extended to the woman (as with John Stuart Mill), she obviously may exercise more control over the size of the family. Smaller families, the most probable choice, mean increased affective or emotional ties. Increased affective ties mean greater attention to the individual child, and this implies a lower childhood mortality rate. A moment's reflection on the widespread practice of abandonment and infanticide in the eighteenth and nineteenth centuries, and its gradual diminution, suggests the possible direction here. So, too, if divorce is a possibility, a small number of children as against a large brood facilitates it. One possibility tends to go with another.

As for birth control itself, in the long run the introduction in either or both parents of attitudes emphasizing conscious decision, control, and the "mechanical" (i.e., artificial means) would favor family limitation, although, paradoxically, at least in the short run, increased child care and affection would lead to the survival of more children, and thus to an increased population at large.[31]

In short, the modern conjugal family, increased affective ties, and birth control appear to go together, psychologically as well as logically. How does the Mill family look in the light of such a development (it is an "ideal" development, for we do not yet have the detailed historical data to sustain this thesis as fact)? One observation that immediately springs to our attention is the unusualness of James Mill's being at home constantly with his family (at least until he entered the employ of the East India Company). Whereas the "model" father presumably goes out to work during the day, and thus cannot serve as a work model or educator for his children, James Mill resembled more the rural, extended family ideal. Unlike the latter, however, James Mill was also "intrusive," and his intrusion took the form of teaching the "mechanical" and Puritanical values of Utilitarianism to his children. As for John Stuart Mill, good Utilitarian though he was, he stayed within the bosom of his family, living with them until he was about forty-five! (In his case, of course, he worked at the East India Company offices for six hours a day, from the age of about seventeen.)

We have already remarked frequently about the divergence in James Mill's theory and practice concerning birth control. His son, however, practiced what he preached, and had no children of his own. (We cannot say surely what would have happened if John Stuart Mill and Harriet Taylor had been free to marry at a young age, but, as we shall show later, all the signs pointed to a small or childless family.)

In short, the Mill family presents an imperfect, partial instance of the presumed trend to the modern conjugal family as we have described it. Until better family history is written, however, even that trend is merely a supposition on our part. What we can say with certainty is that John Stuart Mill is much closer in his attitudes to the modern conjugal ideal than was his father; his newer ideals stemmed in part from currents of thought and feeling afloat in his time, but, more importantly, from his own personal development, with its attendant parental conflict.

An Autobiography

LET US TURN now briefly to the document that tells us most about Mill's development: his *Autobiography*. An autobiography is meant to reveal and to conceal, and often conceals best where it claims to reveal most. In this sense the autobiographer may be likened to a magician who distracts our attention from the real trick taking place. However, with an autobiographer the trick is generally on himself as well as us, and he is as much a spectator as we are of the performance he puts on.

Why does one write an autobiography? It may be to record significant events in which one was a participant or observer; John Stuart Mill presented himself as a microcosm of an "age of transition in opinions." It may be to describe one's own education, as a pedagogic example; John Stuart Mill offers this reason, too. He also adds an unusual reason: "to make acknowledgment of the debts which my intellectual and moral development owes to other persons." Correctly translated, this meant that John Stuart Mill wished his autobiography to serve as homage to his father, James Mill, and to Harriet Taylor, who later became his wife.

Autobiography is always a looking back over one's life from a particular vantage point; Chateaubriand, for example, wrote his memoirs at three separate times, and the results are quite different. Thus, autobiography is always a matter of perspective. Erik Erikson has brilliantly extended this idea to the reader as well as to the writer of autobiography, and worked out a typology of the "moments" in which an autobiography should be viewed. With great subtlety he has shown how the writing and reading of an autobiography is not a timeless process, but embedded in ongoing history and the search for identity of both the individual writer and reader, and the communities in which they live.[32]

For whom did John Stuart Mill write? Ostensibly it was for his contemporaries. A moment's reflection, however, shows that he was also writing for posterity, in whose progress he wished to believe. Later readers would then look back on John Stuart Mill's life as one "stage" in mankind's development. He was also writing for himself, trying to understand the "stages" in his own personal development, and placing his little dot in the greater picture of the progress of humanity.

As nearly as we can ascertain, Mill began writing his *Autobiography* in 1853–1856, starting when he was forty-seven, two years after his marriage to Harriet Taylor. The original draft seems to have "contained a complete account, as Mill would then have given it, of his life up to his marriage."[33] Harriet appears to have read the entire manuscript and to have made numerous suggestions and corrections. Thus, in addition to himself and posterity, Mill was obviously writing for Harriet's eye. It was apparently she who counseled him to tone down or eliminate some of the passages most critical of his parents. (She does not seem, however, to have advised him to tone down his fulsome praise of her; more of this anon.)

Within this early draft, Mill's revisions seemed to move relentlessly, as Stillinger says, "from private to public, and from public to more public, voice." Mill is increasingly prudential both about himself and others—revealing now only to conceal the better? He stands more detached from his material, and thus from his self. As he wrote Harriet on February 10, 1854: "Of course one does not, in writing a life, either one's own or another's, undertake to tell everything." In pursuit of this dictum, Mill increasingly came to write the "history of my mind" rather than of his feelings.[34] That he knew the possibilities of a better balance can be seen in an early letter (1833) to Thomas Carlyle, in which he wrote:

> This letter will be as you desire, extremely biographical: I was conscious myself of a deficiency in that department, in my last: which however was

wholly *auto*biographic; for what is *my* life made up of, in the main, but my thoughts and feelings?[35]

But it was only with friends such as Thomas Carlyle and Auguste Comte, who had undergone crises of feeling similar to his own, or John Sterling and Robert Barclay Fox, whose religious sensibilities guaranteed an emphasis on the feelings, that John Stuart Mill could ponder the state of his self-consciousness. To Carlyle he could write in 1834 that "truly I begin to think that instead of being as I once thought I was, the most self-conscious person living, I am much less self-conscious *now*" (although here he seems to be equating self-consciousness with awkwardness or being ill-at-ease); to Sterling he wrote in 1840, "for though there is nothing that I do not desire to shew, there is much that I never do shew, and much that I think you cannot even guess"; and to Fox in 1840:

> For you have not, nor have even those of your family whom I have been so fortunate as to see more of, as yet seen *me*, as I really & naturally am, but a *me* artificially made self-conscious, egotistical, & noisily demonstrative by having much feeling to shew & very little time to shew it in.[36]

Even more significant is Mill's letter of 1843 to Comte, in which he expresses his awareness that it is only through self-knowledge that one achieves the life of reason itself:

> He who has not arrived at an exact consciousness of his own character will not know how to conduct himself according to reason. He will remain under the sway of his habits, whether of action, sentiment or thought. I believe that this self-examination, unhappily too rare everywhere, is at least as much so for the male as the female sex. An intimate knowledge of self, and the dominion over self which results from it, are very exceptional facts with both. . . .[37]

Such self-knowledge, however, seems increasingly to have been rejected by Mill. Having put his early draft aside around 1856, he only resumed the writing of his *Autobiography* after Harriet's death, apparently during the last five years of his life. At his death on May 8, 1873, the manuscript was still unfinished. Shortly thereafter, however, Harriet's daughter, Helen Taylor, edited the manuscript (deleting some further passages) and published the *Autobiography* in London in 1873. Whereas the early draft stopped with Mill's marriage in 1851, the published version reordered some of the earlier material and added a chapter called "The Remainder of My Life," offering an ever more public and desiccated account of Mill's later mental and mainly political life (he had a brief spell in Parliament). It is clear that, with

Harriet dead, Mill was trying to say that his own life had effectively, and certainly affectively, ended.

The account of the *Autobiography*'s composition and editing should put us on our guard. We must compare the published 1873 version with the early draft (now fortunately available in print). This, of course, is relatively easy. More difficult is to read all the versions with an eye to what is being concealed, both from us and from Mill himself, as well as ostensibly revealed. That is what psychohistory claims to do. It is helped, of course, by revelations other than the merely autobiographical: letters, diaries, second-person accounts, even novels and historical descriptions from the period. Yet, when all this is said, we must still give special attention to the autobiography. It, of all the genres, offers us the picture of a subject as he would like to see himself and to be seen. Both by what it says and what it does not say, it seeks to establish the author's identity as he himself views it. In seeking to understand John Stuart Mill's development "from the inside," as well as in correspondence with external processes, we must pay rapt, but not blindfolded attention to the *Autobiography*.

8

Childhood

Father to the Man

CHILDREN have always been with us. But, it is now argued, the notion of the child as distinct from the adult, of childhood as a definite stage, with its own special characteristics and dynamics, is of late appearance, coming into Western consciousness somewhere near the end of the eighteenth century and flowering in the nineteenth.

The glaring omission of children in traditional history is well captured by Peter Laslett in *The World We Have Lost.* He wonders why the

> crowds and crowds of little children are strangely absent from the written record. . . . There is something mysterious about the silence of all these multitudes of babes in arms, toddlers and adolescents in the statements men made at the time about their own experience. . . . We cannot say whether fathers helped in the tending of infants. . . . We do not know very much about what they played, or even about what they were encouraged to play or to do. . . . Nothing can as yet be said on what is called by the psychologists toilet training. . . . We do not even know for certain how babies were carried about. It is in fact an effort of the mind to remember all the time that children were always present in such numbers in the traditional world, nearly half the whole community living in a condition of semi-obliteration. . . .[1]

Such omission by historians, of course, accords well with our individual repression of childhood memories, a cardinal tenet of Freudian psychology. Only now do we seem "mature" enough to face our beginnings candidly.

8 / Childhood

Childhood history differs from family history in its concentration on parent-child relations and its desire to see those relations mainly from the point of view of the child. Needless to say, there is an overlap of the two fields. Yet the difference of central focus and perspective needs constantly to be remembered.

Attention to the child in the terms we have indicated seems to have arisen strongly as a result of romanticism. It appeared first, at the end of the eighteenth and beginning of the nineteenth century, in poetry—though the critical exception of Rousseau's prose *Emile* (1762) must always be noted—and then shifted by the middle of the century to novels.

As Peter Coveney points out, the child, now perceived as unique in its innocence and spontaneity, became a *symbol* of all that was wrong in the new, industrializing world.[2] It was Wordsworth who called attention to "the child as father of the man," and reminded his contemporaries that the child came "trailing clouds of glory" from Heaven. Again and again he lamented the "loss" of innocence as the "prison house" of adult life closed upon the growing child. The other theme he sounded was the breaking of ties, and the need to "connect" things again. On the personal level we can interpret the sense of loss in part as Wordsworth's reaction to the death of his mother when he was eight. On the public level he is pointing to a loss of innocence and goodness caused by the hard-hearted, mechanical oppression of the new industrial society blotting out the promptings of maternal Nature, as well as to the loss in society of "connection," of affective ties, between man and man, class and class, and man and the universe.

Other poets joined Wordsworth in voicing the romantic sensibility. Then came the novelists, epitomized by Charles Dickens, who counterposed the symbol of childhood innocence to the reality of the victimized child of Victorian society. Much of that reality came out of the excrescences of laissez-faire industrialism, seemingly justified by the Manchester and Utilitarian philosophies. More specifically, even in a nonindustrial setting, child rearing in many homes was blighted by the strict and joyless tenets of Puritanism.

This last assertion poses something of a problem for us. It seems to run counter to the view that the Puritan family, anticipating the Utilitarian family, tended to encourage increased affective ties, both between the parents and between them and their offspring. How can this view be reconciled with the idea of strict Puritan child rearing? The answer must be sought in the psychological rather than merely logical realm. Puritan ministers, and theology, preached incessantly that the child was born evil and willful, out of sinful lust, and needed to have its will curbed from the beginning. The good and caring parent was the strict parent. As seventeenth-century Puritanism came increasingly to be aligned with the "Puritan Ethos" behind capitalistic expansiveness, as depicted by Max Weber, it put its child-rearing beliefs more and more in the service of the new work discipline. By the nineteenth century the "Puritan" parent had become the "intrusive parent," spurring himself and his child on joylessly toward achievement, the new secular equivalent of religious salvation. Affective ties can make for more watchfulness rather than less, and, ironically, the somewhat neglected child may have a freer and more spontaneous childhood.

With both the Puritan and the Romantic, the child is more symbol than reality. In the former case he represents original sin; in the latter, original innocence. Throughout the nineteenth century these two views of the child fought one another. Only at the end of the century, with Freud and his coworkers, did the child as social symbol give way effectively to the child as object of scientific attention.[3] In his theory of infantile sexuality, Freud claimed that the child was not the innocent of Romantic fancy. But equally was he not the depraved character of Puritan belief, whose every impulse was to be subjected to savage repression.

Ultimately it was Freud who took seriously the notion that "the child is father of the man," and then showed in detail how this development actually took place. Although his original informants about childhood were adult patients, Freud placed the greatest stress on those early years up to about six or seven. As is well known, he postulated that the child went through stages of "sexual" development, from oral to anal, and then a phallic stage (later to be reawakened as the genital stage of puberty, around thirteen or fourteen, after a latency period of "forgetting"). In the phallic stage the child undergoes the vicissitudes of the Oedipus complex, which, for Freud, was the nucleus of all future neuroses.

Since Freud, his disciples have placed more stress on the pre-Oedipal stage, especially its oral qualities. Freud's own daughter, Anna Freud, followed a strong hint of her father's later in his life that more attention be paid to ego processes—for example, defenses—than to id. She, and many others, began to study children directly, and not only as reflected through adult memories. Seeking to avoid the "originology fallacy" on the edge of which Freud teetered (and into whose abyss lesser workers without his genius tumbled), these disciples of Freud gave increasing attention to the numerous stages in human development when significant change and adaptation might take place, though each was naturally affected by the earlier experiences. The child *was* father to the man, but the man was not *merely* a grown-up version of the child; he was something different. To think otherwise would simply be to reverse the earlier view that children were merely miniature adults.

One of the most exciting recent developments in psychoanalysis has been the work of Erik Erikson. His work more than anyone else's, though building on the contributions of others (e.g., Anna Freud, his teacher; Heinz Hartmann; and Harry Stack Sullivan, with his emphasis on inter- as well as intrapersonal dynamics), has prepared the way for the development of psychohistory.[4]

There is no need here to go into further details about Erikson's system, now so well known.[5] Having worked out his psychosexual schema with patients in the clinic and in the field (e.g., Sioux Indians), Erikson then applied it to historical figures, and with *Young Man Luther* (1958) and *Gandhi's Truth* (1970) contributed to the new discipline, or interdiscipline, of psychohistory. In Erikson's work the child is still central and unique; but it is a child that must grow up, undergoing hopefully creative vicissitudes, and take on adult roles and character.

Analysts such as Erikson, as well as many other child psychiatrists, have provided us with the developmental schemata by which we can understand an individual child. Historians such as Philippe Ariès in his *Centuries of Childhood* are beginning to give us the detailed historical data by which we can understand an "average" child, in different countries and times. Thus for the first time we begin to possess the requisite tools and materials for the study of childhood as it prepares a child to become an adult. We have, in short, a sketchy kind of general context for our observations about John Stuart Mill's childhood.

A Missing Childhood?

THE FIRST THING that must be said of John Stuart Mill is that he seems never to have been a child, or to have had a childhood. As Caroline Fox remarked, he was a boy who "never was a boy."[6] Of playmates his own age, from whom he might have learned what it is to be a child, he had none. Like Rousseau's *Emile*, but for Utilitarian reasons, he was deprived of peer-group company and, fittingly, given *Robinson Crusoe* to read. What "friends" he had were all adults: his father's friends, such as Bentham and Place.

Yet John Stuart Mill *was* at one time a child, although his father never treated him as one, thus stunting and blighting, as John himself eventually realized, certain parts of his growth. In fact, John Stuart Mill never really grew up, never really left off being a child, as we see in his extraordinary adulation of his father and, later, of Harriet Taylor. Although a paradox, we can firmly assert that John Stuart Mill never was a child, and yet in large part remained one, although in a twisted fashion, all his life.

What we have in the *Autobiography* is the story not of a child, but of an education. It is the education of a "prodigy," or so he struck many around him. As Francis Place remarked: "John is truly a prodigy, a most delightful fellow," warning in the next breath that he would probably grow up selfish and morose. Such a view is given support by a modern estimate which places John Stuart Mill around the top in innate ability of 300 eminent geniuses. We ourselves are a little overwhelmed by the first preserved letter of young John, to Bentham, in 1812 (at age six); while the handwriting is a bit childish, the short text is unsettlingly mature.[7]

By now, the content of John Stuart Mill's early education has passed into the folklore of achievement. Even those who have not actually read his *Autobiography* have heard how he learned to read Greek at three and prattled in Latin at eight. At the latter age, he tells us he had read

> a number of Greek prose authors, among whom I remember the whole of Herodotus, and of Xenophon's Cyropaedia and Memorials of Socrates; some of the lives of the philosophers by Diogenes Laertius; part of Lucian, and Isocrates's ad Demonicum and ad Nicoclem. I also read, in 1813, the first six dialogues (in the common arrangement) of Plato, from the Euthyphron to the Theaetetus inclusive: which last dialogue, I venture to think, would have been better omitted, as it was totally impossible I should understand it.

An even more extended list is given in a letter of July 30, 1819, to Samuel Bentham, in which to the classics are added geometry, algebra, Newton's Universal Arithmetic, and so on, as part of John Stuart Mill's staple diet of childhood education.[8]

Was it really a unique education? Was it merely an education of "cram"? Comparative childhood history suggests that we—and Mill—have tended to exaggerate the uniqueness of his early training. Material from seventeenth-century England, for example, suggests that such classical accomplishments at a tender age were relatively frequent. John Evelyn, who considered the commencement of his own learning of Latin at four as late, made sure that his son would do better. As he informs us:

At two years and a half old he could perfectly read any of the English, Latin, French or gothic letters pronouncing the first three languages exactly. He had before the fifth year, or in that year not only skill to read most written hands but to decline all the nouns, conjugate the verbs regular and most of the irregular; learned out *Puerilis*, got by heart almost the entire vocabulary of Latin and French primitive verbs . . . began to write legibly and had a strong passion for Greek. The number of verses he could recite was prodigious. . . . He had a wonderful disposition to mathematics having learned all his catechism early and understood the historical part of the Bible and New Testament to a wonder. He had learned by heart divers sentences in Latin and Greek which on occasion he would produce even to wonder. . . .[9]

In short, John Stuart Mill's education was prodigious, but it hardly proves, as indeed his father often cautioned him, that he was a prodigy.

But such an education ran the real danger of being merely a cramming process. As Samuel Coleridge warned:

It was a great error to cram the young mind with so much knowledge as made the child talk much and fluently: what was more ridiculous than to hear a child questioned, what it thought of the last poem of Walter Scott? A child should be child-like, and possess no other idea than what was loving and admiring.[10]

John Stuart Mill rejected the first part of the accusation, and we have no reason not to agree with him in his view:

There is one cardinal point in my education which more than anything else, was the cause of whatever good it effected. Most boys or youths who have had much knowledge drilled into them, have their mental faculties not strengthened but overlaid by it. They are crammed with mere facts & with the opinions or phrases of others, & these are accepted as a substitute for the power to form opinions of their own. And thus the sons of eminent fathers, who have spared no pains in their education, grow up mere parroters of what they have learnt, incapable of any effort of original or independent thought. Mine, however, was not an education of cram. My father never permitted anything which I learnt, to degenerate into a mere exercise of memory. He strove to make the understanding not only go along with every step of the teaching but if possible precede it. His custom was, in the case of everything which could be found out by thinking, to make me strive & struggle to find it out for myself giving me no more help than was positively indispensable.[11]

But what of the last part of Coleridge's warning? Here, alas, John Stuart Mill's education, as he himself frequently tells us, failed. "A child should be child-like." John Stuart Mill's education was solely an education in books and in rational analysis. Of the feelings, especially of love, there was nothing made available. Externally, John Stuart Mill seemed the successful product of a careful and caring education, designed to produce the epitome of the rational, happy man. The "Mental Crisis" would show how hollow were the foundations on which his life had been built. Only in late adolescence, or early manhood, did John Stuart Mill set out to acquire an education of the feelings to match his earlier education of the mind. The emptiness which he carried with him from childhood, however, could not be redeemed; it could only be made tolerable, and then the basis for new intellectual accomplishment.

Sibling Relations

AS A CHILD, John Stuart Mill was not only a pupil; he was also a teacher. When eight years old he was set to work tutoring his sister, Wilhelmina, and then each succeeding sibling (though helped by the intermediate ones). Thus, in addition to being responsible to his demanding father for his own lessons, he was also held responsible for the correctness of his siblings' answers. It was a task over which he suffered acutely. It must also have spoiled any real possibility of normal childlike sibling relations, for John Stuart Mill was perpetually acting as a substitute father to his sisters and brothers. Indeed, a strange remark by Bain suggests that, in teaching his siblings, John may have identified fully with his father as an aggressor: "For while he scolded them freely for their stupidity and backwardness, he took pains to explain their lessons, which their father never did."[12] As we have noted, James Mill also scolded his first son for "stupidity," leaving indelible marks on the young psyche. There is one last speculation we might venture as to the effect of John Stuart Mill's teaching his own siblings while a child or young boy. It may have made him less eager, at least unconsciously, to have children of his own; he had already had them in the form of his siblings.

One can sympathize with James Mill—overwhelmed with his own tasks, devoting hours each day to his first-born, unable to afford a tutor even if he had wanted one (which is doubtful), obsessed with the need of his children for "Utilitarian" education—for setting young John to work in his place. A consequence, however, was that between young John's own education and having to educate his siblings, there was not much space left for a normal childhood even if James Mill had wished to provide one for his child. John's lack of a true childhood, therefore, may well have been merely the exaggerated prototype of his brothers' as well. In any case, perhaps oppressed with their own dismal experiences, none of the four boys married or begot children of their own; only the girls did. As for John's future relations with his siblings, these seemed to have become increasingly cold and distant in his young manhood. Although he loved his brother Henry and deeply lamented his early death at age nineteen, the more typical relation was with his brother George, with whom he quarreled and eventually broke off completely (over Harriet Taylor); a similar pattern manifested itself with his sisters as time went on.

In sum, John Stuart Mill, as the substitute father for his siblings, tended to imitate James Mill and to withhold or withdraw love from his brother and sisters. Even before this he had learned to withdraw it from his own father, the "most wonderful man in the world." The reasons are clear. In spite of the extraordinary attention showered on him, John Stuart Mill's sense of self-esteem was badly damaged by his father's alternating offerings of love and scorn. The young boy came, in some part of his psyche, to fear his father as well as to admire him. It is an ambivalence that runs throughout John Stuart Mill's life and relations.

We catch the full flower of the blows to self-esteem suffered by Mill at the hands of his father in a passage written for the *Autobiography*, but not included in the published version. Giving way to his feelings over forty years after the event, he remembers:

> I was utterly unobservant: I was, *as my father continually told me*, like a person who had not the organs of sense. . . . My father was the extreme opposite in all these particulars: his senses and his mental faculties were always on the alert . . . both as a boy and as a youth *I was incessantly smarting* under his severe admonitions on the subject. He could not endure stupidity, nor feeble and lax habits . . . and I was perpetually exciting his *anger* by manifestations of them. *From the earliest time I can remember* he used to reproach me, and most truly, with a general habit of inattention; owing to which, he said, I was constantly acquiring bad habits, and never breaking myself of them; was constantly forgetting what I ought to remember, and judging and acting like a person devoid of common sense; and which could make me, he said, *grow up a mere oddity*, looked down upon by everybody, and unfit for all the common purposes of life [italics added].[13]

"Unfit" for life. The sense of being "unprepared," unequipped by his parents—for his mother, too, had not even prepared him to take care of his own domestic needs—joins the absence of love in John's remembrance of his childhood. In one area only, the intellectual, had he been adequately trained. The price, as we have already noted, was the absence of a fulfilling and independent childhood.

III / *John Stuart Mill*

A One-Sided Picture

THE PICTURE we have thus far painted of John Stuart Mill's childhood is gloomy. It needs to be corrected. We must remember that his mother was "tender hearted," and it is hardly likely that her inability to have the children obey her was a source of complaint for the six-year-old John, as it was to become for the sixty-year-old author of the *Autobiography*. James Mill, for all of his intrusiveness, did not whip or maltreat his son in the ways familiar to readers of *Oliver Twist*. Life was hard for the Mills, but it was not a life of unmitigated privation.

In addition to the good side of his thoughtful and caring parents, young John gained much from another "member" of his family: Jeremy Bentham, his honorary grandfather. As a prodigy himself (who had suffered from a pushing, intrusive father), Bentham may well have empathized with the younger version presented by John. In any case, as early as the summer of 1809 he had invited the entire Mill family to visit with him at Barrow Green, a splendid mansion which he was renting, and then to live near him in the city as well. It was, however, at Ford Abbey, a huge house in Somerset which Bentham began renting in 1814, and to which the Mills repaired for about six months each year, that his effect on young John can be seen as most pronounced. In the spaciousness and grandeur of his house, he opened a new vista for the boy, freeing him from the narrow limits of his existing "home." Even in the understated prose of the *Autobiography* we can see that it is still a golden memory for John Stuart Mill:

> This sojourn was, I think, an important circumstance in my education. Nothing contributes more to nourish elevation of sentiments in a people, than the large & free character of their habitations. The middle age architecture, the baronial hall & the spacious & lofty rooms of this fine old place, so unlike the mean and cramped externals of English middle class life, gave the feeling of a larger & freer existence & were to me a sort of poetic culture, aided also by the character of the grounds in which the Abbey stood; which were riant & secluded, umbrageous, & full of the sound of falling waters.[14]

Young John here had a foretaste of what a "poetic culture" could be (of course, the memory is colored by his later development). Against "mean and cramped" middle-class life (*the* praised class of his father), John could now place "elevation of sentiments." It is then Bentham, the very source of John Stuart Mill's supposedly arid and mechanical Utilitarianism, who also offered the antidote. As we shall see shortly, the paradox will be repeated, for Jeremy Bentham not only provided young John with the expansive halls of Ford Abbey in childhood, but opened the door to a more independent life in adolescence. In any case, not to anticipate, Bentham had planted at least one seed of sentiment, even if only inadvertently, in the soil of John's childhood.

A Lacuna

BEFORE leaving John's childhood, there is one extraordinary fact we must notice. Though at the very beginning of this book we postulated, indeed asserted, the existence of a major Oedipal conflict in John Stuart Mill which would exhibit itself virulently during his mental crisis, we have offered no evidence for its earlier manifestation in his childhood. Did it emerge full-blown at age twenty, like Minerva from Jove's forehead? This hardly seems likely. Did young John say to his father, as so many of our own children (if we observe them closely), "Let *me* get into bed with Mommy, and you move out"?[15] Did he masturbate, for example, and was he severely reprimanded and perhaps threatened? It seems almost *lèse majesté* to ask such silly questions about that great intellect, John Stuart Mill, yet these questions are the stuff of childhood. What appears extraordinary at first is that we have no evidence whatsoever of the child's attitudes and feelings toward his mother and father *at the time*. Our only evidence comes from the memory of the adult John Stuart Mill, and that gives us only the carefully selected words of a mature man about his recollected, and repressed, childhood. On second thought, then, it is hardly surprising or extraordinary that we have no evidence one way or the other about an Oedipal stage of development in the child, John Stuart Mill.

9

Adolescence

The Concept

WHAT HAPPENS to the child? Does he become "father to the man" at one bound? The Associationalist psychology of Bentham and both Mills did not concern itself with such a problem. Only as psychology became truly *developmental* in its perspective did it direct its attention to such matters. Unintentionally and indirectly, by his stress on personal development, John Stuart Mill helped prepare the way for the new attitude.

By the end of the nineteenth century the new developmental view prevailed. Due recognition was given to the fact that, uniquely among animals, the human animal entered a period of "latency" after childhood per se. That is, the child goes through all the stages of development leading to full sexuality by the time he is somewhere between six and eight, except that he stops at phallic rather than genital (i.e., reproductive) performance. From about eight to twelve he is in a latency period, during which sexual urges still exist but are increasingly subordinated to ego activities—sublimative, adaptive, and defensive—and superego control. This is the time when learning activities seem freest from the threat of the impulsive life. Whereas other animals, such as a cat or a dog, go directly from infanthood to adult behavior, including ability to forage for themselves and to reproduce, humans experience a lengthy pause.

The pause ends with the onset of puberty. Puberty means literally the appearance of pubic hairs, one of the outward signs that the human animal is entering upon true sexual and physical maturity;

thus puberty is a biological stage. While its incidence may vary over time and culture—for example, the onset of menarche in girls in Western countries has dropped from about age seventeen in the 17th century to about twelve or thirteen today, probably due to diet—puberty itself is a genetic constant. As such, it must be recognized and dealt with in some fashion by all societies, and the passing of the threshold into physical "maturity" from childhood, via latency, to adulthood, is almost everywhere marked by ritual celebration and social initiation.

In modern society a new concept (and therefore reality?) has taken its place beside the fact of puberty. This is the concept of "adolescence." First given classic expression by G. Stanley Hall in the 1890s, he then stated the concept emphatically in 1904 in his two-volume work, *Adolescence*.[1]

Hall's perspective was Darwinian, although he saw man's evolution as having shifted from the physical to the psychological plane. His thought was a strange combination of mysticism and science, and it is not always easy to be sure of his message. He seems, however, to be saying that man's evolution from prehuman to a human stage is preserved in the latency period, which "suggests the culmination of one stage of life as if it thus represents what was once, and for a very protracted and relatively stationary period, the age of maturity in some remote, perhaps pigmoid stage of human evolution, when in a warm climate the young of our species once shifted for themselves independently of further parental aid." [1: ix–x] Today, our young in their latency period still exhibit strong "nativistic and more or less feral instincts." [1:xi]

It is in this evolutionary context that Hall placed his concept of "adolescence" (which literally means "growing up"):

> Adolescence is a new birth, for the higher and more completely human traits are now born. The qualities of body and mind that now emerge are far newer. The child comes from and harks back to a remoter past; the adolescent is new-atavistic, and in him the later acquisitions of the race slowly become prepotent. Development is less gradual and more saltatory, suggestive of some ancient period of storm and stress when old moorings were broken and a higher level attained. [1:xiii]

The "new birth," however, is not easy. It involves a good deal of difficulty and even despair, and is attended by depression and melancholy. Hall's initial explanation for the increased "morbidity" is rather ingenious, though not very convincing. He claims that it occurs because the individual is still liable to the diseases peculiar to childhood, though these are abating, but is also now susceptible to the diseases of maturity. In this concurrence, somehow, depression is to be expected. [1:xiv]

Hall is better on this point when he goes into details about the problem of sex and the dangers of perversion and degradation surrounding it. Clearly, one of the distinguishing features of puberty is the torrential onrush of awakened sexual feeling. In a society in which marriage is not encouraged at the age of puberty, how are these impulses to be dealt with? Hall is advanced in his thinking when he lightens the burden of guilt on the young man by declaring that nocturnal emissions are normal, and not to be regarded as sinful. In fact, the danger is that young men, condemned for nocturnal emissions *supposedly within their moral control*, as they were told by so many Victorian sexual and medical moralists, would turn guiltily to quacks, and undergo lasting harm.

On the subject of masturbation Hall took a more conventional position. Aware that it did not lead directly and immediately to insanity (as the Swiss doctor, Tissot, had insisted in his landmark work of 1758, *Onania, or a Treatise upon the Disorders Produced by Masturbation*), Hall warned: "Current impression to this effect has much to do in causing terror, shamefacedness, and some of the bashfulness and solitude sometimes seen." [1:439] Having said this, Hall immediately added to the terror by asserting strongly that frequent indulgence in the vice inhibits the growth of the individual and "causes the race to deteriorate." [1:438] The other result is psychological: depression. In Hall's terms:

> Perhaps the most common psychic result is a sense of unworthiness, sin, pollution, and the serious diminution of self-respect, often instinctively covered or resisted by whimmish and boisterous self-assertion, or occasionally hidden by almost morbid scrupulousness and convictions of foreboding disaster or penalty. In what theologians have described as the conviction of sin, this plays an enormous and hitherto unappreciated role. Consciousness of a vice so hated and despised is a potent factor in youthful melancholia, taking away the joy of life, and sometimes plunging the victim into discouragement culminating in a sense of utter despair. It is one of the causes of most of the morbid types of self-consciousness or introspection. [1:439]

Inner sin also manifests itself in outward signs: "baldness, a stooping and enfeebled gait" [1:444], moodiness, laziness, lack of interest, and so on. [1:447] One can imagine the anxious youth of seventeen or eighteen looking at himself in the mirror and examining his conduct to see if the telltale signs of self-abuse have emerged in Dorian Gray fashion! (For women the habit of self-abuse is less frequent and less hurtful, Hall tells us.) In the face of such dangers, what should the individual do? How can society help to protect the individual against himself? The cure, Hall seems to imply, is to stigmatize self-abuse as dirty and to shame youth into hard work, early rising, cold baths, and energetic achievement—in short, the Puritan ethic—as a defense against the unnatural temptations of sex.[2]

At this point we can see that Hall has come dangerously close to making adolescence a testing time for the Puritan character. Thus, in the end, his notion of adolescence is part scientific concept and part value symbol. Freud, while recognizing the importance of the onset of true genitality at around fourteen, had concentrated on the vicissitudes of infantile sexuality. Hall repaired this omission, and made "adolescence" a period of complex psychological as well as physical growth, to be studied "scientifically." But he also made it a symbol of the "pure" life of childish innocence suddenly exposed to the dangers of sexual perversion and criminality.

Besides viewing adolescence symbolically and scientifically, Hall seems also to have located it within the tradition of religious conversion. As Joseph Kett puts it:

> Hall himself, born in 1844, belonged to one of the last generations of New England boys expected to go through an elaborate ritual of conversion during adolescence. When he and his co-workers at Clark University in the 1890s were developing the modern concept of adolescence, they resurrected the old adolescent-conversion nexus by establishing a practically automatic connection between puberty and a kind of ultimate concern which manifested itself specifically in religious conversion.[3]

Evangelists long before Hall had been aware that adolescence, the period between fourteen and twenty-four, was the ideal time to effect a religious conversion. Hall at the turn of the century metamorphosed this religious conception into a "scientific" one, and reconstructed it in terms of the notion of adolescence as a "second birth," leading to a higher mental life. Closer to our time, Anna Freud has talked of adolescence as the period of "intellectualization," of commitment to a new ideology, and Erik Erikson has linked ideology to identity and seen adolescence as an "identity crisis." Whatever the precise nature of the change in the individual from around fourteen to twenty-four, however, we are all now aware that, *in our society* at least, puberty has become adolescence, and religious conversion, in general, been turned into the forging of a new, secular identity. Or such, at least, is the ideal.

III / *John Stuart Mill*

Why Now and Here?

EARLIER we insisted that adolescence is a time-bound and culturally limited phenomenon. What factors favored its emergence as a reality, a concept, and a symbol in the modern period, i.e., starting in the late eighteenth and culminating in the twentieth century? Two needs or impulses loom large in any answer: *Liebe und Arbeit*, as Freud referred to them. It is the conditions under which these necessities could be filled in modern Western society that created the phase of individual development that we now call adolescence.

Sex is awakened at puberty in all cultures. What seems critical for the concept of adolescence is the Puritan-Victorian constraints surrounding it in the West. It is primarily in a "Puritanical" (and even post-Puritanical) atmosphere that sex becomes truly problematic, laden with sin and guilt, and leading in our culture to the raging purgation of a "storm and stress" period. Depression or melancholia becomes the expected experience. As we have suggested earlier, the sexual problem is made even more acute at this time by the continued evolution toward the conjugal family, in which increased affective ties prepare the way for a heightened Oedipal struggle.

The other drive involves work and a "career." In simple societies there is little to choose from, and in traditional, ascriptive societies the choice is generally made by society, not the individual. It is only in rapidly changing, modernizing societies that career choice becomes a serious problem for relatively large numbers, evoking great anxiety and effort at self-definition. And it is, of course, during adolescence that the choice must be made. (Until recently this was less of a problem for girls, and adolescence seemed less traumatic for them.) Generally, in modern Western societies, allowing for local variations, it has been at about age fourteen that the boy has had to decide (or have decided for him) whether to go on to high school or out to work. For working-class youth there was usually little choice, and their job was determined by the condition of the labor market. For those bright working-class youth who left their class, or for the middle- and upper-class youth who went on to further schooling, an eventual choice of career loomed. Sometime in their early twenties they would be expected to choose their vocations. Less and less was their work choice a "given," determined by family and social necessity rather than by individual decision.

Admittedly, as we have already suggested, adolescent work choice was still indirectly but strongly dominated by or influenced by social and family pressures, especially in the form of the "achievement motive." Middle-class values, generally of a "Puritan" cast, were expected to dictate successful resolution of the adolescent dilemma; as Hall reminds us, adolescent sexuality was to be curbed and placed in the service of the Puritan work ethic.

The introduction of age-grading made "achieving" adolescents more and more conspicuous and self-aware of their status. Before industrialization there had been no set age for being in a particular level of education, or for going off to work. A Jeremy Bentham at age twelve was not unique in being at Oxford University in the same class as a twenty-four-year-old. A farm boy was at work from an early age, with occasional time out for schooling. Age-grading, the insistence that biological age set the lock step in which all youth will march, seems a relatively new invention of the increasingly mechanized and mechanical West. It also prepared the way for a highly visible group of young people passing through a stage in which they had to grapple with sex and work as problematic entities.

There was another aspect to adolescent turmoil and struggle, one, as we have noted, to a certain extent neglected by Freud. It involved aggressive impulses and a conflict over authority. Just as in the initial Oedipus complex, around age four to five, during which the child unconsciously desired not only the father's wife but his power, in adolescence, even when any actual Oedipus complex was muted, free choice of sex and work often meant rebellion against parental authority. Frequently this might take the form of ideological strife, and, if manifested by sufficient numbers of young people, a fueling of the conflict of generations. In fact, as the nineteenth century wore on into the twentieth, the aggressive aspects of the adolescent "crisis" seemed at least as important, if not more so, than the classic libidinal drives of Freud's original formulation. Looked at closely, the two aspects operate concomitantly.

In any event, the upshot of all these concurrent factors was threefold: First, by the end of the nineteenth century, adolescence became a conceptually recognized stage in a development perspective applied to modern Western youth, covering the ages fourteen to twenty-four. Second, by the twentieth century adolescence had become more or less a "way of life" of an age-group, rather than a lonely, transitory stage of a single individual. Third, we can now see that modern Western society (and other modernizing societies) has made adolescence into a second kind of latency period, only this time the latency is social rather than sexual (as it is at ages eight to twelve).[4]

With all of this said, we must also take due recognition of the assertion that empirical studies show that most youth of fourteen to twenty-four do *not* experience the syndrome we have ascribed to adolescence![5] Such data, in fact, suggest that adolescence as we have conceptualized it is an "elite" experience, a "storm and stress" phenomenon undergone only by certain unusually sensitive and troubled youth. Just as ours may be a unique society in conceptualizing puberty as a time of adolescence, so may only certain unique youth within our society be "called" to the struggle. For most, even in our society, sexual resolution (including marriage and the "choice" of a partner), settling into a work pattern, and acceptance of parental authority may still be "givens," comfortably provided by their family and the larger society. Thus, while adolescence has come to be a scientific concept, an ideal type, and a symbol for everyone in our culture, as an intense experience it appears to be reserved for a small company of the "twice born." Like the Oepidal struggle, it is potential for the many, but meaningful actuality for the few. Yet we must not overlook the fact that those few illuminate the inner experience of themselves and their society in a way that is important beyond mere numbers.

Visit to France

IS IT MEANINGFUL to look at John Stuart Mill as a typical "adolescent"?[6] I think not. It is more important to see him in the context of romantic "storm and stress"—not seen as a "way of life," but perceived as the demoniacal experience of an isolated person—unexpectedly impinging on a Utilitarian character taught to ignore such emotions or possibilities. Awareness of the modern concept of adolescence, however, can bring to our study an eye sharpened to look for certain features of puberty and growing up ignored by Mill and his contemporaries, and an emphasis on the developmental perspective beyond that even of Mill and his nineteenth-century followers. On the other hand, the study of Mill can bring to the concept of adolescence a useful reality and a historical perspective on *its* development.

We can start our study of Mill's "growing up" with a major experience at fourteen, frequently called his *Boyhood Visit to France*.[7] As we said earlier, it was Jeremy Bentham, John's "honorary grandfather," who opened the door to his protégé. In 1820 he wrote to his brother Samuel, who was residing in France, at Pompignan, proposing to send him a "pet-boy" for six months or so.

The "pet-boy" was John Stuart Mill. James Mill, in spite of his proudful independence, was "much gratified" at the suggestion. He himself had thought a few years earlier of removing his entire family to France for a while, in the fantasy of living cheaply and giving a Continental education to his children. Now the fantasy could be made reality in the person of John. The visit would allow the young boy to learn French, and his general acquaintance with French culture would serve admirably as part of his intellectual education. Moreover, James Mill had decided emphatically against sending his son to Cambridge University (though Sir John Stuart had explicitly set aside the money for this purpose). The ostensible reason was that John already knew more than he could learn there, and that the universities of Cambridge and Oxford were centers of cant and ignorance (relatively true at the time).[8] Instead of sending John off to University at age fourteen for a number of years, James Mill could substitute a short visit to France of six months (it actually became a year, with John conniving with the Benthams to extend his trip), whereby the experiment at youthful independence could be made limited and carefully controlled. Or so James Mill thought.

In any case, James agreed to let his son visit the Samuel Benthams in France in 1820. It was a momentous decision. Before the departure, father took son for a walk in Hyde Park and informed him how different he was from other less precocious boys. Yet he made clear that this was not something to be prideful about, for it was a matter of his education, not his personal accomplishments. We have John Stuart Mill's own account of this little lecture in the *Autobiography*:

I remember the very place in Hyde Park where, in my fourteenth year, on the eve of leaving my father's house for a long absence, he told me that I should find, as I got acquainted with new people, that I had been taught many things which youths my age did not commonly know; and that many persons would be disposed to talk to me of this, and to compliment me upon it. What other things he said on this topic I remember very imperfectly; but he wound up by saying, that whatever I knew more than others, could not be ascribed to any merit in me, but to the very unusual advantage which had fallen to my lot, of having a father who was able to teach me, and willing to give the necessary trouble and time; that it was no matter of praise to me, if I knew more than those who had not had a similar advantage, but the deepest disgrace to me if I did not.[9]

Let us look a little more closely at this passage. It is an important memory for John Stuart Mill, of an event occurring at the moment when he is about to make his first independent foray into the broader world. He recalls the "very place" in Hyde Park, though he claims to remember only "very imperfectly" (in an early draft he had written "too imperfectly to *risk* [italics added] writing them down") what other things his father said on the topic. The basic message that comes through is twofold: John Stuart Mill has no merit of his own, and he owes everything of merit to his father. The subterranean message is, of course: You will miss me in France, for I am vital to you; without me, you are nothing. This was the challenge that young John encountered on the eve of his trip to France.

James Mill made sure, though perhaps unconsciously, that his presence remained with his son, for he demanded from him a strict and continuous accounting. The result, an unexpected dividend for our study of John Stuart Mill, was the Journal and the Notebook. As John writes in his very first letter from Pompignan on June 2, 1820: "I arrived at the Chateau last night, or rather this morning, at about 2 o'clock, and according to your injunctions, I write you immediately an account of my journey. I have kept a pretty accurate journal, as you will see." Money is accounted for in the Journal, e.g., "I had 16 shillings to pay for luggage," but more important is the moral accounting: "In this letter [July 11, 1820], I have divided my day according to the number of hours employed on each particular study, to show you that I do not throw away my time." There is a touch of the confessional, too, for on a number of occasions John writes how he "lay in bed late, not knowing the hour," "lay in bed *purposely* late, having nothing to do [italics added]," and "Slept till past the time for going to Madame Boulet's; *lost thus* my music lesson [italics added]."[10] Surely young John knew how angry these confessions of weakness would make his father. Do we have here both a conscious conscience "speaking only with the voice of my father," and at the same time an unconscious rebellion and a speaking out against the father's insistent "accountability"?

In any event, John Stuart Mill carefully accounted for the minutae of his lessons and public learnings to his father. What he did not account for, certainly to his father, or consciously to himself, was the formative influence on him of key members of the Bentham family, and especially the effect of one outsider, a young boy his own age, named Balard.

It was George Bentham who wielded the first influence over the young John almost from the moment of his arrival. A young man of nearly twenty, he was the first such person whom Mill had encountered. Instead of John teaching his siblings, a person who could have been his sibling was teaching him. George Bentham corrected John Stuart Mill's lessons, involved him in sports such as swimming, and, more importantly, taught him botany. It became a lifelong interest for Mill. (In the psychological literature on adolescence, we might note that "collecting" is regarded as a typical event of this phase of development, a sublimation of sexual curiosity, and a substitute for aggressive feelings. Mill's later comment to Herbert Spencer that his "murderous propensities . . . are confined to the vegetable world" seems unexpectedly to give color to these assertions as they fit young John.)[11] Bentham, who was on the verge of becoming an eminent botanist, took young John on many of his field trips, with the result that the outdoors was suddenly opened wide to the young boy by the nephew of old Jeremy.

There seems little question that George Bentham also served as a potential model for John, an alternate identification to that with his own father. The dedication to botany is one sign of that possibility being realized. Something, however, seems to have short-circuited the relationship. It may have been doomed from the start by John Stuart Mill's presumptuous precocity, for there is a faintly negative tone to George Bentham's diary entry on the third day of young John's visit: "Went early with J. M. [John Mill] to Toulouse, on the road he conversed a good deal in French about crops, the country he has passed &c though he has been but a fortnight in France and had learn[ed] but a month or six weeks before from Richard, gave him an algebra su[m] that I had not been able to do, which he resolved in a few minut[es]."[12]

Perhaps the relationship was also influenced by James Mill's growing coolness with Jeremy Bentham after 1818, with all the Benthams becoming distant from all the Mills. Unfortunately, we have no hint of the relations of John with George Bentham after 1820 until 1828, when we have a cold and critical letter by Mill on George Bentham's work on logic. Asked by John Bowring, Bentham's assistant and hardly a friend of the Mills, though a Utilitarian, to review it for the *Westminster Review*, John Stuart Mill explained his initial refusal:

> I will now tell you exactly what I think of Mr. George Bentham's book—and what I am ready to say of it, if you think that it would be more satisfactory to Mr. Bentham than an entire omission. I do not think that Mr. G. B.'s book affords any proof of want of talent—far from it—but many of haste, and want of due deliberation. This mistake was, as it seems to me, that of supposing that he was qualified to write on such a subject as Logic after two or three months' study, or that so young a logician was capable of maintaining so high a ground as that of a critic upon Whately. . . . Mr. George Bentham seems not to be aware, that Dr Whately is a far greater master of the science than *he* is, and that the people will think the dispropor-

tion still greater than it is. It would therefore have been wiser in him not to have assumed the tone of undisputed and indisputable superiority over Whately, which marks the greater part of his critique.[13]

Whether or not Mill's sharp words got back to George Bentham—and given Bowring's general maliciousness to the Mills, this is certainly a possibility—Bentham retorted to an overture from Mill a few years later, in 1832, in equally cold terms:

I should be very sorry were you to imagine that we attribute to you any [remissness?] towards us and we shall always feel great pleasure in seeing you whenever our respective occupations admit of our meeting. I am however now so much engaged with my legal and other pursuits that I really cannot fix any time when you would be likely to find me at home. Indeed I seldom return till late at night and in my absence my mother never sees any one but a few of her most intimate friends. . . . I therefore fear I must trust to meeting you at the Athenaeum or calling on you at the India House when I can get so far. In the meantime I shall always be most happy if I can in any way be of any use to you.[14]

As late as 1843, John Stuart Mill seems to have remembered the echoes of this letter. In that year he had a copy of his own *Logic*—a nice touch—sent to George Bentham, who had then acknowledged it. Mill wrote, in turn, "I was very glad to see your handwriting again, though the mere fact of sending my book did not require or merit any acknowledgment from you," and then offered to secure some plant specimens for his former botany teacher if Bentham would merely mark what he wanted in an enclosed catalog. Bentham sent back the catalog unmarked, but mentioned in his letter a few species he would like to have. Mill replied that he would be on the lookout for them, and then listed a few others in his possession, adding: "If any of the two or three I have mentioned would be of the least value to you I should feel really obliged by your saying so, as I should try anything else however trifling which you would put it in my power to do for you or yours." Then, in what seems an obvious, though probably unconscious, remembrance of Bentham's letter of ten years earlier, Mill concluded: "I am always to be seen or heard of here at 18 Kensington Square and though I am not often at the Athenaeum without some special cause, your being to be met with there would be cause sufficient."[15]

It appears that over twenty years after his trip to France, Mill still had mixed feelings, colored by fondness, for his youthful teacher of those times, enough to send him his *Logic*, to offer to collect plants for him, and to meet him at the Athenaeum. The earlier rebuff, it would seem, had come from George Bentham (had the 1832 letter perhaps also been inspired by disapproval of John Stuart Mill's recent involvement with Harriet Taylor, the wife of another man?). Whatever the complete and true explanation, it seems that the French trip gave the fourteen-year-old John a teacher and model close to his own age, from whom he then became rapidly estranged. Alas, the first excursion into "feelings" apparently came too quickly to grief.

There was, however, another Bentham who had a strong influence, in its way more lasting, on young John. This was Sir Samuel's wife, Lady Bentham. She stood in marked contrast to John's own mother. The latter, as we know, was never mentioned in the published *Autobiography*; as we shall see, Lady Bentham is given much praise there for her "parental" role in John Stuart Mill's life. Our concern with her, then, is not merely because she figured in Mill's boyhood experiences, but because of the real and symbolic effect she had on the future course of his life, especially as it related to women as "mother" figures.

Lady Bentham had two qualities whose absence John Stuart Mill lamented in his mother: she was intelligent, and she could make herself obeyed. In the Journal John tells how she proposed to him a subject for a dialogue on "the question whether great landed estates and great establishments in commerce and manufactures, or small ones, are the most conducive to the general happiness?"[16] There are evidences throughout of the lady's compelling way—*she* decides when and where and how they are to stop on their trips—but none more than in the authoritative tone with which she faced down James Mill, and insisted that John be allowed to stay for an additional six months (meanwhile attending the University of Montpellier—shades of Cambridge University!). In a letter of September 14, 1820, inserted in John Stuart Mill's Journal, she announced:

> We [the Benthams] have been considerably successful in getting the better of his inactivity of mind and body when left to himself—Upon all occasions his gentleness under reproof, and thankfulness for correction are remarkable; and as it is by reason supported by examples we point out to him that we endeavour to convince him [sic], not by command that we induce him to act so or so, we trust that you will have satisfaction from that part of his education we are giving him to fit him for commerce with the world at large—Unless therefore we receive immediately your orders for his return forthwith we shall take him on with us to Montpellier.[17]

The implied criticism of James Mill's method of education is breathtaking, and the preemptory "we shall take him" (little watered down by "unless . . . we receive immediately") noteworthy. James Mill meekly concurred in the decision taken by Lady Bentham.

At a number of places in the Journal, John confessed how he was bored without books. "As all my books are locked up in the trunk . . . I am afraid I shall be a little troubled with ennui today" and "starved for books" are fairly typical entries. Lady Bentham set herself to rectify this situation wherein the young boy's life consisted only of books. She arranged for lessons for John in riding, fencing, dancing, and music; she made sure that her son George took the "inactive" body of John out into the open, botanizing, mountain climbing, walking, swimming; and together, the whole family took him to the circus. One glance at the Journal shows how eagerly, in spite of himself, young John responded. It is sheer nonsense to say, as Packe does, that he "hated these gentlemanly pursuits [e.g., "the foppery of dancing"], but was made to continue." In fact, when Miss Clara, one of the Bentham daughters, slept late, John tells us how he "took a lesson in her stead," and one constantly senses his willingness to engage in his new way of life (in spite of falling during one of his dancing lessons). There is no question of his eagerness to follow Lady Bentham's lead, and "not by command."[18]

In the same letter to James Mill just quoted, Lady Bentham made clear her insistence on an outward, symbolic change to go along with the new, inner education." "Should John remain with us," she announced, "I must beg your permission to order for him a new coat at Montpellier, partly because he has *outgrown* [italics added] his present ones, partly because seeing the variety of company he must with us [sic], and be amongst those who dress well. . . ."[19] The indirect criticism of the dowdy Mill's way of life is evident. In any case, once again James Mill acquiesced docilely.

In contrast to Lady Bentham's competence and care, John's own mother must have suffered badly in his mind. There is one short letter to her in the Journal, signed "Your affectionate Son," and he does record at one place having received letters from her and his sisters.[20] Otherwise there is no mention of Harriet Mill, even though she bore her seventh child, Henry, John's second male sibling, while he was away. We seem on the way to his complete dismissal of her in the published *Autobiography*.

In the *Autobiography*, however, we have his mature estimate of Lady Bentham and her influence on him. He speaks there of her as Sir Samuel's "wife, a daughter of the celebrated chemist, Dr. Fordyce . . . a woman of strong will and decided character, much general knowledge, and great practical good sense of the Edgeworth kind: she was the ruling spirit of the household, as she deserved, and was well qualified, to be. Their family consisted of one son (the eminent botanist) and three daughters, the youngest about two years my senior. I am indebted to them for much and various instruction, and for an almost parental interest in my welfare."[21] As we have seen earlier, James Mill had had his various "family romances"; in a way we sense that his son had come to have a similar experience.

There is one other personal experience, the importance of which for him John does not reveal to his father. It is his friendship with a boy of about his own age, Antoine-Jérôme Balard (or Ballard). For the first time John made a friend of his own, independent of his father's choice. As he explained to Comte in a letter written twenty years later, his friendship in Montpellier with Balard was part of "the happiest six months of my life."[22]

John's first mention of Balard is in his Notebook entry of December 7, 1820, where he notes for his father: "M. Ballard, a young man well known by M. Bérard, and who is getting ready to take the public courses at the Faculty of Sciences, has been kind enough to give me some of the local plants. M. Bérard has spoken very well of him; he is very well educated, especially in chemistry."[23] The emphasis here is on M. Bérard's approval, for Bérard would be respected by James Mill, and also on the chemistry, in which the father's interest and personal involvement (interestingly, his best friend, Thomson, had been a chemist) could be expected to be high. In Balard, of course, John had found an echo of George Bentham's interest in botany, as well as his father's in chemistry.

All in all, there are only about half a dozen references to Balard, generally rather offhanded, in the Notebook. If we did not have four later letters from Balard to Mill, and John Stuart Mill's testimony in his letters to Comte of the importance of the friendship, we might be misled (as James Mill undoubtedly was) as to the significance of the relationship.[24] Indeed, as it is we are left in an unsatisfactory position. As F. A. Hayek says in his introduction to *The Earlier Letters of John Stuart Mill*: "If, for instance, good fortune had somewhere preserved the letters which for some years after his visit to France as a boy Mill wrote to his 'first friend' Antoine Jérôme Balard, later a distinguished chemist, these would probably tell us more about his early development than any document which might still be found in England."[25]

The first letter from Balard to Mill is dated June 27, 1822, and talks mainly about botany, chemistry, and scientific societies. It assumes that John's future "career," unstated here, will prevent him from occupying himself with the science of botany.

The second letter is dated a little over two years later (July 1824). Balard confesses that he has not answered Mill's last letter immediately, as requested, and then goes on to congratulate him for being on the "road to success" (i.e., in the East India Company). "My friend," Balard exhorts him, "advance there rapidly, in order to reach quickly that state of independence to which all men aspire . . ." Much of the rest of Balard's letter is then occupied with a recital of his own ambitions: "Only when I shall arrive at that state will I be perfectly happy; now I live only for the future." For Balard "that state" of the happy future turns out to be his wish to be a successful and wealthy pharmacist. As he concludes the letter, "Adieu my friend. I hope to make amends by writing you soon, and perhaps then I will be able to sign myself Balard apothecary instead of simply Balard. . . ."

There is a disturbing note of crass middle-class ambition in Balard's letter, and we can suspect that Mill began to wonder if his dear friend's interest in "independence" meant the same thing as his own increasing absorption with the subject. Nor could Mill have taken heart from Balard's response to his effort to convert him to Utilitarianism. On Mill's advice, Balard had read the *Traité de Legislation civile et pènale*, but, as he concludes, "I might have aspired to become a utilitarian, but I limit myself to wishing your Society well, feeling myself without the necessary means of contributing to its renown."

The next letter of April 4, 1827, makes the situation even clearer. Balard begins, "Our correspondence has already been so long interrupted that I do not know whether to offer reproaches or excuses. . . . In such a state of uncertainty, I embrace the simplest choice, that of forgetting the past and concerning myself with the present." Balard blithely goes on to talk at great length about his successes in commercial pharmacy, although he has still not arrived at his expected fortune. Similarly, most of his news about mutual friends is about their careers. He concludes that he will insure a quick reply from Mill this time by asking him a favor: to put him in touch with chemical merchants in London, who will help him sell his new discovery, bromine (with which, in fact, Balard eventually did make a success). His comment, "It would be very advantageous for my fortune and reputation to distribute this substance," suggests a certain insensitivity on Balard's part to Mill's attitudes.

Balard's last letter is dated January 19, 1831. He announces that the Royal Society of London has awarded him a medal, and asks Mill's help in having it forwarded to him. With the medal he wants Mill to include a long letter informing him of his "social position," his "progress," his "hopes," and so on. Balard's own position, he announces, is improving, though he must work from morning till night. Other mutual friends, he tells Mill, are "rapidly marching to fortune" and "earning a great deal of money." Of ideas, scientific thought, or Balard's intimate feelings, there is no mention whatever.

No more correspondence between Mill and Balard has been preserved. After 1831 there seems to have been none. Almost all observers, while puzzling over the lapsed correspondence, seem to feel as does Anna Jean Mill, editor of the Journal and Notebook, that "The friendship is not written off."[26] As evidence, they cite Mill's letter to Comte on August 12, 1842, in which he writes:

> I am very glad to hear you are a native of Montpellier; it is another bond of sympathy, for I myself passed the happiest six months of my youth in that town, in the winter of 1820–21. It was also there that for the first time I found a friend, that is to say a friend of my own choice, as opposed to those given me by family ties. This friend I have never seen since; for a long time we kept up a correspondence which finally ended a little by the fault of both of us, and I do not even know if he is still alive.[27]

On Comte's assurance that Balard was still alive and a successful Professor in Paris, Mill tried to arrange to meet his youthful friend. As he wrote Comte on August 30, 1843, "If you see M. Balard in Montpellier, I would be delighted to hear about him. I wrote to him, I believe, three months ago. Unless something unforseen occurs, I anticipate the realization of a fraternal visit which I have long desired."[28] The desired meeting, however, never took place, and the chapter in Mill's life involving Balard was forever closed, at least outwardly.

Now, in effect, I believe the friendship *was* "written off." I think Mill suffered great disappointment in it, just as with George Bentham. Gradually he seemed to perceive that this friend chosen by himself was, in fact, only another version of the grasping, parvenu Englishman increasingly characteristic of the English scene. Again his early venture into independent feelings seems to have turned out poorly. We may, in fact, be witnessing the beginnings of a pattern here.

But this was in the future. In 1820, when John Stuart Mill was fourteen, Balard, like George Bentham, represented human possibilities beyond those offered by his father. James Mill had hitherto "made" his son; now John was "making" a part of his life for himself. In all ways, then, the boyhood trip to France was a major formative experience for John Stuart Mill. His father had told him how different intellectually he was from other boys; John was learning how similar he was to other boys in his emotional needs.

On John's return to England, his father noticed only a physical change. In August 1821 James Mill wrote to Ricardo: "John has been at home for some weeks, very much grown; looking almost a man, in other respects not much different from when he went."[29] James Mill was satisfied that his son had learned fluent French, and he could probably guess that this would involve John in a future intense interest in French political and intellectual affairs. His intentions, then, had been fulfilled. Only a cranky and slightly cracked psychologist might read significance into John's Journal notes that the paintings that pleased him most in the Luxembourg gallery were of "David of Leonidas and the Spartans at Thermopylae, and another of the Queen of France *giving liberty to slaves* [italics added]," or that what most pleased the "shy and awkward" youth (to use his father's terms) in a *Cabinet* display was "a suit of ancient armour."[30] Perhaps a bit more obviously plausible was young John's sudden interest on his return home in reading all the books he could about the French Revolution, a subject we shall deal with in greater detail later.

John Stuart Mill, however, knew inwardly that he had gone to France as a child or youth, and had come back on his way to being a man. The fact is put rather coldly and objectively in the *Autobiography*, where he tells us in one place: "When I was about fourteen I left England for more than a year and after my return though my studies went on under my father's general direction *he was no longer my schoolmaster* [italics added]." About twenty pages later he makes the situation even clearer: "But the greatest advantage which I derived from this episode in my life was that of having breathed for a whole year the free and genial atmosphere of Continental life. This advantage I could not then judge and appreciate, *nor even consciously feel*, but it was not the less real [italics added]."[31] It is a judgment with which we concur heartily.

Back Home

WITH JOHN back in England, James Mill set to work again on his education. He took advantage of his son's newly acquired ability to read French, and put in his hands Condillac's *Traité des Sensations* and other works. More importantly, he set him to reading Jeremy Bentham's principal speculations as interpreted by Dumont in the *Traité de Legislation*. The result was unexpectedly traumatic. As Mill informs us in the *Autobiography*: "The reading of this book was an event in my life; one of the turning points of my mental history."[32] True, he reminds us, his previous education by his father "had been, in a great measure, a course of Benthamism." But now:

> In the first few pages of Bentham it [the "greatest happiness" standard] burst on me with all the force of novelty. . . . The feeling rushed upon me that all previous moralists were superseded, and that here indeed was the commencement of a new era. . . . When I laid down the last volume of the Traité I was a different being. The principle of utility, understood as Bentham understood it, and applied in the manner in which he applied it through these three volumes, fell exactly into its place as the keystone which held together the detached and fragmentary portions of my knowledge and beliefs. It gave unity to my conceptions of things. I now had opinions; a creed, a doctrine, a philosophy; in one (and the best) sense of the word, a religion; the inculcation and diffusion of which could be made the principal outward aim of a life. And I had a grand conception laid before me of changes to be made in the condition of mankind by that doctrine.[33]

What had happened to young John? He tells us that he had become a "different being," and we sense from his words that we are in the presence of a "conversion" episode, though the creed is secular. In short, it sounds as if he were experiencing a "new birth" in adolescence, as described by G. Stanley Hall. John had reached a higher moral plane, and had achieved, seemingly for himself, an aim in life and a possible career.

To this I would add a further interpretation and then a qualification. The episode also sounds as if, having consciously flirted with independence from his father, young John is now retreating to a reaffirmation of identity with James Mill and his beliefs. This time, however, the identification is modulated through the words and inspiration of his "honorary grandfather," Jeremy Bentham, who incidentally was responsible for John's trip to France. John could feel that he had acquired an ideology of his "own" while at the same time damping down the threatening desires for rebellion and independence by reaffirming at this critical stage in his life his father's beliefs and way of life. In short, as would be demonstrated decisively five years later in John's mental crisis, the "new birth" was really abortive, or rather a false pregnancy.

The Austins, Especially Sarah

JAMES MILL had his own ideas as to his son's possible career. "At this time," John Stuart Mill informs us, "my father, notwithstanding his abhorrence of the chaos of barbarism called English law, had turned his thoughts towards the bar as on the whole less ineligible for me than any other profession."[34] In furtherance of this aim, he set

John to work (in the winter of 1821–1822) reading Roman law with John Austin, an admirer of Bentham (who, we must remember, was also deeply interested in reforming the "barbarism" called English law).

John Austin (1790–1859) at the time was thirty-one and a neighbor of the Mills in Queen Square. He had gone into the army at age sixteen, seeing service in Sicily, but upon the death of a brother in 1812 had resigned his commission at the urging of his parents. Studying for the bar in Norwich, he met Sarah, the beautiful and vivacious youngest daughter of the important and well-connected Taylor family of the area. Spurred on by her hopes, he was called to the bar in 1818, and then married her the next year.

It was a strange and unexpected marriage. When he met her Sarah was nineteen, lively, and something of a flirt. He was gloomy and given to introspection and chronic depression. Yet, to the amazement of her friends, she waited for him until she was twenty-six. Obviously impressed with his mental genius, she believed that she would be his salvation, and it seemed that she was. As for John Austin, his nervous malady caused him to give up practice at the bar in 1825. Chosen in that year for the newly created Chair of Jurisprudence at the London University, he took his wife and four-year-old child, Lucie, to Germany for two years in order to improve his knowledge of Roman law and thus better prepare himself to teach. Alas, as he discovered a few years after his return to London, by 1830 there were not enough students willing to pay the tuition fees on which his chair depended (it was unendowed), and he resigned in that year. For the rest of his life he was often in financial difficulties, never, it seems, writing the great book that would fulfill his tremendous promise. Fortunately, Sarah was able to help with the finances, for she had profited from the two years in Germany by becoming fluent in the language, and now helped eke out their existence with translations.

In 1821, when John Stuart Mill began studying law with John Austin, all of this was ahead. For young Mill the connection with John Austin was significant, and their friendship lasted until Austin's death. In the *Autobiography* Mill devoted some pages to summing it up. There is a strange echo in one passage of Mill's own mental crisis, when he says of Austin: "The dissatisfaction with life and the world, felt more or less in the present state of society by every discerning and conscientious mind, was in his case, I think, combined with habitual dissatisfaction with himself, giving a generally melancholy cast to the character, very natural to those whose passive moral susceptibilities are much more than proportioned to their active energies." It sounds as if John Austin served both as a partial model for Mill's melancholy of 1826 and as a frightening warning example. On the surface, however, Mill summed up Austin's effect on him as follows:

On me his influence was most salutary. It was moral in the best sense. He took a sincere and kind interest in me, far beyond what was to be expected towards a mere youth from a man of his age, standing, and what seemed austerity of character. My intercourse with him was the more beneficial to me owing to his being of a different mental type from any of the other intellectual men whom I frequented, and his influence was exerted against many of the prejudices and narrownesses which are almost sure to be found in a young man formed by a particular school or a particular set.[35]

It is clear that John Austin served at a crucial point in John's life as a broadening influence and as an alternate type of intellectual to James Mill.

On an emotional level, however, it was Sarah Austin who proved critically important. While John was in France she took over the task of instructing his sisters. When he returned, Sarah Austin had just had her only child, Lucie (later Lady Duff Gordon), and John rapidly became one of her chief playmates; she shortly came to call him "Bun Don," a childish mispronunciation of "Brother John." The "brother" theme took on further meaning when in 1825, at the age of nineteen, John started to take German lessons with Sarah Austin, and addressed her henceforth as "Mütterlein," or "Little Mother."

At this point I wish to suggest two outrageous interpretations. The first is that Sarah Austin, like Lady Bentham, was perceived by John as a kind of substitute mother. His own mother was a "Hausfrau"; Sarah Austin was a gifted intellectual in her own right, whose salon in later life was admired by all. Harriet Mill merely slaved for her children physically; Sarah Austin, like his father, taught both John and his siblings. The suspicion arises that John Stuart Mill could only admire a woman who in some important ways reminded him of his father![36]

The maternal relation seems to have waxed and waned. We have a rather formal letter of 1830, addressed to "Mrs. Austin." Less than a year later John Stuart Mill wrote warmly: "How I wish I were by your side, and could speak to you instead of writing. You may lay down your anxiety, my dear Mütterlein, I hope never to resume it," and signed "ihre Sönnchen." In 1836, with his father slowly approaching death, Mill is still writing in the same vein, adding "What you say about my coming to see you is very kind of you my dear Mütterlein," although he then pleads ill health as a reason for not making the trip.[37] The same tone is maintained in his letter of 1837. There is next a gap in the extant correspondence until October 1841, when we have again a formal letter to "Mrs. Austin," signed "J. S. M." At this point the mother-son relation has broken down completely.

What had happened to the relationship? What was it that led Mill to write in his *Autobiography* of his former admired and beloved "Mütterlein" that: "She laid herself out for drawing round her as many persons of consideration or promise of consideration, as she could get, and succeeded in getting many foreigners, some literary men and a good many young men of various descriptions, and many who came for her remained for him. Having known me from a boy, she made great profession of a kind of maternal interest in me. But I never for an instant supposed that she really cared for me; nor perhaps for anybody beyond the surface; I mean as to real feeling, not that she was not quite ready to be friendly or serviceable."[38]

Before we hazard a guess about what went wrong, we must advance our second outrageous interpretation. It is simply that beneath the mother-son relation ran a potential lover's relation. John Stuart Mill was a handsome boy with delicate, aquiline features. Sarah Austin was a recognized beauty. As one of her friends, M. Barthélmy St. Hilaire, described her: "It was in 1840 that I first knew Mrs. Austin. . . . She was still extremely handsome, and her complexion, which she preserved till the day of her death was dazzling." Her husband, as St. Hilaire said, was "intensely nervous and often ill, he loved solitude, and even in his own house no one saw him until dinner."[39] There is no question of Sarah's devoted love for her ailing husband, but the psychic price for the high-spirited, gregarious, and flirtatious woman must have been high.

At an unrecognized level, a romantic involvement with John Stuart Mill would have held much attraction, especially covered over as it was with maternal solicitude and love. Do we have any evidence for such "insulting" speculation? There is one episode, around 1833, that gives credence to Sarah Austin's romantic susceptibility. She became romantically involved, at long distance, with a German princeling. As Michael St. John Packe describes it: "Although she had never seen Prince Puckler Muskau, she loved him desperately, and began a lengthy correspondence with him in language of the most ardent intimacy."[40] Eventually Sarah Austin recalled her duty to her family, and refused to meet her gallant. The affair remained one of letters only, was never consummated, and ended shortly after it had begun.

In a letter of July 18, 1833, written by Thomas Carlyle from Craigenputtock to Sarah Austin, there is one cryptic statement. Inviting her to come visit at the same time as John Stuart Mill, Carlyle adds: "The journey were no unpleasant thing; the rather if you held

John Mill to his word, who has as good as promised to see us here this autumn. After all, what if you should really take thought of it."[41] Was Carlyle after something? Did he sense the underlying aspect of the mother-son affection?

It was at the Austin's house in 1831, having just become acquainted with Mrs. Austin, that Carlyle first met John Stuart Mill. As he wrote his wife Jane on September 1, 1831:

The Frau Austin herself was as loving as ever—a true Germanised spiritual *screamiken*. We were five of a party: her husband, a lean grey-headed painful-looking man, with large earnest timid eyes and a clanging metallic voice, that at great length set forth Utilitarianism *steeped* in German metaphysics, not dissolved therein; a very worthy sort of limited man and professor of law. Secondly, a Frenchman, of no importance whatever, for he uttered not a word except some compliments in his own tongue. Thirdly, John Mill, "Spirit-of-the-Age." The other two you know already. This young Mill, I fancy and hope, is "a *baying* you can love." A slender, rather tall and elegant youth, with small clear Roman-nosed face, two small earnestly-smiling eyes; modest, remarkably gifted with precision of utterance, enthusiastic, yet lucid, calm; not a great, yet distinctly a gifted and amiable youth.[42]

In Mill, as we shall see, Carlyle thought he had a potential disciple. In both Mill and Mrs. Austin he knew he had made friends of two appealing, intelligent, and interesting people.

The friendship blossomed. Then in May of 1834 Carlyle visited Sarah Austin, involved at the time in extricating herself from her impulsive romance with Prince Puckler Muskau. As Packe tells it: "She greeted him with a volley of tattle, a 'Niagara of gossip,' omitting no detail of the affair of John Mill and Harriet Taylor."[43] This was the first Carlyle knew of Mill's involvement with Mrs. Taylor. As Carlyle immediately wrote in his Journal to his wife (May 24, 1834) about Mill:

Let me now treat thee to a budget of small news. . . . Mrs. Austin had a tragical story of his having fallen *desperately in love* with some young philosophic beauty (yet with the innocence of two sucking doves), and being lost to all his friends and to himself, and what not; but I traced nothing of this in poor Mill; and even incline to think that what truth there is or was in his adventure may have done him good.[44]

Jane Carlyle promptly relayed the news to her husband's brother, Dr. John Carlyle: "The most important item [of news learned from Mrs. John Austin] was that a young Mrs. Taylor, though encumbered with a husband and children, has ogled John Mill successfully so that he was desperately in love."[45]

This, then, is the context in which Carlyle may have sensed an incipient emotional relationship between Mill and Sarah Austin, or at least on the part of the latter. Packe has told us that Mrs. Austin had prattled to Carlyle about the Mill-Taylor affair "to cover her own traces" with Puckler Muskau. Perhaps. But is it not more plausible to believe that she was also acting as "the woman scorned"? John Mill was surely a more interesting fantasy romance to Sarah Austin—I do not believe her capable of anything more than that, for she still loved her husband deeply—than Puckler Muskau, that choice of psychic desperation. Wasn't Sarah Austin as beautiful and intelligent as Harriet Taylor? Wasn't Mrs. Taylor, like Mrs. Austin, also encumbered with husband and child? Why, then, had John chosen the former? At some even deeper level, was Sarah Austin aware that John had fallen in love with a younger version of herself, *of the same name* (Sarah's maiden name was Taylor; see further p. 284), with the identical claims to intellectuality, beauty, and strength of will?

From such "evidence" one can build a castle in the air. Yet, in the labyrinthian ways of the underground life, such are the threads we must follow, hoping they will lead us out of the psychic maze. In any case, Mill's actual romance was with Mrs. Taylor, not Mrs. Austin. We can speculate that any possible feelings on his side toward the beautiful older woman would have been immediately suppressed as incestuous in nature. Was she not his "Mütterlein"? When he came to know about her tattling interference in his life—"a very mischievous tongue," he attested—he would turn against her even in this role, and write, scornfully and scorned, about her professed "kind of maternal interest in me." At the end, as with George Bentham and Balard, another kind of emotional relationship had collapsed for John Stuart Mill. It is only in hindsight that we can see that it helped prepare the way for his more important relationship with Harriet Taylor.

A Career Choice

WE HAVE mainly been discussing John Stuart Mill's youthful affective relations. It might be well now to say a word about his work and career choices. There was no traumatic youthful agitation here, or at least not until the mental crisis (and really not even then). When his father set him to prepare for the law by reading under John Austin, John dutifully concurred. As we have seen, upon reading Bentham for himself, he also hoped to become a legal and moral reformer. In accordance with this desire, he turned to writing as the means of promulgating and circulating his ideas. Thus, in the summer of 1822 he wrote his first argumentative essay (on the fact that the rich were not morally superior to the poor). In that same year his first published writings appeared in the *Traveller* newspaper. John Stuart Mill was launched on his long writing career.

In the very next year John's daily occupation and means of material security were provided for him. "In May 1823," he tells us, "my professional occupation and status *were decided by my father's* obtaining for me an appointment from the East India Company, in the office of the Examiner of Indian Correspondence, *immediately under himself* [italics added]."[46] At that time his father's promotion in the Examiner's office opened up a vacancy that the directors gave to John "on a footing," as James Mill wrote a friend, "on which he will in all probability be in the receipt of a larger income at an early age than he would be in any profession: and as he can still keep his hours as a student of law, his way to the legal profession is not barred, if he should afterwards prefer it."[47] Although for the first three years John received no salary as such, and only an annual gratuity of £30, he was soon recipient of a salary that made him affluent and which he enjoyed, with increases, until his retirement from the East India Company in 1859. His father had thus put at his disposal a sizable financial heritage.

The work itself, though somewhat pedestrian, was not arduous, and John Stuart Mill was expected to dispatch it within six hours a day. In fact, as Bain informs us, he "probably never gave more than half of that time to his office routine. His two great works—the *Logic* and the *Political Economy*—were, I may say, written during his office hours."[48] It was not that John Stuart Mill scanted his work—he was too moral and serious for that—but simply that, as Bain points out, in a regular business establishment his "efficiency" would have brought no reward in terms of free time for his own work. Thus the East India Company not only gave him professional status and financial security; it also allowed him to continue easily as a writer and reformer.

Thus we can see that work and career were relatively untroubled areas in John Stuart Mill's life, at least at the time of his youth. He had decided early to be a reformer and writer, and, as we shall soon see, after the subsidence of the mental crisis, with its challenge to all he believed in, he continued unwaveringly in this decision. There was, of course, what at one point he called the "drudgery" of the East India Company, but a few hours of this a day seem a small price to have paid in order to pursue his chosen career in tranquillity and relative affluence.

III / *John Stuart Mill*

Mill's Peer Group

IN PURSUIT of his youthful Benthamite ambition to be a "reformer of the world," John Stuart Mill turned not only to writing, but to becoming a founder of small societies of like-minded individuals. In the winter of 1822, aged sixteen, he organized a "little society," originally composed of three members and never expanding in its three and one-half years of existence beyond about ten, which he called the Utilitarian Society (taking the word from John Galt's *Annals of the Parish*, a book about Scottish life much admired by James Mill). It met in Jeremy Bentham's house. "The chief effect of it," Mill tells us, "was its bringing me in contact with young men less advanced than myself, among whom, as they professed the same opinions, I became a sort of leader or chief."[49] William Eyton Tooke, George Graham, and, later, John Arthur Roebuck were the chief figures with Mill.

Here Mill could begin to reform the world by leading a band of disciples. On a less intellectual plane, we can see that it also fulfilled a normal boyhood inclination: to band together with other young men in a group. Mill at last had his own peer group! When the Utilitarian Society disintegrated (as such youthful societies have a habit of doing), Mill was central in replacing it with a new society which met at the house of George Grote, where Mrs. Grote sympathetically watched over them as they met for an hour and a half, twice a week in the morning, before proceeding to their various offices. Whereas the Utilitarian Society had discussed abstract, metaphysical issues, the new grouping took a set text, such as Ricardo's book on economics, Hobbes' on logic, and in 1829, as their last work, James Mill's *Analysis of the Human Mind*, to serve as a catalyst of discussion. While this sect was flourishing, John Stuart Mill had also become involved (in 1825) with a weekly meeting of Owenites, and debates between Utilitarians and Owenites raged fiercely for a few months. Out of these debates the Utilitarians drew a plan to establish in London a replica of the Edinburgh Speculative Society, and this new Debating Society embraced all ages. It numbered about one hundred names, including some M.P.s, a few Lords, and many of the bright and aspiring young politicians and intellectuals of London. Alas, the debates were not very successful, and the illustrious members failed to attend regularly.

Whether for this reason, or for others, John Stuart Mill seemed to lose his taste for societies. Shortly after the collapse of the Debating Society, under the specific inspiration of reading Condorcet's *Life of*

Turgot, Mill resolved to break away from his previous groups: "This book [Condorcet's] cured me of my sectarian tastes. The two or three pages beginning 'Il regardait toute secte comme nuisible,' and explaining why Turgot always kept himself distinct from the Encyclopedists, sank deeply into me. I left off designating myself and others as Utilitarians, or by the pronoun 'we,' or any other collective denomination: I ceased to *afficher* sectarianism."[50] We can also speculate that Mill was entering upon the period of his mental crisis. With his faith in his aims as a reformer shaken, with his new doubts as to the sufficiency of his father's doctrines, it is hardly likely that Mill could be more than half-hearted as a Utilitarian debater. The zeal and true faith were gone. His youthful intellectual friends would, in most cases, have to give way to new, more affectively linked friends, or at least they would have to be intellectuals with a keener appreciation of the emotions.

Yet among his early companions there was one, John Arthur Roebuck, who would have seemed suitable to bridge the gap. The two youths had first met in 1824. Roebuck, who had just come from the wild spaces of Canada to study for the bar in England, presented himself to Thomas Love Peacock, a family friend, and a fellow examiner with James Mill at India House. Peacock immediately introduced him to John Stuart Mill, and the two fell into prolonged conversation. Mill told him about Bentham and the Utilitarian Society, and put into his hands "a small octavo manuscript, which was a description of the principles of the Utilitarian Society, and its rules." As Roebuck recalls, "He offered to introduce me, and if, upon consideration, I acquiesced, he would propose me as a member."[51] Roebuck quickly became a convert, and John Stuart Mill also had a new friend.

The third member of the triumvirate was George Graham, and together the three of them walked and talked through the streets of London and roamed in the countryside, where they botanized as well. They had become inseparable, forming what they laughingly called the "trijackia," all of them being named John (this was also Graham's middle name). John Mill, proud of his new and self-chosen friends, then made the mistake of presenting them to his father at the Mills' summer lodgings. We give Roebuck's version and interpretation of what happened:

I found that [John] Mill, although possessed of much learning, and thoroughly acquainted with the state of the political world, was, as might have been expected, the mere exponent of other men's ideas, those men being his father and Bentham; and that he was utterly ignorant of what is called society; that of the world, as it worked around him, he knew nothing; and above all, of woman, he was as a child. He had never played with boys; in his life he had never known any, and we, in fact, who were now his associates, were the first companions he had ever mixed with. His father took occasion to remark to myself especially, that he had no great liking for his son's new friends. I, on the other hand, let him know that I had no fear of him who was looked upon as a sort of Jupiter Tonans. James Mill looked down on us because we were poor, and not greatly allied, for while in words he was a severe democrat, in fact and in conduct he bowed down to wealth and position. To the young men of wealth and position who came to see him he was gracious and instructive, while to us he was rude and curt, gave us no advice, but seemed pleased to hurt and offend us. This led to remonstrance and complaint on the part of John Mill, but the result was that we soon ceased to see John Mill at his home.[52]

Bain continues the story after remarking that John Stuart Mill "seemed unconscious of his father's dislike to his having them for friends: The reason of the dislike I can only surmise." (Unfortunately, Bain does not let us in on his surmise.) According to Bain, the aftermath of the quarrel was this:

On Monday morning, Roebuck and Graham went up to London, by the regular coach; Mill stayed behind, and then walked to town (from Croydon). On next seeing his friends, he told them what happened between him and his father; he had, he said, "vindicated his position". The scene left a great impression in the family. The children have a recollection of their mother being, on one occasion, in a state of grief, saying, "John was going to leave the house, all on account of Graham and Roebuck".[53]

The issue, a fairly typical adolescent episode of independence and personal choice, was obviously a draw. John Stuart Mill, although for the first time openly opposing James Mill, did not leave his father's house. But neither did he give up his friends. Henceforth he met them only outside the parental grounds, and it is on this occasion that the Utilitarian Society dissolved as such, stopped meeting at the house of James Mill's neighbor, Bentham, and resumed at the Grote's.

Having claimed Roebuck for himself, within a few years John Stuart Mill chose to break with him. This is odd, because Roebuck was a person of feeling who gave a strong place to the poetic side of life, the lack of which Mill was to become so aware of during his mental crisis. As we shall see, Mill turned after 1826 to Wordsworth for his "cure." Roebuck, given to vigorous action as well as poetic feeling, preferred Byron. In 1828 they opposed each other on the issue in the Debating Society, the first time they had appeared on opposite sides. From then on the friendship, already cooling, weakened considerably (though it did not end until a few years later, over Roebuck's caution to John Stuart Mill about Harriet Taylor; see pp. 289–290).

Roebuck's version is as follows:

When Mill began to think for himself, he was anxious to show that his mind was no longer under the dominion of his father, or of Bentham. He therefore placed himself before the world as an independent critic, and took every occasion that offered to enter into disquisition upon the views of Bentham, and consequently of his father, who always agreed with Bentham, and was deemed his chief disciple and exponent. . . .

Among other things, in order to show his severance from his old ideas and mode of thought, he now professed to be greatly swayed by the influence of Poetry. [Mill thus] took to reading and criticising poetry. But in reality he had no poetic emotions, and the lessons of his early childhood and youth had chilled his heart and deadened his spirit to all the magnificent influences of poetry.[54]

In short, for Roebuck, Mill never was able successfully to make the leap to feelings. Mill, in his version, turns the accusation around:

My disputes with Roebuck in the early part of our discussions turned mainly on the culture of the feelings; and in these he who had certainly the quickest feelings took the unfeeling side. But this, instead of a paradox, is the explanation of the whole matter. Like most Englishmen who have feelings, he found his feelings stand very much in his way: he was much more susceptible to the painful sympathies than to the pleasurable, and looking for his happiness elsewhere, wished that his feelings should be deadened rather than quickened.[55]

In the end we are left with a paradoxical conclusion: Mill claims to reject Roebuck, earlier rejected by his father, because Roebuck, like his father, and all Englishmen, was unable to feel! For us there is an addendum to that conclusion. Again John Stuart Mill has exhibited the pattern of having a friend chosen by himself in whom he becomes disappointed, and in his disappointment then chooses to break with. Personal relations are clearly a difficult matter, at a difficult point in his life, for the youthful John Stuart Mill.

Nevertheless, however difficult they may have been, his personal relations were now his own, with his own peers. He had formed his own societies and chosen his own friends. Although outwardly subservient to his father after the trip to France, and then under his watchful eye at the East India House, John Stuart Mill was beginning inwardly to question and challenge his father's paternal and intellectual authority. The flare-up of independence over Roebuck as a friend was, in fact, an unusual outward sign of deeper inward changes, of the sort that today we might characterize as evidence of adolescent struggle. Was this tentative effort at independence also accompanied by ambivalence and feelings of guilt? Mill's difficulties with personal friendships seem to suggest that this was the case. It is the mental crisis occurring in John Stuart Mill's twentieth year, however, which reveals the full magnitude of struggle as well as the price exacted for his affirmation of self against his father. We must now turn directly to that tormenting experience, which has haunted all our work up until this moment, and which must at last be exorcised, or at least confronted boldly.

10

The "Mental Crisis"

A Classical Case

JOHN STUART MILL'S mental crisis was a profound spiritual experience. It welled out of his deepest emotional needs and called into question his firmest intellectual commitments. It is also an experience that demands our most enlarged psychological understanding (a young man going through this crisis today might well seek professional assistance). On this subject, psychohistory presumably should have something special to say—in fact, an obligation to speak—in overtly psychoanalytic terms, without falling into the trap of becoming mere psychopathology.

Let us, then, begin our "treatment" of the mental crisis as if we had before us what psychoanalysts call the "presenting symptoms." What is it that bothers a patient when he first starts treatment? What are his complaints? His symptoms? Some may seem purely physical—headaches or partial paralysis, for example—some purely mental—depression or unhappiness, for example—and most a combination of the physical and mental. Of course, John Stuart Mill is not a patient presenting himself to us, and we are not psychoanalysts about to offer him therapy. Yet it seems useful to look at his own record of his mental crisis, suffered when he was about twenty years old, *as if* it were a form of "presenting symptom," introducing us to all the ever-widening ramifications of "The Case of James and John Stuart Mill."

Bearing constantly in mind that we are imagining John Stuart Mill presenting himself to an analyst, as if he were entering therapy, we shall proceed with an initial presentation and analysis of his mental crisis. It is crucial to remember that throughout this initial account, and at this point in our work, we shall be only on the outermost edges of psychohistory, really practicing a form of psychopathology rooted in the "Classical" (i.e., 1920s) application of psychoanalysis to historical figures. Hopefully, the limitations of that approach, as well as its fascination and strengths, will become readily apparent as we proceed in our work.

Presenting Symptoms

JOHN STUART himself tells us the story; it comprises what we are calling the "presenting symptoms":

But the time came when I awakened . . . as from a dream. It was in the autumn of 1826. I was in a dull state of nerves, such as everybody is occasionally liable to; unsusceptible to enjoyment or pleasurable excitement; one of those moods when what is pleasure at other times, becomes insipid or indifferent; the state, I should think in which converts to Methodism usually are, when smitten by their first "conviction of sin." In this frame of mind it occurred to me to put the question directly to myself: "Suppose that all your objects in life were realized; that all the changes in institutions and opinions which you are looking forward to, could be completely effected at this very instant: would this be a great joy and happiness to you?" And an irrepressible self-consciousness distinctly answered, "No!" At this my heart sank within me: the whole foundation on which my life was constructed fell down. All my happiness was to have been found in the continual pursuit of this end. The end had ceased to charm, and how could there ever again be any interest in the means? I seemed to have nothing left to live for. At first I hoped that the cloud would pass away of itself; but it did not. A night's sleep, the sovereign remedy for the smaller vexations of life, had no effect on it. I awoke to a renewed consciousness of the woeful fact. I carried it with me into all occupations. Hardly anything had power to cause me even a few minutes oblivion of it. For some months the cloud seemed to grow thicker and thicker. The lines in Coleridge's "Dejection"—I was not then acquainted with them—exactly describe my case:

A grief without a pang, void, dark and drear,
A drowsy, stifled, unimpassioned grief,
Which finds no natural outlet or relief
In word, or sigh, or tear.

In vain I sought relief from my favourite books; those memorials of past nobleness and greatness from which I had always hitherto drawn strength and animation. I read them now without feeling, or with the accustomed feeling *minus* all its charm; and I became persuaded, that my love of mankind, and of excellence for its own sake, had worn itself out. I sought no comfort by speaking to others of what I felt. If I had loved any one sufficiently to make confiding my griefs a necessity, I should not have been in the condition I was. I felt, too, that mine was not an interesting, or in any way respectable distress. There was nothing in it to attract sympathy. Advice, if I had known where to seek it, would have been most precious. The words of Macbeth to the physician often occurred to my thoughts. But there was no one on whom I could build the faintest hope of such assistance. My father, to whom it would have been natural to me to have recourse in any practical difficulties, was the last person to whom, in such a case as this, I looked for help. Everything convinced me that he had no knowledge of any such mental state as I was suffering from, and that even if he could be made to understand it, he was not the physician who could heal it.[1]

This mental crisis or "nervous breakdown," as one writer describes it (others ascribe it to overwork), persisted through "the melancholy winter" for about six months, according to Mill, who, nevertheless, went on outwardly with his normal working habits.[2] In the spring, however, a "small ray of light" broke the gloom. (Michael St. John Packe, Mill's latest and most thorough biographer, claims that Mill compressed four years of his life in the telling.)[3] In Mill's account:

I frequently asked myself, if I could, or if I was bound to go on living, when life must be passed in this manner. I generally answered to myself, that I did not think I could possibly bear it beyond a year. When, however, not more than half that duration of time had elapsed, a small ray of light broke in upon my gloom. I was reading, accidentally, Marmontel's "Memoires," and came to the passage which relates his father's death, the distressed position of the family, and the sudden inspiration by which he, then a mere boy, felt and made them feel that he would be everything to them—would supply the place of all that they had lost. A vivid conception of the scene and its feelings came over me, and I was moved to tears. From this moment my burden grew lighter. The oppression of the thought that all feeling was dead within me, was gone. I was no longer hopeless: I was not a stick or a stone. I had still, it seemed, some of the material out of which all worth of character, and all capacity for happiness, are made. Relieved from my ever present sense of irremediable wretchedness, I gradually found that the ordinary incidents of life could again give me some pleasure; that I could again find enjoyment, not intense, but sufficient for cheerfulness, in sunshine and sky, in books, in conversation, in public affairs; and that there was, once more, excitement, though of a moderate kind, in exerting myself for my opinions, and for the public good. Thus the cloud gradually drew off, and I again enjoyed life; and though I had several relapses, some of which lasted many months, I never again was as miserable as I had been.[4]

Let us look more closely at these accounts. It has been obvious in the last few decades to a number of observers that Mill was suffering from a classic case of the Oedipus complex.[5] Mill's tears on reading Marmontel were an "abreaction." The larger context, of course, is that

Mill at twenty was going through a kind of "Sturm und Drang" (in modern terminology, as we have seen, a late adolescence) experienced by many of his contemporaries (e.g., Wordsworth, Matthew Arnold). Thus, some of Mill's distress was merely symptomatic of his age and time.[6] The thick "cloud" of melancholy was one that hovered over many of his contemporaries.

Certain key elements, however, characterize the first part of Mill's account. He tells us that he "awakened (from his 1821 convictions) as from a *dream* [italics added, as in all the quotes that follow]." He could find no cure in "*a night's sleep*," though suffering from a "drowsy . . . grief." Surprisingly, no commentator has stressed Mill's confession that "The words of Macbeth to the physician often occurred to my thoughts" (in the original draft, Mill says "recurred incessantly").[7] The words occur in Act V, Scene III. Macbeth asks of the physician:

> *Canst thou not minister to a mind diseas'd,*
> *Pluck from the memory a rooted sorrow,*
> *Raze out the written troubles of the brain,*
> *And with some sweet oblivious antidote*
> *Cleanse the stuff'd bosom of the perilous stuff*
> *Which weighs upon the heart?*

The physician, a good Freudian, responds with what is a frustrating answer, then as now:

> *Therein the patient*
> *Must minister to himself.*

We must remember that the "mind diseas'd" is not Macbeth's (at least not directly), but *Lady* Macbeth's. It is she, in Scene I, who cannot sleep. Her thoughts are filled with images of blood, and the murder on her hands cannot be cleaned away: "Who would have thought the old man to have had so much blood in him?" To the Doctor's utterance, "This disease is beyond my practice," she answers "To bed, to bed, to bed." As Mill found out, this was not a possible cure. The last word is with the physician: "Unnatural deeds do breed unnatural troubles; infected minds to their deaf pillows will discharge their secrets."

Mill describes his state, as we have seen, as like that "in which converts to Methodism usually are, when smitten by their first conviction of sin" (interestingly, this is not in the original draft, ca. 1853–1856, but was presumably added in either 1861 or 1869–1870). How had he sinned? Was it that he was unable to have "loved any one sufficiently"? Or that he loved too much, but in a way that he could not understand or acknowledge? Did he also hate so much that he would have liked to kill (as had the Macbeths) and, unconsciously wanting to kill, turned the unacceptable desire back on himself, saying "I seemed to have nothing left to live for"?

This feeling, of course, corresponded on the conscious, rational level with Mill's sense of loss emanating from the collapse of faith in the Benthamite doctrines as a guide to the good life. "The end"—of being a Benthamite reformer of the world—"had ceased to charm," a fact disclosed to him by a newly awakened "irrepressible self-consciousness." The result was dark, drear dejection, with no one to whom to turn (least of all his father, from whom, as we can see, Mill had "turned away"). Stoically, he tried to accept his self-imposed isolation and to effect a self-cure.

The cure presumably came with the reading of Marmontel's *Mémoires*.[9] Instead of his own death, Mill acts out his feeling about his father's imagined death (or murder?). A. W. Levi has had the common sense to look up the account in Marmontel, a minor French writer of the nineteenth century. As Levi records: "Marmontel, a young man at school, has just finished a successful course of study, and his disputation being over, was celebrating with his friends and his professor." But he is surprised that the former are not more joyous. The *Mémoires* continues:

"Ah, if I had done well" said I "you would not all be so sad." "Alas," said the professor, "the sadness which surprises you is most deep and sincere; and would to Heaven it had no other source than the brilliancy of the success which you have experienced. I have a much more cruel misfortune to announce to you. You have no longer a father." I fell under the blow, and was a quarter of an hour without color and without voice. . . .

In the middle of the night I arrived at my mother's door; I knock, I pronounce my name, and instantly I hear a plaintive murmur and a mixture of groaning voices. All the family get up, the door is opened; and on entering, I am encircled by my weeping friends; mother, children, old helpless women, all almost naked, dishevelled, resembling spectres, and extending their arms to me with cries that pierce and rend my heart. I know not what force, a force that nature surely reserves for extreme misery, suddenly displayed itself within me. I never felt so superior to myself. I had to raise an enormous weight of grief; I did not sink under it. I opened my arms, my bosom to these wretched creatures; I received them all with the assurance of a man inspired by heaven, and without manifesting weakness, without shedding a tear—I who weep so easily. "Mother, brothers, sisters, we experience" said I "the greatest of afflictions; let it not overcome us. Children, you lose a father, and you find one; I am he, I will be a father to you; I adopt all his duties; you are no longer orphans." At these words, rivers of tears, but tears much less bitter, flowed from their eyes. "Ah," cried my mother, as she pressed me to her heart, "my dear boy, I knew you so well." And my brothers, my sisters, my good aunts, my grandmother, fell on their knees.

This touching scene would have lasted through the night, had I been able to support it. I was faint with fatigue; I asked for a bed. "Alas" said my mother, "there is no other in the house than that of—" Her tears stifled her voice. "Well, give me that; I will lie in it without reluctance." I did lie there. I did not sleep; my nerves were too much shaken. The whole night long I saw the image of my father as vividly as strongly impressed upon my soul, as if he had been present. I sometimes thought I really beheld him: it did not alarm me. I extended my arms, I spoke to him. "Ah, why is it not true?" said I. "Why are you not what I seem to see? Why can you not answer me, and at least tell me whether you are satisfied with your son?" After this long watching and this painful disorder of the fancy, which was scarcely a dream, it was grateful to me to see daylight. . . .

Levi's analysis is as follows:

What happened was that by an act of empathy Mill identified himself with the bereaved Marmontel. Through the very similarity of circumstance this was no difficult matter. Marmontel also was the eldest of a great number of children, and his father too was prudent and severe and with "a rough and stern exterior." In reading Marmontel's account, Mill could in the process of identification and without guilt bring to full consciousness the idea that his father in the natural course of things would some day die, and that he himself would then assume the dominating role of the dead. "Mother, brothers, sisters" says Marmontel "we experience the greatest of afflictions: let it not overcome us. Children, you lose a father, and you find one: I am he, I will be a father to you: I adopt all his duties." The voice is the voice of Marmontel—but the wish is the wish of Mill! And the episode of the father's bed is, indeed, also deeply symbolic. "I was faint with fatigue; I asked for a bed. 'Alas' said my mother 'there is no other in the house than that of. . . .' Her tears stifled her voice 'Well give me that; I will lie in it without reluctance.' " Could ever symbolism be more relevant? In experiencing his father's death and the freedom which this would mean to his own ego, but under the literary and imaginative circumstances which would absolve him of the guilty wishes themselves, Mill brought to the surface of consciousness what had hitherto been laboriously repressed, and by this cathartic act spontaneously found the real solution for his mental crisis.[8]

I find Levi's analysis persuasive. It is even more persuasive—and more Oedipal—if one peruses the book, and reads of an earlier passage in which young Marmontel, enamored of a Mlle. B****, runs into his mother's anxious opposition to the girl. Through an intermediary the mother accuses the girl of indecency and of seducing her son. Furious, the son locks himself in his room, experiencing for the first time "agitation and ecstasy," but opens to his mother's entreaties, to be folded in her arms and bathed with tears.

To fill out Levi's account we give the remainder of the passage he quotes: "My mother, who had slept no more than I had, believed that she was waiting for me to wake up. At the first sound she heard me making, she came to me, and was terrified at the transformation [révolution] which had taken place in me. My skin seemed to have been dyed in saffron." The doctor who is called in diagnoses it as "a sign of intense melancholy" and advises an immediate absence, a trip.

The "revolution" that brought illness to Marmontel brought relief to Mill. Whereas Marmontel, who generally wept so easily, shed no tears, Mill "was moved to tears"; he could now feel again. While Marmontel and his mother, like the Macbeths, could not sleep, Mill felt his burden grow lighter and, we can assume, his nights less troubled with dreams from which he had to awake. But while the effects differed, the cause in both cases was the same: for both Marmontel and Mill, the father, as he had existed, was dead. The overshadowing cloud was gone.

John Stuart Mill had surmounted, or at least survived, his mental crisis. Intellectually, he explained it as a realization that the cold, dry analysis offered by Utilitarianism was not enough; it needed to be supplemented by "the internal culture of the individual," the "passive susceptibilities"—in short, the life of emotion. In his "new way of thinking" he turned to Wordsworth, who showed him "a source of inward joy, of sympathetic and imaginative pleasure, which could be shared in by all human beings." Thus, John had grown past his father, broadening his beliefs to include convictions and *feelings* outside his father's narrow purview.

What had occurred emotionally in the Marmontel episode that allowed Mill to move forward intellectually? The evidence indicates that by experiencing the death of his father imaginatively and by displacement to Marmontel's father, John was able to "work through" his ambivalent and hitherto unexpressed feelings of love and hate for his father. On one side, we may conjecture that he could face the possibility of his father's death as the loss of the loved object on whom he most depended, by means of an imagined period of mourning and melancholy. On the other side, we can see that he came to terms with his feelings of rivalry toward his father by vicariously killing him and then replacing him.

In this strange and "accidental" way John Stuart Mill was able to assert his independence. He passed not only through a reawakened Oedipal crisis but also through a work and career crisis. His identity as a reformer—the Utilitarian's pursuit of "changes in institutions and opinions"—was challenged and shaken; in the end, however, it was not destroyed, but broadened and made more humane. The identification with his father's career, both as an intellectual and a civil servant, was also eventually reaffirmed, but in the new terms. In short, to the civilized training of the mind given him by his father, John added the cultivation of the emotions.

Let us close our "Classic" account of the case with the details of James Mill's actual, rather than fantasied, death, and John Stuart Mill's reaction to it. In 1836 James Mill had become an invalid. Having suffered from recurrent attacks of gout all his life, he now had "an attack of gout in the eyes, of which we can dimly imagine the horror," Bains tells us. He also had a "sick headache," and chest seizures, with spitting of blood. Though he could still lash out in irritable attacks on his children, James Mill, that strong, overpowering father, had become terribly weak; as he himself wrote his son James, "My great complaint now is weakness."[10]

What was John Stuart Mill's reaction to his father's weakness? It seems that he could not face it. John himself suffered a "general physical collapse" at this time. I quote his biographer, Packe, as to the symptoms: "*weakened lungs, a deranged stomach*, and a *nervous twitching of the right eye*, complaints from which he suffered more or less for the remainder of his life. . . . He was [also] seized with *violent pains in the head* [italics added]."[11] Neither Packe nor any other commentator seems to have noticed the resemblance of John's symptoms to those of his father. In any case, John Stuart Mill was judged so "dangerously ill" that he was ordered off to Brighton.

There he stayed while his father died on June 23, 1836. Well could the words of his brother Henry, who *did* attend the father's deathbed, have applied to John's inflamed imagination: "You will not have had the torment of seeing him get weaker and weaker every day . . . [he] used to say to me or George [another brother] that he would very willingly die, if it were not that he left us too young to be sure how we should turn out."[12] Do we have here one of the clues to John's illness and his strange absence from the father's deathbed? The details are different, but the atmosphere is the same as in Marmontel's *Mémoires*. John Stuart Mill had already lived through his father's death in 1826, and he could not bear to reactivate the scene in actual fact ten years later.

We have some confirmation for this view in what followed. Throughout the rest of 1836, John Stuart Mill could not work or write effectively. Packe's account reminds us of the prescription of Marmontel's physician: "Brighton having failed, it was decided that he should go abroad to see what the 'free and genial' atmosphere of his beloved France could do for him." The India House gave him a three months' leave of absence. On his return he was still very sick, but, with his father dead, he was "promoted again in the India office and was now Third Examiner with a salary of £1,200. . . ." As Packe so well puts it, "there was also his father's estate to be cleared up and his family to be provided for . . . it was to John they turned."[13] Gradually, John Stuart Mill improved in health, and returned to his work. The son had taken over from the father.

Freud's Melancholia

IF MILL had been able to turn to an analyst, such as Sigmund Freud, what could he have learned about his mental crisis? Let us see what form Freud's analysis might have taken. Freud's first tentative explanation of melancholia, a term under which he included what is generally described as states of depression, occurred in a manuscript of 1897 which he sent to his friend Wilhelm Fliess. In this manuscript, where, incidentally, Freud first foreshadowed the Oedipus complex, he commented:

> Hostile impulses against parents (a wish that they should die) are also an integral constituent of neurosis. They come to light consciously as obsessional ideas. . . . They are repressed at times when compassion for the parents is active—at times of their illness or death. On such occasions it is a manifestation of mourning to reproach oneself for their death (what is known as melancholia) with the same states (of illness) that they have had. The identification which occurs here is, as we can see, nothing other than a mode of thinking, and does not relieve us of the necessity for looking for the motive. It seems as though this death-wish is directed in sons against their father and in daughters against their mother.[14]

Having cast this flickering light over the subject, Freud laid it aside until 1915, when he finished a draft of his paper, "Mourning and Melancholia," itself not published until 1917. In this paper Freud went well beyond his original formulation. He proceeded by establishing the similarities between mourning and melancholia, and then their crucial differences. "Mourning," he informs us, "is regularly the reaction to the loss of a loved person or to the loss of some abstraction which has taken the place of one, such as one's country, liberty, an ideal, and so on." As for melancholia, he tells us, its distinguishing mental features are "a profoundly painful dejection, cessation of interest in the outside world, loss of the capacity to love, inhibition of all activity, and a lowering of the self-regarding feelings to a degree that finds utterance in self-reproaches and self-revilings, and culminates in a delusional expectation of punishment." Freud concludes: "With one exception the same traits are met with in mourning. The disturbance of self-regard is absent in mourning; but otherwise the features are the same."[15] In fact, as Freud himself notices later, there is another difference: mourning is for an actual death, whereas melancholia can be occasioned by an imagined loss of the love object.

How can we explain the crucial difference in regard to the disturbance of self-regard? In the mourner we can readily see, or think we see, what is causing him grief. (Actually, as Freud shows us, the mourner also has ambivalent feelings about the death of a loved one.) The melancholic, on the other hand, as Freud says, "seems puzzling to us because we cannot see what it is that is absorbing him so entirely." What we do see in the melancholic is "an extraordinary diminution in his self-regard, an impoverishment of his ego on a grand scale. . . . The patient represents his ego to us as worthless, incapable of an achievement and morally despicable; he reproaches himself, vilifies himself and expects to be cast out and punished. . . . In mourning it is the world which has become poor and empty; in melancholia it is the ego itself."[16]

Why? Freud's explanation is tentative and complicated. He surmises that the complaints against the self, the self-reproaches, are disguised reproaches against the loved object: "We perceive that the self-reproaches are reproaches against a loved object which has been shifted away from it on to the patient's own ego." This occurs when, for various reasons, the libido attached to a particular person is withdrawn—because of a real or fancied slight or disappointment—and instead of being attached to a new object is displaced onto the ego, where it establishes what Freud calls an "*identification* of the ego with the abandoned object."[17] This identification is a regression to narcissism, or self-love. Ambivalence toward the love object, however, which is now incorporated into the melancholic's own ego, leads to a self-hate as well. Thus we have the reproaches against the self and a feeling of worthlessness, of total depression.

In terms used by Otto Fenichel, Freud's disciple, "Hostility toward the frustrating objects has been turned toward one's own ego," and this intense self-hatred can culminate in thoughts of suicide.[18] As Fenichel further widens the account:

> Experiences that precipitate depressions represent either a loss of self-esteem or a loss of supplies which the patient had hoped would secure or even enhance his self-esteem. They are either experiences which for a normal person would also imply loss of self-esteem, such as failure, loss of prestige, loss of money, a state of remorse, or they imply the loss of some external supplies, such as a disappointment in love or the death of a love partner; or further they may be tasks which the patient has to fulfill and, which, objec-

tively or subjectively, make him more aware of his "inferiority" and narcissistic needs. . . .[19]

Such is the classical clinical picture and etiology. What is the cure or treatment that might have been tended to Mill? As for melancholia, Freud would have told him:

> The fact that it passes off after a certain time has elapsed without leaving traces of any gross changes is a feature it shares with mourning. We found by way of explanation that in mourning time is needed for the command of reality-testing (the object is really dead) to be carried out in detail, and that when this work has been accomplished the ego will have succeeded in freeing its libido from the lost object. We may imagine that the ego is occupied with analogous work during the course of a melancholia.[20]

In short, as Macbeth's physician had put it, "Therein the patient must minister to himself."

Depressions: Mental and Otherwise

APPLICATION of Freud's analysis to Mill is too obvious to need further explication. It ought to be pointed out, however, that there is another, complementary way of looking at the same materials. Contemporary psychoanalysts would tend to stress the reality factors and ego involvement rather more than in the classical libidinal picture we have just offered. The emphasis would be on depression stemming from the ego's awareness of its helplessness, or at least difficulty, in achieving independence and an identity of its own. Thus Mill's awareness of his father's shortcomings, arrived at intellectually, and his need to redefine his relations to his family, made acute by social changes manifesting themselves in family structure and dynamics, are seen as being at the conscious level of conflict. If experienced by many others at the time, this conflict becomes a generational conflict brought about as much, if not more, by reality factors as by a supposedly idiosyncratic Oedipal conflict.[21] Such an extension of Freud's theories, of course, does not refute the role of the Oedipus complex; it builds on it. In short, our materials on Mill allow us—nay, force us—to emphasize *both* the Oedipal struggle and the changing social and intellectual situation.

By emphasizing the latter factor we can speculate more readily on the ways in which Mill's "psychopathology" begins to form a part of a larger psychohistorical study. The argument goes something as follows.

Melancholia, as described by Freud and classic psychoanalytic theory, is a universal trait. Its manifestations, however—that is, its severity and frequency of occurrence (and in passing let us note that we have dealt with it only in masculine terms)—will be strongly influenced by cultural and historical circumstances. The precipitating factors, as we have noted, are loss of self-esteem or loss of narcissistic supplies. These can come from internal causes, which is why the trait is potentially universal, but in the main are undoubtedly facilitated by external events.

In dealing with this conjunction of internal and external events, Fenichel can help show us the way when he remarks:

> Under difficult social circumstances and in unstable times the number of depressions and depressive suicides increases [the latter point is one developed by Emile Durkheim]. . . . It may suffice to state that a society that cannot provide necessary satisfactions for its members necessarily creates a vast number of persons with an orally dependent character. Unstable times, and economic depressions, by depriving people of their satisfactions as well as of their power and prestige and habitual ways of regulating self-esteem, increase their narcissistic needs and their oral dependence. On the other hand persons who, as a result of childhood experiences, have developed an orally dependent character are worse off under such social conditions, since they are unable to take frustrations without reacting in a depressive way.[22]

Such a statement can open exciting prospects before us. "Unstable times and economic depressions" are matters known to historians; can they now be linked more directly, through a study of *mental depressions*—mental crises?—to psychohistory? Thus, for example, the early nineteenth century may have been a period of unusually "unstable times" (or so at least it appeared to contemporaries), when, as Matthew Arnold was to say later, Western man seems to have been caught "between two worlds, one dead, the other powerless to be born." And in England, for example, dejection and depression *appear* increasingly to have been present as part of the growing pains of poets, novelists, social critics, and intellectuals in general; in Germany, *Weltschmerz* and *Sturm und Drang* periods *seem* increasingly to have characterized the advanced youth groups. As I sought to argue in Chapter 2, on the Oedipus complex in the nineteenth century, the changes involved in the "modernization" of Europe affected family relations as well as general social relations, and issued in a heightened and more blatant father-son conflict than hitherto. With increased prevalence and seriousness of outcome to the Oedipal struggle, emphasizing both its libidinal and aggressive aspects, is it not possible to postulate a link between it and the spread of the black cloud of grief and dejection that hovered over the pillow of John Stuart Mill and so many of his contemporaries?

So, too, with Fenichel's "childhood experiences" and "an orally dependent character." If, for example, as Phillipe Ariès claims in his book, *Centuries of Childhood*, it is only in the nineteenth century that the typical "nuclear" family emerges (see, however, p. 160 for our qualification of this notion), with its highly individual and "narcissistic" attention to its now recognized "child," we may dimly perceive a child-rearing experience fostering strong oral dependency. The removal of such narcissistic supplies, under the impact of reality or an acute Oedipal conflict, may foster greatly the tendency to a melancholic crisis.

To return to John Stuart Mill, he did experience the unstable times surrounding him, on top of the intense narcissistic attention (though without love) showered on him by his father in his early years. The result seems to have been a reasonably typical "romantic" melancholia, solved in part by a turn to romantic cultivation of the feelings. On the intellectual plane, as we shall see, his experience led John Mill to a synthesis of various political and philosophical doctrines. On the emotional plane, his mental crisis appears to have left him strengthened—a strength that, I suspect, was part of his power to impress by his honesty and fearlessness those who knew and read him. In his melancholia he had mastered what for most people is a terrifying threat: the threat of a psychotic breakdown, attended by enormous death wishes and death anxieties. Having overcome, even if only partly, the threat of madness and the terror of wishing to destroy his beloved father, John Stuart Mill could go on to a partly new life of his own, which could offer fresh sustenance to others.

Utilitarian Analysis

THERE IS a poignancy in John Stuart Mill's recognition during his mental crisis that even achievement of all his reforming aims would not bring him "happiness," for happiness was the touchstone of Utilitarian philosophy and psychology. The Utilitarian motto, in fact, was "the greatest happiness of the greatest number." The Utilitarian measure for all legislative reforms was the Felicific Calculus: Would an act produce more pleasure for more people than it would produce pain? In the face of a "right" to happiness (*vide* the Declaration of Independence), failure to achieve it was a doubly intolerable feeling.

John Stuart Mill knew he was suffering pain when he should be experiencing pleasure; thus personal pain and philosophic disillusionment were conjoined. It seemed a catastrophe for him.

If he were to turn to Utilitarian psychology to explain his condition, what would be the answer? Would he find therapy there? The fact is that John was deeply involved with the composition of his father's *Analysis of the Phenomena of the Human Mind*—his fundamental work on Associationalist psychology—during a period of time that overlapped completely the mental crisis. In the summer of 1822, on six week's holiday at Dorking in Surrey, James Mill began to compose his *Analysis*. As his biographer, Bain, puts it, it "cost him six of those holidays, being published in 1829."[23] In the *Autobiography* John tells us further that his father "allowed me to read the manuscript, portion by portion, as it advanced."[24]

What did it tell him? A brief and oversimplified statement of Associationalist tenets is in order here, to give the context. The starting point is John Locke (in fact, James Mill begins his work with a quotation from the *Essay on Human Understanding*). Sensations are the origin of all that is in the mind. The copies of the sensations which remain in the mind are ideas. Thus, all ideas are derived from experience. Ideas are combined in the mind according to what John Stuart Mill in 1869 was to call "The great fundamental law of Association" [1:x]; hence the name, Associationalist psychology. Indeed, James Mill's two-volume *Analysis* is largely devoted to the way in which these associations occur, with the basic mechanism being a deterministic linking of the sensations and ideas in a train, reoccurring in memory as they were earlier experienced in reality.

Some sensations, probably the greatest number, James Mill tells us, are what we call indifferent; they are not considered painful or pleasurable. But many sensations are associated with pain or pleasure. A man knows whether they are painful or pleasurable simply "by feeling it; and this is the whole account of the phenomenon." [2:184] The wise educator, by seeking to utilize pleasurable or painful associations, i.e., by providing the correct "experiences" for his pupil, can lead him into the paths of virtue and civic duty. James Mill identified the major causes of our pleasures as wealth, power, and dignity (because they procure us the services of our fellow creatures), although he stressed that our fellow creatures offered us pleasure directly through friendship, kindness, family, and so on. [2:208–215ff.]

The Associationalist system seems rather pat and contrived to us today. Yet, as enunciated by James Mill in his clear, forceful prose, it carries with it a kind of unexpected conviction. One almost believes in the system while reading about it. And when one recalls how undeveloped physiological research was at the time, and how slight any real progress in psychiatry or general psychology, one is impressed by James Mill's accomplishment. Thus we can share John's approbation, even as late as 1869, of his father's psychology. Though John Stuart Mill, Bain, and Grote at that time, editing a new edition of the *Analysis*, qualified and expanded some of James Mill's simplicities, they held to the general theory.

But in 1826 John was undergoing a depressive fit. What did his father's Associationalist psychology have to say about that? The answer, basically, was in terms of sensations in the alimentary canal, connected to the state of digestion! James Mill began by stating: "The complicated sensations in the intestinal canal, like those in the muscles, though obscure, and even unknown, as individual sensations, often constitute a general state of feeling, which is sometimes exhilarating, and sometimes depressing." [1:46] He continues: "In the state of wretchedness, which accompanies indigestion, and which sometimes proceeds to the dreadful state of melancholy madness, it is difficult to say how much is sensation, and how much association." [1:47] As an instance of association, however, he mentions the horrible dreams which indigestion produces in sleep.

At this point Mill drops the subject. He has partly echoed the ancient notion of "humors," wherein psychic states, e.g., the bilious, take their rise from the digestive functions. When he resumes the subject about fifty pages later, it is in terms of association of ideas. Although he does not intend it, he seems to offer us a striking, Freudian-type association of his own. As his example of how, as he puts it, the consequence of a sensation absorbs all our attention and causes us to forget the antecedent, he offers the following illustration: "A friend arrives from a distant country, and brings me the first intelligence of the last illness, the last words, the last acts, and death of my son. The sound of the voice, the articulation of every word, makes its sensation in my ear; but it is to the ideas that my attention flies. It is my son that is before me, suffering, acting, speaking, dying." [1:100] Why *this* example here? It seems an odd and melancholy choice. So, too, does a later illustration of how memory works according to a law of association: "After a lapse of many years, I see the house in which my father died. Instantly, a long train of the circumstances connected with him rise in my mind: the sight of him on his death-bed; his pale and emaciated countenance; the calm contentment with which he looked forward to his end; his strong solicitude, terminating only with life, for the happiness of his son; my own sympathetic emotions when I saw him expire. . . ." [1:326]

These personal illustrations seem odd choices for the generally cold and reserved James Mill. The theme of death runs strong in them. Did he sense, in some unconscious way, what his son was going through in the period around 1826? Such a speculation seems far-fetched, yet it is haunting because of James Mill's odd choice of examples. In any case, two paragraphs after the example of the dying son James Mill resumes his discussion of the psychic causes and effects of indigestion:

> Anxiety, in most people, disorders the digestion [here he has reversed his earlier order]. It is no wonder, then, that the internal feelings which accompany indigestion, should excite the ideas which prevail in a state of anxiety. Fear, in most people, accelerates, in a remarkable manner, the vermicular motion of the intestines. There is an association, therefore, between certain states of the intestines, and terrible ideas; and this is sufficiently confirmed by the horrible dreams to which men are subject from indigestion; and the hypochondria, more or less afflicting, which almost always accompanies certain morbid states of the digestive organs. [1:101]

To this statement John added an interesting note in 1869:

> It is true that the sensations in the alimentary canal, directly produced by indigestion, though (as everyone knows) in some cases intense, are in others so slight as not to fix the attention, and yet may be followed by melancholy trains of thought, the connection of which with the state of the digestion may be entirely unobserved: but by far the most probable supposition appears to be, that these painful trains are not excited by the sensations, but that they and the sensations are joint or successive effects of a common organic cause. It is difficult to comprehend how these obscure sensations can excite the distressing trains of ideas by the laws of association. . . . [1:103]

It would seem, therefore, that John had *not* suffered seriously from indigestion during his melancholia, and that his father's connection of the two was not correct.[25] Both, according to John, came from a common cause. With this said, however, John then, disappointingly from our point of view, claims that the two states, poor digestion (even unobserved) and melancholic trains of thought, originate in a common *organic* cause.

How had he explained his melancholia to himself in 1826, when no obvious organic cause appears to have presented itself? Surely he must have been puzzled that his father's explanation, rooting his melancholia in his alimentary canal, did not seem to apply to him. Yet no other explanation was at hand in terms of the Associationalist psychology in which he believed.

The Non-Utilitarian Cure

IT WAS to Wordsworth and poetry that John Stuart Mill turned for his cure. In the *Autobiography* he remarks that he still believed during his mental crisis that "the pleasure of sympathy with human beings and the feelings which made the good of others, and especially of mankind on a large scale, the object of existence, were the greatest and surest of sources of happiness."[26] Alas, "to know that a feeling would make me happy," he admits, "did not give me the feeling." Worse, he acknowledges, "the habit of analysis had a tendency to wear away the feelings," and his entire education had been aimed at giving him the habit of analysis.

Wordsworth helped teach Mill how to break the habit, or at least moderate it, and how to cultivate the feelings. As John put it:

> What made Wordsworth's poems a medicine for my state of mind, was that they expressed, not mere outward beauty, but states of feeling, and of thought coloured by feeling, under the excitement of beauty. They seemed to be the very culture of the feelings, which I was in quest of. In them I seemed to draw from a source of inward joy, of sympathetic and imaginative pleasure, which could be shared in by all human beings; which had no connexion with struggle or imperfection, but would be made richer by every improvement in the physical or social condition of mankind. From them I seemed to learn what would be the perennial sources of happiness, when all the greater evils of life shall have been removed. And I felt myself at once better and happier as I came under their influence.[27]

In this passage we have one of the most useful keys to the intellectual aspect of Mill's depression. Mill is saying, or at least implying, that the Utilitarian means of reform, employed in order to eliminate the positive evils in the way of reaching the end—happiness—do not in themselves bring happiness (in fact, Utilitarianism may stand in the way of that end by its narrow-minded concentration on means). We must still examine the nature of "happiness" itself. If we do this, we discover that it depends on "inward joy . . . sympathetic and imaginative pleasure"—in short, aesthetic rather than analytic qualities. It follows that pushpin, to paraphrase Bentham, is *not* as good as poetry. Implied, too, is the notion that one must seek the meaning of life both logically and experientially even *before* the Utilitarian end of happiness is to be achieved, and that life's meaning lies in an ongoing openness to sympathetic and imaginative experiences. It is some such awareness as this that seems to have enveloped Mill, intellectually as well as emotionally, in his mental crisis.

In Wordsworth Mill found a fellow seeker—and finder. Mill announced that in the "Intimations of Immortality" the poet "had had similar experience to mine; that he also had felt that the first freshness of youthful enjoyment of life was not lasting; but that he had sought for compensation, and found it, in the way in which he was now teaching me to find it. The result was that I gradually, but completely emerged from my habitual depression, and was never again subject to it."[28]

A glance at Wordsworth's Preface to the *Lyrical Ballads* suggests why, philosophically, he was so suited as a poet to appeal to John Stuart Mill. In the Preface we find the basic ideas animating Wordsworth's poetry. He grounded his poetry in Associationalist psychology. He talks of "certain known habits of association," of "the manner in which we associate ideas in a state of excitement," and takes as his poetry's task "to illustrate the manner in which our feelings and ideas are associated in a state of excitement." Thus, Wordsworth accepts sensationalism as his epistemology.[29]

Wordsworth, however, is not concerned with the abstract ideas, or their personification, that arise on the basis of our sensations. He wishes to keep his reader close to "the company of flesh and blood" and to describe the feelings of ordinary men in ordinary language. In a famous passage, he defines all good poetry as "the spontaneous overflow of powerful feelings," but this definition must be qualified, because the poet must also have thought "long and deeply," for "our continued influxes of feeling are modified and directed by our thoughts, which are indeed the representations of all our past feelings."[30] Thus the poet avoids simple, commonplace sensationalism and language by allowing for thought as recollected feeling. His appeal for Mill, therefore, could be in terms of both feeling and thought.

Mill could also be happy with Wordsworth's views on pleasure and pain. Thus the poet speaks of "the native and naked dignity of man . . . the grand elementary principle of pleasure by which he knows, and feels, and lives, and moves. We have no sympathy but what is propagated by pleasure. . . ." Then, almost in a direct glance at Mill's problem, Wordsworth continues: "The knowledge both of the Poet and the Man of Science is pleasure; but the knowledge of the one cleaves to us as a necessary part of our existence, our natural and inalienable inheritance; the other is a personal and individual acquisition, slow to come to us, and by no habitual and direct sympathy connecting us with our fellow beings."[31] It is the Poet who gives "immediate pleasure to a human being" and links man with man.

Connection with his fellow beings is exactly what John Stuart

Mill had been lacking. Wordsworth showed him the way in which he might rejoin the human race, and *feel* at one with his fellow beings. Indeed, I suspect it is because Wordsworth wrestled so hard with this crucial problem for himself, and finally succeeded, that he could offer Mill a convincing solution. Wordsworth, in fact, was acutely aware of the break in generations, the lack of connection everywhere. He speaks of "the revolutions, not of literature alone, but likewise of society itself," and admits that such changes have "cut me off from a large portion of phrases and figures of speech which from father to son have long been regarded as the common inheritance of Poets."[32]

The imagery of lack of connection—of man with man, man with society, and man with nature—is rampant in the period and in Wordsworth's poetry. Only "connect/ the landscape with the quiet of the sky," he implores us, in "Lines Composed a Few Miles Above Tintern Abbey," and the result will be "that blessed mood,/ In which the burthen of the mystery,/ In which the heavy and the weary weight/ Of all this unintelligible world,/ Is lightened. . . ." In the poem that struck Mill most forcefully, "Intimations of Immortality From Recollections of Early Childhood," he perceived Wordsworth as having gone through a similar sense of loss, of a discontinuity with his past, as himself. As Wordsworth intoned: "There was a time when meadow, grove, and stream,/ the earth, and every common sight,/ To me did seem/ Apparelled in celestial light,/ The glory and the freshness of a dream." When the dream vanished, or turned to a nightmare, Wordsworth was able to fight off his depression through the cultivation of his deeper feelings and the powers of recollection, and to recapture the links with the past while letting go of it in actuality. As a result, he could conclude: "We will grieve not, rather find/ Strength in what remains behind;/ In the primal sympathy/ Which having been must ever be,/ In the soothing thoughts that spring/ Out of human suffering;/ In the faith that looks through death,/ In years that bring the philosophic mind."

John Stuart Mill was also able to find strength in what was left behind from his original Utilitarian dream. To its single-minded devotion to logical analysis, he now added the poetic cultivation of feelings. As he later wrote Carlyle on July 5, 1833, he took as his task "to make those who are not poets, understand that poetry is higher than Logic, and that the union of the two is Philosophy."[33] Mill, in short, had become aware of the complexity of the human condition. To put the claim at its highest, in the words of critic Thomas Woods, "Mill's importance as a thinker derives mainly from his awareness [of this complexity], and that awareness was due in a large degree to the influence on him of poetry and, in particular, of the poetry of William Wordsworth."[34]

A Look Back

IN RETROSPECT, we can now see that John Stuart Mill's mental crisis was a kind of "growing pain." By 1830–1831 he was emerging as a "developed" young man. The image of growing pains, however, is partially misleading, because it suggests something outgrown. In fact, John Stuart Mill retained all that had gone before in his life—the melancholia runs henceforth like a dark stain through his existence—reworking almost compulsively his earlier experiences and the illumination that had come to him in the mental crisis.

It is the mental crisis itself, however, that lights up Mill's life like a flare dropped over a battlefield "where ignorant armies clash by night" (as Matthew Arnold put it in "Dover Beach"). By its light we can now take a broad and synoptic view of John's self-assertion, looking back to his boyhood and ahead to the "finished" figure of "Young Man Mill."[35] The surge to independence started with Mill's boyhood trip to France. We noted there his "accountability" to his father for almost every moment of his time, while also suggesting that his inner life went unrecorded and unconfessed, at least overtly, in the Journal and Notebook. Shortly after his return to England there occurred a trivial incident of great symbolic import which we have not yet discussed. It was the loss of John Stuart Mill's watch. It occurred in the autumn of 1822, when John accompanied his new teacher in Roman Law, John Austin, and Mrs. Austin, on a visit to Norwich, where all the Taylors, her family, lived. After giving his father an account of his studies and visits, John adds a last paragraph:

> I wish I had nothing else to tell you, but I must inform you that I have lost my watch. It was lost while I was out of doors, but it is impossible that it should have been stolen from my pocket. It must therefore be my own fault. The loss itself (though I am conscious that I must remain without a watch till I can buy one for myself) is to me not great—much less so than my carelessness deserves. It must, however, vex you—and deservedly, from the bad sign which it affords of me.[36]

In a Freudian context, such a loss of a watch is no "accident."[37] It was intended. Of course, the intention is unconscious, but nonetheless it symbolizes John's desire to stop being accountable to his father for every moment of his life. Moreover, the watch itself is the prime symbol of the mechanical aspect of life, of the Newtonian clockmaker's universe in microcosm, so dear to the heart (hard-heartedness?) of Utilitarians. Jean-Jacques Rousseau understood this well when he deliberately threw away his watch as he retired from artificial society to his isolation in nature. The watch stood for discipline and control, mechanical and unvarying. In "losing" his watch John was unconsciously rebelling against his father's rigid control.

Consciously, of course, he was conscience-stricken. Had he not, as he told us, "acquired a habit of leaving my responsibility as a moral agent to rest on my father and my conscience never speaking to me except by his voice"? In any event, his father seemed satisfied by his son's "manly" confession, and perceived only continuing dutifulness in his holding himself "accountable." John Staurt Mill inwardly knew better. As Bain informs us, when, on the death of James Mill, John was willed his father's precious watch (made more precious because it had been the gift of the father's only beloved friend, Ricardo), he refused to keep it and hastily turned it over to his younger brother, Henry.[38]

We are using the loss of the watch as a symbol of the opening stage in John Stuart Mill's growth toward independence. We must also note that it was in the company of the Austins—and we recall John Stuart Mill's tribute to the role of John Austin in his development—that the incident had occurred. It was now another Austin, John Austin's younger brother Charles, who helped John Mill take another step forward. A gifted and attractive youth, Charles Austin was but six years older than Mill, and at the time of their meeting had just left the University of Cambridge. They became friends, and Mill now, through Charles Austin, met many who would later shine in politics or literature, men such as Macaulay, Hyde and Charles Villiers, Strutt, and others. As Mill tells us:

> None of them however, had any effect on my development except Austin: whose influence over me differed from that of the persons whom I have hitherto mentioned, in being not that of a man over a boy but of an older contemporary. It was through him that I first felt myself not a pupil with teachers but a man among men. He was the first person of intellect whom I met on a ground of equality, though obviously and confessedly my superior on that common ground.[39]

"A man among men." This is the point of development Mill had finally reached in his twenties, with the aid of the Austins.

III / *John Stuart Mill*

Liberty versus Necessity

MILL RECOGNIZED Austin's role fully, but in his statement of the influence he erred in saying that none of those to whom Charles Austin had introduced him had had any effect upon him. Thomas Babington Macaulay, though indirectly and perhaps negatively, had an approximately equal effect. Charles Austin had shown John Stuart Mill that he was a "man among men"; Thomas Macaulay brought home forcefully to him that his father, James Mill, was a lesser man than he had thought. Both the emotional and intellectual consequences were to be profound.

According to John Stuart Mill, for a long time he had been defending the theory of government laid down in Bentham's and his father's writings, but had become increasingly aware of its limitations. Macaulay's attack on James Mill's *Essay on Government* in the March 1829 number of the *Edinburgh Review* crystallized John Stuart Mill's doubts. As Mill puts it, "This gave me much to think about."[40] Macaulay, in his slashing critique, as we saw in Chapter 4, had accused James Mill of looking "only at one-half of human nature." He insisted that James Mill ignored the way in which man actually differed from man (and, indeed, from woman), "generation from generation," and treated them as if they were fixed, universal figures. John Stuart Mill was sympathetic to these criticisms, yet of course he could not go the whole way with Macaulay. His solution—a *resolution* of his difficulties, really—was to eschew both men, and to offer a compromise position embodying the best of the two sides. Macaulay's empirical mode of treating political phenomena, seeking to go from historical observations to some general theory of government, was invalid as a method. Only the deductive method was correct. His father embraced the deductive method, but took the wrong example, the geometric mode. What was required was the appropriate "Physical or Concrete Deductive Method" (we shall go into further details when we discuss John Stuart Mill's *Logic*; here we are interested only in his attitudes).

Thus, John Stuart Mill partly reaffirmed and then transcended his father's beliefs. At the same time, he could not but agree with several of Macaulay's strictures, and especially "That my father's premises were really too narrow." More boldly, John Stuart Mill for the first time took an openly critical stance toward his father:

I was not at all satisfied with the mode in which my father met the criticisms of Macaulay. He did not, as I thought he ought to have done, justify himself by saying "I was not writing a scientific treatise on politics. I was writing an argument for parliamentary reform." He treated Macaulay's argument as simply irrational; as an attack on the reasoning faculty; an example of the remark of Hobbes that when reason is against a man a man will be against reason. This made me think that there was really something more fundamentally erroneous in my father's conception of philosophical Method, as applicable to politics, than I had hitherto supposed there was.[41]

At this point John Stuart Mill was as willing to be critical of his father as his father had always been of him. John had discovered that his father had clay feet, and was only a "man among men"; John Stuart Mill was now also a man in his own right.

This emotional emancipation took intellectual form, as John Stuart Mill tells us, in his work on the *Logic*, which he began in the early part of 1830. Here, in the part on the Moral Sciences, he worked out his disagreement with his father on the correct deductive nature of political science. He also wrestled with the philosophical issue of Liberty versus Necessity, struggling in highly abstract terms with the powerful emotions which were constricting his own most intimate life. That this is not mere speculation is borne out by John Stuart Mill's precise, personal description of what was happening:

During the later returns of my dejection, the doctrine of what is called Philosophical Necessity weighed like an incubus on my existence. I felt as if I was the helpless slave of antecedent circumstances; as if the character of all persons had been formed for them by agencies beyond their control, and was wholly out of their power. I often said to myself what a relief it would be if I could disbelieve the doctrine of the formation of character by circumstances. . . . I pondered on the subject till gradually I saw light through it; I saw that the word necessity as a name for the doctrine of cause and effect applied to human action, carries with it a misleading association; and that this association is the main cause of the depressing and paralyzing influence which I had experienced. I perceived that though character is formed by circumstances, our own desires can influence those circumstances; and that what is really inspiriting and ennobling in the doctrine of free will, is the conviction that our will has real power over the formation of our character; that our will, by influencing some of our circumstances, can modify our future habits or capacities of willing.[42]

What could be clearer than that the "dejection" of Mill's mental crisis, the "depressing and paralyzing" nature of that experience, was intimately connected to his feeling that he had been "made," *completely determined*, by his father? Only by vindicating the possibility of free will, or liberty, could Mill explain and justify his own assertion of independence. To say this is *not* to reduce Mill's complex philosophical thought to psychology—Mill's philosophy had its own independent history, and judgment on its worth is independent of its origins—

but to suggest the way in which intellectual and emotional development took place correspondingly, and the way in which the latter lent passion and commitment to the enterprise of the former.

Mill himself later glimpsed the connection when he wrote Tocqueville in 1843, warmly thanking him for his approbation of the views in the *Logic* on human liberty. "I myself consider that chapter as the most important in the book; it is the faithful expression of the ideas which I have held for almost fifteen years, which I have never written down, but, I can say, in which I have found tranquility, since they alone have fully satisfied in me my need to harmonize intelligence and conscience, placing the feeling of human responsibility on solid intellectual grounds." Having traced the issue back to his 15th year [!], Mill then concludes, this solution "has been for me *a veritable lifesaver* (my italics)."[43]

The Straining of the Links

OUR THESIS is that by 1830–1831, Mill had gone through the worst of his mental crisis and had achieved both a form of independence and a kind of health, or recovery. The doctrine of Liberty and Necessity is one sign of that struggle and resolution.

Another, infinitely more trivial, but no less symbolically important, is the imagery of—his jacket![44] It can help conclude our account of John Stuart Mill's "adolescence." We remember that toward the end of his boyhood trip to France, Lady Bentham had insisted on buying him a new jacket, "because he has outgrown his present ones." In the article "The Spirit of the Age" (in the *Examiner*, January 6–May 29, 1831), which more than any other marked in writing John Stuart Mill's intellectual break with his father and Benthamism, we see this same jacket reappear, now metamorphosed into an intellectual simile. Informing us that his Age is now one of change and transition, inhabited by "new men, who insisted upon being governed in a new way," Mill goes on to say: "Mankind have outgrown old institutions and old doctrines, and have not yet acquired new ones. When we say outgrown, we intend to prejudge nothing. A man may not be either better or happier at six-and-twenty, than he was at six years of age: but the same jacket which fitted him then, will not fit him now."[45] In 1831, of course, Mill was just about twenty-six.

The assertion of independence, the separation from his father, was plainly made, but it was not, and was not intended to be, a complete break. Mill was still "between two worlds," and would always remain in that position. The jacket imagery (as well as the fact that he published "The Spirit of the Age" anonymously) confirms this fact for us. Thus, in the *Autobiography* Mill summarizes the compromise nature of his "transition" in 1830–1831 as follows:

> I found the fabric of my old & taught opinions giving way in many fresh places, & I never allowed it to fall to pieces, but was incessantly occupied in weaving it anew: I never, in the course of my transition, suffered myself to remain confused & unsettled. When I had taken in any new idea I could not rest till I had adjusted its relation to all my old opinions, & ascertained exactly how far its effect ought to extend in modifying or superseding them. [For this compromise, John Stuart Mill thought he really even had his father's blessings.] Though I could not speak out my whole mind at this time without coming into conflict with my father. . . . [t]here are things however which incline me to believe that my father was not so much opposed as he seemed, to the modes of thought in which I supposed myself to differ from him. . . .[46]

In short, even speaking to himself with the voice of his father's conscience, John Stuart Mill could feel himself relatively conscience free.

Yet, though one voice conveyed to him his father's blessing, another voice reminded him how half-hearted that blessing really was. In his deepest emotions John Stuart Mill knew this, and knew thereby that the death of his father in 1836 had "freed" him from a part of his thralldom. A few month's after James Mill's death, John wrote Edward Lytton Bulwer, admitting that the same event which "has deprived the world of the man of greatest philosophical genius it possessed," as well as the most powerful writer for the *Westminster Review*, "has made it far easier to do that, in the hope of which alone I allowed myself to become connected with the review—namely to soften the harder & sterner features of its radicalism and utilitarianism, both which in the form in which they originally appeared in the Westminster, were part of the inheritance of the 18th century."[47] We can now see, too, that in "softening" the hard and stern features of Utilitarianism, John Stuart Mill was changing not only the inheritance from the eighteenth century, but the visage of his father.

We can also see that John Stuart Mill never completely escaped from his father. Even in death, the father spoke constantly to his son; we have already described John's immediate reaction—an almost physical identification, taking on the symptoms of his father—in 1836. The emotional identification was even stronger, and persisted throughout John Stuart Mill's life.

Out of Mill's struggle for independence from this identification emerges a fairly clear pattern of relationships to others. Again and again he allows himself to appear as the true disciple of some intellectual leader—a Carlyle, or a Comte, as we shall see—only to surprise and disappoint him by gradually asserting his independence. The assertion of independence never rejects completely the "master's" doctrine, but simply weaves it as one new thread into the fabric of John Stuart Mill's opinions. In this Mill is epitomizing the "liberal" position, which advances cautiously by a "tolerant" hearing of other views, and then partial incorporation of what is "good" in them into the mainstream of its own thought.

Mill's personal development, marked by great emotional distress, as made glaringly clear in the mental crisis, corresponds with the seemingly serene dialectical synthesis of ideas that go to make up his liberal political and social philosophy. Thus, a character in depression and turmoil, rebelling against the eighteenth century in the form of son versus father, emerges with an ideology of apparent calm and placid rationality. The overall result is that John Stuart Mill is a reformer, occasionally even a radical reformer, but not a revolutionary. The ideology, too, is an ideology of reform, not revolution. The link between the generations is attenuated and remolded; it has not been snapped. The conflict has not been to the death.

11

Intellectual Development

An Intellectual Accouchement

JOHN STUART MILL was an "intellectual," though not a professional intellectual in the sense of earning his living by his pen and thoughts (professionally he was a civil servant). As such he lived mainly by ideas, and it is his ideas that cause most of us to be interested in him. If all we had was the record of his emotional struggles, his mental crisis, we would think it an interesting human story, but of no real consequence for history (and thus psychohistory). Only in the light of John Stuart Mill's importance as a thinker does his emotional life take on a significant historical interest.

Up to now we have been analyzing the way in which Mill's emotional life dovetails with his intellectual life. We have been maintaining that the psychological development corresponds with, or even influences, the logical development. The reverse, however, is also true. Ideas and ideology do not exist in a vacuum, sealed off from the rest of one's life (though this may occur under intense repression). They are the result of adaptive needs, and help adapt us to life itself. They can and do both correspond with and exert an influence over our emotional life. Intellectual convictions can push one, logically, toward certain emotional commitments, which then take on a psychological life of their own. In the case of John Stuart Mill, I believe that something like this did occur. His mind, as well as his heart, told him that something was wrong, some element missing from his father's conceptions about philosophy and politics. As a thinker, John Stuart Mill proceeded to search for the necessary correctives, the needed elements. Thus, when he experienced his "new birth" it was as much an intellectual as an emotional *accouchement*, and we must constantly bear that fact in mind.

To best understand this concept, we shall proceed in two ways. The first is to study Mill's intellectual development in the 1830s and 1840s primarily in terms of his personal relations: to Carlyle, the Saint-Simonians, Coleridgians, and Tocqueville. Here, the friends and the thoughts, the personal and the theoretical, mix in an intriguing manner. The second is to examine his thought in terms of the subjects he treated: economics, government, social science, and so on. We shall begin with the first way now.

A Mental Evolution

JOHN STUART MILL perceived his own mental development as occurring in three definite stages. The first stretches to about 1830–1831, what he calls "the old Westminster Review period." The second period terminates in around 1844, with the success of the *Logic* (1843), which led to publication the next year of the political economy essays (though these had actually been written in 1830–1831). After this, he informs us, "*The Principles of Political Economy* and all subsequent writings belong to a third and different stage of my mental progress which was essentially characterized by the predominating influence of my wife's intellect and character." Most commentators have seen Harriet Taylor as taking John Stuart Mill farther and farther away from his father's opinions. It is interesting, therefore, to note John Stuart Mill's view of the matter: "In this (as it may be termed) third period of my mental progress, which still [ca. 1854] continues and which now went hand in hand with hers, my opinions gained equally in breadth and depth. . . . One of the earliest changes which occurred in this stage of my progress was that I turned back from what there had been of excess in my reaction against Benthamism."[1]

Ought we to accept Mill's own view of his mental evolution? We are certainly prepared to accept 1830–1831 as the end of the first phase, a "new birth" for Mill both emotionally and intellectually. It was also in 1830 that John Stuart Mill first met Harriet Taylor. According to his own testimony, her influence on his intellectual life was slow in developing, for it was not until around 1844 that he signalizes her dominating influence. As he explicitly tells us in the *Autobiography*, during the 1830s her "influence was only one among many which were helping to shape the character of my future development. . . . *the only actual revolution which has ever taken place in my modes of thinking was already complete* [italics added]." After this "actual revolution" (ca. 1830), the only substantial changes yet to come were, as Mill tells us, "on one hand, in a greater approximation, so far as regards the ultimate prospects of humanity, to a qualified Socialism, and on the other, a shifting of my political ideal from pure democracy, as commonly understood by its partizans, to the modified form of it, which is set forth in my Considerations on Representative Government." At this point Mill does *not*, like many later commentators, credit his qualified shift to socialism to Harriet Taylor, but passes over the subject in silence and deals only with the other shift which, he tells us, "took place very gradually, [and] dates its commencement from my reading, or rather study [in 1835] of M. de Tocqueville's 'Democracy in America.' "[2] The end of this change, according to Mill, was his *Considerations on Representative Government* (1861).

The organization of Mill's published *Autobiography* suggests a slightly different periodization to his mental development. The first six chapters, comprising three-quarters of the book, bring us to about 1840, after which he offers us a "General View of the Remainder of My Life" as his last chapter (written after Harriet's death). Is it 1840 or 1844 which marks the end of the second stage? My own view is that around 1848 is probably a more significant watershed in John Stuart Mill's intellectual evolution. It is marked by the publication of his *Principles of Political Economy*, which, with the *Logic*, he thought his major contribution to thought. Whatever Harriet's share in the book—a point to be argued in another chapter—it is clear that the work was John Stuart Mill's own treasured conception, nurtured since the days when his father lectured to him on Ricardo's economics. 1848 is also the year of Revolution, and for Mill, as for Marx and so many others of the time, it demonstrated, or rather confirmed, a new possibility *and* a new limit to politics and political philosophy. Lastly, it is the year in which John Taylor is dying (though he lingered on until 1849), thereby freeing Harriet to marry John Stuart Mill a few years later, with all that that meant for his emotional life with his remaining family and friends, as well as its implications for her expanding influence over his intellectual life.

Development is a key idea for John Stuart Mill. It does not matter what precise dates we assign to these stages, as long as we remain aware that qualitative changes did occur at some points in time. John Stuart Mill began life, almost literally at age three, as a Utilitarian, shaped and made almost wholly by his father. By the time he was twenty-six John had managed to struggle toward his own remaking—toward the only "actual revolution" in his opinions. By engaging in a baffling and depressing Oedipal conflict with his father, he managed also to fight his way clear of many of his former beliefs. As he wrote Carlyle in 1832, "On the whole there are scarcely any left of the old narrow school of Utilitarians." The old generation was gone. Of the new generation, John Stuart Mill says: "None however of them all has become so unlike what he once was as I myself, who originally was the narrowest of them all, having been brought up more exclusively under the influence of a peculiar kind of impressions than any other person ever was. Fortunately however I was not *crammed*; my own thinking faculties were called into strong though but partial play; & by their means I have been enabled to *remake* all my opinions."[3]

We agree with John Stuart Mill in this view of his own development (though not about *all* his opinions). What were his new opinions? How, in detail, had they been remade, whether in a second stage ending in 1840, 1844, or 1848, or in a third stage lasting from the mid 1840s to the end of his life in 1873? It is to tracing and analyzing some of the highlights of this development (in this chapter restricted to the changes during the crucial 1830s) that we now turn. In doing so, we can see to what intellectual consequences his "new birth" brought him, and therefore many of us.

The Practical Intellect

INTELLECTUALITY, for Mill, was always in creative tension with practicality. To put it another way, his main interest was in combining discussion of abstract questions of moral philosophy with practical political problems of his time. In this he was true to his earliest aim of being a moral reformer. He was also following the footsteps of his father, who believed that theory and practice must always be conjoined.[4]

It is true that, increasingly disappointed at the possibility of realizing his reforming aims immediately in politics, Mill turned more and more to the theory side of his interests. As he wrote John Sterling in 1831: "You will perhaps think from this long prosing rambling talk about politics, that they occupy much of my attention: but in fact I am myself often surprised how little I really care about them." With this disclaimer, Mill then continues:

The only thing which I can usefully do at present & which I am doing more & more every day, is to work out *principles*: which are of use for all times, though to be applied cautiously & circumspectly to any: principles of morals, government, law, education, above all self-education. I am here much more in my element: the only thing that I believe I am really fit for, is the investigation of abstract truth, & the more abstract the better.[5]

We sense Mill's self-estimate of the rightness of his own administrative vocation (in the East India Company) when he remarks, in an essay on Alfred de Vigny, that the true genius, whether in poetry or philosophy, cannot expect to be fully rewarded in his own time; nevertheless, he must earn his own keep in this world, seeking "worldly honor and profit . . . in the way others do." If such men cannot, Mill adds, "it is usually from something ill regulated in themselves—something, to be cured of which would be for the health even of their own minds."[6]

Perhaps Mill had worked this problem out in his mental crisis, along with his relations to his father. In any case, the dominant mode of almost his entire life was a combination of theory and practice, of applying abstract principles to current political and social problems (and vice versa). Only by understanding this and bearing it in mind can we best understand Mill's mental development. Just as his ideas were in correspondence with his personal development, so they evolved in conjunction with his practical experiences.

Revolutions

THE PRACTICAL experience that had the greatest effect on John Stuart Mill's thinking in this period appears to have been the French Revolution of 1830. As he informs us, the July events "roused my utmost enthusiasm, and gave me as it were a new existence."[7] Behind this Revolution, however, stood the French Revolution of 1789, and we must consider both together in order to understand the idea of what "revolution" meant to John Stuart Mill, and why it offered him a "new existence."

Utilitarianism, certainly in the person of Jeremy Bentham, had not been enthusiastic about the French Revolution of 1789. For Bentham the Revolution had been based on the wrong principles: abstract, airy natural rights instead of utility. True, he was willing to advise the

French Assembly on how to draw up a new code of laws (on Utilitarian principles, of course), and for this assistance was made an honorary French citizen. But his advice was not taken, and gradually Bentham lost interest in the events in France. Besides, England, led by Burke, was turning against the Revolution, and Bentham, primarily concerned with reforming English law and society, wished in any case to dissociate himself from the visionary ideology of the French revolutionaries, and the resultant violence, and to offer a sober, home-grown justification for reform.

But what of James Mill? According to Bain, we are totally in the dark about how Mill viewed the Revolution. In my view, however, Bain exaggerates our lack of knowledge. While it is true that we do not have James Mill's written record of how he felt at twenty (in 1793), we do have his *Commonplace Book*, composed over an extended period (there are no dates of entry) of his life. This provides a number of observations on the French Revolution which, taken together, give us an indication of his attitude toward 1789.

In Volume I, James Mill quotes Madame de Staël, to the effect that "the fury of the rebellion was always in proportion to the injustice of the servitude." Then, after a number of other quotes, he remarks: "Holland, the Netherlands, Switzerland, Italy, were revolutionized by the French: was there any revolution of property?" His interests are clearly in the economic as well as political changes, and he follows this question with a quotation attributed to Destutt-Tracy: "The revolution of France gave a prodigious impulse to the productive powers of the country—increased the population, improved the agriculture, etc.—and how? By [converting?] suddenly that immense unproductive consumption which was produced by a [useless?] court, church, and aristocracy into productive consumption." There is one last comment on the subject: "French Revolution frightens fools."

James Mill was no fool. We can assume that at age twenty he was even more radical than at the time he was writing his *Commonplace Book*.[8] We know how opposed he was to the parasitic upper class of England; we can be sure that he welcomed, at least initially, a revolution across the Channel that swept away the pernicious privileges of the hated aristocracy (presumably without disturbing middle-class property).

Whatever the truth about James Mill, John Stuart Mill discovered the French Revolution of 1789 for himself. It was on his return from France in 1821; during the trip he seemed not to be concerned with the subject.[9] As he tells us in the *Autobiography*:

I am not sure whether it was in this winter or the next that I first read a history of the French Revolution. I learnt with astonishment that the principles of democracy then apparently in so insignificant & hopeless a minority everywhere in Europe, had borne down everything before them in France thirty years earlier, and had been the creed of the nation. As may be supposed from this, I had previously had a very vague idea of that great commotion. I knew nothing about it except that the French had thrown off the absolute monarchy of Louis 14th & 15th, had put the king & queen to death, guillotined many persons, one of whom was Lavoisier, & had ultimately fallen under the despotism of Bonaparte. But from this time the subject took an immense hold of my feelings. It allied itself with all my juvenile aspirations to the character of a democratic champion. What happened so lately, seemed as if it might easily happen again: & the greatest glory I was capable of conceiving was that of figuring, successful or unsuccessful, as a Girondist in an English Convention.[10]

Mill's stress is on his public aspiration to be a "democratic champion." We have already suggested that the boyhood trip to France had also sown the first seeds of personal rebellion, the assertion of some sort of autonomy from his father. A revolution that put a king (and queen) to death, and threw off absolute monarchy, would quite naturally take "an immense hold of [the] feelings" of a boy seeking to assert his own independence from a powerful and domineering father. What had happened so "lately" (1789?) in the political realm might well encourage the juvenile Mill to think it might happen again in the personal sphere. The inner and outer aspirations corresponded.

It is at this point that John Stuart Mill began his extensive reading in the literature of the French Revolution, and eventually even contemplated doing a book on the subject. The book was not to be. Instead it was Mill's friend, Carlyle, who wrote on the Revolution. Nevertheless, Mill, as we shall see, had definite views of the Revolution. Here we are only positing the personal nature of the Revolution of 1789 as context for Mill's "new existence" in 1830.

Upon the fall of Charles X in July 1830, Mill, with his friends Roebuck and Graham, hastened to France. His account in the *Autobiography* is extremely laconic; he merely states: "I went at once to Paris, was introduced to Lafayette, and got acquainted with several of the active chiefs of the popular party."[11] After his return, Mill goes on, he entered warmly into English politics, while continuing to write on French subjects.

If it were not for Roebuck we might never have known that, for example, Mill and his two friends, on the occasion of Louis Philippe's first visit to the opera, had aroused the audience to shout for "La

Marseillaise," and then shouted "Debout, debout! until the whole audience, including the King himself, actually stood up during the playing of the revolutionary tune."[12] In addition to Lafayette, they also met the Saint-Simonian leaders Enfantin and Bazard, and were properly impressed by them. It is only in his letters from Paris to his father that Mill is more revealing of himself and his reaction to the Revolution. What impressed him most was the behavior of the Parisian workmen. "Surrounded by every temptation that perfect license could offer," Mill informs his father, "not one excess was committed. Vast treasures passed through their hands untouched. . . . These men were actually starving, and yet they would take no recompense. Having effected their glorious objectives, they calmly retired to their homes and resumed their accustomed avocations." There can be no question that the selfless behavior of the revolutionaries affected John Stuart Mill's later views, for example, on the events of 1832 in England and on the question of democracy.

In contrast to the people or "the mob," the middle and upper class showed itself badly. As Mill further reports to his father:

> The *educated* and the *rich* now came upon the stage. The hour of danger passed, one government was overthrown, another was to be framed. Compare the conduct of this party with that of the people, the mob, who had fought during the ever memorable three days.
>
> No sooner was it ascertained that all danger was really past, than a hungry crowd appeared, eager for place and careless of public interests.[13]

Iris Mueller, in her book *John Stuart Mill and French Thought*, describes how John Stuart Mill became increasingly disillusioned with the results of 1830. In a series of articles in *The Examiner* from 1830 to 1834, he recorded his observations at the failure of "reform" efforts in France. The Revolution had overthrown one oppressive regime, only to introduce another. The key problem was "Representation," and once the middle class had gotten a regime to their taste they blocked any further effort to broaden or make valid the franchise. For Mill, it was a shock to discover that his father's vaunted middle class could be as selfish and reactionary as the hated aristocrats. According to Mueller, Mill, still basically a Benthamite in 1830, now became open to the notion of a Saint-Simonian elite as an alternative to the failed middle class.

Mueller's detailed analysis is persuasive. There seems little question that the experience of the French Revolution of 1830 had a profound effect on Mill's mental development. Coming as it did at the time of his personal "new birth," it predisposed him even further to question his father's Benthamism, and to seek new sources for new ideas that he could make his own.

Further, it seems to have made him both more willing to sanction violence during the Reform Bill agitation in 1832, and to expect less from the tepid, middle-class reform he saw being prepared around him. Whereas his father was horrified at the potential violence and socialism lurking in the working-class movement, and threw himself with great energy into organizing and inspiring the moderate reform of the Bill as the alternative to revolution, John Stuart Mill could write his friend John Sterling in October 1831 that:

> If the ministers flinch or the Peers remain obstinate, I am firmly convinced that in six months a national convention chosen by universal suffrage, will be sitting in London. Should this happen, I have not made up my mind what will be best to do: I incline to think it would be best to lie by and let the tempest blow over, if one could but get a shilling a day to live upon meanwhile; for until the whole of the existing institutions of society are levelled with the ground, there will be nothing for a wise man to do which the most pig-headed fool cannot do much better than he. . . . If there were but a few dozens of persons safe (whom you and I could select) to be missionaries of the great truths in which alone there is any well-being for mankind individually or collectively, I should not care though a revolution were to exterminate every person in Great Britain and Ireland who has £500 a year. Many very amiable persons would perish, but what is the world the better for such amiable persons?[14]

The Reform Bill was passed, though John Stuart Mill did mainly "lie by." He also played down his bloodthirsty and aberrant willingness to "exterminate" every person of large wealth. The sentiment was uncharacteristic of Mill, and so, in fact, was his unreserved approval of revolution. It is a measure of his personal and political rebelliousness in 1830–1831 that he could entertain such notions. Gradually, however, he found his way back to a reaffirmation of his original impulses and identifications, though in a highly developed and dialectical form.[15] It is to that intricate intellectual and emotional development that we now turn in the form of Mill's close "friendships" with men such as Carlyle, Comte, and others.

Carlyle: The Friend in Hero's Clothing

IT WAS through his "Spirit of the Age" that Mill met Carlyle. As he tells us in the *Autobiography*, the article was a result of his initial enthusiasm over the French Revolution of 1830. In a series of five short articles published in *The Examiner* under the title "Spirit of the Age," Mill sought publicly (though anonymously) to embody his new opinions. Looking back at them in later life, Mill thought them "lumbering in style" (our own view is that they are among the liveliest of Mill's writings) and ill-timed. Their only virtue for Mill was that they caught the attention of Carlyle, then living in solitude in Scotland, and determined him to inquire after the unknown author when next in London.

The actual introduction took place in London on September 2, 1831, with Sarah Austin as the intermediary. Again we must note the critical role of the Austins in Mill's life—private and intellectual.

As Carlyle wrote his wife on September 4: "We had almost four hours of the best talk I have mingled in for long. The youth [John Stuart Mill was, in fact, only eleven years younger than Carlyle] walked home with me almost to the door; seemed to profess, almost as plainly as modesty would allow, that he had been *converted* by the head of the Mystic School, to whom personally he testified very hearty-looking regard [italics added]."[16]

Carlyle thought he had a disciple whom he had converted. Charles Buller was delighted at how well the two had gotten along, but tried to warn Carlyle that Mill was still a Utilitarian. He wrote Carlyle on September 12:

Conceive how great was my pleasure at learning from her [Sarah Austin] that you had called on her; that you had come for the purpose of making acquaintance with John Mill; and that you had met him to your mutual delight. I knew well that to make you esteem one another, nothing was wanting but that you should understand each other. But I did not do sufficient justice to the Catholicism of both of you to feel quite confident that this would be the certain effect of your meeting. In this world of sects people rarely talk to each other for any purpose but to find out the sectarian names which they may fasten on each other; and if the name but differs, they only spend their time in finding out the various ramifications of each other's dissensions. In names and professed doctrines you and John Mill differ as widely as the poles; but you may well meet on that point where all clear spirits find each other, the love of truth, which all must attain in their road to truth.

Then Buller added emphatically, "to you without any fear I point out John Mill as a true Utilitarian."[17]

Carlyle refused to heed Buller's warning. There was ground for his illusion, besides his own ardent wish for a disciple. John Stuart Mill at first displayed what to us is by now a familiar pattern of behavior: putting himself in the position of supine pupil before a superior teacher, and then gradually asserting his independence while retaining some of his teacher's ideas. It was the way both his personality and his mind worked. Moreover, Carlyle had the very words of the "Spirit of the Age" before him, and these certainly brought into doubt the "trueness" of Mill's Utilitarianism.

The "Spirit of the Age," as we have already suggested, was filled with the spirit of Mill's personal rebellion. Especially in the first article, Mill seems to project onto the public scene his personal crisis. "Thousands awoke as from a dream," he tells us, to discover that in this new age of transition "Mankind will not be led by their old maxims, nor by their old guides." "Do the young respect the old, or adopt their sentiments?" he asks rhetorically. But what is to take the place of the discarded past? Here Mill becomes more cautious. "Before I compliment either a man or a generation upon having got rid of their prejudices, I require to know what they have substituted in lieu of them."[18]

The personal note diminishes as Mill goes on to the next four articles. (Having established the changing and rebellious nature of his "age," he is more concerned to explore the directions in which a new truth might be found.) The main routes in his map for the future seem heavily influenced by Saint-Simonian construction, and much of the "Spirit of the Age" adumbrates the *Logic* with its call for a new moral science, and, on that basis, emergence of a new elite which shall lead with certainty the age of transition from its present discord to a new state of order. In passing, Mill indicates how the new means of communication have diffused knowledge and prepared the way for elimination of the present higher classes, which "instead of advancing, have retrograded in all the higher qualities of mind." One of the clear directions of history, in fact, is the abolition of hereditary distinctions. Having said all this, it comes as a bit of a surprise to see Mill, in his penultimate article, suddenly praise the "authority of ancestors." Only at a time of transition, we are now told, are the old to be disregarded. Mill informs us:

> Narrowness of mind, and obstinate prejudice are not the necessary, or the natural concomitants of old age. Old men have generally both their opinions and their feelings more deeply rooted than the young; but is it an evil to have strong convictions, and steady unfluctuating feelings? It is on the contrary, essential to all dignity or solidity of character, and to all fitness for guiding or governing mankind. It constitutes prejudice, only when society is at one of those turns or vicissitudes in its history, at which it becomes necessary that it should change its opinions and its feelings.[19]

Mill was at one of those "turns" or "vicissitudes" in his personal history. We can see, however, how basically unrevolutionary his attitude was. He wished independence from his father, only in order that he might feel he had incorporated "freely" in himself that which he judged good in his father's beliefs. At no point did he wish to reject root and branch what his father, and his father's generation, stood for. Reading the "Spirit of the Age" without knowing John Stuart Mill or his personal development, Carlyle could be forgiven for not seeing this.

On the other side, we can see how Mill might have been partially misled as to Carlyle's "true" position. Although Carlyle was older than Mill, he had published less at the time of their meeting. Writing to John Sterling on October 20, 1831, Mill reports that he had "long had a very keen relish for his [Carlyle's] articles in the Edinburgh and Foreign Reviews" (though he adds cryptically, "which I formerly [when, we would like to know?] thought to be such consummate nonsense"), and goes on:

> I think he improves upon a nearer acquaintance. He does not seem to me so entirely the reflexion or shadow of the great German writers as I was inclined to consider him; although undoubtedly his mind has derived from their inspiration whatever breadth of life is in it. . . . He has by far the largest and widest liberality & tolerance (not in the sense which Coleridge justly disavows, but in the good sense) that I have met with in any one; & he differs from most men who see as much as he does into the defects of the age, by a circumstance greatly to his advantage in my estimation, that he looks for a safe landing *before* and not *behind*: he sees that if we could replace things as they once were, we should only retard the final issue, as we should in all human probability go on just as we then did, & arrive again at the very place where we now stand.[20]

Where did Mill get this view of Carlyle as liberal and tolerant, which was as far from the mark as Carlyle's initial view of the young "baying"? Carlyle's first contribution to the *Edinburgh Review* was in 1827, on Jean Paul Richter; in 1829 he published an article on Voltaire and one on Novalis in the *Foreign Review*. The Richter and Novalis would reflect the largely "German" shadow that Mill had detected over Carlyle's works. On August 5, 1829, Carlyle noted in his Journal: "Also just finished an article on the 'Signs of the Times' for the Edinburgh Review."[21] Undoubtedly it is this work which gave Mill his new view of Carlyle, especially of Carlyle as a progressive thinker with an eye to the future. We know that Mill read it, and he even uses the phrase "signs of the times" in his own "Spirit of the Age."

What was Carlyle's message in his "Signs of the Times"? It is that his age was not an Heroical or Moral Age, but a "Mechanical Age." "Men," as he tells us, "are grown mechanical in head and in heart, as well as in hand." The prime mechanics, of course, are the Utilitarians. Was John Stuart Mill put off by this attack on his father and his school? It seems not, for Mill himself was making the same attacks on them as was Carlyle.

Along with Mechanical Science, Carlyle cried out, men need the "science of Dynamics," which treats of "the mysterious springs of Love, and Fear, and Wonder, of Enthusiasm, Poetry, Religion, all which have a truly *infinite* character." When Carlyle goes on to say that "it seems clear enough that only in the right coordination of the two, and the vigorous forwarding of *both*, does our true line of action lie," Mill could only nod his head in agreement, and feel that here indeed he had encountered a man of "liberality and tolerance."

There was more to agree with, without offense to Mill's former Utilitarian friends. Carlyle speaks about "a cry which, everyone now sees, must and will be answered. . . . Give us a reform of Government!" If one ignores Carlyle's satirizing this notion as mechanically providing happiness, and focuses on "must and will be answered," all is conformable. His view of the French Revolution as having "something higher in it than cheap bread . . . an Idea," would give no offense, and his assertion, "Doubtless this age also is advancing," would fit him comfortably next to the Utilitarians.

A second feature that both John Stuart Mill and Carlyle had in common was a somewhat similar father-figure in their background. Like Mill, Carlyle could write at his father's death:

> For a true and brave man, such as there are too few left, I must name my father. If we think what an element he began in, how he with modest unwearied endeavour turned all things to the best, and what a little world of good he had created for himself, we may call his life an honorable, a noble one. In some respects there is perhaps no man like him left.

Yet Carlyle, too, earlier had written: "We had all to complain that we dared not freely love our father. His heart seemed as if walled in. . . . It seemed as if an atmosphere of fear repelled us from him, me especially."[22]

Even more importantly, Carlyle, like Mill, had gone through a deep mental depression whose effects constantly lingered over him. In 1833, years after the initial outbreak, he was still writing that "The accursed, baleful cloud that has hung over my existence *must* (I feel it) dissipate. . . ."[23] John Stuart Mill could have written these same words, and more or less did in 1826. Though the causes and content of the melancholic episodes may have been different, they served as a powerful bond of sympathy between the two (indeed, the same bond existed between Mill and Comte). With such an empathetic person Mill could explore his new personal needs for feeling in terms of intellectual sustenance. While most of their correspondence was about books and ideas, the personal surfaced significantly, as when Mill confessed in 1833: "My case must be left to Nature, I fear: there is no mind-physician [shades of Freud?] who can prescribe for me, not even you, who could help whosoever is helpable: I can do nothing for myself, and others can do nothing for me; all the advice which can be given (and *that* is not easily *taken*) is, not to beat against the bars of my iron cage." Turning to Carlyle's fellow situation, Mill continues:

> You see it is cold comfort which I can give to any who need the greatest of comforts, sympathy in moments of dejection; I, who am so far from being in better mental health than yourself, that I need sympathy quite as much, with the added misfortune that if I had it, it could do me no good. . . . But this is enough for the present, in this strain; perhaps I may say more another time.

"Another time" came quickly. A month later Mill wrote:

> I have allowed myself to be paralysed more than I should, during the last month or two by these gloomy feelings, though I have had intervals of comparative brightness but they were too short. I have therefore a poor account to render of work done.[24]

"Work done" was the enduring bond that held the two men together, even when the emotional connection began to fray (as, in the pattern of Mill's relations, it was bound to do, even if other reasons had not existed). Writing had first brought the two men together, and it was the exchange of ideas and intellectual assistance that provided the bricks and mortar of the relationship.

With all the elements of connection that we have mentioned, and others, there were fundamental differences, ignored or played down at first by the two men, which eventually washed away the friendship and disclosed how mistaken each had been in his hopes about the other. One of the most critical was in their estimate of women. Mill, who ignored his mother and felt no love for her, was a champion of women's rights. Carlyle, who deeply loved his mother, writing to her constantly, was a male chauvinist. Thus, Carlyle could write, "I have seen no woman in the whole world whom I would have preferred as a mother"—there are no Lady Bentham's or "Mütterleins" in Carlyle's life—and at the same time announce to his future wife, Jane, "The man should bear rule in the house, and not the woman. This is an eternal axiom, the law of nature, which no mortal departs from unpunished. . . . I must not, and I cannot live in a house of which I am not the head."[25]

Though generally discreet, Carlyle appears occasionally to have been unguarded with Mill on the touchy subject of women. Thus, we have Mill writing to him:

> There was one thing in what you said of Madame Roland which I did not quite like—it was, that she was almost rather a man than a woman; I believe that I quite agree in all that you really meant, but *is* there really any distinction between the highest masculine & the highest feminine character?[26]

Carlyle seems to have let the subject drop, as did Mill. In the end, however, it was bound to be a source of unspoken discord (exacerbated, as we shall see, by what the Carlyles thought was Harriet Taylor's role in the loss of the French Revolution manuscript).

It was, of course, not only about women—that was simply the most "personal" matter—that Mill and Carlyle disagreed. Religion was another major point of division. Although occasionally swayed by friendship and his habit of parroting the voice and substance of his "teachers" (till he turned against them) into saying things sympathetic to religious feeling, Mill was basically unfeeling on the subject, if not actually atheistic and hostile. Carlyle, though he rejected the outward forms of his family's Calvinism, was deeply religious. An intellectual (and emotional) divergence of such import between the two men was bound to color all of their thoughts. The issue became joined over German metaphysics.

At first Mill was taken with the notion of holism, and with the view that morals were based on an insight into the whole, not on an analysis of mental laws. The German view of religion, Mill wrote approvingly, seemed to be one "of poetry and feeling with little, if anything, of positive dogma."[27] "I tried," Mill said, "to go *all round* every object which I surveyed, and to place myself at all points of view, so to have the best chance of seeing all sides. . . . I became catholic and tolerant in an extreme degree."[28] It was this sort of "tolerance" that Mill had praised in Carlyle.

Gradually, however, Mill reverted to his earlier Utilitarian attitudes. Mystical feeling for the whole gave way to cold analysis of parts (though seen in a new and broader light). In praising Carlyle's *French Revolution* in 1837, Mill added that the author had underestimated the importance of general principles:

> The essence of past experience lies embodied in those logical, abstract propositions, which our author makes so light of:—there, and no where else. From them we learn what has ordinarily been found true, or even recall what we ourselves have found true, in innumerable unnamed and unremembered cases, more or less resembling the present.

Logical method, not just mystical insight, is needed. "Without a hypothesis to commence with," Mill argued, "we do not even know what end to begin at, what points to enquire into. Nearly every thing that has ever been ascertained by scientific observers, was brought to light in the attempt to test and verify some theory; to start from a theory, but not to see the object through the theory; to bring light with us, but also to receive other light from whencesoever it comes; such is the part of the philosopher, of the true practical *seer* or person of insight."[29] Against Carlyle's prophet, Mill poses the "true practical *seer*," himself.

In a letter to Carlyle of March 2, 1834, Mill had already indicated the direction of his thoughts:

> Is not the distinction between Mysticism, the Mysticism which is of Truth, & mere dreaming, or the substitution of imaginations for realities, exactly this, that mysticism may be "translated into logic?" I mean in the only sense in which I ever endeavour to translate it. You will understand what I mean. Logic proves nothing, yet points out clearly whether and how all things are proved. This being my creed, of course none of my mysticism, if mysticism it be, *rests* on logic as its basis; yet I require to see how it looks in the logical dialect before I feel sure of it. And if I have any *vocation* I think it is exactly this, to translate the mysticism of others into the language of Argument.[30]

Similarly, Mill believed that his vocation was to translate the poetry of others into the language of logic. In the *Logic* he tried to accomplish both these tasks (neither the poetry nor the mysticism would be very recognizable). In the process he sought to offer a defense of scientific empiricism and deduction against the German supernaturalists and idealists.

On a more political level, Mill also found himself coming to see Carlyle's "tolerance" for what it was: intolerance. Starting with a clash over Irish and colonial questions in 1848, the two came to polemics over the article, "Occasional Discourse on the Negro Question," which Carlyle wrote for *Fraser's Magazine* the next year. In his article Carlyle poured scorn on "Exeter Hall Philanthropy" and "The Dismal Science" for their defense of "Black Quashee," the stupid, lazy nigger who, he claimed, was the source of the troubles in the British West Indies. Mill answered him in the next issue of *Fraser's* with a typical liberal defense of humaneness. The argument lay simmering until the Jamaica Riots and the ensuing controversy over Governor Eyre in 1865 reawakened the quarrel and ruthlessly exposed the different meanings of "tolerance" for the two erstwhile friends.[31]

There is one last difference that widened between Mill and Carlyle. Originally, their respective mental crises had pulled them together. Gradually, their growing divergence on how to deal with such internal matters pushed them apart. Carlyle came to deny the validity of any kind of introspective psychology, and, as John Robson puts it, "advocated a drowning of the individual in extrapersonal moral purposes, known and accepted through intuition."[32] He could combine both his "anti-self-consciousness" theory and his "Gospel of Work." Mill was more tolerant of introspection, and did not favor "work for work's sake" (the Puritan version of "Art for Art's Sake"?), but only as it contributed to the self-development and moral growth of the individual.

In the end, the factors that had brought Mill and Carlyle together turned out not to be strong enough to resist the forces dissolving the relationship. Worse, some of the supposed positive factors—a common liking for tolerance, a common experience of introspection—turned out to be illusory. These matters would have been enough to attenuate the friendship. When coupled with Mill's pattern of initial overevaluation of a "teacher," and then gradual perception of clay feet, they effectively eroded the union of minds hoped for on both sides.

The French Revolution *Episode*

AS WE have noted, shortly after his return from France, aged fifteen, John Stuart Mill had begun an interest in the literature of the French Revolution, which he maintained thereafter. By 1828 he was in a position to write a magisterial review (for the *Westminster Review*) of Sir Walter Scott's *Life of Napoleon*. As Mill describes it in his *Autobiography*, this article

> cost me more time and trouble than any previous; but it was a labour of love, being a defence of the early French revolutionists against the Tory misrepresentations of Sir Walter Scott in his Life of Napoleon. For this the number of books which I read, making notes & extracts, even the number which I bought (for in those days there was no public or subscription Library from which books of reference could be taken home) far exceeded the worth of the immediate object; but I had a half formed intention of writing a History of the French Revolution.[33]

In 1833 Mill also reviewed the first two volumes of Alison's *History of Europe*, focusing his observations on the French Revolution. Here he underlined the universalistic nature of the French Revolution—it was not "peculiarly French," but part of a "progressive transformation embracing the whole human race"—and called special attention to the fact that the political revolution had originated as a "moral revolution."[34]

There could be few subjects more worthy of extended treatment than a history of the French Revolution. Yet John Stuart Mill, admirably prepared as he was, did not write it. Instead, Thomas Carlyle, whose expertise and initial interests had been in German letters and metaphysics, did. Why? Carlyle had become increasingly curious about France, after an initial dislike of the *philosophes*, and was aware of what a promising and financially profitable subject the Revolution might be. Thus, after reading Mill's review of Alison, he wrote to him:

> To me, it often seems as if the right *History* (that impossible thing I mean by History) of the French Revolution were the grand Poem of our Time; as if the man who *could* write the *truth* of that, were worth all the other writers and singers. If I were spared alive myself, and had means, why might not I too prepare the way for such a thing? I assure you the attempt often seems among my possibilities.[35]

Mill, who was already sending Carlyle packets of books on the subject, and sharing his knowledge and views of the French Revolution with his friend in long letters, replied:

> You suggest to me, what I have many times thought of, the advisableness of my writing something more elaborate than I have yet written on the French Revolution: it is highly probable I shall do it sometime if you do not; but besides the difficulty of doing it tolerably, there is a far greater difficulty of doing it so as to be read in England, until the time comes when one can speak of Christianity as it may be spoken of in France; as by far the greatest and best thing which has existed on this globe, but which is gone, never to return, only what was best in it to reappear in another and still higher form, some time (heaven knows when). One could not *now* say this openly in England, and be read—at least by the many; yet it is perhaps worth trying. Without *saying out* one's whole belief on that point, it is impossible to write about the French Revolution in any way professing to tell the *whole* truth.[36]

Carlyle, of course, would not suffer from this disability. He himself was a "religious" man. With this said, however, one must question Mill's professed reason for not writing a history of the French Revolution. It sounds like a rationalization based on the inevitable grain of truth. Surely Mill was clever enough to mask his anti-Christian message in acceptable terms, if necessary. How else could he have written his reviews? Something deeper than the difficulty of pronouncing the "whole truth" about religion in the French Revolution suggests itself. In fact, Mill, who from the earliest moment that he could hold a pen had tried to imitate his father's history of British India, never wrote any sort of full-scale history. As we have seen, the *History of British India* was his true sibling—"I was born the son of James Mill, author of the *History of British India*"—and Mill could not, it seems, bring himself to rival father and "brother" in a history of the French Revolution. Far-fetched as such an explanation seems on first glance, it makes more sense of the matter than any other. Although he collected an immense amount of work on the subject, and thought deeply about it, he could not bring himself to make a philosophical history out of the "grand Poem of our time." Instead he left it to his friend Thomas Carlyle, helping him immensely in the task, though again, as I shall seek to show, with ambivalent feelings.

Carlyle, as he wrote his brother John in 1834, had found his subject:

I have fixed on my book, and am labouring (*ohne Hast, ohne Rast*) as yet afar off to get it ready. Did I not tell you the subject? The French Revolution. I mean to make an artistic picture of it. Alas! the subject is high and huge. *Ich zittre nur, ich stottre nur, und kann es doch nicht lassen.* Mill has lent me above a hundred books; I read continually, and the matter is dimly shaping itself in me.[37]

By the beginning of 1835 he had finished the first volume and given the manuscript to Mill to read. Then on March 6 occurred a dreadful event: The manuscript was accidentally burned. We are still not entirely clear as to how it happened. Packe's account, for example, is as follows:

As was his habit, Mill had read much of it aloud to Harriet, and had discussed with her the observations he proposed to make upon it. In the meantime he had laid it out in his room at his father's house; and there, while clearing out old papers for kitchen use, he had swept it off to limbo.[38]

Other sources are more precise, and tell us that "a servant of the Mills used the pages as fire-lighters, mistaking them for discarded notes."[39] Or, as Mill's sister Harriet wrote in 1873 (after Mill's death): "As far as my recollection goes, the misfortune arose from my brother's own inadvertence, in having given your papers amongst waste paper for kitchen use. I can perfectly well remember our search, and my dear brother's extreme distress, and I fancy, tho' of this I do not feel so sure, that some pages were found."[40]

There is no question of Mill's obvious distress. Immediately he rushed off to the Carlyles to break the terrible news, taking Harriet Taylor with him for support. Seeing the distraught Mill, the Carlyles thought he was eloping with Harriet and had come to tell them about it. When they found out the real cause of the visit, they were partly relieved; in any event, they behaved with great nobleness, seeking to comfort Mill for *his* sorrow. As Carlyle wrote him the next day:

My dear Mill, How are you? You left me last night with a look which I shall not soon forget. Is there anything I could do or suffer to alleviate you? For I feel that your sorrow must be far sharper than mine: yours bound to be a *passive* one. . . . I have ordered a *Biographie Universelle*, this morning;—and a better sort of paper. Thus, far from giving up the game, you see, I am risking another £10 on it. Courage, my Friend![41]

Then, to show his forgiveness and trust, Carlyle offered to lend him the manuscript of part of the second volume of the *French Revolution.*

Mill's response was to say that he would

not be able to cease thinking of it until it is ascertained how far the loss is capable of being repaired—or rather reduced to a loss of time and labour only—There are hardly any means I would not joyfully take, if any existed by which I could myself be instrumental to remedying the mischief my carelessness has caused—That however depends not upon me. But there is one part of the evil—though I fear the least part—which I could repair—the loss to yourself of time and labour—that is of income.

In another letter the following day, he speaks of "that which can buy peace of conscience is precious." He adds that if Carlyle really wishes to give him the manuscript of the second volume, he should entrust it to Mrs. Taylor for "in her custody no harm could come to it."[42] This suggestion would certainly seem to clear Harriet Taylor of any complicity in the loss, yet oddly enough the Carlyles, as Hayek puts it, "seem to have conceived the idea that Mrs. Taylor was responsible [though not deliberately] for the destruction of the manuscript."[43] While this suspicion did not immediately color their relationship with her, it helped prepare the way for the ultimate break.

As for John Stuart Mill, he supported Carlyle during the rewriting of Volume 1, though Carlyle would take only £100 of the £200 offered. And, in spite of the accident, the friendship continued. But was it really an "accident"? No one could possibly accuse John Stuart Mill of deliberately wishing to destroy Carlyle's manuscript. Yet how can we explain his incredible carelessness in "inadvertently," as his sister remembered, placing the entire manuscript as "waste paper for kitchen use" (after all, the careful John Stuart Mill *had never* misplaced any *other* manuscript)? Do we have here an "accident" similar to the loss of the watch, in which unconscious motives conflict with conscious ones? Mill's position vis-à-vis Carlyle and the French Revolution was necessarily ambiguous. Mill, in one part of himself, had deeply wished to write the history of the French Revolution, and yet, as we have suggested, was unable to do so. Next he plays the role to Carlyle *that Bentham had played to his father*. Thus, although Carlyle is older, it is John Stuart Mill who lends him books and guides him on his way. (After the burning of the manuscript it is again Mill who "patronizes" Carlyle by giving him financial support, as Bentham had with James Mill.) What feelings did the reversed roles—Mill as the patron—awake unconsciously?

Mill felt that he could have (and therefore should have?) written a better book than Carlyle. As he wrote Comte in 1842:

> Carlyle is famous for various works, among others for a History of the French Revolution, written from a point of view which is imperfect but progressive in this country, and remarkable for a truly epic genius, although this genius can develop without any other general doctrine than what one can call the criticism of criticism.[44]

"Without other general doctrine": this was also the crux of Mill's intellectual break with Carlyle, first publicly argued in his review of the *French Revolution*. It was Mill who was the "true practical *seer* or person of insight," as he wrote there, who perceived that "the essence of past experience lies embodied in those logical, abstract, propositions" which Carlyle made "so light of." Yet he had allowed, nay consciously helped, Carlyle to write the book he, Mill, should have written. There was even more, then, on Mill's "conscience" than we have suggested up to now. In sum, the incident of the loss of the French Revolution manuscript symbolizes much of both the intellectual and personal dimensions that underlay Mill's friendship with Thomas Carlyle.

Saint-Simonians and Comte: The Friendly Enemies

WITH THE SAINT-SIMONIANS, and then Auguste Comte, Mill entered into another long and involved affair. As with Carlyle, the effect on Mill was powerful but almost incalculable because of its complexity. Mill had seen Henri Saint-Simon during his boyhood trip to France; at the time it meant nothing to him, and he did not even record it in his Journal, but only came to realize its importance in the *Autobiography*. He seems to have read little, if any, of Saint-Simon's works at first hand. Then on May 30, 1828, Mill met Gustave d'Eichtal, through their mutual friend Eyton Tooke, at the London Debating Society. D'Eichtal, the son of a rich Jewish banking family, had become acquainted with Saint-Simon's writings through the recommendation of his mathematics teacher, Auguste Comte.[45] D'Eichtal quickly became a good friend of John Stuart Mill, and as one of his first acts of friendship pressed on him a copy of Comte's *Système de politique positive*, which formed a part of Saint-Simon's *Catéchisme des Industriels* (1823).

When Comte had written this piece, he was still a disciple of Saint-Simon. Indeed, he was also his secretary and a sort of adopted son. Controversy over Saint-Simon's apparent effort to claim the *Système* as his own—publishing it without separate recognition of Comte—led to the "father-son" relation dissolving in acrimony. Thus, by 1828 Comte had broken with Saint-Simon and was beginning to set forth his own system. It was not, however, until 1837, with the publication of the first volumes of Comte's major opus, the *Cours de philosophie positive*, that Mill would become fully aware of the differences between Comte's scheme and the Saint-Simonian one, from which Mill had already separated himself around 1832. In any event, in the late 1830s and early 1840s Mill was exposed to another dose of Saint-Simonianism, in Comtean form. It was not until 1841 that the intellectual connection also became a "friendship"—opening up all the gains along with the dangers of that relation—with the two men entering into extensive correspondence at that time.

In the beginning, however, it was, as noted, d'Eichtal who presented Mill with the initial version of Saint-Simonianism. Though interested, Mill was at first dubious. As he wrote d'Eichtal on October 8, 1829:

> When I read the "Opinions Littéraries, Philosophiques et Industrielles" [by various writers, including Saint-Simon] which I took up with some expectations, I was perfectly astonished at the shallowness of it. It appeared to me the production of men who had neither read nor thought, but hastily put down the first crudities that would occur to a boy who had just left school. . . . When, however, I read Comte's "Traité de Politique Positive," I was no longer surprised at the high opinion which I had heard you express of the book, & the writer, and was even seduced by the plausibility of his manner into forming a higher opinion of the doctrines which he delivers than on reflexion they appear to me at all entitled to. I find the same fault with his philosophy, that he does with the philosophy of the eighteenth century. . . . It is a great mistake, a very common one too, which this sect seem to be in great danger of falling into to suppose that a few striking and original observations, are sufficient to form the foundation of a *science positive*.

More importantly even, in Mill's mind, Comte was making the same mistake that Macaulay had so recently and so justly accused James Mill of making:

They deduce politics like mathematics from a set of axioms and definitions, forgetting that in mathematics there is no danger of partial views: a proposition is either true or it is not, & if it is true, we may safely apply it to every case which the proposition comprehends in its terms: but in politics & the social science, this is so far from being the case, that error seldom arises from our assuming premisses which are not true, but generally from our overlooking other truths which limit, & modify the effect of the former.[46]

We should bear this passage in mind. Later we shall see Mill's assertions that Benthamism was actually the best preparation for Positivism, Comte's mature doctrine; here the connection is first presented as a criticism. By 1837 Mill believed that Comte had gone well beyond the position criticized here and had, in fact, placed the *science positive* on sound foundations; but by 1844, Mill, while still believing in the positive science, had reverted to the criticisms voiced in his first comment on Comte's work. Thus, this passage almost prophetically sums up Mill's reaction to Positivism. His first reaction was also his last, dialectically rephrased.

What, however, were the abstract "ideas" to which the Saint-Simonians gave what Mill called "order and system"? One of them is presented in Mill's very first letter to d'Eichtal. It embraces the notion of elitism, of an intellectual (and industrial) class leading the masses for their own good. "The intelligent classes," Mill approvingly wrote apropos of the Catholic Emancipation bill, "lead the government, and the government leads the stupid classes." This was also good Benthamite doctrine. In fact, however, Mill did not believe his own observation, for as he quickly wrote d'Eichtal in his next letter, "There are no men of talents among us." It had only been his enthusiasm for d'Eichtal that had led him to his first assertion. Nevertheless, belief in the desirability of leadership and power over government by the "intellectual classes" persisted, as an idea given order and system by Saint-Simonianism.[47]

What d'Eichtal did, on behalf of the Saint-Simonians, was to offer an air of certainty about his doctrines which initially appealed to the searching Mill. Mill, having just given up one "conviction," Benthamism, was vulnerable to another conviction. He was also cautious. Thus, though Mill was tempted to join the Saint-Simonians, the temptation was never serious. He wished certainty, but feared it mightily. Intellectually, this position corresponded with his personal need to obey a strong teacher and then oppose to him his own autonomy. In the case of the Saint-Simonians, he tried to combine the attraction of their certainty with a judgment that they were also tolerant and liberal (we have already seen this assertion made in the case of Carlyle). Thus, he claimed that the second service rendered by the Saint-Simonians—the first being their emphasis on the Pouvoir Spirituel, the intellectual elite—was their

having . . . paid more attention & attached more importance than other philosophers to the fact, that institutions which if we consider them in themselves, we can hardly help thinking it impossible should ever had produced any thing but the most unqualified mischief (the Catholic church for example) may yet, at a particular stage in the progress of the human mind, have not only been highly useful but absolutely indispensable; the only means by which the human mind could have been brought forward to an ulterior stage of improvement.

On this Saint-Simonian form of historicism, Mill added praisingly:

They [Saint-Simonians] have, and their system tends to produce even as it appears to me in excess, that eclecticism, and comprehensive liberality, which, as it widens the range both of our ideas and of our feelings, is far more pardonable & less mischievous even when most *exagéré*, than the opposite fault.[48]

It was not only Saint-Simonian ideas that appealed to John Stuart Mill. It was also the role of the Saint-Simonians in the French Revolution of 1830. In the presence of middle-class opportunism and corruption, only the Saint-Simonians seemed to offer leadership to the working classes, who had behaved so well (as Mill had written his father). What is more, they proclaimed, as Mill put it, "The perfect equality of men and women, and an entirely new order of things in regard to their relations with one another," to coexist with the new order of industrial relations.[49] In Mill's eyes, the only good thing to come out of the events of 1830 was the example of the Saint-Simonians. Whatever his later criticisms of their doctrine, he never forgot their early behavior.

The Revolution of 1830, however, had sad consequences for Saint-Simonianism as a movement. It first distorted it, and then destroyed it. The distortion was through government persecution after 1830, when the Saint-Simonians continued their attack on the disappointing results of the Revolution. Partly as a result of the government repression, the more sober group of Saint-Simonians were pushed aside by a more radical and flamboyant group around a charismatic leader, Enfantin. Then the movement was destroyed, both by Enfantin's putative communitarian excesses—his "retreat" at Ménilmontant became a public spectacle—and by the trial in 1832 at which, despite his efforts to hypnotize and convert the court, he was condemned to prison and the movement consequently to dissolution.[50]

By 1832, the Saint-Simonians as a group were in disarray. Mill was still sympathetic to their cause, although, as he wrote Carlyle in April 1833:

Such part of the St Simonians as remain faithful, or at least a large body of them headed by Barrault, have as I find from the French newspapers, set out for the East (Constantinople I was told was their first destination) *pour chercher la femme libre*. This seems greater madness than I had imputed to them. It is among the inmates of a harem that they expect to find a woman capable of laying down or as they say *revealing* the new moral law which is to regulate the relations between the sexes! it will be lucky for them if the search is attended with no disagreeable personal consequences to them except only that of not finding.[51]

Even Enfantin still retained Mill's respect. The influence would remain, though the immediate impetus of the group was gone.

Even if the group had been preserved intact, however, Mill would never have enrolled himself as one of its members, though repeatedly urged to do so by d'Eichtal. Although he helped d'Eichtal in his "truly apostolic work" by distributing Saint-Simonian literature and suggesting possible converts in England, he made their differences clear. He wrote:

St Simonism is all in all to you, St Simonians, but to me it is only *one* among a variety of interesting and important features in the time we live in, & there are other subjects & other occupations which have as great a claim upon me as it has.[52]

Comte: The Positive Friend

MILL'S encounter with the Saint-Simonians came toward the end of his "new birth," the outcome of the struggle depicted in his mental crisis. Thus, the Saint-Simonian ideas became part of his new synthesis rather than a cause of his generational break. By the time he entered into a serious relationship in 1841 with Comte, he was almost at the end of what he labeled his second stage of mental development (which he concludes around 1844, though we suggested 1848 as a more significant date). After 1844, as we have noted, Mill claims to enter a stage dominated by his wife's intellect and character.

The renewed Saint-Simonian cum Comtean influence actually began in 1837, when John Stuart Mill read the first two volumes of

Comte's *Cours de philosophie positive.* Mill had just resumed the writing of his *Logic*, halted in 1832, and was ripe for Comte's work. While Mill claimed that most of his ideas had already been worked out, he admitted that he "gained much from Comte with which to enrich my chapters in the subsequent rewriting, and his book was of essential service to me in the parts which still remained to be thought out."[53] The remaining parts mainly concerned the logic of the moral sciences, but Mill really gained more from Comte than he admits here.

According to Mill, he had been prepared by his whole Benthamite past to benefit from Comte's work. As he wrote Comte in 1841, when their correspondence began:

> Although Benthamism can remain, doubtless, far removed from the true spirit of the positive method, yet this doctrine appears to me now the best preparation existing today for true positivism, applied to social doctrines.[54]

Thus, Mill's shift to positivism was perceived by him not as a break, but as part of a continuum. There appears also to be a latent personal dimension in Mill's initial fascination with Comte, as is suggested by the remark of John Austin, writing to Mill (in 1845), when he describes the author of the *Cours* as "like Mr. Bentham (of whom he constantly reminds me), he is so wedded to his own devices and so full of presumptuous contempt for all which has been done by other. . . ."[55]

It seems, therefore, that Mill was attracted to Comte for both intellectual and personal reasons. One of the most important intellectual things that he got from Comte was an expanded and more convincing version of the Saint-Simonian law of the three stages. Comte had the detailed scientific training to demonstrate concretely how first astronomy, then physics, chemistry, and biology had all moved from the theological via the metaphysical to the scientific, i.e., positive, stage. Now Comte added a last science to the list: sociology. He coined the name in the fourth volume of his *Cours*, forty-seventh lesson, and placed under it both social statics and social dynamics.

By "positive" Comte meant that explanation had reached the point where scientific "laws" existed, explaining the constant relationships of phenomena and not their presumed "cause" (whether theological, as with spirits or God, or metaphysical, as with Nature). With simpler phenomena, such as astronomical or physical, these invariant relations lent themselves readily to mathematical expression. As the phenomena became more complex, other methods than the mathematical had to be invoked, such as the comparative. With sociology, the most complicated of all phenomena, the comparative method over time—the synchronic or dynamics—and over space—the diachronic, or statics—had to be employed to bring the data into positive form.

Comte's series not only offered an historical description of the development of the sciences, i.e., a history of science, but a philosophy of history as well, i.e., a scientific explanation of the way progress had and must take place, for Comte indicated what social structures had to accompany the mental states of the three stages. This overpowering vision of the unity of thought and practice had great appeal to Mill. Moreover, Comte's series purported to be an educational scheme, too, for clearly one ought to study astronomy in order to understand physics, and physics to understand chemistry, and so on. Thus, pedagogy took its place next to philosophy of history as being scientifically grounded. What Benthamism had tried to do, in a metaphysical way, Comte's Positivism appeared to be doing successfully in a scientific way. Mill might well feel himself personally moving from a metaphysical to a positive stage of his mental development under the guidance of his new mentor. Thus, Mill's personal ontology both recapitulated and prepared the way for the race's putative phylogenetic development.

Comte's air of certainty about the nature and direction of history —what Austin called his "presumptuous contempt"—backed up by impressive knowledge of each science, was calculated initially to appeal to Mill. So, too, was Comte's replacement of the religious viewpoint by the strictly scientific one. As Mill wrote to him, it was

> the basic idea of your work, that is to say, the substitution of the scientific point of view for the religious, and the application to social studies of the philosophical method which today irrevocably presides over all other studies.

Mill was even willing, at least at first, to follow Comte in the latter's effort to replace existing religion with his new science. Thus, as Mill explained it to his friend John Pringle Nichol, there were good grounds

> for believing that the *culte de l'humanité* is capable of fully supplying the place of a religion, or rather (to say the truth) of *being* a religion—and this he has done, notwithstanding the ridiculousness which everybody must feel in his premature attempts to define in detail the *practices* of this *culte*.[56]

Comte's positive philosophy not only supplied a new and secularized "religion" to go with its philosophy of history, it also offered a reconstructed society, which could be called "socialist," as a practical counterpart. Thus, in the same letter to Nichol, Mill added that, though he had reservations about Comte's political ideas, he favored his "socialist" views, that is, those "calling for an entire renovation of social institutions and doctrines, in which respect I am entirely at one with him."

Mill, after the French Revolution of 1830, had turned increasingly from day-to-day politics to a search for a science of politics. If this could be found, then the "rule" of an enlightened elite over the masses of men could be justified, for it would be "knowledge" rather than will ruling over them (and Mill at this stage was becoming disillusioned over the possibilities of democracy). Mill, like his father before him, believed that the masses would voluntarily follow their betters once the latter could claim disinterested scientific knowledge. After all, one did not quarrel with a mathematician's assertion that "2 + 2 = 4."[57] This was not a mere matter of "opinion," and when social scientists could reach such certain knowledge, one would not quarrel with them either.

The problem, of course, was to develop such a scientific sociology. Mill acknowledged openly that this was his basic interest in writing the *Logic*. He also admitted that he had borrowed from Comte the method of inquiry advocated in the *Logic*, which was to discover the principles of moral science (Mill's term for Comte's sociology): the method of inverse deduction. Put simply, historical evidence—Macaulay's empiricism—would show us the laws of human development (social dynamics), that is, the law of the three stages (which could not have been discovered by pure deduction). Once we have these laws, we can then apply them deductively—thus following James Mill's preferred method—to establish the laws of existing society (social statics).[58] What Mill modestly thought he had added in his *Logic* to Comte's formulation was a method of verifying the laws reached by Comte's method of inquiry: "Comte is always profound on the methods of investigation but he does not even attempt any exact definition of the conditions of proof," Mill commented.[59]

From the beginning Comte thought he had a disciple in Mill, and Mill had certainly flattered him in this belief at the start of their epistolary friendship. Mill's constant acknowledgement of his indebtedness to Comte seemed to confirm this view. Comte was pleased with his supposed disciple, and honored him by breaking the rule of his "cerebral hygiene," that is, of not reading anyone else's writings lest he be distracted from or influenced in his own thinking. For Mill's *Logic* he made an exception; Mill was duly flattered.

For four or five years the intellectual connection between Mill and Comte was strong, and they wrote to each other often and at length. There was another bond between them as well: an emotional one. Both had suffered through emotional disturbances, so-called "mental crises" (Comte, in fact, more seriously disturbed than Mill, even suffering confinement in a mental institution). Just as with Carlyle, Mill felt he could unburden himself in the presence of an empathetic friend. Thus, typically, he wrote to Comte:

Without any well-defined complaint, I experience chronically a nervous weakness and a quasi-febrile malady which I have, moreover, experienced at various times earlier in my life, and which was familiar enough to me so that I knew it would not last long. The best complete cure would be, I know, a trip of several months, but failing such a remedy, which in fact is almost impossible, I am sure to recover my usual health little by little if nothing happens further to weaken me. Meanwhile the doctors advise me to work as little as possible, but I follow their recommendation only so far as my own experience causes me to recognize its necessity, medicine in my view not having arrived at a sufficiently perfect positive state so that liberty of conscience no longer exists in this class of ideas.[60]

As Bain summarizes the relation correctly: "It was Comte's nature to be very frank, and he was circumstantial and minute in his accounts of himself and his ways. Mill was unusually open; and revealed what he seldom told to anybody, all the fluctuations in his bodily and mental condition."[61]

But just as with Carlyle, Mill came gradually to reveal to Comte not only his "mental condition," but the fact that he was not a true disciple. As always, the withdrawal manifested itself overtly in growing intellectual differentiation and differences. Again as with Carlyle, Mill came to realize that his own "liberality" was not the same as that which he had presumed Comte to possess.

The break points occurred over a number of issues. Mill, from the very beginning of his Saint-Simonian involvement in 1829, while attracted to the law of the three stages, hesitated over its possible deterministic nature. He objected to the notion that progress had to occur uniformly "by a sort of fatality or necessity" in which the mind of man "grows and unfolds its different faculties always in one particular order, like the body," and insisted that

different nations, indeed different minds, may & do advance to improvement by different roads; that nations & men, nearly in an equally advanced state of civilization, may yet be very different in character, & that changes may take place in a man or a nation, which are neither steps forward nor backward, but steps to one side.[62]

While it is true that Comte brought Mill a long way toward the certainty of a single line of progress, the latter still resisted the full force of positive determinism.

This became especially clear over Comte's views on the desirable society. Increasingly Comte emphasized, if only by implication, the hierarchic and authoritarian nature of positive politics; the word of the positive savants was not to be questioned, and, if necessary, their authority would be enforced by the state. Mill recoiled from such intended interference with the individual's right of judgment. His personal experiences, his desperate need to assert individual autonomy and the right of the individual to free development, reasserted themselves. By 1848 he made crystal clear his differences with Comte. As he wrote then, Comte's principles,

> when reduced to practice, would be the most contrary to human liberty of any now taught or professed; for it seems to me that he would make everybody's way of life (or at all events after one choice) . . . inexorably closed against all change of destination or purpose.[63]

Fundamental to Mill's differences with Comte was their opposed positions on psychology. Comte, in spite of his personal experience, refused to recognize its existence as a possible positive subject. After biology there was sociology; psychological phenomena simply disappeared or were resolved into biology or sociology. In fact, when pressed by Mill, Comte suggested that phrenology was the true science—a physiological one—which explained all of the phenomena supposedly imputed to a so-called psychological domain; Comte pressed on Mill the reading of Gall's works. Mill dutifully read six volumes of the latter, and tentatively confessed himself unable to judge the validity of his theories. At the time, however, Mill was really temporizing. His final judgment on Comte's neglect of psychology, and on his suggested substitute, phrenology, was astringent:

> With all his science he is characteristically and resolutely ignorant of the laws of the formation of character; and he assumes the differences which he sees between women and men, philosophers and men of action, rich people and proletarians (or rather between the limited specimens of each class which come within the scanty means of knowledge of a recluse, whose knowledge even of books is purposely restricted)—all these differences he assumes as ultimate, or at least necessary facts, and he grounds universal principles of sociology on them.[64]

The argument over psychology also involved the views of Mill and Comte on women. And it was on this issue above all, with all its personal ramifications in the lives of the two men, that the friendship broke apart. Comte, like Carlyle, thought women inferior by nature. Indeed, belief in their inferiority and weakness found a scientific basis in the findings of physiology—and phrenology! From these facts, it followed naturally for Comte that women's place was in the home. There he would gallantly protect them, for example, by prohibiting divorce.

At first Mill tried to play down their differences, and to stress their possible future agreement. Thus, in a long letter of October 30, 1843, devoted almost entirely to the women question, he wrote:

Our difference of opinion on the question that you correctly characterize as the most fundamental in social speculation certainly ought not to give rise to any anxiety about the ultimate possibility of a sufficient convergence of opinion among educated people, established on purely rational bases.[65]

In Mill's view, his future work on Ethology would show that women's presumed "nature" was tied to their education and to the circumstances imposed by existing society on their individual development. With changed education and circumstance, we cannot tell what women will be and how they will behave. Anticipating his later work on the *Subjection of Women*, Mill expressed himself optimistically about the result. To all these arguments Comte returned a negative, and continued to advocate the reading of Gall. By 1846, Mill, on this most important of all points, had had enough, and expressed himself in haughty and nondisciple-like tones:

But finally, whether my anatomical and physiological notions correspond or not to the idea that you have formed from your point of view, from my view I may be permitted to believe that I have studied more, and better appreciated, in certain regards, the theory of intellectual and moral phenomena neglected by you, given the scorn that you profess for psychology, in which you include all direct study of mental phenomena, while abstracting them from their organic state.[66]

Effectively, Mill had anticipated one of the central arguments of Freud: that the life of the mind, and therefore of character, was not bound by "organic causes," but had a psychological existence and laws of its own.

If the women question was the visible rock on which the remnants of Mill's discipleship to Comte had shattered, the rending of that relation had taken place earlier over a different issue, with both men averting their eyes from its overt recognition. At some point around 1844, the two men reversed roles. Comte, older by eight years, became the dependent one, and Mill his patron. In place of Mill's intellectual debt to Comte, we now have Comte's financial debt to Mill. Comte, in greater and greater trouble with his superiors at the Ecole Polytechnique, where he tutored in mathematics, lost his position and thus most of his small income. He turned to Mill for support. Mill, first offering his own assistance, was able to arrange for his friends Grote, Molesworth, and Raikes Currie to make up the deficiency in Comte's income for the year. In the next year they also supplied much of the deficit, but indicated their subvention would not continue. Instead of being thankful for the support he had received, Comte lectured Mill in a long letter on the obligations of rich men to penniless philosophers. Mill's reaction was one of increasing exasperation with Comte's importunities.

Nevertheless, in spite of the shattering reversal of the personal relation, it would be foolish to underestimate the intellectual contribution of Comte to Mill. Building on the Saint-Simonian influence, Comte offered Mill a creed which carried within it a comprehensive philosophy of history, a fecund conception of scientific method, and an inspiring glimpse of the possession of a moral or social science. Mill took these, while rejecting the "credal" aspects of Comte's system. Intertwined with the intellectual contributions was a more personal aspect: the shared feeling of what it was to suffer from a nervous breakdown and its aftermath, and to work out one's doctrines in the light of this revelation about the irrationality of reason. In the case of John Stuart Mill, the working out of his mental crisis had also left him with heightened feelings about the need for free individual development, and for the possibility of women sharing this need. On these, and on other emotionally tinged issues, Mill clashed with Comte. When to this was added the changed relationship with Comte, who, at first a Benthamite-like mentor, now suffered reversal into a patronized dependent, the friendship was clearly at an end. The psychological pattern, as with Carlyle, had been repeated and completed. The intellectual results lingered on powerfully in Mill's tolerant and liberal effort to fashion a moral science, and to construct a political system and society inspired by the image of such a science.

Men of Feeling: The "Germano-Coleridgians"

IN THE *Autobiography*, speaking of his mental crisis, Mill makes reference to the poetry of Samuel Taylor Coleridge:

> Two lines of Coleridge, in whom alone of all writers I have found a true description of what I felt, were often in my thoughts, not at this time, but in a later period of the same mental malady.
>
> *Work without hope draws nectar in a sieve*
> *and hope without an object cannot live.*[67]

At the time of the crisis, of course, in 1826, Mill had been affected by Wordsworth's poetry, rather than Coleridge's, and we must therefore mentally qualify Mill's praise of the latter as alone giving a true description of his state. In fact, it was not so much Coleridge's poetry as his prose that played a later and critical role in Mill's mental development.

The influence of Coleridge, unlike that of Carlyle and Comte, was not directly projected through a personal relationship and, in that sense, it is of a different order. As Mill described the situation in a letter to his friend John Pringle Nichol,

> Few persons have exercised more influence over my thoughts and character than Coleridge has; not much by personal knowledge of him, though I have seen and conversed with him several times, but by his works, and by the fact that several persons with whom I have been very intimate were completely trained in his school.[68]

In sum, the personal knowledge of Coleridge's ideas was mediated through others.

Of these others, the first and outstanding figure was John Sterling. Mill and Sterling met in 1828 at the London Debating Society. Sterling and his friend Frederick Maurice appeared to be on the completely opposite side of all issues from Mill and his Utilitarian friends. In this case, opposites attracted each other. Recalling the beginning of the relationship, Mill tells us in the *Autobiography*:

> One vehement encounter between Sterling & me, he making what I thought a violent & unfair attack on the political philosophy I professed, to which I responded as sharply, fixed itself particularly in my memory because it was immediately followed by two things: one was, Sterling's withdrawing from the society; the other, that he & I sought one another privately much more than before, & became very intimate.[69]

It was Sterling's frank, affectionate, and expansive character that attracted Mill, and through that attraction of character he was then attracted to Sterling's mentor, Coleridge.

Mill's first letter to Sterling, in April 1829, makes the situation clear. It is uncharacteristically revelatory (and Mill only wrote this way with "friends" such as Carlyle and Comte, and a few others later). Mill begins:

> I have given a greater number of perusals to your note than I believe I ever gave to any epistle before. I should not however have troubled you with any answer to it, if you had not seemed to take sufficient interest in what concerns me, to lead me to believe that I might talk to you upon a subject so entirely personal as the state of my own mind without your considering it a bore or an intrusion. I was unwilling that you should leave the London

Debating Society without my telling you how much I should regret that circumstance if it were to deprive me of the chance not only of retaining such portion as I already possess, but of acquiring a still greater portion of your intimacy—which I value highly for this reason among many others, that it appears to me peculiarly adapted to the wants of my own mind; since I know no person who possesses more, of what I have not, than yourself, nor is this inconsistent with my believing you to be deficient in some of the very few things which I have.[70]

Then Mill speaks to Sterling of his "comparative loneliness" and of some of his extremely painful states of mind. Mill, it seems, had at last found a "pillow" on which he could discharge his fearful secrets.

By all accounts, Sterling was a most attractive soul. He must have been to get Mill to unburden himself to a relative stranger, though by the strange ways of the psyche it was only to a comparative stranger that Mill could reveal himself. In his short life of thirty-eight years, Sterling exerted a long influence on others, not because of anything he wrote (though he did write a novel, *Arthur Coningsby*, and various essays), but because, as Mill put it, his mere existence benefited the world, irrespective of what he did. "I shall never think of you," Mill wrote Sterling in 1844, "but as one of the noblest, and quite the most loveable of all men I have ever known or look to know."[71]

It was under this heavy emotional influence that Mill was drawn to what he called the "Germano-Coleridgian" school. How far the emotion could carry him is shown in a long letter to Sterling in 1831 where, apropos of Wordsworth, Mill remarks, "All my differences with him, or with any other philosophic Tory, would be differences of matter-of-fact or detail, while my differences with the radicals and utilitarians are differences of principle."[72] Such a sweeping repudiation of his erstwhile friends was uncharacteristic. In general, it was in an effort to secure balance, a broader view of truth than was provided by the half-truths of the Utilitarians, that Mill turned to the "philosophic Tories," or Coleridgians, while retaining elements of his former allegiances.

We see this clearly in his famous articles on Bentham (1838) and Coleridge (1840) as the two seminal minds of their time. As Mill remarks in the essay on Coleridge, "It is hardly possible to speak of Coleridge, and his position among his contemporaries without reverting to Bentham." Mill's conclusion in this regard is equally revealing of the real measure of Coleridge's effect on his thought: "We hold that these two sorts of men, who seem to be, and believe themselves to be, enemies, are in reality allies. The powers they wield are opposite poles of one great force of progression."[73] Mill could say this with such conviction because he had already experienced the union of "enemies" in his personal relations with Sterling, and worked the results into the development of his own character and thoughts.

True to his pattern, Mill moved enthusiastically to embrace the new doctrines, and to enroll himself as a seeming disciple in the new school. In a short time, of course, a cooling would occur. In this case the new discipleship was complicated by the fact that Mill had to come to terms with his feelings and views about Bentham (his "grandfather"), and thus indirectly with his father, as a matter of intellectual accounting. He tried to do this first in 1833 (shortly after Bentham's death) with a short essay on Bentham published anonymously as an appendix to Edward Lytton Bulwer's book, *England and the English.* The essay was critical (though fair), and John Stuart Mill knew it. Therefore, as he wrote Nichol, "It is not, and must not be, known to be mine."[74] The father's shadow still stood over his son's public mental development.

In his 1833 "Remarks on Bentham's Philosophy" Mill argued that what Bentham needed was "a much deeper insight into the formation of character, and knowledge of the internal workings of human nature" than was provided by his simple "interest" theory of human motivation.[75] Without this Bentham was bound to fail in the consideration of the great social questions and the formation of national character. Moreover, he would erroneously conclude that law should be the same for all times and places, and ignore the different requirements of different peoples—a tribe of North American Indians, a body of emancipated Negroes—at different times in history.

Such was Mill's intellectual charge against Bentham, overshadowing completely any emotional charge except for one brief disclosure. The effect of such writings as Bentham's, Mill declared, "if they be read and believed," has as one of two possible consequences (the other is self-seeking) "hopeless despondency and gloom."[76] This, of course, was the consequence for Mill, as he so poignantly revealed in his account of his mental crisis. In 1833 that consequence was enough to embitter Mill to the point that his estimate of Bentham's philosophy, his intellectual worth, was largely negative.

By 1838, and after the death of his father, Mill could write more freely and publicly on Bentham, and could balance the critical charges with more positive estimates. His effort, as he points out, was "the first attempt at an impartial estimate" of Bentham's character as a philosopher.[77] The distance between this essay and the one of 1833 is a measure of Mill's emotional return to a pre-1830 commitment, as well as of his progress toward the desired fusion of ideas.

Two men, Mill argues in the essay, have introduced a "revolution" in the general modes of thought and investigation in their time: Bentham is one, Coleridge the other. Mill then classifies all writers into Movement and Conservative types, and places Bentham in the first category ("the same division with ourselves," Mill added) and Coleridge in the second.

Admittedly, Mill says, Bentham's role in the Movement is as a "critical" thinker; of course, Mill is referring to Comte's division into critical and organic periods. If Bentham's criticism was, like so many of the eighteenth-century philosophers, merely destructive, it would not deserve our approbation. But, Mill insists, Bentham's criticism was "positive"; his character was "synthetic." The major achievement of Bentham's positive criticism was in the realm, not of opinions, but of method. His was "the method of *detail*; of treating wholes by separating them into their parts, abstractions by resolving them into things." By a mere accident this method became linked for Bentham with Utilitarianism. This linkage meant that many of Bentham's opinions were unsound (as we shall see, Mill thought that Coleridge had the better opinions), but it left unimpaired the value of his method. By his method, Bentham "for the first time introduced precision of thought into moral and political philosophy" and, Mill declared, "this is nothing less than a revolution in philosophy."[78]

Having praised Bentham in these terms, Mill turned to his limitations. These are the same as limned in 1833, but the phrasing is more gentle and the shortcomings appear in a more favorable context. Bentham's peculiar use of his method—the exhaustive method—gave little assurance that his materials would be complete. The result was half-truths. The paucity of materials showed to worst advantage in Bentham's treatment of human nature, where Bentham dismissed what was vague and romantic, the whole kingdom of the Imagination. At this point Mill's personal passion flamed anew, as it had in 1833. Bentham, he charges,

> never knew prosperity and adversity, passion nor satiety: he never had even the experiences which sickness gives,—he lived from childhood to the age of eighty-five in boyish health. He knew no dejection, no heaviness of heart. He never felt life a sore and weary burthen. He was a boy to the last. Self-consciousness, that daemon of the men of genius of our time, from Wordsworth to Byron, from Goethe to Chateaubriand, and to which this age owes

most both of its cheerful and its mournful wisdom, never was awakened in him.[79]

The flaw in Bentham was a flaw in his generation, and Mill's passion leads him into both a stylistic fault and a bitter boast: "His [Bentham's] own lot was cast in a *generation* [italics added] of the leanest and barrenest men whom Europe had yet produced, and he was an old man [we had just been told "He was a boy to the last"] when a better race [!] came in with the present century."[80] Mill, it is clear, felt himself to be of the "better race," those who had gained wisdom from "dejection" and "self-consciousness." He was right, but it is nevertheless unworthy self-praising.

After this outburst, however, Mill quickly lapses back into an "impartial" analysis of Bentham's ideas. Bentham's other limitations, Mill tells us, are his ignoring of motives in human nature other than mere Interest, and of the need by individuals for self-culture and self-formation.

To Bentham's credit, Mill informs us, must be placed his awareness of the historical nature of law—Bentham accepts the view of the German Historical School of Law that law is an accretion over time. But Bentham avoids the conservatism of such a view by insisting that the law must be reformed, according to rational criteria, to fit our age of progress and transition. In contrast to his 1833 essay, Mill defends Bentham against the imputation that he ignored the influence of time and place in matters of legislation (Bentham, in fact, had written a pamphlet with that title); it is only the lack of a philosophy of national culture that gives Bentham this appearance. To us, the distinction must seem subtle.

Mill had finally settled his intellectual accounts with Bentham, and thus partly with his father. Although not generally looked at this way, the 1838 essay is a generous account, especially when seen, first against the 1833 estimate, and more importantly, against the general picture of John Stuart Mill's emotional as well as mental development. Unlike Bentham, Mill felt he had grown up, had gone past the stage of being a boy. He could afford now to take the broad view and amend his own "half-truths" about Utilitarianism, while incorporating them into a greater synthesis.

For the other half of that synthesis, however, he had to turn to his portrait of Coleridge. Coleridge, Mill informs us, "has contributed more to shape the opinions of . . . [the age's] younger men" than any other thinker. Whereas Bentham asks about an opinion, "Is it true?"

Coleridge asks "What is the meaning of it?" Whereas Bentham simply dismisses an idea long held by men, but now shown false, Coleridge asks "Why had men believed in it so strongly?"

Both attitudes are necessary, Mill claims, for it is only in the conflict of "antagonist modes of thought" that intellectual progress will be made. Implicit in Mill's view is a faith in the eventual reconcilability of such antagonistic modes of thought, and we see how he links his belief in intellectual liberalism with that in political liberalism when he declares that the conflicting types of thought "are as necessary to one another in speculation as mutually checking powers are in a political constitution."[81]

Mill now turns to the epistemological basis of Coleridge's philosophy, and locates it in Kant's idealism. He labels this position false and declares "that truth, on this much debated question, lies with the school of Locke and of Bentham." Yet the doctrines of Locke can (and did) lead to "the shallowest set of doctrines which perhaps were ever passed off upon a cultivated age as a complete psychological system—the ideology of Condillac and his school [i.e., the *idéologues*, led by Destutt de Tracy]." This ideology resolved all the phenomena of the human mind into sensation by simply *calling* all states of mind by that name. "That men should begin by sweeping this away from them," Mill declares "was the first sign, that the *age of real psychology* [italics added] was about to commence."[82] Coleridge, who had first been an enthusiastic Hartleian, was one of the leaders in sweeping away the debris of the old system.

Abruptly, Mill turns to the topic of civilization. It is Coleridge and his school, he asserts, who have reminded us how precarious civilization is, and "what a host of civilizing and restraining influences" are necessary for the existence of "a state of things so repugnant to man's self-will and love of independence." For civilization to be preserved "demands the continuance of those influences as the condition of its own existence." This is the foundation belief and justification of conservatism. It calls our attention to the need for Authority and Obedience, to counter "the natural tendency of mankind to anarchy."[83] Such a need, along with the need for loyalty and nationality, was overlooked by the *philosophes* of the eighteenth century.

Coleridge and his school repaired the omission. Though the Economistes, Mill asserts, were "the first to form the idea of a Social Science," it was the Germano-Coleridgians who made the real breakthrough to such a science. "They were the first [Mill had given this credit earlier to Tocqueville, whose *Democracy in America* he reviewed in 1835] who inquired systematically into the inductive laws of the existence and growth of human society." In doing this, they made "a contribution, *the largest made by any class of thinkers* [italics added], toward the philosophy of human culture."[84]

This was heady praise. Mill seems to have forgotten the contributions of other thinkers, and he is distressingly vague about who besides Coleridge was in the Germano-Coleridgian school. Elsewhere he had said the same things about the Saint-Simonians and about Comte. It is clear that he is using Coleridge as a symbol for an entire new direction in thought. We also know that at this time he was finishing his own work on the *Logic* (though it was not published until 1843), in which the major interest was in establishing the correct method and aim of a social or moral science. It seems equally clear, then, that he was reading some of his own thoughts into Coleridge.

In any case, Mill gives Coleridge the credit for developing a philosophy of sociology, history, and culture. To this he added credit for a matching philosophy of education, whose direction would be based on a scientific understanding of "the causes of influencing the formation of national character."[85] In charge of this education would be a Coleridgian "Clerisy," and Mill, to the consternation of his Utilitarian friends, wrote in friendly fashion about Coleridge's notions concerning the Church and the uses to be made of its holding, which he calls "national property." Coleridge, according to Mill, had revived the idea of land as a trust.

For the early John Stuart Mill and his father, James Mill, the landholding aristocracy was *the* enemy. Now John Stuart Mill is prepared to accommodate himself to a new conception of the British Constitution put forth by Coleridge. In Coleridge's theory of the Constitution, there is a balance of powers between, as Coleridge put it, "the two antagonist powers or opposite interests of the State, under which all other state interests are comprised. . . . Those of *permanence* and of *progression*." The permanence interest is represented in and representative of the land, the progressive in and of trade and manufacturing. On this basis Coleridge opposed the Reform Bill of 1832 as upsetting that balance. It comes as something of a shock to see John Stuart Mill excusing, and accepting, Coleridge's position because "The Reform Bill was not calculated materially to improve the general composition of the Legislature."[86]

Why, at the end of his essay on Coleridge, had Mill tilted so far in his favor? The answer seems to lie in Mill's effort at *political* realism. He concludes by saying that "we hope we may have proved to some, not previously aware of it, that there is something both in him [Coleridge], and in the school to which he belongs, not unworthy of their better knowledge." In other words, the antagonistic mode of thought is here a worthy, and furthermore permanent, opponent. Interest in the land, and thus Conservatism, Mill asserts, is a permanent feature of the English political landscape and it cannot be dismissed out of hand:

> To suppose that so mighty a body can ever be without immense influence in the commonwealth, or to lay plans for effecting great changes, either spiritual or temporal, in which they are left out of the question, would be weakness itself. Let those who desire such changes ask themselves, if they are content that these classes should be, and remain, to a man, banded against them; and what progress they expect to make, or by what means, unless a process of preparation shall be going on in the minds of these very classes; not by the impossible method of converting them from Conservatives into Liberals, but by their being led to adopt one liberal opinion after another, as a part of Conservatism itself.[87]

We would offer a complementary explanation. Mill's personal need to tolerate and embrace antagonistic modes of thought—a need we have tried to explain as stemming from his entire psychological development and manifesting itself after the mental crisis as a search for autonomy from his father—is here extended to a political need to encompass his Conservative opponents. Liberal ideology of the Millian type grows out of his effort to forge a liberal identity. That is his major interest. It conditioned his whole approach to Coleridge and to the Germano-Coleridgian doctrines which Coleridge symbolized.

Tocqueville: An Alter Ego?

THERE IS one last figure we wish to consider in our effort to understand John Stuart Mill's intellectual development in the 1830s. It is Alexis de Tocqueville. He is unique in that he primarily confirmed Mill in certain of his ideas, rather than provoking him to a dialectic and then a new synthesis. As Mill commented to Tocqueville: "If there was any one of the leading intellects of this age to which I could flatter myself that my own had a kind of analogy it was probably yours."[88]

The intellectual relation began in 1835. In April of that year, Mill wrote Joseph Blanco White that:

> I have begun to read Tocqueville. It seems an excellent book: uniting considerable graphic power, with the capacity of generalizing on the history of society, which distinguishes the best French philosophers of the present day, & above all, bringing out the peculiarities of American society, & making the whole stand before the reader as a powerful picture.[89]

By May Mill had met Tocqueville, who had been visiting London. We have no record of his reaction to Tocqueville personally. But the correspondence between the two men suggests strongly that Mill was tempted at first to raise "introspective" as well as intellectual questions with Tocqueville, as he had with Sterling, Carlyle, and Comte. In his letter of April 27, 1836, from Brighton, for example, Mill writes:

You must be surprised that I did not immediately answer your letter—& so I would, if it had not found me ill & in bed—I have been in indifferent health all the winter & have lately had a short attack of rather a sharper kind. I now write to you from Brighton where I have come to try to get well—& I am just now too tired to write in French.[90]

What was the "attack"? We, if not Tocqueville, recognize its link to the imminent death of James Mill, and in his letter of June 15 John Stuart Mill hinted of this link:

My father is sinking to his grave under a lingering pulmonary complaint—I fear there is no chance of his recovery. My own complaint does not cause me any uneasiness, it is slight, & not painful, & there is nothing serious in it but its obstinacy. It has hitherto resisted all remedies—if I should be obliged to travel, which I think not unlikely I must I fear go further off than Paris or any part of the north of France—not so much for climate as for a complete change of scene—.[91]

How did Tocqueville respond to these overtures? It was, in fact, Tocqueville who wrote the first letter (or at least, no earlier letter between the two men has survived), requesting Mill to read his *Democracy in America*, which, he said, at least had the merit "of being the work of one of your good friends, for I hope that you now so regard me." Again in a letter of July 12, 1835, he declared, "I assure you, I do not regard you solely as an *acquaintance*. I believe that we have begun a true friendship. . . ." It was also Tocqueville who sought to elicit from Mill an account of his illness, while suggesting that he could empathize because of the loss of one of his own parents. As Tocqueville wrote Mill on February 10, 1836:

I have learned, my dear Mill, by a letter from Mrs. Austin, that you are anxious about your father. I hope that your fears have since been dissipated, and that his health is now reestablished. I am all the more interested in your anxieties for having myself recently endured the distress of losing my mother and thus experienced the full extent and bitterness of this kind of grief.

Tocqueville could hardly be expected to know the quality and depth of Mill's involvement with his father, which might make it far different from Tocqueville's relation to his mother and her death. In any case, it was to this letter that Mill replied in April with the brief and non-committal description of his illness quoted above. Tocqueville responded on June 5, 1836:

The state of your health distresses me. What is the matter with you? You appeared to me to enjoy vigorous health when I left you less than a year ago. Would this not be the case of a change of air? Consider that and think of France and the friends you have there. For my part I would be very happy to see you again.

Mill finally replied on November 9 with a fuller medical description of his case. To this Tocqueville responded, practically by return mail, on November 19:

I thank you for giving me news of your health; I confess that I was very anxious about this prolonged affliction whose cause I could not perceive. Be sparing of yourself this winter and, whatever it costs you, do not work so as to tire yourself.[92]

What is puzzling is that, after all of this concern about Mill's health and condition and Mill's own circling about the issue in his letters, nothing more revealing came from it. In spite of Tocqueville's warm overtures of friendship, Mill did not, at any time, disclose to Tocqueville the true nature of his mental crisis as he had to Sterling and Carlyle, and would to Comte. There is no confession of his recurring depression.

Why Mill held back is a question we cannot comfortably answer. Tocqueville was about Mill's own age (actually a year older), whereas Carlyle and Comte were older men; but Sterling was also Mill's age. Was Tocqueville "too healthy," i.e., not one of those men of irrepressible self-consciousness, "that daemon of the men of genius of our time"? This seems to get us closer to the mark, for while Sterling had no evident nervous breakdown, his Germano-Coleridgian sympathies seemed to predispose him in the right direction. Above all, Tocqueville was too close to Mill in *external* character, too "analogous" *intellectually* for Mill to reveal himself to Tocqueville and thus *to himself*.

Only in the later draft of his *Autobiography* did Mill talk at any length about Tocqueville, concerning the way in which the French writer had influenced him in his considerations on democracy. According to Mill, Tocqueville strengthened him in his belief in democracy, while emphasizing the dangers implicit in the tyranny of the majority, especially in the form of public opinion. Tocqueville also gave Mill the courage to oppose Comte's stress on centralization with an equal stress on decentralization, and thus to be able to steer "carefully between the two errors."[93] Starting with his review of Tocqueville's *Democracy in America* in 1835, and a second review in 1840, Mill tells us that he wrestled with these problems continuously until 1861 and the publication of *Considerations on Representative Government.*

The value of *Democracy in America* was that, by analyzing it, Mill could come to grips with the problem that had agitated his father so much: the relations of aristocracy to democracy. In Tocqueville John Stuart Mill encountered a true aristocrat who nevertheless believed that democracy was the wave of the future. Yet Tocqueville did not slavishly prostrate himself before history, but coolly and critically analyzed the drawbacks in democracy itself. And he did so in terms of a "science" of politics which combined induction and deduction, thus meeting Macaulay's criticism of James Mill on government, as well as offering a test of Comte's general propositions about the course and pattern of social progress, exemplified in one specific society, America. In a sense, then, Tocqueville was also presenting Mill with a "positivist" defense of democracy to go along with his father's Utilitarian justification.

Mill begins his first review of Tocqueville's *Democracy in America* with a long quote, establishing Tocqueville's view that "the general equality of conditions" in America has a "prodigious influence" over "the whole course of society": politics, law, public opinion, and so on. For Tocqueville, America presents the rest of the world with a picture of its own future, for democracy, whether one approves of it or not, is the direction in which all societies are tending. In that democracy, all being equal, "all must be alike free, or alike slaves." The outcome depends on the fitness of the people for self-rule.

For Mill, two more major points were made by Tocqueville. The first touched on a constant concern of Mill's own personal development. As Mill remarks: "It is a tyranny exercised over opinions, more than over persons, which he [Tocqueville] is apprehensive of. He dreads lest all *individuality of character* and *independence of thought and sentiment* should be prostrated under the despotic yoke of public opinion [italics added]." It seems not to have occurred to Mill that the introduction of a positive social science might, logically, have the same result as a nonscientific public opinion, in an unintended and unexpected way. The second point, introduced at the very end of Mill's account of Tocqueville, is the latter's claim that "democratic institutions, combined with the physical character of the country, are the cause . . . of the prodigious industrial prosperity observable in the

United States."[94] Mill quotes Tocqueville to this effect, without further comment. As we shall see, however, it is a point to which he will return, more critically, in his second article on *Democracy in America.*

Democracy *Revisited*

THE SECOND article was published in 1840 in the *Edinburgh Review* (a Whig periodical) rather than in the now defunct Radical *London Review.* Having had five years in which to ponder his earlier views on democracy and on Tocqueville's treatment of the subject, Mill begins with a brief recapitulation of how Tocqueville's book has constituted "the beginning of a new era in the scientific study of politics." As such, it offers "an impartiality without example," and though some of Tocqueville's "practical conclusions lean towards Radicalism, some of his phrases are susceptible of a Tory application." In fact, the value of Tocqueville's book is not in its conclusions, but in the mode of arriving at them. To use modern terminology, the work employs a kind of multivariate causal analysis rather than metaphysical assertion. In Mill's terms:

> It is not risking too much to affirm of these volumes, that they contain the first analytical inquiry into the influence of democracy. For the first time, that phenomenon is treated of as something which, being a reality in nature, and no mere mathematical or metaphysical abstraction, manifests itself by innumerable properties, not by some one only; and must be looked at in many aspects before it can be made the subject even of that modest and conjectural judgment, which is alone attainable respecting a fact at once so great and so new. . . . His method is, as that of a philosopher on such a subject must be—a combination of deduction with induction: his evidences are laws of human nature, on the one hand; the example of America and France, and other modern nations, so far as applicable, on the other. His conclusions never rest on either species of evidence alone; whatever he classes as an effect of Democracy, he has both ascertained to exist in those countries in which the state of society is democratic, and has also succeeded in connecting with Democracy by deductions *a priori*, showing that such would naturally be its influences upon beings constituted as mankind are, and placed in a world such as we know ours to be.

Though Mill can not say so, we seem to have an anticipation of Max Weber's ideal type in the last part of this assertion. In any case, as Mill concludes, this is "the true Baconian and Newtonian method applied to society and government."[95] These statements contain one of Mill's most significant observations on the nature of his projected social science; it echoes others that we shall encounter in his *Logic*.

Democracy, in Tocqueville's definition, is not a question of the form of government—he can conceive of Democracy under an absolute monarchy—but of equality of conditions, toward which all of history is tending. As Mill puts it: "The progress and ultimate ascendency of the democratic principle has, in his eyes, the characteristic of a law of nature." For Tocqueville this unintended yet necessary course of history is by that very quality marked out as "a providential fact," wherein "all have been blind instruments in the hands of God."[96]

A contemporary of Mill and Tocqueville's, Karl Marx, observed this same movement and direction of history. For Marx, of course, it would end in the classless society. Mill took a different view. He did not foresee an end of classes, but of upper-class power. "We do not maintain that the time is drawing near," he remarked, "when there will be no distinction of classes; but we do contend that the power of the higher classes, both in government and in society, is diminishing; while that of the middle and even the lower classes is increasing, and likely to increase." In fact, it was really the *middle* classes who, leading the lower classes, were entering upon the actual exercise of power. "America is *all* middle class," Mill asserted, but even England is under the sway of that same class. Their rule is made possible, in democratic form, by the new technology, for "the Newspapers and the Railroads are solving the problem of bringing the democracy of England to vote, like that of Athens, simultaneously in one *agora*."[97]

The rule of the middle class, however, made possible as it is by the means of communication, also makes possible the tyranny of the majority, and Mill returns to this compelling subject. He dismisses the idea that it is from the material, selfish interests of the majority that the minority or even an individual must fear oppression; the interests of both in this area are concomitant. It is rather from the "antipathies of religion, political party, or race," as American experience shows, Mill prophetically declares, that tyranny of public opinion, rather than law as such, must be expected.[98]

Mill next takes up a point in Tocqueville, the treatment of which must leave us disappointed. It is Tocqueville's analysis, not of the "province of intellect," but of "Sentiments and Morals." Here the argument is that the gradual progress of social equality has brought a "general softening of manners and the remarkable growth, in modern times, of humanity and philanthropy." Having agreed with this, Mill then adds: "The general equality penetrates also into the family relations: there is more intimacy, he thinks, than in Europe, between parents and children, but less, except in the earliest years, of paternal authority, and the filial respect which is founded upon it." For us the disappointment is acute when Mill peremptorily concludes: "These, however, are among the topics which we must omit," thus leaving us with little direct assistance in one of the key tasks to which our own book is devoted.[99]

Mill passes on instead to a rather complicated critique of Tocqueville's views on the causal relationship of democratic and economic development (or what Mill calls Civilization). As we recall, Mill had ended his 1835 consideration of *Democracy in America* with an uncritical acceptance of Tocqueville's view that democratic institutions are the cause of industrial prosperity. In 1840 he asserts that Tocqueville has "at least apparently, confounded the effects of Democracy with the effects of Civilization." Mill resorts to the comparative method to make his point:

Consider, for instance, the French of Lower Canada. Equality of conditions is more universal there than in the United States; for the whole people, without exception, are in easy circumstances, and there are not even that considerable number of rich individuals who are to be found in all the great towns of the American Republic. Yet do we find in Canada that *go-ahead spirit*—that restless impatient eagerness for improvement in circumstances—that mobility, that shifting and fluctuating, now up now down, now here now there—that absence of classes and class-spirit—that jealousy of superior attainments—that want of deference for authority and leadership—that habit of bringing things to the rule and square of each man's own understanding—which M. de Tocqueville imputes to the same cause in the United States?[100]

There is also an example on the other side, a reverse of this mental experiment. It is England, where there is the same and indeed greater "progressive commercial civilization" as in America, without the equality of conditions, yet with the same air of restlessness and mobility. Mill's tone is approving when he comments: "The mobility and fluctuating nature of individual relations—the absence of permanent ties, local or personal; how often has this been commented on as one of the organic changes by which the ancient structure of English society is becoming dissolved?" We hear no echo here of Carlyle's lament over the dissolution of all personal ties into "Cash Payment as the sole nexus." Mill is too pleased at the dissolution of the ancient structure of English society by the progressive forces of economic development. In his analysis, against Tocqueville's, the causal weight seems to be placed on industrial progress bringing about democracy, rather than the other way.

Having said all this, Mill then seems to retreat from his position, or at least to qualify it. He is now worried that a single class—the middle class—will impose a homogeneous community, a tyranny of the majority, over society. Such homogeneity, for Mill, implies, as in China, a stationary society. Progress results from individual differences. "The unlikeness of one man to another is not only a principle of improvement, but would seem almost to be the only principle," Mill announces rather extravagantly. Thus, the class that wields the strongest power in society must be prevented from exercising its full strength. How can this be done? Mill calls into question his and Tocqueville's earlier assertion about the necessary direction of history, the law of nature whereby both democratic and economic development proceed causally linked:

But human affairs are not entirely governed by mechanical laws, nor men's characters wholly and irrevocably formed by their situation in life. Economical and social changes, though among the greatest, are not the only forces which shape the course of our species; ideas are not always the mere signs and effects of social circumstances, they are themselves a power in history. Let the idea take hold of the more generous and cultivated minds, that the most serious danger to the future prospects of mankind is in the unbalanced influence of the commercial spirit—let the wiser and better-hearted politicians and public teachers look upon it as their most pressing duty, to protect and strengthen whatever, in the heart of man or in his outward life, can form a salutary check to the exclusive tendencies of that spirit—and we should not only have individual testimonies against it, in all the forms of genius, from those who have the privilege of speaking not to their own age merely, but to all time; there would also gradually shape itself forth a national education, which, without overlooking any other of the requisites of human wellbeing, would be adapted to this purpose in particular.[101]

Here, at last, Mill has been able to attempt a fusion of his Germano-Coleridgian ideas with his positive science, whether of Comte or of Tocqueville. Other sentiments than the commercial—might we say the utilitarian?—must prevail if European society is not to decline, a victim of its own economic progress. Specifically, Mill tells us, "an agricultural class, a leisured class, and a learned class" are necessary to check the commercial class. In this manner England might avoid the overhomogenization of American society, and its tyranny of the majority. Yes, Mill agrees, "The ascendency of the commercial class in modern society and politics is inevitable," but its evil features can be eliminated if the intellectual stands true to his calling and exercises correctly the power of the mind.[102] While Mill's specific instance—intellectual recognition of the necessity of a leisured, learned agricultural class—seems limited in conception and bound to English conditions, his general conceptions as to the nature of democracy, economic development, and moral progress are worthy of more serious consideration. These conceptions were foreshadowed in the essays on Bentham and Coleridge. They are brought into balance with Mill's other intellectual commitments, developed in the course of his personal development, during the friendship with and in the two essays on Tocqueville.

The Union of Mind and Spirit

THERE IS small need to summarize the course of Mill's intellectual development in his "second stage"; the extended materials should speak for themselves. As we have seen, in 1828, two years after the onset of his mental crisis, Mill fell under the influence of the Germano-Coleridgians, initially in the person of John Sterling, and of the Saint-Simonians, through the intermediacy of Gustave d'Eichtal. By 1831, when he met Carlyle, he had aligned himself with the new "Spirit of the Age." That spirit represented, in part, a generational revolt. It allowed Mill to work out in intellectual terms some of what he had experienced in emotional terms in his mental crisis; Carlyle seems mainly to have supported the emotional side of Mill's commitment. The intellectual change was not a mere "reflection" of the emotional change, but another and related way of dealing with the same problems: How much tutelage and how much autonomy are needed by an individual in his development from child to man? How much are needed by a people in their development toward a free yet responsible society? Appended to these fundamental questions were more precise subheadings, such as: the nature of democracy—delegation or representation; the role of elites—aristocratic or Saint-Simonian; the function and power of the middle classes; the lower classes; the danger of the tyranny of a majority; and so on.

At the same time as he was raising these questions in his new spirit, Mill was also, as a good Utilitarian intellectual, seeking to establish the correct nature of moral and social science. The answer to this task also entailed a philosophy of history. The Saint-Simonians, including the youthful Comte, offered him pertinent inspiration. The Germano-Coleridgians contributed their views on the balance of progressive and permanent forces in the weaving of history. Was that history inevitable? Could Saint-Simonian social science offer a total and certain explanation of future progress? If it could, would this serve as a justification of a new elite, which could thus avoid the uncertainties and vagaries of unenlightened democratic rule?

11 / Intellectual Development

By 1833 there are signs that Mill had absorbed the influence of the Saint-Simonians, the Germano-Coleridgians, and Carlyle, and was turning back, erratically and intermittently, to a reaffirmation of his earlier Utilitarian commitments without letting go of his new insights. The "tolerant" and "liberal" synthesis which he sought to effect was a "new birth" of his father's brand of "liberalism," not a complete rejection of it. At this point came his encounter with Tocqueville and *Democracy in America*. As we have seen, Tocqueville gave Mill a specific example of the inductive-deductive method of social science at work. He also presented him with a reaffirmation of democracy, which nevertheless was critical enough to point up the dangers of a tyranny of the majority (and thus to reaffirm the crucial need for a moral and social science, whose presuppositions Mill was seeking to establish at this time in his *Logic*).

By 1840 Mill had tried to synthesize the two spirits that had warred in his breast throughout the 1830s. He initially made the attempt in his articles on Bentham and Coleridge, as well as on Tocqueville's *Democracy in America*. The beginning, in 1841, of his epistolary friendship with Comte both reawakened some of the earlier influences and pushed him on to a tested reaffirmation of some of his political and scientific views. Thus, in the 1840s, and certainly by their end, Mill had worked through the "only revolution" in his intellectual development. If we take 1848 as a terminal date, Mill was then forty-two years old.

Had Mill also worked through his emotional revolution? We know that the virulence of his mental crisis had subsided around 1830, when, at age twenty-four, he was entering on his new intellectual positions. At this point we can be permitted to say that he had ended his "adolescence." The death of his father in 1836 reawakened, in great intensity, the emotional conflict of ten years earlier. While this, too, subsided, there seems little reason to believe that Mill was at any time free from the emotional turmoil of his generational struggle. By the 1840s, and his own forties, he had learned to live with it. The results in his own life were a mixture of resignation and low-keyed contentment. In his intellectual life, as we have tried to show, the result was a momentous transmutation of the philosophy of "greatest happiness" into a philosophy of political liberalism, characterized by a new realism and breadth, and an effort at a moral-social science the aspirations of which went well beyond the dogmatic simplicities of the generation of Utilitarians who had given first birth to the young John Stuart Mill. Thus, out of Mill's mental crisis had come a true "second birth," with the umbilical cord still loosely tied to the original parental creators.

12

Harriet: Love Unto Death

Sex

AT THE HEART of generation, and generations, is the sex act, requiring the coming together of a man and a woman (or at least such was the case in Mill's time). Sex may or may not involve love. In fact, it may even involve hate and serve aggressive, warlike purposes, as in the battle of the sexes. Conversely, love may or may not entail sex.

Freud, in declaring that the good life was based on "Liebe und Arbeit"—love and work—implicitly pointed to another connection, that *between* love and work. In this extrapolation, work is sublimated love, or sex; on this transformation of impulse is built the whole edifice of civilization. As we may recall, with James Mill we began an inquiry into the way the "investment" of libido in work could create a "homo economicus." One consequence for Victorians seems to have been what I shall call the "economization" of sex, with the way open to further exploitation in two major directions: (1) prostitution, or the direct sale of women's sexuality; and (2) admittedly a later development, the sale of products by investing them with the aura of eroticism (e.g., using a pretty woman to sell a product). In this economization, sex is not sublimated in work, but is itself directly put to work in the economical process. Beyond even these "free" market arrangements, marriage itself is seen by some as a form of legalized prostitution.[1]

Where in this tangle of sex, love, and work does John Stuart Mill stand? We are faced initially with two striking paradoxes. One is the fact that John Stuart Mill, who scorned his mother in the *Autobiography* and in life, became the pioneer advocate of the emancipation of women. The other paradox is equally startling: Mill, it is claimed, knew less about women and sex than almost any man; however, it is also claimed (by different critics, needless to say) that Mill was more advanced in his knowledge of the psychology of women than any other person of his sex (though guided thereto by another man's wife, Harriet Taylor).[2]

Can we resolve these paradoxes? And can we answer such further questions as: What were Mill's own sexual experiences, if any, and his attitudes toward sex? How did he, raised in an "unloving family" and convinced of his inability to love, reconcile the possibilities of sex and love in his relation to the woman of his life, Harriet Taylor? Was there a special relationship between work and sex for Mill, touching especially on the question of creativity? The answer to such questions is given "on the pulse," in terms of his turbulent and "scandalous" relation to Harriet Taylor, where it takes a vibrant shape ultimately transformed into the abstract assertions of Mill's writings on women.

A Romance

THE STORY of the romance between Mill and Harriet Taylor is quickly told. Sometime in 1830—we are not sure of the exact date, but the meeting seems to have occurred in the summer or early autumn—John Stuart Mill met Harriet Taylor at a dinner party at her home. The meeting of Mill and Mrs. Taylor, the wife of John Taylor and the mother of his two children, had been arranged by her friend, William Johnson Fox, a Unitarian minister and publicist. After four years of marriage to her well-meaning but boring husband, Mrs. Taylor had complained to Fox of the intellectual vacuity surrounding her life, and he had decided on John Stuart Mill as the cure. It was a dangerous piece of pastoral advice. Harriet Taylor was twenty-three, beautiful, fiery, and in search of a soul mate. John Stuart Mill was twenty-five, handsome, highly intelligent, open to new experiences by 1830, and unknowing about women. The result was an intense involvement of the two for the rest of their lives.

Was it love at first sight? We cannot tell for sure, for there are no surviving reminiscences. We do know that by the summer of 1831 the two were intimately involved, even though Harriet Taylor was delivered of her last child, Helen, on July 27, 1831.[3]

Every evidence, and all the psychology involved, points to the relationship as Platonic, though with intense emotional undertones. Whatever sensual elements existed appear to have been sublimated in a very special sort of "friendship." This situation undoubtedly made it possible for John Taylor to agree to a kind of *ménage à trois*.

The "love affair" itself underwent the usual ups and downs. In the summer of 1832 Harriet wrote Mill that they must not meet any further. Reluctantly, he agreed. But a few weeks later they were seeing one another again, and he was again visiting the Taylor home. Meanwhile, on the intellectual plane, sometime during 1831 or 1832 they were also exchanging essays on marriage and divorce, on women and their position in society. These essays were to form the basis of the later "Enfranchisement of Women" and "The Subjection of Women." Concurrently, on the emotional plane, it seems that a temporary withdrawal by Mill from active pursuit of Harriet caused her to become the more positive one in the relationship. The romance thus spurred on, by 1833 Harriet and her husband agreed to a trial separation of six months. The separation was at his request, for he hoped she would get over her infatuation and realize the impropriety of the relationship. Instead, after a short interval, Mill joined Harriet in Paris, and the two were together there for over six weeks. On their return the *ménage à trois* was formally institutionalized, with Harriet living with her husband, having Mill at her home when John Taylor was out, and spending summer weekends with Mill. Mill, who seems to have alternately feared (ostensibly because of public opinion) and hoped for a complete break of Harriet with her husband, continued to live at home with his parents and siblings, and went on with his writings and his work at the East India Company. We must not forget that the intellectual development we have described Mill undergoing from 1830 on was taking place concurrently, and correspondingly, with his emotional and spiritual involvement with Harriet Taylor.

For almost twenty years this state of affairs persisted. The romance had become an agreed-upon convention. Yet it never lost its excitement for the two lovers, perhaps because of the constant threat of public condemnation. Then, in 1849, John Taylor died of cancer. Two years later Mill and Harriet Taylor married; one consequence, as we shall see, was that Mill, finally leaving his parental home, quarreled with his family. At last John Stuart Mill and Harriet Taylor were husband and wife. Though hampered by their mutual increasing illness, especially on Harriet's side (consumption), they intensified their intellectual collaboration, creating a number of "joint productions," as

Mill referred to them, such as *On Liberty*. Then in 1858, while on a trip to France, Harriet died in Avignon. Desolate, Mill dedicated the rest of his life to her worship. Having just retired from the East India Company before her death, he bought a house in Avignon with a view of her grave. Here he prepared for publication the essays and writings on which they had both labored. His life, Mill said, only had meaning henceforth as it existed in her service. Even in death, Harriet was Mill's constant spiritual companion. So ends their romantic story.

Why Harriet?

WE HAVE only told a story, briefly and concisely.[4] What is the meaning of this story—its psychological significance, and, more importantly, its psychohistorical interpretation?

In his mental crisis, John Stuart Mill tortuously broke with his father psychologically, partly in terms of a severe Oedipal crisis. He was now free to lament the absence of feeling, and of love, in his own life, and to go in search of them. In Mill's loneliness, in his teetering on the edge of misanthropy, he was ready for the emotional entrance of someone into his life. We have already suggested a kind of latent possibility with Sarah Austin, but this, as we saw, was psychologically impossible for him. Were there other possibilities of female companionship and love open to him besides Harriet Taylor? Our information is extremely cloudy. One source suggests that Mill was an "aspirant for Eliza Flower's hand."[5] Eliza Flower was Harriet's best friend. She was also romantically involved, as we shall see, with W. J. Fox, and any possible intimacy with Mill seems highly unlikely.

There is another intriguing story. As Bain tells it:

> Mill for a time (I suppose during the thirties) went to the receptions of Lady Harriet Baring, afterwards the first Lady Ashburton, whom he was said to admire very much. He was introduced, I believe, by Charles Buller, a great favourite with her ladyship, herself remarkable for wit and brilliancy. He broke off this connexion abruptly; various reasons were afloat. Of course, Mrs. Taylor's name came up in the explanation.[6]

Whatever the intricate truths of Mill's various other romantic possibilities, it was Harriet Taylor who became his choice. I want to suggest now that this choice was not accidental; that, in fact, it was heavily overdetermined. One of the most obvious evidences of this overdetermination is her name, Harriet Taylor. The prevalence of Harriets in Mill's emotional life is astounding, and cannot be explained away simply on the basis of the commonness of the name in mid-nineteenth century Victorian England (after all, Marys and Annes were at least as common). Thus, while realizing the limitations of this sort of orthodox Freudian analysis, we cannot allow ourselves to dismiss it.[7]

The psychological mechanism involved is that of displacement. Love that has as its original object the parent is displaced onto a person unconnected by family relationship. Often, however, in the selection of the new object of love, one can trace the influence of similarity or of some other connecting link between it and the original. One type of similarity manifests itself in names.[8]

In the case of John Stuart Mill, his mother was named Harriet Burrow (note the similarity to Harriet Baring, lending plausibility to the story about her and Mill). She was twenty-three years old when she married James Mill; Harriet Taylor (whose mother, in turn, was named Harriet) was the same age when John Stuart Mill met her. Like John Stuart Mill's mother, Harriet Taylor was also married; in winning her from John Taylor, Mill was unconsciously victorious in his Oedipal struggle with his father. (Indeed, the replacement, if not the displacement, had already been prefigured in the Marmontel episode.) We must also notice the name of Harriet's husband, John Taylor; Mill could identify with the "John." Moreover, an early neighbor of the Mills at Newington Green, when John Stuart Mill was growing up, had been John Taylor's grandfather. As John Stuart Mill tells us, this man had lived in the next house to James Mill and had sometimes invited young John to play in his garden. Yet another neighbor a little later, at Queen Square, had been John Austin, who was married as we know to Sarah, née Taylor. Mill admired and partly identified with Austin, and entered into a "motherly" relation with Sarah Taylor, now Austin. We have already noted the latent significance of that relationship; it is now possible to see how Harriet *Taylor* took the place of Sarah, who, in turn, serves as the intermediary link to John Stuart Mill's mother.[9]

Improbable as all this may seem, it is less improbable than that so many "coincidences" of name could have centered around John Stuart Mill's emotional attachments, even in a society in which Harriets, Johns, and Taylors were common appellations.

Another aspect of the overdetermination involved in John Stuart Mill's relations with Harriet Taylor may at first glance seem even more improbable than the assertion about names. It is simply that, in Harriet Taylor, John Stuart Mill was able to love and possess not only his mother, but his father as well. Probably only Harriet Taylor could have filled these joint necessities of John Stuart Mill's emotional life. They were the requirements of what, for want of a better term, I shall call John Stuart Mill's bisexuality. As we shall see, this explanation helps us to understand one of the reasons why he "overvalued" her so extravagantly.

We have already tried to explain how Harriet would represent his mother in John Stuart Mill's unconsciousness, as the Oedipal displacement. (The "girlish petulance" noticed by Carlyle would add to this transference.) The relation of Harriet to her husband, John Taylor, however, reverses the relation of Mill's mother to his father. As Mill tells us in the *Autobiography*, John Taylor was "a most upright, brave, and honourable man . . . but without the intellectual or artistic tastes which would have made him a companion for her [his wife]."[10] Moreover, the unfolding of their marriage duplicates, with the players changed, his parents' marriage: Harriet, in the first year or so of the marriage, was a doting, loving wife, as James Mill was a loving husband; both then rapidly fell out of love with their respective spouses. Thus, in coming to the rescue of Harriet Taylor, John Stuart Mill rescued *both* his father and his mother. Of course, it was only as an unconscious process, kept unconscious by a whole range of psychoanalytic defenses and maskings, that John Stuart Mill's "bisexual" needs could achieve satisfaction.

If this is accepted, we can see that John Stuart Mill's relations to his mother are even more complicated than so far stated. Not only is Harriet identified with his mother; John Stuart Mill *himself* is so identified.[11] In this aspect of his unconscious he takes his mother's place as the one loved by his father. When this happens—and in the peculiar logic of the psyche it can coexist with the identification of Harriet with his mother!—John Stuart Mill is the "feminine" soul, obeying and accepting the dominance of the more "masculine" Harriet. That Mill could entertain this notion even on the conscious level is made clear in a number of passages, but especially in his letter to Thomas Carlyle (October 1833) in which, having asked "*Is* there really any distinction between the highest masculine and the highest feminine character?" Mill answers:

The women, of all I have known, who possessed the highest measure of what are considered feminine qualities, have combined with them more of the highest masculine qualities than I have ever seen in any but one or two men, & those one or two men were also in many respects almost women. I suspect it is the second-rate people of the two sexes that are unlike—the first-rate are alike in both—except—no, I do not think I can except anything—but then, in this respect, my position has been and is, what you say every human being's is in many respects "a peculiar one."[12]

Although Mill often modestly complained how second rate he was, we do not really believe his disclaimer of being first rate; as the latter, he was also "peculiar."[13] While we would like to know what he had in mind by his "except," which he then rejected, we are nevertheless safe in saying that Mill accepted his own bisexual nature, with its combination of feminine and masculine traits. The feminine could permit him to identify with his mother, while at the same time the masculine side wished her, in the person of Harriet, for himself.

In Mill's unconscious, Harriet was not only his mother as a desired Oedipal object. She was also his mother as maternal figure. Everyone has noticed Mill's dependence on her in practical and household affairs—and we remember how Mill had complained that having everything done for him in domestic matters had been a fatal flaw in his upbringing—and how he constantly noted down for Harriet the symptoms of his illnesses, as if he were a child with its mother.

But, as we have contended, Harriet was not only John Stuart Mill's mother, both as Oedipal and maternal object; in his unconscious she was also his father. Like his father, Harriet supervised his work and helped him revise it. Having started out as his pupil, she dramatically reversed roles, certainly by 1833, and began to be his teacher. Again like his father, she alternately praised and scorned him. For example, in one letter of 1854 she said: "I thought so exactly as you did about that trash in the Ex[aminer] . . . ," and then in almost the same breath reprimanded him about the autobiography he had begun to write, parts of which he had submitted to her: "I feel sure dear that the Life is not half written and that half that is written will not do."[14]

Indeed, Harriet went beyond the real-life James Mill and displaced him as the greatest person John Stuart Mill had ever known. She became the idealized incarnation of all James Mill's virtues, without any of his vices, combining a "character . . . of feeling . . . with a vigorous and bold speculative intellect." She also had "the perfection of a poetic and artistic nature," along with an eminent "practical capacity." As Mill avers in the *Autobiography*, "she possessed in combination the qualities which in all other persons whom I had known I had been only too happy to find singly." Is it any wonder that Mill concludes:

> She became to me a living type of the most admirable kind of human being. I had always wished for a friend whom I could admire wholly, without reservation & restriction, & I had now found one.[15]

In stepping into the father's shoes, Harriet had avoided having his clay feet.

As father and mother, masculine and feminine, Harriet was also able to combine for John Stuart Mill the worlds of intellect and feeling, and thus to heal the schism that had so frighteningly disclosed itself in the mental crisis. In his essays on Bentham and Coleridge, Mill had intellectually delineated the two yearning halves of his existence. Harriet represented Bentham and Coleridge combined. Like the latter, she stood for the world of poetry and feeling. It is more surprising to see that in Mill's imagination she also stood for the world of prose and rationality of the former. Thus, in a striking passage of an 1853 letter to Harriet, he exults: "I should like everyone to know that I am the Dumont and you the originating mind, the Bentham, bless her!" It is an assertion such as this that must have led Hayek to make this surprising statement: "Far from it having been the sentimental it was the rationalist element in Mill's thought which was mainly strengthened by her influence."[16] But Hayek's statement is only partially true; as Mill has already told us, Harriet synthesized in one person all that he had ever admired previously in many persons.

That synthesis, as we have been suggesting, fused the masculine and feminine needs of Mill's psyche as well as of his mind. The Platonic relationship with Harriet allowed him to enjoy and fulfill the Platonic ideal of bisexuality.

Freud, though influenced, one suspects, by the Platonic ideal, had derived the concept of bisexuality directly from his friend Wilhelm Fleiss. Thus, in an early version of his work, Freud recognized the fact that man's (and woman's) sexuality rotated between two magnets: the masculine and feminine inclinations. On one side, for a man, was the normal declination to the masculine, and to heterosexuality. On the other, carried to the extreme, was homosexuality (with all its complications of who plays the masculine and who the feminine "roles"). Mill, we suspect, stayed almost completely in the middle of the Freudian picture. As Bain remarked rather discreetly: "I am not singular in the opinion that in the so-called sensual feelings, he was below average; that, in fact, he was not a good representative specimen of humanity in respect of these; and scarcely did justice to them in his theories." As a result, Bain tells us, John Stuart Mill "made light of the difficulty of controlling the sexual appetite," and thought birth control for married couples easy, through mere continence.[17] For Mill, the masculine and feminine were wedded within himself; he seems not to have needed their wedding together outside himself, in a sexual union with a woman. Or, rather, he needed another person like himself, and he found "her" in Harriet Taylor.

In Harriet Taylor, Mill also found the solution to the problem of his mental crisis. He could now fuse his masculine and feminine needs in one person who also represented for him the possession of, and possession by, his father and mother. Harriet allowed him to return to his childhood desires for a perfect father and an ideal mother. She embodied a regression to childhood dependency, while at the same time she sustained him in the assertion of independence from his father and the whole school of Bentham. She gave him the faith that he could love and be loved—as she wrote to him in 1833, "for me I *am* loved as I desire to be," and added, "O my own love"—that he had passions and could invoke them in others.[18] Yet, just as important, their relationship did not require Mill to make a commitment to sexual love and to possible responsibility for a family and children of his own, since Harriet was already married. Thus Harriet allowed him his Oedipal victory without his having to consummate it. Only on these terms could Mill enter into an intimate relation with a member of the "opposite" sex.

Nevertheless, Mill could not help having strong feelings of guilt. His father, who had always been his "conscience," soon heard of his son's connection to Harriet. Bain describes what happened: James Mill "taxed him with being in love with another man's wife. He [John Stuart Mill] replied, he had no other feeling toward her, than he would have towards an equally able man. The answer was unsatisfactory, but final." In the light of our discussion about John Stuart Mill's "bisexuality," we can see that the answer was not all that unsatisfactory. On the unconscious level, it touched the truth, though not the whole truth. However, James Mill could hardly be expected to find satisfaction in the answer. As Bain puts it, James Mill "could do no more, but he expressed to several of his friends, his strong disapproval of the affair."[19]

John Stuart Mill was therefore made directly aware that he did not have his father's blessings, a fact of which his conscience had undoubtedly already made him indirectly aware. The weight of his superego was heavy, and it goes a long way toward explaining both his constant changes of attitude in the early years with Harriet, and his break later with his friends and family over her. In 1833, when Harriet had essayed the trial separation from John Taylor and was advocating a permanent liaison in the form of a *ménage à trois*, the problem became acute. We can see from the correspondence between the two lovers that John Stuart Mill was having doubts and suffering from pronounced feelings of guilt. In September 1833 Harriet is forced to write to him:

The most horrible feeling I ever know is when for moments the fear comes over me that *nothing* which you say of yourself is to be absolutely relied on—that you are not sure even of your strongest feelings. Tell me again that it is not.

As Hayek suggests, we see what is bothering Harriet in a letter John Stuart Mill wrote to W. J. Fox only a day after her letter:

If she is ever out of spirits it is always something amiss in *me* that is the cause—it is so now—it is because she sees that what ought to be so much easier to me than to her, is in reality more difficult—costs harder struggle—to part company with the opinion of the world, and with my former modes of doing good in it, however, thank Heaven, she does not doubt that I can do it.

It was Harriet who supplied the strength and sought to allay his fears. In 1835, for example, she had to cope with Mill's feeling that public opinion condemned them, and that if they continued their love affair he would have to resign himself to obscurity. Harriet responded angrily to his doubts:

Dear one—if the feeling of this letter of yours were your *general* or even *often* state of mind it would be very unfortunate for—may I say *us*—for *me* at all events. . . . Good heaven have you at last arrived at fearing to be "*obscure & insignificant*"*!* What *can* I say to that but "by all means pursue your brilliant and important career". Am *I* one to choose to be the cause that the person I love feels himself reduced to "obscure & insignificant"! Good God what has the love of two equals to do with making obscure & insignificant. if ever you *could* be obscure & insignificant you *are* so whatever happens & certainly a person who did not feel contempt at the very idea the words create is not one to brave the world.

Having told him he is a coward, Harriet adds disdainfully, "There seems a touch of Common Place vanity in that dread of being obscure and insignificant."[20]

The psychic pressures on Mill from all sides were intense. Harriet was telling him he was vain and cowardly; his father, slowly dying in 1835, was a "living" reproach to him; and John Stuart Mill's exaggerated symptoms at the time of his father's death in 1836 were overdetermined anew. Some of his "liberated" friends, such as W. J. Fox, were annoyed with him for not living up to his principles, openly avowing to the world his liaison with Harriet, and insisting that she live with him. His reactions to those who thought he should break completely with Harriet were very sharp, for here his desires and guilt feelings conflicted. When his friend John Roebuck tried to remonstrate with him, John Stuart Mill repulsed him coldly. Roebuck, who had been at that first dinner at which Mill had met Harriet, had been unaware of their growing intimacy until, as he tells it:

On the occasion of an evening party at Mrs. Charles Buller's, I saw Mill enter the room with Mrs. Taylor hanging upon his arm.

The manner of the lady, the evident devotion of the gentleman, soon attracted universal attention, and a suppressed titter went round the room. My affection for Mill was so warm and so sincere that I was hurt by anything which brought ridicule upon him. I saw, or thought I saw, how mischievous might be this affair, and as we had become in all things like brothers, I determined, most unwisely, to speak to him on the subject.

With this resolution I went to the India House next day, and then frankly told him what I thought might result from his connection with Mrs. Taylor. He received my warnings coldly, and after some time I took my leave, little thinking what effect my remonstrances had produced.

The next day I again called at the India House, not with any intention of renewing the subject, but in accordance with a long-formed habit of constantly seeing and conversing with Mill. The moment I entered the room I saw that, as far as he was concerned, our friendship was at an end. His manner was not merely cold, but repulsive; and I, seeing how matters were, left him. His part of our friendship was rooted out, nay, destroyed. . . .[21]

Roebuck was not the only one of his friends to whom Mill turned cold. All who ventured the slightest criticism of his relation to Harriet, or were even suspected of having gossiped about it, incurred his enmity henceforth. Mrs. Grote, Harriet Martineau, Sarah Austin all received, to greater or less degree, the same treatment as Roebuck. Mill persisted in this pattern throughout the years of his liaison with Harriet; after his marriage he even extended it to his intimate family, as we shall see. Such an overreaction can only be explained on the basis of an oversensitive conscience, a highly acute sense of guilt. Mill reacted so violently to the slightest breath of criticism by his friends largely because the criticisms were also his own, in his unconscious, where his internalized father still possessed him.

The other way Mill reacted was to overvalue Harriet extravagantly, for only if she were the most perfect being could the moral imperfections of his attachment to her be justified. Freud has written at some length about the overvaluation of a loved one. Mill is a prime example of the type. There is a kind of "Methinks the lady doth protest too much" effect on us as we read his encomiums to Harriet. We are embarrassed, as were his friends, by his abasement before her and his overlush praise of her. What are we to make of his New Year's greeting to Harriet in 1855, in which he calls her "The only person living who is worthy to live," or of his words, written to introduce the republication of "The Enfranchisement of Women" (originally published in *West-*

minster Review, 1851) in his *Dissertations and Discussions*, after her death, in which he declares, "So elevated was the general level of her faculties, that the highest poetry, philosophy, oratory, or art seemed trivial by the side of her"?[22] Such examples could easily be multiplied. We sense that Mill's compulsion—really an obsession—to praise her served two needs: In praising her he was unconsciously praising himself (Harriet's instinct was right in constantly criticizing his vanity), an otherwise forbidden confession; even more significantly, he was justifying his terribly complicated Oedipal "sin" to himself and the world.

Who Is Harriet?

WHO, in fact, was Harriet, this paragon of virtues? What was she like in her own person? Mill himself was not sanguine about the possibilities of understanding Harriet psychologically. As he wrote an American champion of women's rights in 1870:

> Were it possible in a memoir to have the formation and growth of a mind like hers portrayed, to do so would be as valuable a benefit to mankind as was ever conferred by a biography. But such a psychological history is seldom possible, and in her case the materials for it do not exist. All that could be furnished is her birth-place, parentage, and a few dates, and it seems to me that her memory is more honoured by the absence of any attempt at a biographical notice than by the presence of a most meagre one.

In order to understand Mill's relation with Harriet, we must disregard his good advice about her. Without denying the paucity of materials, or wishing to dishonor her memory, we shall make what efforts we can at comprehending Harriet's "psychological history."[23]

Harriet was born to Harriet (Hurst) and Thomas Hardy on October 8, 1807. Her parents seem to have had some pretensions to social importance (which may have left Harriet an inherited tendency to snobbishness). Her father at the time of her birth was a "surgeon and man-midwife," that is, an early obstetrician, and a member of the Royal College of Surgeons.

Dr. Hardy was apparently a stern and authoritarian man, and we can presume a typical Victorian rule over his brood of five boys and two girls (Harriet was the middle child of the seven). In her letters Harriet referred to him as "The Governor." We do not know what his relations were like with his wife, nor do we know anything about Harriet's early life. According to Packe, "Caroline, her younger sister, lived at home with their mother, and there developed between the three women an emotional triangle which on occasion drove Harriet to the edge of exasperation."[24]

At eighteen and a half, in March 1826, she was married to John Taylor, a prosperous wholesale druggist eleven years her senior. Exactly how that marriage came about—the Hardys and Taylors lived distant from one another—we do not know. There is some possibility that Hardy *père*, as a Doctor, might have known the Taylor family in their professional capacity as druggists; or perhaps he knew them as fellow Unitarians. There is also a story that Dr. Hardy arranged the match for financial reasons, but we have no evidence that he suffered from monetary difficulties. However, that he arranged the match seems almost certain, and Harriet seems merely to have followed her father's wishes.

Nevertheless, the marriage began as a happy and satisfying one. John Taylor was active in the affairs of the Unitarian congregation, of which W. J. Fox was the minister, and he took part in radical politics. While not handsome, he was certainly kind and amiable, surely a welcome contrast at first to Harriet's domineering father. When a child, Herbert, was born a little over a year after the wedding, the couple seemed bounteously happy. Harriet wrote to her husband on July 7, 1828, from Ryde, Isle of Wight, where she was on vacation with the baby:

My dearest John, Though I knew that I must not send you another letter for some days, as I only wrote yesterday, yet I cannot bear to defer the pleasure of writing, even tho' you should not see it at present. I received your letter my dearest by Edward last night—every letter you send me the mere sight of your writing, gives me great pleasure but the happiness the delight I have received from this can scarcely be imagined—every question I asked you, all that I have said is answered in the very words I would have chosen. . . . I put it under my pillow that I might read it to our dear little one as soon as he awoke this morning. . . . Oh my dear John each hour that passes brings us nearer the day when we shall meet and I think from my present feelings that I shall never again consent to our parting. . . .[25]

Two years later another son, Algernon, invariably called "Haji," was born. Sometime that year, as we know, Harriet went to Fox and complained about her lack of an intellectual and artistic companion in her husband. Shortly thereafter occurred the fateful—and fated?—meeting with John Stuart Mill. Yet in the midst of her growing dissatisfaction, presumably even after meeting John Stuart Mill, Harriet became pregnant once again with her last child, Helen (usually called Lily).

What had happened in those few short years? Had she simply become bored with the person, John Taylor, whom Carlyle described as "an innocent dull good man"?[26] Was it simply that her own intellectual and artistic gifts began to flower? At hand in the Unitarian circle around W. J. Fox was a perfect hothouse for forced growth of any romantic yearnings that Harriet might have now had. It is therefore requisite that we pause to say something about the setting in which Harriet's mental development and her romance with John Stuart Mill began to blossom.

The Circle: Fox and Eliza

AT THE CENTER of this circle was William Johnson Fox.[27] Born in 1786 of a peasant farmer and the daughter of the village barber, by 1830 Fox had risen, by dint of his native abilities and hard work, to a position of intellectual and journalistic leadership in London. Though deprived of formal education during his early years, in 1806 Fox had managed to enter an academy for the training of Dissenting ministers, where he was educated in orthodox Calvinism. Quite soon after his graduation and after he had taken his first parish, Fox began to have religious doubts. Within a relatively short time he moved from Calvinism to an advanced version of Unitarianism. Called to London in 1816, he began to contribute to various periodicals on cultural and political topics, and attracted a good deal of favorable notice for his oratorical ability. His visibility was aided by expanded literary pursuits. In the course of his activities he formed a connection with some of the followers of Bentham, and began to contribute to the Utilitarian journals. He also wrote for the Unitarian journal, the *Monthly Repository*, becoming its editor in 1828 and purchasing it in 1831. Thus, when Harriet and John Stuart Mill each met him separately, he was a successful and active participant in the intellectual, artistic, and political life of London, as well as a Unitarian minister of advanced views.

Some of these views were in the area of marriage and women's rights. Like a number of other Unitarians, Fox advocated better education for women, their right to the franchise, generally greater equality between the sexes, and even liberalization of the divorce laws. It was in acting on his views about women's rights in his own life that Fox went beyond even most of those who shared his advanced views.[28]

Fox's own marriage was not happy. Before being called to London, he had served as Unitarian minister for five years in Chichester.

There he became involved with Eliza Florance, daughter of a local barrister. Although Fox recognized that Eliza would "never excite an enthusiastic passion," as he wrote in his diary, loneliness led him to believe she might "be very well loved." Nevertheless, in 1815, just before he was to leave for London, the semiengagement was broken off (apparently at the instigation of Eliza's father, who did not regard Fox as a suitable match). In 1819, however, Eliza Florance came to London, ostensibly to work as a teacher. By this time her father's fortunes had suffered a reverse, and Fox's successes had made him a good catch. There is some suspicion that the renewal of the "engagement" was not done, as Mineka puts it, "without pressure from Miss Florance and her parents." Fox acquiesced, though without enthusiasm, and the couple were married on April 20, 1820. By August 1821 a boy was born—alas, a deaf mute. This seems to have occurred at about the time Fox was becoming increasingly disillusioned with his marriage. In February 1822 he suffered a severe breakdown, which incapacitated him from preaching for a year; when he met John Stuart Mill this was bound to provide an unspoken emotional link between the two men, in spite of their differences in age.[29]

In any case, Fox recovered and went on to greater accomplishments. He also produced two more children in the now loveless marriage. During this same time, a friendship developed with the family of Benjamin Flower, a radical editor, and his two motherless daughters. Fox became increasingly not only companion and religious teacher to the two Flower girls, Eliza and Sarah, but their mentor and guide in literary and artistic matters. The two girls were highly talented, Eliza composing hymns and tunes, and Sarah contributing poems and articles to the *Monthly Repository* as well as writing hymns (one of which, "Nearer, My God, to Thee," achieved enduring fame). Eliza (or Lizzie, as she was called), almost from the beginning, assisted Fox in his work by researching materials and copying out his speeches and articles. Gradually the teacher-assistant relation turned into a romantic attachment. When Eliza's father died in 1829, Fox was appointed executor and trustee for his friend's children; the relationship became even more intimate. By 1832 Mrs. Fox was openly complaining to her husband about his involvement with his ward, seventeen years his junior.

There can be no question about Fox being romantically involved with Eliza Flower (we must note here, too, the overdetermination of names, Eliza Flower and his wife's maiden name, Eliza Florance). On the other hand, neither can there be any question about the physical propriety; it was a meeting of souls, not of bodies. Fox was not a prepossessing man; he has been described as a "tubby little man . . . with a moon-like face." Indeed, he was only five feet tall, and not at all handsome in figure or face. Eliza, on the other hand, was "frail, and slim," beautiful with "the unnatural bloom and burning eyes" of the consumptive disease from which she suffered.[30] Strange physically as a pair (Beauty and the Beast?), they seemed made for each other emotionally; it was on this plane that they conducted their love, and set an example for others.

Divorce in England of the 1830s was out of the question, and Fox and his wife, therefore, though continuing to live together, entered into an agreed-upon separation. But Mrs. Fox, unhappy with the arrangement, told of her troubles to some of her husband's congregation in 1834. A great hullabaloo followed. Asked to resign, Fox fought back and was upheld by a majority of his congregation, though forty-six out of a total of one hundred and twenty members withdrew. Shortly afterward, Fox negotiated a formal separation from his wife and set up a separate household with Eliza, in the suburb of Bayswater, taking with him two of the children (at their request). Here they lived, defying the conventions of society, Eliza helping Fox tirelessly with work and children until her death in 1846.

The Reason Why

THIS VICTORIAN domestic drama surrounded Harriet Taylor and John Stuart Mill as they pursued their own romance. Harriet and Eliza Flower were devoted friends at the beginning. In fact, an air of unconscious eroticism hung over their love for one another. Thus, Eliza wrote to Harriet:

> If it were not for fear of accidents and making Mr. Taylor jealous, I could say how "I would I were a man" to have laid my heart at your feet while you were talking yesterday.[31]

Perhaps Harriet sensed the emotional dangers involved; in any case, in 1833 she wrote, as romantic couple to couple, about her joy in John Stuart Mill:

> Why do you not write to me my dearest Lizzie? (I never wrote that name before) if you w^{d} say on the merest scrap what you are talking about what the next sermon is about where you walked to, & such like, how glad I should be! You must come here—it is a most beautiful paradise. O how happy we might all be in it. You will see it with me, bless you! won't you?[32]

As for the male side of the couples, their relations were more restrained. Needless to say, however, John Stuart Mill and W. J. Fox had intellectual interests as well as emotional fellow-feeling to share, and Mill also thought of Fox as his one confidant in his affair with Harriet.

Obviously, there was a tremendous excitement stimulated in each couple by the affair of the other. They were companions in social boldness, defying the conventions of their time. The group that surrounded them gave them increased inspiration and confidence. Sarah Flower in 1834 married W. B. Adams, a writer (under the name "Junius Redivivus") and engineer, who had been married before to a daughter of Francis Place, and was a notable exponent of women's rights. There was also ardent feminist Harriet Martineau (who, nevertheless, was later scandalized when Fox and Eliza Flower began to live together, and shunned them), and two other gifted sisters, Margaret Gillies, a painter of miniatures, and Mary Gillies, a novelist, who also advocated less conventional relations between the sexes. Thus, Mill and Harriet Taylor found themselves members of a comforting ideological band who preached a new view of marriage and the relations of the sexes, and some of whom practiced what they preached. Harriet in particular had all sorts of external encouragement to proceed in her personal development by whatever means necessary, however unconventional.

Did she also have "internal" encouragement? Were there psychological dynamics involved of which she was unconscious? Here we are of necessity on less certain ground. To secure any hints, we must return to Harriet's relations to her own parents. Through the mists of time we seem to glimpse an initial love of and identification with the mother, later turning into acrimonious dislike. In what appears to be a letter of 1839 to John Taylor (the exact date is unclear), Harriet describes her visit to her parents at Birksgate, and says: "I should like you to come . . . both Papa and mama want you to come very much . . . mama is as usual all warmth and kindness." A mother perceived as warm and kind might explain Harriet's rivalry with her sister, Caroline, for her affection. About ten years later, however, responding to her mother, who has reproached her for not writing immediately on John Taylor's death, Harriet gives us another indication of how she perceives her mother. Defending herself hotly, Harriet retorts: "*You* who have passed your whole life in denouncing forms and saying how you never would act upon them."[33] Do we see here the early model for Harriet's 1832 "Essay," in which she declares:

Whether it would be religious conformity, Political conformity, moral conformity or Social conformity, no matter which the species, the spirit is the same: all kinds agree in this one point, of hostility to individual character. . . .

The remedy, Harriet concludes, "is, to make all strong enough to stand alone; and whoever has once known the pleasure of self-dependence, will be in no danger of relapsing into subserviency."[34]

By the 1850s, if not before, Mrs. Hardy is revealing herself as a complaining woman, twisting Harriet's words and irritably accusing her of "unmerited aversion" to her sister Caroline, of not responding to her (Mrs. Hardy's) birthday greetings, and of not writing for a year (to which Harriet retorts, "False—I wrote in February and again in September '56"). Mrs. Hardy asks back a picture that Harriet has had for twenty years, laments that she is "a neglected mother," and asks rhetorically: "In what respect I have ever failed as a mother, it is for you to decide."[35] Harriet will have none of this, and indignantly spurns all the accusations.

What has happened? We do not really know, and can only guess that 1849 is a turning point for both Harriet and her mother. In that year both lost their husbands. What is absolutely extraordinary is that we seem not to possess one single reference by Harriet Taylor to her father's death. Did it awaken *any* feelings in her? Was she so overcome by John Taylor's death that she could spare no thought for her father's, or was her rather extravagant mourning for John Taylor partly because she was also mourning, unconsciously, for her father *in* her husband? All is hidden from us.

Is there anything more we can say? Only that Harriet's negative feelings seem to be directed to both parents; before 1849 they were directed mostly to her father. By the late 1840s she was obviously trying to avoid going to Birksgate. Ill health on her part was her constant excuse to her father and mother. The real reason, as she writes John Taylor in December 1848 (incidentally, before she realizes how sick he is), is that:

The near relationships to persons of the most opposite principles to my own produces excessive embarrassments, and this spring it must be *far* worse than usual owing to the constant presence in London of A[rthur] [her sister's dissolute husband], whom I must either neglect (which is very disagreeable to me) or admit into a degree of intimacy which must inevitably lead to an interference on the part of Birksgate and either a rupture with them or to discussions & dissentions which I have not the strength to bear.[36]

Although she is a mature woman of forty, she confesses to "intense anxiety" about seeing her parents. As she writes John:

I am obliged to leave very indefinite *what* it is that I dread in going to Yorkshire, because I cannot [deny?] or hint the truth, which is *their ways* —But as I never say anything *but* the truth, I told them the fact that I *require* regular *early* hours and simple diet—*Two things* which of all things on earth they both *most abominate*.[37]

What specifically of Harriet's father? As the "Governor" he would seem the most obvious threat to her "self-dependence." We have no direct evidence of her feelings toward him, only the general rumor that she resented his domineering ways. If the general tradition is correct, however, and we have every reason to believe it is, then we may have our thread to Harriet's falling out of love with John Taylor as early as 1829. In July of that year Harriet was on holiday at the seashore, pregnant with her second child. John, worried about her, consulted his obstetrician father-in-law, and wrote Harriet accordingly:

Papa told me that sea bathing will suit you on a warm day if you feel quite disposed for it and if you only just dip and out again; you must on no account remain in longer than just time enough to get one dip, and if you feel the least cold or shivering afterwards you must not repeat the bath.— Attend to all this and you have your husband's full permission to bathe.— Excuse this Lordly way of putting the affair, but you know it is his love and affection for his sweet girl that alone make him appear dictatorial.[38]

From what we know of Harriet Taylor a year later, that was the wrong tone to take with her. It was ideally calculated to arouse all her resentments toward her father, and now, by unconscious identification, her husband. Harriet's response was an assertion of romantic independence. On the back of her husband's letter she scribbled a poem:

MERMAID'S SONG

In chrystal caves of Ocean's deep
I make my pearly home
The rocking surges soothe my sleep
With wild and plaintive moan.

Sometimes I roam where glist'ning sands
Reflect bright Hesper's ray
Or bend to distant sunny lands
My happy cheerful way.[39]

As is evident, we are on extremely thin ice in all of the above. What we know for sure is that by 1830 Harriet was ready for an involvement with John Stuart Mill. Further, we can be certain, as far as such matters ever can be certain (and we will present the very strong evidence in a moment), that Harriet had one more child by her husband, and then renounced all further sexual relations with any man, including either her husband or John Stuart Mill.

Needless to say, this is an unusual state of affairs requiring an unusual explanation. Why did Harriet Taylor allow herself to become pregnant again by her husband while she was obviously falling in love with John Stuart Mill? We can speculate as follows. Harriet Taylor, like a good Victorian woman, did not really like sex, but faithfully fulfilled her duties to her husband.[40] Or at least she did so for a time. The last childbirth must have clinched the matter, finally symbolizing dominance by her "dictatorial" and "Lordly" husband, identified at some level of Harriet's unconscious with the "Governor," her father (who, moreover, was an obstetrician). In addition, she had fallen in love with another man, and to continue to make love with her husband was a betrayal of that other attachment, Platonic though it was. In the midst of such emotions, we can speculate that Harriet turned "frigid," denying her sexuality at the same time as she affirmed her mental as well as physical independence. One required the other, in her "peculiar" psychodynamics.

We said earlier that the evidence for Harriet having renounced all sexual relations after 1832 was very strong. What is this evidence? There is, first, John Stuart Mill's own account in his *Autobiography*. As he explains there:

> Our conduct, during these years, gave not the slightest ground for any other supposition than the true one, that our relation to each other was one of strong affection & confidential intimacy only. For though we did not consider the ordinances of society binding on a subject so entirely personal, we did feel bound that our conduct should be such as in no degree to bring discredit on her husband nor therefore on herself; & we disdained, as every person not a slave of his animal appetites must do, the abject notion that the strongest & tenderest friendship cannot exist between a man & a woman without a sensual relation, or that any impulses of that lower character cannot be put aside when regard for the feelings of others, or even when only prudence & personal dignity require it.[41]

We have no reason to doubt Mill; the tone conveys authenticity, and the whole pattern of his life lends conviction.

So do his intellectual beliefs. As he wrote later in his essay on Utilitarianism (1861; reprinted 1863), the Epicureans, though they correctly named pleasure as the aim of life, did not intend mere animal gratification: "The comparison of the Epicurean life to that of beasts is felt as degrading, precisely because a beast's pleasures do not satisfy a human being's conceptions of happiness. Human beings have faculties more elevated than the animal appetites; and, when once made conscious of them, do not regard any thing as happiness which does not include their gratification."[42] Thus, the intimacy that Mill speaks of is an intimacy (and in his early draft Mill had added "entirely apart from sensuality," a phrase later eliminated by Harriet) of spirit and not of body: that is all he admits between the two lovers. Their disdain for the merely "animal," the impulses of a "lower" character, coinciding with their generally elitist feelings, would have prevented anything more, even if prudence had not. The imagery of control is the same imagry as in Mill's advocacy of birth control, now applied to sexual intercourse itself.

Harriet's response to reading Mill's early autobiographical draft version of their relationship is contained in a letter to him of February 14–15, 1854:

> Should there not be a summary of our relationship from its commencement in 1830. . . . This ought to be done in its genuine truth and simplicity—strong affection, intimacy of friendship, and no impropriety. It seems to me an edifying picture for those poor wretches who cannot conceive friendship but in sex—nor believe that expediency and the consideration for feelings of others can conquer sensuality.[43]

It strains credulity to believe that, in a private letter to John Stuart Mill, Harriet would act out a charade about their true relations.

Such views by Harriet coincide with her earlier statements on the position of women and their role in nineteenth-century English marriage. As she wrote around 1831:

> No institution that could possibly be devised seems to me so entirely tending to encourage and create mere sensualism as that of marriage. In the first place it makes some mere animal inclination respectable and recognized in itself. . . .[44]

The note of "mere animal inclination" is heard once more. That Harriet exempted herself from such base appetites is clearly implied in the notes on marriage and divorce which she wrote out for John Stuart Mill. As she says there:

> Whether nature made a difference in the nature of men & women or not, it seems now that all men, with the exception of a few lofty minded, are sensualists more or less—women on the contrary are quite exempt from this trait, however it may appear otherwise in the cases of some.

Harriet is obviously not among the "some." Where sex is required of such disinterested women in marriage, however, marriage becomes merely a form of legalized prostitution, and we hear Harriet's echo of a prevalent view of the proponents of women's rights of her time (to be made famous by Karl Marx) when she adds:

Women are educated for one single object, to gain their living by marrying —(some poor souls get it without the churchgoing. It's the same way—they do not seem to be a bit worse than their honoured sisters).[45]

Such a statement in 1831 or 1832 strongly suggests to us that Harriet Taylor's emotional and intellectual resistances to further sexual intercourse were reinforcing one another intensely.

What are the evidences from outside? First, the evidence for physical intimacy is slim. Harriet was observed publicly to lean on John Stuart Mill's arm; they apparently held hands, and Carlyle tells of seeing them eating grapes together from the same vine. In short, there *was* a possibly strong sensual attraction between the two lovers. Did it proceed to physical intercourse, in spite of their disclaimers to the contrary? Almost all of their contemporaries automatically assumed it did, and some advocates of women's liberation today obviously wish it had (as proof that companionship of sentiment and intellect is not necessarily at the expense of sex).

Carlyle, at least, thought he knew better than his gossiping contemporaries. As he wrote to John Sterling in 1837: "His *Platonica* and he are constant as ever: innocent I do believe as sucking doves, and yet suffering the clack of tongues, worst penalty of guilt."[46] Carlyle's intuition coincides with what a foreign observer, Theodore Gomperz, later tells us. Gomperz, having attached himself to the Mills in the 1850s, was one of the few persons at that time admitted to intimacy with them. He records in astonishment how Mrs. Mill proudly asserted that "since her first meeting and loving Mill she had never been more than an 'intimate friend' to either him or John Taylor."[47] Though this statement is uncharacteristically public in its frankness for Harriet Taylor Mill, it nevertheless has the ring of truth to it.

There is one more piece of indirect evidence which relates to the problem of whether, after marriage, John Stuart Mill and Harriet entered upon a more perfect union. From about 1841 Harriet was an invalid, suffering from paralysis of her legs for a number of years. Without going into the details here (see pp. 318–320), we quote Bain's description:

At this time, she was suffering from spinal injury, and had to remain on the sofa for several years. She ultimately recovered the power of walking, but was delicate in other ways, being liable to attacks of hemorrhage from the lungs. During all the years of her marriage with Mill, she was properly described as an invalid.[48]

While it *is* possible that, though ailing and an invalid, and with her strong feelings against sexuality, Harriet, at age forty-three, engaged in physical intercourse with John Stuart Mill, it is hardly likely. The whole tenor and pattern of our psychohistorical analysis suggests that "existence" for them simply no longer included sex between man and woman.[49]

Mill's "Royal Road"

WE SHALL conclude this consideration of sexuality in Mill and Harriet with an extraordinary private statement. It is John Stuart Mill's account of a dream he has had, one of only two specimens he has left us of that "royal road" to the unconscious, as Freud called it, so dear to the heart of psychoanalysts and, therefore, presumptively, psychohistorians. Mill recorded it in a letter of February 17, 1857, to Harriet. He had accompanied her on a trip as far as Edinburgh, and while she proceeded north he turned back toward London. We quote the whole of his account:

> On Saturday night at York I slept little & dreamt much—among the rest a long dream of some speculation on animal nature, ending with my either reading or writing, just before I awoke, this Richterish sentence: "With what prospect then, until a cow is fed on broth, we can expect the truth & nothing but the truth to be unfolded concerning this part of nature, I leave to" &c. &c. I had a still droller dream the same night. I was seated at a table like a table d'hote, with a woman at my left hand & a young man opposite—the young man said, quoting somebody for the saying, "there are two excellent & rare things to find in a woman, a sincere friend & a sincere Magdalen". I answered "the best would be to find both in one"—on which the woman said "no, that would be too vain"—whereupon I broke out "do you suppose when one speaks of what is good in itself, one must be thinking of one's own paltry self interest? no, I spoke of what is abstractedly good & admirable"—how queer to dream stupid mock mots, & of a kind totally unlike one's own ways or character. According to the usual oddity of dreams, when the man made the quotation I recognized it & thought that he had quoted it wrong & that the right words were "an innocent magdalen" not perceiving the contradiction. I wonder if reading that Frenchman's book suggested the dream. These are ridiculous things to put in a letter, but perhaps they may amuse my darling.[50]

We do not know if Harriet was amused, but we are fascinated. The manifest content is clear; the latent meaning, alas, is unavailable to us through Mill's possible free associations. As with most dreams, we can guess that something in Mill's experience the previous day suggested some of the surface elements of his dream; but we do not even know what these might have been. Had he, for example, read something by Jean Paul Richter (as well as by "the Frenchman")? The focus in the first dream sequence is on "animal nature," but what this means we do not know (does it refer to man's "real" nature, or, in fact, to nonhumans, i.e., cows, and so on?). Again, according to the general laws of dream production, the second dream sequence should take up the work of the first dream. Here the manifest material is more ample. The subject is the nature of a woman (animal nature?): Is she friend or Magdalen, i.e., fallen, sensuous woman? Mill wishes "to find both in one."[51] The woman, sounding suspiciously like Harriet, chides him for his vanity (a frequent criticism of Mill by Harriet). Against this charge, Mill (and we wonder who is the other person present, the young man) defends himself, denying that he is self-interested. Then he seeks to dismiss the whole business by laughing at his "stupid mock mots" (a habit at first of almost all patients in analysis) and dismissing them as out of "character" for him. Lastly, he rescues the whole situation by summoning up the image of "an *innocent* magdalen," thereby having his virtue and yet enjoying it. (Who is the Frenchman? If only we knew this latter-day equivalent of Marmontel for us psychohistorians!)

Was Mill, in the deepest recesses of his being, giving voice to more sexual longings than any permitted in his waking movements, or in the course of his life? Have we, and others such as Bain, underestimated the latent force of his sensuality? The dream of Mill as a middle-aged man—he was fifty-one—forces us to entertain this suggestion. Whatever its truth, however, all our other evidence points to a complete repression and sublimation of any sexual impulses that might have surged through the frame and mind of John Stuart Mill. In Harriet Taylor, he had found his Platonic friend; there was no role, at least in his consciousness, for a Magdalen.

Triangles and Guilt Feelings

HARRIET'S renunciation of sexuality involved not only John Stuart Mill, but also her husband, John Taylor. What did it mean for Harriet's husband? Did he live in abstinence for the next seventeen years of their marriage? We must postulate either tremendous self-control and renunciation, a liaison with another woman, or resort to "legalized prostitution's" alternative, that is, prostitution itself. Somehow, the last two seem unlikely for the moral and high-minded John Taylor (though some similarly "moral" Victorians did resort to that characteristic vice of the age), and renunciation more in character. But we have no evidence in the matter; surprisingly, we don't even have gossip of any sort.

Was there some special need in Harriet for triangles? Triangles seem to surround her. We recall Packe's description of her relations with her mother and sister in these terms, and we are reminded, too, of her initial relation to her friend Eliza Flower, and then the latter's entanglement with Fox, who had a wife. Did this need also operate in John Stuart Mill?

Freudian psychoanalysis has some general observations on the subject. Thus, for example Flügel, in his *Psychoanalytic Study of the Family*, informs us:

> Just as the child's love activities in relation to its earliest love object were impeded by the fact that this object was already bound by affection, law or both, to a third person (i.e. the parent of the same sex as that of the child), so in adult life the individual's choice may fall only on objects who are similarly not at liberty in the disposal of their affections. There are indeed some men and women who can only fall in love with married or betrothed persons, and who are doomed therefore either to become dangerous enemies to the harmonious married life of others or else themselves to suffer successive repetitions of the unsuccessful love of their childhood.

Then, telling us that the need for triangular love relations finds its complement in the desire for obstacles in the way of love (because of guilt over the incestuous desires), Flügel cites an example from the life of Schiller (who, incidentally, fell in love with several persons of the same first name: Charlotte von Wolzogen, Charlotte von Kolb, and Charlotte von Lengefeld):

> On the occasion of the publication of the banns for the marriage between the poet and Charlotte von Lengefeld, the former is said to have remarked jokingly to his bride that it would be a pity if no one came to raise some objection to the marriage or to dispute his right to Charlotte's hand![52]

Now, clearly, the general description given by psychoanalysis cannot be expected to fit exactly any one case. Its applicability to the Mill-Taylor affair, as to any other, must be mainly suggestive. On Harriet's side, as we have seen, we are not very clear as to her motives, though there is no question that it is she who insists on keeping both John Taylor and John Stuart Mill attached to her. However, by not separating from her husband, and thus not being free to "marry" (i.e., live with) John Stuart Mill, Harriet could avoid the sexuality she now found repugnant. (By 1851, the situation, of course, was no longer threatening in the same way.) For Mill, similar factors seem to apply. Was it sheer accident that he fell in love with a married woman (and one with the same name as his mother)?[53] And accepted a triangular relationship that blocked not only marriage, but sexual consummation? The Oedipal explanation in these circumstances carries additional conviction.

Mill's strange behavior at his own marriage, when it finally occurred, adds fire to this conviction. The story is best told in his own lengthy letter to Harriet, written almost a month after the marriage:

My dearest wife/Though I am persuaded it is unnecessary for any practical purpose, it will be satisfactory to me to put into writing the explanation of an accidental circumstance connected with the registry of our marriage at the Superintendant Registrar's Office at Weymouth on the 21st of April 1851.—Our marriage by the Registrar Mr. Richards was perfectly regular, and was attested as such by Mr. Richards and by the Superintendant Registrar Mr. Dodson, in the presence of both of whom, as well as of the two witnesses, we signed the register. But I was not aware that it was necessary to sign my name at full length, thinking that as in most other legal documents, the proper signature was the ordinary one of the person signing: and my ordinary signature being J. S. Mill, I at first signed in that manner; but on being told by the Registrar that the name must be written at full length, I did the only thing which occurred to me and what I believe the Registrar suggested, that is, I filled in the remaining letters of my name. As there was not sufficient space for them, they were not only written very small and close, but not exactly in a line with the initials and the surname, and the signature consequently has an unusual appearance. The reason must be at once apparent to any one who sees it, as it is obvious that J. S. Mill was written first, and the remainder filled in afterwards. It is almost superfluous to say that this is not stated for your information—you being as well aware of it as myself, but in order that there may be a statement in existence of the manner in which the signature came to present this unusual appearance. It cannot possibly affect the legality of our marriage, which I have not the smallest doubt is as regular and valid as any marriage can be; but so long as it is possible that any doubt could for a moment suggest itself either to our own or to any other minds, I cannot feel at ease, and therefore, unpleasant as I know it must be to you, I do beg you to let us even now be married again, and this time in a church, so that hereafter no shadow of a doubt on the subject can ever arise. The process is no doubt disagreeable, but I have thought much and anxiously about it, and I have quite made up my mind that however annoying the fact, it is better to undergo the annoyance than to let the matt[er] remain as it is. Therefore I hope you will comply with my earnest wish—and the sooner it is done the better.[54]

Here, surely, we are in the presence of another version of the Schiller example. Mill's protest that he has "not the smallest doubt" rings hollow, especially as he then goes on to convey his doubt and anxiety vividly. With the Freudian conception in mind, we are even made suspicious that, on the unconscious level, Mill wished there *were* doubts about the marriage, so that the forbidden gratification, even if only partial, of his Oedipal wishes—still strong even at that remove of time—might not take place. However, there was no second marriage ceremony to allay Mill's doubts. We can guess at Harriet's no-nonsense reply to her spouse's apprehensions.

Shortly before the marriage itself, however, Harriet also exhibited rather strange and erratic behavior. She seems increasingly to have demonstrated affection for John Taylor, and, when she learned that he was dying, anger for John Stuart Mill. Her anguish at John Taylor's suffering and the inevitable loss ahead was real. Devotedly she nursed and cared for him. When John Stuart Mill innocently, but apparently inappropriately, wrote to her, she snapped back at him:

> You talk of my writing to you "at some odd time when a change of subject of thought may be rather a relief than otherwise"! *Odd time!* indeed you must be ignorant profoundly of all that *friendship* or *anxiety* means when you can use such pitiful narrow hearted expressions. The sentence appears to have come from the pen of one of the Miss Taylors. It is the puerility of thought & feeling of any utterly headless & heartless pattern of propriety old maid.
>
> As to "odd time" I *told* you that I have not a moment unfilled by things to be done when not actually standing by the bedside or supporting the invalid—& as to "change of subject of thought a relief"! Good God shd you think it a relief to think of somebody else some acquaintance or what not while I was dying? If so—but I will say no more about this—only after such a mode of feeling on your part I feel it sacrilegious to enter into any account of what I feel & suffer in this most dreadful & most melancholy & most piteous case—my heart is wrung with indignation & grief.[55]

Gradually, however, her tone moderated, or perhaps Mill had apologized abjectly. A month later, she was writing him that "The certainty of being really of the greatest use & quite indispensable to him (or to any one) gives me a quantity of strength and life—. . . ." The "any one" seems to have allowed room even for Mill, especially as she added, "Take care of yourself for the world's sake."[56] With the death of John Taylor on July 18, 1849, Harriet turned back to Mill and, uncharacteristically, asked his advice about funeral arrangements. Four days later, on July 22, she wrote to him:

> Of feelings & thoughts there is far too much to be said in a note—I must see you soon—it occurs to me that it might be well to go down to Walton to spend next Sunday & that in that case you might come down for the Sunday.[57]

Obviously their relationship had survived the end of the triangle. Henceforth it was to go on as a "Joint Production," but, at least on the conscious level, without the shadow of doubt cast by John Taylor.

The Character of Harriet

WHAT traits and qualities did Harriet bring to the "Joint Production"? Her own intellectual and literary accomplishments when she met John Stuart Mill were only incipient. Still, they were above the ordinary, especially for a twenty-three-year-old girl, mainly self-educated. Her anonymous contributions to the *Monthly Repository*—Mineka says a total of eleven and Hayek claims three poems, six book reviews, and one small essay—show a small but real talent.

After 1832 Harriet published nothing more on her own; her literary ambitions were sublimated in John Stuart Mill's writings. The 1851 *Westminster Review* article, "The Enfranchisement of Women," presumably grew out of the early exchange of views between Mill and Harriet on marriage and divorce. Mill, in his introduction to the reprint of the article in *Dissertations and Discussions*, claimed that all the papers in the two volumes were "joint productions of myself and of one whose loss, even in a merely intellectual point of view, can never be repaired or alleviated." The essay on women, however, was "hers in a peculiar sense, my share in it being little more than that of an editor and amanuensis." The hyperbole of Mill's feelings suggests the magnitude of her loss, but also (incorrectly as we shall see, 336–338) calls into doubt his judgment as to her role in "The Enfranchisement of Women."[58] In any case, it is clear from a glance at their correspondence that Mill and Harriet were constantly exchanging ideas on this subject, as well as on the material that would eventually become *On Liberty*, and that Harriet continuously served as his editor, if not more.

What would Harriet have gone on to without Mill? We have no way of knowing. Would Mill have done what he did without her? Again, we cannot be sure of the answer. My own view is that he would have done substantially the same things (though perhaps a little less publicly in the area of women's rights and socialism); Harriet was the consequence of the resolution of his 1826 crisis, worked out in the early 1830s, and not its cause. Having said this, however, I would also add that Harriet was a gifted woman in her own right, though not above the circle of emancipated women in which she placed herself.

While I do not discern signs of unusual genius—how many such individuals are there, of either sex?—she certainly exhibited marked traits of a superior intellect and a sensitive heart. For Mill she was a unique and flawless "fellow traveller"; he was the same for her. In this sense, theirs was not only a "peculiar" but also a perfect romance.

Other noteworthy though perhaps less praiseworthy traits in Harriet's character shed valuable light on the relationship between her and Mill. From the very first meeting, it seems, she exercised an almost hypnotic effect on him. He felt he had to obey her. As he wrote in July 1832, after she had declared they must not meet again, "She will be obeyed. . . . To obey her is for me a necessity." Of course, Mill, as we suggested in discussing his relationship to Lady Bentham, seemed able to respect only women who commanded him about. Harriet was unusually suited for this requirement. Her hypnotic quality is captured vividly by Carlyle's comment, echoing many other observers, about Harriet's "great dark eyes, that were flashing unutterable things" at Mill. Instances of Mill's immediate obedience to her are abounding. In 1849 he wrote: "The Political Economy packet came on Monday for which a thousand thanks. I have followed to the letter every recommendation." In 1854, giving the reasons pro and con why he should review Comte, he concludes: "You dearest one will tell me what your perfect judgment and your feeling decide." In the same year he wrote: "About the matter of my mother's inheritance, of course as your feeling is so directly contrary, mine is wrong, and I give it up entirely."[59]

Tennyson in his poem "The Princess" depicted the Victorian ideal of the man-woman relation:

> *Man for the field and woman for the hearth;*
> *Man for the sword and for the needle she;*
> *Man with the head, and woman with the heart;*
> *Man to command, and woman to obey;*
> *All else confusion.*

In this light, the Mill-Taylor relation was almost a parody of the patriarchal family, but with Harriet commanding and Mill obeying. A curious note jotted down by Mill in his account of a trip to Cornwall in 1832 symbolizes his entire attitude. He records the story of "St. Michael's Chair," which overhangs a precipice. It is

> a trial of courage to sit in it with your feet hanging down. . . . You cannot get into the chair from the inside, and must therefore perform at that height a complicated process of turning round both in getting in and out . . . the vulgar saying is that whoever sits in the chair ensures the prerogative of rule during the married state. I know not whether this be an ancient superstition, or a joke founded on the very probable supposition that a woman who has

boldness enough to brave so much apparent danger (it is chiefly *apparent*) will by exercise of the same boldness obtain (as it is ten chances to one she will deserve) the government of her husband. At the hazard of passing for cowards, and at the sacrifice of our prospects of conjugal preeminence, we [he and his male friends] unanimously forbore to fill St. Michael's Chair.[60]

Mill's words were prophetic. Conjugal male preeminence was not a prominent trait in his relation to Harriet. Rather, the reverse was true, and willed as such by Mill himself. He deprecated himself before Harriet, declaring: "I am but fit to be one wheel in an engine not to be the self moving engine itself—a real majestic intellect, not to say moral nature, like yours, I can only look up to and admire." Mill, who prided himself on independence, exhibits himself as heavily dependent on his loved one. She led, and he followed. She afforded him security. As Mill said: "What a sense of protection is given by the consciousness of being loved." She took care of him maternally, as we have already pointed out, and Mill laughingly acknowledged his helplessness when Harriet told him how to take care of himself during his trip to Greece in 1855:

You might well say that some other person's savoir faire was wanted "in addition" to mine—I could not help laughing when I read those words, as if I had any savoir faire at all. . . .[61]

In short, whereas Harriet took on the role of her own domineering father, coupling it with a maternal solicitude, Mill regressed in regard to her into the dependent, obedient role he had played as a child with his father. It was a psychologically perfect symbiotic relation.

There is no question as to where the strength lay. From the moment in 1833 when Harriet decided on the *ménage à trois*, even in the face of a hesitant John Stuart Mill, the roles were set. Harriet wrote him in those trying days:

Yes, these circumstances *do* require greater strength than any other—the greatest—that which you have, & which if you had not I should never have loved you, I should not love you now.

By quoting Mill's letter a few sentences later, however, Harriet showed that she was not really sure of her lover's strength. "It is false," she assures him (and herself), "that 'your strength is not equal to the circumstances in which you have placed' yourself." Then Harriet continues:

Would you let yourself "drift with the tide whether it flow or ebb" if in one case every wave took you further from me? Would you not put what strength you have into resisting it? Tell me—for if you would not, how happens it that you will to love me or any (?).[62]

Mill, as we know, rose to this occasion. But from then on it was clear who was really the firm, strong, decisive one, as a glance at their correspondence after 1833 confirms.

In addition to strength, there is some evidence that Harriet had her fair share of intellectual and social snobbery. In her early essay of 1832 she speaks of how Society "is a combination of the many weak, against the few strong; an association of the mentally listless to punish any manifestation of mental independence." Mill, of course, was willing to join her in this Nietzschean affirmation, and, as in sexual restraint, both felt themselves far above the multitude. Thus Mill responded by talking about "the best popular morality" as that "which attains this general pacification [of conflicting desires] with the least sacrifice of the higher natures." By the "higher natures," he explained, "I mean those characters who from the combination of natural & acquired advantages have the greatest capacity of feeling happiness, & of bestowing it." In turn, Harriet spoke of those who shared their views, especially on the women's question, as "always the best people."[63]

Harriet's snobbery, though apparently not John Stuart Mill's, went beyond the merely intellectual and became increasingly strident and social as time went on. In 1848, for example, she wrote John Taylor from Dover:

> This place is not at all attractive after the better places—it is thoroughly cockney in every sense, and not very pretty to compensate for the sort of company. I shall return to Walton on Monday. . . . There is really nothing to do in this stupid place.

At Walton, the sight of "a vulgar row of poor peoples' houses in front" makes Harriet decide to look for a new place to stay. Back in Dover, she wrote:

> I liked Dover better at the end of our stay than at first—the place is even pretty—and altho [sic] the people one sees here are decidedly vulgar, one is much less mixed up with them than at Ryde or Brighton because there is no particular promenade or promenade hour.[64]

Besides exhibiting occasional signs of social snobbery, Harriet has also been accused of being selfish. Thus, for example, Hugh Elliot refers to her as "selfish and somewhat conceited."[65] Mill took a completely opposite view, recalling in the *Autobiography*:

> Her unselfishness was not that of a taught system of duties, but of a heart which thoroughly identified itself with the feelings of others, often went to excess in consideration for them by imaginatively investing their feelings with the intensity of its own.[66]

It is, needless to say, difficult to decide in such a matter. There does seem to be one piece of implicit selfishness in her treatment of her daughter's ambition to be an actress. For years Harriet opposed this wish (partially, it seems, because of the "low" social status of the theatre), and only gave in upon condition that, as Hayek puts it, "great secrecy was to be observed." Thus:

> Helen Taylor not only assumed the name of "Miss Trevor", under which alone she was known during the eighteen months or two years of her stage career, but all possible precautions were taken to prevent the reason for her absence from home becoming known or her correspondence with her mother giving any clue to her identity.[67]

Here, it seems, snobbery and selfishness combined.

But the accusation of selfishness, as in Elliot, obviously goes beyond Harriet's behavior in relation to her daughter's career. It points at the consequences of her assertion of personal independence and the right to self-development on those around her. When Harriet entered into her affair with John Stuart Mill, did she identify with the feelings of her children? Did she consider, empathetically, its effect on her husband? The evidence suggests she did not. As a "higher nature" and one of the "best" people, Harriet (and John Stuart Mill?) placed herself above common, or popular, morality. "Unconscious fine natures," she wrote in an unpublished note, "are intensely egoist—at first unknowingly—I refer to their relations to others."[68] The line between the necessary assertion of one's own autonomy and aspirations to development and destructive egoism is a fine one; each reader must draw it for him or herself, and then pass judgment as to how it applies to John Stuart Mill and Harriet Taylor.

Children

WHAT WAS the effect of this "egoism" on Harriet's three children? Herbert, the oldest, who was six when Harriet first separated from her husband, seemed more and more to take his father's side. Of all the children he saw the least of his mother. At age seventeen he entered his father's business, eventually to succeed him. In 1849, when he was planning a trip to the New World, he did not even bother to write and inform his mother about it. Herbert, apparently, had taken the triangular relationship hard.

"Haji," the next boy, seems to have been caught in the middle. He appears to have seen more of his mother during holidays and in excursions to the seashore than did his brother. There is a small piece of evidence suggesting that Haji, during puberty, may have been resentful toward his mother. Harriet writes her husband in 1848 about the young man's cough, adding, "He systematically refuses to pay any attention to my advice on that subject—or on any other."[69] But this appears to describe a mere youthful attitude. In general, Haji seemed to accept John Stuart Mill as his substitute "father," and to side with Harriet rather than his real father. In 1849, for example, he was willing to have Mill use his influence to try to get him a post in the East India Company, though nothing came of it. When Mill and his mother married, Haji took their side in a bitter exchange with Mill's brother George, who thought it ill-advised. After their marriage in 1851, along with his sister Helen, Haji went to live with the Mills, staying with them for five years. The rest of his life is a story of failure, unto the second generation. He tried his hand as a farmer, and then temporarily joined a monastery in Rome. Finally, in 1860, he married, still without a career or even a job (he had, however, his father's inheritance). Packe observes:

> It was not to be a fortunate alliance. The wife died four years later. Of the three children, the eldest daughter became a religious fanatic, and went to live with pious friends in Canada. The son, Cyprian, joined the Navy, but soon afterwards went mad and had to be confined. While Mary, after nursing Haji for the last thirty years of his life, in the course of which time he almost starved them both to death by an excessive addiction to vegetarianism, performed the same function for her Aunt Helen, retrieving her from her querulous senility.[70]

We can only guess at how much of Haji's unfortunate life was owing to his parents' separation.

Both the Taylor boys, for better or for worse, married.[71] Helen, the girl, never did. Her whole life, with the possible exception of a few years, was spent with her mother, and then in taking her mother's place in caring for John Stuart Mill. Helen identified completely with Harriet. From the moment of her birth in 1832 she was her mother's constant companion. She never went to school, picking up her education from her mother and presumably from Mill's conversation, and her own strenuous reading in English, French, and German. At around fourteen or fifteen she became infatuated with the subject of religion, especially the Catholic, for Harriet had insisted on this possibility as part of her children's emotional development—a far cry from her husband's Unitarianism. Helen's other infatuation, as we have noted, was the theater, but it was not until she was twenty-four (in 1856) that, as "Miss Trevor," she was allowed by her mother to try out for the stage. With the death of Harriet two years later, Helen's dramatic career, never all that promising, came to an end as she decided to live with and take care of her stepfather at Avignon.

Helen had loved her mother dearly. Her letters are filled with such appellations as "my darling, my sweetest Mama," "my sweet one," "my precious Mama," repeated endlessly, and with phrases such as "that beautiful and loving face," "I send you a thousand Kisses . . . and I kiss your dear letters." One letter, of 1858, ends with a childlike "Mama, your Lily (I like Lily to be close to Mama)." After her mother's death, Helen transferred some of this affection to Mill, and took her mother's place with him. She also took on the psychological relation, it seems. Thus, by 1868 she was writing in her mother's tone, criticizing Mill's reply to Bradlaugh on the question of his religious beliefs:

> I do not know which I dislike most—the assertion that to be called an Atheist is calumny, that you are as much one as Gladstone is a Catholic, or that dignitaries of the Church of England have spoken for you ! ! ! Surely to use such arguments is to sacrifice all that it is worthwhile to be elected for. . . . I cannot tell you how ashamed I feel . . . makes me literally blush for you and must lower the opinion entertained of you by everyone who knows you and sees it.[72]

The peremptory tone sounds almost from the grave.

Mill worried about Helen sacrificing her life for him. As he wrote her in 1860:

> It would be very painful to me to think that I should always continue to be the only one, as I must necessarily fail you some day and I can never be at ease unless, either by means of persons or of pursuits you have some other resource besides me.

He need not have been concerned, as he put it, at "drying up her springs of life" in sacrifice to him. As early as 1844 Helen had been reading Mary Wollstonecraft and becoming imbued with the spirit of woman's emancipation. The next year she recorded her view of *Romeo and Juliet*:

> And what is this love which is to work such miracles? Admiration of one another's good looks! And then, just met, they "are already arranging how to be married! There's nature!" I do not believe that people do fall in love with one another after this fashion—and if they do at all I am sure it is not in the teeth of every possible tie which can bind weak or strong, bad or good people.

Clearly, the romantic Helen was highly skeptical about "romantic" love, and the possibility of falling in love at first sight. Her mother's romance with John Stuart Mill apparently did not occur to her. In any case, aside from a ludicrous if sad courtship by Theodor Gomperz (see p. 343), Helen seems not to have had or wanted any suitors. Reading Mrs. Inchbald, she noted in 1846 that "she seems to have had nevertheless in most matters a great deal of *good* sense. . . . She evidently took good care to keep herself out of marrying—she had had enough of that."[73] It appears that the unsuccessful marriage of Harriet and John Taylor may also have left its mark on their daughter. In any case, Helen's only love was her mother. Then, in part transference, she turned to John Stuart Mill. Together with him she invested much of her emotional life in fighting for the cause, in the image of which her mother had lived, and to the defense of which she had consecrated her life: women's rights.

Can Helen be considered John Stuart Mill's child as well as Harriet's? Only in a very special sense. As to children of their own, Mill and Harriet, at least in their correspondence, never raised this question, probably for obvious reasons. Did Mill miss having his "own" children? We know he liked playing with youngsters, but there is no evidence that he wished to generate any of his own. His work and writings apparently satisfied his urge for creativity. These, as he wrote to Robert Barclay Fox in 1842, were his "mental offspring."[74] By sublimating his generative powers in the creation of ideas and books, Mill had fulfilled his father's injunctions about birth control, even if in a way that James Mill had not directly envisaged.

A Family Quarrel

WHEN MILL gained Harriet in 1851, he not only did not acquire a family of his own (except perhaps for Helen), but lost his own natal family. Or rather, he deliberately broke with them. John Stuart Mill's contemporaries were shocked at his callous treatment of his mother and siblings, just as contemporaries of his father had been shocked at James Mill's behavior.

As in all such family squabbles, the details are obscure, disagreeable, and often only of interest to the participants. All observers agree that until 1851, when he left his mother's home, Mill was pleasant and friendly to his family. We must not let his omission of any mention of his mother in his *Autobiography* convince us that he had never cared for her. As Henry Solly, a classmate of his brother James, recalled, John Mill "was evidently very fond of his mother and sisters, and they of him; and he frequently manifested a sunny brightness and gaiety of heart and behavior which were singularly fascinating." Another friend, J. Compton, also remembers that "In those days [ca. 1830] John was devotedly attached to his mother and exuberant in his playful tokens of affection. Towards his father he was deferential. . . ."[75] The fondness persisted, it seems, all through his affair with Harriet.

But with the announcement of his intended marriage to Harriet, the scene of domestic bliss abruptly fades away. In Mill's eyes, his mother and his two unmarried sisters, Clara and Harriet [!], as Hayek puts it, "committed the never to be forgiven offence of not at once calling upon the lady whom until then they had not been allowed to know and to whom they had probably not even dared to allude."[76] Mill's feelings seemed to have changed overnight.

What had really happened? A letter from his married sister Mary Colman (now thirty-one, married for four years, and with a growing family of her own), is our most representative overt evidence. We quote at some length.

My dear John/ In thinking over the strange change which appears to have taken place in your character, which has taken place in your conduct towards your family, during the last six months whilst striving to feel indifferent towards you, I felt that even now I loved you too much for such indifference, and I trust that a worthier feeling had gained possession of me, when I determined honestly to write and remonstrate with you on your present conduct.

Mary then proceeds to talk about Mill's behavior to Clara.

I tell you now and one day you may know yourself that you have cast away a pearl of great price. And for what? What has she done, what has anyone done, what do you alledge [sic]. I can find nothing except that my mother did not call on your wife the day after you had announced your engagement, the propriety of which step as a matter of Etiquette remains to be settled. Anyhow however you know full well, that if you had only expressed a wish to my Mother on the subject anything would have been done. But even supposing that their behaviour had been bad which I cannot believe was that any justification for yours.

She ends her long and obviously hastily and emotionally written letter as follows:

One more word before I close this letter, which may be the last you ever receive from me; As regards the unfortunate estrangement which has taken place between you and George now for some years, and which was increased by some occurrences which took place when I last saw you at Kensington now more than a year ago, you may remember that I was the only one who told you you were unjust in your judgment of him, I knew George better than you did, and I told you you were mistaken. I had known George in his unreserved moments and from childhood and although we had never spoken on the subject I felt convinced that had you not yourself destroyed your influence over him, by showing at some time or other that you were ashamed of him and thought nothing of him, did not love him, you might have led him in any direction, so great was his respect for you as a man. But you must have shown him that you were afraid of his disgracing you. From such a sway he turned away, had you trusted him as a man, with a noble heart and as he deserved, you would never have had occasion to say he "never had a character".[77]

The brother George, for whom, according to Mary, Mill had failed to offer a loving "parental" model, also figured in the developing quarrel. Mill had not informed his younger brother, then in India, of his impending marriage. When he heard about it secondhand, George wrote a note to Harriet Taylor, now Mill, which, while not fulsome, seems harmless enough in its acknowledgment of the union. An accompanying letter to Haji (the two had been childhood chums), however, stirred up a tempest. Haji was indiscreet, or mischievous, enough to show the letter to his mother and his new stepfather. While we do not have that actual letter, we do have a subsequent one of George Mill to Haji which seems to supply the necessary information:

Believing that your mother would generally rather discourage than encourage the marriage of others I certainly was at first surprised to find her giving so deliberate an example of marriage in her own case; in which moreover there seemed to me less to be gained than in almost any marriage I could think of.[78]

George had touched a raw nerve. Harriet was livid, and it was in this mood that she wrote of George's lack of "good breeding" as a "family failing." John Stuart Mill also wrote a very astringent letter, castigating his brother's ill manners.

As for his mother, Mill never really broke fully and openly with her. However, he suggested in 1851 that she go live with his sister Wilhelmina in Germany, although she would not know the language. And, of course, he hurt her by his coldness to his sisters, and thus indirectly to her. As his sister Mary wrote him in 1854:

My Mother is very unhappy, because she thinks that she has not behaved well to your wife. She is constantly urging me to go to Blackheath and call on her, saying that it would please her very much, and nothing will direct her mind from this one point. She is still very weak, unable to stand, and thinks evidently that you are very angry with her and do not come to see her on that account.[79]

All in all, Mill, who was so generous to outsiders seemed rather heartless and insensitive to his own mother.

On June 15, 1854, Mill's mother died. As with his father, John Stuart Mill neither visited his mother during her last days, nor attended the funeral. (He was on the Continent, nursing his own health.) It was also around this time that he seems to have been writing the early draft of his *Autobiography*, with its paragraphs (left out in the published version) about his "unloving" mother and her effect on James Mill. To an outside observer it appears to be John Stuart Mill who was "unloving" in this relation, or rather, who was too threatened by an overloving mother to be able to reciprocate any longer, once married to Harriet. In Harriet (Taylor) he concentrated all his loving and positive feelings, ignoring thereby the life and death of his mother.

Sickness, Unto Death

ALTHOUGH John Stuart Mill seems to have tried to ignore the death of his mother, death, and the illnesses that preceded it, were a constant subject of his concern. His traumatic reaction to the death of Harriet, of course, brought to a head all the feelings on the subject accumulated over a long period of time.

A glance at John Stuart Mill's correspondence, especially his letters to Harriet, shows what an almost compulsive subject illness was. In this, of course, John Stuart Mill and Harriet were at one with their age. In nineteenth-century England a link seemed to have existed between the rapt attention to symptoms of illness and, for example, the public concern with sanitation and cleanliness. Under the omnipresent threat of cholera epidemics (the one in 1832 was massive) and the "white plague," i.e., consumption or TB, such concern is understandable. On the more private level, cleanliness was associated with "higher" things, and sex, for example, was seen as "dirty" and low-minded.

How did Mill and Harriet manifest these concerns? Starting with his mental crisis, an interest in illness was constant and abounding for Mill. His father's death heightened this concern. Characteristically, Mill was convinced that, at age thirty-three, he was already an old man of sorts, doomed to recurrent bouts of ill health. As he wrote a friend in 1839, "hardly anybody continues after my age to have the same vigorous health they had in early youth."[80] Mill's complaints, constantly reiterated in letters to his friends, family, and Harriet, range from a simple cold to carbuncles. The major illness, as we have already seen in detail, was recurring depression and melancholia. It was combined with the definite threat of consumption, which we shall analyze later at some length.

Harriet, too, was from the beginning of their romance frail and subject to illness. In her case, the consumption which was to kill her probably laid the basis for other, earlier difficulties. She did not, however, suffer from Mill's depression. Was she, instead, a victim of an hysterical episode, resulting in paralysis of her legs? What was the cause of the paralysis Harriet suffered in the 1840s? Bain, whom we have already quoted, referred to it as a "spinal injury." Hayek's account is as follows:

> She suffered for a time from some spinal injury suffered in a carriage accident which kept her for long on a sofa and for the rest of her life seems to have been the cause of a recurrent paralysis or at least partial lameness. But her illness seems rarely to have been an obstacle to her travelling, or rather seems to have provided the pretext for moving about restlessly most of the time.

In a footnote he adds:

> It occurred probably early in May 1842, when according to Helen Taylor's diary Mr. and Mrs. Taylor were thrown out of a carriage. Mrs. Taylor was certainly very ill during the following months.[81]

This should dispose of the matter. Harriet's paralysis was of physical origin, the result of an accident. There is only one problem with this explanation. It completely ignores a letter from John Stuart Mill to Sarah Austin (October 4, 1841) in which he informs her:

> Mrs. Taylor bids me tell you how one fine day (it was really not more than a week) she suddenly and with hardly any warning lost the use of her legs almost entirely—this was in June, and since, the little power of moving them that was left has become still less, in spite of all manner of remedies.[82]

While it is admittedly extraordinary that either Harriet Taylor or John Stuart Mill would want to tell Sarah Austin about this episode, it is even more extraordinary that Hayek and others have overlooked it. The paralysis in 1841 is clearly of psychological origin, or at least as clearly as such things can be established. Apparently there were no physical origins, and the "remedies" seem principally to be the traditional "baths" (Mill speaks of Harriet "trying Franzensbad").[83]

What could have triggered an hysterical reaction? Packe's account of what happened in September 1840, a year before Mill wrote his letter to Sarah Austin, is suggestive:

> Harriet, on returning from Brighton in the summer of 1840, was perhaps as well and happy as ever in her life; "we have had the most lovely season and

have enjoyed the sea thoroughly," she told Miss Fox, the daughter of W. J. Fox. But her good state did not continue. Her second visit to her family at Birksgate in September was not the amiable affair that it had been the year before. She fell foul of her sister Caroline, whom she suspected of monopolizing their mother, and of making a league with her brother Edward to rule everybody and everything. Caroline had by this time married her drunken lawyer, Arthur Ley, who had been since the death of the eldest brother Thomas a trustee of Harriet's marriage settlement. Harriet's profound dislike and distrust of him led to a quarrel lasting till her death, becoming more or less violent as Caroline was alternately an object of pity for being bullied by him, or of anger for defending him.[84]

If this, or something like it, is the "cause" of Harriet's delayed paralysis reaction—it would, of course, give her an excuse for not visiting Birksgate again, and we have already noted her feelings on that subject—then the psychological etiology would be not in terms of the classic seduction anxieties (Cf. Freud's "Dora, a Case of Hysteria"), but as a result of threatening aggressive impulses. We need not totally disregard the sexual, for the quarrel with Caroline over the mother is ultimately "sexual" in *its* origins (as we tried to suggest, p. 296), and certainly the anxiety and dismay over the "marriage" elements of the squabble could reasonably be expected to reawaken strong feelings on *that* general subject, itself also "sexually" based. (In fact, of course, the sexual is not itself disjoined from the aggressive impulses, although Freud tended to treat them rather too separately.) In any case, after 1841 Harriet's aggressive and hostile feelings appear to have manifested themselves increasingly in an ever more arrogant, hectoring tone toward Mill and all around her.

Thus a psychological explanation—hysteria—seems more plausible for Harriet's paralysis in 1841 than any purely physiological one. But then what of the "carriage accident"? To begin with, it occurred almost a year later than the original paralysis! The *post hoc* fallacy therefore applies. It may well be that Harriet used the occasion, probably unconsciously, to reinforce her complaint of paralysis, and Helen Taylor and John Stuart Mill's memories conveniently obliged later by forgetting the earlier manifestations of the disease. Freud's early work with hysterical paralysis constantly involved "carriage accidents," that is, railroad carriage mishaps, and only gradually and painstakingly did he discover that the resultant loss of mobility, for which no organic causes could be located, was of psychic origin. While we can never be absolutely sure in the case of Harriet's "spinal injury," the heavy suspicion is that it, too, was of psychic origin. It is regrettable, at least from our point of view, that Sigmund Freud was not available in 1841, instead of just hot baths!

However, it was not paralysis, hysterical or otherwise, that was Harriet's major complaint or the cause of her death. It was consumption, the characteristic disease of her age. In her own family, her eldest brother died of consumption in his twenties. Compared to the Mills, however, the Hardys were relatively exempt from the ravages of the "White Plague." James Mill had it, and died finally of his long-standing pulmonary phthisis. He seems to have passed it, or a tendency to it, on to John Stuart Mill, who was firmly convinced he would die of it, and to his other sons, Henry and George, both of whom did die of it.[85] In the circle surrounding both Harriet and John Stuart Mill, Eliza and Sarah Flower suffered from it, succumbing in the end to the wasting disease. So did John Sterling and Sterling's friend, Dr. Calvert. And Keats, Shelley, Chateaubriand, Schiller, Novalis, and Lawrence Sterne, to name a few more, also fell victim to it. Such famous names merely indicate the visibility of the disease, which, like the Black Plague, from whence it adapted its name, the "White Plague," swept huge numbers of "nameless" people in nineteenth-century Europe to their death.

Rene and Jean Dubos, in their fascinating book, *The White Plague*, give us the best description of the nature, rise, and spread of the disease, and especially of the "mood" created by it around the time of the Mills.[86] Tuberculosis, as they inform us, was a "social disease" which manifested itself almost exclusively in an urban setting, thereby giving ground to the widely held belief that susceptibility to it was increased by the artificialities of city life.

As the Dubos inform us: "A great outburst of the disease followed the Industrial Revolution. The epidemic became the White Plague, giving pallor to the dreariness of the mushrooming cities, and injecting its fever into the romantic moods of the age." It generally "struck hardest among young men and women in their prime, condemning many of them to early death"; Keats and Novalis were typical examples of such victims, and their cases helped foster the notion that sensitive natures fell victim to TB because of contact with a crude world.[87]

In general, consumption was thought mainly to afflict highly spiritual types whose sensitivity was manifested in their physical symptoms, especially noticeable in women: a transparent complexion, a hectic glow, and large, burning eyes. Such frail and delicate-looking women were given to fainting spells and to lying on couches. As one author wrote about his heroine, the disease made her body aspire to "become a spirit," to "move toward the supernatural of spirituality," and the disease itself was "an illness of the lofty and noble parts of the human beings." Consumption was seen as related to genius, and, as the

Dubos say, there was the belief "that the intelligently-gifted are the most likely to contract the disease, and furthermore that the same fire which wastes the body in consumption also makes the mind shine with a brighter light."[88]

Just as tuberculosis was connected to spirituality, so spirituality and spiritual natures were seen as psychically receptive to the disease. As the Dubos suggest:

> [Psychic reactions] also must be given an important place among the conditioning factors of disease . . . case after case in which some severe psychic disturbance, such as caused by an unhappy love affair, a family tragedy, or financial difficulties, is followed a few weeks or a few months later by an attack or a recurrence of tuberculosis.[89]

All in all, in the first half of the nineteenth century consumption was distinctly perceived as a refined, upper-class disease; only in the second half of the century was it recognized as the "great killer and breeder of destitution" among the laboring classes, thus losing much of its "fashionable" quality.[90] In 1830, however, it was clearly the psychosomatic counterpart of the "Spirit of the Age" and of many of the Age's aspirations, at least among the circle surrounding Harriet and John Stuart Mill. It seems unnecessary to spell out its applicability—its "spiritual" correspondence with "higher natures," its heightened emotionalism, its availability as a psychic response to emotional distress—to our two lovers. We need only be aware of consumption's existence as the prime context of illness in which nineteenth-century figures played out their lives.

Harriet Taylor was aware of her consumptive tendencies quite early, and as a result much of her traveling was to warmer climates. She tried, however, not to brood over the mounting disease. As she wrote her son Haji in 1849, "if a person thinks themselves consumptive the effect on the spirits has the utmost possible tendency to produce or to accelerate that fatal disease."[91] By 1854, however, her "power of positive thinking" was no longer enough to prevent a severe hemorrhage at Nice, of which she nearly died. Four years later, in 1858, the disease finally claimed her in Avignon. Starting out as her usual cough with fever, it suddenly got out of hand, and a few days later she was dead.

Mill, too, was convinced that he would die of the "family disease," as he calls it in his *Autobiography*. This conviction had grown upon him at least by 1840 when, attending his brother Henry in Falmouth as the latter lay dying of tuberculosis, he remarked to Caroline Fox, "I expect to die of consumption."[92]

In 1854, Mill, exhibiting apparent symptoms of tuberculosis, was sure that his time was approaching. While we can't help feeling that some of his symptoms were "sympathetic" manifestations brought on by Harriet's state, as symptoms they were all too real. In any case, in February 1854 Mill reported to Harriet that he was again (he had gone before in early January) consulting Dr. James Clark because of "the decided and unmistakable appearance of blood in the expectoration."[93] Though Clark assured him it was not TB, the symptoms grew worse. Finally, in March 1854, Clark admitted "that there is organic disease in the lungs and that he had known this all along."[94] Like Harriet, Clark appears to have believed in "positive" thinking. Once brought to acknowledge the existence of the disease, however, Clark prescribed cod-liver oil and stout clothing. Another doctor, Ramadge, prescribed that Mill breathe through a kind of metal trumpet, three times a day, for half an hour each time. Whether as a result of this treatment or for other reasons, the spread of the infection seemed halted, and Mill temporarily felt better.

Mill had begun to keep a diary on January 8, 1854 (lasting until April 15, 1854). Whether it was started under the premonition of death from tuberculosis is not certain, though it is probable. In any case, coinciding as it did with Mill's discovery of his tubercular condition, it affords us evidence of his state of mind at the time. On January 12, 1854, the same day as he wrote Harriet about his first consultation with Dr. Clark, Mill noted in his diary:

> There is hardly a more striking example of the worthlessness of posthumous reputation than the oblivion into which my father has fallen among the world at large.

On January 19:

> I feel bitterly how I have procrastinated in the sacred duty of fixing in writing, so that it may not die with me, everything that I have in my mind which is capable of assisting the destruction of error and prejudice and the growth of just feelings and true opinions.

A month later, on March 19:

> The belief in a life after death, without any probable surmise as to what it is to be, would be no consolation, but the very king of terrors. A journey into the entirely unknown—the thought is sufficient to strike with alarm the firmest heart.

On March 25:

> The only change I find in myself from a near view of probable death is that it makes me instinctively conservative. It makes me feel, not as I am ac-

customed—oh, for something better!—but oh, that we could be going on as we were before. Oh, that those I love could be spared the shock of a great change! And this feeling goes with me into politics and all other human affairs, when my reason does not studiously contend against and repress it.

And the last entry, on April 15:

The remedies for all our diseases will be discovered long after we are dead; and the world will be made a fit place to live in, after the death of most of those by whose exertions it will have been made so. It is to be hoped that those who live in those days will look back with sympathy to their known and unknown benefactors.[95]

Two themes run strongly through Mill's diary entries. The first is that he has not had time to finish the work that is his claim to immortality, the only life beyond death which he can face without terror. The second is that, in the face of death—of others, as well as his own—he becomes conservative, seeking to hold onto the dead person through retention of what he stood for. This latter feeling seems to relate to the lament for his father's departed glory, and suggests that Mill's mourning for his father's death necessarily involved for him a wish to resuscitate his father's work in a new form; he wished the same would be done for his own exertions on behalf of mankind.

Mill, however, was not to die yet. Although he suffered serious relapses, and "great and rapid wasting of flesh," he survived the death of his mother in June 1854, as we have noted, and went off for a tour of Brittany.[96] Here he spent all day in the open, walking extraordinary distances and enjoying himself immensely. Botany and walking seemed to be Mill's best cures. Resolved to continue his therapy, Mill again obtained leave from the East India Company in December 1854, and undertook an extensive tour of France, Italy, and Greece. Only in June 1855 did he rejoin Harriet (who had been too sick in December to accompany him) in Paris.

It is worth noting that John Stuart Mill and Harriet spent a good deal of time apart during their marriage—for example, six months in 1854–1855, while Mill was in France, Italy, and Greece, and a week's walking tour in the French Jura in August 1855, not to mention the frequent occasions when Mill had to be back at the East India Company offices while Harriet remained on the Continent. Health reasons, of course, accounted for a good deal of this. The pattern of their relationship explains the rest. Having established a spiritual companionship during the triangular days, maintained by letters and only short intervals together, they had grown accustomed to this mode of intercourse. After marriage it was only natural for the pattern of nineteen years to continue, reinforced as it was by Harriet's sickness and Mill's need to take walking tours as his cure.

The strenuous walking tours and mountain climbs—Mill's account of his Greek experiences, for example, is almost unbelievable for a man in his fifties, supposedly suffering from serious consumption—were most effective, for Mill lived on until 1873, when he was sixty-seven. Harriet was not so lucky, or perhaps so strong. Her death in 1858 came when she was only fifty. She and Mill had been married for seven short years.

On her death in Avignon, Mill reacted with extreme grief and extravagant mourning. This time, unlike the situation with his father and mother, he was on the spot. He was to stay there, with intervals of extended return to England and other journeys on the Continent, for the rest of his own life. Within a few weeks of Harriet's death he bought a small house overlooking the cemetery in the suburb of Saint-Veran of Avignon in which she was buried. He insisted on giving numerous sums of money to the Mayor and to the pastor of the local Protestant Church, as if in penance. To the doctor who had been summoned from Nice, but had arrived too late to save Harriet, Mill gave the extraordinary sum of £1000. Over Harriet's grave Mill had erected, at great expense, a monument of the finest Carrara marble, bearing a long inscription extolling the virtues of his beloved.[97]

Mill now ostentatiously dedicated the rest of his life to his dead wife. He would live, he declared, only to give expression to her ideas and to fulfill her ambitions to serve humanity. He had already pledged himself to do this in 1854, that other year of death and malady, when he wrote Harriet:

> I hope we shall live to write together "all we wish to leave written" to most of which your living is quite as essential than mine, for even if the wreck I should be could work on with undiminished faculties, my faculties at the best are not adequate to the highest subjects and have already done almost the best they are adequate to. Do not think darling that I should ever make this an excuse to myself for not doing my very best—if I survived you, and anything we much care about was not already fixed in writing you might depend on my attempting all of it and doing my very best to make it such as you would wish, for my only rule of life then would be what I thought you would wish as it now is what you tell me you wish.[98]

In 1858 he repeated his dedication, it seems, to all who would listen. In November 1858, announcing Harriet's death to W. T. Thornton, Mill declared: "The spring of my life is broken. But I shall best fulfill her wishes by not giving up the attempt to do something useful."[99] To Helen Taylor he wrote a few months later, about Montpellier:

I think it is a delightful place, and should have *felt* it delightful once. *Now*, the contrast with the change in my own life the reverse way, deepens the melancholy which is the ground plan of life and is always in the depths whatever else may be on the surface. . . . But I would not wish it otherwise and would rather seek than avoid any place or circumstance that makes it more so. . . .

And to Alexander Bain, in early 1860, he confessed:

My principal anxiety is to do as exactly as I am able what would have been done if I had still my darling to guide me, not only for the reasons which exist in all cases, but for the special one that all relations with persons should shew her to be as much present as before.[100]

Do we not sense a pattern in all of this? Mill deals with his guilty feelings at having survived Harriet, his great love, in a number of ways: by extravagant signs of his grief, such as large outlays of money and profuse encomiums to her memory; by a denial that, in fact, she is dead; and by a dedication of his own life to her, i.e., by "giving up" his own life as such. Moreover, by emphasizing the "melancholy" which is the ground plan of his life, Mill makes visible the manner in which his mourning will be carried out (and we, of course, recall Freud's "Mourning and Melancholia").

Almost all of Mill's friends were shocked by the exaggerated nature of his lamentations for Harriet and his hyperbolic praise of the virtues and abilities of his dead wife. From our vantage point, perhaps, we can see that Mill's behavior was not so much foolish as therapeutic. He had not mourned openly at the death of his father and mother, or given vent to any of the powerful emotions within him, and had suffered inside accordingly. With Harriet he allowed himself to wail and bewail in romantic and sublime fashion. In mourning Harriet in this fashion, he was at last able to mourn his parents.

In the Fullness of Time

AFTER Harriet Taylor Mill's death in 1858, John Stuart Mill still had fifteen years of a full life ahead of him. Though his mind was now completely formed and subject to no new "revolutions," many of his best productions were yet to come: *On Liberty* (1859); *Considera-*

tions on Representative Government (1861); *Utilitarianism* (1861–1863); *An Examination of Sir William Hamilton's Philosophy* (1865); *Auguste Comte and Positivism* (1865); and *The Subjection of Women* (written in 1861; published in 1869). In 1869 he also edited and published his father's *Analysis of the Phenomena of the Human Mind.* Published posthumously were his *Autobiography* (1873); *Three Essays on Religion* (1874); and *Chapters on Socialism* (1879; 1891). Articles kept flowing in a steady stream, and many of Mill's best pieces date from after 1858. This is hardly the record of a man who had exhausted his creative powers, or had lost belief in his purpose in life.

At the same time, John Stuart Mill's contribution to public life broadened. With his resignation from Indian affairs at the time of the dissolution of the Company in 1858, Mill was free for other tasks. In 1865 he was elected to Parliament on his own terms, for he had refused, openly and as a matter of principle before the election, to be bound by his constituency's specific wishes, or to run or pay for his own campaign. For three years he served in an independent and upright manner, even introducing a bill for woman's suffrage to the consternation of many of his colleagues and followers, until finally his independent and "amateur" stance was too much for his own constituency and they refused him reelection.

Parliament was not Mill's only involvement with the political arena during this time. Throughout the course of the American Civil War he stated publicly and resolutely his position against the South and slavery, and propagated his views vigorously. When the Governor Eyre case broke into the open, Mill took his stand with the Committee to bring him to trial. Elected Rector of St. Andrews in 1866, he seized the occasion of his Inaugural Address to make a major pronouncement on the existing state of education. When a society for the Representation of Women was formed in London, Mill assumed an active part. Indeed, his letters, for example, to Croom Robertson, the secretary, show a certain arrogant proprietorship of the movement, with Mill strongly wishing to dissociate *his* society from the more militant and radical women's groups wishing to coalesce with it. These same letters also show Mill's "practicality," as when he lectures Robertson on the virtue of having "a pretty face" speaking at meetings, to prove to women themselves that the proponents of women's rights are not removed from the rest of their sex by reason of physical disadvantage.

With all his writings and activities, Mill still had time for numerous and lengthy travels, and walking and botanizing trips. As we noted earlier, his consumptive symptoms did not prevent him from leading a vigorous and active physical existence, including a second six-month visit to Greece (this time accompanied by his stepdaughter Helen). So, too, his emotional life seems to have reached a satisfactory plateau, for in those latter years he seems to have made peace with his surviving family, especially his sister Mary. We have the impression, then, of a man who had not been laid low by the death of his beloved Harriet, but rather had gone on freely and even happily—certainly contentedly—with the fulfillment of their joint purposes. His death in May 1873, a few days after a fifteen-mile walk that brought on an unexpected illness, was serene. Greeting death in dignified and patient fashion, we are told that just before the end Mill murmured, half delirious: "You know that I have done my work."[101] That work, as we all know, did not die with him, but took on an independent existence.

13

Sex and Sensibility

A Domestic Revolution

IN 1854, believing that he and perhaps Harriet were about to die, Mill, as we have seen, began his short-lived diary, itself an effort to achieve some sort of continuing "life" in the future. The diary entry of March 26 reflects his mood:

As I probably shall have no opportunity of writing out at length my ideas on this and other matters, I am anxious to leave on record at least in this place my deliberate opinion that any great improvement in human life is not to be looked for so long as the animal instinct of sex occupies the absurdly disproportionate place it does therein; and that to correct this evil two things are required, both of them desirable for other reasons, viz., firstly, that women should cease to be set apart for this function, and should be admitted to all other duties and occupations on a par with men; secondly, that what any persons may freely do with respect to sexual relations should be deemed to be an unimportant and purely private matter, which concerns no one but themselves. If children are the result, then indeed commences a set of important duties towards the children, which society should enforce upon the parents much more strictly than it now does.[1]

In fact, as we know, Mill's life was spared, and he went on to write "The Subjection of Women" (published 1864), giving therein his fully considered views on the "absurdly disproportionate" subject involving "the *animal* [italics added] instinct of sex."

Mill, in his more perceptive moments, realized that sex, or at least the relations of the sexes, was one of the two or three most fundamental problems for human thought and action. Frequently his vision was obscured by his resentment at the Victorian arrangement of sexual relations, leading him to denigrate the whole subject as attracting disproportionate attention. We, however, must not be misled by his statement into overlooking Mill's contribution to a basic reappraisal of sex. The true Mill speaks out in the House of Commons, May 20, 1867, when he points out: "We talk of the political revolutions of the world, but we do not pay sufficient attention to the fact that there has taken place among us a silent domestic revolution. [The parliamentary record at this point has "Hear" from the listeners.]"[2]

What was the nature of this "domestic revolution"? According to Mill, "Men and women for the first time in history are really companions." In the past, "Their lives were apart . . . separate both in their amusements and in their serious occupations. The man spent his hours of leisure among men—with men alone did he converse on any serious subject; the wife was either a play thing or an upper servant." Now, Mill announces sanguinely, "All this among the educated classes is changing." This change is a prerequisite for any further progress of the human race. As Mill puts it in a letter of December 1868 to a Russian correspondent, who asked him his views on higher education for women:

> The equal advent of both sexes to intellectual culture is important not only to women, which is assuredly a sufficient recommendation, but also to universal civilization. I am profoundly convinced that the moral and intellectual progress of the male sex runs a great risk of stopping, if not receding, as long as that of the women remains behind, and that, not only because nothing can replace the mother for the education of the child, but also, because the influence upon man himself of the character and ideas of the companion of his life cannot be insignificant; women must either push him forward or hold him back.[3]

In taking this position, Mill was striking at the whole code of masculinity of his time, and at the notions of duty and empire for which the code served as an underpinning. Here also he at last found himself in direct opposition to his father. Thus the "domestic revolution" was, at this point, revolutionary in two senses.

It is my view that Mill was able to take this revolutionary position for two major reasons: one was mainly personal, and the other intellectual. On the personal level, it was his acknowledgment of his own bisexuality (which he saw as characterizing all superior persons), which allowed him not to fear the "womanly" in himself, or the "masculine" in women. Moreover, whereas other men, such as Freud, could not see the woman as a competitor without thereby also seeing her as malelike and "unmotherly," Mill, because of his bisexuality, and *because he had also come, tragically, to view his own mother as unloving and thus "unmotherly,"* was under no such inhibiting compulsion. A "masculine" woman competing with Mill was not betraying her "maternal" qualities; rather, in his strange psychological underworld, she was fulfilling them.

On the intellectual level, the explanation is simpler. Mill's fundamental methodological position in the social sciences freed him to look at women's character in a fresh light. As a "progressive historicist," if we may coin the term, Mill was aware that statements about "laws" of human nature and society were, in general, merely provisional and time-bound. We cannot tell, he insists, what women are *really like*, or *can be*, from what they are under the present circumstances. The "feminine" nature of woman is not necessarily a "universal and absolute truth," and the present relationship of the sexes is not "immutable." Almost alone among the great thinkers of his time, Mill was able to free himself from the dominance of the "present arrangements" and to speculate freely on what was "nature" and what "nurture" in the formation of the sexes.

Many observers tend to give Harriet Taylor most of the credit for freeing Mill from the typical male presumptions of his time. I believe otherwise. While giving Harriet her due—she undoubtedly stimulated him, and helped push him to a public announcement of his views—I think the seeds of Mill's position were sown much earlier, in his natal family. *The* woman who was "subjected" and needed to be "emancipated," even if against her own desires, was Mill's mother, the wife of James Mill. That emancipation was the real, sublimated object of Mill's Oedipal victory. In my interpretation, Mill had conquered his father, not in order to have his mother for himself as an "upper servant," but to free her and place her beside himself as an equal. In his *Autobiography* Mill gives support to my general view, at least as it applies to Harriet Taylor's role in his "mental growth":

> It might be supposed, for instance, that my strong convictions on the complete equality in all legal, political, social and domestic relations, which ought to exist between men and women, may have been adopted or learnt from her. This was so far from being the fact, that those convictions were among the earliest results of the application of my mind to political subjects, and the strength with which I held them was, as I believe, more than anything else, the originating cause of the interest she felt in me. What is true is, that until I knew her, the opinion was in my mind, little more than an abstract principle.[4]

Our only disagreement with Mill is in his characterization of his opinion as merely an "abstract principle." In our view it was his most fundamentally rooted emotional and psychological commitment. Together, his conscious and unconscious "mental" development pushed him into becoming the foremost champion of women's rights in the nineteenth century.

Origins

THE WOMEN'S RIGHTS idea and movement did not emerge full-blown from Mill's forehead, as Minerva did from Jove's. It had a history behind it, and we ought to say something about that history in order to provide a context for Mill's contribution. Needless to say, we are offering only a sketchy account.

One strand in that history, in Western Europe, came from within religious development—specifically, new attitudes toward the woman within Protestantism. The Protestant Reformation itself, of course, was highly male-oriented. Luther, in breaking with the Pope in Rome and eventually marrying a nun, was thinking of "freedom" for himself, and not for his wife-to-be. Henry VIII, in England, was similarly preoccupied. Yet out of their actions came an unexpected development, expressing itself in the Protestant sects that broke with the official, patriarchal church hierarchies. Thus, while the Puritans maintained the patriarchal family in which the wife was an inferior, they modified it by their conception of marital love (which we have already mentioned as intensifying affective ties; see p. 160). They also raised woman's status by

> their exalted conception of family life, their protests against wife-beating and the double standard of sexual morality, and their denunciation of the churching of women, with its origin in the primitive view of woman as shameful and unclean. . . .

But it was the English Civil War, as Keith Thomas informs us, that worked a major shift. All the separatists who flourished during the war—the Brownists, Independents, Baptists, Millenarians, Quakers, Seekers, Ranters—"laid great emphasis upon the spiritual equality of the two sexes." The Quakers especially placed great stress on the spiritual rights of women, and "All the Friends were allowed to speak and prophecy on a basis of complete equality, for the Inner Light knew no barriers of sex."[5] Some of the sects, at least as viewed by their enemies, were reputed to hold advanced views on marriage and divorce.

But it was only spiritual equality that was claimed and granted; the Quaker family itself remained notoriously patriarchal. Moreover, while the sectarian limitation of the father-husband's authority in the sphere of conscience had implicit political consequences, they were not drawn at the time, and, indeed, did not appear until the late eighteenth century, when the fight was resumed. As Thomas concludes:

> Future feminist's movements were to base their arguments less upon any renewed assertion of women's spiritual equality than upon natural right and a denial of any intellectual differences between the sexes.[6]

It was the French Revolution that, by its espousal of natural rights, inadvertently opened the way to women's claim to equality. The Revolution itself, though women played an important role in it, was not made for them or in their name. The Declaration of the Rights of Man and the Citizen meant exactly that; women were not given the full rights of citizens. Yet the assertion of natural rights was extended, at least in theory, in two directions that had profound consequences for what Mill called "the animal instinct of sexuality." The names of the Marquis de Sade and of Mary Wollstonecraft symbolize the two developments, which seem, at first glance at least, to go in opposite directions.

The Marquis de Sade has become a notorious synonym for sexual perversion. Indeed, "sadism" is a common term for a particular form of sexual gratification. We tend to forget that, in his mad way, the Marquis saw himself as fighting in the sexual realm for the same natural "liberty" and "freedom" that the French Revolutionaries were claiming in the political domain. Thus, for example, in his *Philosophy in the Bedroom* (1795) he advised:

> It is absurd to say that immediately a girl is weaned she must continue the victim of her parents' will in order to remain thus to her dying day. It is not in this age of preoccupation with the rights of man and general concern for liberties that girls ought to continue to believe themselves their families' slaves, when it is clearly established that these families' power over them is totally illusory.[7]

Similarly, in a semiparody of John Stuart Mill's future statements on the nature-nurture dilemma, de Sade remarks perceptively how the world has stupidly confused "social institutions for Nature's divine ordinations." Clearly, we must free ourselves from the former, though in de Sade's sexual revolution, it appears, we are born not so much for liberty as we are "born for libertinage."[8]

What de Sade did, along with his encouragements to perversity (and, surely, much of the world of prostitution and pornography was a world he helped to make), was to shake preconceived notions about sexuality and the "natural" relations of the sexes, and to insist on the absolute equality of right, sexually, of the two sexes.[9] He made the hidden "animalities" of man—and woman—a public matter (in spite of censorship), and asked in a manner that could not be overlooked why our "natural" impulses were to be treated by society in such an "unnatural" way. His shocking, bawdy, half-demented language must not obscure the fact that de Sade was also raising fundamental ethical and psychological questions about man's nature.[10] He thus helped contribute to the general atmosphere in which a "domestic revolution" might take place.

De Sade's specific version of that revolution, needless to say, was not the one envisioned by Mary Wollstonecraft, although both drew their vision from the emancipatory spirit of the French Revolution. In fact, Wollstonecraft first emerged as a significant writer with her reply to Burke's *Reflections on the French Revolution.* Entitling her book *A Vindication of the Rights of Men*, she almost immediately followed it with another, called *A Vindication of the Rights of Woman*, thereby making clear the connection for her of the democratic and domestic revolutions.

The second *Vindication* is a melange of ideas, reflecting its author's unsystematic self-education.[11] Wollstonecraft starts from a Lockean assumption: Political rights are based on the individual's possession of reason. The crucial question, therefore, is "Do women have reason?" and the question quickly answers itself in the affirmative. It follows, of course, that, having reason, women should have political and sexual rights. Instead, as Wollstonecraft has shown, they are in political and sexual servitude, with their servitude used as proof that they do not have sufficient reason! "Brutal force," the author tells us in an inchoate sentence, "has hitherto governed the world," and brutal force becomes enshrined in prescription: "There seems to be an indolent propensity in man to make prescription always take place of reason, and to place every duty on an arbitrary foundation. The rights of kings are deduced in a direct line from the King of Kings; and that of parents from our first parent." In fact, as Wollstonecraft perceives, slavery to parents prepares the way for obedience to kings, "for the absurd duty, too often inculcated, of obeying a parent only on account of his being a parent, shackles the mind, and prepares it for a slavish submission to any power but reason." Such a statement recalls the similar one by de Sade, and anticipates the Freudian view on the origins of political authority. Wollstonecraft's insight into the nature of parental rule also seems to foreshadow Freud when she remarks:

"Parental affection is perhaps the blindest modification of perverse self-love. . . . [and] indeed, in many minds, is but a pretext to tyrannize where it can be done with impunity."[12]

How can women break out of their unjust servitude? By correct education, is Wollstonecraft's answer. Hitherto women have been badly educated—she compares them to aristocrats—and as a result lack strength of mind. Wollstonecraft's model is the middle class and its exertions. In terms that would delight James Mill, she notices how: "Abilities and virtues are absolutely necessary to raise men from the middle rank of life into notice; and the natural consequence is notorious, the middle rank contains most virtue and abilities."[13] The message is clear: Women must emulate the middle class attitudes and attributes if they wish to rise. In sum, as we can see, Wollstonecraft was very bourgeois in her attitudes. In this regard she symbolized the fact that, just as the French Revolution was a "middle-class" revolution, so the "domestic revolution" of the late eighteenth century had also to be middle class in its ideas and aspirations.

Milieu

THE INSPIRATION of the French Revolution as a source of sexual freedom and equality, after finding varied expression in Wollstonecraft and de Sade, dwindled as the Revolution turned conservative. The Code Napoleon, if anything, gave a diminished status to women and provided for increased ascendancy of the father within the family. In the Restoration that followed, the battle of the sexes continued and grew in heightened fashion, even if that of the armies ceased.

Only the romantics, with their stress on self-development and self-expression, and Fourier and the Saint-Simonians, fed directly into the gathering stream of woman's desire for emancipation. Fourier especially, in his notions as to how sex and economics were linked, anticipated Freud. In his willingness to give free play to sexual passions, Fourier seems a kind of de Sade without sadism; his desired outcome appears a kind of communal harmony instead of an individualized libertinage. As for the Saint-Simonians, we need only quote John Stuart Mill's comment in his *Autobiography* to see what effect their views on the relations of the sexes had upon him:

> I honoured them above all for the boldness & freedom from prejudice with which they treated the subject of family, the most important of any, &

needing more fundamental alterations than any other, but which scarcely any reformer has the courage to touch. In proclaiming the perfect equality of men and women, & an entirely new order of things in regard to their relations with one another, the St. Simonians in common with Owen & Fourier have entitled themselves to the grateful remembrance of all future generations.[14]

As we mentioned earlier, the changed view of woman's role and nature could be viewed as beginning to emanate from Protestantism and the sects that emerged from it. The religious impulse in this direction appears to have surfaced again in the 1830s, at least in England, in the Unitarian movement. Mary Wollstonecraft herself had been a Unitarian. Now, thirty years or so later, the Unitarian circle to which Harriet Taylor belonged took up the cause and advanced "radical" views on marriage and divorce, the right of women to vote, and female legal disabilities (for example, not being able to own property when married). Such views, of course, were as much political as religious, and we have already seen how W. J. Fox was prototypic in his evolution from the religious to the political sphere. His link with Utilitarianism makes this connection even more evident, especially if we remember that the *Westminster Review*, Bentham's journal, had been a champion of women's rights almost from its inception.

In such a milieu John Stuart Mill could feel relatively at home. He could see himself as fulfilling certain Utilitarian aims, rather than destroying them. There is also a strange way in which "free love" could be perceived as a counterpart to "free trade." Free love, in this context, did not mean license and libertinage. Rather, it meant the self-regulated but free expression of the "liberal" personality in its sexual relations, unrestrained in any artificial way by society. Free love is not a term that John Stuart Mill used, but the idea is one that would not have been uncongenial to him.[15]

Along with novel ideas about the relations of the sexes, the middle of the nineteenth century saw efforts at legal emancipation and at organization of an actual woman's movement. It was in America that the Women's Movement was first inaugurated, with the Seneca Falls convention of July 1848. The "Statement of Sentiments" composed there harked back not to the French Revolution but, as might be expected in this case, to the American Revolution, and offered a paraphrase of the Declaration of Independence. The real inspiration and impetus, however, was provided by the antislavery movement; indeed, the leaders of the Seneca Falls meeting had been involved with the World Anti-Slavery Convention held in London in 1840 (in fact, they had been excluded from the meeting, which further fueled their ire).

As we shall see, the frequent comparison of women's slavery with Negro slavery was not mere metaphor but ran deep in the history of the woman's movement.

This was the atmosphere of ideas and action in which Mill and Harriet developed their ideas on the desirable relations of the sexes. Laws and social regulations played their part, along with the ideas and values promulgated by Wollstonecraft, the Romantics, the Saint-Simonians, and others, in influencing their conceptions in this area. So, too, did their personal attitudes and feelings toward sex and sexual intercourse. It is only in the light of the confluence of all these factors that we can seek to understand the meaning and significance of their writings on that most momentous of all events, the "domestic revolution."

Essays on Women

WHEN FREUD declared that Mill was one of those who knew least about women, he was basing his judgment on "The Enfranchisement of Women," which he had translated for Theodore Gomperz's collected edition of Mill's works in German. There seems good evidence that much, indeed most, of this article was written by Harriet Taylor, rather than Mill. We are thus faced with the possibility and the paradox that Freud may have been condemning a woman's knowledge of her own sex, rather than a man's. However, this consequence would follow only if Mill's views and those of Harriet Taylor's were in fact distinct.

Even before the "Enfranchisement," Mill and Harriet had written to each other on the women's question. In 1832, as we have already noted, they had exchanged views on marriage and divorce. The existence of these drafts allows one scholar, Alice Rossi, to make a strong case for Harriet as the major author of the 1851 paper; my own reading of the "Enfranchisement" supports her.[16] Internal evidence, stylistic and otherwise, suggests that much of the article, especially the middle parts, came from Harriet's pen. (A computer analysis of Mill's and Harriet's ways of writing might settle the issue.) In any case, the question of the differences between Harriet and Mill ought not to obscure the much greater similarities of view that they shared, worked out over a long period of time. It is a similarity in view that was, as Mill tells us, arrived at independently by each. Without Mill, however, it is doubtful that Harriet would either have written for publication in a journal such as *The Westminster Review*, or been featured in its pages. John Stuart Mill, with his reputation already great and secure, could obtain a significant hearing for advanced views on the women's question. Indeed, it was not so much the originality of his ideas as the fact that John Stuart Mill was promulgating them that made the "Emancipation" and especially *The Subjection of Women* the landmarks they became.

Before dealing directly with those two works, we should refer briefly to Mill's earlier expressions on the subject. His 1832 manuscript essay for Harriet contains two points worth our special attention. The first is Mill's defense of the free exercise of impulse and will on the part of "higher natures," such as Harriet. For such beings, popular morality stands aside. He apostasizes:

> If all resembled you, my lovely friend, it would be idle to prescribe rules for them: By following their own impulses under the guidance of their own judgment, they would find more happiness, and would confer more, than by obeying any moral principles or maxims whatever.

Of course, by "impulses" Mill does not mean sensuality, which he completely scorns. What he really means is that such a person "in case of a strong passion conceived by one of them for a third person" should be free to follow that passion without restraint by popular morality. It also happens that "the highest natures are of course impassioned natures," and therefore galled most by a marriage bond not tied together by continuing affection.[17] Reading all this, we cannot help but feel that Mill, in this particular aspect of the women's question, is indulging in a bit of special pleading brought on by his personal involvement with Harriet in 1832.

The other point of interest in the 1832 manuscript is more briefly noted. Under the intellectual influence of the Saint-Simonians, it was only natural for Mill to think in terms of stages of progress. Instead of mankind, he thought here, however, of womankind. The first stage, Mill tells us, was when women were slaves. The second was when they secured a more "permanent hold upon their masters," i.e., legal marriage. This, however, an advance from slavery per se, was itself only a new form of slavery. "In the progress of civilization," Mill announces, "the time has come when women may aspire to something more than to find a protector."[18] Divorce, embodying true equality at last, is the step ahead.

The first few paragraphs of the "Enfranchisement," presumably Mill's, take up a similar theme foreshadowing much of the polemics of "Sexual Politics" of the future. It is that women's emancipation is on a footing with Negro emancipation: women, by analogy with Negroes, are slaves. The next argument to be noticed, and this is presumably Harriet's (though Mill allowed it to appear under his name), is that women should be allowed to swell the "crowd of competitors" for all sorts of civil and political positions. It is this assertion that obviously caught Freud's eye and aroused his ire against Mill.

The last argument we wish to discuss has a longer chain of reasoning attached to it. The origin of women's subjection, we are told, is in physical force. Man, as the stronger being, simply conquered them. (Interestingly enough, in his 1832 manuscript Mill had said of man's superior bodily strength, "even that admits of doubt.") This alleged strength then becomes the prescribed virtue for men, and the "negative identity," to use modern parlance, for women. In the words of the "Enfranchisement," "self-will and self-assertion form the type of what are designated as manly virtues, while abnegation of self, patience, resignation, and submission to power . . . have been stamped by general consent as pre-eminently the duties and graces required of women."[19]

The discussion then takes an unexpected turn. According to the "Enfranchisement," improvement in the moral sentiments of mankind has led, "for the first time in the world," to a situation in which "men and women are really companions." Unfortunately, while this would be:

> A most beneficial change, if the companionship were between equals; but being between unequals, it produces, what good observers have noticed, though without perceiving its cause, a progressive deterioration among men in what had hitherto been considered the masculine excellences. Those who are so careful that women should not become men, do not see that men are becoming, what they have decided that women should be—are falling into the feebleness which they have so long cultivated in their companions. Those who are associated in their lives, tend to become assimilated in character.
>
> In the present closeness of association between the sexes, men cannot retain manliness unless women acquire it.

This flanking attack on male power, in terms of the very virtue—strength—most prized by men, is clever, though chauvinistic. The "Enfranchisement" goes on to hold out the ideal of companionate marriage: the union of "a strong-minded man and a strong-minded woman." Behind even this union, however, is a hidden threat. In a trial of strength, once equality prevails, women will turn out to be the stronger. This is implicit in the otherwise innocuous passage in which we are told that "Women, in their present physical and moral state" have the "stronger impulses."[20] Is this last the voice of Mill or of Harriet? It could be either or of both. What is striking is that both based the argument for woman's emancipation on a glorification of strength, rather than on an acknowledgment of virtues implicit in abnegation of self, patience, and so on, the so-called "feminine" virtues. For the Mill who extolled bisexuality, this seems an uncharacteristic conclusion; we are forced to believe that it is primarily the voice of Harriet Taylor speaking.

With *The Subjection of Women*, it is definitely Mill's voice we hear, though, of course, always with the possibility that it is echoing Harriet's. Mill wrote the first draft of his treatise in 1860 in Avignon, revised it there in 1868, and published it in 1869. On its publication it became the beacon by which the women's movement henceforth lighted its path.

Mill begins by reiterating the view expressed in his *Autobiography* (not yet published, of course) that inequality of the sexes is not only wrong in itself, but "one of the chief hindrances to human improvement."[21] Thus, from the outset Mill attempts to place his views on the women's question in the context of his entire view as to the history and future progress of the human race. The women's question is not just a problem for women.

Then follows a curious admission that opinions rooted in intense feelings, as is the women's rights question, are the least amenable to reasoned argument. Mill's psychological insight here is sharp, and logically leads him to a less than sanguine view of the short-range possibilities for change. However, Mill does not allow himself to take such a view. Instead he attacks the nineteenth-century glorification of the unreasoning elements in human nature:

> It is one of the characteristic prejudices of the reaction of the nineteenth century against the eighteenth, to accord to the unreasoning elements in human nature the infallibility which the eighteenth century is supposed to have ascribed to the reasoning elements. For the apotheosis of Reason we have substituted that of Instinct; and we call everything instinct which we find in ourselves and for which we cannot trace any rational foundation. This idolatry, infinitely more degrading than the other, and the most pernicious of the false worships of the present day, of all of which it is now the main support, will probably hold its ground until it gives way before a sound psychology, laying bare the real root of much that is bowed down to as the intention of Nature and the ordinance of God.[22]

We seem almost to hear a return to the eighteenth century, and to James Mill, now enlisted in the service of a new and wider cause.

Mill next moves to a restatement of the analogy of women's slavery to Negro slavery, both rooted in the law of the strongest. Without mentioning Darwin, Mill seems to be directing his fire this time against Social Darwinism: "Conquering races hold it to be Nature's own dictate that the conquered should obey the conquerors, or, as they euphoniously paraphrase it, that the feebler and more unwarlike races should submit to the braver and manlier." The resulting relationship is then justified as "natural," and any attempted changes as "unnatural"; but, as Mill scathingly points out, "unnatural generally means only uncustomary." The worst part of women's slavery, however, in contrast to Negro slavery (and here I think Mill underestimates the applicability of his remarks to Negro servitude), is that "Men do not want solely the obedience of women, they want their sentiments."[23] Thus they seek to brainwash them into believing their state of servitude a desirable one, and argue that women voluntarily wish to be as they are.

At this point, Mill declares that the peculiar quality of the modern world is that we are no longer born into customary roles or fixed social positions. Women are the only remaining exceptions to this radical assertion of individualism. Their "nature," too, is not a fixed quality, requiring them to remain in an assigned, customary niche. All "human character" is shaped by external influences, and both history and Associationalist psychology agree in confirming this fact. Thus, the interplay of woman's "nature" and the circumstances shaping its development is a prime subject of a future psychology. Such a psychology, Mill implies, can only be truly based on what women themselves will come to know and reveal about their own character. "It is a subject," Mill declares, "on which nothing final can be known, so long as those who alone can really know it, women themselves, have given but little testimony, and that little, mostly suborned." Only a man here and there, Mill concludes, "has any tolerable knowledge of the character even of the women of his own family."[24] We shall see a little later how Mill is personally involved in this general argument.

Women's slavery, Mill now reiterates, is the worst sort because, in addition to constant attendance on her master, she is forced into the lowest degradation of a human being, "that of being made the instrument of an animal function contrary to her inclinations." As we have seen, marriage for Mill was all too often only a legalized version of prostitution. Only among equals can moral sentiments arise. All else is a relation "of command and obedience," with the family being "a school of despotism." In the equal marriage of the future, there will be community, not domination. This will be the "political" aspect. As for the economic aspect, Mill is willing to have the woman work outside the house, though in a just state of things he does not think it "a desirable custom."[25]

What is women's "nature"? Different nations, he reminds us, hold different conceptions of it: "An Oriental thinks that women are by nature peculiarly voluptuous. . . . An Englishman usually thinks that they are by nature cold," Mill informs us, in an insight, that, alas, he never pursued. In fact, however, Mill concludes:

> We cannot isolate a human being from the circumstances of his condition, so as to ascertain experimentally what he would have been by nature; but we can consider what he is, and what his circumstances have been, and whether the one would have been capable of producing the other.

If we follow this latter procedure, Mill suggests, we shall find that women are as bright and gifted as men, and, once given or allowed the same "eagerness for fame," will achieve the same success.[26] Wollstonecraft's middle-class virtues for women seem to have surfaced again, almost a century later!

Finally Mill asks, rhetorically by now, "Would mankind be at all better off if women were free?" Or is it better to leave the world undisturbed by this new "social revolution"? The answer to the latter question is, of course, a resounding no. The first reason revolves around ". . . the advantage of having the most universal and pervading of all human relations regulated by justice instead of injustice." Injustice is taught to one-half the human race in that "school of despotism," the family. By the mere fact of being born a male, the boy is "by all right the superior of all and everyone of an entire half of the human race," Mill asserts. While we would demur a bit over the factual assertion—Mill ignores race and class, wherein, for example, a white woman or an upper-caste Indian woman would be "superior" to a vast number of men—we can certainly see his general point. It is made vivid and personal for us when he expostulates: "How early the youth thinks himself superior to his mother; owing her perhaps forebearance, but no real respect." Such a training in what Mill calls "the self-worship of the male" runs directly counter to the modern principle of men being respected, not for what they "are, but what they do."[27]

If women were given equality with the man in the family, we should avoid this contradiction in the boy's training. If boys and girls were afforded common and equal upbringing, they would also be prepared for a truly companionate marriage. Such a marriage, in turn, would be truly a learning institution in which the "moral regeneration of mankind" would commence. For half the human species, it would mean true liberation. Freedom, Mill tells us, "is the first and strongest want of human nature," after the "primary necessities of food and raiment." The distance between Mill and, say, Freud, is obvious, for there is no mention of sex as a "primary want." Absence of the sexual in Mill's economy of the passions is made equally clear when he reminisces about his own adolescent development:

> Let any man call to mind what he himself felt on emerging from boyhood—from the tutelage and control of even loved and affectionate elders—and entering upon the responsibilities of manhood. Was it not like the physical effect of taking off a heavy weight, or releasing him from obstructive, even if not otherwise painful, bonds? Did he not feel twice as much alive, twice as much a human being, as before?[28]

It is more or less on this note that Mill ends, converting the argument on the relation of the sexes into an argument over power and authority. We are on our way to *On Liberty*. As we can finally see, *The Subjection of Women* is in large part a segment of Mill's views on government; Mill is indeed really concerned with "Sexual Politics" rather than sexual relations.

A Psychology of Women

WHAT ABOUT sex and sexual relations per se? Does Mill's lack of "personal" knowledge on this subject affect his arguments substantially? Whatever the answer to this question, do his abstract arguments deserve respect in their own right, showing an advance over previous conceptions? These are serious questions emerging from a consideration of Mill's life as well as his doctrines, and tempting us thereby into a hazardous inquiry into the "psychology of women."

We shall approach this subject by a brief, but at last full, consideration of Freud's relations to Mill. The actual link between Freud and Mill is Theodore Gomperz, who arranged for the twenty-four-year-old Freud to translate four of Mill's essays. Gomperz himself could well have served as a model Freudian patient. He is typical of so many nineteenth-century characters who behave in a kind of "Alice in Wonderland" fashion, as if compelled to obey the strange rules of a Freudian kingdom. Born in Moravia in 1832, Gomperz entered the University of Vienna in 1849 to study classical philology and philosophy. Dissatisfied with the dominant Hegelian position in German thought, he stumbled on John Stuart Mill's name while reading Grote's *History of Greece*. "In the autumn of 1853," Gomperz tells us, "I bought a copy of

Mill's 'System of Logic' which put me at once into a state of sheer exuberance. I had hardly finished reading it when I began to translate it."[29] So entranced with the book was the young scholar that he wrote Mill an eight-page letter to tell him about his experience. The letter, and Gomperz's interest in translating the book, led to a correspondence and then to a visit to London in 1856. Gomperz was one of the very few admitted to the house and intimacy of Mill and his wife, Harriet; it was in the course of this familiarity that Gomperz heard Harriet remark that since her first meeting with Mill she had never been more than an "intimate friend" to him or John Taylor. The death of Harriet in 1858 broke up this particular domestic familiarity, but Gomperz continued to write at length to Mill.

Mill obviously had a disciple. By accident, he also almost had a kind of son-in-law, for Gomperz convinced himself that he was in love with Helen, and proposed to her. A firm rejection ended the matter, in rather humiliating fashion. After a serious depression—a typical Freudian one, in fact—Gomperz recovered, married another lady, and went on with his work, as advised by Mill. More important for our purposes, in 1867 he agreed to take charge of the production of a complete edition of Mill's works in German. Mill was delighted. The collected edition encountered delays, as all such works do, and it was not until 1880 that the twelfth and final volume appeared, seven years after Mill's death. In this volume, translated by Sigmund Freud, appeared the "Enfranchisement of Women," "Plato," "Thornton on Labour and Its Claims," and "Socialism" (a posthumous work of Mill's).

As we know, Freud admired Mill's general rationality and liberal spirit. Mill, he said, was "perhaps the man of the century who best managed to free himself from the domination of customary prejudices." In one area, however, Freud felt that Mill had gone too far:

His autobiography is so prudish or so ethereal that one could never gather from it that human beings consist of men and women and that this distinction is the most significant one that exists. In his whole presentation it never emerges that women are different beings—we will not say lesser, rather the opposite—from men. He finds the suppression of women an analogy to that of negroes. Any girl, even without a suffrage or legal competence, whose hand a man kisses and for whose love he is prepared to dare all, could have set him right. It is really a stillborn thought to send women into the struggle for existence exactly as men. If, for instance, I imagined my gentle sweet girl as a competitor it would only end in my telling her, as I did seventeen months ago, that I am fond of her and that I implore her to withdraw from the strife into the calm uncompetitive activity of my home. It is possible that changes in upbringing may suppress all a woman's tender attributes, needful of protection and yet so victorious, and that she can then earn a livelihood like men. It is also possible that in such an event one would not be justified in mourning the passing away of the most delightful thing the world can offer us—our ideal of womanhood. I believe that all reforming action in law and education would break down in front of the fact that, long before the age at which a man can earn a position in society, Nature has determined woman's destiny through beauty, charm, and sweetness. Law and custom have much to give women that has been withheld from them, but the position of women will surely be what it is: in youth an adored darling and in mature years a loved wife.[30]

The passage tells us at least as much about Freud as about Mill. Freud offers his conservative and "customary" view of women's place and role in society, thereby almost completely dismissing Mill's radical "politics of women."

Did Freud in his own work (clearly, not in this passage) offer a better, more profound, and truer—at least more human—view of men and women and the significant distinction that characterizes them? We cannot presume here to deal fully with such a vast and intricate subject, but we will single out two aspects of Freud's theories that bear significantly on our discussion of John Stuart Mill, Harriet Taylor, their relation, and their ideas on the psychology of women.

The two aspects concern the concepts of bisexuality and the Oedipus complex. The first obviously related to women as much as to men. For Freud, there was good anatomical evidence underlying the notion of bisexuality. Women possessed the clitoris as a vestigial penis, and men had nipples and vestigial breasts. But what was really involved in such bisexual Platonic beings? In the physical, sexual sense, of course, men and women might have strong elements in their nature of the opposite sex, thereby pulling them away from heterosexual activity. But Freud was more directly concerned with the psychological qualities, with what it meant to have masculine and feminine components in one's nature. By "masculine" he tended to mean the hard-driving, aggressive, strong, competitive traits; these are the "thrusting" qualities associated with the male penis, symbolized in spears, arrows, and other pointed instruments. In society, these traits implied Darwinian struggle. By "feminine" he meant the tender, nurturant, calm, unwarlike traits; these are the "receptive" qualities associated with the female womb, symbolized by circles and enclosures of various sorts. In society, these traits meant the "female" supporting the competitive "male," and keeping his home safe and comforting for him.

All too often, however, Freud betrayed his own best insights, and confused "masculine" psychological traits with male physiques and "feminine" with female; it is this confusion that he was expressing in his criticism of Mill on women. Freud would be right *only if* most males *naturally* had the traits associated with the "masculine," and females the "feminine." Mill's question, of course, was whether this concurrence was a matter of nature or nurture. Were men born aggressive and competitive, and women the opposite, or were these characteristic traits resulting from society's way of educating and socializing the two sexes? The argument still rages today.

At the present, both the view that "masculine" equals male and the glorification of "masculinity" are under serious attack. In late twentieth-century America, young boys wear long hair and girls wear working jeans to show that masculine and feminine have been too long kept apart in our society, with one consequence being a rampant "machismo" that supposedly has led to such blights as Vietnam. The acceptance here of bisexuality, it appears, is connected with Mill's insight that sex and politics are linked.

Yet the scientific, psychological aspects of the subject still remain unsolved. Freud, for example, while accepting the existence of bisexuality (in the spirit we have described), believed that there were fundamental differences between the sexes which were not simply derived from social conventions. These differences, for Freud, revolved around the Oedipus complex, which he called the "nuclear" complex of all the neuroses.

Can the Oedipus complex be applied to women? Put in very simple terms, in his earlier work Freud tended to ignore the pre-Oedipal period (comprising the oral and anal stages), though he was fully aware that all children have the same first love object, that is, the mother. With the onset of the phallic phase, in the Freudian scheme, the boy retains the mother as his love object but, under the fear of castration from the father, gives up his hope of actually attaining her, except by identifying with the father. According to Freud, in this process of coming to terms with his Oedipus complex the boy develops a strong superego (by dealing with castration anxiety), and prepares the way for the sublimation of his sexual energies in work and the elaboration of civilization. As we have suggested, allowing for modifications of society and history (major modifications, as we have seen), we find this description of the psychosexual development of the boy to be acceptable as a universal trait.

What of the girl? Her task, unlike the boy's, is to give up the first love object, and yet eventually to identify with it. Moreover, the girl's discovery, according to Freud, of not having a penis—thus of being castrated—leaves her with a lowered sense of self-esteem, or, technically, with penis envy. The mother, too, is devaluated on the basis of that same discovery. As Freud puts it in "Some Psychical Consequences of the Anatomical Distinction Between the Sexes" (1925):

After a woman has become aware of the wound to her narcissism, she develops, like a scar, a sense of inferiority. When she has passed beyond her first attempt at explaining her lack of a penis as being a punishment personal to herself and has realized that the sexual character is a universal one, she begins to share the contempt felt by men for a sex which is the lesser in so important a respect.

(Incidentally, the boy, too, devalues the woman for her lack of a penis.) The difficulties of identifying with such a devalued creature are clear. It can only be achieved, in Freud's model, by the girl's renunciation of the active and aggressive libidinal instincts. Already "castrated," the girl cannot be expected to develop the strong superego which the boy develops under the *fear* of castration. As Freud puts it:

I cannot evade the notion . . . that for women the level of what is ethically normal is different from what it is in men. . . . Character-traits which critics of every epoch have brought up against women—that they show less sense of justice than men, that they are less ready to submit to the great exigencies of life, that they are more often influenced in their judgements by feelings of affection or hostility—all these would be amply accounted for by the modification in the formation of their superego which we have inferred above. We must not allow ourselves to be deflected from such conclusions by the denials of the feminists, who are anxious to force us to regard the two sexes as completely equal in position and worth.[31]

Devalued, weak, without a respectable superego or its possible resultant achievements, women were indeed creatures not worth evaluating highly!

There are difficulties with this picture. What, for example, is the evidence for penis envy, that bugaboo of present-day women liberationists? The revelations of the unconscious, answer the psychoanalysts, as revealed in the cases of countless women patients in analysis. We must accept this evidence, unless we wish to accuse the analysts (many of them women, incidentally) of bad faith. However, are these revelations the result of what Mill called "social conventions," wherein the male, and male power, is glorified in our society, and women from their earliest days brought up to be inferior, with the penis as the reigning symbol of their servitude? Only extensive comparative psychoanalysis—as yet undreamed of—working with "patients" from many different societies, in some of which women might have a more dominant position, might answer this question "scientifically."

In any case, does it really matter? Even if women by nature did have unconscious penis envy, could the effects, e.g., devaluation, be removed or mitigated by a society whose "conventions" deliberately balanced the virtues of masculinity and femininity? After all, as Freud himself admitted, men envy women their creativity, their ability to produce and nurture children. Is this, in all societies, a major formative influence on men, always causing them to sublimate their envy in intellectual or artistic "creation"? Or is this envy also a matter of social conventions, and not a male "given"?

And if women envy men (to accept this view for a moment) for their penises, do men fear women for their castrating, or other destructive potentialities? Freud obviously saw women as terribly threatening and aggressive. "Wherever primitive man has set a taboo," he wrote in "*The Taboo of Virginity* [*Contributions to the Psychology of Love III*]" (1918), "he fears some danger and it cannot be disputed that a generalized dread of women is expressed in all these rules of avoidance. Perhaps this dread is based on the fact that woman is different from man, forever incomprehensible and mysterious, strange and therefore apparently hostile."[32]

It is all the more surprising, therefore, that Freud, knowing women to be often hostile, threatening, aggressive, and destructive, so rigidly identifies these traits with the "masculine" and the opposite with the "feminine." True, the "Electra complex" supposedly recognizes women's aggressive sexual feelings, *but against the mother only*. In this counterpart to the Oedipus complex, the girl wishes, unconsciously, to remove her mother in order to have sole possession of her father's love. Freud does not seriously conceptualize cases in which the girl's hostility is against the domineering male.

It is worth pursuing this matter a bit. To begin with, Electra is not a good mythical counterpart to Oedipus. Through lack of strength or resolve, she does not try herself to murder her mother, but leaves the deed to her brother, Orestes. Further, it is not Electra, but Clytemnestra who dominates the tragedy. She is the strong and authoritative figure throughout, overpowering her husband in life and eventually murdering him. The reason she wishes to murder him is that Agamemnon, vain and enamored of martial prowess and glory, has sacrificed their daughter, Iphigenia, as an offering to the gods, so that his expedition to Troy (to bring back another troublesome woman, Helen) can proceed. Here the father kills his own daughter, exercising his patriarchal power.

Aeschylus' play, and the myth in back of it, especially as seen in the light of nineteenth-century father-daughter reality, suggests a "complex" at least as important as the supposed "Electra" one. I shall call it the "Iphigenia complex." It is probably time and culture bound in an even more fundamental way than the Oedipus complex. It assumes a society in which the power of the father over his women, especially his daughters, is almost unlimited and yet resented in a newly conscious way. Certainly, daughters have been depreciated in many societies. The form of this depreciation in nineteenth-century Western society is encapsulated in the phrase, the Victorian patriarchical family. The domination of Elizabeth Barrett and her sisters by their father, including his taboo on their marriages, is a good example.[33] The harsh tyranny exercised by the father in the Brontë family is another. So, too, apparently, is the authoritarian rule of Harriet Taylor's father, the Governor. In these situations it is not so much *for* the father's love (though it probably figures initially) as *against* his domination that the daughters struggle, coming later to *hate* these would-be Agamemnons. Such women, consciously or unconsciously, seek to avoid becoming symbolic Iphigenias. Like Iphigenia's mother Clytemnestra, they may try to become stronger and more "masculine" than the male himself. At least such is their unconscious desire, as the case of Harriet Taylor suggests.

In Freud's concept of both the Oedipus and Electra complexes, he emphasized the libidinal elements. A more comprehensive view, as we have suggested in a number of places, would embrace the aggressive as well as the libidinal factor. While Freud came to understand this in theory, he did not let it affect his practice, leaving us as a result no body of case material on aggression in any way equivalent to that on sexuality. Nevertheless, even Freud would agree wholeheartedly with, for example, D. W. Winnicott when the latter remarks that "Aggression is part of the primitive expression of love."[34]

It is in the context of some such suggestion as Winnicott's that the Oedipus complex is best situated. In this form, the complex embodies aggression at least as much as libidinal desires for a particular parent. As we recall, in the original Greek drama, political power and authority, as well as the person of the mother, is involved in the battle of Oedipus with his father. Even Freud's own dreams as he stumbled along the "royal road" to the unconscious inform us of this same fact. As brilliantly analyzed by Carl Schorske, Freud's dreams show us how he moved from frustrated political ambitions, involving an intense conflict over authority, to working out a science of psychoanalysis wherein the conflict over authority is presented in libidinal guise.[35] Thus, in the Irma Dream, the Uncle Dream, and the Dream of the Botanical Monograph, the movement is from the examination of professional and political to parental authority, with the latent content being more aggressive than libidinal in nature. At the end, though, in the Oedipus complex, Freud has reversed this order, and metamorphosed the aggressive political conflict into a primarily libidinal one. Psychological desire anticipates political conflict, i.e., conflict over authority, and at this point all politics is reduced to the primal conflict between father and son. In Freud's own interpretation of his Revolutionary Dream, he informs us:

> The whole rebellious content of the dream, with its *lèse majesté* and its derision of the higher authorities, went back to rebellion against my father. A Prince is known as the father of his country; the father is the oldest, first, and for children the only authority, and from his autocratic power the other social authorities have developed in the course of the history of human civilization. . . .[36]

"For children the only authority"; such is Freud's picture of the father and his autocratic power. Mill would point out that though this is true for much of human civilization, it is, in fact, a matter of "social convention." Where it *is* embodied in the father and is exercised "autocratically," we can expect an acute Oedipus complex (though perhaps made manifest in the culture only where other propitiating factors, such as those discussed in Chapter 2, are present). In my view, we can also expect some form of what I have called the Iphigenia complex, rather than an Electra complex. Different in expression from the man's, the woman's effort to achieve autonomy and independence can be expected to be as real and as important as his. To prove our various points, of course, detailed case studies are needed, both of nineteenth-century psychohistorical figures and of contemporary woman patients. While Harriet Taylor's case seems to point in this direction, we can say nothing with surety until much more theoretical and clinical evidence is at hand.

Meanwhile, we are left with an unsatisfactory picture of the psychology of women.[37] Freud's ideas of bisexuality and of the Oedipus and Electra complexes are major steps forward, of course, but they are extremely partial. In his idea of bisexuality, Freud too often betrays his insight that "masculine" and "feminine" are more psychological than physiological characteristics, and seems to insist, for example, that "boys must be boys," i.e., "masculine," irrespective of their basic bisexual composition. Can we imagine his reaction if his wife Martha insisted on living up to the "masculine" aspects of her bisexuality? As for the Oedipus and Electra complexes, here Freud slights the aggressive component in favor of the libidinal, and even when he allows it does not present it in a sufficiently cultural or historical context. While we do not wish to deny the "given" nature of the aggressive or libidinal "instincts," i.e., as required aspects of psychosexual development, and thus universal in potentiality, we must equally affirm their modifications over time and space.

Freud thought that John Stuart Mill knew nothing about the "given" of women; about the universal elements of sexuality, and thus of the "natural" relations of the sexes. There is a good deal of truth to this judgment if we focus on the sexual component. Mill's "higher nature" never stooped to such basic knowledge. On the other hand, Mill undoubtedly knew more about political authority and autonomy than did Freud, and he was certainly more aware of the role played in these matters by "social convention." Freud, covertly starting from political authority, as Schorske suggests, went deeply into patriarchal authority, and thence into the thickets of libidinal conflict. Mill, starting from intense personal experience of his mother and father, remained on the overt level of political authority, in which he included the subjection of women. As a result, Freud offers us a deep and labyrinthian psychology of women, badly needing the complement of Mill's awareness of the role of social conventions, while Mill offers us a politics of women which is shallow on the depth psychology side. Both Freud's psychology and Mill's politics of women cry out for future experiment and evidence. Only then shall we be able to tell exactly how much in women (and men) is "nature," presumably of some Freudian kind, and how much "nurture." In this effort, as we have seen, the "romance" of John Stuart Mill and Harriet Taylor presents us with only one "peculiar" piece of evidence, and that, as in a looking glass, seen darkly.

14

Economics

Economics and Sex

JOHN STUART MILL was at the center of a revolution in man's (also meaning woman's) dealing with his sexual nature. In the nineteenth century men were engaged, first, in making sex a nonreligious subject by secularizing Christ's injunction to deny the flesh; this they did initially for "prudential," i.e., economic reasons. Second, they were taking unto themselves the greatest possible control, through artificial means, over their own procreation; one consequence was that, psychologically, in denying God or nature's unmitigated creativity, men were also asserting their own potential self-made quality.[1] Then, as the century went on, with additional knowledge of genetics and birth control methods, men took unto themselves even further "blocking" power over sexual generation.

In Mill's time, if not today, these problems of sexuality were intimately related to economics. It is no mere play on words to say that "production" became the central concern of economics at the same time as it did of sexuality, and that the two are directly linked through the concept of population, with productivity in economics threatened by productivity in sex (at the same time as it was the potential cause of it).

It was Malthus who stated this "law" in the most dire terms, and then Ricardo who, with his "Iron Law of Wages," seemed to turn economics into the "dismal science." Because of his belief in birth control, James Mill was apparently more sanguine than his friend Ricardo. And John Stuart Mill carried this optimism even further, embedding economics directly in the expanding progress of mankind, though on the same basis of a faith in population control. John Stuart Mill tackled the problem head on. "Can political economy do nothing," he asks in his *Principles of Political Economy*, "but only object to everything, and demonstrate that nothing can be done?" If this were so, "political economy might have a needful, but would have a melancholy and a thankless task." One seems to hear echoes of Mill's own experience of "melancholy" at twenty when he adds that if the bulk of the human race were to remain as "slaves to toil in which they *have* no interest, and therefore *feel* no interest . . . I know not what there is which should make a person with any capacity of reason, concern himself about the destinies of the human race."

Back in 1826, as we have seen, Utilitarian economics, along with the rest of the doctrine, had suddenly seemed to Mill to offer a bleak picture both to himself personally and to mankind. As we know, he pulled himself out of this "dismal" world and reaffirmed his commitment to being a reformer. Whatever the personal sexual dimensions of that experience, by 1848 and publication of the *Principles* Mill had found a solution to economic melancholy in controlled sexuality. Now, he tells us:

> Poverty, like most social evils, exists because men follow their brute instincts without due consideration. But society is possible, precisely because man is not necessarily a brute. Civilization in every one of its aspects is a struggle against the animal instincts. Over some even of the strongest of them, it has shown itself capable of acquiring abundant control. It has artificialized large portions of mankind to such an extent, that of many of their most natural inclinations they have scarcely a vestige or a remembrance left. If it has not brought the instinct of population under as much restraint as is needful, we must remember that it has never seriously tried.[2]

Freud could not have put the matter better. Clearly, for Mill, men were to be "artificialized" in the sexual realm by "artificial" means of contraception, which would make their procreation "amenable to their own control." Before this could happen, however, men would first have to conquer the prevailing notion that sex was power, and that "masculinity" meant sexual prowess. Mill argues:

> It is not too much to say that over-indulgence is as much caused by the stimulus of opinion as by the mere animal propensity; since opinion universally, and especially among the most uneducated classes, has connected ideas of spirit and power with the strength of the instinct, and of inferiority with its moderation or absence; a perversion of sentiment caused by its being the means, and the stamp, of a dominion exercised over other human beings.[3]

Thus, somewhat to our surprise, Mill's views on bisexuality suddenly surface again, in an economic treatise.

A Heritage Revisited

JOHN STUART MILL'S involvement with economics was early and long. When he was a boy of thirteen, his father had lectured to him on Ricardian economics during their daily walks. By eighteen John Stuart Mill was writing an article on "War Expenditure" for the *Westminster Review*, and from that time on economic articles and reviews came from his pen in a steady flow.[4]

Throughout his writings on economics, Mill worked as a participant in and contributor to a "science." Economics, therefore, is in many ways one of the most "professional" and the least "personal" areas of Mill's efforts. How, then, can we be so bold as to try to use his economic treatises for the purposes of psychohistory? The answer is that we are not attempting to describe, much less analyze and criticize, *all* of Mill's economic ideas, or, indeed, to treat even those we do primarily as *economic* ideas per se. We have neither the desire nor the technical competence to do so. What we are asserting is that Mill's economic writings, like his father's, carry with them a psychological message whose significance we can, however haltingly, try to comprehend.

On the major point of method, Mill seemed to follow his father's deductive vision, yet, in practice, to stray into the paths of empirical qualification. James Mill, as we have seen (Chapter 5), emphatically declared economics to be a deductive science like geometry, and free from the curtailment of historical experience. John Stuart Mill adopted this view in theory—in economics one reasoned "from . . . one law of human nature"—but in practice preferred, at least in his *Principles*, to follow Adam Smith in associating "The principles with their applications."[5] Thus, James Mill's hermetically sealed economic world was opened to history and reality, even if only through a half-open window.

On some other major issues, John Stuart Mill simply disagreed openly and sharply with his father. James Mill had started his *Elements of Political Economy* by declaring that "Political Economy is to the State, what domestic economy is to the family." John Stuart Mill, directly quoting his father, rejects this comparison: Domestic economy is an art, consisting of rules or maxims of prudence, whereas Political

Economy is a science; the difference is critical, and for John Stuart Mill it is essential to disown the notion that economics is in any way a "paternal" science. James Mill had denied the possibility of a glut, of general overproduction.[6] John Stuart Mill accepted the possibility, and adumbrated the general outlines of a trade cycle in which it figured. James Mill did not believe that working wages could go up except at the expense of the capitalist's share in production. John Stuart Mill gradually came to take a more sanguine view, and to believe that the wages fund was not necessarily limited and in strict equilibrium; workers could increase their share, and not necessarily at the expense of the capitalist.[7] Most important, while James Mill believed that those who preached socialism were good only for hanging, John Stuart Mill wished to give them a fair and sympathetic hearing, and even wavered on the edge of enrolling himself in their ranks.

On this last issue, it is clear that he not only disagreed with his father over technical points, even important ones, but entered a whole new world of thought and feeling. Was this transformation, as many observers have believed, largely the result of Harriet Taylor's influence? Let us examine some of the evidence.

John Stuart Mill first showed some sympathy to socialism, in its Saint-Simonian form, during the early 1830s, when he was tugging hardest at his natal ties to Benthamism. Although strained, at that time the ties to Utilitarian economics held. It was through examination of a limited question, the "claims of labor," that Mill seems next to have tested the wider issue. Mill begins his article of 1845:

> There are signs of an increased solicitude for the "Claims of Labour," which of itself is a thing of the highest promise, and more to be rejoiced over than all the mechanical triumphs which both those who would magnify, and those who would depreciate, the present age, would be apt to point to as containing its especial significance and merit.[8]

At this point, however, for John Stuart Mill the "claims of labor" can only be honored in limited fashion: the laborers must control their breeding, and this they will do, he is confident, if correctly educated. Indulging in a bit of acknowledged Utopian thinking, Mill also foresees the possibility of experiments in profit sharing and of small cooperatives. The test of all schemes, however, must be whether they render individuals independent of all assistance, and promote self-help.

By 1848, and the publication of the first edition of the *Principles of Political Economy*, Mill was ready for a more systematic examination that went beyond the claims of labor in its narrow form.[9] In a famous chapter he examined socialism and communism per se. While Mill thought he was being impartial, almost all readers are impressed by the chapter's definitely antisocialist tone. By 1852, and the third edition, however, Mill's tone had changed. He now spoke of socialistic forms of society with enthusiasm and at least moderate hopes.

What had happened in the interval? Well, there was the Revolution of 1848, which made a strong impression on Mill, especially the experiments of Louis Blanc. Then there was the aftermath of Chartism in England, which Mill had earlier acknowledged as "the first open separation of interest, feeling, and opinion, between the labouring portion of the commonwealth and all above them." And lastly, there *was* Harriet Taylor. While John Stuart Mill tried to resist what he saw as her naive hopes for the possibility of rapid transformation—"I cannot persuade myself that you do not greatly overrate the ease of making people unselfish," he wrote—he gradually gave way.[10] Harriet's strong views affected John Stuart Mill; in his hands, her views took on moderation and technical detail. Together they revised Book II, Ch. I "Of Property," of their "joint production" (Mill had wished to dedicate the *Principles* to Harriet publicly, but had to settle for some private copies, appropriately prefaced), and, in the third edition, laid down the somber but balanced estimates by which liberal thought could proceed to democratic socialism.

It is my view that, independently from Harriet Taylor, John Stuart Mill already possessed the prime elements of this transition. Saint-Simonianism, the Revolution of 1830, the "claims of labor" problems, even the teaching of John Austin, of whom Mill remarked that he was not "fundamentally opposed to socialism in itself, as an ultimate result of improvement," all helped make him ready. But Harriet was the catalyst. Without her, the elements would probably never have been fused. As Mill explains in his *Autobiography*:

> Our opinions were now far *more* heretical than mine had been in the days of my most extreme Benthamism. In those days I had seen little further than the old school of political economists into the possibilities of future improvement in social arrangements. Private property as at present understood, & inheritance, appeared to me as to them, the *dernier mot* of legislation: & I looked no further than to mitigating the inequalities consequent on these institutions, by abolishing primogeniture & entails. The notion that it was possible to get rid in any considerable degree of the flagrant injustice involved in the fact that some are born to riches & the vast majority to poverty, I reckoned chimerical; & only hoped that by universal education, leading to voluntary restraint on population, the portion of the poor might be made more tolerable. In short, I was a democrat but not the least of a Socialist. We were now less democrats than I had formerly been, because we

dreaded more the ignorance & especially the selfishness & brutality of the mass: but our ideal of future improvement was such as would class us decidedly under the general designation of Socialists.[11]

With Harriet, John Stuart Mill was willing to stand in the ranks of those terrible socialists whom his father would have hanged.

As we shall see in more detail later on, Mill's views on economics functioned on a number of levels, one of which involved his feelings toward socialism, and thus his relations to his father and toward Harriet, as well as to economic theory per se. There were two other extra-economic purposes to John Stuart Mill's work. One is that economics for Mill was related to the logic of social science. Economics, in this scheme, is part of moral science, which treats of man solely as a being "who desires to possess wealth." The other purpose is that for Mill, economics was not *merely* a science, or even a branch of moral science. It was an art as well; that is, a science with practical applications.[12] As with all of his thought, Mill intended theory and practice always to go together in economics. Personal, philosophical, and practical—on these multiple levels, Mill's economics had meaning for him, and, hopefully, for us.

Economics and Philosophy of History

THOUGH he had long pondered such a work (especially in relation to his thoughts on logic), Mill finally decided to write "a systematic treatise on Political Economy" in April 1844. He began writing in the autumn of 1845 and completed his first draft about eighteen months later, in March 1847. After some rewriting, the first edition was published in April 1848. To have written and prepared for the press two volumes, equaling almost 1,000 pages, in such a short time, was a mighty labor; John Stuart Mill could only do it because he had, so to speak, been babbling economics since puberty.

His basic inspirations, of course, were James Mill, Ricardo, and Adam Smith. But behind them now stood Auguste Comte. 1844 was the time of John Stuart Mill's most intense correspondence with the French Positivist. Even though Comte rejected the possibility of economics as a positive science, Mill persevered in his effort to construct one. Such an economic science was to be part of Mill's greater edifice of social science: ethology (see Chap. 16). Thus, in the Preface to his *Principles* Mill hints at what he has in mind:

It appears to the present writer, that a work similar in its object and general conception to that of Adam Smith, but adapted to the more extended knowledge and improved ideas of the present age, is the kind of contribution which Political Economy at present requires. The "Wealth of Nations" is in many parts obsolete, and in all, imperfect. Political Economy, properly so called, has grown up almost from infancy since the time of Adam Smith: and the philosophy of society, from which practically that eminent thinker never separated his more peculiar theme, though still in a very early stage of its progress, has advanced many steps beyond the point at which he left it. No attempt, however, has yet been made to combine his practical mode of treating his subject with the increased knowledge since acquired of its theory, or to exhibit the economical phenomena of society in the relation in which they stand to the best social ideas of the present time, as he did, with such admirable success, in reference to the philosophy of his century.[13]

According to Mill's letters to Comte, however, "philosophy of society" and "the best social ideas of the present time" are actually a kind of shorthand for Comte's Positive Science (though Mill is never uncritical in using the philosophy). In short, it is the empirically based Comte who is the grey eminence behind Mill's enlarged "philosophy of society," affecting even that bastion of his Utilitarian heritage, economics.

What Comte preeminently supplies to Mill is a philosophy of history. Thus, Mill begins by tracing with broad strokes the accumulation of wealth through time: from the state of savagery, to the shepherd state, to the agricultural state, and so on. From this picture he emerges with the conclusion that inequality is a result of spontaneous progress. As Mill tells us: "There thus [because of the gathering of large flocks and herds "by active and thrifty individuals"] arises, in the shepherd state, inequality of possessions; a thing which scarcely exists in the savage state, where no one has more than absolute necessities." The shepherd state, however, though unequal, is not exploitive; only in the agricultural state, with the emergence of landlords, does exploitation begin. Thus it is that history confirms both John Stuart Mill and his father in their antipathy to landlords and aristocrats. In Mill's analysis, the surplus extorted from dependents is taken either by a single landlord—the government—or by a number of individual landlords. The first is the Asiatic mode, or what today we refer to as the Hydraulic Society. The second is the system of ancient Europe. Both developments resulted from "the spontaneous course of events."[14]

According to Mill, all these stages of human society still coexist, with most having been preserved in their fixed, undeveloping state for centuries. Thus we have a kind of living museum of nations unequal in wealth; within each nation, this fossilized inequality is perpetrated within classes.

Such a comparative situation allows us to identify the causes of the development of wealth—and hence of inequality. We need no longer, Mill implies, be mere victims of spontaneity. The explanation for the development of wealth, however, is not simple. Among the complex causes are moral and psychological factors, and institutional and social relations. In Mill's view:

> In so far as the economical condition of nations turns upon the state of physical knowledge, it is a subject for the physical sciences, and the arts founded on them. But in so far as the causes are moral or psychological, dependent on institutions and social relations, or on the principles of human nature, their investigation belongs not to physical, but to moral and social science, and is the object of what is called Political Economy.[15]

Mill has defined for us the nature of Political Economy. His task is to investigate its workings. As we have seen, Mill believed that history exhibited a progressive accumulation of wealth, at least in some areas of the world. His problem now is to make such accumulation amenable to our control, rather than merely accidental, and to show how, if we wish, we can eliminate, or at least mitigate, inequality.

Production

AS I HAVE already tried to suggest, the nineteenth century is preeminently the Age of Production. Whereas previously it was nature that was seen as providing the fixed, limited product available for man's consumption, now a new, labor-oriented view prevailed. Man's labor, suitably divided, could produce additional wealth.

John Stuart Mill is in this tradition. Wealth is a matter of production, and "The requisites of production are two: labor, and appropriate natural objects." Mill retained vestiges of the old theory by agreeing that nature supplies all the forces and powers necessary to the creation of wealth; men, however, are required to activate them. In the physical world, man puts "objects in motion; the properties of matter, the laws of nature, do the rest."[16] Although the way in which men organize their labor to act upon physical objects is not part of physics, but of economic science, there are laws of production which, though different from physical laws, resemble them in their fixity and certainty. Such laws circle around the entities of labor, capital, and land.

Mill first undertakes the discussion of these laws in terms of productive and unproductive labor, and productive and unproductive consumption. Labor must initially produce accumulated labor, i.e., surplus food, which can then be used to sustain further agriculture. If the produce were immediately consumed, no further production would result. Thus, deferment of gratification is requisite for accumulation of the very first capital. Mill, however, seems to ignore the possibility that a man can eat only so much of an agricultural commodity, and the "surplus" might be just that, and not deferred gratification. The desire to "invest" that surplus by hiring laborers, of course, is another matter. Deferred gratification, in Mill's theory, seems more a psychological than an economic necessity. With this accumulated labor as his basis, Mill proceeds to trace out the other ways in which labor serves as a means of producing further wealth-producing materials, making tools or implements, protecting goods by building warehouses, docks, and so on, conveying the goods to desired places, distributing them, and so on. All of this is "productive labor."

It is with Chapter 3 of the *Principles* that we are informed that there can also be "unproductive labor." Though Mill asserts that "Production not being the sole end of human existence, the term unproductive does not necessarily imply any stigma; nor was ever intended to do so in the present case," we are unconvinced. Why use the pejorative term if this is the case? Why not a neutral, purely "economic" term? In any case, Mill goes on to say that productive labor does not only produce *material* wealth, but also includes training and utility embodied in human beings, or even in inanimate beings; thus, a teacher or government official also labors "productively." For Mill, unproductive labor is that "which ends in immediate enjoyment," rather than in the creation of either material wealth or increase of the accumulated stock of the permanent means of enjoyment.[17] The key concept here is, of course, that of deferred gratification. What is "immediately enjoyed" is ipso facto unproductive, while what makes for the possibility of future "enjoyment" is productive.

Of course, Mill was aware that "Unproductive may be as useful as productive labor"; that even "Productive labor may render a nation poorer (where the wealth it produces is unsalable)"; and that "Though society grows no richer by unproductive labor, the individual may." He also knew how difficult it was in practice to rule that a certain sort of immediate enjoyment might not be "psychologically" requisite for continued productive labor, and thus itself productive. Yet he held onto his classification as a most important one, and extended it to consumption. "Whoever contributes nothing directly or indirectly to production, is an unproductive consumer."[18] It is a view such as this that led Mill to call the labor of a performer on a musical instrument unproductive labor, although the musical instrument and the skill of the musician are both classified by him as the result of productive labor. Economic "analysis," it seems, has been unsuccessfully strained for purposes that would appear to lie more fittingly in the domain of psychological analysis.

Capital

IN DISCUSSING capital, Mill starts with the postulate that the deferment of gratification is the root of all capital. His next proposition is that capital is absolutely essential for industrialization, i.e., "that industry is limited by capital."[19] Capital sets productive labor in motion. It is not consumer demand, Mill announces, but the availability of capital and productive power that sets the limit to wealth (a position since cast in doubt by Keynes).

In fact, Mill, with his usual sophisticated and complicated awareness, allows for another method of capital accumulation. "In a rude and violent state of society," he informs us, plunder and slavery are other sources of capital accumulation (if not immediately consumed in "personal indulgences"); but these, too, he asserts, are based on robbing someone of his savings, i.e., deferred gratification. Thus, later on, he reverts to his basic definition, as when he informs us that "all capital is the product of saving, that is, of abstinence from present consumption for the sake of a future good."[20] It is difficult to see how a slave would agree with him, at least about the "future good," but Mill's psychological dedication to deferred gratification seems to lead him to forget reality, economic or otherwise (Mill, of course, was strongly against slavery).

Mill's position, representative of Utilitarian economics, also raises the interesting question as to what sort of character type corresponds with this view of capital, and its formation. He believed that improvidence was connected with "a low state of intelligence" on the part of both individuals and communities.[21] Increased intelligence, Mill asserted, meant increased concern for the future, and thus increased capital accumulation. Thus, in his view, cognitive factors underlay the psychological commitment to deferred gratification. All of this raises an interesting question: What happens to this preferred character type when capital is generated by government deficits, à la Keynes, rather than by individual savings? Does a shift in character structure follow (or proceed)?

Mill's theories raise another interesting point. Hoarding, he tells us, is *not* a form of capital accumulation. To be capital, it must be consumed, i.e., expended on such things as seeds, tools, or wages for productive laborers. Thus, Mill's saving must be *active* saving, not mere retention of money.

Such a view challenges the stereotype of the early capitalist as an "anal type." Generally, such stereotyping is tied to the emergence of Protestantism and the prevalence of anal references in the sixteenth and seventeenth centuries. A moment's consideration, however, ought to remind us that Luther, that very model of the anal type, was fanatically anticapitalist.[22] (He recommended that capitalists be broken on the wheel.) From our point of view, anality, when it served the purposes of capitalism and industrialism, probably did so mainly in its compulsive attention to time. "Time wasted is money wasted" is good advice from Benjamin Franklin. Work discipline in the factories, based on rigid observance of time, may well have corresponded with an anal characteristic; the award of a gold watch after twenty-five years of faithful service is a fitting symbol. But as for economic *activity*, that would seem to accord poorly with psychological anality. We see this clearly in Karl Abraham's observation:

> If the libido of the male person does not advance in full measure to the stage of genital organization, or if it regresses from the genital to the anal developmental phase, there invariably results a diminution of male activity in every sense of the word. His physiological productiveness is bound up with the genital zone. If his libido regresses to the sadistic-anal phase he loses his productive power, and not only in the purely generative sense. His genital libido should give the first impulse to the procreative act, and therewith to the creation of a new being. If the initiative necessary for this reproductive act is lacking, we invariably find a lack of productivity and initiative in other respects in his behaviour.[23]

Mill, with his stress on "productivity," was alert to the thrusting, generating character of capitalism. In his economic theory he was probably the first to recognize fully the significant role played by the entrepreneur, or what he called the "undertaker," in economic development. Profit, in this case, was a reward for risk and skill, as well as a "remuneration of abstinence."[24] Though he did mix up the functions, Mill at least perceived that the entrepreneur was often a gambler. He realized that not all businessmen were what Max Weber later called "rational" types, but that a large proportion of them "preferred excitement" to "safety" and frequently were of "an irrational or immoderate character."[25] Such men were what Carlyle called "Captains of Industry," an heroic breed.

They were not anal types. They were, to pursue our analysis in these terms, "phallic" types, filled with a desire to achieve and expand, not to hoard and to retain.[26] What Mill does with his concept of the entrepreneur is to remind us of the vapidity of the unexamined notion of the capitalist as primarily an anal character. The miser figure is outmoded both economically and psychologically by the nineteenth century. A more complicated analysis than hitherto offered is necessary.

Mill helps us to pursue this analysis by his concern with "motives" as part of the economic process. "Successful production," Mill lectures us, "like most other kinds of success, depends more on the qualities of the human agents, than on circumstances in which they work: and it is difficulties, not facilities, that nourish bodily and mental energy." In a kind of psychological imperialism, he then adds: "To civilize a savage, he must be inspired with new wants and desires, even if not of a very elevated kind, provided that their gratification can be a motive to steady and regular bodily and mental exertion."[27] Since Mill assumes the spread of economic civilization to be beneficial, it is clear that the "moral" superiority of the West was as important in his eyes as its material superiority, and just as necessary an export to underdeveloped countries as capital.

But the "Protestant Ethic" was not only a matter of national character; within the Western countries themselves it was also a class affair. Mill found the desire to accumulate concentrated in the middle class:

> In the more prosperous countries of Europe the ordinary degree of economy and providence among those who live by manual labor cannot be considered high; still, in a very numerous portion of the community, the professional, manufacturing, and trading classes, being those who, generally speaking, unite more of the means with more of the motives for saving than any other class, the spirit of accumulation is so strong, that the signs of rapidly increasing wealth meet every eye: and the great amount of capital seeking investment excites astonishment, whenever peculiar circumstances turning much of it into some one channel, such as railway construction or foreign speculative adventure, bring the largeness of the total amount into evidence.[28]

These same middle classes, of course, support the free and stable institutions of government, oppose war with its ravages, and generally favor those political and cultural factors that facilitate production and exchange on a large scale. Thus, in the intellectual, economic, political, and military areas, the same middle-class cluster of motives cohere to support the greatest possible industrial growth.

Distribution: Communism and Socialism

UPON TURNING, after almost 200 pages, from the subject of production to the problem of distribution, Mill makes a sharp and highly significant division. "The laws and conditions of the production of wealth," he tells us, "partake of the character of physical truths. There is nothing optional, or arbitrary in them." Distribution, however, is another affair: "That is a matter of human institution solely." In this area, the distribution of wealth, all "depends on the laws and customs of society." Does this mean that distribution forms no part of science? Not so, Mill tells us:

> The opinions and feelings of mankind, doubtless, are not a matter of chance. They are consequences of the fundamental laws of human nature, combined with the existing state of knowledge and experience, and the existing condition of social institutions and intellectual and moral culture. But the laws of the generation of human opinions are not within our present subject.[29]

In short, Mill's *Principles of Political Economy* are only a part of moral science; his work on government and especially on psychology and ethology is needed to complete the subject. For the time being, however, this elaboration was at best sketchy.

Anticipating part of Karl Marx's treatment of the ephemeral and time-bound nature of capitalist economics in the *Economic and Philosophic MSS.*, Mill clearly pointed out what he thought to be the disjunction between the fixed laws of production and the temporary arrangements of distribution:

> It is a case of the error too common in political economy, of not distinguishing between necessities arising from the nature of things, and those created by social arrangements: an error which appears to me to be at all times producing two opposite mischiefs; on the one hand, causing political economists to class the merely temporary truths of their subject among its permanent and universal laws; and on the other, leading many persons to mistake the permanent laws of Production (such as those on which the necessity is grounded of restraining population) for temporary accidents arising from the existing constitution of society—which those who would frame a new system of social arrangements, are at liberty to disregard.[30]

Mill's disjunction of production and distribution in economic theory is today disputed.[31] But whatever the right or wrong in the case—a matter for experts—it did allow him to treat the subject of socialism and communism as a matter of "opinion," as forming part of the "laws and customs of society." What practical results would flow from the particular social arrangement was to be discovered, not by deduction from the fixed laws, but by observation and conjecture.

It is under the chapter heading "Property" that Mill pursues his inquiry.[32] Interestingly, he does not start with a consideration of the principle of individual property—either in terms of a question of social philosophy or of its actual origin in any of the existing nations of Europe—but with an examination of its critics. Socialism and communism are often almost interchangeable terms for Mill, and he is rather too loose in his usage of them. Communism, he suggests, embraces those "whose scheme implies absolute equality in the distribution of the physical means of life and enjoyment"; Mill cites Robert Owen, Louis Blanc, and Etienne Cabet. The adherents of socialist schemes, on the other hand, "admit inequality, but grounded on some principle, or supposed principle, of justice or general expediency, and not, like so many of the existing social inequalities, dependent on accident alone"; here we find Saint-Simonianism and Fourierism.[33] Mill's sympathies are undoubtedly with socialism.

Mill begins his discussion of these various schemes by trying to show that, whatever their merits or defects, they are not necessarily impracticable. The key problem for Mill is how jobs will be apportioned fairly under such schemes. "There are many kinds of work," he reminds us, "and by what standard are they to be measured one against another? Who is to judge how much cotton spinning, or distributing goods from the stores, or bricklaying, or chimney sweeping, is equivalent to so much ploughing?" Besides, he adds, "even in the same kind of work, nominal equality of labor would be so great a real inequality, that the feeling of justice would revolt against its being enforced. All persons are not equally fit for all labor; and the same quantity of labor is an unequal burden on the weak and the strong, the hardy and the delicate, the quick and the slow, the dull and the intelligent."[34] Nevertheless, Mill is willing to believe that even this difficulty is surmountable. As an ideal, Mill concludes, communism, with all its possible faults, must be given the palm when measured against existing capitalist reality. But such a comparison is misleading:

> We must compare Communism at its best, with the *régime* of individual property, not as it is, but as it might be made. The principle of private property has never yet had a fair trial in any country; and less so, perhaps, in this country than in some others. The social arrangements of modern Europe commenced from a distribution of property which was the result, not of just partition, or acquisition by industry, but of conquest and violence: and notwithstanding what industry has been doing for many centuries to modify the work of force, the system still retains many and large traces of

its origin. The laws of property have never yet conformed to the principles on which the justification of private property rests. They have made property of things which never ought to be property, and absolute property where only a qualified property ought to exist. They have not held the balance fairly between human beings, but have heaped impediments upon some, to give advantage to others; they have purposely fostered inequalities, and prevented all from starting fair in the race. That all should indeed start on perfectly equal terms, is inconsistent with any law of private property: but if as much pains as has been taken to aggravate the inequality of chances arising from the natural working of the principle, had been taken to temper that inequality by every means not subversive of the principle itself; if the tendency of legislation had been to favor the diffusion, instead of the concentration of wealth—to encourage the subdivision of the large masses, instead of striving to keep them together; the principle of individual property would have been found to have no necessary connection with the physical and social evils which almost all Socialist writers assume to be inseparable from it.[35]

Until such a comparison is made, Mill declares, we cannot intelligently decide between the two systems.

But if we must choose now, he continues, "the decision will probably depend mainly on one consideration, viz., which of the two systems is consistent with the greatest amount of human liberty and spontaneity." Mill's lingering distrust of communism is based on his fear of its latent authoritarianism. Having struggled through his mental crisis to achieve a kind of independence and autonomy, Mill was not about to place himself consciously under any new despotism. Perhaps his intellectual and psychological fear of dependency (coupled with a psychological attraction to it as well, making for greater fear of giving way) led him to play down the elements of mutuality present in communism. In any case, he was highly sensitive to any threats of outside control. Under communism:

The question is whether there would be any asylum left for individuality of character; whether public opinion would not be a tyrannical yoke; whether the absolute dependence of each on all, and surveillance of each by all, would not grind all down into a tame uniformity of thoughts, feelings, and actions. This is already one of the glaring evils of the existing state of society, notwithstanding a much greater diversity of education and pursuits, and a much less absolute dependence of the individual on the mass, than would exist in the Communistic *régime*. No society in which eccentricity is a matter of reproach, can be in a wholesome state. It is yet to be ascertained whether the Communistic scheme would be consistent with that multiform development of human nature, those manifold unlikenesses, that diversity of tastes and talents, and variety of intellectual points of view, which not only form a great part of the interest of human life, but by bringing intellects into a stimulating collision, and by presenting to each innumerable notions that he would not have conceived of himself, are the mainspring of mental and moral progression.[36]

Though Mill offers no judgment here, it is clear that his fears as to communism (which is *not* equivalent to Marxism for him) are deep and troubling.

In the first edition Mill claimed that his arguments against communism were not applicable to socialism, and especially not to Saint-Simonianism, which was of "far higher intellectual pretensions," but by the third edition he was no longer making this invidious distinction. Mill's principal objection to Saint-Simonian socialism was to the notion of a small Comtean elite dispensing distributive justice to everyone else. As he declared:

A fixed rule, like that of equality, might be acquiesced in, and so might chance, or an external necessity; but that a handful of human beings should weigh everybody in the balance, and give more to one and less to another at their sole pleasure, and judgment, would not be borne, unless from persons believed to be more than men, and backed by supernatural terrors.

By the third edition, Mill's highest praise had come to settle on the Fourierists. Their scheme for retaining private property, and even inheritance, and combining them with work based on the law of attractions, seemed to him to hold out the greatest promise for a real equality, resulting "not from the compression, but, on the contrary, from the largest possible development, of the various natural superiorities residing in each individual."[37] With this said, however, Mill returned to his original position that only time and experiment will tell which of the schemes, individual or community property, is best. His final conclusion is very judicious:

In the meantime we may, without attempting to limit the ultimate capabilities of human nature, affirm, that the political economist, for a considerable time to come, will be chiefly concerned with the conditions of existence and progress belonging to a society founded on private property and individual competition; and that the object to be principally aimed at in the present stage of human improvement, is not the subversion of the system of individual property, but the improvement of it, and the full participation of every member of the community in its benefits.[38]

Dynamic Laws

IN BOOK IV of the *Principles*, Mill takes up a subject not treated in James Mill's *Elements*: the "Influence of the Progress of Society on

Production and Distribution." Until now, he tells us, we have been considering the "Statics" of the science. To these "economical laws of a stationary and unchanging society" we must now add the "laws" concerning "the economical condition of mankind as liable to change, and indeed in the more advanced portions of the race, and in all regions to which their influence reaches as at all times undergoing progressive changes."[39]

But how can one reconcile the presumably fixed laws of economic production with the effort to work out fixed laws of the dynamic evolution of society as a whole, when, as he admits, there are no fixed laws of distribution, because these relate too much to the uncertain areas of customs, mores, and psychology? Mill by-passes this problem, it seems, because of his faith in the Comtean scheme of dynamics and his unquestioned belief, most of the time (cf., however, p. 368), in the inevitability and virtue of "progress." On this basis he offers an early theory of economic development. According to Mill, in the advanced countries of the world, and those under their sway:

> There is at least one progressive movement which continues with little interruption from year to year and from generation to generation; a progress in wealth; an advancement in what is called material prosperity. All the nations which we are accustomed to call civilized, increase gradually in production and in population: and there is no reason to doubt that not only these nations will for some time continue so to increase, but that most of the other nations of the world, including some not yet founded, will successively enter upon the same career.[40]

But continued progress is not inevitable. Mill, of course, acknowledges the unfavorable side of population increase. But he believed that this problem would be mitigated by the tendency of laborers to spend the higher wages made possible by progress to satisfy newly acquired tastes rather than merely to feed new mouths.

Another, equally serious threat to continued progress is contained in the tendency of profits to fall to a minimum, what economists today call "Diminishing Returns."[41] As Mill summarizes:

> The field of employment for capital is twofold; the land of the country, and the capacity of foreign markets to take its manufactured commodities. On a limited extent of land, only a limited quantity of capital can find employment at a profit. As the quantity of capital approaches this limit, profit falls; when the limit is attained, profit is annihilated; and can only be restored through an extension of the field of employment, either by the acquisition of fertile land, or by opening new markets in foreign countries, from which food and materials can be purchased with the products of domestic capital.[42]

This economic theory would later be used to explain the necessity of capitalist imperialism. At the turn of the century, the latter idea was taken up and given supposed empirical support in a book by J. A. Hobson, which then became the basis for Lenin's famous treatise on "Imperialism."

For Mill, however, there were possible short-run alternatives. Inventions could lead to lowered money wages, and thus increased profits. So, too, could declining food costs, resulting from a particular event, such as the end of the Corn Laws. But these were only temporary expedients; sooner or later the tendency of profits to a minimum would assert itself in the advanced countries.

Nevertheless, Mill was not pessimistic. He believed that the first result of the "law" of diminishing returns would be investment by the "have" countries in the "have-not" countries; this was a step to equality, yet this, too, was merely postponing the inevitable. "The increase of wealth is not boundless," Mill announced as a truth known to most political economists (would he have included his father in this group?). "When the progress ceases, in what condition are we to expect that it will leave mankind?" Surprisingly, Mill states flatly that the stationary state is good for mankind:

> I cannot, therefore, regard the stationary state of capital and wealth with the unaffected aversion so generally manifested towards it by political economists of the old school. I am inclined to believe that it would be, on the whole, a very considerable improvement on our present condition. I confess I am not charmed with the ideal of life held out by those who think that the normal state of human beings is that of struggling to get on; that the trampling, crushing, elbowing, and treading on each other's heels, which form the existing type of social life, are the most desirable lot of human kind, or anything but the disagreeable symptoms of one of the phases of industrial progress. It may be a necessary stage in the progress of civilization, and those European nations which have hitherto been so fortunate as to be preserved from it, may have it yet to undergo.[43]

Only the stationary state can be cultured and just. The progressive is necessary to raise man's material well-being; leveling institutions before that point is reached "may lower the heights of society, but they cannot, of themselves, permanently raise the depths."[44] But once this necessary progressive stage has accomplished its purpose, we ought to welcome the stationary.

Of course, this ultimate stationary state is good only if population is made stationary. Since Mill assumes this will be the case, he rejoices in what we can call the "end of civilization," i.e., of material progress, and the onset of the age of culture. In Mill's words:

It is scarcely necessary to remark that a stationary condition of capital and population implies no stationary state of human improvement. There would be as much scope as ever for all kinds of mental culture, and moral and social progress; as much room for improving the Art of Living, and much more likelihood of its being improved, when minds ceased to be engrossed by the art of getting on. Even the industrial arts might be as earnestly and as successfully cultivated, with this sole difference, that instead of serving no purpose but the increase of wealth, industrial improvements would produce their legitimate effect, that of abridging labor. Hitherto it is questionable if all the mechanical inventions yet made have lightened the day's toil of any human being. They have enabled a greater population to live the same life of drudgery and imprisonment, and an increased number of manufacturers and others to make fortunes. They have increased the comforts of the middle classes. But they have not yet begun to effect those great changes in human destiny, which it is in their nature and in their futurity to accomplish. Only when, in addition to just institutions, the increase of mankind shall be under the deliberate guidance of judicious foresight, can the conquests made from the powers of nature by the intellect and energy of scientific discoverers, become the common property of the species, and the means of improving and elevating the universal lot.[45]

As we know, in Mill's day this was a Comtean notion. Today it is discussed under the heading of "zero growth" policy.

"Lower" Classes

MILL TURNS next to "The Probable Futurity of the Laboring Classes." He announces:

When I speak, either in this place or elsewhere, of "the laboring classes," or of laborers as a "class," I use those phrases in compliance with custom, and as descriptive of an existing, but by no means a necessary or permanent state of social relations. I do not recognize as either just or salutary, a state of society in which there is any "class" which is not laboring; any human beings, exempt from bearing their share of the necessary labors of human life, except those unable to labor, or who have fairly earned rest by previous toil. So long, however, as the great social evil exists of a non-laboring class, laborers also constitute a class, and may be spoken of, though only provisionally, in that character.[46]

We shall see in a moment why this is disingenuous, given Mill's psychological attitudes to the laboring class. First let us consider Mill's treatment of the subject in overtly economic terms.

There are, according to Mill, two theories about the laboring class. One is "the theory of dependence and protection, the other that of self-dependence." The dependence is a paternalistic theory. It sees the poor workers as "children" to be allowed no spontaneous action.

Mill dismisses this theory—Tory benevolence—peremptorily. The "superior classes" are not sufficiently improved to govern in the tutelary manner, and by the time they were so improved, supposing this possibility, "The inferior classes would be too much improved to be governed." In an advanced, secure society in which the working class can read, it can organize itself and will no longer accept "parental" rule, although it can be educated and guided in the right direction. Such an education, while shunning the training in "deferential awe or religious principles of obedience," can still be expected to leave them with a "respect for superiority of intellect and knowledge" freely given. Mill believes that "such deference is deeply grounded in human nature."[47]

Such independent workers (and Mill includes among them women, who should also no longer be dependent, and should have all occupations opened to them) will also no longer consent to being "hired" by others. The solution is for them to form associations of laborers. (When Russian populist Nicholas Chernyshevsky translated Mill's *Principles*, it was clearly this idea which most appealed to him, and which he then enshrined in his novel, *What is to be Done.*)[48] Mill did not believe that expropriation of existing capital was necessary; the workers would pool their own resources and then add to it by raising capital from outside in the normal way.

Even in his associations, Mill believed in the necessity of competition—and here he broke with most other socialists—and advocated piecework, above a guaranteed minimum, as the only really fair system. (As he wrote his wife, "One of the most discreditable indications of a low moral condition given of late by the English working classes is the opposition to piece work.")[49] Mill reprimanded socialists because they "overlook the natural indolency of mankind; their tendency to be passive, to be the slaves of habit."[50] Moreover, "Wherever competition is not, monopoly is," i.e., Mill advocated competition among the associations as well as among the workers in them. Thus, while foreseeing a future for the laboring class in which they were no longer dependent, but working in freely formed associations, Mill insisted on retaining the competitive element. Otherwise, indolence would persevere, though dependence was at an end.

So much for the economic picture. What about Mill's psychological attitudes toward the laboring class? They are unconsciously built into such synonyms as "lower class" or "inferior classes," mentally set in contradistinction to "higher natures," prevalent among Mill and all his "class" contemporaries. These attitudes are most powerfully persuasive because they are seemingly part of the nature of things.

The basic imagery involved is spatial: lower versus higher. "Lower" is equated with the body, and especially the "baser" parts, the region of impulses and passions of a mere "animal" nature, of a "low moral state." Thus, in speaking of the "lower classes," the implication was clear that one was referring to the "baser" elements of humanity, not just to an economic class. It was the class that had to work with its body (often just its "hands") and not its mind. Against its low moral state, one placed the figure of the "upright" man, naturally a person of the "higher" classes.

Lower was also directly related to sex. We have already seen how Mill prided himself and Harriet as being "above" the animal appetites, the "impulses of that lower character." It was a commonplace of Victorian times that the lower classes had dissolute sexual habits and were promiscuous. Being members of the "lower" classes, they were bound to have "low" impulses as well, and low in this case meant sexual.

As we know, this fantasy of the middle and upper classes had strange psychological repercussions. Freud, for example, writes about men who can only have sexual intercourse with prostitutes or women of the lower class, for sex is "dirty" and cannot be practiced with their clean, pure wives (who, in the unconscious, are also equated with their mothers). Something of this attitude is reflected in the recently discovered life of Arthur J. Munby, a member of the English Victorian middle class who seems to have had a lifelong obsession with working women, and in fact married one of them and lived in secret with her for years.[51]

Lower was not only intimately connected with sex, it also was related to savages and the savage state of man. Savages were seen as "impulsive" and unable to control their passions, sexually or otherwise. Mill fully shared in this view, as when he typically remarked: "The savage cannot bear to sacrifice for any purpose the satisfaction of his individual will. His impulses cannot bend to his calculations."[52] It was inevitable, therefore, that the equation was made in the psyche: lower-class sexuality and savagery, low in the scale of human evolution, are one and the same.

In the early nineteenth century a true revolution in spatial perspective had been attempted by the romantics. They sought to validate the images of downward versus upward, and inner versus outer. Through their efforts—which I equate in significance with Francis Bacon's change of time perspective, whereby he viewed the "moderns" as actually "older" than the "ancients," and therefore more mature and advanced—the way was opened to Freud's treatment of lower and inner (deeper) life as being of equal worth and importance with higher and outer experience (though even Freud exhibited vestiges of the traditional perspective in his scheme of the id, ego, and superego). Owing, too, to the romantics, who were aware that the inner was also the seat of the secret sexual life, the way was also prepared for Freud to make sex respectable.[53] As a result, the unconscious elements of the disdain for the lower and the inner were brought to the surface and these aspects now given equal validation as well as continuity with the higher and the outer.

The romantic revolution, however, was only partially successful, and Freud was still in the future. The Victorians by and large rejected the proposed change in attitudes. Mill, as a fairly typical Utilitarian in this matter, shared the unconscious assumptions of his time and class. As a result, his almost automatic assumption of lower class and lower impulses going together lay underneath his conscious statements about the laboring class and its role in government and economics, and often undermined these statements. As we shall see, Mill's feelings about the lower classes comfortably supported his elitist notions that those qualified to rule, i.e. "higher natures," had also a right to guide the untutored and impulsive masses. While this warred with Mill's commitment to equality, it fitted well with his psychological disposition, typical of his time, society, and class.

In his economics Mill might seek to uplift the laboring classes, and to defend their claims to high wages and even to independent associations of their own. Yet without calling into question the sincerity of these positions, one must again ask how they correspond to Mill's psychological attitudes to the lower classes. Mill could write that the correct way of raising up (note the spatial image) the mass of the people was:

> . . . not in the vulgar way of "rising in the world," so often recommended to them—not by endeavouring to escape out of their class, as if to live by manual labour were a fate only endurable as a step to something else; but by raising the class itself, in physical well-being and in self-estimation.[54]

He could hardly realize the unconscious disparagement involved. It was "vulgar" for the individual worker to rise, yet if the whole class rose, but was still "lower," the pejorative meanings were still attached to them in the unconscious. If Mill really meant what he said, he would have had to share in the revolution in spatial imagery of the romantics, as well as in the economic evolution he was advocating. There is no sign that he ever did mean it on that "lower" level.

Economic Functions of Government

FINALLY, Mill explores from the economic side the same problem he would deal with in *On Liberty* and other works on government. One by one he takes up the necessary functions of government. The first and major one is taxation. Mill does not favor taxation "as a means of mitigating the inequalities of wealth," and he is opposed, for example, to the graduated income tax. In fact, Mill is convinced that the whole notion of a direct tax on income is unfair and should only be resorted to during great national emergencies. On the other hand, Mill favors inheritance taxes, even graduated inheritance taxes. He also approves of taxes on rent, though he believed that a tax on profits is "in a state of capital and accumulation like that in England, extremely detrimental to the national wealth."[55] In general, Mill's yardstick is whether a tax penalizes the hard-working and thrifty—the man who works and earns his money directly and productively—or merely takes away from the individual gains that he has not himself worked for, e.g., rent and inheritance.

The next function of government is to provide protection of person and property. Without this security, economic development is hampered. Yet, for Mill, free institutions are even more important than security. He observes:

> Insecurity paralyzes, only when it is such in nature and in degree, that no energy, of which mankind in general are capable, affords any tolerable means of self-protection. And this is a main reason why oppression by the government, whose power is generally irresistible by any efforts that can be made by individuals, has so much more baneful an effect on the springs of national prosperity, than almost any degree of lawlessness and turbulence under free institutions.[56]

When the chips are down, Mill almost invariably opts for a version of governmental functions which does not sacrifice the individual or his just rights. He is emphatic, for example, that government should not choose opinions for people; that freedom of thought is essential for economic development.

In the last chapter of the *Principles* Mill specifically explores "The Grounds and Limits of the Laissez-Faire or Non-interference Principle." He distinguishes between two kinds of intervention: the authoritative and the advisory-exemplar. Authoritative intervention occurs when the government tries to control the free agency of individuals. Advisory-exemplar intervention occurs, for example, when:

> [A] government, instead of issuing a command and enforcing it by penalties, adopts the course so seldom resorted to by governments, and of which such important use might be made, that of giving advice, and promulgating information; or when, leaving individuals free to use their own means of pursuing any object of general interest, the government, not meddling with them, but not trusting the object solely to their care, establishes, side by side with their arrangements, an agency of its own for a like purpose.[57]

Though both forms of intervention may be required on various occasions, it is clear which Mill favors. Adamantly, he takes his stand on the rock of individual freedom:

> Whatever theory we adopt respecting the foundation of the social union, and under whatever political institutions we live, there is a circle around every individual human being, which no government, be it that of one, or a few, or of the many, ought to be permitted to overstep: there is a part of the life of every person who has come to years of discretion within which the individuality of that person ought to reign uncontrolled either by any other individual or by the public collectively.[58]

Where the limit should be placed is open to debate; that it should be placed is not. "Letting alone, in short," Mill concludes, "should be the general practice: every departure from it, unless required by some great good, is a certain evil."[59]

Among the departures required by "some great good" is the provision by the government of education for the people. But Mill insists that while government can—and should—require education for its citizens, it must not control the content of that education. Government also can interfere with the power of parents over their children, by such measures as laws against child labor. Women, however, are not children, and government should leave them alone—and equal. Mill also believes that government can give assistance to the poor through such measures as the Poor Law, can support colonization (though curiously, Mill never directly addresses himself to a discussion of imperialism), and can back geographical and scientific expeditions. All in all, his list is small; the motto, as he says, is "Letting alone." The touchstone of government activities is concurrently to free man from artificial restraints and to help him in the "legitimate employment of the human faculties, that of compelling the powers of nature to be more and more subservient to physical and moral good."[60] On this note, and with this phrase, Mill ends his *Principles of Political Economy*.

14 / Economics

The Purposes of Economics

IT OUGHT to be clear by now that Mill's economics was subservient to two purposes: his belief in the possibility of a general social science, and his desire for the maximum fostering of free individual development. Thus, on one hand he sought to place Utilitarian economics in the service of an effort at establishing a Comtean dynamic "science," while on the other hand he made the conclusion of his economics the prologue for his inquiry, *On Liberty*.

In a more limited sense, Mill was not so much opposed to government intervention per se as he was to unnecessary intervention. Seen in the context of his time, his work can be viewed as an effort to tear down an outmoded bureaucratic and authoritative interference and then to reintroduce a more effective government. Perhaps we can get at this problem best by quoting D. R. McGregor:

> The Free Trade Movement is coming to be seen as having achieved not merely the repeal of a rusty, mercantilist apparatus of commercial and industrial regulation but also the creation of a new administrative framework within which the factors of productivity were rendered mobile and rational and industrialism freely expansive: The decades after the first Reform Act saw not a contraction but a redefinition of the functions of government.[61]

Such a redefinition and restructuring were carried out in England by Utilitarians such as Hume at the Board of Trade, Southwood Smith in public health, Chadwick in public administration, and many others. Mill was of this band.

This aspect of Mill's laissez-faire attitudes, however, must not blind us to his larger intent. His eye was always on the self-development of the individual, and thus of the society made up of such individuals. Autonomy and liberty, under a fostering protection and education, were requisite for that development. Mill knew this, not only as an abstract piece of knowledge, but as something pulsing through his own being, embedded in his nerves. It was for this reason —as well as changes in historical circumstances—that Mill could go well beyond his father in the subject that had engaged them during their daily walks. While James Mill's economics had been arid, out of time, and "elemental," his son's was warm in human feeling, immersed in history, and "complicated." While the father's economics had been strictly in the service of increasing material wealth, John Stuart Mill's was made into a handmaiden of liberty and the expansion of human self-realization. For all of these reasons, and more, we can say that in the generational change between James Mill and John Stuart Mill we moved from one "economic world" to another, and that this new "economic world" is one in which economics is only part, though a very important part, of a larger universe of human values.

15

On Government

Government: Political and Personal Themes

PROBLEMS of government and governance were at the heart of John Stuart Mill's life and work. The compulsive themes around which his thought revolved were those of liberty and obedience, domination and development, individual and society, democracy and elitist expertism, coercion and tolerance, and "sentimental" custom and "scientific" reason. These themes, of course, were not unique to Mill; they were the common concern, certainly of his generation, and probably of most generations. What is unique is the special juxtaposition of these themes in Mill's synthesizing mind, and the particular way in which the political and psychological dimensions of these "primal" topics fused in Mill.

Let us cite a few instances. Mill's personal openness to suggestion —his suggestibility—was deeply rooted in the authoritarian education imposed on him by his father. As John Stuart Mill confesses in a rejected page of his *Autobiography*, as a result of his father's moral domination:

> I thus acquired a habit of backwardness, of waiting to follow the lead of others, an absence of moral spontaneity, an inactivity of the moral sense and even to a large extent, of the intellect, unless roused by the appeal of some one else. . . .[1]

It was this trait that led Mill into the characteristic pattern of initial discipleship and then assertion of independent opinion that we have noted earlier. It also led Mill to be unusually open to other views, parts of which he internalized and then worked into a many-sided synthesis of his own. Thus he weighed the claims, for example, of Bentham and Coleridge, order and progress, and the eighteenth and nineteenth centuries, and ended up placing some of each in the common balance of his mind (and heart). It is this "many-sidedness," this tolerant, open, and receptive hearing of many points of view, that is at the heart of the liberal political position. Often charged with being changeable or weak, the liberal commitment to political and psychological openness requires a peculiar sort of strength of its own. John Stuart Mill won through to this strength out of the trauma of his mental crisis and his conflict with his father. As a result, he said what he had to say on the subject with unusual force and meaning.

Mill was intensely concerned with the question of domination. Who rules? This standard topic in political philosophy Mill extended in all directions. He not only dealt with the traditional problems of despotism, aristocracy, and so on, but broadened the analysis to include the rule of custom.[2] At a time of rapid social change carried out in the name of "scientific" reason, Mill asked what legitimate scope should be accorded to custom. He then linked this topic to the rising domination of public opinion—the despotism of social rules—and dealt with the subject in the broadest possible way by tying this issue to the issue of development, both the individual's and society's. In one majestic sweep he examined the entire problem of domination: of one interest group over the general interest; of custom and public opinion over all individuals; of men over women; of parents over children; and called all such domination into question in the name of principle and reason. As Maurice Cranston perceptively describes the situation:

> Mill published his *Essay on Liberty* at a time and in a place when the constraints of the state were few, but the constraints of society, many and onerous. The battle for freedom in Locke's sense of "freedom" had been won in England. Mill's Victorian contemporaries were seldom ordered about by their government, but nearly all of them were constantly being ordered about by fathers, husbands and masters; and these fathers, husbands and masters in their turn were dominated by social taboos and conventional ideas.[3]

The terms of domination had changed, but domination still persisted, in new and perhaps stronger form. John Stuart Mill knew this intimately. His own development had been a constant struggle to escape from parental domination made more difficult because of the very seductiveness of that domination, with its appeals to narcissism and even "loving" concern. Isaiah Berlin catches a part of this concern when he remarks: "The *Essay on Liberty* deals with specific social issues in terms of examples drawn from genuine and disturbing issues of its day, and its principles and conclusions are alive in part because they spring from acute moral crises in a man's life."[4]

What Berlin calls "moral" I prefer to call "psychological." Indeed, in Mill the political, the moral, and the psychological are inextricably mixed. He is a man, not just a mind. His life experiences on the key questions of liberty and authority underlie and correspond with his ratiocinations about such reified topics as liberty and authority. Only if we constantly bear this in mind can we make the greatest sense, on all levels, of his writings on government.

The Ambivalences

JOHN STUART MILL'S views on the great questions of government and governance did not remain static but developed and changed, along with his personal development. As we have seen in an earlier chapter (Chap. 11), Tocqueville's *Democracy in America* stimulated Mill during the 1830s to review his positions on a number of critical issues. Mill's Utilitarian heritage had predisposed him to a belief in "democracy." The influence of Coleridge, Carlyle, and the Germanic school encouraged him toward "holism" and the acceptance of other aspects of the truth. Mill responded by trying to synthesize Bentham and Coleridge, the radical and the conservative positions. Tocqueville, on the other hand, strengthened Mill in his belief in democracy, but now in a modified form, "from pure democracy, as commonly understood by its partisans, to the modified form of it, which is set forth in my 'Considerations on Representative Government.'" Mill, following Tocqueville, became increasingly aware of the dangers of pure democracy, while more and more convinced that some form of it was inevitable, and therefore increasingly constrained to see that it should be the "modified" version.

Mill recognized with growing clarity that the growth of communications, and especially of the press, prepared the way for increased domination by public opinion. But, unlike Karl Marx, he realized that the consequence was, not a classless society, but a society dominated by the middle class. Alas, that class, in which his father and John Stuart Mill himself originally had had such faith, was now betraying its mission. It was imposing the tyranny of the majority (coopting, in the process, the laboring class), and, as a further result, threatening to bog down modern society in a stationary manner. In his *Principles of Political Economy* Mill was willing to scoff at the dangers of a stationary society, and even to sing its praises, once progress had already occurred. But psychologically and politically, stationary meant stagnation for Mill, and was not acceptable. Robson has collected a number of Mill's comments on stagnation:

> "stagnation [is] the greatest of our dangers, and the primary source of almost all social evils"; only the Civil War could bring an end to "the intellectual and moral stagnation that previously prevailed" in the United States; the "danger of American democracy was stagnation—a general settling into a dead level of low morality and feeling"; "the real ultimate danger of democracy" is "intellectual stagnation"; "the greatest danger of a settled state of society" is "intellectual stagnation"; one result of the fear of public opinion is "a general torpidity and imbecility"; there is "a relaxation of individual energy" in such a state; "the most serious danger is that the national mind should go to sleep."[5]

These quotations represent Mill's conscious thought. In the tortuous realm of the unconscious, I believe the equation in the early 1830s went something as follows: The tyranny of middle-class public opinion leads to stagnation; stagnation is the reign of moral fear and the end of energy and independence; this stagnation is what I am tempted to give into, by giving up Harriet Taylor in the face of public opinion. First hammered into his soul in the 1830s, this searing equation stayed with John Stuart Mill the rest of his life. Political reality seemed to confirm it more and more. The Reform Bill of 1832 had done little to elevate the moral life of England, though it had partly shifted power to the middle classes. By 1859 Mill was convinced that further extension of suffrage without extensive safeguards would merely strengthen the tyranny of the majority. In France, the Revolution of 1848 had promised freedom but instead had brought about a middle-class despotism, followed by and enshrined in the very visible despotism of Louis Napoleon. It is with the shadow of these realities over his basic psychological commitment that Mill felt himself increasingly compelled to speak out on the problem in terms of both his personal behavior—defying public opinion in many areas, such as the woman's question—and his political writings, especially *On Liberty*.

While Mill's views on the tyranny of public opinion did not so much change as develop steadily, his position in another key area, the relation of liberty to social science, seems to have shifted to and fro. Under the influence of his father and Bentham, Mill had believed in Utilitarianism as a "science" of morals and legislation, entailing political activity to put its principles, and adherents, in actual power. The personal events of the late 1820s, and the failure of the French Revolution of 1830, disillusioned Mill with both Utilitarianism as a social science and politics as an activity. In the 1830s and early 1840s he turned increasingly to a form of Comtean sociology, seeing in it the basis of a true science of politics. As he expresses himself in a rejected passage of his *Autobiography*:

I had always identified deference to authority with mental slavery and the repression of individual thought. I now perceived that these indeed are the means by which adherence is enforced to opinions from which at least a minority of thinking and instructed persons dissent; but that when all such persons are as nearly unanimous, as they are in the more advanced of the physical Sciences, their authority will have an ascendancy which will be increased, not diminished, by the intellectual and scientific cultivation of the multitude, who, after learning all which their circumstances permit, can do nothing wiser than rely for all beyond on the knowledge of the more highly instructed. I did not become one atom less zealous for increasing the knowledge and improving the understanding of the man; but I no longer believed that the fate of mankind depended on the possibility of making all of them competent judges of questions of government and legislation. From this time my hopes of improvement rested less on the reason of the multitude, than on the possibility of effecting such an improvement in the methods of political and social philosophy, as should enable all thinking and instructed persons who have no sinister interest to be so nearly of one mind on these subjects, as to carry the multitude with them by their united authority.[6]

In this antidemocratic mood, never really given up by Mill, he wrote his *Logic*, and concentrated mainly on analyzing the basis on which a true social science could be established. Though in the 1830s he resumed some of his political activity, his main faith was in the possibility of an agreed-on social or moral science. By the late 1840s and early 1850s, Mill's belief in the possibility or efficacy of such a social science was ebbing fast, though it always stayed with him residually. At the same time his distrust and fear of pure democracy were greater than ever. Where was he to turn? Part of the answer is in *On Liberty* and *Considerations on Representative Government*, as we shall soon see. Here, tipping against social science, Mill sought to indicate the permissible range of political power and activity by measuring them against the principle of liberty. In these books the great questions of authority and liberty, coercion and tolerance, "sentimental" custom and "scientific" reason, and all the others, are given a classic, overt treatment in "artistic," not "scientific," terms.

These shifts from social science to liberty and back and forth again and again corresponded, it seems, to his own personal shifts from a yearning for certainty, first centered on the figure of his father and the latter's deductive science of Utilitarianism, to a desperate search for autonomy and self-development, in order to escape from that same overbeloved and hated father. Political events such as those of 1830, 1832, 1848, and 1852 constantly forced upon Mill the need to tip the balance in one direction or the other. So did his basic intellectual commitments. Underlying, corresponding with, and giving passion to his utterances on these great and momentous problems, however, were his own pulsating ambivalences. It is these ambivalences that make Mill pronouncements so intensely human, and fix them forever in the mind and psyche of anyone else who has glimpsed, even dimly, what Mill called "self-consciousness, that daemon of the men of genius of our time." On the question of social science and liberty, Mill's views did not so much develop steadily as rotate compulsively, with each rotation, however, giving off a brilliant light.

A Joint Production

VIEWED FROM one vantage point, *On Liberty* is the despairing attempt by a political thinker who has lost his faith in a social science that could serve as the basis and justification of the rule of a philosophical elite to defend the individual and his right to free self-development against the impending tyranny of the "mass." *On Liberty* is less a call to rule than a denial of domination. As such, it is an essay whose organization is poor, and many of whose arguments are vague and inconclusive. Nevertheless, in spite of its obvious flaws, *On Liberty* is a classic because of the agonizing nature of the dilemma that is perplexing Mill, and because we sense the intensely human aspect of the argument, both for him and for ourselves. In the end, exactly because of its ambiguities and ambivalences, it becomes the classic statement of liberalism.

In his *Autobiography* Mills tells us that he had "first planned and written it as a short essay in 1854."[7] That date, as we know, marked the height of John Stuart Mill's fears of both his own and Harriet's impending death. It was also in that year that he had begun his *Diary*, and was working hard on the draft of his *Autobiography*. In short, *On Liberty* takes its place alongside the other most "self-conscious" products of Mill's mind; it is, as they are, an unusually "personal" work.

In the *Autobiography* Mill writes:

It was in mounting the steps of the Capitol [in Rome], in January, 1855, that the thought first arose of converting it [the original short essay] into a volume. None of my writings have been either so carefully composed, or so sedulously corrected as this.

More than any of his other works, Mill informs us, the essay was a collaborative effort with Harriet:

The "Liberty" was more directly and literally our joint production than anything else which bears my name, for there was not a sentence of it that was not several times gone through by us together, turned over in many ways, and carefully weeded of any faults, either in thought or expression, that we detected in it.[8]

Together, he and Harriet were to have undertaken its final revision in the winter of 1858–1859, but her death placed the whole burden of revision on Mill's shoulders. On publication, he dedicated the essay to "her who was the inspirer and in part the author, of all that is best in my writings."

Again we are faced with the question of Harriet's true role in Mill's writings. My view is that she caused John Stuart Mill to emphasize the "romantic," expansive strain in his views, and to strike "strong" poses not generally natural or congenial to him. For example, in the *Diary*, on January 13, Mill deplores that:

Those who should be the guides of the rest, see too many sides to every question. They hear so much said, or find that so much can be said, about everything, that they feel no assurance of the truth of anything. But where there are no strong opinions there are (unless, perhaps, in private matters) no strong feelings, nor strong characters.[9]

Here Mill had really described his own situation. A few weeks later, however, on February 6, he was writing in another mood:

Not symmetry, but bold, free expansion in all directions is demanded by the needs of modern life and the instincts of the modern mind. Great and strong and varied faculties are more wanted than faculties well proportioned to one another; a Hercules or a Briareus more than an Apollo. Nay, at bottom are your well-balanced minds *ever* much wanted for any purpose but to hold and occasionally turn the balance between the others?[10]

This, if I am not mistaken, is the voice of Harriet. Such ambiguity and ambivalence compound the problem, for in *On Liberty*, too, there are passages which suggest the same kind of alternating mood as in the *Diary*. Yet we must not overvalue Harriet's contribution. The themes are Mill's, though Harriet shared in some of them, and the arguments and the writing are overwhelmingly his contribution. Harriet, like James Mill, figures as a major psychological source of John Stuart

Mill's *On Liberty*; the essay itself, however, is the distillation of his entire life and ratiocinations.

Liberty and Development

LET US now follow Mill's somewhat convoluted argument more or less step by step. He begins in Chapter 1 by declaring that his subject is not Liberty of the Will, but Civil or Social Liberty, although we know that in his *Logic* he had to struggle desperately to escape from the nightmare of "Philosophical Necessity" in order even to perceive the possibility of individual and social liberty. Here, however, he simply ignores the connection between the philosophical and the political questions. The latter, he tells us, is "the vital question of the future."[11]

According to Isaiah Berlin, the doctrine of liberty embraces two separate concepts: negative and positive liberty. Negative liberty deals with the question: How far can government (or society) legitimately interfere with me? Positive liberty deals with the question: Who governs me? In Berlin's view, Mill confused these two distinct notions of liberty. We shall see whether we agree with Berlin as we proceed, noting only that his analysis of liberty as compounding two concepts is brilliant and fruitful.[12]

In the first part of his work Mill sticks rigorously to the first concept. Modern society, he tells us, has replaced ancient political and religious despotisms by democracy, a new form of potential social tyranny. Thus the old question of what are the limits to government interference with the individual must be answered in terms of the new context. Hitherto, under the prevailing democracy, Mill informs us, the boundaries encircling society's interference with the individual have been set by custom. Now it is time to set them by reason, by a recognized principle. That principle, according to Mill, is:

> That the only purpose for which power can be rightfully exercised over any member of a civilized community, against his will, is to prevent harm to others. His own good, either physical or moral, is not a sufficient warrant.[13]

In this principle Mill locates the citadel of liberty.

Mill will only breach the citadel, and make exceptions, in the cases of young children below the age of maturity, and of barbarians, for in such a backward state as barbarism "the race itself may be considered as in its non-age." (We shall see later what an opening in his theory is thus made by Mill's belief in stages of progress.) At this juncture Mill introduces a subsidiary principle: "Liberty, as a principle, has no application to any state of things anterior to the time when mankind have become capable of being improved by free and equal discussion."[14] What Mill clearly has in mind is that, though we cannot force people to do something for their own good, we have the possibility of convincing them by reason, and this requires reaching the age of reason. Thus, his desire for development pushes him toward Berlin's second, positive concept of liberty, but by Mill's own path and logic.

Both principles, incidentally, are rooted for Mill in utility, and not in the idea of abstract right. In his version of utility, moreover, it is:

> . . . grounded on the permanent interests of man as a progressive being. Those interests, I contend, authorize the subjection of individual spontaneity to external control, only in respect to those actions of each, which concern the interest of other people.

The key words here are "progressive being," "interests," "subjection," "spontaneity," and "control"; taken together, they encapsulate much of Mill's personal and intellectual development. Around that individual development he now draws certain inviolate spheres:

> [First,] the inward domain of consciousness; demanding liberty of conscience, in the most comprehensive sense; liberty of thought and feeling; absolute freedom of opinion and sentiment on all subjects, practical or speculative, scientific, moral, or theological.
>
> [Second,] liberty of tastes and pursuits; of framing the plan of our life to suit our own character; of doing as we like, subject to such consequences as may follow: without impediment from our fellow creatures, so long as what we do does not harm them, even though they should think our conduct foolish, perverse, or wrong.
>
> [Third,] from this liberty of each individual, follows the liberty, within the same limits, of combination among individuals; freedom to unite, for any purpose not involving harm to others.[15]

Taken together, these define the realm of liberty.

In the past this realm has been violated by political and religious bodies, ranging from the ancient commonwealth to "the ambition of a hierarchy, seeking control over every department of human conduct," such as the Puritan divines. So, too, some modern reformers, though opposed to the religions of the past, seek to impose their own doctrines as a form of spiritual domination. Mill singles out his old friend Comte as one who aims to establish a "despotism of society over the individual, surpassing anything contemplated in the political ideal of the most rigid disciplinarian among the ancient philosophers."

The real threat, however, derives less from any specific philosopher than from the general tendency of society:

> The disposition of mankind, whether as rulers or as fellow citizens, to impose their own opinions and inclinations as a rule of conduct on others, is so energetically supported by some of the best and by some of the worst feelings incident to human nature, that it is hardly ever kept under restraint by anything but want of power; and as the power is not declining, but growing, unless a strong barrier of moral conviction can be raised against the mischief, we must expect, in the present circumstances of the world, to see it increase.[16]

In this passage Mill echoes his father's belief in the Hobbesian notion of man's unlimited lust for domination over others while recognizing that, as in his father's imposition of opinion over him, some of the best and some of the worst motives are confounded in this desire. Having reached this "liberal" and "many-sided" view, Mill then goes beyond it by promulgating the need for every individual to develop freely and according to his own inner needs.

Free Inquiry

MILL MOVES to his next argument by declaring that defense of the "liberty of the press" (which his father had undertaken) against government control is no longer necessary; the arguments have been conclusive and are accepted by all. Control by social coercion—the tyranny of the majority—is, however, another matter. Mill's task is to combat this new despotism by its own weapon, "opinion," i.e., reasoned argument. His position here reflects his deepest conviction that ideas, opinions, are the ultimate forces in human history, and that the moral reformer is, therefore, the moving power in mankind's development.

Mill's arguments are not particularly original, as he is the first to admit. He asks, how can we be sure that the opinion we seek to stifle is false? We can know only by trial and error. For Mill, the "source of everything respectable in man either as an intellectual or as a moral being" is that "his errors are corrigible."[17] But it is solely by discussion, which is a mental form of experience, that we can avoid the blunders inherent in action, where the error is paid for by human misery.

At no time, however, according to Mill, can we have anything but partial certainty:

The beliefs which we have most warrant for, have no safeguard to rest on, but a standing invitation to the whole world to prove them unfounded . . . and in the meantime we may rely on having attained such approach to truth, as is possible in our own day. This is the amount of certainty attainable by a fallible being, and this is the sole way of attaining it.[18]

Of course, Mill is always prepared to admit his own fallibility. Thus, in his "Thoughts on Parliamentary Reform," he confesses his error on the question of the secret ballot. His former argument, he tells us, "is specious, and I once thought it conclusive. It now appears to me fallacious."[19] Willing to admit error and frailty in himself, Mill is also thereby ready to see more correct views in his opponent; the two attitudes must go together.

Where these attitudes do not prevail, men will be persecuted for holding divergent views. Fixed dogmas, which do not allow for admission of error, will crush all who dissent from them. Such was the case with Socrates, the most eminent thinker of all time, put to death by an Athenian tribunal on the grounds of having subverted the necessary dogmas. The specific charge on which he was tried was that of corrupting the young. Commenting on this charge in his essay on "Grote's Plato," published seven years after *On Liberty*, Mill makes a most revealing statement about both the nature of generational change and his own experience:

When the charge of corrupting youth comes to be particularized, it always resolves itself into making them think themselves wiser than the laws, and fail in proper respect to their fathers and their seniors. And this is a true charge: only it ought to fall, not on the Sophists, but on intellectual culture generally. Whatever encourages young men to think for themselves, does lead them to criticize the laws of their country—does shake their faith in the infallibility of their fathers and their elders, and make them think their own speculations preferable. It is beyond doubt that the teaching of Sokrates, and of Plato after him, produced these effects in an extraordinary degree. Accordingly, we learn from Xenophon that the youths of rich families who frequented Sokrates, did so, for the most part, against the severe disapprobation of their relatives. In every age and state of society, fathers and the elder citizens have been suspicious and jealous of all freedom of thought and all intellectual cultivation (not strictly professional) in their sons and juniors.[20]

Does progress automatically emerge, however, out of such generational "shaking" of received authority? In the essay on "Grote's Plato," Mill, unlike Freud, was not sanguine. The Platonic dialectic, he tells us, imposes upon us a twofold obligation:

This twofold obligation, to be able to maintain our opinions against the criticism of opponents and refute theirs, and never to use a term in serious discourse without a precise meaning, has always been odious to the classes who compose nearly the whole of mankind; dogmatists of all persuasions, and merely practical people. Hence it is that human intellect improves so slowly, and, even in acquiring more and more of the results of wisdom grows so little wiser. . . . In things that depend on natural sagacity, which is about equally abundant at all times, we are not inferior to our forefathers; in knowledge of observed facts we are far beyond them; but we cast off particular errors without extirpating the causes of error; the Idols of the Tribe, and even of the Den, infest us almost as much as formerly; the discipline which purges the intellect itself, protecting it from false generalization, inconclusive inference, and simple nonsense, on subjects which it imperfectly knows, is still absent from all but a few minds.[21]

In *On Liberty* Mill was either more optimistic, or unwilling to weaken his own argument by admitting its fundamental deficiency in practice. He seems to be saying that the new social tyranny works in more subtle fashion than did the spectacular trials of Socrates and Christ. For example, the middle-class revival of religion is, in fact, merely the latest version of "the strong permanent leaven of intolerance in the feelings . . . which at all times abides in the middle classes of this country." Mill's indictment of his father's favorite class is scathing and penetrating. He points out:

Our merely social intolerance kills no one, roots out no opinions, but induces men to disguise them, or to abstain from any active effort for their diffusion. With us, heretical opinions do not perceptibly gain, or even lose, ground in each decade or generation; they never blaze out far and wide, but continue to smolder in the narrow circles of thinking and studious persons among whom they originate, without ever lighting up the general affairs of mankind with either a true or a deceptive light. And thus is kept up a state of things very satisfactory to some minds, because without the unpleasant process of fining or imprisoning anybody, it maintains all prevailing opinions outwardly undisturbed, while it does not absolutely interdict the exercise of reason by dissentients afflicted with the malady of thought.[22]

Mill, however, is not satisfied. He suffers from the "malady of thought." The great ages, he declares, are those of free inquiry. Even when we are right we need to know the true grounds of our own opinions, and these can only be supplied by free discussion. Remembering his own "conversion" experience, Mill remarked in another of his essays, "On Genius":

Everyone, I suppose, of adult years, who has any capacity of knowledge, can remember the impression which he experienced when he *discovered* some truths which he thought he had known for years before. He had only believed them; they were not the fruits of his own consciousness, or of his own observation; he had taken them upon trust, or he had taken upon trust the premises from which they were inferred.[23]

Living beliefs, on the other hand, are discoveries revivified and confirmed by the test of disputation, the probing of one's opponent's case to see if perhaps *he* has the correct opinion. Even on undisputed matters, dissident discussion is useful.[24] The Socratic dialectic is a perennial necessity, even though it is essentially a "negative" approach:

It is the fashion of the present time to disparage negative logic—that which points out weaknesses in theory or errors in practice, without establishing positive truths. Such negative criticism would indeed be poor enough as an ultimate result; but as a means to attaining any positive knowledge or conviction worthy the name, it cannot be valued too highly; and until people are again systematically trained to it, there will be few greater thinkers, and a low general average of intellect, in any but the mathematical and physical departments of speculation.[25]

This again is a direct slap at Comte, and we perceive increasingly that his erstwhile friend and "teacher" is Mill's real opponent in this "discussion."

Mill seeks to transcend the negative-positive dichotomy—of two opinions, both may be partly true and partly in error. He recognizes this situation, not only in scientific or intellectual matters, but in political matters as well, where it often happens that:

A party of order or stability, and a party of progress or reform, are both necessary elements of a healthy state of political life; until the one or the other shall have so enlarged its mental grasp as to be a party equally of order and of progress, knowing and distinguishing what is fit to be preserved from what ought to be swept away. Each of these modes of thinking derives its utility from the deficiencies of the other; but it is in a great measure the opposition of the other that keeps each within the limits of reason and sanity.

Here, in the practical realm of politics, Mill reaffirms the position he had taken in his articles on Bentham and Coleridge. Many-sidedness was a political as well as intellectual necessity.[26]

Mill defended the value of many-sidedness on many fronts: intellectual, political, and if we remember our discussion of bisexuality, personal. There is little left for him to do except add that free discussion is good for the contestants, and, what is more, for the third parties listening to the debate. As Mill concludes: "We have now recognized the necessity to the mental well-being of mankind (on which all their other well-being depends) of freedom of opinion, and freedom of expression of opinion."[27] Recalling Mill's mental crisis, we cannot help feeling that "mental well-being" is a matter of personal salvation as well as of the development and progress of the human race.

Free Action

HAVING DEFENDED freedom of opinion and discussion, Mill turns to the question of whether the same reasons require that men should be free to *act* upon their opinions. It is largely a rhetorical inquiry. Men must be entirely free to act unless their actions unnecessarily make them "a nuisance to other people." This position is argued by Mill not only on Utilitarian grounds, but because the free development of the individual is a good in itself. Mill goes well beyond the position of his father and Bentham, and offers a highly "romantic" defense of liberty. Although this position occasionally conflicted with Mill's elitism, as when, in "Thoughts on Parliamentary Reform," he defended weighted voting on the ground that "there is no one who, in any matter which concerns himself, would not rather have his affairs managed by a person of greater knowledge and intelligence, than by one of less [i.e., himself],"[28] it did represent his basic stance. More typically, as in *On Liberty*, he would rather have the individual mismanage his own affairs, and act badly and foolishly perhaps, in order to forward his self-development, than have some wise teacher, no matter how good his motives, decide and act for him.

According to Mill, ". . . it is only the cultivation of individuality which produces, or can produce, well-developed human beings."[29] This is a terribly important idea in Mill, underlying his views on the possibility and direction of human progress. Earlier we saw how, in "Grote's Plato," he was pessimistic about generational conflict *in fact* being meaningful and destroying the Idols of the Tribe. In the *Autobiography* Mill explains how "I had learnt from experience that many false opinions may be exchanged for true ones, without in the least altering the habits of mind of which false opinions are the result." Here his conclusion is phrased in terms of a required change of consciousness. He announces:

> [Though the English public] have thrown off certain errors, the general discipline of their minds, intellectually and morally, is not altered. I am now convinced, that no great improvements in the lot of mankind are possible, until a great change takes place in the fundamental constitution of their modes of thought.[30]

In *On Liberty*, however, Mill realized that the change in consciousness could only come about through a changed experience of the entire person. What was needed was a new kind of self-development, or individuality. Isaiah Berlin gets at the issue splendidly:

James Mill and Bentham had wanted literally nothing but pleasure obtained by whatever means were the most effective. If someone had offered them a medicine which could scientifically be shown to put those who took it into a state of permanent contentment, their premisses would have bound them to accept this as the panacea for all that they thought evil. Provided that the largest possible number of men receive lasting happiness, or even freedom from pain, it should not matter how this is achieved. Bentham and Mill believed in education and legislation as the roads to happiness. But if a shorter way had been discovered, in the form of pills to swallow, techniques of subliminal suggestion, or other means of conditioning human beings in which our century has made such strides, then, being men of fanatical consistency, they might well have accepted this as a better, because more effective and perhaps less costly alternative than the means that they had advocated. John Stuart Mill, as he made plain both by his life and by his writings, would have rejected with both hands any such solution. He would have condemned it as degrading the nature of man. For him man differs from animals primarily neither as the possessor of reason, nor as an inventor of tools and methods, but as a being capable of choice, one who is most himself in choosing and not being chosen for; the rider and not the horse; the seeker of ends, and not merely of means, ends that he pursues, each in his own fashion: with the corollary that the more various these fashions, the richer the lives of men become; the larger the field of interplay between individuals, the greater the opportunities of the new and the unexpected; the more numerous the possibilities for altering his own character in some fresh or unexplored direction, the more paths open before each individual, and the wider will be his freedom of action and thought.[31]

Free development requires spontaneity, and this cannot be planned for by reformers, who therefore abhor it. Similarly, the interpretation of experience by the individual must be his interpretation, and not that imposed by mere custom. As Mill puts it:

It is the privilege and proper condition of a human being arrived at the maturity of his faculties, to use and interpret experience in his own way. It is for him to find out what part of recorded experience is properly applicable to his own circumstances and character.

Character itself interprets experience, and is continuously formed by that experience; such is Mill's message. The nature of that character, of the actor, is as important as the acts he carries out, and here Mill goes well beyond received Utilitarian doctrine: "It really is of importance, not only what men do, but also what manner of men they are that do it." Then in a strikingly un-Benthamite metaphor, Mill declares that "Human nature is not a machine . . . but a tree, which requires to grow and develop itself on all sides, according to the tendency of the inward forces which make it a living thing." And he adds: "One whose desires and impulses are not his own, has no character, no more than a steam-engine has a character."[32]

It is extraordinary after such an admission that Thomas Carlyle, who once referred to Mill as a "steam-engine" intellect, should refuse to see how Carlylian Mill was being here. Instead he focused on Mill's refusal to force people to be free and better. Growled Carlyle: "As if it were a sin to control or coerce into better methods, human swine in any way . . . Ach Gott im Himmel!"[33] Clearly, here was the vital difference between the authoritarian Carlyle and the liberal Mill. Mill could say:

No government by a democracy or a numerous aristocracy, either in its political acts or in the opinions, qualities, and tone of mind which it fosters, ever did or could rise above mediocrity, except in so far as the sovereign Many have let themselves be guided (which in their best times they always have done) by the counsels and influence of a more highly gifted and instructed One or Few.

But Mill hastened to add:

I am not countenancing the sort of "hero-worship" which applauds the strong man of genius for forcibly seizing on the government of the world and making it do his bidding in spite of itself. All he can claim is, freedom to point out the way. The power of compelling others into it, is not only inconsistent with the freedom and development of all the rest, but corrupting to the strong man himself.[34]

Mill was, in fact, not opposed, as he put it, to the "stuff of which heroes are made." But his heroes were not Carlyle's. They were men of strong impulses and energy, but their strong susceptibilities and feelings were guided by an equally strong conscience of a "liberal" caste.[35] Such a person, wishing to express his own character, would also respect the right of others to free self-development.

The threat to such "heroes" came from the despotism of custom. Could it also come from the spirit of improvement? In an important and paradoxical statement, Mill recognized a problem which on most occasions he wished to neglect:

The spirit of improvement is not always a spirit of liberty, for it may aim at forcing improvements on an unwilling people; and the spirit of liberty, in so far as it resists such attempts, may ally itself locally and temporarily with the opponents of improvement. . . .

Nevertheless, Mill concludes, "The only unfailing and permanent source of improvement is liberty." Without liberty, there is only Chinese stagnation; indeed, there is no history. The terrible paradox is that improvement itself is making for greater homogeneity, for advancement "toward the Chinese ideal of making all people alike." Thus, liberty must assert itself anew, against the very improvement, or progress, made possible by liberty. And it must do so immediately:

> If the claims of Individuality are ever to be asserted, the time is now, while much is still wanting to complete the enforced assimilation. It is only in the earlier stages that any stand can be successfully made against the encroachment. The demand that all other people shall resemble ourselves, grows by what it feeds on. If resistance waits till life is reduced *nearly* to one uniform type, all deviations from that type will come to be considered impious, immoral, even monstrous and contrary to nature.[36]

For Mill, of course, it is the despotism of custom that is "contrary to nature," but he believes this because his "nature" is "human nature," variegated and with the right and need to develop freely.

On Limits to Authority

THOUGH SOCIETY is not founded on a contract, Mill argues that we are bound by the social relation itself to certain conduct: we must not injure the interests of one another insofar as these are rights, and we must bear our share of the labor and sacrifices necessary for defending the society. Aside from these conditions, however, the individual should be free to think and act as he pleases insofar as his conduct affects only his own interests, and not that of others. Mill's argument here is couched not in terms of self-development, but in terms of self-interest. "I am the last person," he tells us, "to undervalue the self-regarding virtues; they are only second in importance, if even second, to the social."[37] The individual, not society, is most interested in his own well-being, and must be left free to act on that interest.

In doing so, of course, the individual may incur considerable loss of esteem and regard from those around him. This is the price he must pay for his eccentricity, or obstinacy, or self-conceit. However, with all his interest in psychology, Mill does not analyze what may be involved in loss of social esteem and how this leads to loss of self-esteem—or how this threatened loss, in fact, functions as a prime form of social coercion. Yet he is aware of the issue. Neither does he really examine the way in which custom—the social mores and morals—filters into our beings and unconsciously shapes our opinions and acts. Yet in his own life he "knew" that internal controls might be as binding as external ones; that, for example, fear of yielding to "lower impulses," itself a reflection of social control, could lead to rigid self-control. This sort of "knowledge," however, never rose fully to the surface in Mill. As a result, his arguments today have a kind of superficial ring to them, being restricted to the nature of external controls.

Still, *On Liberty* is a book on political, not psychological matters, and it is only because Mill himself runs the two together by talking of self-development that one hopes for more from him. Much of his remaining discussion is quite specific. He deals with religious practices, such as the Mohammedan prohibition against eating pork, which violates the right of the individual to his own personal taste, and the Puritan regime of morals, forbidding harmless amusements. He laments the disposition in the United States for democracy to inhibit wealthy individuals from lavish display for fear of popular disapprobation (Mill was obviously writing before the "gilded age" of the late nineteenth century!), and he fears that future socialism will seek to level wages and work through a kind of "moral police" (i.e., union control). Mill concludes this chapter by defending the right of the Mormons, whose beliefs (especially their belief in polygamy) he opposes, to exist, asserting: "I am not aware that any community has a right to force another to be civilized."[38] How are we to reconcile this statement with his defense, in his book *Considerations on Representative Government*, of colonial rule, which he describes:

> . . . as legitimate as any other if it is the one which in the existing state of civilisation of the subject people most facilitates their transition to a higher stage of improvement. There are, as we have already seen, conditions of society in which a vigorous despotism is in itself the best mode of government for training the people in what is specifically wanting to render them capable of a higher civilisation.[39]

Clearly there are two sides to Mill. One favors self-development, with society's right to interfere carefully limited. The other favors development and progress of societies, with intellectual elites and superior societies possessing a historical mission to uplift and enlighten the natives (domestic or colonial). This split is deep in Mill's own soul. It is also a dilemma of Western civilization in the nineteenth century (continuing into the twentieth). Unable to deal with the problem effectively in *On Liberty*, Mill ignores it, and lamely concludes that civilization need fear little from barbarism, which it has already conquered. If it does fear the vanquished enemy, civilization is so degenerated that it deserves to go under. Mill's conclusion, as can be seen, is curiously off the mark—and inconclusive.

What more can we say of *On Liberty*? Mill's ambivalences, his changes of attitude, his awareness of the need for balance and for the reconciliation of theory and application, often weaken his argument; but they strengthen our admiration for the integrity of the man. He emerges from the pages of his essay as the living exemplar of what it is to be and think like a liberal human being. He extols the individual as a "vital power" that differs from and is more important than a "machine." The machine, we realize, is the state, or "society," or custom. It is also the "mechanical personality" which denies the spontaneity and uniqueness of each individual's self-development. Mill gained this knowledge out of the intense experience of his own life; he had lived *On Liberty* before he wrote it. In fact, though cast in the form of intellectual argument, *On Liberty* is most important for the example it provides of how a man who has achieved "liberty" thinks and feels. Its power over us stems at least as much from the strength of Mill's personal identity—his self in action—as from his ideological persuasions.

Choice of Government

IF *On Liberty* was Mill's most personal work, *Considerations on Representative Government*, published two years later, was one of his most formal productions. In fact, after the first few chapters, which are exceptionally revealing, it is also one of his most pedantic and pedestrian works.

Nevertheless, for a full picture of Mill's view on the problem of government, it is indispensable. In it Mill seeks to fulfill the message of *On Liberty* by turning "toleration" and "many-sidedness" into higher synthesis. Thus in the Preface he declares:

> From various indications, and from none more than the recent debates on Reform of Parliament, . . . both Conservatives and Liberals (if I may continue to call them what they still call themselves) have lost confidence in the political creeds which they nominally profess, while neither side appears to have made any progress in providing itself with a better. Yet such a better doctrine must be possible; not a mere compromise, by splitting the difference between the two, but something wider than either, which, in virtue of its superior comprehensiveness, might be adopted by either Liberal or Conservative without renouncing anything which he really feels to be valuable in his own creed.[40]

Modest as he is, Mill obviously thinks "superior comprehensiveness" to be a worthwhile goal.

Mill entitles his first chapter, "To what Extent Forms of Government Are a Matter of Choice." His real argument is over whether government is to be regarded as a mechanical or spontaneous entity; we immediately recall his discussion of human nature in *On Liberty*.

Some minds, Mill says, regard government "as wholly an affair of invention and contrivance." Opposed to them are those "who are so far from assimilating a form of government to a machine, that they regard it as a sort of spontaneous product, and the science of government as a branch (so to speak) of natural history." Both doctrines, in Mill's view, when held as an exclusive theory, are absurd. They "correspond to a deep-seated difference between two modes of thought [and he might have added "character"]," neither of which is entirely right or wrong. Mill's task is to avail himself "of the amount of truth which exists in either."[41]

Note that Mill's problem here is really one of *generation.* Is government made, as is a machine, so that a people can seek to create itself *de novo*, for example, through a constitutional convention, just as an individual (James Mill?) claims to create himself? Or is government a matter of spontaneous growth, emerging in seemingly happenstance fashion out of the mists of time? Though Mill had declared human nature to be like a tree, not a machine, he could not carry this analogy all the way into his speculations on the origins of government. He was too aware that his "tree" of life, his own "spontaneous" development, had been carefully tended and nourished by the contrivances of his father, just as he was aware that such nurturance could quickly become a mechanical trap, an iron cage, preventing true growth. Intellectually, Mill was too clear about the way in which governments were "The work of men, and owe their origin and their whole existence to human will," at the same time as he recognized that will was constrained by organically evolved conditions which would prevent it from successfully choosing just *any* form of political institutions.[42]

In this way, Mill arrived at his synthesis. Government *is* a matter of choice, but that choice is circumscribed by history, i.e., the stage in development and the characteristic nature of a particular people. Specifically, free government depends on a great variety of existing dispositions, and Mill gives a pioneering analysis of the conditions necessary for representative government.[43] Nevertheless, he concludes that within these necessary historical limits, "Institutions and forms of government are a matter of choice."[44]

Are such choices a matter of science or art? Mill believed that political philosophy, in the form of Utilitarianism, provides the end to which all political institutions must aim. Implementation of this aim, in the form of morals and legislation, however, is a matter of political art. While this art, for Mill, infringes on science—for example, it bases itself upon a scientific psychology—it starts from a moral law given by argumentation rather than from empirical data given by observation.

Though Mill is, of course, interested in what men *do* do in the political realm, he is much more interested in what they *should* do; his intent is normative, rather than descriptive, or even analytical, as in modern political science.

Only in this very qualified sense, therefore, can we actually talk about Mill's work on government as being part of a "political science," or a branch of his general sociology. This becomes clear when he announces: "To inquire into the best form of government in the abstract (as it is called) is not a chimerical, but a highly practical employment of scientific intellect."[45]

Because he believes in the efficacy of a political science, or art, Mill also believes in the role of the intellectual in politics. Such an individual has employed his "scientific intellect" in examining the problems of politics; he therefore has a right to guide and lead his fellow men. Without such "disinterested" knowledge, he would be merely another person fighting for self-interested power.

Mill, however, believed forcefully in the power (now justified) of the intellectual, and in the efficacy of ideas. "Speculative Thought," he declared, "is one of the chief elements of social power," and opinions stronger than interests: Thus, "a monk of Wittenberg, at the meeting of the Diet of Worms [was] a more powerful social force than the Emperor Charles the Fifth, and all the princes there assembled." So, too, "It was not by any change in the distribution of material interests, but by the spread of moral convictions, that negro slavery has been put an end to in the British Empire and elsewhere."[46] In short, "It is what men think that determines how they act," and not mere physical or economic power. It is for this reason, we can now see, that government for Mill is a matter for philosophy, not science; at least so it is in his *Considerations on Representative Government*.

Marks of a Good Government

IN HIS second chapter, "The Criterion of a Good Form of Government," Mill resorts to an historicist position. Whereas a Rousseau, for example, in the *Social Contract* had offered eternal, abstract criteria, such as increased population, Mill declared that "The proper functions of a government are not a fixed thing, but different in different states of society."[47]

Mill next considers the constituents of social well-being under two headings frequently proposed by contemporary political philosophers:

"Order and Progress (in the phraseology of French Thinkers); Permanence and Progression in the words of Coleridge." Seductive as this neat division is, Mill judges it "unscientific and incorrect." We have a toleraby distinct notion about Progress, Mill tells us: it means improvement. But what is Order? It involves obedience, or preservation of peace by cessation of private violence. As such, it is essential for Progress, according to Mill, but it can also be placed in the service of Permanence (and even Despotic Permanence, he implies). Thus he concludes:

> [The best government] is that which is most conducive to Progress. For Progress includes Order, but Order does not include Progress. Progress is a greater degree of that of which Order is a less. Order, in any other sense, stands only for a part of the pre-requisites of good government, not for its idea and essence.[48]

Some minds are predominantly bold and wish progress, while others are cautious and desire stability. In his usual judicious fashion, Mill reminds us that we need both, so that "the tendencies of each may be tempered, insofar as they are excessive, by a due proportion of the other." At this point Mill identifies these two tendencies with the generations, and remarks:

> The natural and spontaneous admixture of the old and the young, of those whose position and reputation are made and those who have them still to make, will in general sufficiently answer the purpose, if only this natural balance is not disturbed by artificial regulation.[49]

By "artificial regulation" did he have in mind, for example, his father's desired restriction of the suffrage to those over forty? As so often in Mill, we have the feeling that his own generational experience motivates and supplies the passion behind his abstract political discussion. The true psychology underlying Mill's political philosophy is his own life experience, and not merely Associationalist psychology.

Having abandoned the Comtean-Coleridgean classification and criteria, Mill announces his own:

> If we ask ourselves on what causes and conditions good government in all its senses, from the humblest to the most exalted, depends, we find that the principal of them, the one which transcends all others, is the qualities of the human beings composing the society over which the government is exercised.[50]

From this it follows that we judge government primarily on its successful promotion of certain desirable moral and intellectual traits; we know what these traits are from Mill's essays *On Liberty* and *Utilitarianism*. A second criterion, Mill tells us, is the "quality of the machinery" for achieving this ultimate end. For Mill, representative government is clearly the best "machinery." In part this is because such government, as "an agency of national education," develops its citizens' powers of self-development as they exercise them.[51] However, as Mill has already insisted, not all people may be ready for the advanced education of representative government. For them more primitive instruction, and thus political institutions, may be needed "according to the stage of advancement already reached." Speaking of what the "*pupils* [italics added]" in "this stage of their progress, require," Mill is even led to argue that slavery itself may be educational *at a given stage*:

> A slave, properly so called, is a being who has not learnt to help himself. He is, no doubt, one step in advance of a savage. He has not the first lesson of political society still to acquire. He has learnt to obey. But what he obeys is only a direct command.

He must learn self-control, i.e., self-government, before he can become a free man. Intermediary between slavery and representative government, he may require "a paternal despotism or aristocracy, resembling the St. Simonian form of Socialism." Whatever the stage, however, and whatever the external control required, the existing form of government must allow for progress to the next stage. This, for example, the Egyptian hierarchy and the paternal despotism of China did not do. Because the Jews and Greeks did, they were "The most progressive people of antiquity . . . the starting point and main propelling agency of modern cultivation."[52] Once again we cannot help feeling that Mill's best government bears a suspicious resemblance to the idealized picture of his father: first controlling the young savage, then inciting and training the young man to self-control, and finally letting him develop into full freedom.

Even a good despotism—an enlightened one—he avers in his next chapter on representation in government, would not be an ideal government. It would leave the people mentally passive. If it attempted to educate the people, it would end by undermining itself, for "any education which aims at making human beings other than machines, in the long run makes them claim to have the control of their own actions." Mill is fully aware that many see this as a doctrine of universal self-interest and selfishness. To this charge he offers a most interesting response:

> We may answer, that whenever it ceases to be true that mankind, as a rule, prefer themselves to others, and those nearest to them to those more remote, from that moment Communism is not only practicable, but the only defen-

sible form of society; and will, when that time arrives, be assuredly carried into effect. For my own part, not believing in universal selfishness, I have no difficulty in admitting that Communism would even now be practicable among the *élite* of mankind, and may become so among the rest.[53]

Here Mill's moral elitism joins hands with the most sweeping equalitarianism—communism—and causes him temporarily to forget his strictures in *Principles of Political Economy*.

In general, however, Mill based his view of government, as well as economics, on interest theory. What he really meant by "interest politics" is spelled out in a later chapter when he says:

When we talk of the interest of a body of men, or even of an individual man, as a principle determining their actions, the question what would be considered their interest by an unprejudiced observer is one of the least important parts of the whole matter. As Coleridge observes, the man makes the motive, not the motive the man. What it is the man's interest to do or refrain from depends less on any outward circumstances than upon what sort of man he is. If you wish to know what is practically a man's interest, you must know the cast of his habitual feelings and thoughts.[54]

In short, not being a "machine," man does not vote his purely "mechanical," i.e., materialistic interests. This point is of great importance. Since the aim of good government is the cultivation, or rather the fostering of conditions for the self-cultivation and development of the individual, we can assume that a "cultured" individual will not vote his crass "mechanical" interest, but rather the general interests of his society, and indeed of humanity. This is still an "interest" theory, but it is a lofty and unselfish one.

In his 1859 article, "Recent Writers on Reform," Mill put his "cultivated interest" theory in this way:

As regards interests in themselves, whenever not identical with the general interest, the less they are represented the better. What is wanted is a representation, not of men's differences of interest, but of the differences in their intellectual points of view. Ship-owners are to be desired in Parliament, because they can instruct us about ships, not because they are interested in having protecting duties. We want from a lawyer in Parliament his legal knowledge not his professional interest in the expensiveness and unintelligibility of the law.[55]

Obviously he thought such individuals existed and could be elected to Parliament. His own election to Parliament in 1866 must have, momentarily at least, confirmed him in this view.

Realist that he was, however, Mill was prepared to load the scales as much as possible for his version of "cultivated interest." A major step in the direction of securing "cultivated interest" politics is Mill's proposal for weighted voting; that is, educated persons, though not property, should be given additional votes.[56] Other devices against the uncultivated masses (mainly the middle classes) and their selfish interests are: requirement of minimum literacy; open rather than secret ballot, an issue on which Mill drastically reversed himself in order to insure that the weight of disinterested opinion could be brought to bear on each individual (ignoring thereby, in this cause, his own fear of coercive public opinion); provision for two legislative chambers, rather than one, to block hasty actions, to represent more cultivated minds, and so on; and no payment for M.P.s to insure that only disinterested persons will run for office. Mill, who believed firmly in universal suffrage, for educational purposes if no other, nevertheless insisted on curbs to universal domination. He demanded representation of the minority, and thought that Thomas Hare's scheme of Proportional Representation was the most important contribution to the art of politics in modern times.[57] In advocating these measures and others, Mill had one constant motive: to block the tyranny of the majority, and to ensure that the "interests" of the cultivated individual, society, and humanity would be honored. Often flawed in the particulars, his work is a noble transfiguration of the Utilitarian "interest" theory.

A Moral Reformer

LOGICALLY, Mill's work on government should have been part of his general sociology. It should have been empirical and inductive, or at least inductive-deductive (as he had complained about his father's work, agreeing thereby with Macaulay's criticism, it was too entirely deductive). But John Stuart Mill did not write a *Democracy in America*, empirically examining the way in which the actual political institutions of a particular democracy functioned in a given historical situation; that task was left to his friend Tocqueville. Nor did Mill produce an empirical study of a despotism, an aristocracy, a nationality, or a colonial dependency, or even a history of India or the French Revolution. An elitist of sorts himself, Mill did not study actual elites, or even seek to analyze their role in government by a comparative study. The leader, as an actual political actor, he ignored. Himself a "psychologist," he never even approximated a psychological study of politics.

Now many of these remarks are obviously present-minded and reflect contemporary concerns. Even so, it is remarkable that Mill made singularly little effort to do for political matters what he did and knew had been done in economic affairs: to construct in detail an explanatory scheme that was inductive-deductive, and thus scientific, or at least to advance the empirical basis on which such a science could be erected, and which his own general theory of social science dictated. The reasons why he did not pursue this path are undoubtedly mixed. The effort at such a political science itself would have been singularly difficult, and Mill's view of the nature of *Geisteswissenschaften*, the "moral sciences," as against the natural sciences, in this area itself mitigated against the inductive method. I believe there was, however, a stronger reason: It is simply that Mill wished to be a moral reformer. This had been his deepest wish from his earliest days. Shaken during his mental crisis, the desire and ambition reasserted itself ever more strongly thereafter. The result was that, in *On Liberty*, *Considerations on Representative Government*, and Mill's other political writings, we hear almost entirely the voice of a dedicated moral reformer rather than of a cool, calculating political scientist. As we know, Mill himself would have been pleased at this verdict, though ambivalently so.

16

Social Science

A Failed Effort

A *System of Logic* was considered by Mill to be, along with *On Liberty*, the work which he was best fitted to write. It is also his most difficult, and, for us, perhaps boring; yet it is crucial to an understanding of Mill. In any case, as early as 1831, when he had begun to work on the subject, he was writing his friend John Sterling: "If there is any science which I am capable of promoting, I think it is the science of science itself, the science of investigation—of method."

Mill's hope was that by his *Logic* he would be able to still the clamor of mere opinion, and substitute true knowledge. Here we shall be primarily concerned with Book 6, in which Mill strove to establish the correct method for social science, to delineate its parts, and to analyze what kinds of knowledge would result from such an approach. We are making no pretense of treating the *Logic* as a whole, or even as a grand philosophical work.[1] What interests us in the *Logic* is the light shed on Mill's idea of a general sociology.

Chronologically, of course, the *Logic* came well before *On Liberty*. Started in 1831, it was finished in 1841, though not published until two years later. Why, then, did we not deal systematically with it, or rather the social science part of it, before *On Liberty*? There are essentially two reasons. First, the general sociology should be seen as replacing Utilitarian "science," and capping Mill's achievement in the fields of political economy and government, with the latter fields being merely parts of the overall accomplishment. Of course, logically, a case could be made for the presentation as well as the execution of the general sociology at the beginning with the more limited fields being fitted into it afterwards. This, in fact, was Mill's original intention. Thus, after finishing the *Logic*, he projected a new book on "ethology," the science which was to serve as the cornerstone for sociology and whose outlines he had sketched in the *Logic*. "There is no chance for social statics at least," he wrote Alexander Bain in 1843, "until the laws of human characteristics are better treated." A few months later, however, he was writing him that "I do not know when I shall be ripe for beginning 'Ethology.' The scheme has not assumed any definite shape with me yet."[2] But by 1845 he had turned instead to work on the *Political Economy*. Though in a letter to Comte of March 26, 1846, defending his efforts in political economy as forming part of a general sociology, Mill still alluded to his intentions concerning his "grande tentative," ethology, he never systematically developed the subject further. As Bain puts it, "His failure with 'Ethology' fatally interfered with the larger project, which I have no doubt he entertained, of executing a work on Sociology as a whole."[3]

If our first reason for dealing with Mill's sociology only now is its implicit capstone position, our second reason is the failure of that last effort itself. As we shall see, it shows the limits of his break with his father and his father's generation—the eighteenth century—and thus makes a fitting conclusion to our analysis of Mill's work. We need, therefore, to look closely at that "failure."

Character Formation and National Character

ETHOLOGY for Mill was "the theory of the influence of various external circumstances, whether individual or social, on the formation of moral and intellectual character."[4] To this subject Mill devoted an entire chapter in the *Logic*. It is really the scientific expression of his lifelong interest in the "formation of character" (*Selbstbildung*), whose nonscientific expression we have already analyzed in *On Liberty*. Mill wanted, first of all, to know how his own character had been formed. This was *the* most pressing and constant question of his life. Had he simply been *made* by his father, as some of his friends mocked him? Was the explanation in Associational psychology? As we have seen, although Mill accepted his father's psychology as correctly laying down the universal laws of the formation of individual character, he could not accept the doctrine of Philosophical Necessity, and fought manfully to leave room for individual liberty. The individual, he concluded, could learn from experience and react in a creative way. Out of manifold motives, he insisted, could come a result which was subject to the laws of causation, but not simply necessitarian.

Mill's interest in character formation was intensely intellectual, in the sense of realizing that only a "science" of national character could justify an intellectual elite seeking to guide the "masses," or serve as a basis for understanding the ephemeral, limited shapes assumed in political economy. It was also intensely personal in its concern with *self*-formation, and, especially, its relation to his strong feelings about the position of women (and the women in his own life). How could one know the true nature, or character, of women, he asked, on the basis of their present education and circumstances? He pointed out:

> What is now called the nature of women is an eminently artificial thing, the result of forced repression in some directions, unnatural stimulation in others. It may be asserted without scruple, that no other class of dependents have had their character so entirely distorted from its natural proportions by their relation with their masters.[5]

It was on this issue, as we know, that he broke most sharply with Comte. In heart and mind, formation of character is the master theme for Mill.

In the case of women, Mill wished to know how their character had been distorted. In the case of nations, he wished to know how it had been formed. In all cases, he wanted to know how we can foresee and control the formation of character to better purposes (a desire that implicitly runs counter to his desire for spontaneous development, and creates a tension in Mill's thought with which he wrestled all his life). The answer was to come from his new science of ethology. Alas, as we have seen, he was never able to give "definite shape" to that science. All he seemed able to do was compulsively to circle about his theme, and to make numerous but unsystematic remarks about various national characters.[6]

As was to be expected, most of his comments were on the English character. Though mixed, they tended to be unfavorable. We have already seen how he excused his father's behavior in the family by putting the blame on the Englishman's habitual shame at expressing his feelings. The result was an atmosphere void of tenderness and affection. So, too, while admitting English superiority in the productive and commercial sphere, Mill called attention to "the very worst point in our national character, the disposition to sacrifice every thing to accumulation and that exclusive & engrossing selfishness which accompanies it." The greatest fault of Englishmen, he believed, was not bigotry but "indifference, moral insensibility":

It is a just charge against the English nation, considered generally, that they do not know how to be kind, courteous, and considerate of the feelings of others. It is their character throughout Europe. They have much to learn from other nations in the arts not only of being serviceable and amiable with grace, but of being so at all.[7]

Occasionally Mill differentiated among classes. Thus, he declared:

Our middle class moreover have but one object in life, to ape their superiors; for whom they have an open-mouthed & besotted admiration, attaching itself to the bad more than to the good points, being those they can most easily comprehend & imitate.[8]

As for the English working class, they were:

. . . in conduct the most disorderly, debauched and unruly, and least respectable and trustworthy of any nation whatsoever. . . . As soon as any idea of equality enters the head of an uneducated English working man, his head is turned by it. When he ceases to be servile, he becomes insolent.[9]

In statements such as these, we seem to detect the tones of an angry and scorned lover. Mill's scathing remarks on his countrymen arise more out of disappointment and frustration than out of "objective" observation and analysis. His heart still belonged to England. As he admitted in 1855: "The nuisance of England is English: on every other account I would rather live in England passing a winter now & then abroad than live altogether anywhere else."[10]

England and France, and their respective national characters, lived in perpetual tension and dialectic in Mill's soul. He alone, he felt, understood the two countries. As for others, he wrote d'Eichthal, "There is something exceedingly strange and lamentable in the utter incapacity of our two nations to understand or believe the real character and springs of action of each other." To Comte he wrote:

I am, like you, deeply persuaded that the combination of the French with the English spirit is one of the most essential requirements for intellectual reorganization. The French spirit is necessary in order that conceptions be general, and the English spirit to prevent them being vague. . . .[11]

It was Comte, however, who generally provoked Mill to a defense of the English character. As was to be expected, it was over the character of women that Mill first reacted. Although in an earlier letter he had praised the role allowed exceptional women in France, in his follow-up letter of October 30, 1843, he insisted that Englishwomen were less constricted by their social position and development than their French counterparts, and concluded that "I believe the English milieu more favorable than the French, all in all, for understanding women."

Similarly, by 1846, as he was beginning to break with the French positivist, he wrote sharply:

> Contrary to general opinion on the Continent, I believe that there is less nationalism among the English than among all other civilized people. They have today far fewer prejudices and national biases than the peoples of the Continent. . . .[12]

One could go on and on citing such comments in Mill. Most of them were on English and French characters. Others were on the Germans (as he wrote Sarah Austin, "much more to your taste [as to mine] than the English"); on contemporary Greeks ("brainless stupidity"); and on Americans (where he specially noted their belief that one man was as good as another). Mill even flirted with a kind of racial theory of character. Thus he wrote on September 14, 1839, to d'Eichthal:

> I have long been convinced that not only the East as compared with the West, but the black race as compared with the European, is distinguished by characteristics something like those which you assign to them; that the improvement which may be looked for, from a more intimate & sympathetic familiarity between the two, will not be solely on their side, but greatly also on ours; that if our intelligence is more developed & our activity more intense, *they* possess exactly what is most needful to us as a qualifying counterpoise, in their love of repose & in the superior capacity of animal enjoyment & consequently of sympathetic sensibility, which is characteristic of the negro race.
>
> I have even long thought that the same distinction holds, though in a less *prononcé* manner, between the nations of the north & south of Europe; that the north is destined to be the workshop, material & intellectual, of Europe; the south, its "stately pleasure-house"—& that neither will fulfil its destination until it has made its peculiar function available for the benefit of both—until our *work* is done for their benefit, & until we, in the measure of our nature, are made susceptible of their luxury & sensuous enjoyment.[13]

Here, of course, Mill's stereotyping—typical of his time (and since?) —was ostensibly harmless; in his typical liberal manner, he looked forward to a fusion of the two character types. He seems never to have recognized the dangers inherent in this sort of "characterology," exemplified, for example, in Tocqueville's friend, Gobineau, whose *Essay on the Inequality of Races*, published in 1853, Mill appears to have passed over in silence.[14] Yet, in *Representative Government*, when he contrasts the admirable "self-helping and struggling Anglo-Saxons" with the inert and envious Orientals and, next to them, the Southern Europeans, he comes perilously close to ethnic prejudice.[15] We seem to hear again the voice of James Mill, castigating the Hindoos for their supine and lascivious characters.

Thus in spite of all Mill's liberalism, and his bisexuality, he was moved in this matter by his father's and his nation's spirit toward a fundamentally "masculine," prejudiced stance, perhaps worse because unrecognized. Perhaps, also, it was partly for this same reason—his father's voice, speaking to him intellectually and psychologically—that Mill was unable ever to rise above his impressionistic views on national character, and therefore to work out a systematic ethology.

But at least Mill knew that the basic explanations for the formation of human character lay in the psychological and social realm, not in the merely physical, and thus, in this case, "racial." Although he could not supply the details and "laws" operative in this matter, he felt sure about the correctness of his general theory. Comte, on the other hand, was more hospitable to a physicalistic explanation, indeed, to a phrenological explanation of character, although his major objection to Mill was of a different sort: He believed (thereby echoing Mill's criticism of Bentham, incidentally) that in his ethology Mill was seeking to subordinate explanation on sociological grounds to explanation in terms of individual psychology, i.e., the laws of human nature. For Comte, in short, Mill's views were basically inimical to the elaboration of a true sociology. To estimate the worth of Comte's charge we must turn to Book 6 of Mill's *Logic*, and a full examination of his views on social science.

Physical and Moral Science

MILL BEGINS Book 6, "On the Logic of the Moral Sciences," with a quotation from Comte's *Cours de Philosophie Positive*. The passage claims that science is the only solid basis for social reorganization, for curing the social crisis of the civilized nations, and asserts the necessity of a stable, commonly held social doctrine to prevent revolution. As Mill had put it in the Preface:

> [Book 6] is an attempt to contribute towards the solution of a question, which the decay of old opinions, and the agitation that disturbs European

society to its inmost depths, render as important in the present day to the practical interests of human life, as it must at all times be to the completeness of our speculative knowledge: viz., Whether moral and social phenomena are really exceptions to the general certainty and uniformity of the course of nature; and how far the methods, by which so many of the laws of the physical world have been numbered among truths irrevocably acquired and universally assented to, can be made instrumental to the gradual formation of a similar body of received doctrine in moral and political science.[16]

In short, Mill places his "practical" political aims in trying to establish a moral science clearly before us at the beginning.

Mill's initial concern is to reject the notion of a basic division between the natural and moral sciences. As he says rather long-windedly:

If on matters so much the most important with which human intellect can occupy itself, a more general agreement is ever to exist among thinkers; if what has been pronounced "the proper study of mankind" is not destined to remain the only subject which Philosophy cannot succeed in rescuing from Empiricism; the same processes through which the laws of simpler phenomena have by general acknowledgment been placed beyond dispute, must be consciously and deliberately applied to those more difficult inquiries.[17]

Mill's view of the progress of the natural sciences was typical of his time. As he remarked in "The Spirit of the Age":

The physical sciences, therefore, (speaking of them generally) are continually *growing*, but never *changing*: in every age they receive indeed mighty improvements, but for them the age of transition is past.[18]

If natural science was cumulative, though unchanging, why not the moral sciences? In 1831, reviewing the physicist Herschel's book *The Study of Natural Philosophy*, Mill was sufficiently impressed by the following statement to reprint it:

"The successful results of our experiments and reasonings in natural philosophy, and the incalculable advantages which experience, systematically consulted and dispassionately reasoned on, has conferred in matters purely physical, tend of necessity to impress something of the well weighed and progressive character of science on the more complicated conduct of our social and moral relations. It is thus that legislation and politics become gradually regarded as experimental sciences; and history, not as formerly, the mere record of tyrannies and slaughters . . . but as the archive of experiments, successful and unsuccessful, gradually accumulating towards the solution of the grand problem—how the advantages of government are to be secured with the least possible inconvenience to the governed . . . why should we despair that the reason which has enabled us to subdue all nature to our purposes should . . . achieve a far more difficult conquest."[19]

It was this inspiration that carried over into the writing of the *Logic*.

In fact, however, matters were not that simple, as Mill himself knew. In his "Definition of Political Economy" (in my view a more subtle and succinct treatment of the logic of the moral sciences than the *Logic* itself), Mill acknowledged the differences between the natural and moral sciences in a forthright manner:

If we contemplate the whole field of human knowledge, attained or attainable, we find that it separates itself obviously, and as it were spontaneously, into two divisions, which stand so strikingly in opposition and contradistinction to one another, that in all classifications of our knowledge they have been kept apart. These are, *physical* science, and *moral* or psychological science.

In physical science, laws of matter obtain; in the moral sciences, laws of mind. To illustrate, Mill offers the example of growing corn, which combines the two:

The laws of matter are those properties of the soil and of vegetable life which cause the seed to germinate in the ground, and those properties of the human body which render food necessary to its support. The law of mind is, that man desires to possess subsistence, and consequently wills the necessary means of procuring it.

His conclusion is striking:

Laws of mind and laws of matter are so dissimilar in their nature, that it would be contrary to all principles of rational arrangement to mix them up as part of the same study. In all scientific methods, therefore, they are placed apart.[20]

But in the *Logic* Mill plays down the differences between the physical and moral sciences. He is aware that the best way to prove his point is actually to construct a moral science, along the lines of the physical. But from this he begs off:

I am not unmindful . . . how vague and unsatisfactory all precepts of Method must necessarily appear, when not practically exemplified in the establishment of a body of doctrine. Doubtless, the most effectual way of showing how the sciences of Ethics and Politics may be constructed, would be to construct them: a task which, it needs scarcely be said, I am not about to undertake.

Instead, he will be like Bacon, and merely point the way. In fact, Mill claims, this is what he has already done:

In substance, whatever can be done in a work like this, for the Logic of the Moral Sciences, has been or ought to have been accomplished in the five preceding Books. . . .[21]

16 / Social Science

A "Free Character"

THE FIRST essential question concerning the moral sciences is: "Are the actions of man, like all other natural events, subject to invariable laws?"[22] An affirmative answer implied the denial of man's uniqueness, his special position in God's creativity. Descartes, for example, had refused to take this step, and by his mind-body dualism exempted man from the natural laws governing all other phenomena. Others, however, such as d'Holbach and La Mettrie, embracing man in their materialism, prepared the way for a view of man's actions as being subject, at least in principle, to invariable laws. Montesquieu seems to have been the first, skirting and abstaining from the religious implications, to claim man's actions for science of a kind we recognize as social science.[23] It was Auguste Comte, however, who definitely made good the claim and established once and for all the legitimacy of sociology, the effort to treat man's social actions as subject to invariable laws. John Stuart Mill followed Comte in this view.

Mill, however, had an additional problem. He had to reconcile science, which establishes necessary and invariable relations, with his desire for moral reform, which implies some degree of free will. More importantly, from his personal view, he had to secure the certainty offered by science with the freedom for self-development and character formation so imperiously required by his own psychic history. As we have seen in detail, Mill's mental depression was inextricably connected for him with the fear of laboring under the yoke of Philosophical Necessity; of being completely "made" by his father, without any hand in his own determination.

Mill devoted the whole of the second chapter of Book 6 to extricating himself from this dilemma. First he affirms the scientific side. The doctrine of Philosophical Necessity, correctly conceived, states that:

> Given the motives which are present to an individual's mind, and given likewise the character and disposition of the individual, the manner in which he will act may be unerringly inferred; that if we knew the person thoroughly, and knew all the inducements which are acting upon him, we could foretell his conduct with as much certainty as we can predict any physical event.[24]

Mill agrees with this formulation. The problem, however, is that human beings *feel* free. They are conscious of their own volition, and convinced that they are not under "this mysterious constraint." Mill goes about solving this problem, whose "depressing consequences" he admits, as follows. Necessity is but mere uniformity of order, capable of being predicted. Rightly named, it is simply causation. Associated with the notion of Necessity, however, is "irresistibleness," and this Mill vigorously negates: "When we say that all human actions take place of necessity, we only mean that they will certainly happen if nothing prevents." There is much, however, in human action to "prevent" mere mechanical behavior. Human actions are ruled by many motives, any one of which itself can be changed. For Mill, the argument is intensely personal at this point, in spite of the formalism and ponderousness of his utterance:

> [A necessarian,] believing that our actions follow from our characters, and that our characters follow from our organization, our education, and our circumstances, is apt to be, with more or less of consciousness on his part, a fatalist as to his own actions, and to believe that his nature is such, or that his education and circumstances have so moulded his character, that nothing can now prevent him from feeling and acting in a particular way, or at least that no effort of his own can hinder it.[25]

Mill, without saying it, was describing the views of his father, or at least the caricature of his father (as well as, of course, the views of people such as Robert Owen).[26] For such a necessarian, "character is formed *for* him, and not *by* him." This position, Mill avers, is a "grand error":

> [A man has,] to a certain extent, a power to alter his character. Its being, in the ultimate resort, formed for him, is not inconsistent with its being, in part, formed *by* him as one of the intermediate agents. His character is formed by his circumstances (including among these his particular organization); but his own desire to mould it in a particular way, is one of those circumstances, and by no means one of the least influential. . . . When our habits are not too inveterate, [we] can, by . . . willing the requisite means, make ourselves different. If they could place us under the influence of certain circumstances, we, in like manner, can place ourselves under the influence of other circumstances. We are exactly as capable of making our own character, *if we will*, as others are of making it for us.[27]

With these words, Mill has vindicated his own self-formation.

Mill now adds that fresh experience constantly remakes us, and thus gives us new volitions. We must, of course, not merely have the wishes, but act on them. This version of the free will doctrine, Mill tells us, has fostered "especially in the younger of its supporters, a much stronger spirit of self-culture." Then, in a last break with his father's doctrine, Mill asserts that motives are not always linked to the anticipation of pleasure and pain; they become habitual, and we eventually come to will a particular course of conduct whether it is, in fact, any longer pleasurable or not. He concludes:

It is only when our purposes have become independent of the feelings of pain or pleasure from which they originally took their rise, that we are said to have a confirmed character.[28]

Thus Mill is able, so to speak, to have his cake and eat it. Human actions are under laws, but these laws of causation are not necessary in the sense of being irresistible.

The Laws of Mind

IN HIS third chapter Mill poses the question of what *kind* of a science a science of human nature would be. The science of human nature, according to Mill, is like Meteorology and Tidology (the science of tides), an inexact science. But this does not mean that it cannot be scientific:

It falls far short of the standard of exactness now realized in Astronomy; but there is no reason that it should not be as much a science as Tidology is, or as Astronomy was when its calculations had only mastered the main phenomena, but not the perturbations.

Although we cannot predict human actions with scientific accuracy, because we cannot foretell all of the circumstances in which individuals will be placed, we can make approximate generalizations, and these are sufficient "for the purposes of political and social science." In fact, "an approximate generalization is practically, in social inquiries, equivalent to an exact one; that which is only probable when asserted of human beings taken individually, being certain when affirmed of the character and collective conduct of masses." With this comforting statement, Mill is then able to conclude:

In other words, the science of Human Nature may be said to exist, in proportion as those approximate truths, which compose a practical knowledge of mankind, can be exhibited as corollaries from the universal laws of human nature on which they rest. . . .[29]

In short, the task is now to establish the "Laws of Mind."

Laws of Mind, for Mill, are restricted to those cases in which a state of mind is produced by a state of mind, not by a state of body, i.e., sensations. If the latter were the sole cause, then mind would be a subject of physical science, and Comte would be right in his decision to eliminate psychology as a separate science: "Mental Science would be a mere branch, though the highest and most recondite branch, of the Science of Physiology." For Mill, however, "The successions . . . which obtain among mental phenomena, do not admit of being deduced from the physiological laws of our nervous organization";[30] hence, psychology deals with the effect of a state of mind on the mind itself. Though originating in sensation, ideas take on a life of their own once inside the mind. The laws governing this mental life are the Laws of Association, and Mill proudly refers his reader to the "masterly" exposition set forth by his father in *The Analysis of the Phenomena of the Human Mind.*

John Stuart Mill adds only that "The laws of the phenomena of mind are sometimes analogous to mechanical, but sometimes also to chemical laws." In the latter state, ideas, instead of merely being added to one another, melt and coalesce into one another. In this "mental chemistry," Mill tells us, "it is proper to say that the simple ideas generate, rather than that they compose, the complex ones." For this reason, complex mental phenomena cannot be understood by first understanding the simpler forms (based on mere sensations, and laws of body). Complex phenomena must be studied in their own right:

> The generation of one class of mental phenomena from another, whenever it can be made out, is a highly interesting fact in psychological chemistry; but it no more supersedes the necessity of an experimental study of the generated phenomenon, than a knowledge of the properties of oxygen and sulphur enables us to deduce those of sulphuric acid without specific observation and experiment.[31]

Thus the autonomy of psychology, the Laws of Mind, has been defended, and, provisionally, its model seen as chemistry, rather than physiology or mechanics.

A "Science" of Ethology

MILL NOW feels able to turn at last to his "Ethology, or the Science of the Formation of Character." What, in fact, is ethology? It is that science concerning character whose laws are

> . . . derivative laws, resulting from the general laws of the mind; and they are to be obtained by deducing them from those general laws; by supposing any given set of circumstances, and then considering what, according to the laws of mind, will be the influence of those circumstances on the formation of character.

While the name ethology could be used to cover the entire science of our mental and moral nature, Mill prefers to use the traditional name psychology for the science of the elementary laws of mind, and ethology for the subordinate science concerning the kind of character produced by these general laws in given physical and moral circumstances. As such, it is an "Exact Science of Human Nature," for its truths are not mere empirical laws, i.e., approximate generalizations, but "real laws."[32]

Empirical laws are uniformities of succession or of coexistence which hold true in all instances within our limits of observation; that is exactly their limitation. Like the example of day succeeding night, they are based merely on observation. Really scientific laws are the causal laws which explain the empirical ones. Such causal laws may be very few and simple, while their effects are various and complicated. By investigating the latter, the multitudinous circumstances, we shall find few propositions respecting behavior or feelings true for all mankind. Every nation and every generation differs in its circumstances from every other. The conclusion Mill draws from all of this is that "mankind have not one universal character, but there exist universal laws of the Formation of Character."[33]

Such laws are to be discovered, or investigated, by the deductive method, which, setting out from general laws, verifies their consequences by specific experience. Such verification in ethology is hampered by the fact that direct experimentation into the formation of character is impossible (e.g., how can we isolate the elements involved in the education of a human being from infancy to maturity?). We are thrown back, then, on observation, but now as a method of confirmation rather than generation of causal laws. In perhaps the fullest description of what he has in mind, Mill says:

> But if the differences which you think you observe between French and English, or between persons of station and persons of no station, can be connected with more general laws; if they be such as would naturally flow from the differences of government, former customs and physical peculiarities in the two nations, and from the diversities of education, occupations, and social position in the different classes of society; then, indeed, the coincidence of the two kinds of evidence justifies us in believing that we have both reasoned rightly and observed rightly. Our observation, though not sufficient as proof, is ample as verification. And having ascertained not only the empirical laws but the causes of the peculiarities, we need be under no difficulty in judging how far they may be expected to be permanent, or by what circumstances they would be modified or destroyed.[34]

Yet Mill gives not one example of how a particular general law interacts with a specific set of conditions, but contents himself with an allusion to the need for some kind of incipient anthropology.

Before us, then, we have the vague entity known as ethology. The ideal is clear enough: We are to take general laws from psychology, deduce their consequences when conjoined with particular circumstances, and emerge with exact laws whose status is causal rather than merely empirical. We are left, however, with two major problems. One is that the scheme more or less stands on the validity and usefulness of the psychology involved. In the event, Associational psychology could not bear the burden placed upon it. There is, of course, the entrancing possibility that, taken up into psychoanalysis, Associational psychology in its new form might offer a sounder and more fecund ground on which to proceed. Indeed, the new field of psychohistory can be looked at in this way. The second problem, reverting directly back to Mill, is that actual implementation of the new science is not worked out. We desperately need a convincing example to go with the ideal, and this Mill never offers us.[35]

Ethology and Politics

THE CHAPTER that follows that on ethology does not really clarify matters. Mill begins:

> After the science of individual man, comes the science of man in society: of the actions of collective masses of mankind, and the various phenomena which constitute social life.

This is puzzling, because we have already been told that ethology also dealt with collective man as well as individuals. The difference, apparently, is that ethology dealt with formation of character, and the science that Mill will now talk about deals with actions. Thus, Mill here wishes to raise the possibility of "giving a scientific character to the study of politics, and the phenomena of sociology." Only recently have men entertained any notion:

> that there were limits to the power of human will over the phenomena of society, or that any social arrangements which would be desirable, could be impracticable from incompatibility with the properties of the subject matter: the only obstacle was supposed to lie in the private interests or prejudices, which hindered men from being willing to see them tried.[36]

Again Mill only adumbrates this science, but gives no details as to how it might be articulated; one thinks ahead to *On Liberty* and *Repre-*

sentative Government to see how far he was himself from such an effort at a political science.

Mill doesn't say so, but one might have thought that the science of politics should proceed in the fashion of political economy by making "entire abstraction" of some one human motive, say, the desire for power or domination.[37] James Mill seems to have been close to such a conception, but in rejecting his father's deductive method in this area, Mill placed himself far from this possibility. Instead he subsumes speculative politics under a general social science—indeed, he seems to confuse the two completely—and relates only the latter, in the form of "social economy," to the prototypic political economy. So, at the end, we are left wondering what is the real difference between ethology and social science. Has Mill merely confused psychology (now extended to ethology) with sociology, thus reducing the latter effectively to the former? This is the criticism leveled at Mill by, for example, Karl Popper. According to Popper, Mill fell victim to psychologism, the doctrine that:

> Society being the product of interacting minds, social laws must ultimately be reducible to psychological laws, since the events of social life, including its conventions, must be the outcome of motives springing from the minds of individual men.[38]

If true, this would go far toward explaining why Mill never worked out a true, autonomous sociology. It would also accord with our view that Mill's compulsive attention to the formation of character, oriented to his individual problems, prevented him from paying independent attention in his theory to external social phenomena.

The Method of Sociology

IN THE REST of Book 6 of the *Logic*, Mill reverts to the subject of method. His views here are among his most famous. There are, he declares, two erroneous methods in the social sciences: the chemical, or experimental, and the geometrical, or abstract. Although Mill had talked earlier about "mental chemistry" in the individual mind, he now insists that:

> Men are not, when brought together, converted into another kind of substance, with different properties; as hydrogen and oxygen are different from water, or as hydrogen, oxygen, carbon, and azote, are different from nerves, muscles, and tendons. Human beings in society have no properties but those

which are derived from, and may be resolved into, the laws of the nature of individual man. In social phenomena the Composition of Causes is the universal law.[39]

There seems no hint here that men in groups might behave differently from men as individuals.[40]

As for the geometrical or abstract method, while deductive, it is nevertheless the wrong model for deductive social science, for it leaves no room for "the case of conflicting forces; of causes which counteract or modify one another."[41] In social science, Mill informs us, the geometrical method manifests itself in the school of abstract rights, where deductions, such as from a social contract, are made in a causal vacuum. Among such "chimerical" attempts Mill also places Bentham's effort to deduce a science of politics from the single abstraction of selfish interest. In Mill's view, since selfish interests are only one among a myriad of conflicting forces, the geometrical method simply doesn't work in such cases.

In social science (which, following Comte, he declares he will call sociology), Mill argues that effects are produced by a complex set of circumstances, and a particular effect "amounts precisely to the sum of effects of the circumstances taken singly." We must follow, therefore, the "Physical or Concrete Deductive Method" of the higher physical sciences:

[We] infer the law of each effect from the laws of causation upon which that effect depends; not, however, from the law merely of one cause, as in the geometrical method; but by considering all the causes which conjunctly influence the effect, and compounding their laws with one another.

Mill is quite candid about the difficulties of doing this in practice, and aware that the results are not positive predictions but only tendencies. He also realizes that all social phenomena, in fact, are one "great case of intermixture of laws," so that the same cause can never be said with certainty to have the same tendency in one people or age as in another.[42] Each people or age must be studied separately and anew.

At this point Mill presents the case for studying fairly simple, immediate influences in semi-isolation. Political economy is his prime example, and we have already commented on his treatment of this subject. Mill also alludes, in this context, to "Political Ethology, or the science of the causes which determine the type of character belonging to a people or to an age." The laws of national character, he now tells us, "are by far the most important class of sociological laws."

Knowing as we do the centrality of the subject of opinions and customs for Mill, we can see easily why ethology is so important for him. Indeed, it is so important that the science of politics, which he elsewhere accords separate recognition, here gets swallowed up in sociology. The reason given in this case is that, unlike political economy, where the diversity of character among different nations at different times enters as an influencing cause only in a secondary degree (though, in fact, Mill seems to anticipate Max Weber in some of his comments on the need for a competitive character), the "Science of Government," i.e., political phenomena:

of all others, is most mixed up, both as cause and effect, with the qualities of the particular people or of the particular age. All questions respecting the tendencies of forms of government must stand part of the general science of society, not of any separate branch of it.[43]

We are left, therefore, with political ethology.

So far, however, it turns out that we have mainly been discussing only one part of sociology, the part that will tell us "what effect will follow from a given cause, a certain general condition of social conditions being presupposed," e.g., the effect of the Corn Laws in nineteenth-century England. In the second part of sociological inquiry:

[We ask] not what will be the effect of a given cause in a certain state of society, but what are the causes which produce, and the phenomena which characterize States of Society generally. In the solution of this question consists the general Science of Society; by which all the conclusions of the other and more special kind of inquiry must be limited and controlled.[44]

But what, in fact, is a "State of Society"? In a definition which is almost equivalent to that for sociology or even ethology, Mill tells us:

What is called a state of society is the simultaneous state of all the greater social facts, or phenomena. Such are, the degree of knowledge, and of intellectual and moral culture, existing in the community, and in every class of it; the state of industry, of wealth and its distribution; the habitual occupations of the community; their division into classes, and the relations of those classes to one another; the common beliefs which they entertain on all the subjects most important to mankind, and the degree of assurance with which those beliefs are held; their tastes, and the character and degree of their aesthetic development; their form of government, and the more important of their laws and customs. The condition of all these things and of many more which will spontaneously suggest themselves, constitute the state of society or the state of civilization at any given time.[45]

Looked at another way, this is the closest Mill comes to offering us an agenda for actual social science inquiry. In any event, only certain combinations of these social facts are possible at a given time, e.g., only certain class divisions can coexist with certain states of industry, and so on. This is what Mill calls "Uniformities of Coexistence," which we can recognize as the sociological expression of his heritage of organicism and holism from the Germano-Coleridgean school.

But what laws govern the way any given state of society emerges from the state before it, and produces the state which succeeds it? For Mill, such a consideration "opens the great and vexed question of the progressiveness of man and society." Of the existence of progressive change "both in the character of the human race, and in their outward circumstances so far as moulded by themselves," Mill had no doubt. Following Comte, he declared:

> The periods at which these successive changes are most apparent are intervals of one generation, during which a new set of human beings have been educated, have grown up from childhood, and taken possession of society.[46]

Here Mill seems rather simplistically to equate generational change with mere biological change, but it is a view that the reality of the nineteenth century seemed to be supporting, and to which Mill's own life bore evidence.

This progress, generational in character, was only an empirical law. To be converted into a scientific law, it must be connected with "the psychological and ethnological laws which govern the action of circumstances on men and of men on circumstances." As society advances, the influence exerted over each generation by the generation which preceded it becomes both more significant and more uniform:

> since the evolution of each people, which is at first determined exclusively by the nature and circumstances of that people, is gradually brought under the influence (which becomes stronger as civilization advances) of the other nations of the earth, and of the circumstances by which they have been influenced. History accordingly does, when judiciously examined, afford Empirical Laws of Society. And the problem of general sociology is to ascertain these, and connect them with the laws of human nature by deductions showing that such were the derivative laws naturally to be expected as the consequences of those ultimate ones.

Today we seek to analyze that general "influence" affecting all nations in terms of the concept of "modernization"; Mill did not have the term, but he seems to have had the general concept in mind. Such an influence, i.e., "modernization," is a derivative law made manifest in the course of history. It must, according to Mill, be linked with the laws of mind, and to deductions from the latter shown to accord with the derivative law. Such is what Mill calls the Inverse Deductive Method. In practice, he admits, we cannot demonstrate a priori that "such was the only order of succession or of coexistence in which the effects could, consistently with the law of human nature, have been produced."[47] But we can come close to this ideal.

In one area, the requisites of stable political union, Mill is willing to offer some specific general truths, or generalizations, of social science. On the assumption that "obedience to a government of some sort" is the first element of the social union, society requires, first, a system of education whose main ingredient is a "restraining discipline"; in modern terms, we would call this a socialization process. The second condition of permanent political science is the "feeling of allegiance or loyalty," but Mill leaves this undeveloped. The third essential condition is "a strong and active principle of nationality," again unanalyzed in any specific depth. Still, we can see that later sociology would develop and extend these conditions in a manner that Mill would presumably have welcomed and wished to follow himself. The illustration he offers of a social dynamic law—that "the military spirit gradually gives way to the industrial," as society becomes progressively more engaged with productive pursuits—carries far less conviction after the experiences of the first half of the twentieth century than at the time Mill was writing.[48]

In the area of social dynamics, Mill was eager to essay one further specific empirical law. It is the "law of successive transformations of religion and society" in a positive, i.e., Comtean, direction. As he tells us:

> The evidence of history and the evidence of human nature combine, by a most striking instance of consilience, to show that there is really one social element which is thus predominant, and almost paramount, among the agents of the social progression. This is, the state of the speculative faculties of mankind; including the nature of the speculative beliefs which by any means they have arrived at concerning themselves and the world by which they are surrounded.[49]

Even the desire for increased material comfort, which is the impelling force behind most improvements in the arts of life, is itself dependent on the progress of knowledge. Thus, Mill reverses Marx's order of influence. Mill admits that most members of society are animated by the desire for material gain; it is only the "exceptional individuals" who are concerned with knowledge. But it is on this handful that progress depends, for it is the state of knowledge that determines the physical, moral, and political state of the community. Thus history confirms Mill's basic elitist disposition. This confirmation, however, he points out, is only visible now, for the law can only manifest itself over long stretches of time. It has been the glory of Comte that he has been able to distinguish it, in terms of his law of the three stages. As Mill triumphantly declares: "The Science of History has only become possible in our own time."[50] Mill has finally been able to connect his laws of mind—the speculative faculties, as spelled out in Associational psychology—with the empirical law, derived from history, showing intellectual progression. Together, the two demonstrate the correctness of Mill's inductive-deductive method (incorporating the concrete deductive method), as well as its practical usefulness in establishing the possibility of social statics and social dynamics. Or so Mill believed. In his own mind he had demonstrated the possibility of sociology, its nature, and the lines on which further inquiry in it must proceed.

The Light of the Future

HOW HAS time dealt with Mill's ideas on sociology? Did the *Logic* vindicate the possibility of a "Moral Science"? Did Mill generate a method and an agenda that influenced the direction in which further inquiry in social science would proceed? These are extended questions whose answers would require a full-scale work on the history of the social sciences. Here we can offer only a short summary of the problem and make a few scattered observations.

Mill, as we have seen, vindicated the effort to treat man as a social being under laws ascertainable by the human mind through ratiocination and observation. He went further, however, by insisting on the unity of the natural and moral sciences. The same methods and principles that applied in the one were applicable in the other. Here his view entered into a growing controversy, which took shape in the later nineteenth century in terms of a presumed opposition between the *Naturwissenschaften* and the *Geisteswissenschaften*, in which the names of German philosophers such as Dilthey, Rickert, and Windelband figure largely. In much of this debate, Mill's name was forgotten, and the fight raged mainly against Comte and positivism.[51]

Mill's roots, however, were deeper than positivism, running straight to his Utilitarian background. As we know, he began from the Associational psychology handed him by his father, and never really swerved from it. John Stuart Mill's major interest was in the formation of character, and his logical efforts to defend the validity and establish the nature of moral science were, in our view, subordinated to, or at least perturbated by, this pressing concern. Moreover, he made formation of character and its psychology the basis of his sociology, often, if one follows Popper's view, reducing the latter to the former. Whatever the truth of this charge—and I believe it just—the limitations of Mill's psychology became critical to his work. Ignoring the unconscious dynamics of the mind as his work does, it appears extremely shallow, and thus to our twentieth-century minds a fragile base for social science.

In any case, Mill linked his Associational psychology, unmodified, to another element of his Utilitarian heritage—conjectural history—only this time updating the latter view. What he did was transmute his conjectural history into Comte's positive philosophy of history, with its law of the three stages, and emerge, under Comte's inspiration, with a form of social dynamics. Unlike Comte, however, Mill left room in the total entity of sociology—both statics and dynamics—for a subscience, political economy. It was in this synthetic manner that, in the area of social science as elsewhere, he effected his generational rebellion.

There was a distinct limit to Mill's generational shift. As he indicated in the *Logic*, in the course of a generation, "a new set of human beings have been educated, have grown up from childhood, and taken possession of society."[52] Mill and his thought were subject to the same "law." By the 1860s, certainly, and perhaps a short time before, Mill's "generation" (and one must use the term loosely here) had exhausted itself. Mill's mind and character were formed in a generation—and in the course of a generational conflict—totally uninfluenced by the two seminal ideas of the period after the mid-nineteenth century: Marxism and Darwinism. Separately, as well as together, they changed the ways in which men thought and felt, as well as making Mill's kind of effort in social science largely outdated.

Marx was apparently totally unknown to Mill.[53] This is really not surprising. Although *The Communist Manifesto* had appeared in 1848, and Marx had published his *Critique of Political Economy* in 1859, the same year as Mill's *On Liberty*, he was still unknown and without influence in England; he was a minor sectarian in the socialist world. Publication of *Capital* in 1872, a year before Mill's death, could hardly have influenced the latter, even if it had been widely recognized by contemporaries; in fact, it was ignored at the time. Thus, Marx's major influence came only toward the end of the nineteenth century, when his categories and attitudes permeated all further work in the social sciences. In sum, though of the biological generation immediately following Mill—Marx was only twelve years his junior—Marx was sociologically of the generation following, i.e., two generations removed, at least in terms of influence. That influence, when it came to bear, gave substance and detail—particularity—to sociological analysis that was undreamt of by Mill.

Darwin was Mill's close biological contemporary, born only three years later (1809). However, by the time that Darwin's major work, *The Origin of the Species*, appeared in 1859, Mill's mind was set, and his own major work—the *Logic*, the *Political Economy*, and even *On Liberty*—finished. Thus the tremendous transformation of thought effected by the theory of evolution passed Mill by. What Freud was to call the second great shaking of man's ego (the first was the work of Copernicus, and the third Freud's own) meant nothing to Mill. He was still in the school of progressivism, compounded of the teachings of his father and Comte, and not of evolution. Between the two concepts, however, a revolution had taken place.

In the case of Darwin, unlike that of Marx, Mill was aware of his work. Thus in the fifth edition (1862) of the *Logic* he adds the observation:

> Mr. Darwin's remarkable speculation on the Origin of Species is another unimpeachable example of a legitimate hypothesis. What he terms "natural selection" is not only a *vera causa*, but one proved to be capable of producing effects of the same kind with those which the hypothesis ascribes to it: the question of possibility is entirely of one degree. . . . He has opened a path of inquiry full of promise, the results of which none can foresee. And is it not a wonderful feat of scientific knowledge and ingenuity to have rendered so bold a suggestion, which the first impulse of every one was to reject at once, admissible and discussable, even as a conjecture?[54]

Yet Mill never either pursued the new path of inquiry opened by Darwin, or even speculated in terms of its bearings on other inquiries, especially in social science.

Could Mill have done so before 1859 and a time when his own mind was already too fully formed? That the possibility was there is suggested by the work of his friend and younger contemporary, Herbert Spencer. Spencer, indeed, with his *Principles of Sociology*, shows the way in which the generation following Mill would construct a theoretical sociology, heavily influenced by evolutionary concepts.[55]

At the same period of the 1860s, a few individuals were also making outstanding theoretical and empirical contributions to the emerging science of anthropology. The names of Sir Henry Maine, Sir John Lubbock, J. F. McLennan, and E. B. Tylor illustrate this development. Moreover, their work gradually began to be supported in institutional fashion. Mill in the *Logic* had asked for "increased study of the various types of human nature that are to be found in the world." In 1843, the same year as the first appearance of Mill's book, an Ethnological Society was founded. Its interests were classificatory, descriptive, and antiquarian, and no effort was made to detect social or psychological laws. But by 1863 some of its members, influenced by evolutionary considerations, broke away to establish the Anthropological Society of London. Its purpose, though vague and mixed, allowed for and encouraged inquiry into "The law of his [man's] origin and progress . . . [attained] by patient investigation, careful induction, and the encouragement of all researches tending to establish a *de facto* science of man."[56] By 1884, the first readership in Anthropology was established at Oxford (E. B. Tylor was the Reader), turning into a chair by 1896 (also first occupied by Tylor).

Thus, we can see that from the 1860s onward, a generation of "anthropologists," increasingly in a professionalized setting, were coming into prominence, thereby joining Spencer, who was laying down the outlines for a sociology on evolutionary principles. Together, the sociologists and anthropologists pushed on in practice with the work Mill had only speculated about haltingly. By the very end of the nineteenth century, anthropology and sociology had been given autonomous and canonical nature as true "sciences" of man and society. If we add the name of Sigmund Freud, we can see that psychology was also about to bring forth a fresh branch, psychoanalysis, which offered a whole new view of the "nature" of man and the "laws of mind" presumed to underlay the varied cultures and societies of particular men.

What Is This to Mill?

WHAT IS all this to John Stuart Mill? We cannot expect him to have known about such developments ahead of time, and to have incorporated their ideas and data in his writings. Nevertheless, only in the context of these later developments can we evaluate his own work in the social sciences. A few conclusions are thereby possible.

While Mill cannot be expected to know the future developments in sociology and anthropology (and in the beginning the two were not really separate), he could have made a greater contribution than in his *Logic*, by actually undertaking his work on ethology. He, himself, as we have seen, realized this, yet he did not do anything about the problem. In my view, the reason is twofold. First, Mill's basic interest was in the formation of character. He knew that sociology had a major role in this formation—on the women's question, for example, he was desperate to vindicate the primacy of nurture over nature—yet he could not bring himself to formulate an autonomous sociology whose subject would be society conceptualized as a system independent of the particular individuals comprising it. He appealed, instead, to scattered observations and to history. Second, Mill's Associational psychology, the laws of mind essential to his deductive method, was simply inadequate to bear the burden of actually stimulating research into the way these laws presumably interacted with social circumstances. In a real sense, Mill needed a psychoanalytic psychology, along the lines now being employed by cultural anthropology and by psychohistory. Without an adequate sociology or psychology, Mill was helpless in pursuing his researches into the formation of character. Yet his compulsive interest in the subject, his personal involvement, as I have tried to show, kept him from proceeding in more promising directions. As a result, Mill's science of ethology frittered itself away into idle and unsystematic observations on national character. At the same time, Mill gave up his aim of establishing a secure social science base for his political philosophy, and turned back to his original aim of being primarily a moral reformer.

We can see this fact clearly illustrated in the review of Sir Henry Maine's *Village Communities in the East and West* that Mill wrote in 1871. Mill applauded the book as doing for property relations what Maine had done in his earlier book, *Ancient Law*, for legal relations, for together these relations and the ideas about them, along with religion, were "the great transmitter[s] of influences from a barbarous age to a civilized one." Mill also glimpsed that Maine's detection of the shift from custom as determining land rents, to competition as a rival principle, was fundamental to the development of capitalist society, and thus industrialism. But this was not Mill's main point. What he wanted to stress in Maine was that the latter, in both his books, had been "a most powerful solvent of a large class of conservative prejudices, by pointing out the historical origin not only of institutions, but also of ideas, which many believe to be essential elements of the conception of social order."

Mill, in fact, was more concerned with the possibility of political and moral reform involved in Maine's work than in its character of empirical research. While agreeing that the deduction of "social truth from abstract human nature" was one-sided, he was more afraid of the "tendency to the far worse extreme, of postponing the universal exigencies of *man as man* [italics added] to the beliefs and tendencies of particular portions of mankind as manifested in their history." In short, Mill wished to have no truck with "objective," "relativistic" research—scientific anthropology—which would operate free of Western moral and political thought, even as a mere preliminary empirical posture. We see this clearly when he congratulates Maine for writing "philosophical history," i.e., "the philosophy of the history of institutions."[57]

At this point we can assert that the limits of Mill's generational revolt had been reached. His rebellion had been far-reaching. He had taken Bentham's and his father's Utilitarianism and combined it with the new thought and feeling inundating the early nineteenth century: Carlyle, Saint-Simonianism, the Germano-Coleridgan school, Auguste Comte. Thus he "connected" the eighteenth and nineteenth centuries, responding in this fashion to the desperate sense of alienation experienced by so many in his age, and epitomized by the Romantics. He had also shaped the central nature of mid-nineteenth-century liberalism, exemplifying it in his own character. In this effort he encompassed practically the whole range of thought of his time, making recognizable contributions of his own in numerous areas: the *Logic* as a whole, the *Political Economy*, *On Liberty* and *Representative Government*, the *Subjection of Women*, and so on, not to mention a corpus of articles that is simply breathtaking. It is hardly much of a criticism, then, to say that his achievement did not reach far enough to establish a social science, or even to form a real bridge to it. That was the task of another generation. Mill had done more than enough in his own time. His father could well have been proud of what his son had "made" on his own. Moving back and forth intellectually and psychologically between two worlds, John Stuart Mill had taken the world given to him by his father and "remade" it in his own, more "liberal," image.

17

Conclusion: The Mills in History

A Time for Oedipus

EARLY in the nineteenth century, John Stuart Mill became locked, as we have seen, in a seemingly fated embrace with his father and his father's generation. For James Mill, too, the relation to his son was a central experience, recalling his own rearing and testing the identity he had worked out for himself as a "self-made man." Joined in a momentous father-son relation, the two protagonists sought to define one another's existence, as well as to forge, or reaffirm, their own separate personalities. Though they attempted to fight out their battles as if no one else were involved, it is clear that their struggles—and conciliations—involved the women in their lives, as well as all other members of the family, stretching from grandparents through siblings to children of the next generation. It is in the context of this large "family" that we have tried to treat of James and John Stuart Mill as a father-son conflict.

It was the genius of Sigmund Freud, later in the century, to give scientific form to a key aspect of this struggle, which he called the Oedipus complex. Freud understandably phrased his concept in universal terms; we have tried to analyze it further in terms of a specific historical context, and as a result to suggest some useful qualifications to the concept in theory. Moreover, we have attempted to show why, during the nineteenth century, father-son conflict in Oedipal terms became a compulsive subject in the Western world. As part of this discussion, excursions into the nature and findings of family and childhood history, as well as an examination of the concept of adolescence, became necessary.

Also central to an analysis of the Oedipus complex as it manifested itself in the lives of James and John Stuart Mill was an understanding of the latter's "mental crisis." In turn, this specific episode raised questions concerning the nature of depression or melancholy, as related both to father-son conflict in general, and to Western developments in the nineteenth century in particular. We emphasized the creative aspect of depressive experiences, such as John Stuart Mill's, and the potential for growth and development, for a "new birth" of the individual, arising out of such descent into anguish, such encounters with "loss." Intellectually and emotionally, John Stuart Mill became his own "man" only after the crisis of his twentieth year.

His crisis, we have tried to suggest, was symbolic of what many in his generation experienced. Thus, the Mills' father-son conflict was emblematic of a larger battle: the generational conflict of their time. And it has been our thesis that generational change, almost necessarily through conflict, is a prime mechanism of social change. Everywhere fathers and mothers beget children, generation unto generation. In placid times the emphasis is on continuity and the inheritance of customary ways. But in times of pressing new problems, of required rapid social transformation, a new generation is challenged to shake off part of the burden of the past in order to be free to march into a new future. The break is never more than partial, and should not be; but without the "death" of an existing generation, the "birth" of a new society, or culture, is unlikely, if not impossible. Nature assures human beings of a physical death. History may or may not provide for symbolic death as well.

In the nineteenth century, Western society underwent the massive social transformation we now call "modernization." A democratic and an industrial revolution, conjoined, swept over men and cultures, loosening traditional ties and connections. These revolutions were experienced by individuals as well as by the abstraction "society," and for them it often took the form of generational conflict. In turn, their personal struggles gave shape and meaning to the larger social transformation. As we have tried to suggest, a key aspect of these struggles was a father-son conflict, deriving much of its motive force from, and crystallizing around, an Oedipus complex. Seen in this light, we can say that the conflict of generations involved in the modernization of

Western society in the nineteenth century was uniquely a "time for Oedipus."

Thought and Feeling

JAMES MILL was not only a father, and John Stuart Mill a son; both were thinkers of contemporary renown, and, in part, of lasting importance. We have taken seriously their work as intellectuals. Both stood in a tradition of Western thought that has its own internal logic, and their thought cannot be reduced to their personal dispositions. It is also clear, however, that their personal dispositions should not be disregarded. It was two specific individuals—James and John Stuart Mill—who produced their intellectual systems, and not some nonhuman abstraction. As living, feeling beings, they were part and parcel of the formation of their thoughts; we gain, therefore, by studying the psychological as well as the intellectual component of their ideas.

Both Mills wrote treatises on politics and political science. In these works the problems of freedom and authority, independence and dependence, custom and reason, were personal issues as well as foci of social discussion and decision. So, too, in economics, problems of free trade, production, and rent, to take only a few "technical" points, were equally problems for James and John Stuart Mill in relation to their personal feelings about individual development, hard work, and aristocratic snobbery.

Each spent much of his life working for the East India Company, where each exerted enormous authority over the administration of many millions of other human beings on the great subcontinent. Yet the nature of authority itself, as we have suggested, was a crucial personal issue for the Mills. For James Mill especially, it became involved with intense feelings about control over impulse, masculinity, sensuality, and related issues. In legislating for India, it was the whole man, James Mill, and not some mechanical contrivance—though this became the caricature—who was at "work." His vision of life, and colonial life, in turn became a formative element in the development of British attitudes toward the "lower" breeds everywhere.

Even in their efforts at a science of legislation or, better yet, a social science, the Mills could not leave behind their conflicts over freedom, authority, and related topics. Thus, John Stuart Mill in his *Logic* tortuously worked over the problem of philosophical necessity, not merely as a matter of cold philosophy but of intense, heated concern about his all-too-human self-development. On this basis he then offered a highly intellectualized fabric of argument concerning the methodological foundations of any possible effort at ethology, or social science.

If even logic is not free from the Mills' concern with freedom and authority, it should come as no surprise that their attitudes to the "domestic revolution" of their time should be colored with a similar absorption. Although they treated the subject of birth control as a matter of pure economics, it is obvious that the issue was part of their attitudes toward "control" in general, especially control over any and all impulses. The sexual, of course, was a central impulse, threatening always to break out. Both for James Mill, who had nine children, and John Stuart Mill, who had none (and indeed probably had no experience of carnal intercourse in his life), the psychological issue was similar, though the actual outcome quite different. For both men, too, the sexual were "lower" impulses psychologically conjoined to the "lower" classes and "lower" races. We have tried to show how these impulses, though ignored in the overt, higher reaches of thought, existed for the Mills in the latent, lower passages of their thought-worlds.

In short, wherever possible we have tried to understand the way in which intellectual and psychological processes interacted in actual, living, developing persons. We have, therefore, combined formal intellectual analyses of the Mills' political, economic, and social science systems with efforts at another kind of analysis—psychoanalysis. The result has been a psychohistorical portrait of these two major makers and shakers of modern thought, along with vignettes of those surrounding them: Harriet Taylor, Sarah Austin, Jeremy Bentham, the Unitarian and Utilitarian circles of the time, Thomas Carlyle, Alexis de Tocqueville, the Saint-Simonians, and the Germano-Coleridgians, to mention the most prominent. In understanding the intellectual production of the Mills, therefore, we hope as well to have gained increased and deeper insight into the general currents of thought and feeling in nineteenth-century Western society.

Liberalism and Liberty

INTELLECTUALLY the Mills, and especially John, occupy a position that is at the heart of nineteenth-century liberalism. Although liberalism emerged with the rise of the middle class to power as a result of the democratic and industrial revolutions, it also has claims as a "universal" ideology, offering values that transcend the limited historical context in which it first took shape. We take these claims seriously. Nevertheless, it is also necessary to examine their historical "fit," and the way in which particular character structures and social settings correspond with the ideology.

On the most limited terrain, it is important to see, through the eyes of the Mills, the effect of certain real events—the Revolutions of 1789, 1830, and 1848, the Reform Bill of 1832—on their evolving conception of liberal doctrine, especially in its Utilitarian guise. Believing in the union of theory and practice, both father and son were keenly aware of the relation of pure thought to exigent events; indeed, they show us the way in this matter.

Here certain central issues emerge with compelling power. One such issue is the presumed opposition of the "rational" and the "irrational." For James Mill there was no problem. The rational, which he identified with Utilitarian thought, was the only acceptable realm. The irrational, which he equated with passion and impulse, was the domain of madness, to be vigilantly repulsed at every moment. What was certain for the father became problematic for the son. John Stuart Mill came to realize, out of the mental crisis in his own life, that feelings were as important as thoughts. Thoroughly educated as a rationalist by his father, it was only natural that young John should openly fight out the issue intellectually, especially in his writings on Bentham and Coleridge, but only darkly and in hidden fashion emotionally, in his wrestling with the depression that gripped him throughout his life.

So, too, on the intellectual level, John Stuart Mill was preoccupied with a part of the rational-irrational problem in terms of the conflict between reason and custom. And for Mill, the path of progress in society was to substitute the former for the latter. On the personal level, as we know, such a substitution also vindicated his relation to Harriet Taylor, where the two lovers had braved the pressure of custom and the tyranny of the majority. In turn, their matchless love affair vindicated the rightness of Mill's intellectual position.

Closely related to the rational-irrational, reason-custom conflict for liberalism were two other issues. One was the opposition of mechanical and organic, perceived in part as determinism versus development. James Mill knew which side he stood on, but his son writhed desperately over the issue. His mind and education pulled him, in the name of reason and science, to the mechanical view; his mental crisis and conflict with his father pushed him relentlessly toward his own self-development, and thus the images of organic growth.

The other, related issue was social science elitism versus democratic tolerance (in fact, of course, John Stuart Mill sought to combine the two). If one had an accepted social science, an elite could justifiably lead and rule over the mass of mankind, who were wedded to the tyranny of custom; Mill was strongly drawn to this velvet version of the paternalism that had so all-knowingly shaped his early life. But another part of John Stuart Mill realized that no such social science existed, and that the pretense of one led to a kind of Comtean constraint that would make a mockery out of self-development. Mill was encouraged, therefore, to espouse tolerance and freedom of thought and expression, not only as goods in themselves for society, but because they alone could permit the individual to form himself. Such a liberal attitude went well with Mill's wish for "many-sidedness" and his own seemingly bisexual nature, but the major passion for it came out of his efforts to "make" himself as a being separate from his father's tutelage.

His father, of course, thought of himself as self-made. Dependence was the great threat to James Mill. Thus, he wrote and fought for a manly political and economic freedom, which he equated with the dominance of middle-class men like himself. The independence he desired for himself, however, he was loath to extend to his son, and certainly to women. One feels that he feared mightily his own desire to be dependent and passive. John Stuart Mill was able to transcend such fears. While ultimately maintaining his independence against his father as well as the tyranny of the majority, John could even contemplate the possibility of socialism as a way of organizing society. In the personal sphere, he could admit so-called feminine and passive elements as part of his own nature.

Eventually, John Stuart Mill believed that he had gone beyond his father's middle-class liberalism in most areas. John openly scorned the self-righteousness and hypocrisy of the middle-class English and French. He saw their control of public opinion as tyranny, their fear of emotion as constrictive. In the realm of theory, he could entertain a version of cultural politics in place of his father's, and his father's generation's, interest politics, and contemplate a society focused around the working class and socialist organizations.

Yet with all his boldness and vision, John Stuart Mill could never escape remaining true to his father's version of middle-class liberalism. At his core John was a rationalist, using the categories of interest politics and classical economics handed down to him. Immensely broadened and deepened, Mill's liberalism was really an extension, not a true transcendence, of his father's Utilitarianism. As such, however, it allowed for possibilities undreamed of by James Mill, especially in the areas of personal development and social existence. Together, father and son had maintained the bonds connecting them, and forged a powerful, continuous, and developing ideology of liberalism.

The "Lesson" of History

OUR STAGE has clearly been crowded. We have sought to tell the story of James and John Stuart Mill, and of the women and friends in their lives. Indeed, this book rests on the understanding and conviction induced in the reader by actual immersion in the preceding chapters. What counts most are the specific words and experiences that, for example, suggest John Stuart Mill's Oedipal feelings, and the particular way these feelings affect his patterns of thought and behavior. Thus it is the detail, the building up of the fragments into a coherent picture, rather than any generalized statement, such as "John Stuart Mill had an Oedipus complex," or "James Mill was a 'self-made' man," that matters in this sort of work.

Still, on the basis of this story, we have tried to formulate certain statements about significance and meaning, concepts and theories. We have advanced broad theses about the nature of father-son conflict, the Oedipus complex, and generational change in the nineteenth century, about dependence-independence, liberty-authority, masculine-feminine, rational-irrational relations, and a whole host of other such dichotomies, or ambivalences.

Always we have sought to balance the claims of restricted historical context and sweeping universal concept, and to strive toward the correct synthesis. Constantly bearing in mind the fact that social and intellectual changes are enormously complex affairs, inevitably proceeding in subtle accord with personal development and transformation, we have tried to study the correspondence between these two sides of change. For us, a vital fact of history is that men and women are conceived, develop, and then "degenerate," and die; this they do from one generation to the next, sometimes in harmony and sometimes in conflict. Really to understand any one generation, we must accordingly ascend to the generation before it, and then descend to the generation after it. This, in the last analysis, is the most profound historical and psychological "lesson" taught to us by our study of the Mills.

NOTES

Chapter 1

1. When I visited the parish in which James Mill was born, and asked the local people about his parents' original house, I was received with stares of incomprehension. "James Mill," they said, "no one here by that name," or else, "Oh, yes, there was a James Mill; he used to run a garage nearby, but he died a few years ago." Even when I visited in another town the school now standing on the property of the academy James Mill had attended as a boy, I found that no one there had ever heard of him.

2. Generational conflict, of course, can be between sons and mothers, as well as between daughters and fathers, or mothers. Also, the personal family struggle can or cannot mirror a larger struggle over differing ideas and values of different age groups. In the period of the Mills the father-son conflict was obviously crucial, and involved a cultural as well as personal clash.

3. We could wish, of course, for greater material on James Mill. A comparison, however, with Erikson's problem in dealing with Luther's father shows us how fortunate we are. Cf. Erik H. Erikson, *Young Man Luther: A Study in Psychoanalysis and History* (New York: W. W. Norton, 1958), pp. 29–79.

4. See Bruce Mazlish, "What is Psycho-History?," *Transactions of the Royal Historical Society*, 5th ser., vol. 21, 1971.

5. Richard Ellmann, "On Psycho-Biography," *The New York Review of Books*, June 17, 1971, pp. 3–4.

6. For another attempt in this direction, see Arthur Mitzman, *The Iron Cage: An Historical Interpretation of Max Weber* (New York: Alfred A. Knopf, 1970), and my evaluation of it in a review-essay in *History and Theory* 10, no. 1 (1971), pp. 90–107.

7. In Freud's words, "If one succeeds in arranging a confused heap of fragments, each of which bears upon it an unintelligible piece of drawing, so that the picture acquires a meaning, so that there is no gap anywhere in the design and so that the whole fits into the frame—if all these conditions are fulfilled, then one knows that one has solved the puzzle and that there is no alternative solution." ("Remarks on the Theory and Practice of Dream Interpretation," in Sigmund Freud, *The Standard Edition of the Complete Psychological Works of Sigmund Freud*, ed. James Strachey, 23 vols. to date (London: Hogarth Press, 1953–), 19:116.

8. *The Mill News Letter*, started in the Fall of 1965, is published by the University of Toronto Press, John M. Robson, editor. The University of Toronto Press is also publishing the *Collected Works of John Stuart Mill*, now in progress.

9. Bruce Mazlish, ed., *Psychoanalysis and History*, rev. ed. (New York: Grosset and Dunlap, 1971), pp. 18–19. (Originally published in 1963.)

Notes

Chapter 2

1. See, for example, Bronislaw Malinowski, *Sex and Repression in Savage Society* (1927), reprint (New York: The World Publishing Co., 1964), and Anne Parsons, "Is the Oedipus Complex Universal? The Jones-Malinowski Debate Revisited and a South Italian 'Nuclear Complex,'" *The Psychoanalytic Study of Society*, 3, 1964, pp. 278–328.

2. Howard R. Wolf, "British Fathers and Sons, 1773–1913: From Filial Submissiveness to Creativity," *The Psychoanalytic Review*, Vol. 52, No. 2 (Summer 1965), pp. 53–70.

3. The most important comparative treatment, though the emphasis is on German literature, is Kurt K. T. Wais, *Das Vater-Sohn Motiv in Der Dichtung. Bis 1880* (Berlin und Leipzig: Walter De Gruyter & Co., 1931. There is also a second part, 1880–1930.

4. Erik H. Erikson, "Reflections on the American Identity," in his *Childhood and Society* (New York: W. W. Norton, 1950).

5. Cf. E. J. Hobsbawm, *The Age of Revolution* (London: Weidenfeld and Nicolson, 1962).

6. Cf. Herbert Moller, "Youth as a Force in the Modern World," *Comparative Studies in Society and History*, 10, no. 3 (April 1968), pp. 237–260.

7. Erikson, "The Legend of Hitler's Childhood," in *Childhood and Society*, pp. 326–358.

8. John Stuart Mill, "The Subjection of Women," in John Stuart Mill and Harriet Taylor, *Essays on Sex Equality*, ed. Alice S. Rossi (Chicago: University of Chicago Press, 1970), p. 143.

9. R. R. Palmer, ed., *Atlas of World History* (Skokie, Ill.: Rand McNally & Co., 1957), p. 194.

10. For proponents of each argument, see, for example, Philippe Ariès, *Centuries of Childhood*, tr. Robert Baldick (New York: Alfred A. Knopf, 1962), and Peter Laslett, ed., *Household and Family in Past Time* (Cambridge, England: Cambridge University Press, 1972).

11. Fred Weinstein and Gerald Platt, *The Wish To Be Free: Society, Psyche and Value Change* (Berkeley and Los Angeles: University of California Press, 1969). The quotes that follow from their book were on pp. 144, 146–147 and 147.

12. Cf. W. Von Leyden, "Antiquity and Authority," *Journal of the History of Ideas*, 19, no. 4 (October, 1958), pp. 473–492.

13. There is, therefore, a seed of truth in some of the speculations concerning Darwin's ill health as having come from his "killing" psychologically, his own father.

14. This was, of course, a reciprocal process. Lessened respect for the father, in his authoritarian form, was conducive to lesser reverence for and greater questioning of an authoritarian God the Father.

15. The subtitle of Strindberg's book is "The Story of the Evolution of a Human Being 1849–67." Though this confirms the strong influence on him of Darwin, it also suggests that Strindberg, like many others, may have misappropriated the term "evolution"; man may "develop" in the course of his life, as does a tree from a seed, but he does not, as an individual, "evolve." (Or does he?) The quotation is from August Strindberg, *Son of a Servant*, tr. Evert Sprinchorn (London: Jonathan Cape, 1967), p. 17.

16. Weinstein and Platt, *The Wish To Be Free*, pp. 141–142. The quotation in the next paragraph is on p. 148. For my views on the difference between scientific and literary efforts at psychological insight, see "Freud and Nietzsche," *The Psychoanalytic Review*, 55, no. 3 (1968).

17. True, Arthur Schnitzler has been suggested as a Doppelgänger for Freud—indeed, by Freud himself—but a glance at Schnitzler's work shows how trivial such a comparison really is if what is at issue is scientific discovery. For a most interesting treatment of Schnitzler, see Carl E. Schorske, "Politics and the Psyche in *Fin de Siècle* Vienna: Schnitzler and Hofmannstahl," *The American Historical Review*, 66, no. 4 (July 1961), pp. 930–946.

18. See, for example, Ernest Jones, *The Life and Work of Sigmund Freud*, 3 vols. (New York: Basic Books, 1953–57), and for a more synoptic treatment, O. Mannoni, *Freud*, tr. Renaud Bruce (New York: Pantheon, 1971).

19. Not all hysterics, as Freud pointed out, were female (in spite of the word "hysteria" being the Greek for womb). Nevertheless, Freud's own *Studies in Hysteria*

concerned only women. For the study of hysteria, see Ilza Veith, *Hysteria: The History of A Disease* (Chicago: University of Chicago Press, 1965); Aaron Lazare, "The Hysterical Character of Psychoanalytic Theory," *Archives of General Psychiatry* 25 (August 1971), pp. 131–137 and Carroll Smith-Rosenberg, "The Hysterical Woman: Sex Roles and Role Conflict in 19th-Century America," *Social Research* 39, no. 4 (Winter 1972), pp. 652–677.

20. In fact, according to a study done by one of my students, the ratio of men to women patients seems to be both equal and constant throughout Freud's medical practice. Thus, it is mostly a question of what cases he chose to write up. By and large, however, this subject needs further scrutiny. See Wayne Zafft, "A Report on Freud's Patients," Unpublished paper, M.I.T., October 29, 1971.

21. Cf., however, James Strachey's editorial to Freud's "Mourning and Melancholia," in Sigmund Freud, *The Standard Edition of the Complete Psychological Works of Sigmund Freud*, 239–242. Also, according to Strachey, "The actual term 'Oedipus complex' seems to have been first used by Freud in his published writings in the first of his 'Contributions to the Psychology of Love (1910)'" (SE, 4:263).

22. Cf. Gregory Rochlin, *Man's Aggression: The Defense of the Self* (Boston: Gambit, 1973), pp. 328–347 and Carl E. Schorske, "Politics and Patricide in Freud's Interpretation of Dreams," *The American Historical Review* 78, no. 2 (April 1973).

23. See Franz Kafka, *Letter to his Father* (New York: Schocken Books, 1966) and Arthur Mitzman, *The Iron Cage: An Historical Interpretation of Max Weber* (New York: Alfred A. Knopf, 1970).

24. For a more detailed discussion, see p. 347, Chap. 13.

25. Freud, *Standard Edition*, 9:237.

26. Ibid., 13:244.

27. Parsons, "Is the Oedipus Complex Universal?," passim.

28. For example, see Otto Rank, *The Myth of the Birth of the Hero and Other Writings*, ed. Philip Freund (New York: Vintage Books, 1964).

29. For a possible explanation of how the Oedipus complex is grounded in biology and the theory of evolution, see Alex Comfort's fascinating chapter, "Darwin and Freud," in his *Darwin and the Naked Lady* (New York: George Braziller, 1962), pp. 23–42.

30. For a reexamination of the relationship in clinical terms, see David Levi, Helm Stierlin, and Robert J. Savard, "Fathers and Sons: The Interlocking Crises of Integrity and Identity," *Psychiatry* 35 (February 1972), pp. 48–56.

31. Wolf, "British Fathers and Sons," p. 64.

32. Tentative data relating to these questions are beginning to emerge from the work of such scholars as E. A. Wrigley and Peter Laslett at the Cambridge Group for the History of Population and Social Structure, but we are still only at the inception of such efforts.

33. Erik E. Erikson, *Identity, Youth and Crisis* (New York: W. W. Norton, 1968), pp. 95–96.

34. The actual title of Turgenev's book in Russian should be translated as *Fathers and Children*, but the usual translation as *Fathers and Sons* does point to the centrality of sons rather than daughters in the book. In our account, all quotations are from *The Vintage Turgenev*, tr. Harry Stevens, vol. 1 (New York: Vintage Books, 1950).

35. Cf. the discussion of the aggressive component of the Oedipus complex on p. 388 and also note 34.

36. Cf. the notion of a rebirth by a "second father," discussed on p. 35.

37. See, too, Bruce Mazlish, "Are We Ready for an American Lenin?," *Horizon* 13, no. 4 (Autumn 1971), pp. 48–55) and my forthcoming book, *Revolutionary Ascetics*, to be published by Basic Books, for a full portrait of Chernyshevsky and others in these terms.

Chapter 3

1. Alexander Bain, *James Mill. A Biography* (London, 1882; reprinted New York: Augustus M. Kelley, 1966). All quotations are from the 1966 edition, unless otherwise stated.

2. James Mill's pride is confirmed for us by his son's comment about his father's "unwillingness to invite any persons to his house who he could not, as he said, make as comfortable as they were at home." *The Early Draft of John Stuart Mill's Autobiography*, ed. Jack Stillinger (Urbana, Ill.: University of Illinois Press, 1961), p. 185 (hereafter referred to as *Early Draft*).

3. James Mill's *Commonplace Book*, London Library, in 3 vols, folio and 1 vol. quarto, presented by John Stuart Mill Esq., January 1872. No pagination in the ms. Vol. 1.

4. See p. 169.

5. Charles Dickens, *Hard Times* (New York: Rinehart and Co., 1958), p. 13.

6. David Ricardo, in a letter to James Mill of October 14, 1821, in regard to the latter's "Liberty of the Press," found Mill too favorable to one exception to the need for complete truth: "Why should a vain man be protected in the concealment of the poverty and lowness of his birth, because an undue regard is paid to rank and riches. . . ." Piero Sraffa, ed., *The Works and Correspondence of David Ricardo*, 10 vols. (Cambridge, England: Cambridge University Press, 1951–1955).

7. *Early Draft*, pp. 58–60.

8. Francis Place to James Mill, October 20, 1817. British Museum Addenda 35,153.

9. James Mill to Francis Place, December 7, 1814, quoted in Graham Wallas, *The Life of Francis Place, 1771–1854* (London: George Allen and Unwin, 1951), pp. 70–71.

10. O. Mannoni, *Prospero and Caliban. The Psychology of Colonization*, trans. Pamela Powesland (New York: Praeger, 1964), p. 145. Cf. Bertram D. Lewin, *Dreams and the Uses of Regression* (New York: International Universities Press, 1958) for an interesting analysis of Descartes' famous dreams of November 10, 1619.

11. Mannoni, *Prospero and Caliban*, p. 101.

12. Judith Shklar, "Subversive Genealogies," *Daedalus*, Winter 1972, pp. 129–154. The quote following is on p. 135.

13. Bain, *James Mill*, p. 37.

14. See, for example, Everett Mendelsohn's account of the professionalization of the natural sciences, "The Emergence of Science as a Profession in Nineteenth-Century Europe," in *The Management of Scientists*, ed. Karl Hill (Boston: Beacon Press, 1964), pp. 3–48.

15. The term "crisis of identity" is inspired, of course, by Erik Erikson's work. Nevertheless, I have refrained from using his term "identity crisis," because I am not referring to that crisis which arises at a particular stage, generally in adolescence, when the somatic, ego, and social development come together and provide the material for a specific "identity crisis." Indeed, for James Mill, it would be difficult to deal with this developmental stage adequately because of a shortage of material. The notion of a continuing and cumulative "crisis of identity" is, however, intrinsic to Erikson's theory of the developmental stages of man. See further, Erik H. Erikson, *Childhood and Society* (New York: W. W. Norton, 1950).

16. John Stuart Mill, *Autobiography*, ed. Currin V. Shields (New York: Liberal Arts Press, 1957), pp. 68, 70.

17. Bain, *James Mill*, pp. 421–422.

18. Ibid., p. 397.

19. Ibid., p. 162.

20. Wallas, *The Life of Francis Place*, p. 74.

21. The quotations, in order, are from the Macvey Napier Papers, at the British Museum: James Mill to Macvey Napier, July 20, 1816, Brit. Mus. Add. 34,612, pp. 117–118; October 23, 1816, Brit. Mus. Add. 34,612, p. 161; and May 7, 1824, Brit. Mus. Add. 34,613, p. 245.

22. James Mill to Henry Brougham, September 24, 1827, University College Library #10,762.

23. James Mill, *An Essay on Government*, ed. Currin V. Shields (Indianapolis-New York: Bobbs-Merrill, 1955), p. 53.

24. Ibid., p. 90.

25. Bain, *James Mill*, p. 63.

26. The threat of sickness reducing James Mill to absolute want, or to death, with the same consequences for his family, was real and constant. Starting around 1812, it seems, Mill was afflicted with severe attacks of the gout (ironically enough, thought then to be from overeating and overdrinking, neither indulged in by the abstemious Mill;

today, we know that gout is an arthritic condition, brought on by a disturbance of the uric-acid metabolism which can be caused by infection.) Hands, and even eyes, were afflicted by the disease, and Mill's writing was periodically interrupted as a result. Thus, we see him writing to a friend in 1828, "It is chiefly because writing has been a very painful operation to me that you have not heard from me sooner. My lumbago has been so bad that it is only by lying on my back, or being bolt upright in slow motion that I have any ease." [September 2, 1828, James Mill to Henry Brougham, University College Library, #9443]

Consumption, however, was the real threat, and eventually took Mill's life. It was endemic in his family. His mother died from it at a fairly young age, and so did his brother William. Mill passed on the disease to many of his own children, including, as we shall see, John Stuart. Consumption, in fact, was *the* disease of the nineteenth century, coloring the entire emotional scene. It is a fit subject for psychohistorical treatment, and we shall attempt to discuss it in those terms when we deal with its presence in John Stuart Mill's life. (see pp. 320–324). In any case, in 1836, at fifty-four, James Mill finally succumbed to pulmonary phthisis, after painful and recurrent hemorrhaging of the lungs. He met his death bravely and with the same self-control, with the exception of his treatment of his family, that had characterized most of his life.

27. Wallas, *The Life of Francis Place*, pp. 68–69.

28. For details see Bain, *James Mill*, pp. 166ff.

29. James Mill to Macvey Napier, April 30, 1818, Brit. Mus. Add. 34,612, p. 193.

30. Bain, *James Mill*, p. 306.

31. Michael Walzer, "Puritanism as a Revolutionary Ideology," *History and Theory* 3, no. 1 (1963): 81; also, *The Revolution of the Saints* (New York: Atheneum, 1968).

32. Bain, *James Mill*, p. 334.

33. Cf. Peter T. Cominos, "Late-Victorian Sexual Respectability and the Social System," *International Review of Social History*, 8, 1963, Parts 1 and 2, pp. 18–48; 216–250.

34. Bain, *James Mill*, p. 64.

35. Quoted in Wallas, *The Life of Francis Place*, p. 74.

36. James Mill to Francis Place, September 3, 1827, in the Place Papers, Vol. 75. Presented by F. C. Miers. British Museum Additional MS, 35.144, p. 114.

37. Mill, *Commonplace Book*, Vol. 1, no pagination.

38. Sigmund Freud, *Group Psychology and the Analysis of the Ego*, trans. James Strachey (New York: Bantam Books, 1960), p. 71. Freud adds that "the great majority of people have a strong need for authority, to which they can submit and which dominates and sometimes even ill-treats them."

39. J. S. Mill, *Autobiography*, p. 33.

40. Bain, *James Mill*, p. 422.

41. Otto Fenichel, *The Psychoanalytic Theory of Neurosis* (New York: W. W. Norton, 1945), p. 44.

42. Mill, *Commonplace Book*, Vol. 4, no pagination.

43. Ibid., Vol. i, no pagination.

44. James Mill to Etienne Dumont, December 13, 1814, and December 28, 1833. India Office Records (originals in Collection Dumont, Bibliothèque Publique et Universitaire de Genéve, Switzerland); and James Mill to Macvey Napier, April 30, 1818, Brit. Mus. Add. 34,612, pp. 192–193, detailing the relations of Mr. Playfair and Mill's History. See, too, Ricardo's comment to Mill, in a letter of September 26, 1811: "At the very moment that you are using the most delicate and refined flattery, you declare that you are no flatterer." Sraffa, *Works*, 6:51.

45. Bain, *James Mill*, p. 139. Needless to say, patronage was a commonplace in Mill's time, though beginning to disappear. Nevertheless, the psychological effect on Mill had its own uniqueness.

46. Cf. Lionel Robbins, *The Theory of Economic Policy in English Classical Political Economy* (London: Macmillan, 1952), and D. R. McGregor, "Social Research and Social Policy in the Nineteenth Century," *The British Journal of Sociology* 8, no. 2 (June 1957), 146–157.

47. Erikson, *Childhood and Society*, p. 37.

48. Elie Halévy, *The Growth of Philosophical Radicalism*, trans. Mary Morris (Boston: Beacon Press, 1955), p. 255, 306; Bain, *James Mill*, pp. 326 and 137.

49. Halévy, *Philosophical Radicalism*, p. 307.

50. James Mill to Macvey Napier, July 10, 1821, Brit. Mus. Add. 34,612, Vol. 2, p. 429.

51. Bain, *James Mill*, p. 74.

52. Wallas, *The Life of Francis Place*, p. 82.

53. Bentham's note is quoted in Michael St. John Packe, *The Life of John Stuart Mill* (London: Secker & Warburg, London: 1954), p. 22, and Mill's reply in Bain, *James Mill*, pp. 119–120.

54. Bain, *James Mill*, p. 73.

55. Wallas, *The Life of Francis Place*, p. 68.

56. Bain, *James Mill*, pp. 136–140.

57. Ibid., p. 141.

58. James Mill to Jeremy Bentham, February 22, 1827, in Bentham MSS., University College London, Portfolio 10, 186. Bain, *James Mill*, pp. 73–74, alludes to this episode and letter, but, interestingly enough, doesn't publish it.

59. We might also note that James Mill's break with Bentham had the possibility of serving as a model for John Stuart Mill's relations with others. Moreover, it bears comparison to the break in the 1820s between Saint-Simon and Comte, another adoptive father-son, master-disciple relation that broke apart in acrimony.

60. Mill to Dumont, India Office Records.

61. Perhaps in the spirit of his father, John Stuart Mill would further settle accounts in his famous essays on Bentham and Coleridge; but that settlement of accounts would also include many against his own father.

62. Halévy, *Philosophical Radicalism*, p. 309.

Chapter 4

1. James Mill, *An Essay on Government*, ed. Currin V. Shields (Indianapolis-New York: Bobbs-Merrill, 1955), p. 48. All page references in the text are to this edition.

2. See J. H. Burns, "Bentham and the French Revolution," *Transactions of the Royal Historical Society*, 5th ser., 16 (1966):112, for details.

3. Ibid., 113.

4. Before James Mill, it is true, Etienne Dumont began the transition of Bentham's scattered and relatively incomprehensible ideas into a doctrine, Benthamism, but it was Mill who solidified the doctrine and made it the basis of a political movement.

5. Piero Sraffa, ed., *The Works and Correspondence of David Ricardo*, 10 vols. (Cambridge, England: Cambridge University Press, 1951–1955), 8:67. James Mill to David Ricardo, September 11, 1819.

6. Elie Halévy, *The Growth of Philosophical Radicalism*, trans. Mary Morris (Boston: Beacon Press, 1955), p. 420.

7. In F. D. Maurice's novel, *Eustace Conway* (1834), when Morton, the Benthamite, discovers Eustace reading Mill's *Essay on Government* and asks him his opinion of Mill, Eustace replies: " 'I think him nearly the most wonderful prosewriter in our language.' 'That do not I (says Morton) . . . I approve the matter of his treatises exceedingly, but the style seems to me detestable.' 'Oh!' (replies Eustace) 'I cannot separate matter and style. . . . My reason for delighting in this book is, that it gives such a fixedness and reality to all that was most vaguely brilliant in my speculations—it converts dreams into demonstrations." *Eustace Conway* (1834), I, pp. 83–84, quoted in William Thomas, "James Mill's Politics: The 'Essay on Government' and the Movement for Reform," *The Historical Journal* 12, no. 2 (1969): 255–256.

8. J. H. Burns, "The Fabric of Felicity: The Legislator and the Human Condition" (Inaugural lecture delivered at University College, London, March 2, 1967), p. 14.

9. Sraffa, *Works*, 7:204.

10. *The Miscellaneous Writings of Lord Macaulay* (London: Longmans, Green & Co., Ltd., 1860), vol. 2, p. 285, 288. All further references in the text are to this edition.

11. Mill, *Essay on Government*, p. 54.

12. Mill to Ricardo, December 27, 1817, in Sraffa, *Works*, 7:233–234.

13. Erik H. Erikson, *Childhood and Society* (New York: W. W. Norton, 1950), pp. 256, 92, 418.

14. *Miscellaneous Writings*, 1, p. 307.

15. James Mill, *The History of British India*, 2nd ed., 6 vols. (London: Baldwin, Craddock and Jay, 1820), 3: 452.

16. Ricardo to Mill, January 6, 1818, quoted in T. W. Hutchison, "James Mill and the Political Education of Ricardo," *The Cambridge Journal* 7, no. 2 (November 1953): 91.

17. *Miscellaneous Writings*, 1, p. 307.

18. Michael St. John Packe, *The Life of John Stuart Mill* (London: Secker & Warburg, 1954), p. 90.

19. It is interesting to note that John Stuart Mill did not leave his parental home until he was over forty years of age! (His father, however, had died when the son was thirty.)

20. The "numerous" middle class, in terms of those enjoying the franchise after the Reform Bill of 1832, turns out to be an additional 250,000 voters to the existing 435,000 in England and Wales, out of a total population of about 16 million.

21. For a similar view of American blacks as childlike—little Sambos—see Stanley M. Elkins, *Slavery* (Chicago: University of Chicago Press, 1959).

22. Thomas, "James Mill's Politics," 262.

23. An earlier version of most of what follows appeared in the issue of *Daedalus* devoted to "Philosophers and Kings," Summer 1968, pp. 1036–1061.

24. John Stuart Mill, "Reorganization of the Reform Party," *Essay on Politics and Culture*, ed. Gertrude Himmelfarb (Garden City, N.Y.: Doubleday, 1963). This article is a splendid analysis of the situation by one who was in a position to know. In addition to the Tories, of course, there were also the Whigs—the other face of the Privileged Classes—generally from the same social background. As Francis Place remarked about the Whigs in 1807, they were "Tories out of place." Graham Wallas, *The Life of Francis Place, 1771–1854* (London: George Allen & Unwin, 1951), p. 40.

25. See S. MacCoby, ed., *The English Radical Tradition, 1763–1914* (New York: New York University Press, 1957), pp. 7–8; Packe, *Life of John Stuart Mill*, p. 192.

26. John Stuart Mill, *Autobiography*, ed. Currin V. Shields (New York: Liberal Arts Press, 1957), p. 132.

27. Alexander Bain, *James Mill, A Biography* (London, 1882; reprinted New York: Augustus M. Kelley, 1966), p. 458.

28. Ibid., p. 425.

29. Ibid., pp. 180–181.

30. Ibid., p. 446. Is it in this attention to the faults and defects of others that we find the occasional break in Mill's self-control in public and the link to his private tyranny in his home?

31. Ibid., p. 447.

32. Packe, *Life*, p. 102.

Chapter 5

1. An early effort in this direction, though now outdated, is Walter A. Weisskopf, *The Psychology of Economics* (Chicago: University of Chicago Press, 1955).

2. James Mill, *Elements of Political Economy* (1821; 3rd ed. London, 1844; reprinted New York: Augustus M. Kelley, 1965). All page references in the text are to the most recent edition.

3. Ricardo to Mill, January 1, 1821 in Piero Sraffa, ed., *The Works and Correspondence of David Ricardo* (10 vols., Cambridge, England: Cambridge University Press, 1951–1955), 8:331.

4. Thomas Carlyle, "Signs of the Times" (1829), in *Carlyle, Selected Works*, ed. Julian Symons (Cambridge, Mass.: Harvard University Press, 1970), p. 25.

5. Mill does claim that a scarcity of labor will "whet the ingenuity of capitalists to supply the deficiency, by new inventions in machinery and by distributing and

dividing labour to greater advantage" [p. 25]; thus he contributes to the argument whether invention is spurred on most by high wages or surplus capital.

6. Elie Halévy, *The Growth of Philosophical Radicalism*, trans. Mary Morris (Boston: Beacon Press, 1955), p. 278.

7. Mill to Ricardo, August 23, 1821, and Ricardo to Mill, August 28, 1821, quoted in T. W. Hutchison, "James Mill and the Political Education of Ricardo," *The Cambridge Journal* 7, no. 2 (November 1953): 93.

8. Cf. John Stuart Mill's handling of this question, pp. 358–360.

9. Steven Marcus, *The Other Victorians* (New York: Bantam Books, 1967), p. 22.

10. Place to Ensorm, Brit. Mus. Add. MSS, 35,153, quoted in Francis Place, *Illustrations and Proofs of the Principle of Population*, crit. and textual notes by Norman E. Hines (London: George Allen and Unwin, 1930; reissue of 1822 edition), p. 10.

11. Phyllis Deane, *The First Industrial Revolution* (New York: Cambridge University Press, 1965), p. 12.

12. William Langer, "Checks on Population Growth: 1750–1850," *Scientific American* 226, no. 2 (February 1972), pp. 92–99.

13. J. T. Krause, "Changes in English Fertility and Mortality, 1781–1850," *The Economic History Review*, 2nd ser., 11, no. 1 (August 1958): 69 and 68.

14. Quoted in Place, *Illustrations*, pp. 12–13.

15. James A. Field, "The Early Propagandist Movement in English Population Theory," *Bulletin of the American Economic Association*, 4th ser., no. 2 (April 1911): 220.

16. *Ibid.*, 221, quoted in Place, *Illustrations*, p. 10.

17. Place, *Illustrations*, pp. 165, 174.

18. Ibid., p. 308.

19. Graham Wallas, *The Life of Francis Place, 1771–1854* (London: George Allen and Unwin, 1951), p. 169.

20. Michael St. John Packe, *The Life of John Stuart Mill* (London: Secker & Warburg, 1959), p. 58.

21. Quoted in Sraffa, *Works*, 6:xv.

22. Hutchison, "James Mill," p. 81.

23. Mill to Ricardo, November 9, 1815, and December 22, 1815, in Sraffa, *Works*, 6:321, 340.

24. Ricardo to Mill, August 8, 1816, and Mill to Ricardo, September 7, 1819, in Sraffa, *Works*, 7:77; 8:57–58.

25. Mill to Ricardo, October 6, 1816, in Sraffa, *Works*, 7:74.

26. Hutchison, "James Mill," p. 82.

27. Ibid., 88, 92.

28. Mill to Ricardo, August 23, 1815, and January 3, 1816, in Sraffa, *Works*, 6:251; 7:6.

29. Mill to Ricardo, August 24, 1817, in Sraffa, *Works*, 7:182, 184.

30. Ibid., 7:182.

31. Alexander Bain, *James Mill. A Biography* (London: 1882; reprinted New York: Augustus M. Kelley, 1966), p. 211.

Chapter 6

1. John Stuart Mill, *Autobiography* (New York: Liberal Arts Press, 1957), p. 5.

2. Mill to Ricardo, December 3, 1817, in Piero Sraffa, ed., *The Works and Correspondence of David Ricardo*, 10 vols. (Cambridge, England: Cambridge University Press, 1951–1955), 7:210.

3. In fact, two other sons of James Mill were similarly provided for; see p. 143.

4. John Galt, *Annals of The Parish* (London and Edinburgh: T. N. Foucis, 1911), pp. 16, 25, 60.

5. James Mill, *The History of British India*, 2nd ed., 6 vols. (London: Baldwin, Graddock and Joy, 1820), 1:xii. All page references in the text are to this edition, unless otherwise indicated.

6. Eric Stokes, *The English Utilitarians and India* (Oxford: Clarendon Press, 1959), p. 51. The statement by Bentham that follows, from his *Works*, ed. J. Bowring, 11 vols. (London: 1843), 10:490, is quoted in Stokes, p. 68. Stokes' book is an extraordinary piece of historical writing, a model of sorts as well as the indispensable work on its subject.

7. Robert Preyer, *Bentham, Coleridge, and the Science of History* (West Germany: Verlah Heinrich Pöppinghaus Ohg., Bochum-Langendreer, 1958), p. 3.

8. Quoted in Stokes, *The English Utilitarians*, p. 178.

9. Cf. Duncan Forbes, "James Mill and India," *The Cambridge Journal* 5, no. 1 (October 1951), pp. 19–33.

10. Cf. J. Bronowski and Bruce Mazlish, *The Western Intellectual Tradition: From Leonardo to Hegel* (New York: Harper & Brothers, 1960), chap. 13.

11. James Mill, review of Charles James Fox, *A History of the Early Part of the Reign of James the Second* . . . , in *The Annual Review and History of Literature*; for 1808, vol. 7 (London: 1809), pp. 101–102.

12. Cf. Bruce Mazlish, *The Riddle of History: The Great Speculators From Vico to Freud* (New York: Harper & Row, 1966), pp. 60, 80.

13. Forbes, "James Mill and India," p. 30.

14. Mill, review of M. de Guignes, *Voyages à Peking, Manille, et l'ile de France, faits dans l'Intervalle des Années 1784 à 1801*, in *The Edinburgh Review* 14, no. 28 (July 1809): 413–414.

15. See Karl A. Wittfogel, *Oriental Despotism* (New Haven and London: Yale University Press, 1957).

16. Forbes, "James Mill and India," 27.

17. Quoted in C. H. Philips, *The East India Company. 1784–1834* (Manchester, England: Manchester University Press, 1961), p. 213.

18. Stokes, *The English Utilitarians*, pp. 312–313.

19. Erik H. Erikson, "On the Nature of Psycho-Historical Evidence: In Search of Gandhi," *Daedalus* 97, no. 3 (Summer 1968), reprinted in B. Mazlish, ed., *Psychoanalysis and History* (New York: Grosset and Dunlap, 1971).

20. Stokes, *The English Utilitarians*, pp. vii, xiii, 27.

21. Francis G. Hutchins, *The Illusion of Permanence. British Imperialism in India* (Princeton, N.J.: Princton University Press, 1967), pp. 40, 59.

22. Mill to Ricardo, August 14, 1819, in Sraffa, *Works*, 8:51.

23. See T. W. Hutchison, "James Mill and the Political Education of Ricardo," *The Cambridge Journal* 7, no. 2 (November 1953): 89, fn. 3, for the comments by H. H. Wilson, who edited Mill's *History* in 1858.

24. Quoted in Hutchins, *Illusion of Permanence*, p. 74. See Erik H. Erikson, *Gandhi's Truth* (New York: W. W. Norton, 1969), for the way in which Gandhi and India "came of age." See also p. 129 of this chapter.

25. For details see Hugh Tinker, *South Asia: a Short History* (London: Pall Mall Press, 1966), pp. 174–175.

26. Ibid., p. 152.

27. Susanne Rudolph, "The New Courage: An Essay on Gandhi's Psychology," *World Politics* 16, no. 1 (October 1963): 98–117.

28. Quoted in Stokes, *The English Utilitarians*, p. 19.

29. Ibid., p. 324.

30. Penderel Moon, *Warren Hastings and British India* (London: 1947 and 1961), 349–350.

31. Quoted in Stokes, *The English Utilitarians*, p. 31.

32. Ibid., p. 34.

33. Ibid., pp. 150, 247; Kenneth Ballhatchet, *Social Policy and Social Change in Western India. 1817–1830* (London: Oxford University Press, 1957), p. 36.

34. Stokes, *The English Utilitarians*, p. 269. See also pp. 239, 252, 258, 268.

35. Ibid., p. 71.

36. Quoted in Duncan Forbes, "The Rationalism of Sir Walter Scott," *The Cambridge Journal* 7, no. 1 (October 1953): 33.

37. O. Mannoni, *Prospero and Caliban. The Psychology of Colonization*, trans. Pamela Powesland (New York: Praeger, 1964).

38. Philip Mason, *Prospero's Magic* (London: Oxford University Press, 1962).

39. Frantz Fanon, *The Wretched of the Earth,* trans. Constance Farrington (New York: Grove Press, 1966).
40. Hutchins, *Illusion of Permanence*, p. 101. See, in general, Chaps. V and VI.
41. Cf. Susanne Hoeber Rudolph, "Self-Control and Political Potency: Gandhi's Asceticism." (Paper delivered at the Association for Asian Studies, San Francisco, April 1965), for a similar analysis of Gandhi.
42. Cf. Karl Marx, "The British Rule in India," New York Daily Tribune, June 25, 1853, reprinted in Shlomo Avineri, ed., *Karl Marx on Colonialism and Modernization* (Garden City, N.Y.: Doubleday & Company, Inc., 1968), pp. 83–89.
43. Quoted in Stokes, *The English Utilitarians*, p. 303.
44. For details see ibid., p. 50; Philips, *The East India Company*, p. 18; William Foster, *The East India House* (London: John Lane The Bodley Head Ltd., 1924), pp. 195–198.
45. Quoted in Stokes, *The English Utilitarians*, p. 60.
46. Mill to Dumont, December 13, 1819, India Office Library.
47. Stokes, *The English Utilitarians*, p. 51.
48. Ibid., p. 116.
49. Ibid., pp. 49–50.
50. For details see Foster, *East India House*, p. 199.
51. Home Miscellaneous Series, 832, India Office Records.
52. Stokes, *The English Utilitarians*, p. 255.

Chapter 7

1. John Stuart Mill, *The Earlier Letters of John Stuart Mill. 1812–1848*, ed. Francis E. Mineka (Toronto: University of Toronto Press, 1963), vols. 12 and 13 of the *Collected Works of John Stuart Mill* (hereafter referred to as *Letters*), p. 315.
2. John Stuart Mill, *The Early Draft of John Stuart Mill's Autobiography* ed. Jack Stillinger (Urbana, Ill.: University of Illinois Press, 1961) (hereafter referred to as *Early Draft*), p. 132. According to their usefulness, I have cited either the published version or the early draft of the *Autobiography.*
3. *Letters*, p. 473.
4. Cf. J. C. Flügel, *The Psycho-Analytic Study of the Family* (London: 1955), pp. 160ff.
5. Michael St. John Packe, *The Life of John Stuart Mill* (London: Secker & Warburg, 1954), p. 9.
6. John Stuart Mill, *John Mill's Boyhood Visit to France, Being a Journal and Notebook Written by John Stuart Mill in France, 1820–1820*, ed. Anna Jean Mill (Toronto: University of Toronto Press, 1960) (hereafter referred to as *Boyhood Visit*), p. 11.
7. *Letters*, p. 6.
8. Harriet Mill to the Rev. J. Crompton, October 62, 1873. MS. letter, King's College, Cambridge, quoted in Packe, *Life*, p. 25.
9. John Stuart Mill, *Autobiography*, ed. Currin V. Shields (New York: Liberal Arts Press, 1957) (hereafter referred to as *Autobiography*), p. 26.
10. Alexander Bain, *James Mill. A Biography* (London, 1882; reprinted New York: Augustus M. Kelley, 1966), p. 59.
11. Cf. ibid., where she is said to be "small," and Packe, *Life*, p. 76, for Henry Solly's view of her as "tall."
12. Bain, *James Mill*, p. 59.
13. Quoted in Packe, *Life*, p. 76.
14. The comment of John Stuart Mill's sister, Harriet, is in a letter to Rev. J. Crompton, October 26, 1873, King's College, Cambridge, that of Mrs. Grote is in Bertrand and Patricia Russell, eds., *The Amberley Papers*, 2 vols. (London: The Hogarth Press, 1937). Both are quoted in Packe, *Life*, p. 33.
15. Quoted in Packe, *Life*, pp. 33–34, 32.
16. *Early Draft*, p. 184.
17. Ibid., pp. 65–66.
18. Ibid., pp. 179–180, 185.
19. Ibid., pp. 56, 181.

20. *Letters*, p. 144.
21. Ibid., pp. 392, 398.
22. *Early Draft*, p. 37.
23. Ibid., p. 43.
24. The fact that James Mill, with all his other burdens, had the energy to devote so much time to his son seemed to the latter one of the two most striking things about his father's life (the second was how foolish his father was to burden himself with a large family, an action so opposed to his opinions on birth control).
25. John Stuart Mill's comment is in *Early Draft*, p. 13; his sister's in letter to Rev. J. Crompton, October 26, 1873, King's College, quoted in Packe, *Life*, p. 47.
26. *Early Draft*, p. 63.
27. *Letters*, pp. 143–144.
28. See William J. Goode, *World Revolution and Family Patterns* (New York: The Free Press, 1970), pp. 1, 70.
29. After this chapter was originally written, Peter Laslett, ed., *Household and Family in Past Time* (Cambridge, England: Cambridge University Press, 1972), came into my hands. It calls into doubt the notion of evolution in the last thousand years or so from the extended kinship family to the nuclear, claiming that the latter existed as an average over all that time. I have let Goode's argument stand, however, for the moment, partly because of the uncertainty of the dispute, but primarily because the narrowing affective ties and changing values seem to me accepted by both Goode and Laslett, and these, rather than family structure, are what is critical to my argument. Moreover, Laslett's conclusions are themselves called into question in the lead review of *The Times Literary Supplement*, May 4, 1973.
30. This is not to say that people did not become infatuated and fall terribly in love before the late eighteenth century—witness Dante and his Beatrice—but only to point to the support and *meaning* given to such passions by the values of the surrounding time and society.
31. One qualification of this picture may be the prevalence of infanticide. Cf. William L. Langer, "Checks on Population Growth: 1750–1850," *Scientific American* 226, no. 2 (February 1972), pp. 92–99.
32. Erik H. Erikson, "On the Nature of Psycho-Historical Evidence: in Search of Gandhi," in B. Mazlish, *Psychoanalysis and History* (New York: Grosset and Dunlap, 1971), pp. 181–212.
33. *Early Draft*, p. 2. See Stillinger's introduction, pp. 1–33, for a complete account of the probable composition of the *Autobiography*.
34. Ibid., pp. 15, 6, 9.
35. *Letters*, p. 169.
36. Ibid, pp. 208, 429, 437.
37. Ibid., p. 608.

Chapter 8

1. Peter Laslett, *The World We Have Lost* (London: Matheson & Co., Ltd., 1965), p. 104.
2. Peter Coveney, *Poor Monkey. The Child in Literature* (London: Rockliff, 1957). This is a fine, pioneering study.
3. It must also be admitted that the child in Freud's science lent itself quickly to becoming a new social symbol, as well as an object of scientific study.
4. For details of this development, see Bruce Mazlish, "Psychiatry and History," in Silvano Arieti, ed., *American Handbook of Psychiatry, The Foundations of Psychiatry*, 2nd ed., vol. 1, (New York: Basic Books, Inc., 1974), pp. 964–979.
5. The reader wishing more details may usefully consult Lucien Pye, "Personal Identity and Political Ideology," in Dwaine Marvick, ed., *Political Decision Makers* (New York: The Free Press, 1962), pp. 290–313, reprinted in Bruce Mazlish, ed., *Psychoanalysis and History*, rev. ed. (New York: Grosset & Dunlap, 1971), pp. 150–173. One word of caution: It is doubtful that Erikson ever intended his stages to be applied mechanically, yet this is a danger into which many historians are liable to fall.

6. Horace N. Pym, ed., *Memories of Old Friends. Being Extracts from the Journals and Letters of Caroline Fox . . . from 1835 to 1871* (London: Smith, Eider & Cap, 1882), p. 85.

7. Place's remark is quoted in Michael St. John Packe, *The Life of John Stuart Mill* (London: Secker & Warburg, 1954), p. 34. For a study of 300 geniuses, see C. M. Cox, *The Early Mental Traits of Three Hundred Geniuses, Genetic Studies of Genius*, ed. L. M. Hermann, vol. 2 (Palo Alto: Stanford University Press, 1926).

For a facsimile of Mill's childhood letter, see John Stuart Mill, *The Earlier Letters of John Stuart Mill. 1812–1848*, ed. Francis E. Mineka (Toronto: University of Toronto Press, 1963) (hereafter referred to as Letters), pp. 2–3.

8. John Stuart Mill, *Autobiography*, ed. Currin V. Shields (New York: Liberal Arts Press, 1957), pp. 5–6; *Letters*, pp. 6–10.

9. John Evelyn, cited in Arthur Ponsonby, *English Diaries* (London: Methuen & Co., 1923), p. 79.

10. Quoted in Coveney, *Poor Monkey*, p. 49.

11. John Stuart Mill, *The Early Draft of John Stuart Mill's Autobiography* ed. Jack Stillinger (Urbana, Ill.: University of Illinois Press, 1961), (hereafter referred to as *Early Draft*), pp. 54–55.

12. Alexander Bain, *John Stuart Mill. A Criticism with Personal Recollections* (New York: Augustus M. Kelley, 1882), p. 28.

13. *Early Draft*, pp. 179–180.

14. Ibid, p. 68.

15. See, for example, the Marmontel episode in Chapter 10, pp. 209–210.

Chapter 9

1. G. Stanley Hall, *Adolescence. Its Psychology and its Relation to Physiology, Anthropology, Sociology, Sex, Crime, Religion and Education*, 2 vols. (New York: D. Appleton & C., 1904). All references in the text, unless otherwise stated, are to this edition. For Hall, see Dorothy Ross, *G. Stanley Hall: The Psychologist as Prophet* (Chicago: University of Chicago Press, 1972).

2. It almost seems as if the concomitant of self-help in the nineteenth century was self-abuse, strange bedfellows!

3. Joseph Kett, "Adolescence and Youth in Nineteenth-Century America," *The Journal of Interdisciplinary History* 2, no. 2 (Autumn 1971): 290–291.

4. As a "social" latency, the concept of adolescence can even be extended to the early thirties, as in Kenneth Keniston's notion of "post-adolescence" as a further stage today of adolescence. Cf. ibid., p. 293, for a recognition of this extension in the nineteenth century.

5. Dorothy E. Eichorn, "Adolescence," *International Encyclopedia of the Social Sciences*, vol. 1 (New York: The Macmillan Co. and The Free Press, 1968), pp. 84–96. As her authoritative discussion sums up the issue: "Put very baldly, without qualification for sex, class, or caste, the average American adolescent is not anxious, emotionally unstable, unhappy, aggressive, or rebellious."

6. It is interesting to note that John Stuart Mill himself used the term in his 1837 article, "Armand Carrel," in the *London and Westminster Review*, which is reprinted in *Dissertations and Discussions*, 5 vols. (New York: 1874): "The national intellect seemed to make a sudden stride from the stage of adolescence to that of early maturity. It had reached the era corresponding to that in the history of an individual mind, when, after having been taught to think (as every one is) by teachers of some particular school, and having for a time exercised the power only in the path shown to it by its first teachers, it begins, without bandoning that, to tread also in other paths. . . ." [1:258] The autobiographical note is evident.

7. This is the title given to Mill's Journal and Notebook, as we have already seen, by the editor, Anna Jean Mill (no relation, incidentally).

8. Cf. Alexander Bain, *John Stuart Mill: A Criticism With Personal Recollections* (New York: 1882), p. 29. Incidentally, John Stuart Mill was to echo his father's strictures

in an 1835 article in the *London Review* on Sedgwick, a professor there, whose backward views on the role of the university Mill attacked rather savagely (see *Dissertations and Discussions*, vol. 1).

9. John Stuart Mill, *Autobiography*, ed. Currin V. Shields (New York: Liberal Arts Press, 1957), pp. 23–24.

10. John Stuart Mill, *John Mill's Boyhood Visit to France*, ed. Anna Jean Mill (Toronto: University of Toronto Press, 1960) (hereafter referred to as *Boyhood Visit*), pp. 3, 42, 19, 25, 44.

11. Cited in Herbert Spencer, *Autobiography*, 2 vols. (New York: D. Appleton and Co., 1904), 2:213; quoted in Michael St. John Packe, *The Life of John Stuart Mill* (London: Secker & Warburg, 1954), p. 486.

12. *Boyhood Visit*, University of Toronto Press, p. 116.

13. John Stuart Mill, *The Earlier Letters of John Stuart Mill*, 1812–1848, ed. Francis K. Mineka (Toronto: University of Toronto Press, 1963) (hereafter referred to as *Letters*), 23. It is amusing to compare Mill's judgment here with that of George Bentham on him, in the diary entry cited earlier.

14. George Bentham to John Stuart Mill, June 16, 1832, in the Mill-Taylor Collection in the British Library of Political and Economic Science (London School of Economics) (hereafter referred to as MT Coll., e.g., MT Coll 7/4 = Mill-Taylor Collection, vol. 7, folio 4), MT Coll. 1/22–23.

15. *Letters*, pp. 577–578.

16. *Boyhood Visit*, pp. 52–53.

17. Ibid., p. 69

18. Ibid., pp. 24, 74, 34. Packe's comment is on p. 44 of his book.

19. *Boyhood Visit*, p. 70.

20. Ibid., pp. 50, 79.

21. *Autobiography*, p. 37.

22. *Letters*, p. 540. Mill to Comte, August 12, 1842.

23. *Boyhood Visit*, p. 88.

24. All four of Balard's letters are in MT Coll. 1/1–3, 4–5, 6–7, 20–21.

25. *Letters*, p. xxiii.

26. *Boyhood Visit*, p. xxiv.

27. Quoted in translation in Packe, *Life*, p. 47.

28. *Letters*, p. 595. Anna Jean Mill's comment is in *Boyhood Visit*, p. xxiv.

29. Mill to Ricardo, August 23, 1821, in Piero Sraffa, ed. *The Works and Correspondence of David Ricardo*, 10 vols. (Cambridge, England: Cambridge University Press, 1951–1955), vol. 9, p. 43.

30. *Boyhood Visit*, 7, 8.

31. John Stuart Mill, *The Early Draft of John Stuart Mill's Autobiography*, ed. Jack Stillinger (Urbana, Ill.: University of Illinois Press, 1961) (hereafter referred to as *Early Draft*), pp. 53, 70.

32. It was obviously this work that John later recommended to his friend Balard, and we shall see in a moment why Mill's disappointment at its reception would be heightened beyond the ordinary.

33. *Early Draft*, pp. 75–76.

34. Ibid., p. 74.

35. Ibid., pp. 81, 81–82.

36. We shall say more about this hypothesis later; see p. 284—286.

37. *Letters*, pp. 53, 71–72, 292.

38. *Early Draft*, pp. 147–148.

39. Quoted in Janet Ross, *Three Generations of English Women* (London: J. Murray, 1893), pp. v, viii.

40. Packe, *Life*, pp. 178–179.

41. Quoted in J. Ross, *Three Generations*, p. 105.

42. James Anthony Froude, *Thomas Carlyle. A History of the First Forty Years of His Life. 1795–1835*, 2 vols. (New York: Charles Scribner's Sons, 1882), 2:153–154.

43. Packe, *Life*, p. 179. Actually, Carlyle used the phrase "Niagara of gossip" about Sarah Austin in a letter written a couple of months later than the event described; see Froude, *Thomas Carlyle*, 2:358.

44. Froude, *Thomas Carlyle*, 2:347.

45. F. A. Hayek, *John Stuart Mill and Harriet Taylor* (Chicago: University of Chicago Press, 1951), p. 80.

46. *Early Draft*, p. 85.

47. Alexander Bain, *James Mill. A Biography*. (London, 1882; reprinted New York: Henry Holt & Co., 1966), p. 207.

48. Bain, *John Stuart Mill*, p. 147.

49. *Early Draft*, p. 84.

50. Ibid., p. 104.

51. John Arthur Roebuck, *Life and Letters of John Arthur Roebuck*, ed. Robert Eadon Leader (London and New York: Edward Arnold, 1897), p. 26.

52. Ibid., pp. 28–29. In fact, Roebuck's social background was far more pretentious than Mill's humble origins.

53. Bain, *John Stuart Mill*, pp. 39–40.

54. Roebuck, *Life and Letters*, pp. 37, 38.

55. *Early Draft*, p. 129.

Chapter 10

1. John Stuart Mill, *Autobiography*, ed. Currin V. Shields (New York: Liberal Arts Press, 1957), pp. 86–88.

2. Freud himself looked upon "overwork" as an etiological factor in diminishing the "strength of the ego," thereby allowing the instincts to overwhelm it. See "Analysis Terminable and Interminable," in Sigmund Freud, *The Standard Edition of the Complete Psychological Works of Sigmund Freud*, ed. James Strachey, 23 vols. to date (London: Hogarth Press, 1953–), 23:226.

3. Michael St. John Packe, *The Life of John Stuart Mill* (London: Secker & Warburg, 1954), p. 79.

4. *Autobiography*, pp. 91–92.

5. Cf. A. W. Levi, "The 'Mental Crisis' of John Stuart Mill," *Psychoanalysis and Psychoanalytic Review* 32 (January 1945): 100; and Howard R. Wolf, "British Fathers and Sons, 1773–1913: From Filial Submissiveness to Creativity," *The Psychoanalytic Review*, Summer 1965, esp. p. 59.

6. Whether this distress was more widespread in Mill's period and place is an interesting and difficult question. See, however, Chapter 2 for some suggestive data.

7. John Stuart Mill, *The Early Draft of John Stuart Mill's Autobiography*, ed. Jack Stillinger (Urbana, Ill.: University of Illinois Press, 1961), p. 118.

8. Levi, "The 'Mental Crisis,'" pp. 86–101. Could one add the notion that Mill must have been much affected—the matter is overdetermined—by the "ghostly" appearance of the father in the Marmontel story, à la Hamlet's father? Mill's reference to Macbeth as continually in his thoughts is probably, then, a condensation of a general reference to a number of Shakespeare's plays concerning the displacing of a father figure.

9. *Mémoires de Marmontel* (Paris: firmin—Didot et cie, 1891), pp. 37–38, 51.

10. Alexander Bain, *James Mill. A Biography* (London, 1882; reprinted New York: Augustus M. Kelley, 1966), pp. 391, 408.

11. Packe, *Life*, p. 205.

12. Bain, *James Mill*, p. 408.

13. Packe, *Life*, p. 208.

14. Freud, *Standard Edition*, 1:254–255.

15. Ibid., 14:243, 244.

16. Ibid., 246.

17. Ibid., 248, 249.

18. Otto Fenichel, *The Psychoanalytic Theory of Neurosis* (New York: W. W. Norton, 1945), p. 392.

19. Ibid., pp. 390–391.

20. Freud, "Mourning and Melancholia," *Standard Edition*, 14:253.

21. See, for example, Greta Bibring, "The Mechanism of Depression," in Phyllis Greenacre, ed., *Affective Disorders* (New York: International Universities Press, 1953), and Willard Gaylin, *The Meaning of Despair* (New York: Jason Aronson, 1968). In

technical language, Bibring sees the ego's awareness of its helplessness as stemming from the need to be independent of narcissistic supplies (oral), the inability to control interfering objects coupled with the inability to see oneself as good (anal), and the inability to be competitive and successful (phallic). For this paragraph, in general, I owe much to my friend Fred Weinstein, whose discussion of the subject was highly useful.

22. Fenichel, *Psychoanalytic Theory*, p. 406.

23. Bain, *James Mill*, p. 205.

24. *Autobiography*, p. 45. The text of the *Analysis* we shall use is James Mill, *Analysis of the Phenomena of the Human Mind . . .*, ed. John Stuart Mill, 2 vols. (London: Longmans Green Reader & Dyer, 1869). All references that follow in the text, unless otherwise stated, are from this edition.

25. At one point, in 1839, Mill does refer to his suffering from indigestion: "I am coming back not at all cured, but cured of caring much about cure. I have no doubt I shall in time get accustomed to dyspepsia, as Lafontaine hoped he should to the region below." (Mill to John Robertson, May 31, 1839, in John Stuart Mill, *The Earlier Letters of John Stuart Mill, 1812–1848*, ed. Francis E. Mineka (Toronto: University of Toronto Press, 1963), p. 400. There is no reference, however, in the *Autobiography* to such a cause, and the absence of such comments in general points to the triviality of indigestion in Mill's own explanation for his mental crisis. For a comparison with someone who did suffer from dyspepsia and attributed his melancholia to it, see James Anthony Froude, *Thomas Carlyle. A History of the First Forty Years of His Life. 1795–1835*, 2 vols. (New York: Charles Scribner's Sons, 1882), passim.

26. *Autobiography*, p. 90.

27. Ibid., p. 91.

28. Ibid., p. 92.

29. Wordsworth's position was quite complicated, and different scholars view him on this matter in different lights. Thus, as Peter Coveney reminds us, Alfred North Whitehead saw Wordsworth as reacting against the mentality of the eighteenth century, while a more recent scholar, Arthur Beatty, saw him "as a poet rigidly Hartleian, an exponent of the central associationist philosophy of the century." For Coveney, both views are partly right, but he nevertheless concludes that "In Hartley, he clearly considered himself possessed of the means to effect a fusion of motion and thought, by displaying the organic growth of human consciousness from infancy and childhood according to the principles of associationism." Peter Coveney, *Poor Monkey. The Child in Literature* (London: Rockliff, 1957), p. 33. For a similar discussion, see Basil Willey, *The Seventeenth Century Background* (Garden City, N.Y.: Doubleday, 1953), chap. ii, "Wordsworth and the Locke Tradition." To the claim that Wordsworth was Platonic and idealistic, rather than sensationalist, in his epistemology, we can quote Mill in a statement that implicitly, if indirectly, refutes this view: "His [Plato] doctrine is related to that of Wordworth's ode, erroneously called Platonic, not as identical, but as opposite: with Wordsworth our life here is 'a sleep and a forgetting,' with Plato it is a recollecting." ("Grote's Plato," *Edinburgh Review*, April 1866, reprinted in John Stuart Mill, *Dissertations and Discussions*, 5 vols. (New York: Henry Holt & Co., 1874), 4:303.

30. William Wordsworth, "Preface to the *Lyrical Ballads*," in Eugen Weber, ed., *Paths to the Present* (New York: Dodd, Mead & Co., 1960), p. 20.

31. Ibid., p. 24.

32. Ibid., p. 22.

33. Mill to Carlyle, July 5, 1833, *Letters*, p. 163.

34. Thomas Woods, *Poetry and Philosophy* (London: Hutchinson, 1961), p. 18.

35. Cf. Erik H. Erikson, *Young Man Luther: A Study in Psychoanalysis and History* (New York: W. W. Norton & Co., 1958).

36. *Letters*, 14.

37. See Sigmund Freud, "The Psychopathology of Everyday Life," in Freud, *Standard Edition*, 6:279.

38. Alexander Bain, *John Stuart Mill. A Criticism with Personal Recollections* (New York: Henry Holt & Co., 1862), pp. 43–44.

39. *Early Draft*, pp. 82–83.

40. Ibid., p. 134.

41. Ibid., pp. 134–135.

42. Ibid., p. 141.

43. *Letters*, p. 612.

44. For a most serious and developed philosophical context for our concern with Mill's jacket, cf. Thomas Carlyle's philosophy of clothes in *Sartor Resartus*.

45. John Stuart Mill, "The Spirit of the Age," in *Essays on Politics and Culture*, ed. Gertrude Himmelfarb (Garden City, N.Y.: Doubleday, 1963), pp. 1, 3. See, too, Mill's renewed use of the jacket imagery in his essay, "Bentham," p. 104.

46. *Early Draft*, pp. 133–134, 158–159.

47. *Letters*, p. 312.

Chapter 11

1. John Stuart Mill, *The Early Draft of John Stuart Mill's Autobiography*, ed. Jack Stillinger (Urbana, Ill.: University of Illinois Press, 1961), pp. 169, 172.

2. John Stuart Mill, *Autobiography*, ed. Currin V. Shields (New York: Liberal Arts Press, 1957), p. 123.

3. John Stuart Mill, *The Earlier Letters of John Stuart Mill, 1812–1848*, ed. Francis E. Mineka (Toronto: University of Toronto Press, 1963), p. 128.

4. See, for example, James Mill, *Commonplace Book*, London Library, in 3 vols. folio and 1 vol. quarto. No pagination given in the ms., vol. 1, entry under "Speculation and Practice."

5. *Letters*, p. 78.

6. John Stuart Mill, *Dissertations and Discussions*, 5 vols. (New York: Henry Holt & Co., 1874), 1:347.

7. *Early Draft*, p. 143.

8. On the other hand, James Mill was also more of a religious believer at age twenty, but he would hardly favor Catholicism.

9. Cf. Iris Wessel Mueller, *John Stuart Mill and French Thought* (Urbana, Ill.: University of Illinois Press, 1956), p. 10.

10. *Early Draft*, pp. 73–74.

11. Ibid., p. 143.

12. John Arthur Roebuck, *Life and Letters of John Arthur Roebuck*, ed. Robert Eadon Leader (London: Edward Arnold, 1897), p. 30.

13. *Letters*, p. 60.

14. Ibid., pp. 78, 84.

15. For example, as late as 1847 Mill was still writing to John Austin: "In England I often think that a violent revolution is very much needed, in order to give that general shake-up to the torpid mind of the nation which the French Revolution gave to Continental Europe." *Letters*, p. 713. Nevertheless, the fundamental direction of his mind was not toward revolutionary but toward radical, i.e., liberal, reform.

16. James Anthony Froude, *Thomas Carlyle. A History of the First Forty Years of his Life. 1795–1835*, 2 vols. (New York: Charles Scribner's Sons, 1882), 2:152, 154.

17. Ibid., p. 190.

18. John Stuart Mill, *Essays on Politics and Culture*, ed. Gertrude Himmelfarb (Garden City, N.Y.: Doubleday, 1963) (hereafter referred to as *Essays on Politics*), pp. 1, 4, 6.

19. Ibid., pp. 25, 32, 33.

20. *Letters*, p. 85.

21. Froude, *Carlyle*, 2:62.

22. Ibid., 2:205; 1:15.

23. Ibid., 2: 296.

24. *Letters*, pp. 144, 148–149.

25. Quoted in Michael St. John Packe, *The Life of John Stuart Mill* (London: Secker & Warburg, 1954), p. 181.

26. *Letters*, p. 184. See the rest of this letter, quoted on our title page.

27. *Autobiography*, p. 115.

28. Mill to Carlyle, January 12, 1834, *Letters*, p. 205.

29. Quoted in John M. Robson, *The Improvement of Mankind. The Social and Political Thought of John Stuart Mill* (Toronto: University of Toronto Press, 1968), pp. 89, 90.

30. *Letters*, p. 219.

31. For a full account of the Governor Eyre controversy, see Bernard Semmel, *Democracy Versus Empire* (Garden City, N.Y.: Doubleday, 1969). Even after their quarrel, however, Mill and Carlyle continued their correspondence, though in desultory fashion.

32. Robson, *Improvement of Mankind*, p. 92.

33. *Early Draft*, p. 116.

34. Mill, *Dissertations and Discussions*, 1: 82.

35. Quoted in Packe, *Life*, p. 175.

36. *Letters*, pp. 181–182. Cf. pp. 138–139.

37. Froude, *Carlyle*, 2:356.

38. Packe, *Life*, p. 186.

39. Robson, *Improvement of Mankind*, p. 88.

40. *Letters*, p. 252.

41. Quoted in Packe, *Life*, p. 186.

42. *Letters*, pp. 252, 253.

43. Hayek, p. 83. Cf. *Letters*, p. 252, fn. 2, for Carlyle's 1873 view of the incident.

44. *Letters*, p. 562.

45. The "Jewish banking family" background is significant. In Saint-Simon's scheme, bankers would hold power and run society. John Stuart Mill, familiar with the qualities of English bankers, such as his father's friends, David Ricardo and George Grote, might well be sympathetic to this notion. It is also interesting to note that Ricardo, like d'Eichtal's father, was Jewish. To my knowledge, neither John Stuart Mill nor James Mill ever adverts to this fact, nor to the "Jewish question" that so preoccupied many of their contemporaries.

46. *Letters*, pp. 35, 36.

47. Ibid., pp. 27–28, 33. Thus, in his letter to d'Eichtal of November 7, 1829, Mill declared: "I am chiefly anxious at present to tell you of the things which I approve and admire in this school. . . . In the first place then I highly approve and commend one of the leading principles of their system, which they have established to conviction, the necessity of a *Pouvoir Spirituel*. They have held out as the ultimate end towards which we are advancing & which we shall one day attain, a state in which the body of the people, i.e., the uninstructed, shall entertain the same feelings of deference & submission to the authority of the instructed, in morals and politics, as they at present do in the physical sciences." *Letters*, p. 40.

48. *Letters*, p. 41.

49. *Early Draft*, p. 140.

50. For an account of the trial, and of the Saint-Simonians in general, see, for example, Frank Manuel, *The Prophets of Paris* (Cambridge, Mass.: Harvard University Press, 1962), pp. 185–189 and passim.

51. *Letters*, p. 150.

52. Ibid., pp. 108, 109.

53. *Early Draft*, p. 163.

54. *Letters*, p. 489.

55. Ibid., p. 654.

56. Ibid., pp. 691, 738–739.

57. This, in fact, was an assertion of the French conservative thinker, the Vicomte de Bonald, who, with Joseph de Maistre, had an influence on Comte. Their influence suggests the conservative, and even reactionary, aspect of part of Comte's thought, which Mill gradually came to see. For how far Mill's "elitist" views could carry him, see *Early Draft*, pp. 188–189.

58. As Mueller phrases it: "Thus, while one investigates the dynamics of societal development by induction, comparing the members of a series or various societies with each other, the study of a static member in the series can only be pursued deductively with premises derived from dynamics, and the results of the deductive analysis of the static state are used to verify the findings of induction." Mueller, *John Stuart Mill*, p. 105.

59. *Early Draft*, p. 163.

60. *Letters*, pp. 584–585.

61. Alexander Bain, *John Stuart Mill. A Criticism with Personal Recollections* (New York: Henry Holt & Co., 1882), p. 73.

62. *Letters*, p. 43.
63. Ibid., p. 739.
64. Ibid., See John D. Davies, *Phrenology, Fad and Science* (New Haven, Conn.: Yale University Press, 1955), which, among other things, underlines the serious claims of phrenology to be a science in the nineteenth century. Many reputable thinkers, such as Herbert Spencer, in fact, as well as Comte, also believed in the validity of phrenology.
65. *Letters*, p. 604.
66. Ibid., p. 697.
67. *Early Draft*, p. 121.
68. *Letters*, p. 221.
69. *Early Draft*, p. 133.
70. *Letters*, pp. 28–29.
71. Ibid., p. 635.
72. Ibid., p. 81.
73. *Essays on Politics*, pp. 122, 151.
74. *Letters*, p. 236.
75. See Edward Lytton Bulwer, *England and the English*, ed. Standish Meacham (Chicago, Ill.: University of Chicago Press, 1970), p. 409. Lytton Bulwer, more or less a Benthamite at the time, wrote the short appendix on James Mill, which, though critical, was fair.
76. Ibid., pp. 418–419.
77. *Essays on Politics*, p. 119.
78. Ibid., pp. 83, 84, 88–89.
79. Ibid., p. 94. In fact, of course, Mill was quite mistaken in his notion as to the even tenor of Bentham's life, especially in the latter's early years.
80. Ibid., pp. 94–95.
81. Ibid., pp. 121, 125. Coleridge's attitude, as described here, anticipates the so-called "ordinary language" analysis developed in modern analytic philosophy.
82. Ibid., pp. 131, 132.
83. Ibid., pp. 135, 137.
84. Ibid., pp. 142, 143. Bentham, in Mill's essay of 1833, had also been praised for being like Bacon.
85. Ibid., p. 146.
86. Ibid., pp. 159, 160.
87. Ibid., pp. 171, 172.
88. *Letters*, p. 458.
89. Ibid., p. 259.
90. Ibid., p. 304.
91. Ibid., p. 306.
92. Alexis de Tocqueville, *Oeuvres Complètes*, ed. J. P. Mayer. Tome 6. *Correspondance Anglaise* (Paris: Gallimard, 1954), pp. 291, 295–296, 307, 312, 314.
93. *Autobiography*, p. 125.
94. *Essays on Politics*, pp. 213, 215.
95. Ibid., pp. 215, 216, 217.
96. Ibid., p. 217.
97. Ibid., pp. 224, 228, 226.
98. Ibid., p. 239. In general, Mill ignored status and cultural politics; see the discussion on p. 400. Here, however, he seems to be aware, momentarily, of their increasing power.
99. *Essays on Politics*, p. 244.
100. Ibid., pp. 257, 258.
101. Ibid., pp. 259–260.
102. Ibid., pp. 263, 264.

Chapter 12

1. In fact, Freud's "degradation" theory, i.e., that sex is only possible for some men where there is no emotional attachment, or idealization of the woman (wife) as pure,

suggests that the notion of Victorian marriage as legalized prostitution is basically a mistaken notion. It also goes without saying that nonmarital prostitution was not unique to Victorian England; it is rather that its role in the free-market economy takes on a special character, especially given the morality and values of the period.

2. Cf. Ernest Jones, *The Life and Work of Sigmund Freud*, 3 vols. (New York: Basic Books, 1953–1957), 1:176, and Kate Millett, *Sexual Politics* (Garden City, N.Y.: Doubleday, 1970), p. 95. See, too, R. V. Sampson, *The Psychology of Power* (New York: Pantheon, 1965), and the introductory essay by Alice S. Rossi to John Stuart Mill and Harriet Taylor, *Essays on Sex Equality*, ed. Alice S. Rossi (Chicago: University of Chicago Press, 1970) (hereafter referred to as Rossi ed.).

3. The birth of Harriet's child in 1831 has led some scholars to conjecture that the child may have been Mill's. Such a conjecture, however, as we shall see, simply does not fit with all other existing evidence, and is the least likely conclusion. For details of Mill's early involvement with Harriet, see Hayek, pp. 23 ff., and especially p. 37.

4. For more detailed accounts, see, for example, Hayek, and Michael St. John Packe, *The Life of John Stuart Mill* (London: Secker & Warburg, 1954).

5. Hayek, p. 29, basing this supposition on Moncure D. Conway, *Centenary History of the South Place Society* (London: Williams & Norgate, 1894), p. 89.

6. Alexander Bain, *John Stuart Mill. A Criticism with Personal Recollections* (New York: Henry Holt & Co., 1882), pp. 166–167.

7. For the meaning of overdeterminism, see Freud, *The Interpretation of Dreams*, and my explanation in *In Search of Nixon. A Psychohistorical Inquiry* (New York: Basic Books, 1972), pp. 159–161. For a comparable analysis of names in a "classic" manner, see J. C. Flügel, "On the Character and Married Life of Henry VIII," in B. Mazlish, ed., *Psychoanalysis and History* (New York: Grosset & Dunlap, 1971), pp. 124–149.

8. Cf. J. C. Flügel, *The Psycho-Analytic Study of the Family* (London: The Hogarth Press, 1966), p. 106. We have already referred to the importance of names in relation to James Mill. It is, of course, not just displacement that makes names and naming important; for example, names also carry a group identity and a social status with them.

9. In 1836 Sarah Austin is still writing to Mill as follows: "Of course I shall do all I can—I hope I can finish the article for you. . . . You did right to apply to me I should have been jealous if you had not and miserable if you had sacrificed your rest when I could help you—I shall put aside [all?] for this and with pleasure. It is a small [earnest?] dearest John of what I should be glad to do for you if I could. . . ." MT Coll. 2/671–672.

10. John Stuart Mill, *Autobiography*, ed. Currin V. Shields (New York: Liberal Arts Press, 1957), p. 120.

11. It is interesting to note that an interviewer in 1868 said of Mill's voice that it was "not strong but of great clearness, notwithstanding the delicate and almost womanly gentleness of its tones" (*Chicago Tribune*, March 15, 1868). MT Coll. 5/4.

12. John Stuart Mill, *The Earlier Letters of John Stuart Mill, 1812–1848*, ed. Francis E. Mineka (Toronto: University of Toronto Press, 1963), p. 184.

13. This view, incidentally, also raises the question of whether John Stuart Mill perceived his father as "first rate," and, if so, did he see *him* as combining the feminine and masculine? We are inclined to believe that, in some obscure way, John Stuart Mill did so perceive his outwardly very "masculine" father.

14. Hayek, p. 196.

15. John Stuart Mill, *The Early Draft of John Stuart Mill's Autobiography*, ed. Jack Stillinger (Urbana, Ill.: University of Illinois Press, 1961), pp. 199, 152, 198–199.

16. Hayek, pp. 185, 17.

17. Bain, *John Stuart Mill*, pp. 149, 89.

18. Hayek, p. 45.

19. Bain, *John Stuart Mill*, p. 163.

20. Hayek, pp. 48, 49, 99–100.

21. John Arthur Roebuck, *Life and Letters of John Arthur Roebuck*, ed. Robert Eadon Leader (London and New York: Edward Arnold, 1897), pp. 38–39.

22. Hayek, p. 214, and Rossi, ed., p. 92. For more negative contemporary judgments of Harriet Taylor, see *Early Draft*, p. 24.

23. Hayek, p. 15. Hayek and Packe give us the best accounts.

24. Packe, *Life*, p. 116.

25. Ibid., p. 117.
26. Quoted in Hayek, p. 24.
27. See Richard Garnett, *The Life of W. J. Fox* (London: John Lane The Bodley Head, 1910), and Francis E. Mineka, *The Dissidence of Dissent. The Monthly Repository, 1806–1838* (Chapel Hill, North Carolina: University of North Carolina Press, 1944).
28. Fox did not go quite beyond *all* of his friends. Dr. Southwood Smith, for example, eventually separated from his wife and lived out of wedlock with a woman artist.
29. Mineka, *Dissidence of Dissent*, pp. 178, 182. For Fox's depression, see Garnett, *Life of W. J. Fox*, p. 45.
30. Packe, *Life*, pp. 120, 122. Fox's shortness, not untypical at the time, helps explain why some observers could describe John Stuart Mill as "tall," while to us his 5′7″ would not be so considered today (Harriet Taylor, incidentally, was between 5′ and 5′1″). We must always bear in mind, as we try to envision the circle of John Stuart Mill and Harriet, how small in stature so many of their friends actually were.
31. Packe, 123–124.
32. Hayek, p. 54.
33. MT Coll. 27/115–117.
34. Hayek, pp. 275, 276.
35. MT Coll. 27/142–143.
36. Hayek, p. 130.
37. MT Coll. 28/218.
38. Packe, *Life*, p. 126.
39. Ibid.
40. As William Acton, the physician, expressed the typical Victorian conviction in his book, *The Functions and Disorders of the Reproductive Organs* (1857): "The best mothers, wives, and managers of households, know little or nothing of sexual indulgences. Love of home, children, and domestic duties, are the only passions they feel. As a general rule, a modest woman seldom desires any sexual gratification for herself. She submits to her husband, but only to please him and, but for the desire of maternity, would far rather be relieved from his attentions. Quoted in Steven Marcus, *The Other Victorians* (New York: Bantam Books, 1967), p. 32.
41. *Early Draft*, p. 171.
42. John Stuart Mill, *Dissertations and Discussions*, 5 vols. (New York: Henry Holt & Co., 1874), 3:329.
43. Hayek, p. 196.
44. Packe, *Life*, p. 125.
45. Hayek, pp. 75–76.
46. Hayek, p. 86.
47. Adelaide Weinberg, *Theodor Gomperz and John Stuart Mill* (Geneva, Switzerland: Librairie Droz, 1963), p. 17. For Gomperz' recollections in general of Mill, see "Zur Erinnerungen John Stuart Mill," *Essays und Erinnerungen* (Stuttgart and Leipzig: 1905).
48. Bain, *John Stuart Mill*, pp. 164–165.
49. For most of us, the state of affairs just described may seem unusual. It is obviously, however, a more common occurrence than generally acknowledged. W. J. Fox and Eliza Flower, John Stuart Mill and Harriet, are probably joined in their renunciation by Thomas and Jane Carlyle in their time. Closer to our own period, G. B. Shaw never consummated his marriage, and neither did Max Weber. Mahatma Gandhi renounced sex in his mid-thirties, and so, apparently, did Sigmund Freud in his mid-forties. Whether "intellectuals" are more liable to live without sexual intercourse than others is a difficult point to establish from nonclinical sources; after all, we tend to know more about the private lives of literary and intellectual figures.
50. Hayek, pp. 253–254. The other dream specimen is recounted in Hayek, p. 247, where Mill writes Harriet: "I had a horrible dream lately—I had come back to her & she was sweet and loving like herself at first, but presently she took a complete dislike to me saying that I was changed more for the worst—I am terribly afraid sometimes lest she should think so, not that I see any cause for it, but because I know how deficient I am in self consciousness and self observation, & how often when she sees me again after I have been even a short time absent she is disappointed. . . ."
51. The source of Mill's Magdalen image is not clear. There is, however, one other

reference to Magdalen worth citing. It is in his letter to Harriet of January 26, 1855, when he tells her about his visit to the Doria gallery, and how he saw there ". . . the Magdalen of Titian, a splendid picture, perfectly satisfactory & pleasurable in execution (conception apart) but as a Magdalen ridiculous. I have seen many Titians at Rome & they all strengthen my old feeling about him—he is of the earth earthy." Hayek, p. 219.

52. Flügel, *Psycho-Analytic Study*, pp. 107–108.

53. It is odd, too, that Greville had insisted, in reference to Lady Harriet Baring, that "Two men were certainly in love with her. . . . One was John Mill." See p. 283.

54. Hayek, pp. 169–170.

55. Hayek, pp. 153–154.

56. MT Coll. 29/250–251.

57. Hayek, p. 164.

58. Rossi, ed., p. 91.

59. Hayek, pp. 38, 287, 144, 188, 210.

60. MT Coll. 37/4.

61. Hayek, pp. 165–166, 187, 234.

62. Ibid., pp. 47, 48.

63. Ibid., pp. 275–276, 59, 77.

64. MT Coll. 28/157–158, 161–162.

65. Letter of Hugh Elliot to Lord Courtney, May 8, 1910. Ms. at London School of Economics. Quoted in *Letters*, xx.

66. *Autobiography*, p. 121.

67. Hayek, p. 252.

68. MT Coll. 3/101.

69. MT Coll. 28/176.

70. Packe, *Life*, p. 420.

71. Interestingly enough, this is the reverse of Mill's family, in which none of the boys except John married, and only the girls married and had children.

72. MT Coll. 53/149–153.

73. MT Coll. 53/131–132; 55/142–144; and 44/42–43, 157.

74. *Letters*, p. 521.

75. Hayek, pp. 32, 33.

76. Ibid., p. 169.

77. Ibid., pp. 171, 173, 174.

78. Ibid., p. 179.

79. MT Coll. 47/58–59.

80. *Letters*, p. 395.

81. Hayek, pp. 112, 296.

82. *Letters*, p. 486.

83. In a letter of March 4, 1859 to William E. Hickson, Mill recounts an additional attempt at cure: "I include directions for taking the Bromide of Potassium. I should think the two cases somewhat similar, as the temporary paralysis was caused in my wife's case by an injury to the spine, suffered in a carriage. It is right to say that she took iodine [shades of Mill's childhood friend, Balard!] at the same time, according to the prescription I send. But the iodine did not apparently do any good until she added the bromine to it." John Stuart Mill, *Later Letters, 1849–1873*, ed. Francis E. Mineka and Dwight N. Lindley (Toronto: University of Toronto Press, 1972), 15:602.

84. Packe, *Life*, p. 288. Packe actually notices the 1841 episode referred to by Mill in his letter to Sarah Austin, but passes it by without comment (p. 289).

85. In fact, George, in the last stages of TB, committed suicide rather than await the end.

86. Rene and Jean Dubos, *The White Plague. Tuberculosis, Man and Society* (Boston: Little, Brown & Co., 1952).

87. Ibid., pp. viii, 10. See pp. 11–17 for a full description of Keat's experience with consumption. Cf. William Langer's account of the Black Plague in his "The Next Assignment," reprinted in Bruce Mazlish, ed., *Psychoanalysis and History*, rev. ed. (New York: Grosset & Dunlap, 1971), pp. 87–107, for a description of how a different disease produced a different widespread mood. A major psychohistorical study of disease remains to be written.

88. Dubos, *The White Plague*, p. 53, quoting the Goncourts, and p. 59. The fact seems to be that rather than TB breeding genius, eagerness to achieve often led to unhealthy regimes that were conducive to infection. Cf. Dubos, pp. 64–65.

89. Ibid., p. 127.

90. Ibid., p. 66.

91. Hayek, p. 140.

92. *Memories of Old Friends. Being Extracts from the Journals and Letters of Caroline Fox. . . . from 1835 to 1871*, ed. Horace N. Pum (London: Smith, Elder & Co., 1882), p. 79.

93. Hayek, p. 193. Packe, incidentally, believes it was Mill who first infected Harriet; see *Life*, p. 360. As for Clark, he is described by Dubos as having been "the most distinguished physician of the English colony" at Naples, who treated Keats, advising exercise on horseback. Dubos, *The White Plague*, p. 16. At the time Mill was consulting him Clark was Physician in Ordinary to Queen Victoria.

94. Hayek, p. 203.

95. Elliot, 2:358, 361, 380, 381, 386.

96. Hayek, p. 206.

97. For the inscription, see Hayek, p. 267.

98. Hayek, p. 199.

99. Ibid., p. 264.

100. MT Coll. 53/94–95, 124–125.

101. Packe, *Life*, p. 507.

Chapter 13

1. John Stuart Mill, *The Letters of John Stuart Mill*, ed. Hugh S. R. Elliot, 2 vols. (London: Longmans, Green, & Co., 1910) (hereafter referred to as Elliot), 2:382.

2. MT Coll. 45/53 (Mill's "Suffrage for Women" speech in House of Commons, May 20, 1867).

3. Ibid., and 45/85.

4. John Stuart Mill, *Autobiography*, ed. Currin V. Shields (New York: Liberal Arts Press, 1957), p. 158.

5. Keith Thomas, "Women and the Civil War Sects," in Trevor Aston, ed., *Crisis in Europe, 1560–1660* (Garden City, N.Y.: Doubleday, 1967), pp. 318, 320, 324.

6. Ibid., p. 339.

7. *The Marquis de Sade*, trans. Richard Seaver and Austryn Wainhouse (New York: Grove Press, 1966), p. 218.

8. Ibid., pp. 237, 186.

9. It might be remarked in passing that de Sade's pornographic writings, as any other, while extolling the passions and advocating free vent for them, actually "depassionize" sex. Sex, for example in his novel *Justine*, becomes a purely mechanical act, with no affective ties between the partners involved. Unless one means by "passion" only an impersonal, knee-jerk type of stimulus-response mechanism, there is no passion left in a sadistic world. Cf. Steven Marcus, *The Other Victorians* (New York: Bantam Books, 1967), pp. 182, 286.

10. At Charenton asylum de Sade was in direct contact with the most advanced thinkers in psychology of his time.

11. Mary Wollstonecraft, *A Vindication of the Rights of Woman* (New York: W. W. Norton & Co., 1967).

12. Ibid., pp. 72, 229, 230, 225, 226.

13. Ibid., p. 100. Wollstonecraft's admiration for the middle class is in sharp contrast to much of the later women's rights movement, which viewed that class with distaste. See, for example, Christopher Lasch, *The New Radicalism in America. 1889–1963* (New York: Vintage Books, 1967), p. 57.

14. John Stuart Mill, *The Early Draft of John Stuart Mill's Autobiography*, ed. Jack Stillinger (Urbana, Ill.: University of Illinois Press, 1961), p. 140.

15. Bertrand Russell, drawing inspiration from his godfather, John Stuart Mill, openly espoused free love in the twentieth century.

16. See John Stuart Mill and Harriet Taylor, *Essays on Sex Equality*, ed. Alice S. Rossi (Chicago: University of Chicago Press, 1970) (hereafter referred to as Rossi ed.), pp. 42, 43 for her specific arguments.

17. Hayek, pp. 59, 74, 60. Mill, of course, had no doubt that he and Harriet were "higher natures." In his mature essay, "Utilitarianism," he sounds exactly the same theme when he says: "A being of higher faculties requires more to make him happy, is capable probably of more acute suffering, and certainly accessible to it at more points, than one of an inferior type; but, in spite of these liabilities, he can never really wish to sink into what he feels to be a lower grade of existence." John Stuart Mill, *Dissertations and Discussions*, 5 vols. (New York: Henry Holt & Co., 1874), 3:31.

18. Hayek, p. 74.

19. Rossi ed., p. 108.

20. Ibid., pp. 110, 112, 114.

21. Ibid., p. 125.

22. Ibid., p. 128.

23. Ibid., pp. 138, 141. Cf. Stanley M. Elkins, *Slavery* (Chicago: Grosset & Dunlap, 1959), for the way in which white slave owners in the American South wanted the love as well as the obedience of their slaves.

24. Rossi ed., pp. 150, 151.

25. Ibid., pp. 160, 173–174, 176.

26. Ibid., pp. 201, 203, 212.

27. Ibid., pp. 216, 217, 218, 219, 220.

28. Ibid., p. 236.

29. Adelaide Weinberg, *Theodor Gomperz and John Stuart Mill* (Geneva, Switzerland: Librairie Droz, 1963), p. 11. For full details of Gomperz's life, see this book.

30. Ernest Jones, *The Life and Work of Sigmund Freud*, 3 vols. (New York: Basic Books, 1953–1957), 1:176–177.

31. Sigmund Freud, "Some Psychical Consequences of the Anatomical Distinction Between the Sexes," in Sigmund Freud, *The Standard Edition of the Complete Psychological Works of Sigmund Freud*, ed. James Strachey, 23 vols. to date (London: The Hogarth Press, 1953–), 19:253, 257–258.

32. Sigmund Freud, "The Taboo of Virginity (Contributions to the Psychology of Love III)," in *Standard Edition*, 11:198.

33. See R. V. Sampson, *The Psychology of Power* (New York: Pantheon Books, 1968), pp. 59–69 for the story of how Elizabeth broke through the taboo and married Robert Browning.

34. D. W. Winnicott, "Aggression in Relation to Emotional Development," in *Collected Papers* (New York: Basic Books, 1958), 205; Cf. Gregory Rochlin, *Man's Aggression* (Boston: Gambit, 1973), pp. 98–99, 105, 109.

35. Carl Schorske, "Politics and Patricide in Freud's *Interpretation of Dreams*," *The American Historical Review* 78 (April 1973), pp. 328–347. See the critique and extension of Schorske's work in Stanley Rothman and Philip Isenberg, "Sigmund Freud and the Politics of Marginality," in *Central European History* (forthcoming). Their critique, however, does not call into question the particular assertions of Schorske that we are utilizing here.

36. Sigmund Freud, *The Interpretation of Dreams*, in *Standard Edition*, 4:217, fn. 1.

37. I must confess myself dissatisfied with the existing literature on the subject of the psychology of women (my dissatisfaction, of course, may simply express my limitations). For one of the better discussions see the essays in J. Chassequet-Smirgel et al., *Female Sexuality. New Psychoanalytic Views* (Ann Arbor, Mich.: University of Michigan Press, 1970).

Chapter 14

1. Cf. Marx's "Man makes himself" and Nietzsche's "God is dead."

2. John Stuart Mill, *Principles of Political Economy. With Some of their Applications to Social Philosophy*, intro by Arthur T. Hadley, 2 vols., rev. ed. [6th ed. of 1865] (New York: The Colonial Press, 1900) (hereafter referred to as *Principles*), 1: 357, 357–358.

3. Ibid., pp. 359, 362.

4. For our purposes, the most important of Mill's economic works are the following: the *Essays on Some Unsettled Questions of Political Economy*, which, written in 1830 and 1831, were first published in 1844; of these *Essays*, "Of the Words Productive and Unproductive" and "On the Definition of Political Economy" are most interesting to us. The popular reception of these *Essays* encouraged Mill to write and publish his *Principles of Political Economy*, which we shall be analyzing at great length. In addition to the *Essays* and the *Principles*, two papers, "The Claims of Labour" (1845) and "Thornton on Labour and Its Claims" (1869) are especially pertinent for us. A glance at Volumes 4 and 5 of the Collected Works of John Stuart Mill, however, will show how much more extensive than our citations was Mill's work in economics. In the earlier essays and reviews, we can see that he tended to "youthful combativeness and occasional arrogance," gradually however, mellowing, and become broader and more tolerant in his views. See John Stuart Mill, *Essays on Economics and Society*, intro. by Lord Robbins, ed. J. M. Robson (Toronto: University of Toronto Press, 1967) (hereafter referred to as *Essays on Economics*), p. xiv. After this chapter was written, Pedro Schwartz' important book *The New Political Economy of J. S. Mill* (Durham, No. Carolina: Duke University Press, 1972), appeared.

5. John Stuart Mill, *Principles of Political Economy*, intro. by V. W. Gladen, ed., J. M. Robson, 2 vols. (Toronto: University of Toronto Press, 1965) (hereafter referred to as *Principles*, Toronto ed.), 1:xxxi; and *Principles*, 1:ix.

6. See Chapter 5, p. 104 of this book, and cf. *Essays on Economics*, p. x.

7. See *Essays on Economics*, p. xxix. Incidentally, I pass no judgment here as to who was right or wrong; see Robbins' introduction, however, for a critique of John Stuart Mill's conclusions.

8. *Essays on Economics*, p. 365.

9. On the "claims of labor" question per se, John Stuart Mill in later life changed his views of 1845 for technical reasons. Thus, in his 1869 essay on "Thornton on Labor and its Claims," Mill admitted that the question involved *both* an issue of economic science and of justice. On the first, economic science, he confessed to his earlier error: "The doctrine hitherto taught by all or most economists (including myself), which denied it to be possible that trade combinations can raise wages, or which limited their operation in that respect to the somewhat earlier attainment of a rise which the competition of the market would have produced without them,—this doctrine is deprived of its scientific foundation, and must be thrown aside. The right and wrong of the proceedings of Trades' Unions becomes a common question of prudence and social duty, not one which is peremptorily decided by unbending necessities of political economy." John Stuart Mill, *Dissertations and Discussions*, 5 vols. (New York: Henry Holt & Co., 1874), 5:52. On the second, justice, he proceeded to explore the limits to which he thought trade unions could press the claims of their members.

10. *Essays on Economics*, p. 369; *Principles*, Toronto ed., 2:1030.

11. John Stuart Mill, *The Early Draft of John Stuart Mill's Autobiography*, ed. Jack Stillinger (Urbana, Ill.: University of Illinois Press, 1961), pp. 147, 172.

12. *Essays on Economics*, p. 321; *Principles*, 1:ix. Cf. John Stuart Mill, *The Earlier Letters of John Stuart Mill, 1812–1848*, ed Francis E. Mineka (Toronto: University of Toronto Press, 1963), p. 631.

13. *Principles*, 1:x.

14. Ibid., 1:5, 11, 12.

15. Ibid., 1:21–22.

16. Ibid., 1:23, 26.

17. Ibid., 1:44, 49.

18. Ibid., 1:49, 50, 51.

19. Ibid., 1:62; see also 1:78.

20. Ibid., 1:69, 160.

21. Ibid., 1:163.

22. See Erik H. Erikson, *Young Man Luther: A Study in Psychoanalysis and History* (New York: W. W. Norton, 1958), and Norman O. Brown, *Life Against Death: The Psychoanalytic Meaning of History* (Middletown, Conn.: Random House, Modern Library, 1959).

23. Karl Abraham, "Contributions to the Theory of the Anal Character," in *Selected Papers* (London: The Hogarth Press, 1948), p. 379.

24. *Principles*, 1:388; cf. Joseph A. Schumpeter, *History of Economic Analysis* (New York: Oxford University Press, 1954), pp. 556–557.

25. *Principles*, 2:171. Cf. Anne Jardim, *The First Henry Ford: A Study in Personality and Business Leadership* (Cambridge, Mass.: The MIT Press, 1970) for an analysis of the "immoderate" entrepreneur.

26. Cf. Erik H. Erikson, *Childhood and Society* (New York: W. W. Norton, 1950), for a characterization of the phallic stage as embracing the child's efforts at initiative.

27. *Principles*, 1:103.

28. Ibid., 1:170.

29. Ibid., 1:196, 197.

30. Ibid., 1:420.

31. Cf. Schumpeter, *History of Economic Analysis*, p. 543.

32. We shall offer Mill's most favorable views of socialism and communism, starting with the third edition. Most of what he describes as communism and socialism is the same in both the first and the third editions; it is mainly the tone and inclination that shifts dramatically in the later. For the first edition version, see *Principles*, Toronto ed., 2: App. A.

33. *Principles*, 1:199, 199–200.

34. Ibid., 1:204.

35. Ibid., 1:205.

36. Ibid., 1:206, 207–208.

37. Ibid., 1:212. In the first edition Mill believed the impediment to Fourierism's success was the "unmanageable nature of its machinery" (*Principles*, Toronto ed., 2:984), requiring a better human nature than we now possess.

38. *Principles*, 1:212–213.

39. Ibid., 2:210.

40. Ibid., 2:211.

41. See Schumpeter, *History of Economic Analysis*, pp. 259–260, for Turgot, and pp. 652–654 for Ricardo and a discussion of Mill's gyrations around this problem.

42. *Principles*, 2:242.

43. Ibid., 2:260, 261–262.

44. Ibid., 2:263.

45. Ibid., 2:264–265.

46. Ibid., 2:265.

47. Ibid., 2:266, 267, 271.

48. See S. P. Turin (Tyurin), "Nicholas Chernyshevsky and John Stuart Mill," *Slavonic Review*, 9, no. 25 (June 1930). Chernyshevsky, although he accepted Mill's definitions of productive and unproductive labor, also divided labor into that which is profitable to society and that which is not profitable to it. As is well known, Lenin was tremendously influenced by Chernyshevsky's novel, *What is to be Done?*—he named his own 1902 tract, "What is to be Done?"—but it was the kind of hard, controlled "Utilitarian" type of hero in the book rather than the laborers' associations that Lenin took as his model and inspiration. See further my book, *Revolutionary Ascetics* (forthcoming).

49. Quoted in Hayek, 307—308.

50. *Principles*, 2:298.

51. On her part, she kept addressing him as "Massa" and confided to her diary that "i made my mind up that it was best and safest to be a slave to a *gentleman*, nor wife and equal to any vulgar man." Quoted in *The New York Times Book Review*, October 29, 1972, p. 7.

52. John Stuart Mill, *Essays on Politics and Culture*, ed. Gertrude Himmelfarb (Garden City, N.Y.: Doubleday, 1963), p. 49.

53. The author of *My Secret Life* was not a romantic, but he, too, understood this connection well. See Steven Marcus, *The Other Victorians* (New York: Bantam Books, 1967), p. 88.

54. *Essays on Economics*, p. 368.

55. *Principles*, 2:311–312, 329.

56. Ibid., 2:384.

57. Ibid., 2:443.
58. Ibid., 2:443–444.
59. Ibid., 2:451.
60. Ibid., 2:480.
61. O. R. McGregor, "Social Research and Social Policy in the Nineteenth Century," *The British Journal of Sociology* 8, no. 2 (June 1957): 150.

Chapter 15

1. John Stuart Mill, *The Early Draft of John Stuart Mill's Autobiography*, ed. Jack Stillinger (Urbana, Ill.: University of Illinois Press, 1961), p. 185.
2. It should be noted, of course, that with the emergence of anthropology as a separate field, professional interest in custom was growing at this time. One thinks also of Walter Bagehot's work, *Physics and Politics* (Boston: Beacon Press, 1956).
3. Maurice Cranston, *John Stuart Mill* (London: Longmans, Green & Co., 1958), p. 18. To put the matter in another context, as Philip Rieff says, discussing the sexual rebellion: "The theme of liberation from a repressiveness more serious than that of any merely political regime was everywhere in the haunted air of the nineteenth century." Philip Rieff, *Freud: The Mind of the Moralist* (Garden City, N.Y.: Doubleday, 1961), p. 374.
4. Isaiah Berlin, *Four Essays on Liberty* (New York: Oxford University Press, 1969), p. 202.
5. John M. Robson, *The Improvement of Mankind. The Social and Political Thought of John Stuart Mill* (Toronto: University of Toronto Press, 1968), pp. 183–184.
6. *Early Draft*, pp. 188–189.
7. John Stuart Mill, *Autobiography*, ed. Currin V. Shields (New York: Liberal Arts Press, 1957), p. 155.
8. Ibid., and p. 161.
9. John Stuart Mill, *The Letters of John Stuart Mill*, ed. Hugh S. R. Elliot, 2 vols. (London: Longmans Green and Co., 1910), 2:359.
10. Ibid., 2:368. Cf. Robson, *Improvement of Mankind*, p. 57–58.
11. John Stuart Mill, *On Liberty*, ed. Alburey Castell (New York: Appleton-Century-Crofts, 1947) (hereafter referred to as *On Liberty*), p. 1.
12. See "Two Concepts of Liberty" in Berlin, *Four Essays*, pp. 118–172.
13. *On Liberty*, p. 9.
14. Ibid, pp. 10, 6.
15. Ibid, pp. 11, 12.
16. Ibid., pp. 13, 14.
17. Ibid., p. 19.
18. Ibid., p. 21.
19. John Stuart Mill, *Dissertations and Discussions*, 5 vols. (New York: Henry Holt & Co., 1874), 4:41–42.
20. Ibid., 4:262–263.
21. Ibid., 4:284–285.
22. *On Liberty*, pp. 30, 31, 32. Cf. Herbert Marcuse, *An Essay on Liberation* (Boston: Beacon Press, 1969), for a similar position on this issue. A comparison of the two books, however, shows how far the discussion of the subject of liberty has changed in the course of one hundred years.
23. Quoted in Robson, *Improvement of Mankind*, p. 187.
24. Mill seems almost to trench on Popper's notion of scientific truth (see Popper's *The Logic of Scientific Discovery* (New York: Science Editions, Inc., 1961)—that we can never fully verify but only fail to disconfirm a statement—but Mill's purpose is quite different from Popper's, and he passes by this insight.
25. *On Liberty*, pp. 44–45.
26. Ibid., p. 47.
27. Ibid., p. 52.
28. *Dissertations and Discussions*, 4:24.
29. *On Liberty*, p. 63.

30. *Autobiography*, pp. 152, 153.
31. Berlin, *Four Essays*, pp. 177–178.
32. *On Liberty*, pp. 57, 59, 60.
33. Quoted in Michael St. John Packe, *The Life of John Stuart Mill* (London: Secker & Warburg, 1954), p. 405.
34. *On Liberty*, pp. 66, 66–67.
35. Ibid., p. 60.
36. Ibid., pp. 70, 71, 74.
37. Ibid., p. 76.
38. Ibid., p. 94.
39. John Stuart Mill, *Considerations on Representative Government*, ed. with an intro. by R. B. McCallum (London: Oxford University Press (hereafter referred to as *Considerations*), p. 313.
40. Ibid., p. 107.
41. Ibid., pp. 109–110.
42. Ibid., p. 111.
43. Cf. Seymour Martin Lipset, *Political Man* (Garden City, N.Y.: Doubleday, 1963), especially part 1.
44. *Considerations*, p. 115.
45. Ibid., p. 115.
46. Ibid., p. 118.
47. Ibid., p. 119.
48. Ibid., pp. 120, 124.
49. Ibid., p. 125.
50. Ibid., p. 125.
51. Ibid., p. 130. Cf. *Dissertations and Discussions*, 4:60.
52. *Considerations*, pp. 130, 131, 132, 133, 135.
53. Ibid., pp. 140, 142.
54. Ibid., 184.
55. John Stuart Mill, *Essays on Politics and Culture*, ed. Gertrude Himmelfarb (Garden City, N.Y.: Doubleday, 1965), p. 271, and *Dissertations and Discussions*, 4:77–78.
56. In the light of recent experience, Mill's faith in plural votes for more highly educated persons seems more a reflection of his overvaluation of intellect than a realistic estimate of results. One thinks of the behavior of Nazi university students and professors. On the other hand, of course, opinion polls in America show university educated persons as holding far more "liberal" views on a wide range of issues than held by grade school graduates. Education itself, therefore, does not seem to be the determining variable.
57. It is odd, given Mill's admiration for Condorcet, that he had overlooked the latter's advocacy of a similar scheme.

Chapter 16

1. On the *Logic* as a whole see, for example, the pertinent essays in J. B. Schneewind, ed., *Mill: A Collection of Critical Essays* (Garden City, N.Y.: Doubleday, 1968), as well as the relevant items listed in the bibliography. On a particular point, concerning Kepler's laws, see, for example, Mill's exchange with Sir John F. W. Herschel in John Stuart Mill, *The Earlier Letters of John Stuart Mill, 1812–1848*, ed. Francis E. Mineka (Toronto: University of Toronto Press, 1963), pp. 673–676.
2. *Letters*, pp. 613, 617.
3. Alexander Bain, *John Stuart Mill. A Criticism with Personal Recollections* (New York: Henry Holt & Co., 1882), p. 79.
4. *Letters*, p. 604.
5. Quoted in Kate Millett, *Sexual Politics* (Garden City, N.Y.: Doubleday, 1970), p. 95.
6. Before faulting Mill too severely, we should note that more recent efforts have hardly been very much more successful. See, for example, the account in Alex Inkeles and Daniel J. Levinson, "National Character: The Study of Modal Personality and

Sociocultural Systems," in G. Lindsey, ed., *Handbook of Social Psychology*, 2 vols. (Cambridge, Mass.: Addison-Wesley, 1954).

7. *Letters*, pp. 31, 32.

8. Ibid., 32.

9. Maurice Cranston, *John Stuart Mill* (London: Longmans, Green, & Co., 1958), p. 23.

10. Hayek, p. 215.

11. *Letters*, pp. 465, 508.

12. Ibid., pp. 606, 692.

13. Ibid., p. 522; Hayek, p. 243; John Stuart Mill, *Considerations on Representative Government*, ed. with intro. by R. B. McCallum (London: Oxford University Press, 1948) (hereafter referred to as *Considerations*), p. 221; and *Letters*, p. 404.

14. Cf. the exchange of views on this subject between Mill's friend, Tocqueville, and Gobineau, in Alexis de Tocqueville, *"The European Revolution" and Correspondence with Gobineau*, ed. John Lukacs (Garden City, N.Y.: Doubleday, 1959).

15. *Considerations*, pp. 146–147.

16. John Stuart Mill, *A System of Logic* (New York: Harper & Brothers, 1869) (hereafter referred to as *Logic*), p. v.

17. Ibid., p. 520.

18. John Stuart Mill, *Essays on Politics and Culture*, ed. Gertrude Himmelfarb (Garden City, N.Y.: Doubleday, 1963), p. 10.

19. Shirley Robin Letwin, *The Pursuit of Certainty* (Cambridge: Cambridge University Press, 1965), pp. 249–250. Cf. Thomas S. Kuhn, *The Structure of Scientific Revolutions* (Chicago: University of Chicago Press, 1962), for a different view of science.

20. John Stuart Mill, *Essays on Economics and Society*, intro. by Lord Robbins, ed. J. M. Robson (Toronto: University of Toronto Press, 1967), pp. 316–317.

21. *Logic*, p. 520.

22. Ibid., p. 521.

23. Cf. Emile Durkheim, *Montesquieu et Rousseau. Précurseurs de la Sociologie* (Paris: Librarie Marcel Rivière et Cie, 1953).

24. *Logic*, p. 522.

25. Ibid., pp. 523, 524.

26. In passing, we might note that James Mill's "necessarian" attitude was in implicit contradiction to his own view of himself as a self-made man. By denying his father's doctrine, John Stuart Mill was affirming in his own way that he, too, was self-made.

27. *Logic*, p. 524.

28. Ibid., pp. 505, 526.

29. Ibid., pp. 528, 529, 530.

30. Ibid., pp. 530, 531.

31. Ibid., pp. 533, 534.

32. Ibid., p. 543.

33. Ibid., p. 540.

34. Ibid., p. 542.

35. Of course, Mill cannot be expected to offer it in the *Logic*; but he needs to point to it somewhere else, i.e., in his own later projected work on ethology. As we have noted, however, this never took "definite shape" for him.

36. *Logic*, pp. 547, 548.

37. For such an attempt, cf. Bertrand de Jouvenal, *On Power*, trans. J. F. Huntington (New York: Viking Press, 1949).

38. Karl Popper, "The Autonomy of Sociology," in Schneewind, *Mill*, p. 428.

39. *Logic*, p. 550.

40. For the opposite point of view, see, for example, Norman Cohn, *Warrant For Genocide* (New York: Harper Torch Books, 1969), the Conclusion, and especially p. 266. Following Ernst Simmel, "Anti-Semitism and Mass Psychopathology," in Ernst Simmel, ed., *Anti-Semitism: A Social Disease* (New York: International Universities Press, 1946), pp. 33–78, Cohn argues that antisemitism in the individual can be quite different from antisemitism in a group.

41. *Logic*, p. 566.

42. Ibid., pp. 561, 564.

43. Ibid., p. 570.

44. Ibid., p. 574.
45. Ibid.
46. Ibid., pp. 575, 576.
47. Ibid., pp. 576, 578.
48. Ibid., pp. 581, 584.
49. Ibid., p. 585.
50. Ibid., p. 586.
51. For continued discussions of these issues, see, for example, Patrick Gardiner, ed., *Theories of History* (New York: The Free Press, 1959), and Hans Meyerhoff, ed., *The Philosophy of History in Our Time* (Garden City, N.Y.: Doubleday, 1959). Also see the important journal, *History & Theory*.
52. *Logic*, p. 576.
53. Cf. John M. Robson, *The Improvement of Mankind. The Social and Political Thought of John Stuart Mill* (Toronto: University of Toronto Press, 1968), pp. 273–276.
54. Quoted in ibid., pp. 273–274.
55. See J. D. Y. Peel, *Herbert Spencer. The Evolution of a Sociologist.* (New York: Basic Books, 1971).
56. This is the prospectus of the Society, quoted in J. W. Burrow, *Evolution and Society* (Cambridge: Cambridge University Press, 1966), p. 119. Burrow's book is useful for the details of the development in anthropology.
57. John Stuart Mill, *Dissertations and Discussions* 5 vols. (New York: Henry Holt and Co., 1874), 5:143, 144, 168.

PERMISSIONS

Permissions

Excerpts from *The Life of John Stuart Mill*, by Michael St. John Packe, have been reprinted by permission of Curtis Brown Ltd., London, on behalf of the author.

Excerpts from *The Works and Correspondence of David Ricardo*, Volume IX, edited by Piero Sraffa and M. H. Dobb, have been reprinted by permission of Cambridge University Press.

PICTURE CREDITS

Plate IV, The Bettmann Archive; Plates VII, IX, X, The Granger Collection; Plates II, XI, XII, Library of Political and Economic Science, London; Plate VIII, The Mansell Collection; Plate V, National Portrait Gallery, London; Plates I, III, VI, XIII, Radio Times Hulton Picture Library.

NAME INDEX

Name Index

Name Index

Name Index

Name Index

SUBJECT INDEX

Subject Index

Subject Index